T0177270

Lecture Notes in Computer Science   **9190**

Commenced Publication in 1973
Founding and Former Series Editors:
Gerhard Goos, Juris Hartmanis, and Jan van Leeuwen

More information about this series at http://www.springer.com/series/7409

Theo Tryfonas · Ioannis Askoxylakis (Eds.)

Human Aspects of Information Security, Privacy, and Trust

Third International Conference, HAS 2015
Held as Part of HCI International 2015
Los Angeles, CA, USA, August 2–7, 2015
Proceedings

Springer

Editors
Theo Tryfonas
University of Bristol
Bristol
UK

Ioannis Askoxylakis
Institute of Computer Science (ICS)
Foundation for Research and Technology -
    Hellas (FORTH)
Heraklion, Crete
Greece

ISSN 0302-9743 ISSN 1611-3349 (electronic)
Lecture Notes in Computer Science
ISBN 978-3-319-20375-1 ISBN 978-3-319-20376-8 (eBook)
DOI 10.1007/978-3-319-20376-8

Library of Congress Control Number: 2015941353

LNCS Sublibrary: SL3 – Information Systems and Applications, incl. Internet/Web, and HCI

Springer Cham Heidelberg New York Dordrecht London

Printed on acid-free paper

Springer International Publishing AG Switzerland is part of Springer Science+Business Media
(www.springer.com)

Foreword

The 17th International Conference on Human-Computer Interaction, HCI International 2015, was held in Los Angeles, CA, USA, during 2–7 August 2015. The event incorporated the 15 conferences/thematic areas listed on the following page.

A total of 4843 individuals from academia, research institutes, industry, and governmental agencies from 73 countries submitted contributions, and 1462 papers and 246 posters have been included in the proceedings. These papers address the latest research and development efforts and highlight the human aspects of design and use of computing systems. The papers thoroughly cover the entire field of Human-Computer Interaction, addressing major advances in knowledge and effective use of computers in a variety of application areas. The volumes constituting the full 28-volume set of the conference proceedings are listed on pages VII and VIII.

I would like to thank the Program Board Chairs and the members of the Program Boards of all thematic areas and affiliated conferences for their contribution to the highest scientific quality and the overall success of the HCI International 2015 conference.

This conference could not have been possible without the continuous and unwavering support and advice of the founder, Conference General Chair Emeritus and Conference Scientific Advisor, Prof. Gavriel Salvendy. For their outstanding efforts, I would like to express my appreciation to the Communications Chair and Editor of HCI International News, Dr. Abbas Moallem, and the Student Volunteer Chair, Prof. Kim-Phuong L. Vu. Finally, for their dedicated contribution towards the smooth organization of HCI International 2015, I would like to express my gratitude to Maria Pitsoulaki and George Paparoulis, General Chair Assistants.

May 2015

Constantine Stephanidis
General Chair, HCI International 2015

HCI International 2015 Thematic Areas and Affiliated Conferences

Thematic areas:

- Human-Computer Interaction (HCI 2015)
- Human Interface and the Management of Information (HIMI 2015)

Affiliated conferences:

- 12th International Conference on Engineering Psychology and Cognitive Ergonomics (EPCE 2015)
- 9th International Conference on Universal Access in Human-Computer Interaction (UAHCI 2015)
- 7th International Conference on Virtual, Augmented and Mixed Reality (VAMR 2015)
- 7th International Conference on Cross-Cultural Design (CCD 2015)
- 7th International Conference on Social Computing and Social Media (SCSM 2015)
- 9th International Conference on Augmented Cognition (AC 2015)
- 6th International Conference on Digital Human Modeling and Applications in Health, Safety, Ergonomics and Risk Management (DHM 2015)
- 4th International Conference on Design, User Experience and Usability (DUXU 2015)
- 3rd International Conference on Distributed, Ambient and Pervasive Interactions (DAPI 2015)
- 3rd International Conference on Human Aspects of Information Security, Privacy and Trust (HAS 2015)
- 2nd International Conference on HCI in Business (HCIB 2015)
- 2nd International Conference on Learning and Collaboration Technologies (LCT 2015)
- 1st International Conference on Human Aspects of IT for the Aged Population (ITAP 2015)

Conference Proceedings Volumes Full List

1. LNCS 9169, Human-Computer Interaction: Design and Evaluation (Part I), edited by Masaaki Kurosu
2. LNCS 9170, Human-Computer Interaction: Interaction Technologies (Part II), edited by Masaaki Kurosu
3. LNCS 9171, Human-Computer Interaction: Users and Contexts (Part III), edited by Masaaki Kurosu
4. LNCS 9172, Human Interface and the Management of Information: Information and Knowledge Design (Part I), edited by Sakae Yamamoto
5. LNCS 9173, Human Interface and the Management of Information: Information and Knowledge in Context (Part II), edited by Sakae Yamamoto
6. LNAI 9174, Engineering Psychology and Cognitive Ergonomics, edited by Don Harris
7. LNCS 9175, Universal Access in Human-Computer Interaction: Access to Today's Technologies (Part I), edited by Margherita Antona and Constantine Stephanidis
8. LNCS 9176, Universal Access in Human-Computer Interaction: Access to Interaction (Part II), edited by Margherita Antona and Constantine Stephanidis
9. LNCS 9177, Universal Access in Human-Computer Interaction: Access to Learning, Health and Well-Being (Part III), edited by Margherita Antona and Constantine Stephanidis
10. LNCS 9178, Universal Access in Human-Computer Interaction: Access to the Human Environment and Culture (Part IV), edited by Margherita Antona and Constantine Stephanidis
11. LNCS 9179, Virtual, Augmented and Mixed Reality, edited by Randall Shumaker and Stephanie Lackey
12. LNCS 9180, Cross-Cultural Design: Methods, Practice and Impact (Part I), edited by P.L. Patrick Rau
13. LNCS 9181, Cross-Cultural Design: Applications in Mobile Interaction, Education, Health, Transport and Cultural Heritage (Part II), edited by P.L. Patrick Rau
14. LNCS 9182, Social Computing and Social Media, edited by Gabriele Meiselwitz
15. LNAI 9183, Foundations of Augmented Cognition, edited by Dylan D. Schmorrow and Cali M. Fidopiastis
16. LNCS 9184, Digital Human Modeling and Applications in Health, Safety, Ergonomics and Risk Management: Human Modeling (Part I), edited by Vincent G. Duffy
17. LNCS 9185, Digital Human Modeling and Applications in Health, Safety, Ergonomics and Risk Management: Ergonomics and Health (Part II), edited by Vincent G. Duffy
18. LNCS 9186, Design, User Experience, and Usability: Design Discourse (Part I), edited by Aaron Marcus
19. LNCS 9187, Design, User Experience, and Usability: Users and Interactions (Part II), edited by Aaron Marcus
20. LNCS 9188, Design, User Experience, and Usability: Interactive Experience Design (Part III), edited by Aaron Marcus

Human Aspects of Information Security, Privacy and Trust

Program Board Chairs: Theo Tryfonas, UK, and Ioannis Askoxylakis, Greece

The full list with the Program Board Chairs and the members of the Program Boards of all thematic areas and affiliated conferences is available online at:

http://www.hci.international/2015/

HCI International 2016

The 18th International Conference on Human-Computer Interaction, HCI International 2016, will be held jointly with the affiliated conferences in Toronto, Canada, at the Westin Harbour Castle Hotel, 17–22 July 2016. It will cover a broad spectrum of themes related to Human-Computer Interaction, including theoretical issues, methods, tools, processes, and case studies in HCI design, as well as novel interaction techniques, interfaces, and applications. The proceedings will be published by Springer. More information will be available on the conference website: http://2016.hci.international/.

General Chair
Prof. Constantine Stephanidis
University of Crete and ICS-FORTH
Heraklion, Crete, Greece
Email: general_chair@hcii2016.org

http://2016.hci.international/

Contents

Cybersecurity

Privacy, Security and User Behaviour

Security in Social Media and Smart Technologies

Security Technologies

Authentication

Single Trial Authentication with Mental Password Writing

Sarah N. Abdulkader(✉), Ayman Atia, and Mostafa-Sami M. Mostafa

HCI-LAB, Department of Computer Science,
Faculty of Computers and Information-Helwan University, Cairo, Egypt
nabil.sarah@gmail.com, ayman@hci.fci.helwan.edu.eg,
mostafa.sami@fci.helwan.edu.eg

Abstract. This paper presents an authentication system that uses brain waves as a biometric discriminant trait. It utilizes Electroencephalogram (EEG) signals generated from mental writing of the user-owned password. Independent Component Analysis (ICA) and baseline correction has been used for preprocessing and noise removal. The effect of two types of features, multivariate autoregressive (MVAR) model parameters and power spectral density (PSD) features, have been studied for this activity. Performance results based on single trial analysis have revealed that imagined password writing can reach average Half Total Error Rate (HTER) of 5 % for PSD features vs 3 % obtained with MVAR coefficients. The experiments have shown that mental password writing can be used for increasing the user acceptance for enrollment conditions while maintaining high performance results.

Keywords: EEG · BCI verification · Biometric authentication · Mental writing

1 Introduction

Technological revolution that characterizes this era has brought a lot of facilities and comfort to different aspects of human lives. It allows fast information exchange in the form of rapid mail delivery systems, distant communication and overseas transactions. These advantages come at the expense of increasing vulnerability of data secrecy. They cause the growing need for advanced authentication mechanisms. Approving or declining the claimed identity of the user is the responsibility of these mechanisms. There are three fundamental techniques used in authentication mechanisms, which are knowledge based, object based, and biometrics based authentication as stated in [1].

Knowledge based authentication requires the owning of some information exclusive to the user. It includes passwords and personal identification numbers. Different kinds of attacks can take this technique down like shoulder surfing and user carelessness. Some of the weakness associated with passwords can be overcome with object based authentication. In this technique, user possesses physical objects which are given for later identity confirmation as cards or tokens. They cannot be shared with the same freedom as exchanging the passwords. However, this category can still be broken with card-theft.

Biometrics based authentication, which is concerned with the measurement of physical characteristics or personal traits, fights the stealing vulnerability associated with the

© Springer International Publishing Switzerland 2015
T. Tryfonas and I. Askoxylakis (Eds.): HAS 2015, LNCS 9190, pp. 3–12, 2015.
DOI: 10.1007/978-3-319-20376-8_1

previously mentioned types. Biometric characteristics can be divided into two broad categories: physiological and behavioral.

Physiological biometrics depend on the physical features of the human body while behavioral biometrics or behaviometrics depend on the action-based features like gait recognition, hand gestures, keystroke dynamics and voice recognition.

A relatively recent discriminative trait, called Electrophysiology, has been used in behaviometrics authentication. It reflects electrical properties and voltage changes of biological system in response to ongoing activities. There are several electrophysiological readings that show great opportunities as biometrics. They have specific names, referring to the origin of the bioelectrical signals, such as Electrocardiography (ECG) for signals originated from the heart, Electrocorticography (ECoG) for signals originated from the cerebral cortex, and Electroencephalography (EEG) for signals originated from the brain as mentioned in [2].

This paper presents a new mental authentication activity and investigates how well it meets various biometrics evaluation factors. The next section highlights different activities for personal identifications and authentications applied in previous researches along with the used assessment criteria.

2   Related Work

EEG is used to study the differences in brain voltage. They reflect the occurrence of motor or mental activities in various Brain Computer Interface (BCI) applications. The brain responses to certain actions have been used to verify the claimed identity even for people with various disabilities or to convey secret messages through the identification process as implied by Su et al. in [3]. They have designed an identification system with the ability to detect a covert warning expressed as a clenching-teeth muscle activity. The system, that uses power spectral density as features and LDA and KNN classifiers, has obtained an identification accuracy of 90 % versus 93.7 % obtained in a non-warning identification system.

2.1   Personal Identification and Authentication

Several researchers have investigated the use of brain signals in personal identification and verification systems for different motivating actions. Visual evoked potential and graphical stimulation have been widely used in a variety of forms like employing face stimulation via presenting either self-face or non-self-face images, as anticipated by Yeom and his colleagues in [4, 5]. They first have chosen the highly distinctive channels and time components related to each user. Then they utilize the averaged ERP signals over multiple trials in order to compute the corresponding features. They have reached a mean accuracy of 86.1 %. While Ravi [6] and Zúquete [7] have presented black and white pictures from Snodgrass and Vanderwart picture set to 70 individuals. Ravi has achieved an identification accuracy of 95.25 % using 40 Hz EEG oscillations. While Zúquete et al. have been concerned with reducing the consumption of electrodes. The performance of two classifiers, K-NN and SVDD, has been compared and their best attained results for eight electrodes are 95.1 % and 98.5 % respectively.

Ashby et al. in [8] have utilized mental based actions like baseline measurement, limb movement, counting, and rotation to authenticate five subjects. It operates low cost EEG headset from the Emotiv Company to collect 14 channel signals, thus increasing the price-based collectability of the system. They have reached an average accuracy 98.78 % using one-versus-all SVM classifier while discriminating five types of features. On the other hand, Hema and his colleagues [9] pay special attention to the uniqueness of reading and multiplication mental responses. They have extracted PSD features from EEG Beta waves and applied them to feed forward neural classifier. The performance of identifying six subjects has reached an average accuracy of 97.5 %. PSD features of mental spelling and reading activities from different subjects have been classified using feed forward neural networks in [10]. The identification system has gained performance accuracy of 78.6 % based on single trial analysis compared to 90.4 % of multiple trials averaging.

Marcel et al. in [11] has involved the mental generation of words in person authentication. The first letter, chosen randomly, is the same across all subjects. They have proposed a statistical framework based on Gaussian Mixture Models and Maximum a Posteriori model adaptation on word generation as well as motor imagery EEG signal. It has resulted in HTER ranging from 6.6 % to 20.5 % for motor imagery versus 12.1 % to 26.1 % for word generation for various number of gaussians in the mixture in a single day.

In an attempt to combine knowledge based and biometrics authentication, Svogor and Kisasondi [12] have discussed the idea of merging the user's mental state with his own password. The password is divided into smaller elements called pels. The user determines the mental state associated with each element.

2.2 Biometrics Evaluation Factors

The biometrics based authentication systems are evaluated against validation factors like those revealed in [13]. They can be categorized, as shown in Fig. 1, into general, system-related, and user-related factors. General factors include the essential characteristics of the authenticating trait like universality, uniqueness, and permanence. Universality verifies the existence of such trait in every human being, while uniqueness ensures its distinctiveness per individual. Permanence or constancy validates the time-invariance of the measured biological phenomena. The system-related factors guarantee the collectability and quantitative aspects along with the estimated system performance. Finally, user-related factors are concerned with the usability and user acceptance level.

In [7], Zúquete et al. criticize the application of visual stimulation in BCI authentication against general and system related factors. They argue that the universality requirement is not completely met for blind or people with severe visual damages but no evidence for uniqueness violation. According to their findings, constancy has been under certain doubts caused by the variability of the circumstances surrounding cognition activities. EEG recording should also be carefully managed to fulfill the collectability condition and enhance signal-to-noise ratio, especially with the low-power attribute of the EEG signals. Electrodes must be placed always in the same scalp location, but this issue is usually solved by using EEG helmets.

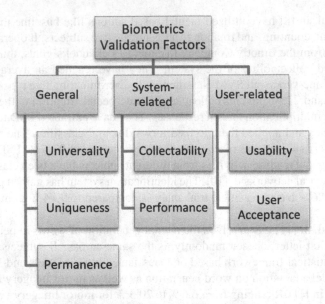

Fig. 1. Biometrics validation factors

According to Chuang et al. [14], the usability issues are related to two main reasons, one regarding EEG hardware, while the other is concerned with the mental tasks. For the recording hardware, less intrusive dry-contact electrode integrated in a wireless headset is preferred over free array of electrodes that must be carefully placed over the scalp. They have assessed mental task usability via a questionnaire filled by the participants in the authentication experiments. The evaluated tasks are closed-eyes breathing, imagined finger movement, sport motion, singing, tone-listening with eye reaction, counting specific color objects, and pass-thought.

The questionnaire has been interested in three factors, difficulty, bore, and the repeating intention. It has been claimed that among the performed tasks, movement imagination and pass-thought represent the most difficult tasks. The subjects have issues with imagining muscle actions without physical respond. Besides, bringing up specific feelings or events accompanying chosen pass-thought has proved hard to repeat on a consistent basis. Subjects have revealed that they consider finger movement as the most boring task. Breathing and counting colors are the highly recommended tasks for repetition. Although the promising usability results offered by breathing task, it is not suitable for sending secret messages opposite to pass, sport, song, and color related tasks. On the other hand, counting colors task faces a problem of recalling the secret attribute compared to the other four mental activities, as the subjects have no difficulty in recalling their personalized sport, song, and pass-thought choices.

In the following section, an authentication system with imagined password writing on a single trial basis is presented. It combines the memory recalling of the conventional password along with the specified mental writing action. This type of mental activities could help sending covert messages. The system enhances usability factors through exploitation of an easy to wear EEG recording headset. It also requires no previous training for dealing with the system. Besides, the system demands only 3 to 4 min for samples' gathering process. The used dataset has been collected from six subjects in normal environmental conditions.

3   System Description

The recorded EEG signals of the participants, as shown in Fig. 2, pass through different phases of manipulation to perform the verification process. They are preprocessing, feature extraction and classification. The following subsections provide details for the involved algorithms in each phase.

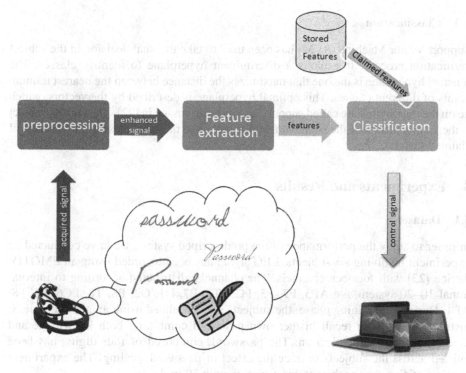

Fig. 2.   Proposed BCI based authentication system

3.1   Preprocessing

The acquired signals from each subject have been modified by ICA. It is a statistical method for blind source separation [15, 16]. It performs spatial filtering for the supplied multidimensional signals to reduce artifacts, enhance SNR and facilitate EEG source localization [17]. In this system, the dimensionality of the output signals is the same as the input. Also, baseline correction has been utilized for this phase as described in [18].

3.2   Feature Extraction

Two types of mental password features have been studied, time analyzing features and spectral analyzing features. Multivariate autoregressive (MVAR) coefficients represent the temporal features. They contribute in modeling EEG multi-channel time series where the prediction for each value of one-channel signal relies not only on the previous values of the same time series but also on the previous values of the signals generated from other channels as well [19]. MVAR of order six has been used and estimated using Vieira-Morf method [20]. Spectral features are also involved in the current experiment. Power Spectral Density (PSD) has been computed using burg method with an autoregressive model of order six [21].

3.3   Classification

Support Vector Machine (SVM) has been used to take the final decision in the subject verification process. It exploits a discriminant hyperplane to identify classes. The selected hyperplane is the one that maximizes the distance between the nearest training points of different classes. This optimal hyperplane is described by the vectors, which lie on the margin that are called support vectors as discussed in [22]. The current subject is then authenticated if the supplied features belong to the same class as the features of claimed identity.

4   Experiments and Results

4.1   Dataset

In order to study the performance of the predescriped system, we have conducted an experiment involving six subjects. EEG signal has been recorded using an EMOTIV device [23] with fourteen channels. The channels, distributed according to international 10–20 system, are AF3, F7, F3, FC5, T7, P7, O1, O2, P8, T8, FC6, F4, F8, AF4. During the training phase, the subjects are stimulated using an auditory cue. It instructs the user to recall his/her own password combining both knowledge and biometric based authentication. The password, composed of four digits, has been unified across the subjects to trace the effect of password stealing. The experiment consists of five runs each contains a session with 20 trials.

4.2   Performance Evaluation

The performance evaluation and enhancement is targeting the reduction of both error types: False Acceptance Rate (FAR) and False Rejection Rate (FRR). FAR is measuring the percentage of the incorrectly authenticated subjects, while FRR is expressing the percentage of refusing the correct identities. In order to consider both errors, Half Total Error Rate (HTER) has been used. It is the average of both FAR and FRR [24].

4.3   Results

The results are obtained using a 10-fold cross-validation repeated over five runs with one-versus-all scheme for each subject. They illustrate that using MVAR model for feature extraction has achieved an error rate 44 %. It's lower than the outcome obtained using PSD features which is 45.08 % with only ICA spatial filtering employed in the preprocessing phase. When correcting baseline of the EEG signal, MVAR modeling parameters and PSD features have achieved reduced error rates of 3 % and 5 % respectively. The detailed results of each feature extraction method are viewed in Tables 1 and 2. The average results for each subject are shown in Fig. 3. ANOVA test has been conducted to trace the effect of baseline power correction on the authentication process. P-value was less than 0.05 for both MVAR model and PSD features. This p-value concludes that there is a noticeable influence of baseline power correction on classification results for both feature types.

Table 1. Authentication performance For MVAR coefficients after baseline correction

	R_1	R_2	R_3	R_4	R_5	Mean
S_1	0.1	0	0.025	0.025	0.025	0.035
S_2	0	0	0	0.075	0.025	0.02
S_3	0.05	0.1	0.1	0.075	0.1	0.085
S_4	0	0	0.025	0	0.025	0.01
S_5	0.025	0	0	0.025	0	0.01
S_6	0.025	0.025	0.025	0	0.025	0.02
Mean	0.033	0.020	0.029	0.033	0.033	0.03

Table 2. Authentication performance for PSD after baseline correction

	R_1	R_2	R_3	R_4	R_5	Mean
S_1	0.15	0.025	0.05	0.025	0	0.05
S_2	0.025	0	0	0.05	0.025	0.02
S_3	0.025	0.075	0.075	0.025	0.075	0.055
S_4	0.075	0.075	0.1	0.1	0.05	0.08
S_5	0.05	0	0	0.05	0.025	0.025
S_6	0.025	0.05	0.05	0.125	0.125	0.075
Mean	0.058	0.037	0.045	0.062	0.05	0.050

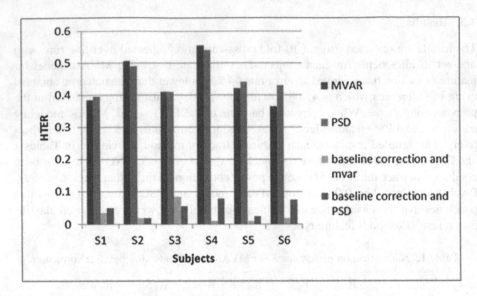

Fig. 3. System performance over five runs

The results have shown the efficiency of mental password writing activity in the authentication process for the same password. The proposed system gives better results than the mental word generation accomplished by Marcel et al. [11] for different words starting with the same letter. Their system has achieved HTER value that equals 6.6 % for motor imagery and 12.1 % for word generation. The effect of employing various passwords will be further examined in future work.

5 Conclusion

In this paper, an EEG based authentication system that utilizes mental password writing activity has been proposed. It aims at considering the user acceptance of enrollment conditions while attaining reasonable performance results. It uses ICA and baseline correction for preprocessing, PSD and MVAR coefficients for feature extraction, and SVM for classification. The final findings have shown that baseline correction has achieved a significant increase in the performance results. They have also revealed that time series modeling features and power spectral density features have offered comparable performance for this type of activity.

References

1. Shanmugapriya, D., Padmavathi, G.: A survey of biometric keystroke dynamics: approaches, security and challenges. arXiv preprint arXiv:0910.0817 (2009)

2. Riera, A., Dunne, S., Cester, I., Ruffini, G.: Electrophysiological biometrics: opportunities and risks. In: Mordini, E., Tzovaras, D. (eds.) Second Generation Biometrics: The Ethical, Legal and Social Context. The International Library of Ethics, Law and Technology, pp. 149–176. Springer, Netherlands (2012)
3. Su, F., Zhou, H., Feng, Z., Ma, J.: A biometric-based covert warning system using EEG. In: 2012 5th IAPR International Conference on Biometrics (ICB), pp. 342–347. IEEE (2012)
4. Yeom, S.-K., Suk, H.-I., Lee, S.-W.: Eeg-based person authentication using face stimuli. In: 2013 International Winter Workshop on Brain-Computer Interface (BCI), pp. 58–61. IEEE (2013)
5. Yeom, S.-K., Suk, H.-I., Lee, S.-W.: Person authentication from neural activity of face-specific visual self-representation. Pattern Recogn. **46**, 1159–1169 (2013)
6. Ravi, K., Palaniappan, R.: Leave-one-out authentication of persons using 40 Hz EEG oscillations. In: The International Conference on Computer as a Tool, 2005. EUROCON 2005, pp. 1386–1389. IEEE (2005)
7. Zúquete, A., Quintela, B., Cunha, J.P.S.: Biometric authentication using brain responses to visual stimuli. In: Proceedings of the International Conference on Bio-inspired Systems and Signal Processing, pp. 103–112 (2010)
8. Ashby, C., Bhatia, A., Tenore, F., Vogelstein, J.: Low-cost electroencephalogram (EEG) based authentication. In: 2011 5th International IEEE/EMBS Conference on Neural Engineering (NER), pp. 442–445. IEEE (2011)
9. Hema, C.R., Paulraj, M., Kaur, H.: Brain signatures: a modality for biometric authentication. In: International Conference on Electronic Design, 2008. ICED 2008, pp. 1–4. IEEE (2008)
10. Hema, C., Osman, A.A.: Single trial analysis on EEG signatures to identify individuals. In: 2010 6th International Colloquium on Signal Processing and Its Applications (CSPA), pp. 1–3. IEEE (2010)
11. Marcel, S., del Millán, J.R.: Person authentication using brainwaves (EEG) and maximum a posteriori model adaptation. IEEE Trans. Pattern Anal. Mach. Intell. **29**, 743–752 (2007)
12. Svogor, I., Kisasondi, T.: Two factor authentication using EEG augmented passwords. In: Proceedings of the ITI 2012 34th International Conference on Information Technology Interfaces (ITI), pp. 373–378. IEEE (2012)
13. Wang, L., Geng, X., Global, I.: Behavioral Biometrics for Human Identification: Intelligent Applications. Medical Information Science Reference, New York (2010)
14. Chuang, J., Nguyen, H., Wang, C., Johnson, B.: I think, therefore i am: usability and security of authentication using brainwaves. In: Adams, A.A., Brenner, M., Smith, M. (eds.) FC 2013. LNCS, vol. 7862, pp. 1–16. Springer, Heidelberg (2013)
15. Hyvärinen, A., Karhunen, J., Oja, E.: Independent Component Analysis. Wiley, New York (2004)
16. Stone, J.V.: Independent Component Analysis. Wiley Online Library (2004)
17. Allison, B.Z., Dunne, S., Leeb, R.: Towards Practical Brain-Computer Interfaces: Bridging the Gap from Research to Real-World Applications. Springer, Heidelberg (2012)
18. Hu, L., Xiao, P., Zhang, Z., Mouraux, A., Iannetti, G.: Single-trial time–frequency analysis of electrocortical signals: baseline correction and beyond. NeuroImage. **84**, 876–887 (2014)
19. He, C., Lv, X., Wang, Z.J.: Hashing the mAR coefficients from EEG data for person authentication. In: IEEE International Conference on Acoustics, Speech and Signal Processing, 2009. ICASSP 2009, pp. 1445–1448. IEEE (2009)
20. Schlögl, A., Supp, G.: Analyzing event-related EEG data with multivariate autoregressive parameters. Prog. Brain Res. **159**, 135–147 (2006)
21. Marple, S.L.: Digital Spectral Analysis: with Applications. Prentice-Hall, Englewood Cliffs (1987)

22. Jian-feng, H.: Comparison of different classifiers for biometric system based on EEG signals. In: 2010 Second International Conference on Information Technology and Computer Science (ITCS), pp. 288–291. IEEE (2010)
23. [Last Visit: 2014.07.08]. http://www.emotiv.com
24. Monroe, D.: Biometrics Metrics Report v3.0. http://www.usma.edu/ietd/docs/Biometrics MetricsReport.pdf

Leap Motion Controller for Authentication via Hand Geometry and Gestures

Alexander Chan[1]([✉]), Tzipora Halevi[2], and Nasir Memon[2]

[1] Hunter College High School, New York, NY, USA
alexanderchan97@gmail.com
[2] New York University Polytechnic School of Engineering, Brooklyn, NY, USA

Abstract. The Leap Motion controller is a consumer gesture sensor aimed to augment a user's interactive experience with their computer. Using infrared sensors, it is able to collect data about the position and motions of a user's hands. This data allows the Leap to be used as an authentication device. This study explores the possibility of performing both login as well as continuous authentication using the Leap Motion device. The work includes classification of static data gathered by the Leap Motion using trained classifiers, with over 99 % accuracy. In addition, data was recorded from the users while utilizing the Leap Motion to read and navigate through Wikipedia pages. A template was created using the user attributes that were found to have the highest merit. The algorithm found when matching the template to the users newly collected data, the authentication provided an accuracy of over 98 %, and an equal error rate of 0.8 % even for a small number of attributes. This study demonstrates that the Leap Motion can indeed by used successfully to both authenticate users at login as well as while performing continuous activities. As the Leap Motion is an inexpensive device, this raises the potential of using its data in the future for authentication instead of traditional keyboard passwords.

Keywords: Security · Biometrics · Authentication

1 Introduction

With the introduction of "motion capture" devices to the consumer market, users have experienced many new ways to interact with computer systems. One of the first of such systems was the Nintendo Wii, which utilized an infrared emitter in the form of a "sensor bar" and an IR receiver in a separate remote. Users moved the remote relative to the IR receiver in order to interact with items on-screen. One significant deficiency of this technology, however, is that the Wii senses only the remote and its movements, rather than the person himself.

As this and similar motion capture technology has progressed, systems have become smaller and more self-contained. Most recently, a gesture sensor called the "Leap Motion controller" (Fig. 1) was released. It uses both optical sensors and infrared light to detect a user's hands. The controller sits flat on a table, with

© Springer International Publishing Switzerland 2015
T. Tryfonas and I. Askoxylakis (Eds.): HAS 2015, LNCS 9190, pp. 13–22, 2015.
DOI: 10.1007/978-3-319-20376-8_2

Fig. 1. The Leap Motion controller is capable of collecting physical and gesture properties of a user's hands.

the sensors pointing up, creating a range of detection in the shape of an inverse pyramid extending up to 600 mm and encompassing a field of view of approximately 150 degrees. The system interprets data from the sensors alongside an internal model of a human hand to determine the position and orientation of a user's hand.

This type of 3D hand gesture motion capture allows for biometric authentication based on two different factors: hand geometry and hand gestures. A large body of literature addresses both hand geometry and hand gesture based authentication, but very little considers gestures in the third dimension, or 3D motion capture devices. In addition to these two types of biometric features, the Leap Motion can also monitor human interactions with a computer, so that it can authenticate both statically, that is, only when access is requested, and dynamically, or continuously, in which identity is continuously verified during device use.

In this study, we assess the feasibility of a 3D gesture device, the Leap Motion controller, for static and continuous authentication based on hand geometry and gestures. Section 2 elaborates on related work and Sect. 3 discusses the features and specification of the Leap Motion controller. Section 4 describes our approach, Sect. 5 presents our results, and Sect. 6 concludes.

2   Related Work

Hand geometry has long been known to be unique among individuals and has already been used as a biometric [7]. Commercial systems, such as the Schlage HandKey, require a user to place his hand around a series of pegs, while a camera takes an image. Such systems measure a set of 30 typical features. That include only physical geometries, and not other physical identifiers such as fingerprints, palm prints, or other markings on the hand.

In addition to simple hand geometry, gesture behavior has been explored on touchscreens and touchpads in both static and continuous contexts [2,5,8,9]. Angulo determined that in a static context, the time taken in drawing a pattern lock contains enough unique information for authentication. Training required drawing at least 250 keystrokes, which makes this method less applicable in a real life situation [5]. Sae-Bae showed that touch gestures are unique to each person, and can authenticate users [9]. In a continuous context, it was also shown that gestures meant for interacting with a device can also authenticate [8]. A Hidden Markov model was shown to be able to ease training while still supporting a high accuracy [2]. In addition, it was shown that a random forest classifier provided the highest identification accuracy, which is supported by other studies regarding gesture data [1]. We apply this work to a 3D gesture device, using a random forest classifier.

3   Leap Motion Controller

The Leap Motion controller is a consumer 3D gesture sensor. Using both optical sensors and infrared light, it detects hand gestures and positions for a novel method of human-computer interaction. Its detection range is in the shape of an inverse pyramid, extending up to 600 mm with a field of view of approximately 150 degrees. Beginning with the v2 Leap software, authentication both receives and interprets data from sensors and compares such data to an internal model of a human hand in order to determine accurately the position and orientation of a user's hand.

The Leap controller generates, on a frame by frame basis, information regarding a user's hands as well as information pertaining to already recognized gestures. A frame typically contains the position of objects, and in the case of a hand, the frame also contains physical properties such as the width and length of the hand and arm as well as the width and length of each digit and the four bones associated with each digit. In addition to these properties, the Leap recognizes certain movement patterns as "gestures". The Leap records gestures for each finger. There are four currently recognized gestures: a circle, a swipe, a key tap, and a screen tap. A circle gesture is simply a single finger drawing a circle; a swipe is a long linear movement of a finger; a key tap is a finger rotating slightly downwards and back up; and a screen tap is a finger moving forward and backward quickly. Figure 2 shows all four gestures in the diagnostic visualizer, with path tracking for visibility. These four gestures, moreover, have their own properties, such as speed.

There has been at least one study analyzing the reliability of the data generated by the Leap controller, and many others analyzing the use of the controller in practical applications such as sign language recognition [3,4,6]. Using an industrial robot capable of providing an accuracy of less than 0.2 mm, meaning it is capable of moving an object in increments of no more than 0.2 mm, Weichert et al. have shown that the Leap has an overall detection accuracy of 0.7 mm, and that the size of "pointable objects", such as fingers, does not affect the accuracy. This high accuracy is complemented by the "hand confidence", a value ranging from 0 to 1 based on the correlation between the observed data and an internal hand model. However, Jakus et al. demonstrate that while static objects are reliably tracked, moving objects are tracked less accurately. Potter et al. also mention that occlusion of parts of the hand negatively affects tracking.

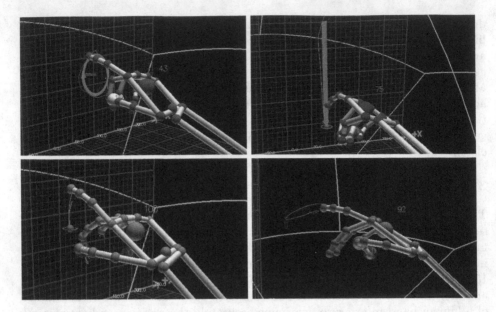

Fig. 2. The Leap Motion controller recognizes four basic gestures out of box. Each of these gestures has inherent properties, such as the time to complete the gesture. Clockwise, from top left, the gestures are: circle, swipe, screen tap, and key tap

Many of these features, such as the hand confidence and the internal hand model, were introduced with v2 of the Leap Software, which also includes skeletal tracking. However, previous research generally used v1, which suffered from poor tracking, especially when part of a hand was occluded. As a result, many previous conclusions of the Leap Motion controller's inconsistency with extensive practical applications might not apply to the updated software.

4   Data Collection

This study is composed of two parts. The first part mimicked a static authentication scenario, where the user would use the Leap for the purpose of login-in authentication. The second analyzed a continuous authentication scenario, where the user performs basic actions using the Leap, i.e. reading web pages online (without performing any explicit user authentication), while simultaneously being authenticated.

4.1   Static Authentication

In this section of the work, 16 participants provided data in two identical sessions. They were asked to place both hands above the Leap Motion controller for 25 s. During this time, only frames where the confidence value of each hand was above 0.9 were recorded. Once the confidence reached this value, the participant was then asked to draw a circle with one finger. The two sessions ensured repeatability of the data.

107 attributes were stored at a rate of 55 frames per second. Three attributes are gesture properties, pertaining to the circle gesture, and the rest are physical properties, consisting of the width and length of both hands and arms, all digits, and the four bones associated with each digit (metacarpal, proximal, intermediate, and distal). For the thumb, the metacarpal bone has length 0. The gesture properties include the radius of the circle, the duration, in seconds, of the gesture, and the acceleration of the finger ($\frac{2\pi r}{t}$, where r is the radius and t is the duration of the gesture).

4.2   Continuous Authentication

For continuous authentication, 10 participants used a program enabling interaction with the operating system through the Leap Motion controller. To move the mouse cursor, users would move their right index finger. Clicking involved a "key tap" gesture with the left hand or a "screen tap" gesture with the right hand, and scrolling involved either a "circle" gesture with the left hand or a "swipe" gesture with the right hand. Subjects were given a few minutes to familiarize themselves with the various controls. Each user was told to navigate from one random Wikipedia page to another, only through clicking links.

Data for this part involved 135 attributes. In addition to the physical properties recorded (the same as those recorded in the previous part), gesture properties were also recorded. These included the orientation of each hand, the speed of each hand and finger, the "grab" and "pinch" strengths of each hand, and various properties pertaining to the four prerecognized gestures.

5   Authentication Algorithms

Two algorithms were implemented for authentication. In the first one, classifiers were used on all of the attributes. In the second algorithm, a template matching approach was adopted to explore the possibility of identifying user's data based on a small number of attributes.

5.1   Classification

A random forest classifier was decided upon for the classification step. It was shown that for such behavioral data sets, random forest classification is superior to other algorithm types, such as linear and kernel density estimation classifiers [1]. For example, a naive Bayes classifier fails, due to high correlation between certain features.

The Waikato Environment for Knowledge Analysis (WEKA) was used for classification. A random forest classifier was used on both data sets. The model was built using a 10-fold cross validation, that is, the data were partitioned into 10 subsamples, and each was used as a test set, while the remainder was used as a training set.

In addition to classification, an attribute selector, in conjunction with the ranker search method, was used to identify which attributes contribute most to the classification. The algorithm tests each attribute and returns a value that indicates how important it is for classification (the higher the value, the more important the feature is).

5.2 Template Matching

For data collected from the second part of the work, further analysis was done to determine the Equal Error Rate (EER), which is the value at which the False Acceptance (FAR) and False Reject Rate (FRR) are equal. First, the data was reduced to a sample size of 4500 instances per user. This data set was then split in half such that 2250 data values were used to build the template for the user, and the rest were used to test the template. Two attributes from the training data were selected to build a template of each user - these attributes were selected based on their relative importance. The template consisted of the weighted averages of these two values.

Every data value from the testing set was compared against the template. A threshold was chosen, and if the distance between the data value and the template value was smaller than this threshold, it was considered an accept. Otherwise, it was considered a reject. If a data value not belonging to that user's template was accepted, the false acceptance rate increased. If a data value belonging to that user's template was rejected, the false rejection rate increased.

A range of thresholds, beginning at 0% and ending at 100% (percentage of maximum possible distance), were tested. The intersection of these two rates was calculated to be the EER. Following are the formulas for these algorithms.

Template creation for user i, when b attribute vectors are used:

$$T_i = Profile(user_i) = average(v_i^1 \ldots v_i^b)$$

Authentication for user i when given attribute vector v_i and a threshold τ:

$$auth(T_i, v_i) = 1 \ if \ |T_i - v_i| > \tau, \ 0 \ otherwise$$

The distance that is measured is the Euclidean distance.

6   Results

During classification, the identification rate, which measures the percentage of correctly classified instances, was used as the main indicator of performance. The closer the identification rate was to 100%, the better the classifier performed. In addition to this metric, WEKA provides more specific information, including the true positive rate, false positive rate, precision, recall, F-Measure, and ROC area.

The true positive rate, or the recall rate, is the ratio of true positives to total positives, while the false positive rate, or false acceptance rate (FAR), is the ratio of false positives to total negatives. Higher TP/recall rates and lower FP rates imply more accurate classifications. The precision, or positive predictive value, is the ratio of true positives to classified positives. F-Measure combines both precision and recall, and is calculated using $\frac{2pr}{p+r}$ where p is the precision and r is the recall. The closer the F-Measure is to 1, the more accurate the classifier is. Finally, the ROC area is the area under a graph of the FP rate versus the TP rate. It represents the probability that the classification algorithm will rank a random positive higher than a random negative. Like the F-Measure, the closer the ROC Area is to 1, the more accurate the classifier.

6.1 Static

Classification accuracy for static authentication using the random forest algorithm was 99.9667 %. Out of 12,006 instances, only 4 were incorrectly classified. The detailed classification is in Fig. 3.

	TP Rate	FP Rate	Precision	Recall	F-Measure	ROC Area
Weighted Average	1	0	1	1	1	1

Fig. 3. Detailed accuracy by class for continuous authentication

Average merit	Feature description
3.765 ± 0	All physical properties
0.478 ± 0.006	Radius of circle gesture
0.134 ± 0.002	Acceleration of hand during gesture
0.127 ± 0.002	Duration of circle gesture
0 ± 0	Length of left and right thumb metacarpal bones

Fig. 4. Calculated average merit for each feature in classification. Merit is a relative measure, and so the higher its score, the more weight it is given during classification. Every single physical property, with the exception of the metacarpal bone length, has a higher merit than the other gesture properties.

All but 5 attributes had the same average merit of 3.765 ± 0. The only attributes that did not have a significant weight were the three gesture properties (radius of the circle, duration of the gesture, and acceleration of the hand), and the lengths of the metacarpal bones in both thumbs. A list of selected attributes and their average merit is presented in Fig. 4.

6.2 Continuous

For continuous authentication, classification accuracy was 98.3862%. The weighted average of the classification is in Fig. 5.

As in static authentication, physical properties have a higher average merit than gesture properties. Figure 6 shows a list of all attributes and their average merit.

A template was constructed for each of the 10 users. Then each individual data value was tested against this template - if the test value was within a certain threshold of the weighted mean of the values, it was considered a success. Each training value was tested against each user template, allowing for both determination of false accept (when an illegitimate user was authenticated) and false reject (when the true user was rejected) rates.

Two features were chosen based on relative weights. The width of the right and left hand were compared against. A plot of the FAR and FRR is shown in Fig. 7.

	TP Rate	FP Rate	Precision	Recall	F-Measure	ROC Area
Weighted Average	0.984	0.001	0.986	0.984	0.984	1

Fig. 5. Detailed accuracy by class for continuous authentication

Average merit	Feature description
2.547 ± 0.001	Physical properties of right hand
1.074 ± 0.002	Physical properties of left hand
0.554 ± 0.001	Number of hands
0.537 ± 0.002	Roll of the right hand
0.452 ± 0.001	Pinch strength of the right hand
0.442 ± 0.002	Yaw of the right hand
0.386 ± 0.001	Pitch of the right hand
0.320 ± 0.001	Yaw of the left hand
0.178 ± 0.001	Roll of the left hand
0.150 ± 0.001	Grab strength of the right hand
0.144 ± 0.001	Pitch of the left hand
0.111 ± 0.001	Pinch strength of the left hand
0.100 ± 0.001	Speed of the right hand and right fingers
0.077 ± 0.001	Grab strength of the left hand
0.050 ± 0.001	Speed of the left hand and left fingers
0.014 ± 0.002	Radius of the circle gesture
0.001 ± 0	Speed of the circle gesture
0 ± 0	Key tap, swipe, and screentap gesture properties
0 ± 0	Length of left and right thumb metacarpal bones

Fig. 6. Average merit for all features for the continuous data. As with the merits calculated in a static context, physical features have a higher merit than all other gesture properties, such as finger speed and hand rotation.

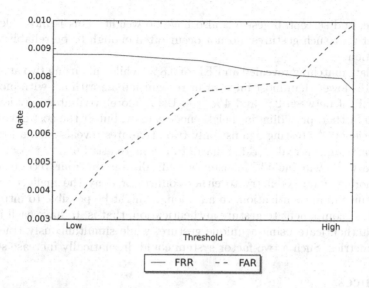

Fig. 7. A plot of error rates as the threshold changes. As the threshold increases, more values are accepted, which increases the false accept rate, but decrease the false reject rate. The reverse is also true for as the threshold decreases. The EER is the point at which the FAR and FRR are equal. Biometric systems aim for the lowest possible EER. Here, the EER is around 0.8 %.

7   Discussions and Conclusions

Based on results of the classification, it is obvious that the Leap Motion, in conjunction with a random forest classifier, is able to distinguish individuals with high accuracy. The ability of the Leap Motion controller to reliably collect data at all times, even in cases where parts of the hand were occluded, shows the improvement of the Leap Motion's software. Therefore, many earlier claims of poor recognition are likely no longer valid. While more rigorous testing must be done, it is safe to assume that the Leap is more capable of complex tasks such as sign-language or handwriting recognition.

In terms of authentication, it is not gestures that matter, but instead simple hand geometry. This is the case for both static, where the only gesture is a circle, and continuous authentication, where there was a greater number of gesture attributes. Because of the greater significance physical properties have, it can be concluded that classification based on physical properties alone is sufficient. Removing gesture attributes will increase the efficiency of the classification while preserving the accuracy, improving performance in a real world scenario.

In both parts, the lengths of the thumb metacarpal bones had no significance whatsoever. This is explained by the fact that the Leap API creates a thumb metacarpal bone, although one does not exist. It assigns this bone a length of 0, and so the length of this bone was the same for all participants. Not only do the lengths of the thumb metacarpals have no weight, but the properties of the key tap, swipe, and screentap gestures also have no weight. This is most likely due to the fact that such gestures did not occur often enough to be reliably used in identification.

Template matching revealed an EER of 0.8 %, while only using two attributes. This EER is lower than most fingerprint recognition algorithms, with most having an EER of between 2 % and 4 % [10]. Using more attributes may lower the EER even further, providing for heightened security, but at the cost of computational efficiency. As testing against only two attributes reveals such a low EER, it is impractical in a real-world scenario to use more attributes.

Future work will include focusing specifically on the four recognized gestures, ignoring hand geometry to either confirm or deny the ineffectiveness of these gestures in authentication. In addition, it might be possible to introduce a "knowledge" component to gesture authentication, that is, to have each individual user authenticate using a unique gesture, while simultaneously tracking of hand biometrics. Such a two-factor system could dramatically increase security.

References

1. Chan, A., Halevi, T., Memon, N.: Touchpad input for continuous biometric authentication. In: De Decker, B., Zúquete, A. (eds.) CMS 2014. LNCS, vol. 8735, pp. 86–91. Springer, Heidelberg (2014)
2. Roy, A., Halevi, T., Memon, N.: An HMM-based behavior modeling approach for continuous mobile authentication. In: IEEE Conference on ICASSP, pp. 3789–3793 (2014)
3. Weichert, F., Bachmann, D., Rudak, B., Fisseler, D.: Analysis of the accuracy and robustness of the leap motion controller. Sensors 13, 6380–6393 (2013). doi:10.3390/s130506380
4. Jakus, G., Guna, J., Tomažič, S., Sodnik, J.: Evaluation of Leap motion controller with a high precision optical tracking system. In: Kurosu, M. (ed.) HCI 2014, Part II. LNCS, vol. 8511, pp. 254–263. Springer, Heidelberg (2014)
5. Angulo, J., Wästlund, E.: Exploring touch-screen biometrics for user identification on smart phones. Priv. Identity Manage. Life 375, 130–143 (2012)
6. Potter, L.E., Araullo, J., Carter, L.: The Leap Motion controller: A view on sign language. Griffith University (2013)
7. Bača, M., Grd, P., Fotak, T.: Basic principles and trends in hand geometry and hand shape biometrics. In: Dr. Jucheng Yan (ed.) New Trends and Developments in Biometrics. InTech (2012). doi:10.5772/51912
8. Frank, M., Biedert, R., Ma, E., Martinovic, I., Song, D.: Touchalytics: on the applicability of touchscreen input as a behavioral biometric for continuous authentication. IEEE Trans. Inf. Forensics Secur. 8(1), 136–148 (2012)
9. Sae-Bae, N., Ahmed, K., Isbister, K., Memon, N.: Biometric-rich gestures: a novel approach to authentication on multitouch devices. In: Conference on Human Factors in Computing Systems, pp. 977–986 (2012)
10. Cappelli, R., Maio, D., Maltoni, D., Wayman, J., Jain, A.: Performance evaluation of fingerprint verification systems. IEEE Trans. Pattern Anal. Mach. Intell. 28(1), 3–18 (2006)
11. Bulatov, Y., Jambawalikar, S., Kumar, P., Sethia, S.: Hand Recognition System Using Geometric Classifiers, DIMACS Workshop on Computational Geometry (2002)

Predicting Graphical Passwords

Matthieu Devlin[1], Jason R.C. Nurse[1(✉)], Duncan Hodges[2],
Michael Goldsmith[1], and Sadie Creese[1]

[1] Cyber Security Centre, Department of Computer Science,
University of Oxford, Oxford, UK
jason.nurse@cs.ox.ac.uk
[2] Centre for Cyber Security and Information Systems,
Cranfield University, Cranfield, UK

Abstract. Over the last decade, the popularity of graphical passwords
has increased tremendously. They can now be found on various devices
and systems, including platforms such as the Windows 8 and Android
operating systems. In this paper, we focus on the PassPoints graphical-
password scheme and investigate the extent to which these passwords
might be predicted based on knowledge of the individual (e.g., their
age, gender, education, learning style). We are particularly interested in
understanding whether graphical passwords may suffer the same weaknesses as textual passwords, which are often strongly correlated with an
individual using memorable information (such as the individuals spouses,
pets, preferred sports teams, children, and so on). This paper also introduces a novel metric for graphical-password strength to provide feedback
to an individual without the requirement of knowing the image or having
password statistics a priori.

Keywords: Graphical passwords · Passpoints scheme · User characteristics · Usable security · Password-strength metric

1 Introduction

As cyberspace becomes more pervasive throughout society, being used by everything from commerce and banking to how we interact with others, the ability
to login securely to a computer or service has become critical to our ability to
reliably use and secure these services. This is particularly true as we increasingly
ask those who are not digital natives to engage with government and local services through the Internet. The most common form of authentication mechanism
is passwords, often called the 'keys' to our digital life. These are an important
technique for protecting both enterprises and individuals alike.

In theory, the textual passwords that are widely used today can provide a
good degree of security, but in practice they are often insufficient due to human
factors such as our inability to memorise a number of 'strong' passwords, typically deemed as a mixture of upper-case and lower-case letters, numbers and
punctuation [1]. Various studies have highlighted that users often use the same

© Springer International Publishing Switzerland 2015
T. Tryfonas and I. Askoxylakis (Eds.): HAS 2015, LNCS 9190, pp. 23–35, 2015.
DOI: 10.1007/978-3-319-20376-8_3

(or very similar), usually 'weak', passwords across multiple accounts [2]. This clearly does not permit the full security potential of textual passwords as an authentication mechanism and potentially poses a risk to the security of the system and the data it contains. Graphical passwords aim to exploit human cognitive processes in order to, arguably, provide a stronger authentication scheme which users find more memorable.

In this paper, we focus on one graphical password scheme, PassPoints, with the aim of investigating the extent to which these graphical passwords might be predictable. Rather than just focus on the choice of click location and image selection as in previous studies, our study considers the relationship between participants' PassPoints passwords and their individual characteristics, such as age, gender, ethnicity, education, risk appetite and learning style. Our work goes beyond current research articles which focus on heat-maps based on image clicks, to consider individuals' characteristics and the possibility of prediction in the same way that users tend to choose textual passwords based upon their spouses, pets, sports teams, children, and so on [3]. Any such relationship provides a good avenue of exploitation for an attacker.

This paper is structured as follows: in Sect. 2 we briefly reflect on graphical passwords, the PassPoints scheme, and related security concerns. Section 3 introduces our study and the user experiment conducted to investigate whether PassPoints passwords might be inferred based on a user's characteristics. Section 4 presents and discusses the key results of the study, before we conclude the paper in Sect. 5.

2   Background

Many graphical-password schemes have been proposed such as PassPoints, PassFaces and PassDoodle which claim to provide enhanced security, memorability and usability. The scheme examined in this paper is a cued-recall scheme called PassPoints which was developed by Wiedenbeck et al. [4]. A user creates a password by clicking (or touching on a touchscreen) an on-screen canvas a prescribed number of times (usually 5). The order and position of these clicks are recorded and establish the user's authentication token. To improve memorability, an image is used as the canvas. To authenticate, the user clicks the same points (within some tolerance) in the same order.

Much like textual passwords, the security of PassPoints passwords can be severely weakened by the predictable behaviour of users. For instance, a common issue with a PassPoints password is that users predominately choose the salient areas of an image as the password points. Golofit [5] showed that over 50 % of user clicks in their study were in areas encompassing only 3 % of the total image area. This demonstrates a huge reduction in the password size space and decreases the password's resilience to 'brute-force' attacks.

Dictionary attacks, where pre-computed lists of likely passwords are used to guess the password in question, have also been proven dangerously effective against PassPoints-style graphical passwords [6,7]. Van Oorschott and Thorpe [6] presented two dictionary-based attacks. The first was a 'human-seeded' attack, which uses experimental data to predict hot-spots of the images (areas with a large number of clicks). The second attack combined dictionaries with click-order patterns to create a first-order Markov model-based dictionary. This dictionary found 7–10 % of passwords within 3 guesses.

Dirik et al. [7] highlighted the importance of image choice on the vulnerability of a PassPoints password to a dictionary attacks. Using image processing techniques, they created a dictionary of the most likely click locations and showed an attack on two images. Their analysis of the two images demonstrated that images with a higher click-point entropy (i.e., an estimate of the number of different likely locations for each click point in the password) are much less vulnerable to dictionary attacks.

While there has been much more research in the area of PassPoints and hotspots generally, to our knowledge, there has been little emphasis on investigating the extent to which PassPoints might be predicted based on a user's characteristics. Considering the possible impact of such an ability, this is the focus of this paper's study.

3 Study and Approach

To examine the predictability of PassPoints, we designed an online user study. A website was developed and deployed that would allow participants to (1) register for the study, (2) to create a PassPoints password based one of three predefined images presented below, and (3) to complete three short surveys, one on their demographics, one on learning styles (motivated by work in [8]) and the last one on their risk appetite (adapted from research by Weber et al. [9]). After the creation of their PassPoints password, each participant was asked to recall the PassPoints on the site on three separate occasions: once immediately after they completed the surveys, the next time three days after the password was created, and the final time seven days after initial completion.

As mentioned in Sect. 2, choice of images for a PassPoints password is extremely important; in the real-world, individuals can actually select their preferred images. To control our experiment however, we decided to present individuals with three images and allow them to select the one to use for their password in the study. The images that were used are shown in Fig. 1, and were chosen because they have different themes (e.g., People[1], Landscape[2], and Animal[3]) that might appeal to different participants. Also, these images have multiple salient points. This was important to the study since images with few salient points are likely to result in similar passwords, making the images the limiting factor in creating similarities between passwords as opposed to the similar characteristics of the participants.

---

[1] 'Marton Mere Swimming Pool' by havenholidays (https://flic.kr/p/4ycWeu).

[2] 'One of the Glens, Scotland' by Chris Ford (https://flic.kr/p/8BumLU).

[3] 'Untitled' by PollyDot (http://pixabay.com/en/chameleon-lizard-multi-coloured-318649/).

Fig. 1. Images which participants used to create their PassPoints passwords. All images were available under the Creative Commons Licence, and sized 620px by 413px.

Recruitment for the survey was carried out using social-media networks and posters around the university campus. For their participation, individuals were entered into a prize-draw with a chance to win a voucher. In total, 236 individuals registered for the study but only 150 individuals completed it; completion was based on whether the participant returned to complete the next phase as necessary, not whether they were (un)able to recall their password.

4   Results and Discussion

Our presentation and discussion of results is structured into five main sections. Each section considers a separate part of the general question of whether passwords can be predicted.

4.1   Which Characteristics Do People Who Chose the Same Image have in Common?

This section questioned whether there were any characteristics of participants that might be used to predict which of the three images they chose to create their password. To answer this question, we used a Fisher's exact test [10] on each attribute to test whether there were any attributes that led participants to choose a certain image. Fisher's exact test is a common statistical method used to determine whether there are associations between two categorical variables.

For the test, the participant attributes (e.g., gender or education), were gathered from the questionnaire data that define a participant's overall characteristics. This has been done since a single characteristic can encompass multiple attributes: for example there are 10 different attributes for the learning styles characteristic. Moreover, all continuous variables such as age or mean of responses to the risk-appetite questionnaire had to be discretised into categories, since the test uses nominal data.

From this analysis, we found that no significant results were obtained when applying the Fisher's exact test to each of the attributes on the three images and therefore, conclude that the choice of image by the user is not dependent of any single attribute.

Next, a multiclass classifier was fit to the attributes associated with the participants. Since the input was a vector of attributes and the output was one of 3 categories, corresponding to the 3 images, a multiclass classifier was an appropriate technique. Backward stepwise regression was used to automatically choose which variables were most relevant to predicting a participant's image choice. At each 'step', the independent variable which has the least impact on how the model fits the data is removed. The remaining independent variables are those that have the most impact on fitting the model to the data.

To avoid overfitting in the model, the data was randomly shuffled and the first 80 % of participants in the shuffled set were used to select and train the model. This process was repeated 50 times. If there existed an accurate model to predict the image that the participant would choose, then the same set of attributes (or a very similar set) would be selected in each model.

The following attributes were in all 50 models: auditoryNorm; tactileNorm; visualNorm; ethical; gambling; health; investment; recreational; social. The auditoryNorm, tactileNorm and visualNorm attributes correspond to normalised scores for the learning styles questionnaire (i.e., auditory learners, tactical learners or visual learners respectively [8]) and ethical, gambling, health, investment, recreational and social correspond to the mean response to sets of questions on those topics in the risk-appetite questionnaire. Therefore a participant's responses to the ethical set of questions (for example) is possibly indicative of their choice of image in some way.

Although there were multiple attributes appearing in the model for each iteration, we found that the models always performed poorly when they were tested on the remaining 20 % of the data in terms of accuracy, precision and recall. The repeated presence of a number of attributes in the model for each iteration provides some suggestion that a multiclass classifier could potentially be used to predict which image the participant chooses. However, the small sample size does not allow for an accurate model to be produced. A larger sample would be needed to explore this claim.

4.2 What Characteristics Do People Who Can Recall Their Password have in Common?

Another interesting question is whether there are any characteristics that act as an indicator for password recall, that is, those participants that are able to reliable recall the PassPoints and the order in which they are required. By fitting a logistic regression model to the data, a set of attributes that can be used to predict whether a participant will pass or fail can be extracted. As in the previous section, the desired model was initially unknown and therefore backwards stepwise logistic regression was used. The ethical, investment and riskMeans attributes appeared in the model on more than 10 of the 50 iterations. riskMeans refers to the mean of the user's responses to all risk appetite questions on the Likert (5-level) scale, and so a higher riskMeans value corresponds to a risk-taker and a lower value to a risk-avoider. Although this is far from unanimous, it may suggest that these attributes do have an influence on a participants' ability to recall their password after 3 days.

In terms of the accuracy, precision and recall performance of the model, these seemed promising (0.728, 0.753 and 0.957 respectively) but upon closer inspection we found that there was clearly a fault with the classifiers; they are very good at predicting if a participant will recall but very poor at predicting if they will not. A classifier can achieve an artificially high level of accuracy if it predicts the most common output for all inputs and this is apparent here.

To determine whether there was a difference in where people who failed to recall their password after 3 days clicked and those that could recall clicked, a Fisher's exact test was used. This involved first discretising the images into 20 px by 18 px boxes and counting the number of clicks in each box separately for those who passed and those who failed.

From our analysis of the images, only with the Animal image was a significant result ($p < 0.05$) found; i.e., the participant's ability to recall their password is dependent on where they clicked. Using Fisher's method to combine the p-values on each of the images yields $p = 0.008$ which is also significant. Therefore the null hypothesis that the participant's ability to recall their password is independent of where they clicked is rejected. This may suggest that the users that fail to recall their PassPoints do so partly because of where they choose to click. There are many potential reasons for this, perhaps they tend or decide to choose points that are harder to remember, or fail to pick out locations that are easy to remember.

To visually compare the difference in where participants who passed and failed clicked, scatter plots were created with the points of participants who passed in green and those that failed in red. These are shown in Fig. 2.

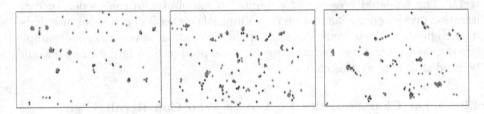

Fig. 2. Pass/Fail scatter plot for the People, Landscape and Animal images respectively; passes are shown in green and fails in red (Color figure online).

It is clear, particularly in the Landscape image in the middle of Fig. 2, that the participants who failed to recall their password after 3 days chose different points to those who can recall. Often the differences in the positions of clicks are small but this may have a large impact on whether the participant can recall the password later on.

A Fisher's exact test was used to determine whether there was a difference in where people who could recall after 3 days but not after 7, and people who could recall after 3 and 7 days clicked. When combined using Fisher's method, $p > 0.05$ suggesting there is not sufficient evidence to reject the null hypothesis that they are independent, suggesting that there is no difference between where participants who could recall after 3 and 7 days clicked and participants who could recall after 3 days but not after 7.

4.3 Where Do People Click and What Characteristics Do People Who Click in the Same Place Share?

To analyse where people clicked, saliency and heat maps where created for each image. Saliency maps provide a visual representation of how much each point of an input image stands out with respect to its neighbouring points. Heat maps show every participant's click-points as well as areas of the images that were popular amongst participants. Previous research [5,6] has shown that users tend to use salient points as part of their password; this was tested as well.

Fig. 3. Saliency map (left) and heat maps (middle and right) for the People image

Fig. 4. Saliency map (left) and heat maps (middle and right) for the Landscape image

Fig. 5. Saliency map (left) and heat maps (middle and right) for the Animal image

Figures 3, 4 and 5 show the saliency maps and heat maps of the People, Landscape and Animal images respectively. There are some similarities between the maps particularly for the People (Fig. 3) and Animal (Fig. 5) images, agreeing with the previous research that some users pick salient points as part of their passwords. On the People image, it can be seen that the children's faces in the top left corner are both salient and a popular region for participants to click, as well as the chameleon's eye, nose and feet in the Animal picture.

The saliency map and heat map for the Landscape image in Fig. 4 are noticeably different. The saliency map focuses on the rocks and stream in the bottom right quadrant of the image, whereas the heat map shows the most popular region as the central mountain. It is not surprising that the mountains were used by many participants as part of their password as they are memorable points; it is perhaps more surprising that the mountain peaks were not picked up as salient points in the saliency maps. This may be due to the Itti-Koch-Neibur algorithm [11] that was used to implement the saliency map. An alternative algorithm might have produced a slightly different saliency map that was more consistent with naively expected salient regions.

Fisher's exact tests were performed on 43 categorical attributes of the participants (obtained from the survey data) against the 'boxes' in which they click on the images (as defined using the same discretisation technique as in the previous section). Of the 43 tests, the only significant value at the $\alpha = 0.05$ level was for the GamblingCats2 attribute when combining the p-values for the three images using Fisher's method, $p = 0.003$. GamblingCats2 corresponds to a participant's responses to questions in the gambling section of the risk appetite survey and thus, their attitude towards gambling may in some way affect where they click.

Fisher exact tests were also done on combinations of attributes, such as being married and having children, and position of clicks; but all results were non-significant. In summary, many participants choose similar points, that are often salient, but the attributes that they possess, at least the ones in this study, seem to have little effect on the locations where they will click.

4.4 Do People Share the Same Pattern of Clicks (i.e., the Order) and if So Which Characteristics Do they Share?

Each participant's click pattern was analysed and classified (similar to Ref [6]) with patterns including: Left-to-right (LR), Right-to-left (RL), Top-to-Bottom (TB), Bottom-to-top (BT), Bottom-left-to-top-right (LR_BT), Clockwise (CW), Anticlockwise (ACW) and None (NONE). From our analysis, we found that in terms of frequency, None (i.e., no pattern) was the most common, followed by LR and TB, occurring 71, 37 and 23 times respectively.

A Fisher's exact test was used to test whether there were statistical differences in the proportion of two patterns; LR versus RL, TB versus BT, CW versus ACW and any pattern versus no pattern (NONE). The findings highlighted significant result for the LR versus RL patterns. This is not surprising, as the vast majority of participants were from countries where reading and writing is performed from left-to-right, so it is to be expected that this pattern would be transferred into other activities such as creating a graphical password.

To examine whether there is a difference in the pattern a participant adopts based on their attributes, a Fisher's test was performed on each attribute and pattern. Three combinations were significant at the $\alpha = 0.05$ level without correction for multiple comparisons: gender with BT pattern ($p = 0.016$), children with TB pattern ($p = 0.014$) and riskCats3 with BT pattern ($p = 0.021$).

The first of these significant results shows that men are more likely than women to use a BT pattern (proportions: $men = 0.16, women = 0.03$). The second shows that participants who do not have children are more likely to use a TB pattern than those with children (proportions: $withoutchildren = 0.19, withchildren = 0.00$). The final result shows that participants with a medium risk average are less likely to use a BT pattern than those with a high or low average and that those with a high average are most likely to use the BT pattern (proportions: $low = 0.20, medium = 0.08, high = 0.36$). It is difficult to qualify these results; it is conceivable that there would be a difference between genders but the other two results are harder to explain.

The final analysis looks at whether the image can influence the participant to create a password with a certain pattern. A Fisher's exact test on counts of the number of participants that used the pattern in question and those who did not against the 3 images, was used.

Table 1. Difference in click-order patterns on the three images

Pattern	p-value	Proportion of pattern on image		
		People	Landscape	Animal
LR	0.911	0.222	0.243	0.273
RL	0.229	0.056	0.143	0.000
BT	0.790	0.138	0.100	0.091
TB	0.028	0.250	0.171	0.045
LR_BT	0.028	0.083	0.000	0.068
RL_BT	0.724	0.028	0.014	0.000
LR_TB	0.545	0.111	0.086	0.045
RL_BT	1.000	0.000	0.000	0.000
CW	0.020	0.000	0.057	0.159
ACW	0.896	0.083	0.129	0.114
NONE	0.587	0.528	0.429	0.500

There were significant results for the TB, LR_BT and CW patterns. Table 1 suggests that the image does have an influence on the patterns in a participant's password. The TB pattern is an example of this with 25 % of participants of the People image having the pattern whereas less than 5 % of participants use it on the Animal image. Grouping the CW and ACW patterns, over 27 % of participants with the Animal image used a 'rotational' pattern whereas only 8 % and 19 % used them on the People and Landscape images respectively. The LR pattern is prevalent in each of the images in similar proportions; 22 %, 24 % and 27 % for the People, Landscape and Animal images respectively. This may be due to the majority of participants being nationals of countries with a left-to-right written language and this pattern creeps into other 'observational' activities.

4.5 Evaluating PassPoints Password Strength

Often when a user is creating an textual password on a website, they are provided with feedback on the strength of their password, usually on a scale from 'weak' to 'strong'. It might be useful if the same feedback were given for graphical passwords, especially as most users are unfamiliar with them and may not understand what is a 'strong' password. To do this, a set of rules were created for scoring passwords based on information taken from saliency maps and click-order pattens. This allows the method to be used on any image and does not require any click-point data for that particular image. These rules were developed after the survey was completed and used the data collected from it, hence participants were not shown the strength of their password during the study.

Using the saliency maps generated for the images, the nth percentile of saliency values for each image was calculated ($n = 90, 95, 97$). These values for n were chosen as Golofit [5] found that 50 % of clicks occurred in only 3 % of an image; the other two levels were included to increase the size of the salient region used, without making it too large. The regions of the saliency maps for each image were then filtered such that only the highest (100-n)% of saliency values remained; the set of these regions is denoted $\phi_{n,i}$ where $n = 90, 95, 97$ and $i = 0, 1, 2$; the image used.

The password weakness score was calculated as follows: (1) $\delta_{sal;n,i}$ = the number of the participant's click-points in the filtered saliency map $\phi_{n,i}$; (2) $\delta_{pat;i} = 1$ if the participant's password exhibits a pattern described in the previous section, else 0; $\delta_{LR;i} = 1$ if the participant's password exhibits a left-to-right pattern as described previously, else 0. The password weakness score, $\Delta_{n,i}$, is then $\Delta_{n,i} = \delta_{sal;n,i} + \delta_{pat;i} + \delta_{LR;i}, (0 \le \Delta_{n,i} \le 7)$ and therefore the lower the value of $\Delta_{n,i}$, the stronger the password. The left-to-right pattern was chosen as an indicator of password strength as over 20 % of passwords had this pattern for each of the three images hence if an attacker prioritises for this common pattern, the password could possibly be obtained faster.

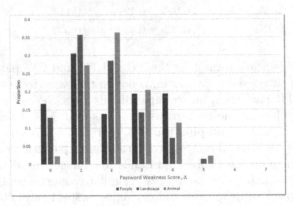

Fig. 6. Bar chart of proportions of password weakness score for each image

The password weakness score, $\Delta_{n,i}$, was calculated for each participant using $n = 90, 95, 97$ however $n = 90$ was chosen as the final percentile value for the saliency maps as it produced a larger distribution of password scores. Figure 6 shows the proportion of passwords with each password weakness score for each image. The Landscape and Animal images have approximately normal distributions of the proportions and the Landscape image has a positive skew. Therefore there are more 'stronger' passwords on the Landscape image than the Animal image. This may be because the Landscape image facilitates 'stronger' passwords than the Animal image or, by chance, the participants that chose the Landscape image pick 'stronger' passwords.

The People image has an approximately uniform distribution but with a larger value for $\Delta_{90,0} = 1$. Therefore, there are approximately equal proportions of each password weakness score for $0 \leq \Delta_{90,i} \leq 4$. This may suggest that the People image promotes more 'weaker' (although also more 'stronger') passwords than the other two images. This may present a weakness as a user that creates a 'weak' password on the People image, may have chosen a 'stronger' password on the Landscape or Animal image because they discourage 'weaker' passwords.

Fig. 7. Weaker passwords: People image password (left) with $\Delta_{90,0} = 4$; Landscape image password (right) with $\Delta_{90,1} = 5$

Fig. 8. Strong passwords: Landscape image password (left) with $\Delta_{90,1} = 0$; Animal image password (right) with $\Delta_{90,2} = 0$

Figure 7 shows passwords that got high ($\Delta_{90,i} \geq 4$) password weakness scores and Fig. 8 shows passwords that got low ($\Delta_{90,i} = 0$) scores. Both passwords in Fig. 7 however, could be considered 'weak' by an observer suggesting that the rules defined can identify a 'weak' password. However, the Animal image-based password in Fig. 8 is given a weakness score $\Delta_{90,2} = 0$ but does not appear to be as 'strong' as the score suggests, especially after comparison with the Landscape image to its left, which also has a score $\Delta_{90,1} = 0$.

It would seem that the only non-obvious point-choice is on the chameleon's body, between its legs. The reason for this anomaly is that calculating the weakness score relies heavily on the saliency maps (5 of the possible 7 points are awarded from the position of clicks), and the saliency map for the Animal image does not recognise the chameleon's nose as one of the most salient points, nor the front knee joint or either foot. However, each of these locations may be considered salient by a human observer. To enhance the accuracy of the password strength metric, the algorithm implementing the saliency maps for the images would have to be improved so that the most 'stand-out' features are identified.

5   Conclusions

In this paper, we have investigated the extent to which the passwords under the PassPoints graphical-password scheme could be predicted based on knowledge of the password setter. In general, the findings have provided little statistically significant evidence that it is consistently possible to do so. While this is encouraging, a larger sample size is needed to confirm these results. This study has confirmed that participants tend to choose similar locations for their password points, thereby creating hotspots, especially around salient points in an image.

There is also some evidence that the click-point pattern that a user's password exhibits is dependent on the image that they choose as their background, exposing a potential weakness in the scheme. However, this evidence was only available after processing the password data on the image, therefore an attacker would need prior knowledge of the image and have data about its usage in order to exploit this information. Finally, this paper has introduced a password strength metric that can provide feedback on a PassPoints password without the requirement of knowing the image or having password data for that image.

References

1. Nurse, J.R.C., Creese, S., Goldsmith, M., Lamberts, K.: Guidelines for usable cybersecurity: past and present. In: Proceedings of the 3rd Cyberspace Safety and Security Workshop at the Network and System Security Conference. IEEE (2011)
2. Das, A., Bonneau, J., Caesar, M., Borisov, N., Wang, X.: The tangled web of password reuse. In: Proceedings of the Network and Distributed System Security Symposium (2014)
3. Brown, A.S., Bracken, E., Zoccoli, S., Douglas, K.: Generating and remembering passwords. Appl. Cogn. Psychol. 18(6), 641–651 (2004)
4. Wiedenbeck, S., Waters, J., Birget, J.C., Brodskiy, A., Memon, N.: Authentication using graphical passwords: basic results. In: Proceedings of HCII (2005)
5. Gołofit, Krzysztof: Click Passwords Under Investigation. In: Biskup, Joachim, López, Javier (eds.) ESORICS 2007. LNCS, vol. 4734, pp. 343–358. Springer, Heidelberg (2007)
6. van Oorschot, P.C., Thorpe, J.: Exploiting predictability in click-based graphical passwords. J. Comput. Secur. 19(4), 669–702 (2011)

7. Dirik, A.E., Memon, N., Birget, J.C.: Modeling user choice in the passpoints graphical password scheme. In: Proceedings of the 3rd Symposium on Usable Privacy and Security, ACM, pp. 20–28 (2007)
8. Bixler, B.: Learning styles inventory. www.personal.psu.edu/bxb11/LSI/LSI.htm (n.d.). Accessed 5 Jan 2015
9. Weber, E.U., Blais, A.R., Betz, N.E.: A domain-specific risk-attitude scale: measuring risk perceptions and risk behaviors. J. Behav. Decis. Making **15**(4), 263–290 (2002)
10. Field, A.: Discovering Statistics Using SPSS, 3rd edn. Sage Publications, Los Angeles (2009)
11. Itti, L., Koch, C., Niebur, E.: A model of saliency-based visual attention for rapid scene analysis. IEEE TPAMI **20**(11), 1254–1259 (1998)

Principles of Persuasion in Social Engineering and Their Use in Phishing

Ana Ferreira[1,2]($\boxtimes$), Lynne Coventry[3], and Gabriele Lenzini[1]

[1] Interdisciplinary Centre for Security Reliability and Trust - University of Luxembourg, Luxembourg, Luxembourg
ana.ferreira@uni.lu
[2] Institute of Cognitive Science and Assessment - University of Luxembourg, Luxembourg, Luxembourg
[3] Psychology and Communication Technology, Northumbria University, Newcastle upon Tyne, UK

Abstract. Research on marketing and deception has identified principles of persuasion that influence human decisions. However, this research is scattered: it focuses on specific contexts and produces different taxonomies. In regard to frauds and scams, three taxonomies are often referred in the literature: Cialdini's principles of influence, Gragg's psychological triggers, and Stajano *et al.* principles of scams. It is unclear whether these relate but clearly some of their principles seem overlapping whereas others look complementary. We propose a way to connect those principles and present a merged and reviewed list for them. Then, we analyse various phishing emails and show that our principles are used therein in specific combinations. Our analysis of phishing is based on peer review and further research is needed to make it automatic, but the approach we follow, together with principles we propose, can be applied more consistently and more comprehensively than the original taxonomies.

Keywords: Social engineering · Principles of persuasion · Phishing emails

1 Introduction

Social engineering consists of persuasion techniques to manipulate people into performing actions or divulging confidential information [1]. How persuasion works is well known in other domains such as marketing where, for instance, Cialdini [2] identifies six principles which are used to influence buyers to purchase goods they may not even like or need to buy. However, less known are the principles of deception usually applied by social engineers to steal confidential information. Uebelacker *et al.* [3] assume that Cialdini's principles work in social engineering as well, but argue that some principles work better depending on the victim's personality traits. Akbhar [4] analyses 207 phishing emails according to what Cialdini's

G. Lenzini—This research is supported by FNR Luxembourg, project I2R-APS-PFN-11STAS.

© Springer International Publishing Switzerland 2015
T. Tryfonas and I. Askoxylakis (Eds.): HAS 2015, LNCS 9190, pp. 36–47, 2015.
DOI: 10.1007/978-3-319-20376-8_4

principles are used therein. However, Cialdini is not the only author to suggest principles of persuasion that can be used in social engineering. Gragg, from reading the literature on persuasion and social-engineering, extracts seven *psychological triggers* [5] which, he claims, make social engineering successful; Stajano *et al.*, from investigating the behaviour of street hustlers, draw seven *principles of scams* and show how these can be used to breach security [6]. All these principles and triggers may be related. Indeed, Gragg's triggers seem to work in some of Cialdini's principles [7]. Still, is unclear what basic principles constitute a clear and complete basis for social-engineering and whether what makes social-engineering persuasive should be found only among Cialdini's, Gragg's and Stajano *et al.* work, or somewhere else.

Contribution. This paper proposes a reviewed list of principles of persuasion that works in social engineering. The list is obtained by comparing and merging Cialdini's, Gragg's and Stajano *et al.*'s principles. In addition, this paper investigates what combination of principles is most commonly used in phishing, a research that can help identify effective and directed countermeasures against this widespread and insidious type of socio-technical attacks.

2 Motivation

Most research about protecting users from phishing emails is about methods to check manually or automatically for keywords, grammatical inconsistencies, typos, or information misplacement [8–10]. All these methods can help the user, but they have not yet changed the fact that people are still falling for phishing emails [10]. Why is phishing so effective? One reason is that phishing e-mails use more or less explicitly deception and persuasion strategies. Some of such strategies, adopted in areas such as marketing, were extensively studied by Cialdini, who grouped them into six basic categories which he called *the six basic principles of influence* [2]. These principles — even if we do not recognize them as such — are used ubiquitously in human interactions to influence and to persuade people to do, act, and think the way one wants. Influence is not only used maliciously but it can also be used ethically to nudge people into a positive behaving; however, surprisingly, it is less effective for this positive purpose unless it is strategically twisted to work [11].

Persuading people and influencing their decisions seems to be not only a matter of human interactions but also of contextual variables. Successful influence is increasingly governed, rather than by cognition, by the context and by the psychological environment where information is presented [11]. In understanding this, social engineers are ahead: they know that to influence and persuade more efficiently they have not only to inform people but also make small shifts in their approach to link their message to deep human motivations. If we were able to identify both the principles of influence and those small shifts, we would be able to understand why these principles make social engineering so persuasive and successful. Moreover, if a small set of agreed principles is developed, studying why human interactions are susceptible and how people react when those principles are in place can be done more orderly and systematically.

3   Methods

We study how Cialdini's [2], Gragg's [5], and Stajano *et al.*'s [6] principles relate one another and from it we produce a reviewed list of more uniform and more general principles of persuasion in social engineering. To relate principles we define three relations, indicated as $=$, $\subset$, and $\sim$. A ssuming that Pa and Pb are two distinct principles, we write that:

$Pa = Pb$, if Pa's and Pb's descriptions use the same keywords or expressions with equivalent meaning and for all scenarios that we can describe where Pa is *successful*, also Pb is, and vice versa. For a principle, to be successful in a scenario means that the application of the principle is what makes the deception work in that scenario. If $Pa = Pb$, they can be used interchangeably.

$Pa \subset Pb$, if for all scenarios where Pa is successful then Pb is also successful, but not vice versa. There are scenarios where Pb is successful but where Pa does not work, so Pa is more specific than Pb.

$Pa \sim Pb = (Pa \cap Pb)$ AND $(Pa \not\subset Pb)$ AND $(Pa \not\subset Pb)$, if Pa and Pb cannot be used interchangeably because there are scenarios where Pa is successful but Pb is not, and vice versa. Then Pa is used to express concepts that partially overlap with principle Pb, but is not a refinement of it.

We use these relations to relate Cialdini's, Gragg's and Stajano *et al.*'s principles, as well as Gragg's and Stajano *et al.*'s principles. Once the relationships are established, we are able to either maintain or combine existing principles and propose a list, which we call *Principles of Persuasion in Social Engineering*. Specifically, we add a new principle for each quotient class defined by the equivalence relation $=$; we have a new principle for each maximal element in the order relation $\subset$. Clusters which are mixed and that include $Pa \sim Pb$ need to be further inspected: we either split Pa from Pb and have two principles or merge Pa and Pb into a new one.

4   Principles of Persuasion in Social Engineering

To easily refer to Cialdini's, Gragg's and Stajano *et al.* principles, we tag each of the principles with the initial letter of the principle author — C for Cialdini, G for Gragg, and S for Stajano *et al.*— and a number, from 1 to 6 or 7, respectively; thus, we have the following IDs: $C1, \ldots, C6$, for Cialdini's principles, $G1, \ldots, G7$ for Gragg's, and $S1, \ldots, S7$ for Stajano, as in the table at the beginning of the next page.

Relating Cialdini's, Gragg and Stajano *et al.'s* Principles. Due to space constraints we can only sketch our findings. We report in Fig. 1 only a few of the obtained relations which shows that (upper part) *Authority* ($C1$ and $G1$) = *Social compliance* ($S1$), which means that the three principles are interchangeable. We can then state that they actually constitute one *Principle of Persuasion in Social Engineering* that we call *Authority* (AUTH).

Figure 1 also shows that (bottom part) *Diffusion responsibility* ($G2$) $\subset$ *Herd* ($S2$) $\subset$ *Social proof* ($C2$), which means that *Social proof* ($C2$) is the most

	C	G	S
1	Authority	Authority	Social compliance
2	Social proof	Diffusion responsibility	Herd
3	Linking & Similarity	Deceptive relationship	Deception
4	Commitment & Consistency	Integrity & Consistency	Dishonesty
5	Scarcity	Overloading	Time
6	Reciprocation	Reciprocation	Need & Greed
7	-	Strong Affect	Distraction

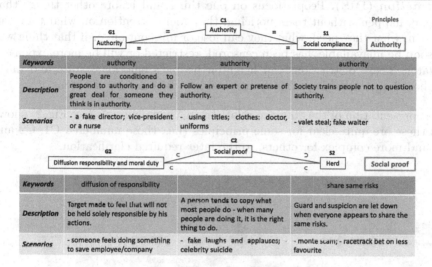

Fig. 1. Example of two relations between the principles.

general including the other two. Since, these three principles also form an independent cluster, we can then state another, more comprehensive, *Principle of Persuasion in Social Engineering*, which we call *Social Poof* (SP). Figure 1 also lists the keywords that characterize the principle (row "Keywords"), quotes the description given by the principle's authors (row "Description") and reports (row "Scenario") the scenarios they gave in describing that principle.

All the relations are represented as a Venn diagram reported in Fig. 2 as well as the proposed five *Principles of Persuasion in Social Engineering*, namely:

Authority (**AUTH**). Society trains people not to question authority so they are conditioned to respond to it. People usually follow an expert or pretense of authority and do a great deal for someone they think is an authority.

Social Poof (**SP**). People tend to mimic what the majority of people do or seem to be doing. People let their guard and suspicion down when everyone else appears to share the same behaviours and risks. In this way, they will not be held solely responsible for their actions.

Liking, Similarity & Deception (**LSD**). People prefer to abide to whom (they think) they know or like, or to whom they are similar to or familiar with, as well as attracted to.

Commitment, Reciprocation & Consistency (**CRC**). People feel more confident in their decision once they commit (publically) to a specific action and need to follow it through until the end. This is true whether in the workplace, or in a situation when their action is illegal. People have tendency to believe what others say and need, and they want to appear consistent in what they do, for instance, when they owe a favour. There is an automatic response of repaying a favour.

Distraction (**DIS**). People focus on one thing and ignore other things that may happen without them noticing; they focus attention on what they can gain, what they need, what they can lose or miss out on, or if that thing will soon be unavailable, has been censored, restricted or will be more expensive later. These distractions can heighten people's emotional state and make them forget other logical facts to consider when making decisions.

The representation of the obtained relations in Venn diagrams (see Fig. 2) shows that these are quite clear for some principles (i.e., those numbered C1, C2 and C3) and more complex for others, so the later required clarification.

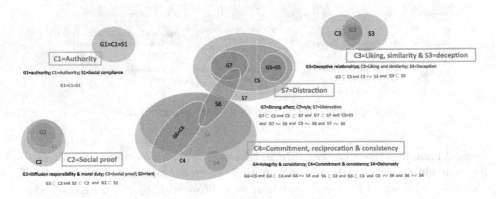

Fig. 2. The Venn diagram showing all relationships among the considered principles.

To assert that *Dishonesty* (*S*4) ⊂ *Commitment & Consistency* (*C*4), as shown in the diagram, we needed to exclude that *Dishonesty* (*S*4) ~ *Commitment & Consistency* (*C*4). Going back to the description and examples of both principles, it is possible to confirm that *Dishonesty* (*S*4) ⊂ *Commitment & Consistency* (*C*4) since the *Dishonesty* (*S*4) principle mainly refers to the fact that people are committed by an illegal action and feel *induced/forced* to finish that transaction and be consistent with the first illegal action they took. This is exactly what the principle of commitment and consistency refers to, but for all types of actions, not only those which include illegal content.

To verify if *Reciprocation* (*C*6) ~ *Commitment & Consistency* (*C*4) or *Reciprocation* (*C*6) ⊂ *Commitment & Consistency* (*C*4) we analyse again the description and scenarios regarding reciprocation by both Gragg *et al.* and Cialdini and conclude that they all fit in Cialdini's *Commitment & Consistency* (*C*4) principle. *Reciprocation* (*C*6) is described as the returning of a favour that someone has made. The receiver feels obliged (committed) to return that favour at some point in time. These examples fit with *Commitment & Consistency* (*C*4) principle as it describes that someone asks something of us, but also the opposite, when we do something that makes us commit and be consistent with the consequences of that previous action. So we believe that, in fact, Cialdini's principle *Commitment & Consistency* (*C*4) integrates the principle *Reciprocation* (*C*6), reducing these to a single principle. However, in this specific case, we leave reciprocation as part of the final principle's name because it is easier to understand its inclusion since it was always identified as a separate principle in other research works.

To clarify if *Scarcity* (*C*5) ⊂ *Distraction* (*S*7), we acknowledge that the *Scarcity* (*C*5) principle is described by people focusing on what they can potentially lose, or miss out on, like limited availability of time, money, goods, etc. The situations are described in a way that focuses people's attention on the lack of those specific things, ignoring all other facts. This is exactly what the principle of *Distraction* (*S*7) described by Stajano *et al.* is about. Making people focus attention on one specific thing while other things go unnoticed and not included in the reasoning.

One final clarification relates to the *Need & Greed* (*S*6) principle which Stajano *et al.* defines as including most cases under the *Dishonesty* (*S*4) principle, so *Need & Greed* (*S*6) ~ *Dishonesty* (*S*4). But what about the other cases inside *Need & Greed* (*S*6), are they all included in the principle of *Distraction* (*S*7) or not? In fact, according to the *Need & Greed* (*S*6) description, people focus attention on what they can gain and forget the other rational facts. This is part of the *Distraction* (*S*7) principle, so the other cases of *Need & Greed* (*S*6) are all included in *Distraction* (*S*7).

5   Persuasion in Phishing Emails

We validated our Principles of Persuasion in Social Engineering by verifying which of them are used in phishing e-mails.

Data Collection and Phishing Elements. We have collected examples of phishing emails from our own mailboxes and from real examples found on the Internet. The inclusion criteria was phishing emails only (we have ignored *SPAM* emails) and, when possible, completed with images, logos and colors, since these can make a difference in the success rate [10]. This type of analysis had to be done manually by a human — there is no tool to automatically associate phishing email elements together with text, images and colors to principles of persuasion — so it was not possible to have a bigger sample at this point.

We organized the collected emails according to their goal, namely (1) *Data Theft*: banking, financial, helpdesk or account deactivation emails asking for confidential or personal information (these emails include attacks such as Man-In-The-Middle, session hijacking, and impersonation); (2) *Malware*: emails with attachments or emails with fake websites such as pharmaceuticals (these websites or attachments can contain Trojan horses, virus, system reconfiguration and malicious software); and (3) *Fraud*: emails offering large sums of money and prizes (this email includes attacks such as the 419 or the Nigerian scams). We have analysed a sample of 52 different phishing emails: 30 from the *Data Theft* category, 15 from *Malware* and 7 from *Fraud*.

There are patterns that recur in phishing emails (e.g., text, images, and colors). We have identified and transcribed them to the table in Fig. 3.

For each element of the phishing email we counted the *Principle(s) of persuasion in Social Engineering* that are used therein. If the same principle(s) appears in consecutive email elements, we counted it(them) as appearing only once.

We have only used phishing emails written in English. Considering other languages is out of scope in this work, but the analysis and comparison between different languages raises interesting questions if some differences are to be found, related to that language/culture.

	Principles of Social Engineering				
	AUTH	SP	LSD	CRC	DIS
Identification (eg. name, email, address, telephone, and similar)	if it is a company, bank or government related		it gives false detailed information to look real		
Details of the service (eg. invoice numbers, requested service details, payment details, and similar)			it gives false detailed information to look real		
Visual cues and restrictions (eg. colors, font, capital letters, big images, exclamation and interrogation marks, time restriction, urgent, must be done, and similar)					focus the attention on these elements
Logos	if it is a company, bank or government related		false but similar images to look real		focus the attention on the elements of the logo
Description of something that concerns the user such as: user's actions, requests, inactivity, and similar	if users actions do not agree with policies and agreements stipulated by the company on the email		it gives false information about what the user did or did not to look real	if it implies that the user must perform an action in return	
as well as information about the user such as: known contacts in CC, referring to friends, colleagues and family, and similar		gives information about how others feel and think about the author of the email	it gives false detailed information regarding the email author to look familiar and real		
Elements that ask the user to perform an action such as: click here, update the form, confirm the form, your tickets are in the attachment, confirm personal details, and similar	press or advise the user to perform an action			ask the user to perform an action in return of what was stated before	focus the attention on specific actions, documents and links present in the email
Actions performed by others such as customers complaints, or others expect your input		other people performed actions that affect the user	it gives false detailed information regarding others to look real		
Elements in the first person stating "I am this and that"			it gives false detailed information regarding the email author to look familiar and real		
Elements in the first person describing behaviour around others		gives information about how others feel and think about the author of the email	it gives false detailed information regarding the email author to look familiar and real		
Asking commitment from the user: "Can I trust you?", "Can you do this for me?", and similar				ask the user to perform an action in return of what was stated before	focus the attention on specific actions or requests
Referring to other elements outside the ambit of the email to look more reliable such as: "You need to have acrobat Reader to read the atached file", and similar			false but similar information about existing products to look real	using existing real information about other companies is consistent to what the user normally sees in real sites	

Pattern elements found within the phishing emails

Fig. 3. Common elements extracted from phishing emails.

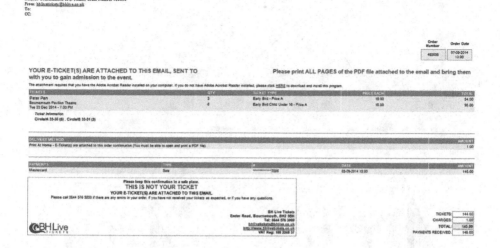

Fig. 4. Peter Pan malware phishing email.

Analysis. We provide an example (e.g., the "Peter Pan phishing email" in Fig. 4) of how we have analysed the phishing emails. As mentioned, we identified the various elements present in the phishing email and counted the *Principle(s) of Persuasion in Social Engineering* therein (see Fig. 5).

The final results are reported in Fig. 6. The graph on the top shows the number of elements that express a specific principle while the graph at the bottom depicts the number of elements that integrate two principles, for the three categories of analysed phishing emails.

	AUTH	SP	LSD	CRC	DIS	Other factors
bhlivetickets@bhlive.co.uk	1		1			color; smaller font
Confirmation of e-tickets order number 480638; Order Date 07-09-2014 13:00			1			smaller font
YOUR E-TICKET(S) ARE ATTACHED TO THIS EMAIL, SENT TO	1		1		1	color; capital letters; bold face
Please print ALL PAGES of the PDF file attached to the email and bring them with you to gain admission to the event	1			1	1	color; capital letters; bold face
The attachment requires that you have Acrobat Reader installed on your computer. If you do not have Adobe Acrobat Reader installed, please click HERE to download and install this program.			1	1		smaller font
A table with clear description of the type of tickets, quantity, seating information, place with date and time of the show and prices per item			1			smaller font
A table with clear description of the delivery method- Print at Home-E-Ticket(s) are attached to this order confirmation (you must be able to open and print a PDF file)	1		1	1		smaller font
A table with clear description of the payment including credit card last numbers			1			smaller font
Please keep this confirmation in a safe place	1			1		smaller font; in a rectangle
THIS IS NOT YOUR TICKET **YOUR E-TICKET(S) ARE ATTACHED TO THIS EMAIL**	1			1	1	bigger font; in a rectangle
Please call number if there are any errors in your order, if you have not received your tickets as expected, or if you have any questions.			1	1		smaller font
BHLiveTICKETS Logo	1		1		1	color; bigger font
BHLiveTICKETS full contact information including: address, telephone number, email, website and VAT Reg. number	1		1			smaller font; bold face; color

Fig. 5. Analysis of the elements of a phishing email and the principles of persuasion in social engineer those elements express.

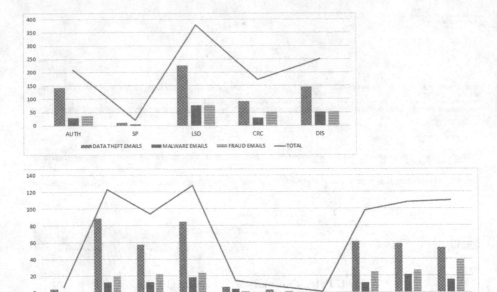

Fig. 6. Number of phishing email elements that express the principles of persuasion in social engineering (authority-AUTH; Social proof-SP; Liking, similarity and deception-LSC; Commitment, reciprocity and consistency-CRC; Distraction-DIS).

Succinctly, the results show that the most common principle of social engineering is the principle of *Liking, Similarity & Deception* (LSD), followed by the principle of *Distraction* (DIS). The next third most common principles are *Authority* (AUTH) for data theft emails and malware, and *Commitment, Reciprocation & Consistency* (CRC) for malware and fraud emails.

When the principles are applied together, the most common pair is AUTH-LSD, followed by AUTH-DIS for data theft emails. For malware emails, the most common pair of principles is LSD-DIS followed by AUTH-DIS, while for the fraud category, the most common pair of principles is CRC-DIS followed by LSD-DIS. Also, some elements of phishing emails include three principles of social engineering and the most common from our analysis are AUTH-CRC-DIS, followed by AUTH-LSD-DIS for both data theft and malware phishing emails. For the fraud category, the three most present principles are AUTH-CRC-DIS, followed by LSD-CRC-DIS.

6   Discussion

Our research shows that previous work had many overlaps in terms of principles and techniques of persuasion and deception in different contexts. We believe in the importance of further study into how these principles relate and are used in social engineering. We believe it will prove useful to have a common list and description of such principles and their identification in social engineering attacks, such as phishing emails. We proposed such a list in this paper which can be reused by other researchers as a common approach for future work. We tested this list by identifying its five principles of persuasion in social engineering in various phishing emails. It was clear that those principles are commonly present in the majority of the elements that constitute phishing emails. However, more analyses need to be performed to verify whether the identified principles are not exclusive (there may be others not yet identified), and also if they are not only present in phishing emails but also in other types of social engineering attacks.

Not surprisingly, the principle of social engineering that is mostly used in all types of phishing emails is the principle of *Liking, Similarity & Deception* (LSD). From all five principles, this is the one that relates more to the way humans interact socially when they try to connect with others by finding characteristics that are more agreeable and similar to them. Humans tend to believe in what other humans do or say, unless they suspect something is really wrong or that some behaviour is completely unexpected.

The second most common used principle is *Distraction* (DIS) we think because it complements the principle of *Liking, Similarity & Deception* (LSD). The human brain is adept at working with images and visual cues have some advantage to any type of verbal expression. However, distraction factors can also be very effective in verbal expression (e.g., open attached file) and so, adding elements that are at the same time familiar, known, and close to what users think is real, together with some extra elements that complement and confirm those characteristics will, it seems, be very effective in the practice of phishing emails. These results confirm the fact that principles of persuasion are not alone. Interfaces, their content and the way they are designed and how the information is presented also have a large impact on users' decisions so more research is required into the effectiveness of persuasive design in the domain of security as well as in the detection and analysis of phishing emails.

Although the principles of *Liking, Similarity & Deception* (LSD) and of *Distraction* (DIS) alone can be important to detect problems in emails we believe that the way they are used together makes them more successful. For instance, when both the principle of *Liking, Similarity & Deception* (LSD) and the principle of *Distraction* (DIS) are paired with the principle of *Authority* (AUTH), which is the majority of times for data theft emails, we can see that this is not a coincidence. Humans respond to authority and requests to make things right, so the principles of *Liking, Similarity & Deception* (LSD) and of *Distraction* (DIS) work better when they contain some authority elements as well. This is also true for malware emails but there are some differences in fraud emails. For fraud emails it seems that the principle of *Authority* (AUTH) is not as common. Instead, the principle of *Commitment, Reciprocation & Consistency* (CRC) is used more because this type of email tends to be more personal and more informal so they replace the sense of authority with the next best possible principle that makes users commit and be consistent with what they are asked. In this case, the emails are very personal, are written in the first person in what appears to be someone who knows the user and seems to have some type of relation within him/her. Asking favours from the user in these circumstances appears more normal. These results show that principles of social engineering are commonly used together so further research is needed to understand in more detail what pairs are used and with what goals. Again, we believe that it will be harder to automatically identify the combination of all these principles so we need new tools that can help us do this.

It is however surprising that the principle of *Social Poof* (SP) is the least used with very low counts. It would be expected, mainly in fraud emails, that these strategies of social awareness, belonging to a group and sharing the same risks could be exploited more frequently. Although we are social beings, when making our decisions, we probably focus more on ourselves, our experiences and how we see the world. We think social engineers target their attacks to appeal to the individual and how important and relevant his/her own actions are to the matter at hand.

While this work identifies which combinations of principles are applied to phishing emails further work is required to explore whether any combinations are more effective in persuading people to act than others. The analysis did not have access to the success rate of the different types of combinations. Now that we have the principles, the next step would be to analyse the success rates of the different combinations.

Other Social Engineering Elements in Phishing. In addition to our principles, phishing emails use more tricks to deceive people and convince them of the authenticity of the email's content. These include, for instance, the repetition of information; the use of bigger and smaller font; the use of bold face; the use of different text colors; or the use of tables. These elements are all about the way information is displayed as specific visual cues can, in fact, influence users' decisions (e.g., Gestalt principles [12, 13]), and are very effective when used in phishing emails. These can probably generate other principles besides the ones studied here and so need to be analysed in future work.

Limitations. There was no previous work that could guide us in the analysis and merging of existing research on principles of persuasion, so we defined a methodology that could, as objectively as possible, focus on text and description provided for each principle. Also, the analysis performed on the phishing emails could not be automated. Although there is software to identify phishing emails, there is no software to verify which principles of social engineering, the elements present in those emails, express. This also explains the small sample since it would not be possible to perform an exhaustive analysis, with a bigger sample, in the available time.

7   Conclusion

By studying the relations among existing principles of influence (Cialdini), psychological triggers (Gragg) and principles of scams (Stajano *et al.*), we propose a synthesized list of principles of persuasion that constitute a basis for principles of social-engineering. We found that our principles are largely used in phishing emails where they mainly appear in specific pairs or triplets. Although the principles of persuasion in social engineering obtained in this paper are not usually used alone (e.g., together with other visual cues and interface dynamics), we consider that the proposed list can help researchers to better recognise and understand how, in what situations and for what purpose those principles are used. With this knowledge, we intend to study and design countermeasures which can be better equipped to target and minimize the success of specific types of social engineering attacks.

References

1. Mitnick, K., Simon, W.: The Art of Deception. Wiley Publishing Inc., New York (2002)
2. Cialdini, R.B.: Influence: The Psychology of Persuasion (Revision Edition). Harper Business, Dunmore (2007)
3. Quiel, S., Uebelacker, S.: The social engineering personality framework. In: Proceedings of 4th Workshop on Socio-Technical Aspects in Security and Trust (STAST 2014), Vienna, Austria, 18 July 2014, pp. 24–30 (2014)
4. Akbar, N.: Analysing persuasion principles in phishing emails. Ph.D. dissertation, Master Thesis, University of Twente, The Netherlands, October 2014
5. Gragg, D.: A multi-level defense against social engineering. Technical Report, SANS Institute - InfoSec Reading Room (2003)
6. Stajano, F., Wilson, P.: Understanding scam victims: seven principles for systems security. Commun. ACM **54**(3), 70–75 (2011)
7. Scheeres, J.W., Mills, R.F., Grimaila, M.R.: Establishing the human firewall: reducing an individual's engineering attacks. In: Proceedings of the 3rd International Conference on Information Warfare and Security (ICIW), Omaha, USA, 24–25 April 2008
8. Fette, I., Sadeh, N., Tomasic, A.: Learning to detect phishing emails. In: Proceedings of the 16th Interenational Conference on World Wide Web (WWW 2007), Banff, AB, Canada, 8–12 May 2008, pp. 649–656. ACM (2007)
9. Kumaraguru, P., Sheng, S., Acquisti, A., Cranor, L.F., Hong, J.: Teaching Johnny not to fall for phish. ACM Trans. Internet Technol. **10**(2), 1–31 (2010)
10. Blythe, M., Petrie, H., Clark, J.A.: F for fake: four studies on how we fall for phish. In: Proceedings of the SIGCHI Conference on Human Factors in Computing Systems (CHI 2011), Vancouver, BC, Canada, 7–12 May 2011, pp. 3469–3478. ACM (2011)
11. Martin, S.J., Goldstein, N., Cialdini, R.B.: The Small BIG: Small Changes that Spark Big Influence. Grand Central Publishing, New York (2014)
12. Arnheim, R.: The gestalt theory of expression. Psychol. Rev. **56**, 156–171 (1945)
13. Geremek, A., Greenlee, M., Magnussen, S.: Perception Beyond Gestalt: Progress in Vision Research. Psychology Press, New York (2013)

Chimera CAPTCHA: A Proposal of CAPTCHA Using Strangeness in Merged Objects

Masahiro Fujita, Yuki Ikeya, Junya Kani,
and Masakatsu Nishigaki[(⊠)]

Graduate School of Informatics, Shizuoka University, Hamamatsu, Japan
nisigaki@inf.shizuoka.ac.jp

Abstract. In this paper, we propose "Chimera CAPTCHA" that requests users to select only a *chimera object*, merged from two 3D objects, in a question image, which consists of some 3D objects and the chimera object. The Chimera CAPTCHA is easy for humans to solve because chimera objects, whose appearance are different from ones judged by common sense, cause a feeling of strangeness. Usability survey suggests that the correct response rate is 90.5 % and the average response time is about 5.7 s. In addition, the CAPTCHA system is able to generate questions countlessly and easily by using 3DCG technologies. We also describe threats to its security.

Keywords: CAPTCHA · A feeling of strangeness · Automatic generation · 3DCG

1 Introduction

With the expansion of Web services, denial of service (DoS) attacks by malicious automated programs (malware) are becoming a serious problem. The Turing test plays an important role in discriminating humans from malicious automated programs and the Completely Automated Public Turing test to tell Computers and Humans Apart (CAPTCHA) [1] system developed by Carnegie Mellon University has been widely used.

Today most Web sites adopt text recognition based CAPTCHA (Fig. 1) or image-based CAPTCHAs such as Asirra (Fig. 2) [2] and YUNiTi's CAPTCHA (Fig. 3) [3] to protect themselves from malware. Many researchers, however, have recently pointed out that the malware with Optical Character Reader (OCR) and/or machine learning could solve those CAPTCHAs [4–6]. In order to take measures against these malware, CAPTCHAs using a human higher recognition ability are needed [7–9]. However, it is not such a straightforward process. This is because CAPTCHAs contain a contradiction: Web servers (computers) should be able to automatically generate the CAPTCHA questions that malware (computers) cannot answer.

Actually, the authors have also proposed the CAPTCHAs using "feeling that something is wrong", one of human higher recognition abilities [8, 9]. When a human faces an unusual situation different from a situation judged by common sense, the scene

© Springer International Publishing Switzerland 2015
T. Tryfonas and I. Askoxylakis (Eds.): HAS 2015, LNCS 9190, pp. 48–58, 2015.
DOI: 10.1007/978-3-319-20376-8_5

Type the characters you see in the picture below.

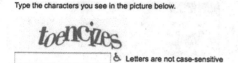

           ✎ Letters are not case-sensitive

Fig. 1. CAPTCHA used by google

Please select all the cat photos:

Score Test

Fig. 2. Asirra

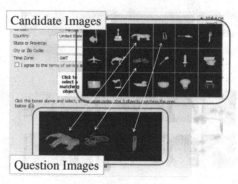

Fig. 3. YUNiTi's CAPTCHA

causes a feeling of strangeness such as unnaturalness or uncanniness. The more we gain experience of something, the better this ability becomes. On the other hand, since even state-of-the-art malware have no common sense, it is expected that malware cannot imitate this ability. Therefore by using "a feeling of strangeness" questions that humans can solve, but malware cannot, might be realized. However, in literatures [8, 9], there remains a problem of difficultly in generating questions automatically.

This paper proposes a new image-based CAPTCHA, called "Chimera CAPTCHA", which satisfies two requirements: (i) using a human higher recognition ability for improving attack tolerance and (ii) easily generating questions automatically. This CAPTCHA consists of some 3D objects and a *chimera object* generated by merging two 3D objects. If a user clicks only chimera objects in a question image, the system identifies the user as a human. It is easy for humans to identify chimera objects, because each chimera object, whose appearance is different from ones judged by common sense, causes a feeling of strangeness.

The organization of this paper is as follows. Section 2 describes related works using "feeling that something is wrong". Section 3 introduces Chimera CAPTCHA and Sect. 4 shows basic experimental results of the CAPTCHA. Section 5 discusses the effectiveness of the CAPTCHA. Finally, Sect. 6 presents our conclusions.

2 Related Works

So far, there have been several CAPTCHAs using "feeling that something is wrong". One is Avatar CAPTCHA [10], which requests users to identify avatar faces from a set of 12 images consisting of human and avatar faces (Fig. 4). According to the phenomenon known as "The Uncanny Valley [11]", humans feel uncanniness for avatar faces. That means it is easy for humans to select only avatar faces from the image set. However the authors of [12] show that using modern object recognition and machine learning, malware can also solve Avatar CAPTCHAs as often as humans can.

Fig. 4. Avatar CAPTCHA

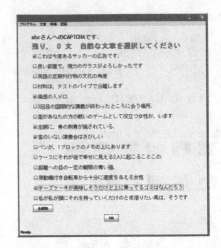

Fig. 5. SS-CAPTCHA

Fig. 6. Four-panel cartoon CAPTCHA (Source: From left: 1st image: 1st panel of four-panel cartoon on p.25 of bibliography [13]; 2nd image: 4th panel; 3rd image: 3rd panel; 4th image: 2nd panel of the cartoon).

Yamamoto et al. proposed SS-CAPTCHA [8], which requests users to distinguish natural sentences by humans from machine-translated sentences (Fig. 5). Although current machine-translation techniques have progressed a great deal, it is impossible even for state-of-the-art machine translators to automatically generate perfect natural sentences that will not make a human feel as though something is wrong. That means it is too difficult for malware to identify whether a sentence is natural or not. However, there has not been a framework for self-production of a sufficient number of natural sentences.

Another interesting CAPTCHA is Four-panel Cartoon CAPTCHA [9], which requests users to arrange the four-panel cartoon rearranged randomly in the correct order (Fig. 6). The four-panel cartoon rearranged randomly causes a feel of strangeness. Then it is easy for humans to arrange the panels in the correct order, since humans can understand the meaning of the pictures and utterances in each panel and hidden humor in the cartoons. Four-panel Cartoon CAPTCHA needs a large volume of four-panel cartoons for generating questions. However, as well as SS-CAPTCHA, Four-panel cartoon CAPTCHA also has the difficulty in self-producing a large number of four-panel cartoons.

3   Chimera CAPTCHA

3.1   Concept

Humans have commonsense through their daily life. "Feeling that something is wrong" is caused by an unusual situation different from a situation judged by common sense. So far computers with common sense have not been realized. Thus feeling that something is wrong must be one of human higher recognition abilities that malware cannot imitate. CAPTCHA systems are able to identify a user, whether a human or malware, by asking a user to discriminate "objects judged by common sense" from "objects different from ones acknowledged by common sense".

However, representing "objects judged by common sense" and "objects different from ones acknowledged by common sense" have been inherently very difficult. To solve this problem, this paper uses 3D models. As services using 3D models have been increasing rapidly in recent years, an indefinite number of 3D models would appear in the future. Most 3D models are generated by modeling objects from the real world. In it, humans are supposed to have seen "the objects that are subject to modeling" at least once. It is expected that humans recognize the objects as a part of common sense. Therefore 3D models function essentially identically to common sense, and 3D models can be used as objects judged by common sense.

Unusual objects which are different from objects judged by common sense are generated by deforming 3D objects. Although there are various ways of deforming 3D objects, this paper uses "merging". In detail, the objects about which humans feel strangeness (described as "chimera objects") are generated by merging two objects picked from a 3D model database. For example, when a dog merges with a chair, a chimera object is generated as seen in Fig. 7.

Question images of Chimera CAPTCHA consist of a chimera object and some ordinary 3D objects. Our CAPTCHA requests users to click the chimera object in the question image. Humans can click it easily, because chimera objects, whose appearance is different from ones judged by common sense, cause a feeling of strangeness. An

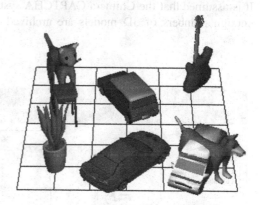

Fig. 7. A chimera object merged from a dog and a chair

Fig. 8. An example question image of Chimera CAPTCHA

example image of Chimera CAPTCHA in the case of one chimera among seven objects is shown in Fig. 8. In the lower right of Fig. 8, there is a chimera object; a dog and an ambulance are merged.

3.2   Automatic Generation of Chimera Objects and CAPTCHA Questions

As Fig. 9 depicts, chimera objects can be generated by putting two 3D objects on the same point. The detail is as follows:

Step 1. The system picks two 3D objects (called "object A" and "object B" respectively)
Step 2. The system puts object A on an arbitrary point P on the three-dimensional plane α
Step 3. The system puts object B on the point P

When the two objects, A and B, are projected onto the two-dimensional plane, the objects merge with each other and humans can recognize them as a chimera object. Therefore our method makes it possible to generate chimera objects easily. In addition, as Sect. 3.1 describes, it is believed that an indefinite number of 3D models would appear in the future. Therefore our method makes it possible to generate chimera objects countlessly.

Once we can assemble chimera objects, the rest is simple. The question images of Chimera CAPTCHA can be produced just by putting a chimera object and a specified number of ordinary objects on a three-dimensional plane. This is how Chimera CAPTCHA has solved the problem of difficulty in generating questions automatically. This is a significant advantage over SS-CAPTCHA and Four-panel cartoon CAPTCHA.

3.3   Automation Procedure

It is assumed that the Chimera CAPTCHA system has a 3D model database, in which enough numbers of 3D models are archived. Authentication procedure of Chimera

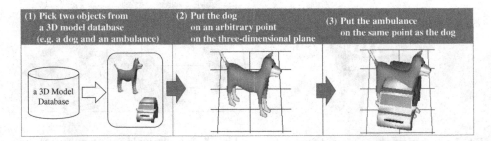

Fig. 9. How to generate a chimera object automatically

CAPTCHA is as follows, where N is the number of 3D objects in an image of Chimera CAPTCHA, or security parameter.

Step 1. The system picks up N objects at random from the 3D model database

Step 2. The system transforms each 3D object picked in Step 1 individually and arbitrarily by Affine Transformation

Step 3. The system puts each object transformed in Step 2 on the three-dimensional plane α

Step 4. The system picks up one more 3D object at random from the 3D model database

Step 5. The system transforms the object picked in Step 4 arbitrarily by Affine Transformation

Step 6. The system selects an object at random out of the N objects put in Step 3

Step 7. The system puts the object transformed in Step 5 on the same position as the object selected in Step 6

Step 8. The system projects the one chimera object and the N-1 ordinary objects, placed on the three-dimensional plane α, onto a two-dimensional plane for the question image

Step 9. The system shows a user (Web page visitor) the question image generated in Step 8

Step 10. The user clicks a part of the question image that feels strange, or the two objects merged with each other

Step 11. If the clicked position on the question image is correct, the user is identified as a human, and if the position is incorrect, the user is identified as malware

In Chimera CAPTCHA, it is difficult for malware, which don't have common sense, to identify the chimera object in the question image. On the other hand, our system knows the position of the chimera object in Step 7. Because this knowledge forms a trapdoor, our system (Web server) can automatically generate the challenges that malware cannot answer, and then the system can determine whether the user (Web page visitor) clicked the correct object or not.

4 A Basic Experiment

We conducted basic experiments to evaluate the authentication rate of the proposed method. After the experiment, we conducted a survey on the subjects for usability.

4.1 Experimental Method

The subjects included seven volunteers, subjects S1 S7, who are all college students majoring in computer security at Shizuoka University. The number of 3D objects in an image (security parameter N) was 24, where the image contained 23 ordinary 3D objects and a chimera object. First each subject could solve as many tutorial challenges as they want. After that, each subject had to solve three challenges. We only evaluated the three trials. The 3D objects used in the tutorials were different from the ones used in the three challenges. Due to an insufficient number of 3D models we had collected, there might have been some objects used more than once in three question images. We instructed the subjects to click on a "merged object (chimera object)" in each question image. For each challenge, we recorded success or failure, the response time and the click position. After completing all of the CAPTCHA challenges, we had the subjects respond to the following questionnaire. Questions 1, 3, 5 were answered on a 5-point scale.

Question 1. Is it easy solving the CAPTCHA? (Easy): Yes (5) – No (1)
Question 2. If you choose 1 or 2 in Question 1, please write why you think that it is not easy
Question 3. Is it user-friendly? (User-friendly): Yes (5) – No (1)
Question 4. If you choose 1 or 2 in Question 3, please write why you think that it is not user-friendly
Question 5. Is it pleasant? (Pleasant): Yes (5) – No (1)
Question 6. If you choose 4 or 5 in Question 5, please write why you think that it is pleasant
Question 7. How many challenges would you be able to consecutively solve? Also, please write why you think that
Question 8. Which would you choose: text recognition-based CAPTCHA or Chimera CAPTCHA in a real Web service? Also, please write your reason

4.2 Correct Response

The experimental results are shown in Table 1, which summarizes the correct response rate and the average response time for each subject. From Table 1, the correct response rate of Chimera CAPTCHA is 90.5 % on average (a total of 21 times, 19 successes, 2 failures).

From Table 1, the average response time per challenge is 5.7 s; the shortest time is 2.7 s, and the maximum time is 12.2 s. The expected response time for text recognition-based CAPTCHAs is around 10 s at the most [14]. From these data, it can be concluded that the proposed CAPTCHA can be solved in a shorter time compared to text recognition-based CAPTCHA.

We analyzed why the two subjects failed. First is a mistake because of overlooking a chimera object. We showed the subject S3 the image he had failed, to which he replied, "I overlooked the answer (chimera) object". Second, in the image the subject S7 had failed, the two objects consisted of the chimera object were almost the same

Table 1. The experimental results for each subject

	Subject							
	S1	S2	S3	S4	S5	S6	S7	Average
Correct response rate	3/3	3/3	2/3	3/3	3/3	3/3	2/3	90.5% (19/21)
Average response time [sec]	3.4	4.6	12.2	5.2	4.5	2.7	7.5	5.7

color and almost the same size. For this reason, it seems to be difficult to find the chimera object in the question image. There is room for improvement in generating chimera objects.

4.3   Usability

The results of the survey are shown in Table 2.

In Question 1, most subjects answered 4 (5 if easy), and the average value was 4.0. The subjects who answered difficult (1 or 2) were asked to write the reason in Question 2. The subject S2 selected 2 and stated "There are some difficult images to find a chimera object". As discussed in Sect. 4.2, this evaluation of S2 might be caused by presenting a difficult question image to solve.

In Question 3, most subjects answered 5 (5 if user-friendly), and the average value was 4.0. In Question 4, no subject answered user-hostile (1 or 2).

In Question 5, most subjects answered 4 (5 if pleasant), and the average value was 3.6. The subjects who answered pleasant (4 or 5) wrote a reason in Question 6. The subject S1 stated, "It is interesting because it likes Quiz" and S3 stated, "It is interesting because it likes Game". The main proposal of Chimera CAPTCHA is to improve attack tolerance and generate questions automatically and easily. However, the result in Question 5 and 6 suggested that Chimera CAPTCHA improved the entertainment value as well. In general, solving CAPTCHA is a chore task for normal users. By improving the entertainment value with our proposed CAPTCHA, users could enjoy solving CAPTCHA. Thus, Chimera CAPTCHA has the potential of contributing to improve usability.

In Question 7, all subjects answered "three challenges". The reasons are as follows: "Challenging three times is comfortable for me. If the number of challenges is greater than three, I may feel chore"; "I solved three challenges, but I required a little effort". The number of challenges (three challenges) may be a good number for users. However, the evaluation may also depend strongly on the experimental condition.

In Question 8, six subjects chose Chimera CAPTCHA, while only one subject chose the text recognition based CAPTCHA. The main reasons for choosing Chimera can be broadly divided into two. First is reducing the response time. For example, the

Table 2. Result of survey

| | Subject | | | | | | | Average | |
	S1	S2	S3	S4	S5	S6	S7		
Q1	5	4	4	4	5	4	2	4.0	
Q3	3	4	5	4	5	4	3	4.0	
Q5	4	4	4	2	2	5	4	3.6	
Q7	3	3	3	3	3	3	3	3.0	
Q8	C	C	C	C	T	C	C	-	

Q1. Easy: Yes (5) – No (1)
Q3. User-friendly: Yes (5) – No (1)
Q5. Pleasant: Yes (5) – No (1)
Q7. How many questions
Q8. Which would you choose?
(T: Text recognition-based CAPTCHA
C: proposed CAPTCHA)

subject S1 stated "This CAPTCHA takes only a short time for response" and S4 stated "This is a fuss-free CAPTCHA". Second is user-friendliness, for example, the subject S2 stated "It is easy because it takes only one click" and S4 stated "It can be done only with the mouse". However, as many Web services uses the text recognition-based CAPTCHA, users are accustomed to solve the text recognition-based CAPTCHA. The subject S5 who chose the text recognition-based CAPTCHA stated "I feel Chimera CAPTCHA is as easy as the text recognition-based CAPTCHA, so I chose the latter".

5 Discussion

5.1 Attack Tolerance

Finding Chimera Objects. A typical attack against the Chimera CAPTCHA it can be considered is that malware extract all objects from a question image and find a chimera object. Namely, malware may try to find "a merged object" in an image. However, for the following two reasons, our CAPTCHA has the tolerance against this attack.

First, there will be occluded objects in a question image. For example, in the upper left of Fig. 8, a cat is occluded by a chair. Humans have spatial reasoning ability. Using the ability, humans could distinguish between "merged objects" and "occluded objects". In contrast, computers do not so far have an adequate level of this ability, so malware may not distinguish between them.

Second, there are many merged objects in the real world. For example, the object shown in Fig. 10 consists of grass and a pot. These objects are "usual" merged objects, in contrast with "unusual" merged objects (chimera objects) that our system generates. Even if the image analysis technologies are advanced and the computers can recognize whether an object is a merged object or not, malware could still not recognize whether the merged object is a usual merged object or unusual one.

Brute Force Attack. In Chimera CAPTCHA, there remains the problem of low tolerance against a brute-force attack. If malware extract all objects from a question image, they can solve the CAPTCHA with a probability of one in N, where N is the sum number of 3D objects used in an image (one chimera object and N-1 ordinary objects).

Increasing the security parameter N or number of questions is the simple way to improve tolerance against brute-force attack. At the same time, however, increasing users' mental load may reduce usability. In addition, if our CAPTCHA system requests users to correct an M number of questions, it is concerned that the answer response rate will be the M power of the rate per question. An ingenuity for reducing response time and increasing correct response rate is needed, such as being easier to find chimera objects.

5.2 Automatic Generation

As shown in Sect. 2, the existing CAPTCHAs using the ability of feeling strangeness have the difficultly in generating questions automatically. On the other hand, as shown

Fig. 10. A usual merged object; grass and a pot are merged

in Sect. 3.2, the Chimera CAPTCHA system makes it possible to generate questions automatically and easily by using 3DCG technologies. In detail, archiving enough 3D models in a 3D database and changing used objects or the parameters such as the scale of object, the system can generate question images countlessly.

6 Conclusion

In this paper, we proposed Chimera CAPTCHA, which is an image-based CAPTCHA focusing on the advanced human-cognitive-processing ability of feeling that something is wrong. The main feature of the CAPTCHA is that computers (Web server) can automatically and easily generate questions that are difficult to solve by computers (malware). While developing a prototype system of the CAPTCHA, we have carried out basic experiments. Seven human subjects solved the challenges of our CAPTCHA in the experiment. The results showed that the correct response rate is 90.5 % and the average response time per one challenge is 5.7 s. Our survey of the results of usability is satisfactory.

It is expected that solving Chimera CAPTCHA is a very difficult task for computers (malware). However, the attack techniques of malware vary and Chimera CAPTCHA's resistance to decipherment is not proven theoretically. We will conduct studies to determine whether our CAPTCHA is truly resistant to malware attacks.

References

1. The Official CAPTCHA Site. http://www.captcha.net
2. Elson, J., Douceur, J., Howela, J., Saul, J.: Asirra: a CAPTCHA that exploit interest aligned manual image categorization. In: 2007 ACM CSS, pp. 366–374 (2007)
3. YUNiTi.com. http://www.yuniti.com/
4. PWNtcha-Captcha Decoder. http://caca.zoy.org/wiki/PWNtcha
5. Yan, J., Ahmad, A.S.E.: Breaking visual CAPTCHAs with naïve pattern recognition algorithms. In: 2007 Computer Security Applications Conference, pp. 279–291 (2007)
6. TechnoBabble Pro: How they'll break the 3D CAPTCHA. http://technobabblepro.blogspot.jp/2009/04/how-theyll-break-3d-captcha.html

7. Chellapilla, K., Larson, K., Simard, P., Czerwinski, M.: Computers beat humans at single character recognition in reading-based human interaction. In: The 2nd Conference on Email and Anti-Spam (2005)
8. Yamamoto, T., Tygar, J.D., Nishigaki, M.: CAPTCHA using strangeness in machine translation. In: The 24th International Conference on Advanced Information Networking and Applications, pp. 430–437 (2010)
9. Yamamoto, T., Suzuki, T., Nishigaki, M.: A proposal of four-panel cartoon CAPTCHA. In: The 25th International Conference on Advanced Information Networking and Applications, pp. 159–166 (2011)
10. D'Souza, D., Polina, P.C., Yampolskiy, R.V.: Avatar CAPTCHA: telling computers and humans apart via face classification. In: 2012 IEEE International Conference on Electro/ Information Technology, pp. 1–6 (2012)
11. Mori, M., MacDorman, K.F., Kageki, N.: The uncanny valley. IEEE Robot. Autom. Mag. **19**(2), 98–100 (2012)
12. Korayem, M., Moharmed, A.A., Crandall, D., Yampolskiy, R.V.: Solving avatar CAPTCHAs automatically. In: 2012 International Conference on Advance Machine Learning Technologies and Applications, pp. 102–110 (2012)
13. Ueda, M.: Shin Kobo-chan 8, Houbunsha (2006). (in Japanese)
14. Kani, J., Suzuki, T., Uehara, A., Yamamoto, T., Nishigaki, M.: Four-panel cartoon CAPTCHA. IPSJ J. **54**(9), 2232–2243 (2013). (in Japanese)

Effects of Password Permutation on Subjective Usability Across Platforms

Kristen K. Greene[✉]

National Institute of Standards and Technology, 100 Bureau Dr, Gaithersburg, MD, USA
kristen.greene@nist.gov

Abstract. The current work examines the effects of password permutation on subjective usability across platforms, using system-generated passwords that adhere to the password requirements found in higher-security enterprise environments. This research builds upon a series of studies at the National Institute of Standards and Technology by testing a previously proposed idea of password permutation: grouping like character classes together in order to improve password usability. Password permutation improves mobile device entry by reducing the number of keystrokes required to enter numbers and symbols. Across platforms (smartphone, tablet, and desktop computer) participants rated the longer (length 14) permuted passwords as easier to type than the shorter (length 10) non-permuted passwords. This demonstrates that the composition and structure of a password are important; people are sensitive to factors beyond simple password length. By combining qualitative and quantitative research, we will ultimately arrive at a more complete understanding of how password construction impacts usability.

Keywords: Passwords · Authentication · Mobile text entry · Typing · Touchscreens · Smartphones · Tablets · Password permutation · Chunking · Usable security

1 Introduction

Although text-based passwords are widely viewed as a problematic mechanism for user authentication [1], they are nonetheless a core element of our current digital society. Large-scale efforts, such as the United States National Strategy for Trusted Identities in Cyberspace (NSTIC), are underway to replace passwords [2]. Yet widespread replacement will take time, and legacy systems may continue to require text-based passwords. It is therefore important that we continue to research and understand passwords in order to improve them, both in terms of their security and usability.

Balancing the security and usability of passwords can be difficult, as the characteristics of password policies intended to make them more secure, such as increasing password length, using numbers, symbols, and mixing uppercase and lowercase letters [3] largely make them less usable. In addition to password requirements and policies [4, 5], there are many other aspects of passwords to study.

One can examine passwords along different phases of their lifecycle [6], from their original generation to later retrieval. One can consider the security and usability of

© Springer International Publishing Switzerland 2015
T. Tryfonas and I. Askoxylakis (Eds.): HAS 2015, LNCS 9190, pp. 59–70, 2015.
DOI: 10.1007/978-3-319-20376-8_6

passwords from different sources, i.e., system-generated [7, 8] versus user-generated passwords [9]. One can evaluate passwords on different platforms, from traditional desktop QWERTY keyboards [10] to smaller mobile touchscreen keyboards [11–13]. Finally, one can examine passwords from the perspective of employees at large organizations [14–16] or web users in general [17].

Of the numerous research possibilities, the current work examines subjective password usability across multiple platforms—desktop, smartphone, and tablet—using system-generated passwords that adhere to the strict password requirements commonly found in higher-security enterprise environments. As the current research builds upon a series of studies at the United States National Institute of Standards and Technology (NIST), this paper begins with a detailed review of the three studies motivating the current work [10].

2   Background

2.1   Usability of System-Generated Passwords on Desktop Keyboards

The first of several NIST studies to examine the usability of system-generated passwords was a desktop study in which participants had to memorize a series of ten different passwords and type them repeatedly [10]. This study was informative in examining the fundamentals of desktop password typing, contributing much-needed baseline data on human performance with complex, system-generated passwords, thereby addressing a critical gap in the literature. Although there was already much research on general memory [18] and memory for passwords [19–22], as well as literature on transcription typing [23] and skilled typing [24–26], those studies did not use stimuli directly analogous to the more complex, system-generated passwords of interest. In particular, prior research did not include stimuli containing the variety of symbols, numbers, and mixed case letters required for passwords in higher-security, enterprise environments.

In [10], system generated passwords were used in order to control for effects of different levels of password meaningfulness. In that study, the researchers set out only to examine effects of increasing password length, wanting to hold other factors—such as password meaning—constant. As is often the case in experimental research, it was necessary to trade external validity for the internal control required to address a specific research question: what are the effects of increasing password length on human behavior with complex passwords? In that study, participants received ten system-generated passwords one at a time. Passwords ranged in length from six to fourteen characters long. For each password, participants progressed through a series of three screens— Practice, Verify, and Entry. Participants were allowed to practice at will on the Practice Screen, then had to enter the target password correctly one time on the Verification Screen, and finally had to type the password ten times on the Entry Screen. After completing this three-phase sequence (i.e., practice, verification, entry) for each of the ten passwords, participants received a surprise recall test.

Not surprisingly, the longer a password was, the more time it took for participants to complete the tasks, with the slope of the timing line increasing around the eight-character password length. Of greater interest was the most prevalent error category:

incorrect capitalization, or shifting, errors. In addition to capital letters, many symbols also require a shift action (e.g., "%" requires pressing the shift and "5" key). Since many enterprises have password policies explicitly requiring the use of uppercase letters and symbols, the high frequency of shifting errors was particularly important.

2.2 Usability of System-Generated Passwords on Mobile Devices

The second of several NIST studies examining the usability of system-generated passwords was a mobile study [11] replicating the aforementioned desktop study [10] with smartphones and tablets. In [11], the research goal was to investigate effects of changing platforms—desktop versus mobile—on human performance using complex passwords. Therefore, the same experimental design and stimuli from [10] were used in the mobile devices study [11].

In [11], device type greatly impacted both the frequency and nature of errors. A total of 2100 errors were made with the smartphone (iPhone 4S[1]) versus only 1289 errors with the tablet (iPad 3). For the smartphone, that corresponds to over four times the number of per-participant group errors as seen in the desktop study, and for the tablet, two and a half times the errors. The percentage of adjacent key errors was significantly higher for the smartphone than the tablet. This makes sense given the smaller target sizes for smartphone keys than tablet keys, especially in the portrait orientation used in [11].

The effects of mobile device constraints on password entry go beyond smaller key sizes; the nature of onscreen keyboards places significantly more demands on working memory for users. Each time a user has to change keyboards to access numbers or symbols, it is akin to a miniature task interruption, incurring interruption costs beyond the additional keystrokes required to change onscreen keyboards. In [11], passwords requiring a number of onscreen keyboard changes, or screen depth changes, had disproportionately large effects across multiple dependent measures (e.g., entry times, error rates). The authors suggested that porting password requirements directly from desktop to mobile platforms may be unwise without consideration of device constraints, such as those imposed by onscreen keyboards.

2.3 Usability and Security of Permuted Passwords on Mobile Devices

The third NIST study of particular relevance to the current work examined the usability and security of permuted versions of the system-generated passwords used in [10, 11]. Given the significant difficulties participants faced in [11] due to the high number of onscreen keyboard changes required for entering complex passwords, it was suggested that password permutation should improve usability for such system-generated passwords [7, 27]. In [7, 27] the authors permuted the stimuli from prior studies [10, 11] by grouping characters into four categories: uppercase letters, lowercase letters, numbers,

---

[1] Disclaimer: Any mention of commercial products or reference to commercial organizations is for information only; it does not imply recommendation or endorsement by the National Institute of Standards and Technology nor does it imply that the products mentioned are necessarily the best available for the purpose.

and symbols. The categories were arranged in that sequence (i.e., uppercase letters first, followed by lowercase, then numbers, and finally symbols) in order to minimize the number of onscreen keyboard changes required. The number of keystrokes saved (i.e., the efficiency gained) via permutation was not necessarily dependent on the length of the original password, but rather on the number of onscreen keyboard changes required. This in turn depended on the frequency and placement of numbers and symbols in the original password, since those are the character categories that necessitate switching back and forth between onscreen keyboards.

Although reducing the number of keyboard changes required improves password usability on mobile devices, introducing the predictable structure of uppercase, lowercase, numbers, and symbols negatively impacts security. In [7, 27] the authors measured the resulting security loss in a series of Monte Carlo simulations evaluating the entropy loss per password length category, as well as determining the number of lowercase letters needed to obtain equivalent levels of security for permuted versus non-permuted system-generated passwords. In [7, 27] also evaluate the length that would be required for an all-lowercase password to have equivalent security as a complex, mixed-character password.

In [7, 27] password permutation reduced the number of keystrokes required on mobile devices, thereby improving at least one facet of usability: efficiency. Although it is possible to count keystrokes (efficiency) without behavioral data, in order to measure improvements in effectiveness (error rates) and satisfaction (subjective usability) for permuted system-generated passwords, human data are needed. The current paper focuses on subjective usability, addressing this gap by testing a subset of the previously described original and permuted passwords across multiple platforms.

3 Experiment

3.1 Method

The current cross-platform[2] study builds upon the previously described NIST studies [7, 10, 11, 27] in several ways. One significant difference was its inclusion of all three devices (desktop computer, smartphone, and tablet) within-subjects. To help address questions raised in [10] that touch-typing ability (the ability to type without looking at the keys) may have contributed to performance differences between participant groups, the current study included a baseline typing test utilizing ten phrases from the MacKenzie and Soukoreff 500-phrase corpus for text entry research [28]. Given the large variability in participant practice repetitions in [10, 11], the current study also implemented forced practice with feedback. To help address questions of whether passwords did not make it out of participants' short term memory in [10, 11], the current study increased the number of practice repetitions required, reduced the number of passwords used, and notified participants about the final recall test (prior studies used a

---

[2] A platform is a unified architecture composed of common hardware and software elements that may manifest in various specific devices. For example, the iPhone and iPad are two devices sharing the iOS platform.

surprise recall test). By significantly increasing the number of repetitions required while simultaneously reducing the number of passwords used, we hoped that passwords would transition from short term memory to motor memory. Finally, the current study also had participants rate their experience typing versus memorizing the passwords, and incorporated a longer debriefing session where participants were queried explicitly about their strategies; these qualitative additions to the prior experimental protocol were most important. Whereas prior work [10, 11] was focused primarily on quantitative data, the current paper is focused on qualitative data, specifically on people's perceptions of permuted versus "jumbled" system generated passwords.

Participants. Participants were recruited from the larger Washington, D.C. metropolitan area. They were paid $75 for their participation in the one and a half hour study session. In order to be eligible for the study, participants had to be at least eighteen years old, have normal or corrected-to-normal vision, own an iOS device, and could not have participated in any of the prior NIST password typing studies [10, 11]. Participants were fairly diverse in terms of age, education, ethnicity, income, and occupation. A total of 83 people participated. Forty-nine were female and 34 were male. Age ranged from 18 to 63 years, with a mean age of 36.5 years ($SD = 11.9$ years). All participants were familiar with onscreen and desktop keyboards. Self-reported keyboard usage frequencies are shown in Table 1.

Table 1. Self-reported frequency of use for onscreen and desktop keyboards

Frequency of use	N Onscreen	N Desktop
Multiple times a day	80	75
Once a day	2	5
Weekly	1	2
Monthly	0	1

Of the original 83 participants, five were pilot participants, and 10 did not complete the entire experiment; only data from the remaining 68 participants were included in the following analyses.

Design. Participants used three devices: traditional desktop computer (PC running Windows 7 Enterprise), smartphone (iPhone, iOS 7.1), and tablet (iPad, iOS 7.1). Device presentation order was counterbalanced. In cases where participants could not complete the tasks with all three devices due to time constraints, they used the desktop computer and one of the mobile devices (either a smartphone or a tablet). Password set was manipulated between subjects: half of all participants received Password Set 1, and the remaining half of participants received Password Set 2. Of the 68 participants included in the following analyses, 37 used password Set 1, and 31 used password Set 2 (details in Materials section). Both password sets contained two passwords: an unmodified password originally used in prior research [10, 11] and a permuted version of a password from prior research. Participants used the same two passwords on all three devices.

Password presentation order was randomized using the randomization function in the data collection software (details in Procedure section).

Materials. Passwords in the current study were a carefully selected subset of the ten system-generated passwords used in the original NIST studies [10, 11]. Both password sets in the current study contained a previously used, non-permuted password of length 10, and a different, permuted password of length 14. Password Set 1 consisted of **q80<U/C2mv** and **Rmofpaf2207#)^**, where q80<U/C2mv was an original length 10 password used in prior studies and Rmofpaf2207#)^ was the permuted version of a previously used length 14 password. Password Set 2 consisted of **p4d46*3TxY** and **QMifnh455230_$**, where p4d46*3TxY was an original length 10 password used in prior studies and QMifnh455230_$ was the permuted version of a previously used length 14 password. For ease of exposition, these passwords may be referred to henceforth as "q80," "Rmof," "p4d4," and "QMif."

The length 14 passwords were selected because they were by far the most difficult passwords from prior work; they took longer to learn and enter and were more error prone as well [10, 11]. They were particularly problematic on mobile devices due to the number of screen depth changes (navigating back and forth between different onscreen keyboards) they required. Therefore, they should benefit most from password permutation.

The length 10 passwords were selected for several reasons. Informal comments from participants in prior studies indicated that "q80" and "p4d4" seemed "easier" and "more memorable." People also previously commented that they were "breaking the password up at the symbols." A desire to explore these qualitative observations more rigorously was one reason for the password selection in the current study. Perhaps more importantly, although the length 10 "q80" and "p4d4" passwords are obviously shorter than the length 14 "Rmof" and "QMif" passwords, they require almost exactly the same number of keystrokes, or taps on a mobile device, to enter as the longer, permuted length 14 passwords. In Set 1 "q80" and "Rmof" both take 19 taps to enter on a mobile (iOS) device. In Set 2 "p4d4" takes 18 taps and "QMif" takes 19 taps. Password sets and tap counts are shown in Table 2. Although only the bold passwords in Table 2 were used in the current study, their permuted or original counterparts are also shown for the sake of comparison.

Procedure. As described in [10, 11] for each password participants saw a series of three screens (Fig. 1) corresponding to practice, verify, and enter phases. Participants completed 20 practice rounds, three verify rounds, and 10 enter rounds for each password. Phase, password number, and round number were always shown at the top of the screen. After completing this sequence for both passwords, participants completed a recall test. During the practice phase, the target password was present, typed text was not masked, and participants received feedback if the password they entered was incorrect. During the verify phase, the target password was no longer present (although participants could go back to the practice screen to see the password), typed text was not masked, and participants again received feedback if the password they entered was incorrect. During the enter phase, the target password was not present, typed text was masked, and no feedback was given; this ensured that one of the three phases was directly analogous to [10, 11]. During practice and verify phases, participants had to type the password correctly in order to move on to the next round. During the enter phase, the password did not have to be correct in order to move on to the next round. During the recall test, typed text was masked, and no feedback was given.

Table 2. Password sets and tap counts

	Original Password	Permuted Password	Length	Taps: Original, Permuted	Screen Depth Changes: Original, Permuted	Taps Saved via Permut -ation
Set 1 (in bold)	q80<U/C2mv	UCqmv802</	10	19, 15	7, 3	4
	m#o)fp^2aRf207	**Rmofpaf2207#)^**	14	24, 19	10, 4	6
Set 2 (in bold)	p4d46*3TxY	TYpdx4463*	10	18, 14	6, 2	4
	4i_55fQ$2Mnh30	**QMifnh455230_$**	14	25, 19	9, 3	6

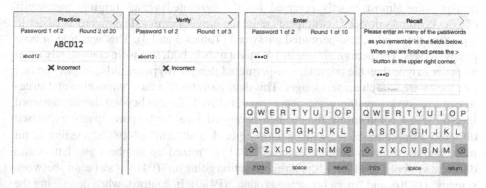

Fig. 1. Example screenshots of practice, verify, enter, and recall screens for iPhone

After participants completed both passwords on the first device, they completed a short questionnaire with four Likert items asking them to rate their experience memorizing and typing each password. Response options ranged from 1 ("Very Difficult") to 5 ("Very Easy"). The moderator then asked them several verbal questions about their typing and memorization strategies for each password. If participants stated they were breaking the password into smaller pieces, they were asked to draw vertical lines between the characters in the password to indicate their break points. These qualitative questions—in particular the typing ratings—were an extremely important part of the current study, and are the focus of the current analyses.

The above procedure was repeated for each of the remaining two devices. After participants completed both passwords on all three devices, they answered a final set of questions about their overall password preferences and strategies. Customized data collection software[3] displayed the passwords on all three devices for the current study. The research software captures a time stamped log of all keyboard actions and button presses while users interact with the data collection application. Although the current study only used two sets of passwords, the software supports any number of sets of passwords via a customizable input file. One can also customize the contents of the ten baseline typing phrases via the input file. Number of practice, verify, and enter rounds required are also customizable via the software settings screen.

3.2 Results: Typing Difficulty Ratings

To simplify tabular presentation of the data, the Likert response options were collapsed from five to three categories. "Difficult" and "Very Difficult" options were collapsed into a single "Difficult" category, while "Easy" and "Very Easy" options were collapsed into an "Easy" category. "Neutral" options were left as they were.

The typing difficulty ratings were extremely telling, especially when examined in conjunction with participants' debriefing comments. The patterns of typing difficulty ratings were almost exactly reversed for the permuted versus original passwords (Table 3). Across devices, participants rated the longer permuted password as easier to type than the shorter, non-permuted password (Tables 3 and 4). This was true in both password sets. The permuted (length 14) passwords in both sets were consistently rated as easier to type than the original, non-permuted (length 10) passwords, despite the fact that they were four characters longer. This demonstrates that the composition and structure of a password are important; people are sensitive to factors beyond simple password length. When commenting on the non-permuted passwords, participants expressed difficulty using phrases like "more jumping back and forth" (P408),[4] "needing to hit more buttons to go to different screens" (P413), "mixed up numbers and letters and different symbols" (P417), "a lot more shift action going on" (P418), "switching between screens" (P420), and "more bouncing around" (P480). In contrast, when describing the permuted passwords, participants made more positive comments such as "I could make a word out of it, and the symbols and letters are all in the same group" (P422), "didn't require shifting through the screens so much" (P423), and "The sequence was easier to remember, it wasn't the juxtaposition of numbers and letters" (P425).

---

[3] Code available at https://github.com/usnistgov/TypingTester. The program was designed to maximize flexibility and opportunity for reuse in future NIST experiments, but we hope that other usable security researchers may also benefit from this research tool.

[4] Participant IDs are denoted as (P###).

Table 3. Per-set typing difficulty ratings

| | Password Set 1 | | | | | |
| | iPhone | | iPad | | PC | |
	Rmof	q80	Rmof	q80	Rmof	q80
N	37	37	37	37	37	37
Mode	5	1	5	1	5	1
	Password Set 2					
	iPhone		iPad		PC	
	QMif	p4d4	QMif	p4d4	QMif	p4d4
N	31	31	31	31	31	31
Mode	5	1	5	1	5	3

Table 4. Per-password typing difficulty ratings

| | iPhone | | | | | | | | |
| | Permuted Passwords | | | | Non-Permuted Passwords | | | | |
		Difficult	Neutral	Easy	Total		Difficult	Neutral	Easy	Total
	Rmof	11	11	15	37	q80	27	6	4	37
	QMif	10	9	12	31	p4d4	23	4	4	31
Total		**21**	**20**	**27**	68	Total	**50**	**10**	**8**	68
	iPad									
	Permuted Passwords				Non-Permuted Passwords				
		Difficult	Neutral	Easy	Total		Difficult	Neutral	Easy	Total
	Rmof	2	10	25	37	q80	22	13	2	37
	QMif	6	9	16	31	p4d4	14	10	7	31
Total		**8**	**19**	**41**	68	Total	**36**	**23**	**9**	68
	PC									
	Permuted Passwords				Non-Permuted Passwords				
		Difficult	Neutral	Easy	Total		Difficult	Neutral	Easy	Total
	Rmof	6	8	23	37	q80	27	5	5	37
	QMif	5	1	25	31	p4d4	8	13	10	31
Total		**11**	**9**	**48**	68	Total	**35**	**18**	**15**	68

4   Discussion

While prior work [7, 27] demonstrated increased objective usability (improved efficiency) from password permutation, that work did not include any qualitative research components, so could not assess whether subjective usability was also improved. The current results strongly suggest that permuting system generated passwords benefits subjective usability as well, nicely complementing [7, 27] and prior NIST quantitative work on the motoric difficulties of complex password entry [10, 11].

Since the purpose of drastically increasing the number of required password repetitions (in comparison to prior studies [10, 11]) was to transition passwords from participants' short term memory to motor memory, the focus of the current paper was on participants' perceptions of typing difficulty (i.e., the motoric component of the password entry tasks). Of particular interest were participants' perceptions of password differences between permuted and non-permuted passwords. It is clear that people are sensitive to the structure and arrangement of characters within a password.

Interestingly, although password permutation was originally proposed specifically to improve ease of entry on mobile devices [7, 27] permuted passwords were rated as easier across both mobile and desktop devices in the current study. This suggests that such permutation may be beneficial regardless of device, having both motoric and cognitive benefits; in addition to reducing the number of keystrokes required on mobile devices, permuted passwords may also be easier to learn and recall. Participants did comment that permuted passwords seemed easier to remember, e.g. "structure was easier to remember, having the three symbols together was helpful" [P480] and "I chunked it into the way it was already organized, it was easier for me to memorize that, and to organize what my fingers were getting ready to do" [P460]. A crucial next step in this line of research will be comparing performance (efficiency and effectiveness) with preference (satisfaction), analyzing the quantitative data to see whether typing and memory improvements correlate with people's subjective impressions of these passwords.

Although the emphasis on qualitative data was one of the biggest differences between the current work and prior NIST password typing studies [10, 11], that does not mean that the quantitative data from the current study are not of interest. On the contrary, the current study provides an extremely rich quantitative dataset that will further complement the qualitative results described here. By combining qualitative and quantitative research, we will ultimately arrive at a more complete understanding of how password construction impacts usability, both for system generated and user generated passwords. Although system generated passwords can benefit greatly from the proposed password permutation, it is not likely that it would offer similar benefits to user generated passwords, as many users already group like character classes together in their passwords (e.g., uppercase first, lowercase next, numbers and/or symbols at the end). Nonetheless, given the higher security enterprise environments for which this research is intended, it is encouraging that we have found a means of making system generated passwords somewhat more palatable to users.

Acknowledgements. The author gratefully acknowledges Brian Stanton at NIST.

References

1. Honan, M.: Kill the password: why a string of characters can't protect us anymore. Wired (2012)
2. National Strategy for Trusted Identities in Cyberspace: Enhancing Online choice, Efficiency, Security, and Privacy. http://www.whitehouse.gov/sites/default/files/rss_viewer/NSTICstrategy_041511.pdf. Accessed on 2011

3. United States Department of Homeland Security: United States Computer Emergency Readiness Team (US-CERT). Security tip (ST04-002): Choosing and protecting passwords. http://www.us-cert.gov/cas/tips/ST04-002.htm. Accessed on 2009
4. Steves, M., Killourhy, K., Theofanos, M.F.: Clear, unambiguous password policies: an oxymoron? In: Rau, P. (ed.) CCD 2014. LNCS, vol. 8528, pp. 240–251. Springer, Heidelberg (2014)
5. Steves, M., Theofanos, M.F.: Password policy interpretation. In: Proceedings of the 3rd International Conference on Human Aspects of Information Security, Privacy and Trust, in the 17th International Conference on Human-Computer Interaction (2015, to appear)
6. Choong, Y.-Y.: A cognitive-behavioral framework of user password management lifecycle. In: Tryfonas, T., Askoxylakis, I. (eds.) HAS 2014. LNCS, vol. 8533, pp. 127–137. Springer, Heidelberg (2014)
7. Greene, K.K., Kelsey, J., Franklin, J.M.: Measuring the Usability and Security of Permuted Passwords on Mobile Platforms. National Institute of Standards and Technology Interagency Report (NISTIR) 8040 (2015)
8. Ploehn, C., Greene, K.K.: The authentication equation: visualizing the convergence of security and usability of system-generated passwords. In: Proceedings of the 3rd International Conference on Human Aspects of Information Security, Privacy and Trust, in the 17th International Conference on Human-Computer Interaction (2015, to appear)
9. Lee, P., Choong, Y.: Human generated passwords – the impacts of password requirements and presentation styles. In: Proceedings of the 3rd International Conference on Human Aspects of Information Security, Privacy and Trust, in the 17th International Conference on Human-Computer Interaction (2015, to appear)
10. Stanton, B.C., Greene, K.K.: Character strings, memory and passwords: what a recall study can tell us. In: Tryfonas, T., Askoxylakis, I. (eds.) HAS 2014. LNCS, vol. 8533, pp. 195–206. Springer, Heidelberg (2014)
11. Greene, K.K., Gallagher, M.A., Stanton, B.C., Lee, P.Y.: I can't type that! p@$$w0rd entry on mobile devices. In: Tryfonas, T., Askoxylakis, I. (eds.) HAS 2014. LNCS, vol. 8533, pp. 160–171. Springer, Heidelberg (2014)
12. Jakobsson, M.: Mobile Authentication Problems and Solutions. Springer Briefs in Computer Science. Springer, Heidelberg (2013)
13. Gallagher, M.A.: Modeling password entry on mobile devices: please check your password and try again. Doctoral Dissertation, Rice University, Houston, TX (2015)
14. Choong, Y., Theofanos, M., Liu, H.K.: United States Federal Employees' Password Management Behaviors – a Department of Commerce Case Study. National Institute of Standards and Technology Interagency Report (NISTIR) 7991 (2014)
15. Shelton, D.C.: Reasons for non-compliance with mandatory information assurance policies by a trained population. Doctoral Dissertation, Capitol Technology University (2014)
16. Choong, Y., Theofanos, M. F.: What 4,500 + people can tell you – employees' attitudes toward organizational password policy do matter. In: Proceedings of the 3rd International Conference on Human Aspects of Information Security, Privacy and Trust, in the 17th International Conference on Human-Computer Interaction (2015, to appear)
17. Florencio, D., Herley, C.: A large-scale study of web password habits. In: Proceedings of the 16th International Conference on World Wide Web, pp. 657–666 (2007)
18. Unsworth, N., Engle, R.W.: Individual Differences in Working Memory Capacity and Retrieval: ACue-Dependent Search Approach. The Foundations of Remembering:Essays in Honor of Henry L. Roedgier III, pp. 241–258. Psychology Press, New York (2007)
19. Forget, A., Biddle, R.: Memorability of persuasive passwords. In: CHI 2008 Extended Abstracts on Human Factors in Computing Systems, pp. 3759–3764 (2008)

20. Vu, K., Cook, J., Bhargav-Spantzel, A., Proctor, R.W.: Short- and long-term retention of passwords generated by first-letter and entire-word mnemonic methods. In: Proceedings of the 5th Annual Security Conference, Las Vegas, NV (2006)
21. Vu, K., Proctor, R., Bhargav-Spantzel, A., Tai, B., Cook, J., Schultz, E.: Improving password security and memorability to protect personal and organizational information. Int. J. Hum. – Comput. Stud. **65**, 744–757 (2006)
22. Yan, J., Blackwell, A., Anderson, R., Grant, A.: Password memorability and security: empirical results. IEEE Secur. Priv. **2**(5), 25–31 (2004)
23. Salthouse, T.: Perceptual, cognitive, and motoric aspects of transcription typing. Psychol. Bull. **99**(3), 303–319 (1986)
24. Coover, J.E.: A method of teaching typewriting based upon a psychological analysis of expert typing. Nat. Educ. Assoc. **61**, 561–567 (1923)
25. Gentner, D.: Skilled finger movements in typing. Center for Information Processing. University of California, San Diego. CHIP Report 104 (1981)
26. Salthouse, T.: Effects of age and skill in typing. J. Exp. Psychol. **113**(3), 345–371 (1984)
27. Greene, K.K., Franklin, J., Kelsey, J.: Tap on, tap off: onscreen keyboards and mobile password entry. In: Proceedings of ShmooCon 2015 (2015)
28. MacKenzie, I.S., Soukoreff, R.W.: Phrase sets for evaluating text entry techniques. In: Extended Abstracts of the ACM Conference on Human Factors in Computing Systems - CHI 2003, pp. 754–755. ACM, New York (2003)

"Too Taxing on the Mind!" Authentication Grids are not for Everyone

Kat Krol[1]([⊠]), Constantinos Papanicolaou[1], Alexei Vernitski[2], and M. Angela Sasse[1]

[1] Department of Computer Science, University College London (UCL), London, UK
{kat.krol.10,constantinos.papanicolaou.12,a.sasse}@ucl.ac.uk
[2] Department of Mathematical Sciences, University of Essex, Colchester, UK
asvern@essex.ac.uk

Abstract. The security and usability issues associated with passwords have encouraged the development of a plethora of alternative authentication schemes. These aim to provide stronger and/or more usable authentication, but it is hard for the developers to anticipate how users will perform with and react to such schemes. We present a case study of a one-time password entry method called the Vernitski Authentication Grid (VAG), which requires users to enter their password in pairs of characters by finding where the row and the column containing the characters intersect and entering the character from this intersection. We conducted a laboratory user evaluation ($n = 36$) and found that authentication took 88.6 s on average, with login times decreasing with practice. Participants were faster authenticating on a tablet than on a PC. Overall, participants found using the grid complex and time-consuming. Their stated willingness to use it depended on the context of use, with most participants considering it suitable for accessing infrequently used and high-stakes accounts and systems. While using the grid, 31 out of 36 participants pointed at the characters, rows and columns with their fingers or mouse, which undermines the shoulder-surfing protection that the VAG is meant to offer. Our results demonstrate there cannot be a one-size-fits-all replacement for passwords – usability and security can only be achieved through schemes designed to fit a specific context of use.

1 Introduction

The pressure to replace passwords with other authentication solutions has been growing. The number of passwords that the user has to create and remember has been steadily increasing leading users to create weaker but more memorable ones, hand their lives over to a password manager, write passwords down or simply reuse the same credential or a variation for multiple systems (Florêncio et al. 2014). Many new authentication schemes have been created with the aim to make authentication easier and/or more secure. But with the exception of the Android Unlock Pattern, none of these replaced passwords – rather, widely adopted solutions have added to the password scheme to create 2-factor authentication, such as Google Authenticator or the 2-factor solutions deployed in online banking (Krol et al. 2015). From the security point of view, a password scheme devised today would need to protect against passwords being collected through malware, phishing and shoulder-surfing. In this paper, we present our preliminary lab-based evaluation of a

© Springer International Publishing Switzerland 2015
T. Tryfonas and I. Askoxylakis (Eds.): HAS 2015, LNCS 9190, pp. 71–82, 2015.
DOI: 10.1007/978-3-319-20376-8_7

scheme that was designed to protect against these types of attacks – the Vernitski Authentication Grid (VAG) (Vernitski 2015).

The VAG was created by one of the authors, the mathematician Alexei Vernitski. Users choose a password consisting of an even number of letters and/or digits. The entry of this password is through a 6×6 grid (the order of characters is random and reshuffled on each authentication) and the user needs to enter the characters of their password in pairs. They need to find the row that contains the first character and the column that contains the second character and enter the letter/digit that is in their intersection. Then this is repeated for each next pair of consecutive characters until the end of the password.

We do not consider the VAG a graphical password since there is no graphical element, such as a picture (Biddle et al. 2012), that the user would need to remember. Instead they are asked to remember a password and then enter it using a grid. The mechanism is a form of challenge-response (C-R) authentication. The aim of the grid is to guard against shoulder-surfing and key-logging. It can protect the password at three stages: (1) at entry in a case when the interface cannot be trusted, for example, when using an unknown computer, (2) at entry when the physical environment is hostile, for example, in the presence of a potential shoulder-surfer and (3) in transit when communication can be eavesdropped on. Capture of the secret password shared between user and system is made more difficult by the characters in the grid being reshuffled each time. If the attacker has a key-logger installed on the users' computer, all they receive will be a set of random-looking characters. A statistical security analysis of the VAG was conducted by Papanicolaou (2013).

Another potential use case for the grid would be as back-up or very infrequent authentication – such as annual tax returns. Long periods of not recalling a password or backup credential lead to high failure rates. To increase memorability of the shared secret, users could pick a password with high personal entropy (Ellison et al. 2000) – a word or phrase that is hard to guess, but meaningful to the user, and strongly embedded in biographical memory.

The remainder of the paper is organised as follows. In Sect. 2, we review relevant existing work. In Sect. 3, we outline the set-up of the study followed by a presentation of both qualitative and quantitative results in Sect. 4. We discuss our findings in Sect. 5, and conclude and provide recommendations in Sect. 6.

2   Related Work

There is a large body of research looking at graphical passwords, a survey by Biddle et al. (2012) provides an overview of the schemes and their evaluations. Although the VAG is not a graphical password, some of the graphical passwords studied were grid-based which can make their findings relevant to our evaluation. GrIDsure is one such example, users are asked to memorise a pattern and then when authenticating they receive a grid filled with digits and need to enter the digits that correspond to their pattern. Brostoff et al. (2010) looked at the usability of GrIDsure and found that in nearly 18 % of usages, participants were trying to enter the PIN on the grid directly instead of typing it. This undermines the security property offered by the grid, namely resistance to shoulder-surfing.

New authentication schemes were also shown to alter user behaviour when accessing systems. Brostoff and Sasse (2000) found that participants logged in with one third of the frequency when they authenticated using a grid of Passfaces® rather than passwords, because the former took significantly longer. In a study by Steves et al. (2014), participants reported they did not follow their natural workflow but batched multiple activities on the same system together to save on authentication time and workload.

With the emergence of touchscreen devices, we are increasingly moving away from a traditional screen and keyboard set-up to virtual keyboards. Previous studies have demonstrated that password entry on touchscreens can be significantly more difficult and time-consuming (Greene et al. 2014). Schaub et al. (2012) investigated the usability and security of six types of virtual keyboards. They showed that the keyboards differed in the usability of password entry (entry time, accuracy) and susceptibility to shoulder-surfing. They found that keyboard designs with poor usability were more resistant to shoulder-surfing. Moreover, research has demonstrated that the entry method affects users' password choice and security as users choose passwords that are easier to enter on touchscreens (Yang et al. 2014).

3 Study Set-up

3.1 Design

The study was conducted in a laboratory with one experimenter and one participant at a time. There were two groups of participants: first one with 31 and the second one with 5 participants. The first stage was the same for both. After being introduced to the scheme, participants were asked to perform six logins. While the first group authenticated six times during one lab session, the second group was asked to return for another session a week later where they were asked to perform another six logins. Each participant in the first group ended their session with a brief interview where the experimenter asked them about their experience.

3.2 Study Goals and Hypotheses

The purpose of the study was to evaluate the user experience of the VAG both quantitatively and qualitatively. The study was meant to be a preliminary evaluation, looking at what users think of the grid, what the learning curve is to use the system and generally explore users' experiences of authentication, their expectations and preferences.

We devised the following hypotheses.

H1: There will be a difference in the time that participants take to enter a password on a PC and a tablet.
H2: The time of entry will decrease the more practice participants have.
H3: Authentication speed will depend on participants' individual characteristics such as age, computer literacy and experience with touchscreens.

3.3 Procedure

Upon arrival, participants received an explanation of what the study will involve, they were asked to read an information sheet and sign a consent form. The workings of the grid were then explained to them using a laminated sheet of paper with a grid on it and a marker pen. Participants were then asked to enrol by setting up a username and password. The password had to be of an even number of characters. Once they were finished, they were asked to perform six logins overall: three on a PC and three on a tablet (order counterbalanced). After having performed these logins, participants were briefly interviewed about their experience and then asked to fill out a brief questionnaire about demographics as well as their computer literacy and cyber-threat exposure Fig. 1.

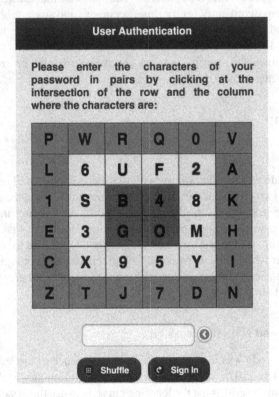

Fig. 1. A screenshot of the login page used in the study. The "Shuffle" option generates a new grid.

3.4 Apparatus

The prototype of the VAG used in the study (Fig. 1) was programmed in Java (using JSP/Servlet technology) and was linked to a MySQL database. The JQuery framework was also used to enhance the interactivity of the prototype and provide a better user experience. The study was performed on a PC running Windows XP using a 22" monitor with a resolution of 1920 × 1080 pixels and a 9.7" iPad 2 with a resolution of 1024 × 768.

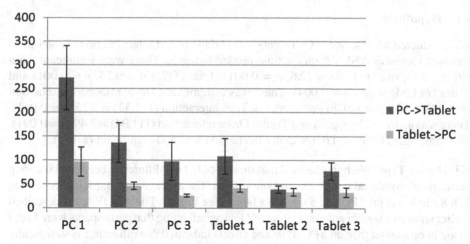

Fig. 2. Login times in seconds presented across different trials.

3.5 Participants

The study was conducted in August 2013. The research was exempted from an ethics committee review. We recruited our participants through a participant pool at University College London. Anyone was welcome to participate as we did not set any requirements. Participants were paid £6 for their participation which took around 30 min. Overall, there were 36 participants in the study, 19 male and 17 female. Mean age was 26.9 years (range: 20–49, $SD = 7.2$). In terms of education, 28 participants had completed a university degree and 7 had A-levels (UK school leaving certification).

4 Results

Overall, across all participants, devices and trials, a login attempt (regardless of if successful or not) took 63.7 s. However, in real life failed attempts to authenticate add to the time needed to access a system, therefore in our analyses we consider the cumulative time needed for a successful login, which means we counted the times of failed attempts too. The cumulative average time for a login using the VAG across all participants, devices and trials was therefore 88.6 s (median = 32.5). This average is skewed by some trials requiring several attempts. Therefore, to illustrate it better, we can say that 45 % of logins took under half a minute, 70 % under 1 min, 79 % under 1.5 min and 85 % under 2 min. Figure 2 shows login times across different trials and treatments. There were six logins and the number of attempts participants needed to successfully log in ranged from the required 6 to 14 ($M = 8.16$, $SD = 2.11$). On average, 1.4 attempts were needed for a successful login ($SD = 0.8$). Passwords chosen by participants were on average 6.7 characters long ($SD = 1.24$, range: 4–10). Out of 36 participants, 22 chose a 6-digit password, presumably influenced by the example password (zebra1) given by the experimenter which had 6 characters.

4.1   Hypotheses

We conducted a 2 (Device: PC, Tablet) × 6 (Trials) × 2 (Order: PC first, Tablet first) repeated measures ANOVA on the time needed to log in. There were significant main effects of Device ($F(1,34) = 12.6$, $p = 0.001$), Trial ($F(2,33) = 9.74$, $p = 0.001$) and Order ($F(1,34) = 9.8$, $p = 0.004$). There was a significant Device × Order interaction ($F(1,34) = 5.24$, $p = 0.028$) and Device × Trial interaction ($F(2,33) = 3.35$, $p = 0.041$). There was a marginally significant Trial × Order interaction ($F(1,34) = 2.49$, $p = 0.091$). The three-way Device × Trial × Order interaction was non-significant ($F < 1$).

H1. Device Type. We hypothesised that there would be a difference between how long participants would take on a PC and on a tablet. On average, our participants needed 118.8 s to log in on a PC and 58.4 s on a tablet (see Fig. 2). The ANOVA test described earlier showed a significant main effect of Device indicating that participants were faster to log in on a tablet than on a PC. Post hoc effects indicated this difference is statistically significant ($U = 319.5$, $p = 0.02$). H1 is therefore supported.

H2. Practice. We hypothesised that login times would decrease the more practice our participants had. We could clearly see the learning curve in that participants' login times were long at the first trial but decreased by the third trial. Upon switching to the other device, the login time was longer at first trial but decreased again with practice (see Fig. 2). Participants who started on a PC were slower in their first trial than those who started on a tablet ($U = 39$, $p = 0.008$). After switching to the other device, participants who used a tablet first and switched to a PC were marginally faster than those who switched from a PC to a tablet but we did not find this difference to be statistically significant. The group that started with a tablet was on average authenticating faster than the group that started on a PC ($U = 3931$, $p < 0.001$). Assignment to these groups was random and we could not find any significant differences between the two groups. For our smaller sample of five participants who authenticated on two occasions, we hypothesised that participants would be faster in their second authentication session. For the first session, the average authentication time was 54.4 s and for the second 39.9 s. Each participant authenticated faster in the second session by an average of 14.6 s. Despite this trend, we found this difference not be statistically significant ($p = 0.4$). A larger sample of participants would be needed to be able to decisively prove or disprove this hypothesis.

H3. Personal Characteristics. We hypothesised that age, computer literacy and experience with touchscreens would influence the speed with which participants authenticated. We found a strong positive correlation between age and authentication time ($r = 0.42$, $p = 0.01$), the older our participants were the slower they authenticated. We found a moderate negative correlation between computer literacy and authentication time ($r = -0.36$, $p = 0.03$), the more computer literate a participant, the faster they authenticated. Finally, we did not find a statistically significant correlation between authentication speed on a tablet and experience with touchscreen devices ($p = 0.095$).

Apart from taking objective performance measures, we also conducted structured observations of participant behaviour while they authenticated. Out of 36 participants,

31 pointed at the grid with their fingers or mouse when they were trying to find the row and the column where the characters of their passwords were. Three participants wanted to write their password down to facilitate breaking it down into pairs of characters.

4.2 Interview Results

After the login tasks, participants were asked to share their experiences with us. The brief interviews were audio-recorded and later transcribed. The transcripts were analysed by one researcher using thematic analysis (Braun and Clarke 2006). In what follows, we describe the themes that emerged from the analysis.

Effort. Out of 31 participants, 16 emphasised the authentication scheme was complicated. Eight participants said it required mental effort with P2 saying it was *"too taxing on the mind"*. P31 explained: *"You do have to give full attention to it, so you can't be doing any other stuff. You can't be on the phone and be like: 'Wait a minute I will just check my email. Oh, I have to login, hold for 5 minutes'"*. As this quote suggests, participants also found the scheme time-consuming to use with overall 13 interviewees stressing it required more time than traditional password entry. P7 emphasised that authentication should be fast especially if it guards access to a critical task: *"If someone is going into cardiac arrest and those seconds matter, you need a procedure that's going to be as quick as possible, not something that's going to complicate things and, potentially, lose a life. I mean I realise logging on a system isn't life and death, but sometimes it is that crucial that you get in as quickly as possible."* Both effort and time needed contributed to the feeling of frustration in some participants. Six of them stressed they found the grid frustrating, P7 explained: *"It just seems like just the password itself is just far easier to remember and quicker to type in than having to find all these different letters and matching up and stuff. Like, if this was a real login for a site that I was on, and especially, you know, a business site or a professional site, it would drive me absolutely up the wall. I mean it would waste a lot of valuable time. So, like I don't understand the purpose of it actually. It's a big time waster."*

Out of 31 participants, 10 emphasised the learning curve for the practice of how to use the grid. They mentioned using the grid became easier with time which we also see in the quantitative data. Nevertheless, P31 stressed that using the grid will never be as easy as entering a password since it cannot be automated: *"Because you have to look at, I mean it's not something you can just memorise. If you just want to check email you memorise a password, or you check in some password, like I memorise the key strokes on my keyboard, that's fine. I hate logging in using tablets and stuff but you know like, it's usually like if I was checking email it's usually just yeah, the pass code and a mobile and everything is there. But there is only your computer that can memorise your keyboard strokes, so you are like whatever, it's muscle memory, you know your password. So that is like, oh no, you actually have to be awake and you have to do like puzzle type thing and then it's annoying to do on an iPad, like say if you've just woken up or are really tired, then you can't log in."* The difficulty P31 described is that a login using the grid requires thinking and focus whereas standard password entry can be done out of muscle memory and the user does not have to concentrate as much.

High-Value Accounts. When asked if they would use this authentication scheme to log in in real life, participants generally gave varied responses. Out of 31 participants, 15 stressed it depended on the context of use. In ten cases, participants emphasised their decision whether to use a grid would depend on what kind of an account they were trying to protect. Participants mentioned that better security would be needed for systems that hold sensitive or confidential information or that could lead to money loss as with access to online banking. P18 explained they would be more likely to use the VAG *"for websites for banks and stock exchanges and all, where the real money is involved and your interest is at stake"*. However, participants were not unanimous on this, four of them stressed their banking was secure enough already, P31 emphasised: *"I'm fine with my bank account I think because I have a key and I have to press one number and then it gives you a number and I do that, so it's not like I have additional mental stress. So, I wouldn't use it for my bank. And anyway my bank is really good because I have had fraud twice and they return it, they block it when I have had fraud, so I am fine."* Nevertheless, P24 stressed they would prefer to use the grid since it does not require them to carry an additional device with them: *"Definitely this one is easier for my bank account than my token because I have to have my token everywhere I go. This way I can do it anywhere in the world, any platform, yeah. So in terms of easier sign-in, it's easier for bank account but in terms of security, I don't know."*

Experience of Fraud. We also saw that prior experience of fraud influenced participants' stated willingness to adopt the VAG. P23 stressed: *"If you could choose, so I would probably want something like this for like my bank account or actually just recently my iTunes password was hacked, someone in Canada got my iTunes password so I had to close my account and cancel my credit card."* Conversely, P24 stressed they did not feel the need to strengthen their authentication through the use of a grid since they had not experienced fraud: *"I might feel more receptive to taking this up if I had ever been a victim of password fraud before, but I haven't. So, let's say if I'd had my account hacked into before I would probably be much more receptive to using this one."*

Frequency of Use. Overall, nine participants made their willingness to adopt the VAG dependent on the frequency of use of the account it would protect. In four cases, participants stressed there was also a link between frequency of use and account importance. They said they logged in to important accounts like banking less often than to their email, thus they would be more willing to put the effort into logging in for something that is high-value and infrequent. P23 explained: *"Logging in to like my email, because I do it so frequently, I probably wouldn't want to go through the hassle of that. But if it's something more secure, I probably would."* P25 expressed a similar view saying: *"I think that would take too long given how often I log into my email account."*

Security. Overall, ten participants stressed the authentication grid was more secure than passwords. Five of them stressed the complexity made it more secure, P26 explained it is difficult to use for the user, so it must be for the attacker too: *"It sounds like it's safer yes, because it's so complex, even for the user themselves."*

5   Discussion

We conducted a preliminary laboratory evaluation of the Vernitski Authentication Grid. A login took 88.6 s on average. We found that the more practice our participants had, the faster they authenticated. Younger participants and those who had higher computer literacy authenticated faster too. We did not find a statistically significant relationship between experience with touchscreen devices and authentication speed on a tablet. Interestingly, we saw that participants authenticated faster on a tablet and subsequently faster on a PC. As mentioned earlier, previous research has shown that authentication on touchscreens poses many usability challenges and it is surprising to see that a login to the VAG was faster on a tablet than a PC.

We also saw that in theory this authentication scheme was meant to guard against shoulder-surfing but participant behaviour undermined this as participants pointed at the screen which might reveal to an attacker what the characters of their password are.

In terms of qualitative feedback, half of our participants thought the authentication grid was complex and over one third described it as time-consuming. Interestingly, when asked about their willingness to use it in the future, 19 participants made their decision dependent on the context where it would be used. They thought the grid could add extra security for systems holding important and sensitive information like banking and systems that they do not access as frequently. They emphasised the notion that for frequent accounts the password is in their muscle memory and they can enter it fast without much thinking. In such a situation, the use of the grid would not be suitable as it requires focus and time. Especially since activities like email or Facebook are quick, users log in for a few minutes just to check if there has been anything new they need to attend to. This is in line with findings from previous studies. Brostoff and Sasse (2000) found that if a login procedure was elaborate and taking longer than password entry, participants logged in less often and once they logged in, they worked on the system for longer than those who logged in just using passwords.

The differentiation that participants made in terms of account importance and frequency of use is very interesting. Passwords were invented for a certain purpose (administering a shared computer), then expanded to all systems as a one-size-fits-all solution and nowadays virtually any Website offering some service requires users to register with a username and password. Context of use is a fundamental HCI concept, however it is often forgotten by security researchers who do not account for differences between individuals and contextual factors such as account type or frequency of use (Bonneau et al. 2012).

We also saw that the stated willingness to use the VAG depended on participants' risk perception. A participant who had experienced fraud stated they would be more likely to use it than a participant who had not. This is in line with previous studies where participants' exposure to cyber-threats made them more cautious in subsequent online interactions (Krol et al, 2012).

Moreover, participants frequently compared using the VAG with entering traditional passwords. With an authentication time of 88.6 s, the grid performed poorly in this comparison. To put this number into perspective, Roth et al. (2004) tested several types of cognitive trapdoor games, that is PIN-entry methods offering resilience to shoulder-surfing.

The longest average entry time for these was around 25 s. To give another example, a standard login where the user has to enter a username and a password (both 8 characters long) was analytically predicted to take approx. 14.8 s (Steves et al. 2014). Additionally, our participants emphasised that using the grid required their undivided attention and they could not enter their password from muscle memory. It is a general problem with one-time credentials that their entry cannot be automated.

5.1 Limitations

The study was a preliminary laboratory evaluation of a new authentication mechanism. Such evaluations are multi-stage processes starting with a lab study, through a real-life deployment to an assessment post-adoption. Being the first stage in a long process our study had a range of limitations. We had a convenience sample of participants who knew what we were studying what might have made them behave in an unnatural way. Also, in real life a login is a gateway to some primary task and users' focus is not on security but on that primary task. This is something we could not recreate in this study since the explanation of the workings of the VAG needed to be quite elaborate and hiding the fact that our study was looking at the grid was not possible. Finally, due to our recruitment through a university participant pool, our study suffers from a volunteer bias and we have a sample of relatively young and well-educated individuals.

5.2 Future Work

Future work could continue with further stages of a usability evaluation of the VAG. Participant responses showed us in what kind of situations and for what types of systems the grid could be used and any future evaluations could focus on testing its deployment in these real-life contexts.

6 Conclusions

As more and more services go online, reliable and efficient authentication will become even more important in the years to come. Our study shows that users are unwilling to use long and elaborate authentication procedures, such as the VAG studied here, unless it is for infrequent and/or high-value accounts. In line with the fundamental security principle saying that a security measure should be proportional to the value of the assets it is protecting, we believe that the strength of authentication should be proportional to the importance/value of the accesses it is protecting. But the need for stronger authentication does not mean increasing the burden on users. The old myth that there is 'usability-security tradeoff' leads security experts to assume that it is OK for stronger security to require more effort. The myth even affects some users: in a recent study (Krol et al. 2015), some of our participants consoled themselves that if the mechanism is demanding, it is secure. But in this current study, the majority of our particpants were frank that they found the mechanism too demanding for regular authentication, and research to date has shown that authentication mechanisms that create too high a burden are circumvented, avoided or abandoned altogether by users (Steves et al. 2014). Performing security tasks can give users the rewarding feeling that they have contributed to making their online interactions secure, but the effort has to be proportionate. The challenge is to be able to strike the right balance between providing users sufficient reassurance and demanding their attention, time and effort.

6.1 Recommendations

In light of the findings of our study, we suggest that grids like the VAG are too complex and time-consuming to use for frequent authentication. Having said that, there are specific contexts of use where the effort is seen to be proportionate. The VAG was faster on touchscreens, so it is more usable there. Most users struggle with infrequently used passwords, and there the use of a more memorable password can offset the longer input times. We also note that the scheme offers better security if used infrequently, since the attacker has to capture many authentication events to increase the likelihood of guessing the password.

There is no usable one-size-fits-all replacement for passwords – rather, mechanisms need to be selected to fit the devices, context of use (primary task, physical and social context), security requirements, and – where possilble – preferences of individual users.

Acknowledgements. We would like to thank Brian Glass, Ingolf Becker and Granville Moore for their help in data analysis. Kat Krol's research was supported by an EPSRC grant to the UCL Security Science Doctoral Training Centre (SECReT) (grant number: EP/G037264/1).

References

Biddle, R., Chiasson, S., Van Oorschot, P.C.: Graphical passwords: learning from the first twelve years. ACM Comput. Surv. (CSUR) **44**(4), 19 (2012)

Bonneau, J., Herley, C., Van Oorschot, P.C., Stajano, F.: The quest to replace passwords: a framework for comparative evaluation of web authentication schemes. In: IEEE Symposium on Security and Privacy (SP), pp. 553–567 (2012)

Braun, V., Clarke, V.: Using thematic analysis in psychology. Q. Res. Psychol. **3**(2), 77–101 (2006)

Brostoff, S., Sasse, M.A.: Are Passfaces more usable than passwords? a field trial investigation. People and Computers XIV — Usability or Else!, pp. 405–424 (2000)

Brostoff, S., Inglesant, P., Sasse, M.A.: Evaluating the usability and security of a graphical one-time PIN system. In: 24th BCS Interaction Specialist Group Conference, pp. 88–97 (2010)

Ellison, C., Hall, C., Milbert, R., Schneier, B.: Protecting secret keys with personal entropy. Future Gener. Comput. Syst. **16**(4), 311–318 (2000)

Florêncio, D., Herley, C., Van Oorschot, P.C.: Password portfolios and the finite-effort user: sustainably managing large numbers of accounts. In: Proceedings of USENIX Security, pp. 575–590 (2014)

Greene, K.K., Gallagher, M.A., Stanton, B.C., Lee, P.Y.: I can't type that! P@$$word entry on mobile devices. In: Tryfonas, T., Askoxylakis, I. (eds.) HAS 2014. LNCS, vol. 8533, pp. 160–171. Springer, Heidelberg (2014)

Krol, K., Moroz, M., Sasse, M.A.: Don't work. can't work? why it's time to rethink security warnings. In: 7th International Conference on Risk and Security of Internet and Systems (CRiSIS), Cork, Ireland, pp. 1–8 (2012)

Krol, K., Philippou, E., De Cristofaro, E., Sasse, M.A.: "They brought in the horrible key ring thing!" analysing the usability of two-factor authentication in UK online banking. In: USEC 2015: NDSS Workshop on Usable Security, San Diego, CA, USA (2015)

Papanicolaou, C.: Novel Authentication Solution. Department of Computer Science, University College London, London (2013)

Roth, V., Richter, K., Freidinger, R.: A PIN-entry method resilient against shoulder surfing. In: 11th ACM Conference on Computer and Communications Security (CCS), pp. 236–245. ACM, Washington, DC (2004)

Schaub, F., Deyhle, R., Weber, M.: Password entry usability and shoulder surfing susceptibility on different smartphone platforms. In: 11th International Conference on Mobile and Ubiquitous Multimedia, p. 13:1–13:10 (2012)

Steves, M., Chisnell, D., Sasse, A., Krol, K., Theofanos, M., Wald, H.: Report: Authentication Diary Study. National Institute of Standards and Technology (NIST). NISTIR 7983 (2014)

Vernitski, A.: Authentication grid. University of Essex, Technical report. http://repository.essex.ac.uk/13231/. Accessed on 21 March 2015

Yang, Y., Lindqvist, J., Oulasvirta, A.: Text entry method affects password security. In: Learning from Authoritative Security Experiment Results (LASER 2014), pp. 11–20. USENIX Association, Arlington (2014)

Human Generated Passwords –
The Impacts of Password Requirements
and Presentation Styles

Paul Y. Lee[✉] and Yee-Yin Choong

National Institute of Standards and Technology,
100 Bureau Drive, Gaithersburg, MD 20899, USA
{paul.lee,yee-yin.choong}@nist.gov

Abstract. The generation stage of the user password management lifecycle is arguably the most important yet perilous step. Fulfilling minimum length and character type requirements while attempting to create something memorable can become an arduous task, leaving the users frustrated and confused. Our study focuses on two areas – password requirements and formatting – and examines the differences in user performance to understand the human password generation space. The results show a clear drop in performance when users generate passwords following a complex rule set as opposed to a simple rule set, with fewer passwords, more errors, and longer times for rule comprehension and password generation. Better formatted presentation helps reduce cognitive load in reading complex password rules and facilitates comprehension. Findings from this study will contribute to a better understanding of the user password generation stage and shed light on future development of password policies balancing security and usability.

Keywords: Password generation · Cyber security · Password policy · Usability

1 Introduction

Password based authentication plays a critical role in information access, controlling everything from bank accounts to web forums and everything in between. Unfortunately, passwords are easy targets and thus are constantly under attack from many cracking methods. The consequences of these attacks can vary from minor annoyances such as having to reset a password, to extremely severe if someone manages to access personal data or financial information. These cracking attempts are made easier by the fact that an overwhelming proportion of users are creating passwords that only contain lowercase letters if no other character types are required [1]. Though many password policies do require users to create passwords containing multiple character types and of a certain length, this introduces usability concerns such as password creation difficulty and memorability.

When creating a password, the user's ultimate goal is to create a text string that is both memorable and sufficiently secure. However, the additional creation criteria can drastically slow down the generation process as the user needs to ponder what items

T. Tryfonas and I. Askoxylakis (Eds.): HAS 2015, LNCS 9190, pp. 83–94, 2015.
DOI: 10.1007/978-3-319-20376-8_8

they can include to satisfy the requirements while still making the password easy to recall [2]. What is needed is an examination of what actions can be taken to alleviate some of the usability issues that arise from stringent password requirements. Here we present lab-based user-generated data and examine the differences in password generation performance when users are faced with different requirements and instruction formats, as well as character distribution patterns in user-generated passwords.

2   Background

As IT-based technologies become more and more integrated in our lives, the number of accounts and passwords a person must keep track of increases. The average person has multiple accounts, ranging from email and banking to the more recent areas of social media and mobile applications. Weak passwords for these accounts could result in increased security risks including unauthorized access to personal information and finances, activity monitoring, and the attacker posing as the legitimate user in online interactions. Consequently, large swathes of research have been dedicated to the area, analyzing not only the security of passwords (e.g., [3–6]), but also users' password selection behaviors (e.g., [7–9]).

Of the three stages in the password management lifecycle [10], our paper focuses on the first – the password generation stage. In this stage, users need to comprehend the password rules presented, explore options of characters to use, and finally compose a text string to satisfy the rules. It is important to understand what factors are at play here, as the subsequent maintenance and authentication stages rely on the generation stage to be both secure and usable. Several methods of facilitating password generation have been proposed, including mnemonics, passphrases, and various probes into graphical authentication. Though research in these areas shows varying levels of promise (e.g., [5, 11, 12]), their real world application is limited.

One of the more commonly implemented methods of regulating the password generation stage is dynamic compliance checking. This approach programmatically checks for adherence of the character-based passwords created by a user to pre-defined rules. These rules often include minimum and maximum string lengths, mandatory inclusion/exclusion of certain character types, and restricting the use of certain words. These password rules are to ensure that users create passwords that fall within a range of acceptable security levels, as users tend to rarely use special characters (non-letter and non-number) unless explicitly required to do so (e.g., [1, 5]).

This study has two objectives. The first is to investigate the password generation space in relation to the length and complexity of password rules. Examining how these rules affect the makeup of passwords such as character distribution and placement patterns will help us better understand how password requirements constrain human-generated passwords. The second is to explore the effects the presentation of the password rules may have on user's password generation performance. Understanding and quantifying the cognitive processes and strategies used during password generation will support the ultimate goal of finding an optimal combination of length and complexity requirements, and presentation style that balances security and usability.

Past research that explores the password generation space asked users to create limited number of passwords (e.g., [5]) or instructed users to create passwords for specific accounts (e.g., [2, 3]). In contrast, this study examines password composition and creation behavior when users are given a longer period of time to generate passwords with only rule complexity and presentation style as factors. Giving participants more time to create passwords allows for an in-depth investigation into generation patterns, while not focusing on creating passwords for specific accounts avoids potential changes to creation behavior due to pre-conceived notions that certain accounts require more secure passwords. A limitation of the study is that users were asked to generate multiple passwords at one time in a lab setting.

Research has found that formatted text can facilitate online reading such as improving comprehension and reading efficiency, compared to block text (e.g., [13, 14]). To understand the potential effects of how password rules are presented, we formed the following hypothesis: users with password requirements presented in a formatted manner will have better password generation performance than users with password requirements presented in an unformatted manner.

3 Method

3.1 Participants

Eighty-one participants were recruited from the metropolitan area of Washington, D.C., the United States. The participants ranged in ages from 18 to 69 years old (*Mean* = 35.1). Approximately 47 % were male and 53 % were female and represented diverse education and occupation backgrounds. Qualified participants had to be familiar with typing using a standard keyboard.

3.2 Apparatus[1]

An experimental program was developed in Python version 3.3.2 for data collection. The program is running on a desktop computer (Windows 7 Enterprise, Intel® Core i7-3770 CPU @ 3.40 GHz, with 16.0 GB RAM) with a 24 in. LCD monitor, a standard keyboard, and a 2-button USB optical mouse with scroll wheel.

3.3 Experimental Design

To investigate the password generation space, we gave each participant two sets of password rules and asked them to generate as many passwords as possible within set time limits. The password rule sets had two levels of complexity. The simple rule set

---

[1] Specific products and/or technologies are identified solely to describe the experimental procedures accurately. In no case does such identification imply recommendation or endorsement by the National Institute of Standards and Technology, nor does it imply that the products and equipment identified are necessarily the best available for the purpose.

only required minimum length of 6 characters. For the complex rule set, we chose stricter rules commonly used in organizations controlling their employees' access or used for personal accounts protecting data of more sensitive nature such as banking or credit cards. The complex rules included minimum length, mixed-case alphabets, numbers, and special characters (Table 1).

Table 1. Experimental design

Presentation style	Password rules	
	Complex	Simple
Formatted	You have 12 min to generate as many passwords as you can	You have 8 min to generate as many passwords as you can
	Your password **must have**:	Your password **must have**:
	• at least 12 characters	• at least 6 characters
	• at least 1 uppercase letter (A to Z)	
	• at least 1 lowercase letter (a to z)	
	• at least 1 number (0 to 9)	
	• at least 1 symbol	
	Your password **must not**:	You can use **any characters** that can be typed on a standard keyboard
	• have 5 occurrences of the same character	Password tip: It is recommended that you use a combination of upper and lower case letters, numbers and symbols
	• contain any dictionary words	
Unformatted	You have 12 min to generate as many passwords as you can	You have 8 min to generate as many passwords as you can
	Your password must be a minimum of twelve characters in length. Each password must contain at least one of each of the following types of characters: uppercase alphabetic (A to Z), lowercase alphabetic (a to z), numeric (0 to 9), and symbols. Your passwords cannot contain any dictionary words. Your passwords cannot have five occurrences of the same character	You need to create a password of minimum 6 characters long
		You can use **any characters** that can be typed on a standard keyboard
		Password tip: It is recommended that you use a combination of upper and lower case letters, numbers and symbols

To test the proposed hypothesis, the password rules were presented in different styles: formatted and unformatted. There are many existing guidelines on text formatting for online reading and comprehension. As a starting point to explore the effects of password requirement presentation styles, we only employed minimal formatting differences by turning unformatted text into bullets and adding line breaks. This condition was between-subjects, i.e., 40 participants were presented with formatted password rules and 41 participants were presented with unformatted password rules. To eliminate potential order effects, the sequence of receiving the two rule sets was counter-balanced, i.e., half of the participants (41) in a between-subjects conditions (formatted or unformatted) started with the complex set, followed by the simple set; the other half (40) started with the simple set, followed by the complex set.

Detailed data were logged programmatically including: number of passwords generated, time spent on password generation, and key presses. All timing data were measured in milliseconds and reported in seconds (s). The final experimental design with different password rule presentation styles is in Table 1.

3.4 Procedure

Participants performed the study individually. Upon arriving at the study facility, the participant was greeted and briefed about the study by the researcher. Each participant was assigned an identification number and randomly assigned to a condition (formatted or unformatted). The researcher started the experimental program, left the testing room, observed the session in an adjacent control room via video feeds, and communicated with the participant using microphones and speakers if necessary.

The experimental program presented the first password rule set and instructed the participant to generate as many passwords as possible according to the requirements within a pre-determined time limit (12 min for the complex rules and 8 min for the simple rules). Participants were informed that they did not have to memorize the passwords generated. Repeated passwords were rejected. Upon finishing the first rule set, the participant received a second rule set and performed the generation task.

After the password generation tasks, participants completed a questionnaire regarding their perception on the difficulty of the password generation tasks and on the strength of the password rule sets.

4   Results and Discussion

4.1   Descriptive Statistics

The 81 participants created 8,165 compliant passwords in total (3,138 complex; 5,026 simple), averaging 100.8 passwords per participant (STD = 57.04). On average, a participant generated 38.74 complex passwords and 62.05 simple passwords. Detailed performance metrics are summarized in Table 2.

The demanding nature of the complex rule set made participants take longer to reach milestones such as hitting the first key or creating their first compliant password. On average, it took participants 82.65 s to create their first compliant complex password. Further breaking down steps taken in these 82.65 s, it took users 23.98 s on average to make their first key press after being presented with the complex rules. Then, it took additional 33.35 s to attempt their first password, and another 25.32 s to create their first compliant password. In contrast, when faced with the simple rules, participants took an average of 14.35 s to press the first key, an additional 7.82 s for first password attempt, and just 0.11 more seconds to complete their first compliant password. Overall it took participants 17.71 s longer to generate a compliant complex password (29.25 s) than to generate a compliant simple password (11.54 s).

Table 2. Password generation performance

Complex Passwords	Mean	STD	Median	Min	Max	Sum
Number of passwords	38.74	21.93	34.00	3	106	3138
Avg. password length	14.23	1.67	13.72	12.03	19.68	n/a
Avg. generation time	29.25	32.00	21.18	6.79	240.00	n/a
Time to 1st key press	23.98	14.58	20.59	4.65	90.00	n/a
Time to 1st password	57.33	58.69	43.96	4.30	351.62	n/a
Time to 1st compliant password	82.65	103.71	50.45	14.93	734.39	n/a
Simple Passwords	Mean	STD	Median	Min	Max	Sum
Number of passwords	62.05	39.57	52.00	8	205	5026
Avg. password length	9.15	2.27	8.74	6.05	20.17	n/a
Avg. generation time	11.54	9.21	9.23	2.34	60.00	n/a
Time to 1st key press	14.35	7.90	12.81	2.15	44.08	n/a
Time to 1st password	22.17	11.20	6.69	58.78	19.86	n/a
Time to 1st compliant password	22.28	11.63	19.86	6.57	58.76	n/a

Finally, due to the differences in length requirements (at least 12 characters for complex; at least 6 characters for simple), the passwords generated from complex rules average 14.23 characters in length while passwords generated from simple rules average 9.15 characters in length.

During the password generation tasks, the experimental program provided instantaneous visual feedback on the compliance of the text string being typed. The text entry field started with a red background (i.e., non-compliant) and changed to a green background (i.e., compliant) at the moment when the password string adhered to the rule set. Once minimum compliance was met, the participants had the option to submit the string or keep typing until they were satisfied. Because of this real-time dynamic compliance checking feature, there were not many non-compliant passwords (i.e., errors) submitted. Twenty-six participants did not generate any non-compliant passwords and the other fifty-five participants generated at least one non-compliant password. We also recorded the number of retry attempts submitted after an error occurred until a compliant password was generated. The results from those fifty-five participants are summarized in Table 3. On average, participants made about twice as many errors with the complex rule set and took three more attempts to recover from the errors, as compared to the performance with simple rule set.

Table 3. Errors and retry attempts

Complex Passwords	Mean	STD	Median	Min	Max
Errors	3.07	4.41	2.00	0	26
Retry Attempts	4.49	7.46	2.00	0	33
Simple Passwords	Mean	STD	Median	Min	Max
Errors	1.45	2.955	1.00	0	15
Retry Attempts	1.44	3.11	1.00	0	17

4.2 Password Generation Space

4.2.1 Character Distribution

To understand the content of the user-generated passwords, we split all characters into four types: lowercase letters, uppercase letters, numbers, and special characters. Table 4 shows the character distribution of the 3,138 complex passwords and the 5,027 simple passwords.

Table 4. Character type distribution

Character type	Complex passwords		Simple passwords	
	Frequency	Percentage	Frequency	Percentage
Lowercase letter	25786	56.38 %	30993	69.39 %
Number	8965	19.60 %	7565	16.94 %
Uppercase letter	5968	13.05 %	3766	8.43 %
Special (non-alphanumeric)	5020	10.98 %	2344	5.25 %

Lowercase letters far outstrip all other character types in both rule sets, representing 56.38 % of characters in complex passwords and 69.39 % of characters in simple passwords. The large proportion of lowercase letters in simple passwords is likely due to the rule set only requiring at least six characters of any type.

Previous research has reported that if character type use is not enforced, users are much more likely to stick to lowercase letters [1]. This rise of lowercase letters in simple passwords does not affect character type frequency ranking, as both datasets have lowercase letters as the most common character type, followed by numbers, then by uppercase letters and special characters. Further, due to the lack of character type quotas in the simple rule set, the occurrences of numbers, uppercase letters, and special characters are all lower than those in complex passwords. More interesting are the results pertaining to the complex dataset, as the rules closely mimic many real world generation guidelines and thus the results are more relevant in today's password creation landscape.

After splitting up the character distribution by character type, we further explored the data by examining the most common characters from each category, as seen in Table 5. We compared specific alphabet frequencies to their occurrences in continuous English text to see if the password generation environment had any effect. Nine of the top ten lowercase letters (e, a, o, s, r, n, t, l, and h) in complex passwords appear in the top ten most common letters in the English language (e, t, a, o, n, i, r, s, and h) [15]. The top ten uppercase letters in Table 5 do not fair quite as well, with only S, L, T, and A matching up. They do match much more closely with the top ten most common starting letters in the English language (t, o, a, w, b, c, d, s, f, and m) [15], with eight matches total. A possible explanation for this difference is that during the study sessions, we observed many participants used English-like words in their passwords. With the need for an uppercase letter in a valid complex password, many participants capitalized the first letter of these English-like words to fulfill the requirement.

The top three numbers are 1, 2, and 3, which follows the natural numerical ordering, followed by 0 which is the last digit of the number row on the keyboard.

Table 5. Ten most common characters in complex passwords, based on character types

Lowercase	Frequency	Percentage	Uppercase	Frequency	Percentage
e	2478	9.61%	S	369	6.18%
a	2006	7.78%	L	354	5.93%
o	1864	7.23%	D	340	5.70%
r	1836	7.12%	T	330	5.53%
s	1831	7.10%	C	319	5.35%
n	1650	6.40%	F	310	5.19%
t	1621	6.29%	W	308	5.16%
i	1468	5.69%	M	305	5.11%
l	1161	4.50%	P	296	4.96%
h	1094	4.24%	A	289	4.84%
Number	**Frequency**	**Percentage**	**Special**	**Frequency**	**Percentage**
1	1328	14.81%	!	895	17.83%
2	1175	13.11%	#	569	11.33.%
3	1146	12.78%	*	525	10.46%
0	1088	12.14%	@	499	9.94%
4	927	10.34%	$	401	7.99%
9	824	9.19%	%	218	4.34%
5	769	8.58%	SPACE	218	4.34%
8	697	7.77%	.	192	3.82%
7	533	6.17%	&	188	3.75%
6	458	5.11%	^	162	3.23%

Special characters follow a similar distribution, with ! (SHIFT-1), @ (SHIFT-2), and # (SHIFT-3) appearing in the top four in Table 5.

4.2.2 Complex Password Patterns

In addition to the character distribution, we examined character type positioning to determine if the generated passwords followed any particular placement pattern. We again focused our analysis on compliant complex passwords. Figure 1 displays the overall character type distribution relative to their position for password lengths of 12 through 18. This range accounts for 92 % of all complex passwords created.

Uppercase letters dominate the first position of the password string, accounting for 66 % of all characters. This correlates with the earlier statement that many participants capitalized the English-like words in their passwords, which were often the first portion of the string. However the rate sharply drops off to 11 % at the second position and slowly decreases toward the last position. Lowercase letters start at a much more modest 19 %, before rising to 71 % in position 2. This 71 % trend holds steady for four positions (2 to 5) before the rate begins to decline at position 6 with an average rate of 5 % per position, before finally ending at 8.6 %. Numbers and special characters begin at about 7 %, but the percentage of numbers begins to increase at position 6, as opposed to special characters which stay relatively steady until position 12 where they begin to rise. Numbers are the predominant character type from position 13 and stay so until the last position in which special characters make up half of the character distribution.

This pattern of uppercase, lowercase, numbers, and special characters positioning was found consistently when examining the data from specific password lengths. We observed that, when generating passwords, participants would exceed the minimum

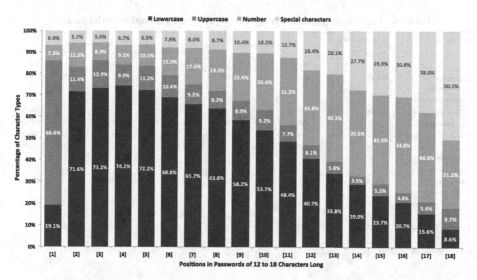

Fig. 1. Character type distribution for specific string positions

12-character requirement. Thus, any particular generation pattern used would hold steady regardless of password length. In addition, we found that this pattern closely follows the rule sequence as presented in the complex password requirements in Table 1. It is of great interest to investigate in future research whether the character positioning changes if the rules are presented in different orders.

4.3   Hypothesis Testing

We set the α of all tests for statistical significance to 0.05 for testing the hypothesis on whether users with formatted rule presentation have better password generation performance over users with unformatted presentation. First, we performed a check on all data against the assumptions for parametric statistical tests. Since all of the data violate the normality and equal-variance assumptions, non-parametric tests were used. Table 6 summarizes the performance for each condition group.

We performed the Mann-Whitney Independent Samples U test to examine the impacts of presentation styles on participants' performance. The hypothesis is partially supported with significant differences found on three performance variables: *Time to first key press for complex passwords* ($U = 584.0$, $z = -2.229$, effect size (r) = -0.25), *Number of simple passwords generated* ($U = 612.5$, $z = -1.96$, effect size (r) = -0.22), and *Average generation time of simple passwords* ($U = 612.5$, $z = -1.96$, effect size (r) = -0.22). The results show that formatted presentation has positive effects on simple password generation, i.e. more passwords and shorter generation time.

Also, when participants were faced with the stringent complex password requirements, it took them 33 % longer to start the password generation activity (i.e., time to 1st key press) with unformatted presentation. This indicates that the formatted presentation helped reduce participants' cognitive load in reading the password rules and facilitated their comprehension.

Table 6. Impacts of presentation styles on password generation performance

Performance	Presentation styles									
	Formatted (n = 40)					Unformatted (n = 41)				
	Mean	STD	Median	Min	Max	Mean	STD	Median	Min	Max
Total number of passwords	108.85	58.26	100.00	29	300	92.93	54.83	82.00	11	253
Complex passwords										
Number of passwords	39.48	21.00	36.00	8	95	38.02	23.02	32.00	3	106
Avg. generation time	25.31	18.02	20.00	7.58	90.00	33.10	41.24	22.50	6.79	240.00
Time to 1ˢᵗ key press[a]	21.20	13.84	18.55	4.65	75.39	26.70	14.95	24.70	8.27	90.00
Time to 1ˢᵗ compliant password	79.78	122.24	47.34	17.48	734.39	85.45	83.23	52.53	14.93	333.58
Simple passwords										
Number of passwords[a]	69.38	41.67	58.00	12	205	54.90	36.51	47.00	8	186
Avg. generation time[a]	9.68	6.84	8.28	2.34	40.00	13.35	10.82	10.21	2.58	60.00
Time to 1ˢᵗ key press	14.67	7.96	13.82	2.70	35.54	14.04	7.93	12.25	2.15	44.08
Time to 1ˢᵗ compliant password	22.56	12.37	20.24	6.57	58.76	21.99	11.00	19.50	9.33	53.92

[a]indicates statistically significant.

4.4   Perceptions on Password Rule Strength and Generation Difficulty

Participants were asked to rate their perception using a 5-point semantic distance scale on: the strength of the password rules in protecting their accounts on (1 – Very Weak and 5 – Very Strong); and the difficulty of password generation (1 – Very Difficult and 5 – Very Easy), for each password rule set. The results are summarized in Table 7.

Table 7. Perceptions on password rule strength and generation difficulty

Perception ratings	Mean	STD	Median	Min	Max
Strength_Complex	4.27	0.73	4.00[a]	2	5
Strength_Simple	2.77	1.13	3.00[a]	1	5
Difficulty_Complex	2.68	1.08	2.00[a]	1	5
Difficulty_Simple	4.19	0.94	4.00[a]	1	5

[a]indicates statistically significant.

We used the Wilcoxon Signed Ranks Test, within-subject comparisons, to examine whether each participant had different perceptions on different password rules. There are significant differences on the perceptions of the strength of the password rules and the difficulty of password generation tasks. In general, participants understand that the complex password rules provide stronger protection (Mdn = 4) over their accounts than the simple password rules do (Mdn = 3). However, it is more difficult to generate passwords that are compliant with stringent and complex password rules (Mdn = 2).

Participants with formatted presentation style tend to perceive the password generation as an easier task than the participants with unformatted style for both the complex rules and the simple rules, as summarized in Table 8. Mann-Whitney U Test was used to examine the impacts of presentation styles on participants' perceptions. Only the perception on the strength of simple password requirements is found statistically significant. Interestingly, participants with the unformatted simple rules perceive the rules as being stronger as opposed to the formatted rules. While more research is needed, a plausible explanation is that the unformatted presentation makes it harder for participants to separate each requirement from the others, which then triggers a false perception of added complexity and strength in the rules.

Table 8. Impacts of presentation styles on participants' perceptions

Perception ratings	Presentation styles					
	Formatted (n = 40)			Unformatted (n = 41)		
	Mean	STD	Median	Mean	STD	Median
Strength_Complex	4.25	0.71	4.00	4.29	0.75	4.00
Strength_Simple	2.50	0.99	2.00[a]	3.02	1.21	3.00[a]
Difficulty_Complex	2.88	1.04	2.50	2.49	1.10	2.00
Difficulty_Simple	4.35	0.77	4.50	4.02	1.06	4.00

[a]indicates statistically significant.

5 Conclusion

Given the near universal reliance on password based authentication methods, our study aimed to better understand the human generated password space as it relates to password requirements and formats. Users' password generation performance with the complex rule set was consistently lower, e.g., longer times for rule comprehension, longer times for password generation and fewer passwords generated, compared to their performance with the simple password rule set. Additionally, participants made twice as many errors when generating complex passwords, and took three times the amount of retries until a valid password. With close examination on the passwords from the complex rule set, it is clear that the stringent nature of the rules does not expand the password generation space much beyond those commonly used alphabetical letters in English language.

This study explored the potential impacts of password rule presentation styles on users' password generation performance. Although the hypothesis was only partially supported, the results show general trends of better performance, e.g., taking shorter time and generating more passwords, from formatted rule presentation. Given the fact that the formatting manipulation in this study was only adding some organization (such as bullets and line breaks) to an unformatted block of text, it would be of great interest to investigate the impacts on password generation performance with more elaborate formatting manipulations such as changing phrasing, plain language, re-ordering rules, and changing text styles (e.g., font family, font size, bolding).

This paper provides findings from our preliminary analyses on the data collected from the study. We intend to perform more in-depth analyses to fully understand how participants approached the password generation tasks when faced with different password rules. It is also of great interest to investigate whether there are relationships between the demographic data (e.g., age, education, self-reported computer proficiency) and participants' password generation performance. We expect the research will shed light on the development of password policies, shoring up the difficulty balancing security and usability.

References

1. Florencio, D., Herley, C.: A large-scale study of web password habits. In: Proceedings of the 16th International Conference on World Wide Web, pp. 657–666. ACM, New York (2007)
2. Proctor, R., Lien, M., Vu, K., Schultz, E., Salvendy, G.: Improving computer security for authentication of users: influence of proactive password restrictions. Behav. Res. Meth. Instrum. Comput. **33**(2), 163–169 (2002)
3. Vu, K., Proctor, R., Bhargavspantzel, A., Tai, B., Cook, J., Eugeneschultz, E.: Improving password security and memorability to protect personal and organizational information. Int. J. Hum. Comput. Stud. **65**(8), 744–757 (2007)
4. Weir, M., Aggarwal, S., Collins, M., Stern, H.: Testing metrics for password creation policies by attacking large sets of revealed passwords. In: Proceedings of the 17th ACM Conference on Computer and Communications Security, pp. 162–175. ACM, New York (2010)
5. Yan, J., Blackwell, A., Anderson, R., Grant, A.: Password memorability and security: Empirical results. IEEE Secur. Priv. Mag. **2**(5), 25–31 (2004)
6. Florencio, D., Herley, C., Oorschot, P.: An administrator's guide to internet password research. In: 28th Large Installation System Administration Conference. Usenix, Washington (2014)
7. Roman, V.Y.: Analyzing user password selection behavior for reduction of pass-word space. In: Proceedings 2006 40th Annual IEEE International, pp. 109–115. IEEE, New Jersey (2006)
8. Jakobsson, M., Dhiman, M.: The benefits of understanding passwords. In: Proceedings of the 7th USENIX Workshop on Hot Topics in Security. Usenix, Washington (2012)
9. Grawemeyer, B., Johnson, H.: How secure is your password? towards modelling human password creation. In: Proceedings of the First Trust Economics Workshop, pp. 15–18 (2009)
10. Choong, Y.-Y.: A cognitive-behavioral framework of user password management lifecycle. In: Tryfonas, T., Askoxylakis, I. (eds.) HAS 2014. LNCS, vol. 8533, pp. 127–137. Springer, Heidelberg (2014)
11. Jermyn, I., Mayer, A., Monrose, F., Reiter, M., Rubin, A.: The design and analysis of graphical passwords. In: 8th USENIX Security Symposium, pp 1–1 (1999)
12. Keith, M., Shao, B., Steinbart, P.: A behavioral analysis of passphrase design and effectiveness. J. Assoc. Inf. Syst. **10**(2), 2 (2009)
13. Walker, R.C., Schloss, P., Vogel, C.A., Gordon, A.S., Fletcher, C.R., Walker, S.: Visual-syntactic text formatting: theoretical basis and empirical evidence for impact on human reading. In: Professional Communication Conference, pp 1–14 (2007)
14. Yu, C.-H., Miller, R.C.: Enhancing web page readability for non-native readers. In: Proceedings of the SIGCHI Conference on Human Factors in Computing Systems, pp 2523–2532 (2010)
15. Bourne, C., Ford, D.: A study of the statistics of letters in english words. Inf. Control **4**(1), 48–67 (1961)

The Authentication Equation: A Tool to Visualize the Convergence of Security and Usability of Text-Based Passwords

Cathryn A. Ploehn[✉] and Kristen K. Greene

National Institute of Standards and Technology, 100 Bureau Dr,
Gaithersburg, MD, USA
{cathryn.ploehn,kristen.greene}@nist.gov

Abstract. Password management is a ubiquitous struggle of the modern human. Despite usability playing a vital role in authentication, many password policies and requirements focus on security without sufficient consideration of human factors. In fact, security and usability needs are often in contention. Until an improved authentication method beyond character input is implemented on a large scale, developing new methodologies for balancing competing requirements is vital.

This research project focused on building a data visualization tool to explore password usability and security metrics. The visualization tool integrates various measurements of passwords, enabling exploration of the intersection of their usability and security components. The tool is based on insight from previously gathered data from usability studies conducted at the United States National Institute of Standards and Technology. It also leverages web technologies to flexibly display data sets computed from sets of passwords. The tool is available at https://github.com/usnistgov/DataVis.

Keywords: Data visualization · Usable security · Keystrokes · Entropy · Password policies · Password permutation

1 Introduction

There is an abundance of usability failures of text-based passwords. Passwords add to the mental strain of users and are managed by counterintuitive requirements. Both personal and work password-protected accounts are impacted by such requirements. Learning and recalling complex passwords for multiple accounts uses mental resources and time [1–4] that can be better applied elsewhere.

Our current research is focused on password requirements from the enterprise perspective. As a result of the cognitive load password management requires, employees must learn to cope with unusable passwords [4–6]. Recent research has surveyed the coping strategies of different groups, such as university members (students and staff), federal employees, and employees in other types of enterprises with regards to password management [1,5–7]. Potentially compromising

© Springer International Publishing Switzerland 2015
T. Tryfonas and I. Askoxylakis (Eds.): HAS 2015, LNCS 9190, pp. 95–106, 2015.
DOI: 10.1007/978-3-319-20376-8_9

password management strategies employees engage in include: using a previous password with minor changes, using an existing password, recycling an old password, using a common name, and using at least one storing method [1,6–8]. Some employees have a false sense of security around their work-related accounts and passwords [1,5,9]. In shifting the locus of control away from their actions and towards the perceived security of the system, employees may continue to use insecure password generation and maintenance methods without the necessary self-scrutiny.

The password policies enforced in many institutions exacerbate the usability weaknesses of passwords, eliciting negative attitudes from employees [7,8]. A recent survey of United States Department of Commerce employees indicates a correlation between employee's negative attitudes towards text-based authentication and the competency of their resulting password management behaviors [1]. Furthermore, employees surveyed felt the passwords required were too long (56.9 %) and too complex (50.7 %) [1]. Previous research reinforces the idea that long, complex character strings are harder to recall and more error prone due to the increased cognitive load [2,9]. The difficulty with using complex character strings is exacerbated on mobile devices due to the constraints of smaller onscreen keyboards [10].

It is widely accepted that the use of text-based passwords is not the ideal authentication mechanism. Research is being done to re-imagine the methods we use to authenticate with the ideal balance of security and usability [11,12]. However, an improved authentication paradigm, such as that envisioned by the National Strategy for Trusted Identities in Cyberspace [13], will take some time to become implemented on a large scale.

In order to improve the usability of text-based passwords in the shorter term, the specific pitfalls of passwords should be explored. An identification of which specific aspects of text-based passwords impact usability is vital. Only with a solid understanding of the mechanisms that affect the usability of passwords can their management be improved. Password requirements can be improved based on this understanding to alleviate some of the cognitive load on password users.

Interactive visual analysis can be an invaluable tool in the pursuit of a more usable password. A quality visualization paradigm can aid in unearthing hidden relationships within a data set, supporting the analysis of large quantities of data very quickly [14]. Ben Schneiderman's **information seeking mantra** is a useful guideline for gleaning insight from data [15]: *Overview first, zoom and filter, then details on demand.* We utilize this concept to guide the design of our own interactive visualization tool.

The main research goal of this project was to facilitate NIST's[1] exploration of where the security and usability of passwords intersect. Although intended to specifically support NIST research, the tool is also available to the wider research community. Reaching this goal involved two major activities: (1) identifying measurable password components, or metrics, to analyze and automating the computation of these metrics for sets of passwords and (2) building a

---

[1] National Institute of Standards and Technology.

visualization tool to allow the dynamic exploration of the computed data sets. The tool should facilitate the comparison of usability and security metrics for sets of system generated passwords[2] and allow dynamic exploration of many different data sets. The visualization tool should also aid in the determination of which password components are significant in regards to usability and security, driving the collection of new data or the formulation of new password metrics for further study. The tool should ultimately give insight into how to better manage passwords with regards to organizational password requirements and password generation.

2 Methodology

2.1 Identification of Password Metrics

The password components initially selected for representation in the tool centered around common measures of security and previous NIST work on usability of system generated passwords. Metrics in the current iteration of the automation code include: linguistic and phonological difficulty (LPD), number of keystrokes, and entropy.

Linguistic and Phonological Difficulty Score. In previous research, a linguistic and phonological difficulty (LPD) scoring system was developed to rate the usability of passwords based on their similarity to spoken or written language patterns [16]. A difficulty score is generated based on the scores of six sub steps: whether the password begins with a symbol; the number of chunks (groups of numbers or letters separated by symbols) a password has; the size of the chunks; whether any letters are capitalized within a chunk; whether the letters, numbers, and symbols are segregated in each chunk or mixed together; and whether the password is pronounceable [16].

Keystrokes. The number of keystrokes needed to enter each password is also measured. For demonstration purposes, the landscape keyboard of the Android Galaxy 3s[3] and the landscape keyboard of the iPad 3 were used to calculate mobile keystrokes. The proliferation of non-desktop devices requiring password entry adds another layer of potential error to the usability equation [17]. Furthermore, due to the introduction of a touchscreen keyboard, symbols are buried in

---

[2] In contrast to the variability that exists in human generated passwords, system generated passwords can be created with more control. Multiple sets of system generated passwords were readily available from previous research. Therefore, system generated passwords were used as a starting point in the current work with a future goal of investigating user generated passwords.

[3] Disclaimer: Any mention of commercial products or reference to commercial organizations is for information only; it does not imply recommendation or endorsement by the National Institute of Standards and Technology nor does it imply that the products mentioned are necessarily the best available for the purpose.

multiple screens instead of persistently visible as they are on desktop keyboards. Depending on the form factor, users need to navigate through multiple screens to type a single character, adding extra keystrokes depending on the device type and operating system. Multiple screens and additional keystrokes add a layer of cognitive overhead to the authentication process, rendering device type a definite usability factor for text-based authentication [10].

Entropy. Metrics for measuring password security fall into two main groups based on how a password was created: user generated or system generated. As the tool was initially created for use with system generated passwords, entropy is the measure of security used in the current iteration of the tool. Information entropy, or randomness, is commonly used to measure password strength for system generated passwords. Use of the term entropy in information theory was coined by Claude Shannon [18]. As bits of entropy measured in a password increase, the predicted measure of security increases. For the purposes of the current iteration of this tool, we used a general formula for entropy from NIST Special Publication 800-63-2, Appendix A [19].

Password Permutation. Password permutation has been suggested as a means of improving complex password entry on mobile devices [20]. By rearranging, or permuting, passwords such that like character classes (i.e., uppercase, lowercase, numbers, and symbols) are grouped together within a password, it reduces the number of keystrokes required to enter the password. Keystrokes are reduced since the user does not have to continually switch back and forth between multiple onscreen keyboards to access the numbers and symbols.

For the sake of the visualization, all previously mentioned metrics were computed for both the original passwords and their permuted counterparts, including: LPD, entropy, and number of keystrokes. It is important to note that the method of computing entropy had to be revised for the permuted passwords, as restructuring the passwords in a predictable format of uppercase, lowercase, numbers, and symbols reduces entropy [20].

2.2   Challenges Automating Metric Computation

The first component of the visualization tool is code that computes usability and security metrics from lists of passwords. The code is written in Python v3.4.0, using a text file as input and a comma separated values file as output.

In the design of the code to compute password metrics, many ambiguities and design questions arose. It was necessary to translate the previously designed LPD score from natural language into a consistent formal language equivalent in order to automate the computation of this score.

Calculating entropy also presented an interesting challenge in terms of prepermutation and post-permutation entropy, since rearrangement of the characters diminishes the resulting information entropy of the password [20].

2.3   Designing the Tool

As the literature evolves concerning password usability, a tool that is dynamic, customizable, and flexible is vital to unearth important relationships between password metrics.

The tool was designed with browser technology (HTML5, CSS3, and JavaScript) to maximize the flexibility, interactivity, and ease of dissemination of the tool[4]. The tool has a low barrier to entry since it is used on a platform independent browser. It can be utilized from any desktop machine on the Chrome browser. We leveraged D3.js, a JavaScript library enabling the altering of documents based on data assigned to different elements within the Document Object Model (which defines the structure of a document) [21].

Based on data sets already in NIST's possession, we determined the visualization tool required the following attributes: scalability for differing data set sizes, display of different tiers of granularity, comparison of different password metrics side by side, and the ability to interact with and customize the view of the data.

Scalability. The sets of NIST passwords to be visualized with the tool could be a range of sizes, in some cases exceeding thousands of passwords. Thus, the tool should accommodate for and display different sizes of data sets. According to Tufte's Shrink Principle, data graphics can (and often should) be shrunk down in size, increasing their data density [22]. To allow the differentiation of entire data sets with individual data points at very small sizes, a heatmap paradigm is employed. The heatmap is a familiar visualization methodology, allowing for easy comparison at varying levels of scale. Furthermore, displaying the data as a matrix prevents data points from being obscured by other data points, such as in parallel coordinates[5]. The columns of the grid represent specific password metrics (entropy, number of keystrokes, etc.). Each row of the grid represents a password, with each block on that row representing a specific usability or security metric of that particular password. Each block is colored darker or lighter according to the value associated with that specific metric. Darker colors indicate a greater value (e.g. higher numbers of keystrokes) while lighter colors indicate lower values (e.g. lower numbers of keystrokes).

Tiers of Granularity. Effective interactive visualizations allow analysis of data at a macro and a micro level. Patterns can arise at any level of granularity in a data set. Three tiers of granularity are provided in the tool, each with a slightly different representation of the data. Figure 1 shows an overview of the tool (including all three tiers). The first tier shows a miniature view of the entire data set (zoomed out). The second tier shows a neighborhood view of the dataset, with about 20 to 50 rows of adjacent passwords. This tier is scrollable, by using

---

[4] The source code for the tool can be found at https://github.com/usnistgov/DataVis.
[5] Parallel coordinates are commonly used to visualize multivariate data. Coordinate axes are placed in parallel with associated data points connected by lines.

the first tier as a scrollbar. The third tier shows password metric results on an individual level, with each metric value of an individual password displayed in detail. All different views of the dataset are simultaneously visible, allowing interactions with the data to include three contexts for the data points explored.

Side by Side Comparison. The grid paradigm provides a simple solution to visually compare different password metrics side by side. Different passwords can be compared based on the changing color saturation of the heatmap. Furthermore, symmetry, particularly bifold reflective symmetry, has a perceptual immediacy in the human mind [23]. We designed the tool to capitalize on this fact, placing the metrics of the permuted passwords to the right of the original password metrics in reverse order (Fig. 1). The locations of the metrics are symmetrical to one another when comparing the original passwords with their permuted counterparts in the grid, allowing different levels of change to be easily detected based on their levels of symmetry.

Interactivity. The tool presents a non-static view of the data, enabling users to change the view of the data based on their interaction. When the mouse hovers over a particular block in the second tier of the visualization, the row and column of that selected block changes color scheme for ease of comparison. The context of any given data point is reinforced visually upon interaction. Furthermore, when blocks are hovered over in the second tier, the corresponding rows and columns are highlighted in the other tiers (Fig. 2). The need to explore patterns based on structural or other password characteristics necessitated the design requirement for dynamic sorting and filtering of passwords in the tool. The ability to subset and rearrange the view of large data sets is a powerful ability in order to hone in on patterns in the underlying data. We equipped the tool to dynamically rearrange, show, and hide grid columns and rows for a fully customizable view (Fig. 2). For example, the tool is equipped to filter passwords by length or by the amounts of numbers, letters, and/or symbols. Any sort and filter technique can be done in conjunction with other customizations on the fly, which update in real time with the tool. Filtering can be done using the controls within the accordion menus on the upper right hand side of the screen (Fig. 2). Using the powerful data selection and manipulation capabilities of D3.js, the amount of further customizations to the sort and filter capability of the tool is only limited by the number of calculations that can be done on the raw data [21].

3   Walkthough

We now give a brief walkthrough of browsing a dataset with the visualization tool using Fig. 2 as an example. The filter controls on the upper right hand side indicate the subset of passwords displayed. As indicated in Fig. 2, passwords of length 8 to 10 are displayed with all other password lengths filtered out. The passwords with the full range of letters are displayed (passwords containing 2 to

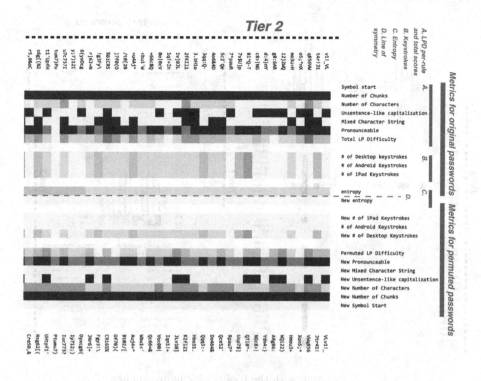

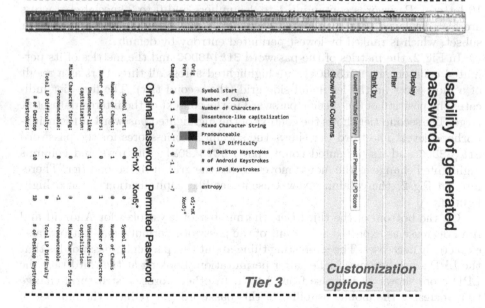

Fig. 1. The visualization tool (annotated) (Color figure online).

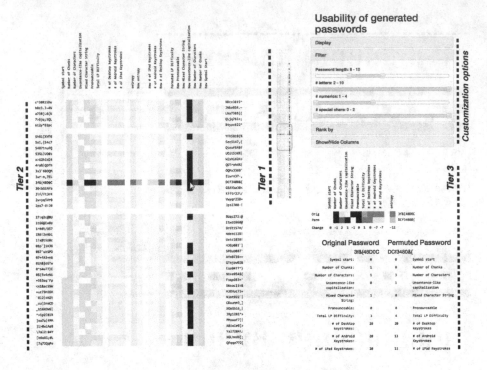

Fig. 2. Filtering with the tool (Color figure online).

10 letters). Passwords containing 1 to 4 numbers and 0 to 2 special characters are also displayed. The highlighted password is in the middle of this particular subset, which is ranked by lowest permuted entropy by default.

In Fig. 2, the metrics of the password 3f&{48DOC and the metrics of its permuted counterpart, DCf3480&{, are highlighted across all three tiers as a result of a mouseover on the left hand side grid (the second tier). The first tier indicates the position of the specific password in the context of the filtered dataset at large. The second tier shows the context of the highlighted password at the neighborhood level. The third tier shows the specific metric scores for the password 3f&{48DOC and its permuted counterpart, DCf3480&{. The rows and columns highlighted change as the mouse moves across the grid in the second tier. Therefore, in Fig. 2, the column "New Unsentence-like capitalization" is also highlighted.

On the bottom of the third tier, the number of keystrokes for Android and iPad decrease as expected as a result of the password permutation. Entropy also expectedly decreases. The interesting thing about this particular password is that the LPD score becomes higher after permutation. Looking at the third tier, the LPD score shows an increase from 3 to 4. In other words, a structural change that increases the mobile usability of this password (i.e. reduces the number of keystrokes necessary on mobile devices) also results in an increase to its LPD

is to show the underlying data. Subsequently, any conclusions derived from a visualization must be backed up with the relevant data sources.

5   Future Work

5.1   Refine Metrics

We created the tool with the ability to evolve and change as the field's knowledge of usability and security regarding text-based authentication grows. As a next step NIST can use the tool to compare password usability metrics with human usability data (such as recall failures, input error rates, time to input, memorization times, etc.). For example, the LPD score could be compared with usability data collected from human subjects. If the human usability data did not correlate with the LPD score, the LPD metric could be revised or discarded from the tool altogether. Such data would inform the refinement of password metrics included in the tool for a more accurate representation of password usability.

As the field moves forward in defining useful password metrics to measure with regard to their impact on usability and security, the tool can easily be modified to accommodate and integrate these measures in its visual comparison paradigm. Entrenched in the tool's genesis is NIST's goal of ultimately understanding which usability components of passwords should inform password management policy.

Expansion of the security metrics included in the tool is another next step. Accurately describing password strength is vital. The trade-offs between theoretical methods and more realistic methods of security measurement have been discussed [24]. Other methods utilizing a source-independent measurement of password resistance to guessing have been developed [25–27], which could potentially be used for human generated and system generated data sets of passwords alike.

5.2   Additional Tool Functionality

The tool can be extended in a number of ways to facilitate and augment NIST's research in exploring password metrics. Analyzing data sets from multiple password generators or the human generated passwords resulting from different password policies side by side is currently impossible, for example, because the color scale used is generated based on the maximum and minimum data values within individual data sets. All data sets to be compared must be loaded into the tool for the color range to be generated correctly for direct comparison. The ability to explore and compare multiple data sets simultaneously would allow an investigator to better explore the trade-offs between one password generator and another, or between one set of password requirements and another.

Adding more visual paradigms to the tool would also serve a beneficial purpose. The grid paradigm is familiar, though the inclusion of other paradigms commonly used for multivariate analysis, such as parallel coordinates, would add layers of sophistication to the level of visual analysis one can accomplish with the tool. It would be useful to see the underlying data displayed in different forms to unearth additional patterns that could be missed in one particular visualization method.

Streamlining the user experience would add a layer of needed usability to the tool. The current tool consists of two separate pieces of code in two languages, requiring a two-step process for users to visualize their passwords. Using the tool requires some knowledge of the command line and code editing, which could be encapsulated from the user and replaced with an easy to use, browser-based graphical user interface. Finally, the tool itself should undergo a more formal usability evaluation, having usable security researchers test it by exploring various data sets.

References

1. Choong, Y.Y., Theofanos, M., Liu, H.K.: United States Federal Employees Password Management Behaviors-a Department of Commerce Case Study. National Institute of Standards and Technology Interagency Report (NISTIR) (2014)
2. Stanton, B.C., Greene, K.K.: Character strings, memory and passwords: what a recall study can tell us. In: Tryfonas, T., Askoxylakis, I. (eds.) HAS 2014. LNCS, vol. 8533, pp. 195–206. Springer, Heidelberg (2014)
3. Cheswick, W.: Rethinking passwords. Commun. ACM **56**, 40–44 (2013)
4. Florêncio, D., Herley, C., Van Oorschot, P.C.: Password portfolios and the finite-effort user: sustainably managing large numbers of accounts. In: Proceedings of the USENIX Security (2014)
5. Adams, A., Sasse, M.A., Lunt, P.: Making passwords secure and usable. In: Thimbleby, H., O'Conaill, B., Thomas, P.J. (eds.) People and Computers XII, pp. 1–19. Springer, London (1997)
6. Grawemeyer, B., Johnson, H.: Using and managing multiple passwords: a week to a view. Interact. Comput. **23**, 256–267 (2011)
7. Shay, R., Komanduri, S., Kelley, P.G., Leon, P.G., Mazurek, M.L., Bauer, L., Christin, N., Cranor, L.F.: Encountering stronger password requirements: user attitudes and behaviors. In: Proceedings of the Sixth Symposium on Usable Privacy and Security, p. 2. ACM (2010)
8. Inglesant, P.G., Sasse, M.A.: The true cost of unusable password policies: password use in the wild. In: Proceedings of the SIGCHI Conference on Human Factors in Computing Systems, pp. 383–392. ACM (2010)
9. Boothroyd, V., Chiasson, S.: Writing down yourPassword: does it help? In: 2013 Eleventh Annual International Conference on Privacy, Security and Trust (PST), pp. 267–274. IEEE (2013)
10. Greene, K.K., Gallagher, M.A., Stanton, B.C., Lee, P.Y.: I can't type that! p@$$w0rd entry on mobile devices. In: Askoxylakis, I., Tryfonas, T. (eds.) HAS 2014. LNCS, vol. 8533, pp. 160–171. Springer, Heidelberg (2014)
11. Hayashi, E., Hong, J., Christin, N.: Security through a different kind of obscurity: evaluating distortion in graphical authentication schemes. In: Proceedings of the SIGCHI Conference on Human Factors in Computing Systems, pp. 2055–2064. ACM (2011)

12. Somayaji, A., Mould, D., Brown, C.: Towards narrative authentication: or, against boring authentication. In: Proceedings of the 2013 Workshop on New Security Paradigms Workshop, pp. 57–64. ACM (2013)
13. National Strategy for Trusted Identities in Cyberspace: Enhancing online choice, efficiency, security, and privacy (2011)
14. Marty, R.: Applied Security Visualization. Addison-Wesley, Upper Saddle River (2009)
15. Shneiderman, B.: The eyes have it: a task by data type taxonomy for information visualizations. In: Proceedings of the IEEE Symposium on Visual Languages, pp. 336–343. IEEE (1996)
16. Bergstrom, J.R., Frisch, S.A., Hawkins, D.C., Hackenbracht, J., Greene, K.K., Theofanos, M.F., Griepentrog, B.: Development of a scale to assess the linguistic and phonological difficulty of passwords. In: Rau, P.L.P. (ed.) CCD 2014. LNCS, vol. 8528, pp. 131–139. Springer, Heidelberg (2014)
17. von Zezschwitz, E., De Luca, A., Hussmann, H.: Honey, i shrunk the keys: influences of mobile devices on password composition and authentication performance. In: Proceedings of the 8th Nordic Conference on Human-Computer Interaction: Fun, Fast, Foundational, pp. 461–470. ACM (2014)
18. Shannon, C.E.: A mathematical theory of communication. ACM SIGMOBILE Mob. Comput. Commun. Rev. **5**, 3–55 (2001)
19. Burr, W., Dodson, D., Perlner, R., Polk, W., Gupta, S., Nabbus, E.: Nist sp800-63-2-electronic authentication guideline. National Institute of Standards and Technology (2013)
20. Greene, K., Kelsey, J., Franklin, J.: Measuring the Usability and Security of Permuted Passwords on Mobile Platforms. National Institute of Standards and Technology Interagency Report (NISTIR) 8040 (2015)
21. Bostock, M., Ogievetsky, V., Heer, J.: D^3 data-driven documents. IEEE Trans. Vis. Comput. Graph. **17**, 2301–2309 (2011)
22. Tufte, E.R., Graves-Morris, P.: The Visual Display of Quantitative Information, vol. 2. Graphics Press, Cheshire (1983)
23. Tyler, C.W.: Human Symmetry Perception and its Computational Analysis. Psychology Press, Hove (2003)
24. Florêncio, D., Herley, C., Van Oorschot, P.C.: An administrators guide to internet password research. In: Proceedings of the USENIX LISA (2014)
25. Kelley, P.G., Komanduri, S., Mazurek, M.L., Shay, R., Vidas, T., Bauer, L., Christin, N., Cranor, L.F., Lopez, J.: Guess again (and again and again): measuring password strength by simulating password-cracking algorithms. In: 2012 IEEE Symposium on Security and Privacy (SP), pp. 523–537. IEEE (2012)
26. Weir, M., Aggarwal, S., Collins, M., Stern, H.: Testing metrics for password creation policies by attacking large sets of revealed passwords. In: Proceedings of the 17th ACM Conference on Computer and Communications Security, pp. 162–175. ACM (2010)
27. Galbally, J., Coisel, I., Sanchez, I.: A probabilistic framework for improved password strength metrics. In: 2014 International Carnahan Conference on Security Technology (ICCST), pp. 1–6. IEEE (2014)

Investigating the Use of Gesture-Based Passwords by the Seniors

Lakshmidevi Sreeramareddy[✉], Pewu Mulbah, and Jinjuan Heidi Feng

Department of Computer and Information Sciences, Towson University,
Towson, MD 21252, USA
{lsreeramareddy,jfeng}@towson.edu,
pmulba1@students.towson.edu

Abstract. Older adults in the US are the fastest-growing demographic group, and also the fastest-growing group of internet users [1]. Many computer related tasks, such as user authentication, could be a challenge for the seniors as their cognitive and physical capabilities decline. To date, the most commonly used authentication method is alphanumeric passwords, which have substantial challenges regarding security and usability [2]. Authentication using traditional alphanumeric passwords can be particularly problematic for the seniors because secure passwords are usually hard to remember [3]. Therefore, due to memory loss, one common problem associated with aging, the traditional alphanumeric passwords could be challenging for the seniors to recall and manage. To address this challenge, we developed a gesture-based password application as an alternative to the traditional alphanumeric passwords [4]. Preliminary studies suggest that users could learn the new password method in fairly short amount of time [5]. In this paper, we report an empirical user study to investigate how the seniors interact with the gesture password application.

Keywords: Usable security and privacy · User security and privacy by design · Accessibility

1 Introduction

User authentication is a crucial area for data security. Numerous authentication techniques have been developed to fit the needs of users in different contexts. The most commonly used authentication method is the alphanumeric password. However, since strong alphanumeric passwords are hard to remember, users tend to choose easy to remember passwords that are vulnerable to dictionary attacks. We developed an alternative gesture-based password method in order to address some of the challenges of the alphanumeric passwords [4]. The motivation behind this method is that people can remember pictures better than text and for longer duration of time [6]. Therefore, gesture-based passwords may require less memory capability than the alphanumeric passwords.

Older adults in the US are the fastest-growing demographic group [1]. As people age, the cognitive capability of the human brain declines, making it harder to remember

© Springer International Publishing Switzerland 2015
T. Tryfonas and I. Askoxylakis (Eds.): HAS 2015, LNCS 9190, pp. 107–118, 2015.
DOI: 10.1007/978-3-319-20376-8_10

and manage the traditional alphanumeric passwords. The gesture-based password may benefit seniors because of its pictorial representation of the password. However, to date, there has been limited research that investigated the usability of different types of passwords as used by the senior. In this paper, we report a user study that evaluated the use of gesture-based passwords by the seniors. In particular, we investigated how the seniors interact with the proposed gesture-based password method, the variations in the behavioral measures while drawing the password, and whether there is any difference in the interaction patterns between the seniors and young users.

2   Related Research

Alphanumeric passwords are the most commonly adopted method for authenticating users online. However, stronger alphanumeric passwords may cause usability problems. Thus, users tend to pick easy to remember passwords that are vulnerable to dictionary attacks [7, 8]. To address the limitations of the alphanumeric passwords, researchers have developed various forms of graphical passwords as alternative authentication methods [6, 9–11]. Research shows that users can remember graphical passwords better than alphanumeric passwords [12]. The limitation of some graphical passwords is that the password space is limited, making the password vulnerable to brute-force attack. Another limitation of graphical passwords is that they are more susceptible for shoulder-surfing attacks than the alphanumeric passwords [13]. More recently, shoulder-surfing defense techniques have been developed and could be adapted to prevent this attack [14].

Graphical passwords can be grouped into two types: recognition-based and recall-based. When using recognition-based passwords, user clicks on regions of a picture or select set of pictures in sequence. Then the system recognizes the selection to authenticate the user. When using recall-based passwords, user draws the password using the memory recall ability. The gesture-based password reported in this paper belongs to the recall-based password group. This method is similar to Draw-A-Secrete (DAS) [9] method developed by Jermyn et al. The DAS method requires the password to cross a sequence of grids to authenticate a user. Nail et al. [15] studied the usability of the DAS method and reported that almost 29 % of password were invalid.

The Passdoodles [16] and gesture-based touch pad system [17] are also recall-based passwords. These methods used password shape, speed of strokes and pauses between strokes in order to authenticate users. Neither method was systematically evaluated through empirical user studies. Furthermore, De Luca et al. [17] and Sae-Bae et al. [18] used specific features of passwords such as pressure, speed, and fingertip dynamics as an additional layer of authentication. Both methods require pre-defined shapes as password. Users must pick their password from system provided catalog of passwords.

Our proposed method differs from existing gesture-based methods [e.g., 6–10] in two perspectives. First, it is grid free, meaning that the drawing area has no grid. Users can freely draw on the canvas provided without any specific limitations. Second, users do not need to use predefined shapes provided by the system. The password content (drawing) is exclusively based on users' imagination.

The number of older adults using technology is growing rapidly [19]. As people age, the biological framework of health would become less efficient [20]. There are chances of declined recall ability. Since complex passwords are hard to remember, seniors tend to use weak passwords for online activities [21]. Those passwords are highly vulnerable for security attacks. Therefore, the seniors would benefit from alternative authentication solutions are easy to remember and, in the meanwhile, offer acceptable security protection.

3   Application Design

The password creation interface is demonstrated in Fig. 1. Once a password is created, we use the $N recognizer algorithm to determine how similar the newly entered password is to the original password [22]. During the authentication stage, in addition to the similarity between the password images, we also consider behavioral measures including drawing speed, pause between strokes, stroke length, password size, and movement angles, to enhance the authentication. The behavioral measures may reflect how well users remember the password and how easy it is to draw the password.

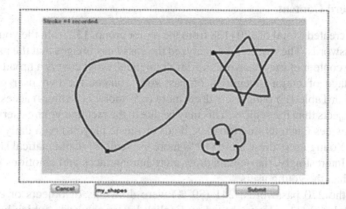

Fig. 1. Demonstration of the password creation interface

4   Participants

Twenty three senior participants took part in the study. Nine participants were females and 14 were males. The average age of the participants was 71, ranging between 65 and 81 (SD. = 4.99). Twenty two young participants took part in the study. Among the 22 participants, 12 were females and 10 were males. The average age of the young participants was 28, ranging between 21 and 38 (SD. = 4.30). All participants have previous experience using computers and the Web. All participants have Web accounts and are familiar with the traditional password authentication process.

5 Task and Procedure

A between-subject design was adopted in this study. Participants in both age groups created and re-entered passwords using a mouse. At the beginning of the study, a researcher explained and demonstrated the gesture-based passwords to the participants. The participants first tried to create one password and re-enter it multiple times. Then they started the formal session and created 6 gesture-based passwords and re-entered each password five times. The application interface used in the study for two groups of users is exactly the same. At the end of the study, participants completed a paper-based demographic questionnaire and a satisfaction survey.

6 Results

According to observation of the researchers and the satisfaction survey, all participants easily mastered the gesture-based authentication method and can comfortably draw the password.

6.1 Password Content

Participants created a total of 270 (138 from the senior group, 132 from the young group) different passwords. The researchers analyzed the password images that the participants created. The content of the passwords varies dramatically and covers a broad spectrum. The percentage of major categories of password content for two user groups are summarized in Table 1. Young users drew more (8 % more vs. seniors) accessories and electronic objects than the seniors. This may be due to the fact that young users use more electronic devices (such as smartphones, iPads or music players) on a daily basis than the seniors. Young users drew more (19 % more vs. seniors) mathematical shapes than the seniors. Interestingly, the seniors drew more human faces and emotions (9 % more vs. young) than the young users.

Among the 270 passwords, 241 (89 %) were drawings of objects or concept or sceneries. Only 29 (11 %) were based on English letters or words, which has positive security implications. Table 2 shows the sample passwords created by the seniors.

6.2 Accuracy of Password Re-Entry

The confidence score (CS) measures the accuracy of the re-entry compared to the original drawing. The CS is calculated by the $N recognizer algorithm and ranges between zero and one. The distribution of the confidence scores for the reproduced passwords entered by both groups are illustrated in Fig. 2. The confidence scores of more than 69 % of the passwords reproduced by both groups are higher than 0.8. 90 % of the passwords reproduced by both groups had confidence scores higher than 0.7. These preliminary results suggest that the participants could reproduce the password with considerable level of accuracy.

Table 1. Categories of password content from young/seniors groups

Category	Seniors (%)	Young (%)
Vegetables, fruits and other food	4.35	5.30
Trees, flowers and other plants	1.45	9.85
Animals	5.07	5.30
Human faces and emotions	19.57	10.61
Buildings	2.17	3.79
Scenery	6.52	6.06
Vehicles	2.17	6.82
Mathematical shapes	13.04	32.58
Numbers	2.90	4.55
Kitchen tools	5.80	1.52
Accessories or electronics or house tools	3.62	11.36
English words or letters	15.42	7.58
Other objects	37.68	42.42

6.3 Comparison Between Seniors and Young Users

One-way Repeated Measures Analysis of Variance (ANOVA) tests were used to compare the performance measures between the two groups of users.

Confidence Score. As discussed in the previous section, the accuracy of password re-entry is obtained from confidence scores (CS). The test result suggests that there is significant difference between the confidence scores of the passwords entered by the two groups of users ($F (1, 43) = 8.16$, $p < 0.007$). The passwords re-entered by senior users have significantly higher confidence score than passwords re-entered by young users (Fig. 3). This may be due to the fact that the seniors perceive security or password more cautiously than the young group. Since they are more cautious, they might pay more attention to the task and re-enter the password more accurately than the young group.

Time to Create and Re-Enter Password. An ANOVA test was conducted using two groups of users as independent variables and the password creation time and re-entry time as the dependent variables. The test result suggests that there is significant difference between the creation time of the passwords by the two groups of users ($F (1, 43) = 13.84$, $p < 0.002$). The passwords created by senior users have significantly longer creation time (M = 23.52 s, SD = 13.37) than passwords created by young users (M = 12.64 s, SD = 8.10) (Fig. 4). The re-entry time of passwords have no significant difference between the two groups of users (F (1, 43) = 1.61, n.s; mean 22.49 for seniors, 13.81 s for young).

Table 2. Sample passwords created by seniors

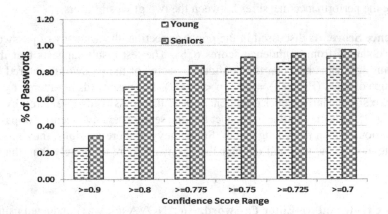

Fig. 2. Distribution of conference scores under young/seniors

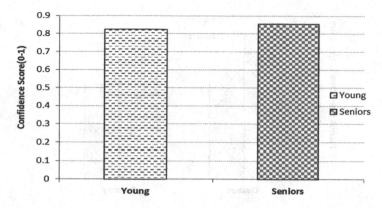

Fig. 3. Confidence score between two groups (number 0–1) young/seniors

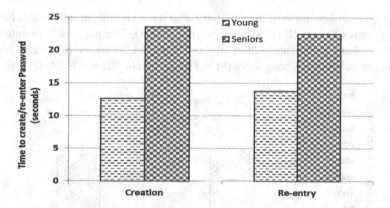

Fig. 4. Average time spent to create or re-enter passwords (seconds) young/seniors

Pauses in Creation and Re-Entry. The test result suggests that there is significant difference between the two groups of users in the pauses between strokes while creating passwords ($F(1, 43) = 24.13$, $p < 0.000$). The passwords created by senior users have significantly lower percentage of pauses ($M = 29.83$ percent, $SD = 4.47$) than passwords created by young users ($M = 40.07$ percent, $SD = 8.88$). The pauses during password re-entry also have significant difference between the two groups of users ($F(1, 43) = 46.44$, $p < 0.000$). The passwords re-entered by senior users have significantly lower percentage of pauses ($M = 25.72$ percent, $SD = 5.58$) than passwords re-entered by young users ($M = 39.08$ percent, $SD = 7.46$) (Fig. 5). Since the seniors spent a longer time during creation and similar amount of time during re-entry, the result suggests that the seniors spent most of the time drawing the strokes rather than recalling the strokes.

Length of Strokes. The test result suggests that there is significant difference in the length of the strokes between the two groups of users ($F(1, 43) = 6.39$, $p < 0.01$). The strokes drawn by seniors users have significantly short length ($M = 664.10$ pixels, $SD = 270.85$) than the strokes drawn by young users ($M = 875.74$ pixels, $SD = 290.51$).

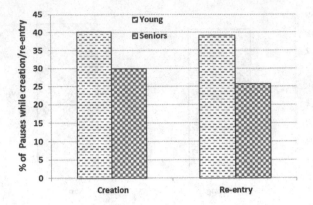

Fig. 5. Percentage of pauses during creation and re-entry for young/seniors

The length of strokes drawn during re-entry also have significant differences between the two groups of users (F (1, 43) = 8.86, p < 0.005). The passwords re-entered by seniors users have significantly short strokes (M = 641.20 pixels, SD = 260.36) than passwords re-entered by young users (M = 894.72 pixels, SD = 309.58) (Fig. 6).

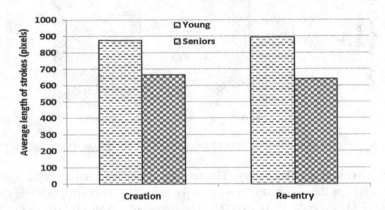

Fig. 6. Average length of strokes during creation and re-entry (pixels) for young/seniors

Password Size. The test result suggests that there is significant difference between the two user groups in the size of the passwords created (F (1, 43) = 7.05, p < 0.01). The passwords created by seniors users have significantly smaller size (M = 2084.1.10 pixels, SD = 14879.76) than passwords created by young users (M = 35811.14 pixels, SD = 22353.22). The size of password during re-entry also has significant differences between the two groups of users (F (1, 43) = 8.24, p < 0.006). The passwords re-entered by senior users have significantly smaller size (M = 19979.84 pixels, SD = 14012.17) than passwords re-entered by young users (M = 38168.45 pixels, SD = 26803.85) (Fig. 7).

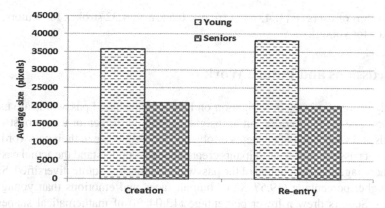

Fig. 7. Average size during creation and re-entry (bounding box pixels) for young/seniors

Drawing Speed. The test result suggests that, there is significant difference in the drawing speed between the two groups of users ($F (1, 43) = 21.69$, $p < 0.000$). The passwords created by seniors users have significantly lower speed ($M = 0.42$ number of pixels per milliseconds, $SD = 0.27$) than passwords created by young users ($M = 1.02$ number of pixels per milliseconds, $SD = 0.55$). The speed of password during re-entry also have significant difference between the two groups of users ($F (1, 43) = 29.76$, $p < 0.000$). The passwords re-entered by seniors users have significantly lower speed ($M = 0.50$ number of pixels per milliseconds, $SD = 0.28$) than passwords re-entered by young users ($M = 1.20$ number of pixels per milliseconds, $SD = 0.54$) (Fig. 8). This result is consistent with the fact that the seniors spent a longer time drawing the strokes.

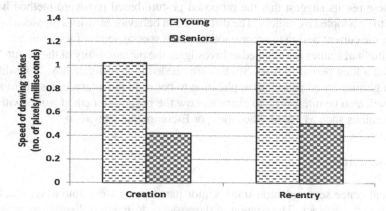

Fig. 8. Average drawing speed of creation and re-entry (number of pixels per milliseconds) for young/seniors.

Number of Strokes in Password. An ANOVA test result suggests that there is no significant difference in the password stroke count between the two groups of users ($F (1, 43) = 0.93$, $p < 0.33$, n.s.; 4.34 stokes for seniors, mean 4.4 strokes for young). The stroke count of password during re-entry also has no significant difference between the two groups of users (F (1, 43) = 0.36, p < 0.54, n.s.; 4.32 strokes for seniors, mean 4.37 stokes for young).

7   Discussions and Future Work

This study is a preliminary investigation on how gesture-based passwords are used by the seniors. The study provides initial insight about how the senior users construct the passwords and what types of concepts or objects they might use in their passwords. The collection of passwords that participants created helps us understand the actual password space. Encouragingly, the content of the passwords seems to be quite diversified. Seniors drew a higher percentage (19.57 %) of human faces and emotions than young users (10.61 %). Seniors drew a lower percentage (13.04 %) of mathematical shapes than young users (32.58 %). Seniors also drew a lower percentage (3.62 %) of electronics or house tools compared to young users (11.36 %). The influence of the traditional alpha-numeric passwords seems to be limited as suggested by the low percentage of passwords based on letters and numbers (18 % for the seniors, 12 % for the young users).

The results demonstrate that there are differences in a number of performance measures between young and senior participants when creating and entering gesture-based passwords. Interestingly, senior users re-entered gesture-based passwords with higher accuracy than young users. The senior participants who spent longer time while creating the gesture-based passwords had significantly lower percentage of pauses when re-enter passwords. It seems that the seniors had easier and smoother transition between strokes, as indicated by the dramatically lower percentage of time pausing between strokes during the re-entries. The senior participants also drew shorter strokes at lower speed than young users. These results suggest that the proposed gesture-based password method has the potential to be adopted by seniors. The difference in behavior measures provides insights to modify the current design to accommodate to the special needs of senior users.

Longitudinal studies are planned to investigate the memorability of the gesture passwords over a long period of time. Studies are needed to investigate how to modify the design of gesture-based password application to better fit the interaction style of senior users. It will also be interesting to examine how the proposed method works with real-life applications such as Email, Facebook, or E-commerce sites.

8   Conclusion

As the confidence scores demonstrate, senior participants were able to reproduce the passwords with accuracy. The content of the passwords drawn is diversified, which has positive implications for security. The seniors and young users also demonstrated different interaction patterns when using the gesture-based passwords. The differences in the performance data between the young and the seniors are very interesting. The seniors preferred passwords with shorter length, the re-entries resulted in higher accuracy, and the passwords have lower percentage of pauses compared to the young users. This research suggests that the gesture-based password method might serve as an alternative authentication solution for seniors.

References

1. Hart, T.A., Chaparro, B.S., Halcomb, C.G.: Evaluating websites for older adults: adherence to 'senior-friendly' guidelines and end-user performance. Behav. Inf. Technol. **27**, 191–199 (2008)
2. Biddle, R., Chiasson, S., Van Oorschot, P.C.: Graphical passwords: learning from the first twelve years. ACM Comput. Surv. **44**(4), 1–41 (2012)
3. Renaud, K., Ramsay, J.: Now what was that password again? a more flexible way of identifying and authenticating our seniors. Behav. Inf. Technol. **26**(4), 309–322 (2007)
4. Sreeramareddy, L., Feng, J., Sears, A.: Poster: preliminary investigation of gesture-based password: integrating additional user behavioral features. In: Symposium on Usable Privacy and Security (SOUPS), pp. 4–5 (2012)
5. Sreeramareddy, L., Janprasert, A., Heidifeng, J.: Evaluating gesture-based password and impact of input devices. In: The International Conference on Security and Management (2014)
6. Gao, H., Guo, X., Chen, X., Wang, L., Liu, X.: YAGP: yet another graphical password strategy. In: 2008 Annual Computer Security. Applications Conference, pp. 121–129 (2008)
7. Adams, A.: Users are not the enemy. Commun. ACM **42**(12), 40–46 (1999)
8. Abdullah, M.D.H., Abdullah, A.H., Ithnin, N., Mammi, H.K.: Towards identifying usability and security features of graphical password in knowledge based authentication technique. In: 2008 Second Asia International Conference Modeling and Simulation, pp. 396–403 (2008)
9. Jermyn, I., Mayer, A., Monrose, F., Reiter, M.K., Rubin, A.D.: The design and analysis of graphical passwords. In: Proceedings of 8th USENIX Security Symposium, pp. 1–4 (1999)
10. Weiss, R., De Luca, A.: PassShapes - Utilizing Stroke Based Authentication to Increase Password Memorability, pp. 18–22 (2008)
11. Owen, G.S.: Graphical passwords: a survey. In: 21st Annu. Computer Security Applications Conference, (ACSAC), pp. 463–472 (2005)
12. Brostoff, S., Sasse, M.A.: Are passfaces more usable than passwords? a field trial investigation. In: McDonald, S., Waern, Y., Cockton, G. (eds.) People and Computers XIV — Usability or Else!: Proceedings of HCI 2000, pp. 405–424. Springer, Heidelberg (2000)
13. Lashkari, A.H., Farmand, S., Zakaria, O.B., Saleh, R.: Shoulder surfing attack in graphical password authentication. Int. J. Comput. Sci. Inf. Secur. IJCSIS **6**(2), 145–154 (2009)
14. Zakaria, N.H., Griffiths, D., Brostoff, S., Yan, J.: Shoulder surfing defence for recall-based graphical passwords. In: Proceedings of Seventh Symposium Usable Privacy and Security - SOUPS 2011, p. 1 (2011)
15. Nali, D., Thorpe, J.: Analyzing user choice in graphical passwords. School of Computer Science, Carleton University Technical report TR-04-01, pp. 1–6 (2004)
16. Varenhorst, C.: Passdoodles: a lightweight authentication method. MIT Res. Sci. Inst. (2004)
17. DeLuca, A., Hang, A., Brudy, F., Lindner, C., Hussmann, H.: Touch me once and i know it' s you! implicit authentication based on touch screen patterns. In: Proceedings of the SIGCHI Conference on Human Factors in Computing Systems, pp. 987–996 (2012)
18. Sae-Bae, N., Ahmed, K., Isbister, K., Memon, N.: Biometric-rich gestures: a novel approach to authentication on multi-touch devices. In: Proceedings of the SIGCHI Conference on Human Factors in Computing Systems, pp. 977–986 (2012)
19. Czaja, S.J., Lee, C.C.: The impact of aging on access to technology. Univers. Access Inf. Soc. **5**(4), 341–349 (2007)
20. Age Related Cognitive Decline. Life Extension Foundation for Long lIfe. http://www.lef.org/Protocols/Neurological/Age-Related-Cognitive-Decline/Page-01

21. CareMonitor, L.: Online Password Security Tips for Seniors, Senior Tech Daily. http://seniortechdaily.com/online-password-security-tips-for-seniors/
22. Anthony, L., Wobbrock, J.O.: A lightweight multistroke recognizer for user interface prototypes. In: Human- Computer Interaction Institute, Carnegie Mellon University (2012)

Password Policy Languages: Usable Translation from the Informal to the Formal

Michelle Steves[1(✉)], Mary Theofanos[1], Celia Paulsen[1],
and Athos Ribeiro[2]

[1] National Institute of Standards and Technology, Gaithersburg, MD, USA
{michelle.steves,mary.theofanos,
celia.paulsen}@nist.gov
[2] Universidale de Brasilia, Brasilia, Brazil
athosribeiro@gmail.com

Abstract. Password policies – documents which regulate how users must create, manage, and change their passwords – can have complex and unforeseen consequences on organizational security. Since these policies regulate user behavior, users must be clear as to what is expected of them. Unfortunately, current policies are written in language that is often ambiguous. To tackle ambiguity, we previously developed a formal language for stating what behavior is and is not allowed regarding password management. Unfortunately, manual translation of the policy to this formal language is time consuming and error prone. This work focuses on providing an interface for policy users to generate accurate models of their interpretations of a password policy. This will aid password policy research, formalization, and ultimately more usable password policies. This paper describes the requirements, design, high-level application features, application validation, user testing, and includes a discussion of how this work is expected to progress.

Keywords: Usable security · Password policy · Question-answer system · Policy workbench · Formal language · XML

1 Introduction

As part of the research and development thrust of the United States' Comprehensive National Cyber-Security Initiative, we undertook an exploration of the relationship between usability and security in password policies. Previous work in this area includes development of a formal language for representing the rules governing user behavior surrounding password creation and maintenance [1]. Having developed a prototype formal representation of password policy rules, we next undertook an effort to map real-world policies onto the formal rule set to validate it and gather users' interpretations of actual password policies. Such a mapping for any policy produces a model of the policy that can be used by analytical tools, including a policy workbench – a set of tools and methods that is used to develop, analyze, and improve policies [2]. Earlier efforts of model generation for policy workbenches have shown only limited success, with resulting models being error-prone, difficult and time consuming to produce [3–6].

© Springer International Publishing Switzerland 2015
T. Tryfonas and I. Askoxylakis (Eds.): HAS 2015, LNCS 9190, pp. 119–130, 2015.
DOI: 10.1007/978-3-319-20376-8_11

These approaches did not show promise in aiding us meet our objective of easily and accurately mapping a policy user's interpretation of a password policy to its formal representation.

We looked beyond these translation methods for an approach that would reduce the learning curve and effort required of the human translator to produce an accurate model. Use of an on-line question-answer system was explored and piloted. While the overall approach of a question-answer system showed promise, our hard-coded prototype made the application impossible to modify without programmer intervention, which would be untenable during the highly-iterative process envisioned to validate the application's user-facing elements, e.g., question and answer wording. Further, we needed the ability to make changes to rules in the underlying set of formal password policy statements as we validate it. A review of question-answer applications showed that no existing applications met our broadest requirement: to construct a set of statements (rules from our formal language) from user-selected, predefined responses to our predefined questions. Therefore, a custom application for our specific requirements was developed. The resulting application provides us with a tool that is highly usable and configurable, including researcher specified content, to present questions and answers to users from which a user's responses are used by the application to construct a set of syntactically correct formal statements that constitutes the user's model of a password policy. Preliminary results show that users with no experience can produce an accurate translation of a real-world password policy in less time and with fewer errors than an experienced translator using the manual translation method.

Why focus on the policy user? Policy users, the end users of policy, are critical components in the ultimate effectiveness of any password policy. A typical user might be governed by multiple policies both at work and at home (e.g., to access corporate email servers, personal financial information, medical records, and e-commerce sites). Ambiguities in these policies, discrepancies between them, and the sheer number of different policies may cause confusion. As a result of this cognitive burden, users may choose weak passwords, write them down, or violate policies in other ways. Consequently, overall security may be weakened. At a minimum, users must be clear as to what is expected of them for a policy to be effective, since these policies attempt to govern user behavior. Ambiguity contained in policies and users' misinterpretation of policy can have complex and unforeseen consequences on organizational security.

Previously, the involvement of policy users in the interpretation of policies to produce formal language models has had a low return relative to the investment of resources needed to produce these models. This was due to the learning curve for policy users associated with manual translation and methods using quasi-natural language approaches, coupled with the error rates in the resulting models. The application described in this paper is anticipated to collect policy user interpretations to generate accurate models of those interpretations to aid password policy research, formalization, and ultimately more usable password policies. This paper describes the broader requirements that drove the requirements, high-level application features, validation of the application, and includes a discussion of how this work is expected to progress.

2 Background

Our overarching goal is to resolve the problem of password policy ambiguity by developing methods and tools for studying and clarifying policy statements. Thus this effort is grounded in research in password usability, password policies, and usability of automatically processing policy texts for the extraction and representation of knowledge and rules. Previous work in each of these research areas will be addressed.

Much research has focused on characterizing passwords that people employ, including [7–11] to name a few. These works rely on lists of passwords and provide insight into the actual passwords that people choose. Since users' password choices are governed in part by policy requirements, these studies are related to our research in password policies.

The relationship between password policy and user behavior has also been studied. Mannan and Oorschot [12] surveyed users of online banks and their understanding of bank's security requirements. They found disconnects between user practice and the banking guidelines. Furnell [13] examined the password-creation guidelines, the enforcement of password-composition restrictions and the reset policy of 10 website policies. In a survey regarding password usage of 32 staff members at a research university and a financial-services organization, Inglesant and Sasse [14] found that password policies which ignore human factors may result in unexpectedly poor security. Choong et al. [15] surveyed approximately 5,000 United States federal government staff members and found that users' password experiences were significantly influenced by password policies.

Others have specifically examined password policies and their content. Summers and Bosworth [16] described what should be in a password policy arguing for user guidance and organizational enforcement of passwords. Spafford [17] argued that the best practices shared by many modern password policies are actually artifacts based on out-of-date risk assessments. Based on his number and use of passwords, Farrell [18] argued that policy writers must acknowledge the increasing burden of password management on their users. Bonneau and Preibusch [19] surveyed the empirical password policies of 150 websites and were able to infer the enforced lengths and complexity requirements by creating accounts and systematically changing the password. Florêncio and Herley [20] surveyed length and complexity requirements for 75 websites according to their password policies and determined that sites that depend on users for revenue have weaker, more accommodating policies. Komanduri et al. [21] performed a large scale study that examined password composition policy and users' password choices. They found that increases in entropy of passwords correlate with decreases in usability but believe that policies can be optimized for entropy and usability.

Some research has attempted to make writing security policies easier. Xu et al. [22] presented a visualization of access-control policies. A list of guidelines for architecting a system for writing security and privacy policies is provided by Johnson et al. [23]. A few have focused specifically on writing password policies. The development of standardized password policies is proposed in [24]. A language for expressing a password-policy scenario in a formal language is presented by AlFayyadh et al., [25]. A measure of system harm resulting from the given scenario can be estimated using simulation. Parkin et al. [26] presented an ontological framework for reasoning about the security and usability costs of different policy decisions.

Finally, several tools have been architected for developing, studying and implementing policy. These systems are referred to as policy workbenches. Policy workbenches generally require that the policy makers interact through a quasi-natural language [2]. Many [2–5] have found that manual translation to the quasi natural language is time-consuming, error prone and thus not necessarily usable. Automated extraction attempts were also shown to be error prone. To address this concern, Michael et al. [2] developed an architecture for mapping policies submitted in a natural language to formats suitable for further processing. However, the approach still required grammar rules for the natural language to ensure accurate semantic interpretation. In [3–5] the researchers also developed a policy workbench for privacy management, again using a constrained natural language as the interface to the tool. They found the manual preprocessing of the policy was time consuming and impacted accuracy. Breaux and Antón [6] also examine policy management. They too use a structured natural language to identify actors, actions and objects in privacy policies.

While our research overlaps that of [19, 20] and the policy workbench efforts in [2–6], the focus of our work differs in important ways. We are focused on how policy users interpret password policies, highlighting the diversity and ambiguities in password policies so that policies can be strengthened. Our specific focus on policy users and their interpretations of password policies versus the machine interpretation of policies has led us to examine an alternative usability driven input approach to a policy workbench.

3   The Application

The functionality of the application centers on collecting an interpretation of a password policy from a user and generating the associated formal rule representation of that policy interpretation. The application design was based on requirements identified through envisioned use case scenarios and established usability principles. To enhance usability of the application, a usability expert reviewed the interface design prior to development. Multiple types of validation testing of the application were performed to ensure effective functionality and usability by the intended user populations. The requirement concerns, system architecture and validation testing are described in this section.

3.1   Application Requirements Considerations

Three main use cases were identified that drove the requirements specification.

1. Collect a policy user's interpretations of the rules in a password policy document and then translate those interpretations into a formal representation of the policy. This yields a model of the policy user's interpretations of the selected password policy. The target user population includes password policy users, specifically those without special password policy expertise. Policy user models are submitted anonymously.

2. Collect a password policy expert's interpretations of the rules in a password policy document and then translate those interpretations into a formal representation of the policy. This yields a model that can be used as the 'ground truth' representation of the selected password policy during analysis. These models must be distinguishable from those produced by policy users. The target user population includes password policy researchers and policy makers.
3. System administration to configure and maintain application software and operations, including configuring and installing new question-answer sets. It was expected that most users having a role of researcher will also have an administrator role for the application.

Finally, the application must support a flexible method for specification of the user-facing content and the formal language onto which user interpretations are mapped.

3.2   Implementation: Architecture and Features

From the requirements considerations related in the previous section, the use of a question-answer system approach was selected to collect user translations of existing policies. The question-answer approach has the advantage that questions and response choices can be crafted such that the mechanics of the translation to the formal rule set are not readily evident to non-expert translators and avoid having translation move beyond the intended scope of the formal rule space. Figure 1 shows an overview of the architecture.

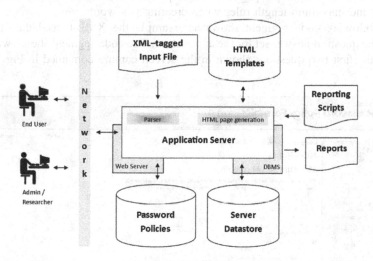

Fig. 1. System overview

In our implementation, policy users and policy makers access the system via a web-based, client-side interface. Once an account is authenticated, the user chooses which policy to review and a browser window provides a document containing the pertinent password policy, while another browser window presents questions and response choices. The user answers each question presented and then completes the review of a password policy. All responses and their corresponding formal language statements are stored by a server-side application. The review can be suspended and resumed at any time by the user.

On the server side, an eXtensible Markup Language (XML) and JavaScript Object Notation (JSON) -tagged input file provides most of the user-facing content used by the system. The tags specify questions, response options, comment solicitation, placement and type of user input, e.g., radio button, textbox options, etc. Further, a mapping of responses to formal statements, along with other user-facing content in the interface, such as text for alert notifications and help page are also specified in this file. The content for each user-facing page of the application is pulled from the XML file by a parser and populated onto the pertinent HyperText Markup Language (HTML) template page.

The application server includes the XML file parser, HTML templates, and a file repository of password policies. Further, the application server uses a web server package and a document-oriented, database management system (DBMS) to manage the datastore containing user account data and policy reviews. The DBMS system chosen supports dynamic schemas, which provides the needed flexibility to support the XML-defined, data-driven nature of the application. The application also accesses a directory of files, each containing a password policy. Finally, a set of scripts is employed to extract data from the datastore to generate spreadsheets and reports used in data analysis by researchers outside of the application.

Figure 2 shows a sample page from the question set regarding questions about minimum and maximum length rules when creating passwords.

The following code segment shows an example the XML-tagged data used to produce the question-answer set for the application. The code segment shown was used to create the first two questions shown in the screen capture contained in Fig. 2.

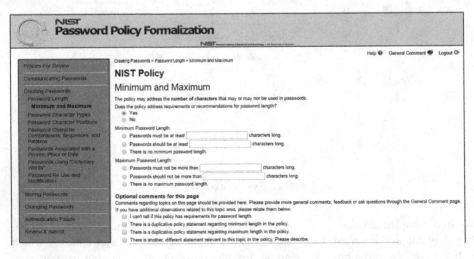

Fig. 2. Example of the user interface

```
<question id="q.2.0">
    <text>Does the policy address requirements or recom-
mendations for password length?</text>
    <response type="select one">
        <option id="q.2.0.A">
            <text>Yes</text>
        </option>
        <option id="q.2.0.B">
            <text>No</text>
        </option>
    </response>
</question>
<question id="q.2.1" display_when="q.2.0.A">
    <text>Minimum Password Length:</text>
    <response type="select one">
        <option id="q.2.1.A">
            <text type="json">Passwords must be at least
                {"cloze": {"validation": {"min": "1"},
                "type": "numerical", "id": "q.2.1.A.a"}}
                characters long.</text>
            <BNF_mapping id="b.35" type="json">Users must
                create passwords with length greater than or
                equal to {"insert": {"qref": "q.2.1.A.a"}}
                characters</BNF_mapping>
        </option>
        <option id="q.2.1.B">
            <text type="json">Passwords should be at least
                {"cloze": {"validation": {"min": "1"}, "type":
                "numerical", "id": "q.2.1.B.a"}} characters
                long.</text>
            <BNF_mapping id="b.36" type="json">Users should
                create passwords with length greater than or
                equal to {"insert": {"qref": "q.2.1.B.a"}}
                characters</BNF_mapping>
        </option>
        <option id="q.2.1.C">
            <text>There is no minimum password length.</text>
        </option>
    </response>
</question>
```

Finally, a second interface is provided for system administrators to set various system parameters such as the number of policies policy users are assigned to review, privileged account management, and similar functions. This interface is served to the client when a user with the appropriate access right authenticates to the system. Users in the role of researcher can use this mode to select a particular policy to review with the same question-answer set that is served to policy users.

3.3   Application Validation

A validation plan was developed to establish that the application and its' question-answer sets are usable and working as intended before the system was deployed to ensure accurate model generation. While identifying validation objectives, efforts were made to isolate concerns to make testing more effective. Identified objectives fall into two broad categories: those for the application itself and those for the data contained in the XML input file, e.g., the wording of the questions and responses. Validation of the system need only be performed once; however, each new input file or one with substantive changes should be validated before deployment. At the writing of this paper, we have completed the first phase of validation – assessing the mechanics of the application with respect to functional correctness and usability objectives.

Validation Objectives. The following validation objectives were excerpted from those identified for the application and its behaviors for any question-answer set:

- The application correctly utilizes the XML input file, e.g., recognizes all defined tags, utilizes tagged data correctly, and renders user-facing content correctly.
- The application correctly captures user responses, including user modifications to previously answered questions.
- For each policy review, the application correctly constructs and returns formal statements based on user responses, and correctly identifies formal statements where the reviewer did not supply all of the responses necessary to completely construct a formal statement.
- The application is usable for intended users.

For question-response sets specifically, the following validation objectives were identified:

- All user-facing content is usable, e.g., question-answer layouts, wording of questions, answers, alerts, button labels, and so on.
- The mapping of responses to formal statements is correctly specified, complete, with no redundancies or inconsistencies.

Validation Strategy. Testing efforts were generally divided along the lines defined by validation objectives, first validating the application and then the input file. Phase I of the strategy tackles the objectives for the application and its behaviors for any question-answer set. Phase II addresses test objectives specifically for question-answer sets.

Phase I: Validating the application. This first phase incorporated many types of tests ranging from black box functionality tests to usability testing of the interface components. Iterative work with the developer addressed issues that were found while testing progressed. Multiple input files were needed for this phase of testing. To assist in developing these input documents, one team member developed a parser which processes minimally-tagged input data and produces an XML file suitable for input to the application. This parser greatly facilitated the process of producing fully-tagged input files while reducing the syntax and typographical errors that would likely be produced if these files were manually generated.

Once the application was assessed to be behaving as expected with respect to the design specification of the XML tag set, usability tests were incorporated. A set of usability tests was developed and used to assess the user's ability to understand the workflow to review a policy, e.g., how to start a policy review, submit a review, and other application mechanics such as navigation within the application, leaving feedback, getting help, and so on. A draft version of the question-answer set and real password polices were used by members of the target end user population to help assess the usability of the application.

Phase II: Validating the input file. During Phase II, testing efforts will focus on assessing the wording of the questions, response options, button labels, alert messages and other user-facing content. To start, the input file will undergo an expert review to ensure that plain language [27] is used throughout and iterative refinements will be made as testing result data are analyzed. Testing will also assess the usability of different question-answer structures and users' feedback on those structures. Finally, the mapping of responses to formal language statements must be assessed for completeness and correctness.

4 Discussion

This work arose from a need to deal with ambiguities in current password policies. These ambiguities not only prevent researchers from comparing and contrasting policy statements, they also could cause users to misinterpret what is expected of them. To tackle ambiguity, we developed a formal language for stating what behavior is and is not allowed when creating, managing, and changing passwords. After developing our formal policy representation, we had several practiced translators perform manual translations of actual password policies. We found that manual translation of existing policies to the formal language to be time consuming and that one translator's set of formal language rules for a given policy might differ from another translator's results. Examination of the differing rules by these translators yielded explanations for the variation which fell into the following categories: (1) translator misread the source policy, (2) translator made a simple syntax error constructing the formal statement, (3) translator had imperfect understanding of the formal rule scope, and (4) translator had difficulty interpreting the source policy in an unambiguous way.

Karat et al. [5] when evaluating privacy rule authoring methods also found that policy makers had trouble writing policy rules without some form of guidance. Performing a usability test comparing interfaces using natural language with guidance, structured lists, and unassisted natural language they found that users performed better with guidance. Users performed faster, preferred the interface, and the quality of the resulting rule was higher with the assisted natural language interface. This encouraged us to develop a question and answer interface that assisted users in translating existing password policies into their formal representation. This user guided approach to translation specifically reduces translator variability due to simple syntax errors constructing the formal statement and translators' understanding of the rule scope.

Phase I testing has demonstrated that the application behaved as expected with respect to the design specification of the XML tag set. Application testing was followed by usability tests for the application. A set of usability tests was developed and used to assess the user's ability to understand the workflow to review and translate a policy, e.g., how to start a policy review, submit a review, and other application mechanics such as navigation within the application, leaving feedback, getting help and so on. A draft version of the question-response set along with real password polices were used by members of the target end user population to help assess the usability of the application. Users easily navigated through the system, followed the workflow, initiated policy translations and submitted translations. User feedback was positive and users felt confident that they could use the system to review and translate password policies.

Now that the application is validated and usable, our user testing will transition to focus on how users interpret the wording of questions and answers. Once this phase is completed, users will use the application to build a collection of translated password policies. This collection will help validate the formal language as well as reveal how policy users interpret current, natural language password statements and which statements lead to misinterpretation within a policy. This analysis results in the identification of ambiguities in current password polices leading to a better understanding of what makes a policy usable from a user perspective. Understanding the usability impact of individual statements and combinations of statements allows organizations to author policies that better support their security concerns.

Future research includes three objectives. The first is translating the formal representation of each statement in a policy to its plain language equivalent and assessing how users interpret a policy presented in a plain language format. Providing policy developers and experts a way to express an existing password policy in a plain language representation is our second goal. Our final goal is to provide policy developers and experts with analysis of security and usability factors for individual and combinations of rules within a policy. We believe that the insights provided by this user-centered approach will enable policy developers and maintainers to improve their password policies, which will, in turn, improve organizational security and the user experience.

Acknowledgements. The authors would like to acknowledge the contributions by James Foti, at the National Institution of Standards and Technology, for his work on the draft question-answer set used during validation of the application. His use of plain language in the text of the questions and answers helped differentiate concerns about the application from concerns about the wording of questions and answers during an early phase of the application's validation. Additionally, the authors would like to acknowledge the contributions of Susanne Furman, also at the National Institute of Standards and Technology, for her contributions to enhance the usability of the application, both during review of the initial design and usability testing.

References

1. Killourhy, K., Choong, Y., Theofanos, M.: Taxonomic rules for password policies: translating the informal to the formal language. Internal report 7970, National Institute of Standards and Technology, Gaithersburg, Maryland (2013)

2. Michael, J.B., Ong, V.L., Rowe, N.C.: Natural-language processing support for developing policy-governed software systems. In: 39th IEEE International Conference and Exhibition on Technology of Object-Oriented Languages and Systems, pp. 263–274. IEEE Press, New York (2001)

3. Brodie, C., Karat, C.M., Karat, J., Feng, J.: Usable security and privacy: a case study of developing privacy management tools. In: ACM 2005 Symposium on Usable Privacy and Security, pp. 35–43. ACM Press, New York (2005)

4. Brodie, C.A., Karat, C.M., Karat, J.: An empirical study of natural language parsing of privacy policy rules using the SPARCLE policy workbench. In: ACM 2006 Symposium on Usable Privacy and Security, pp. 8–19. ACM Press, New York (2006)

5. Karat, C.M., Karat, J., Brodie, C., Feng, J.: Evaluating interfaces for privacy policy rule authoring. In: ACM 2006 SIGCHI Conference on Human Factors in Computing Systems, pp. 83–92. ACM Press, New York (2006)

6. Breaux, T.D., Antón, A.I.: Deriving semantic models from privacy policies. In: Sixth IEEE International Workshop on Policies for Distributed Systems and Networks, pp. 67–76. IEEE Press, New York (2005)

7. Morris, R., Thompson, K.: Password security: a case history. Commun. ACM **22**(11), 94–597 (1979). ACM Press, New York

8. Klein, D.V.: Foiling the cracker: a survey of, and improvements to, password security. In: 2nd USENIX Security Workshop, pp. 5–14. USENIX, Berkeley (1990)

9. Wu, T. D.: A real-world analysis of kerberos password security. In: 1999 Network and Distributed Systems and Security Symposium. Internet Society (1999)

10. Florencio, D., Herley, C.: A large-scale study of web password habits. In: 16th ACM International Conference on World Wide Web, pp. 657–666. ACM Press, New York, (2007)

11. Dell'Amico, M., Michiardi, P., Roudier, Y.: Password strength: an empirical analysis. In: 30th IEEE INFOCOM, pp. 1–9. IEEE Press, New York (2010)

12. Mannan, M., van Oorschot, P.C.: Security and usability: the gap in real-world online banking. In: 2007 ACM Workshop on New Security Paradigms, pp. 1–14. ACM Press, New York (2008)

13. Furnell, S.: An assessment of website password practices. Comput. Secur. **26**(7), 445–451 (2007). Elsevier, Amsterdam

14. Inglesant, P. G., Sasse, M. A.: The true cost of unusable password policies: password use in the wild. In: SIGCHI 2010 Conference on Human Factors in Computing Systems, pp. 383–392. ACM Press, New York (2010)

15. Choong, Y.Y., Theofanos, M., Liu, H.K.: United States Federal Employees Password Management Behaviors a Department of Commerce Case Study. Internal report 7991, National Institute of Standards and Technology, Gaithersburg, Maryland (2014)

16. Summers, W. C., Bosworth, E:. Password policy: the good, the bad, and the ugly. In: WISICT 2004, Winter International Symposium on Information and Communication Technologies, pp. 1–6. Trinity College, Dublin (2004)

17. Spafford, E: Security Myths and Passwords. In: CERIAS Blog, 19 April 2006. http://www.cerias.purdue.edu/site/blog/post/password-change-myths/. Accessed Feb 2015

18. Farrell, S.: Password policy purgatory. IEEE Internet Comput. **12**(5), 84–87 (2008)

19. Bonneau, J., Preibusch, S.: The password thicket: technical and market failures in human authentication on the web. In: 9th Workshop on the Economics of Information Security (2010). http://weis2010.econinfosec.org/papers/session3/weis2010_bonneau.pdf. Accessed Feb 2015

20. Florêncio, D., Herley, C.: Where do security policies come from? In: 6th ACM Symposium on Usable Privacy and Security, article 10. ACM Press, New York. (2010)

21. Komanduri, S., Shay, R., Kelley, P.G., Mazurek, M.L., Bauer, L., Christin, N., Egelman, S.: Of passwords and people: measuring the effect of password-composition policies. In: 2011 SIGCHI Conference on Human Factors in Computing Systems, pp. 2595–2604. ACM Press, New York (2011)
22. Xu, W., Shehab, M., Ahn, G.J.: Visualization based policy analysis: case study in Selinux. In: 13th ACM Symposium on Access Control Models and Technologies, pp. 165–174. ACM Press, New York (2008)
23. Johnson, M., Karat, J., Karat, C.M., Grueneberg, K.: Optimizing a policy authoring framework for security and privacy policies. In: 6th ACM Symposium on Usable Privacy and Security, article 8. ACM Press, New York (2010)
24. AlFayyadh, B., Thorsheim, P., Jøsang, A., Klevjer, H.: Improving usability of password management with standardized password policies. In: 7eme Conférence sur la Sécurité des Architectures Réseaux et Systemes d'Information, 7th Conference on Network and Information Systems Security, SAR SSI 2012. https://sarssi2012.greyc.fr/wp-content/uploads/SAR-SSI-2012_p38-45_AlFayyadh.pdf. Accessed Feb 2015
25. Shay, R., Bhargav-Spantzel, A., Bertino, E.: Password policy simulation and analysis. In: 2007 ACM Workshop on Digital Identity Management, pp. 1–10. ACM Press, New York (2007)
26. Parkin, S.E., van Moorsel, A., Coles, R.: An Information security ontology incorporating human-behavioural implications. In: 2nd International Conference on Security of Information and Networks, pp. 46–55. ACM Press, New York (2009)
27. What is plain language? http://www.plainlanguage.gov/whatisPL/. Accessed on Feb 2015

Usability of Activity-Based and Image-Based Challenge Questions in Online Student Authentication

Abrar Ullah[✉], Hannan Xiao, and Trevor Barker

School of Computer Science, University of Hertfordshire, Hatfield, UK
{a.ullah3,h.xiao,t.1.barker}@herts.ac.uk

Abstract. There has been a renewed interest in secure authentication of students in online examinations. Online examinations are important and high stake assets in the context of remote online learning. The logistical challenges and absence of live invigilation in remote un-supervised online examination makes the identification and authentication process extremely difficult. The authors implemented pre-defined text-based challenge questions for student authentication in online examination using a Profile Based Authentication Framework (PBAF) approach. The pre-defined questions require students to register their answers, which causes distraction and usability challenges. In this study, a non-invasive activity-based learning journey questions approach was implemented combined with the image-based questions, using the PBAF approach. Findings of the study shows significant difference in the efficiency of activity-based and image-based questions during the learning process ($p < 0.01$). There was no significant difference in the accuracy of multiple-choice image-based and activity-based questions ($p > 0.01$). There was a significant difference in the accuracy of activity-based questions and activity-date questions ($p < 0.01$).

Keywords: Online examination · Authentication · Usability · Security

1 Introduction

Online examination or assessment is an essential component of online learning environment. In traditional online learning, examination is an embedded and integral part of the learning environment. Learning and examination are performed remotely and largely rely upon remote authentication protocols for security and invigilation [1].

The UK quality assurance code for practice suggests that online examination are vital for evaluating student skills against the learning goals [2]. The outcome of online examination is used to award grades, and ultimately a certificate or degree. This makes online examination a high stake process. Online examinations are conducted into both supervised and unsupervised locations. The supervised online examinations are invigilated face-to-face or proctored remotely. However, the unsupervised examinations are taken remotely without any physical invigilation. In an ideal scenario, a legitimate student accesses remote online examinations using secure authentication and completing the examination process according to the requisite examination protocols.

© Springer International Publishing Switzerland 2015
T. Tryfonas and I. Askoxylakis (Eds.): HAS 2015, LNCS 9190, pp. 131–140, 2015.
DOI: 10.1007/978-3-319-20376-8_12

However, cheating and academic dishonesty is reported in both face-to-face and remote online examinations [3]. Researchers suggest that online examination provides more opportunities for academic dishonesty [4–6]. Lanier [7] conducted a study on 1,262 college students and found that cheating in online examination is significantly higher than face-to-face examination.

In response to authentication threats. We proposed a "Challenge Questions" approach for authentication of online examinees. A Profile Based Authentication Framework (PBAF) was developed, which utilizes "Login-ID and Password" and "Challenge Questions" for authentication of online students. Challenge questions have been widely used for credential recovery by corporate email service provider, and banks for identity verification. The traditional challenge questions approach implements personal and security questions as authentication token. In the conventional challenge questions approach, users are required to register their answers to challenge questions at the outset for authentication at a later stage. In our proposed method, answers to challenge questions are recorded during the learning process and used for authentication in order to access online examination.

In this study we have evaluated the use of image-based and activity-based learning journey questions in a "six week" online course. The usability analysis of image-based and activity-based learning journey questions is reported in the results section.

2   Background

Authentication is important to prove that a user is, who he claims to be. Threats to online examination due to lack of physical interaction in a remote setting. The authors proposed and developed a Profile Based Authentication Framework (PBAF) [8]. The PBAF approach utilizes challenge questions and login identifier and password for authentication of online students. The method was empirically evaluated for guessing and collusion attacks [9, 10]. However, our previous studies reported usability and security issues with the pre-defined text-based and image-based challenge questions.

The pre-defined challenge questions had inherent usability issues reported by a number of earlier studies [11–13]. In the context of collusion, where a student may share access credentials with third party via email or telephone, pre-defined questions may be stored for sharing. In order to discourage sharing of challenge questions with a third party, we implemented non-invasive activity-based learning journey questions in this study. The activity-based questions integrates the learning and examination process and verify student identity based on the learning footprints. However, the focus of this paper is usability of the image-based and activity-based learning journey questions.

The study is part of an ongoing research to evaluate use of challenge questions for authentication of students in online examinations. In response to our previous studies [9, 10, 14] which reported the usability challenges using pre-defined text-based challenge questions, we implemented image-based and activity-based learning journey challenge questions for authentication purposes. This study aims to:

- Implement the activity-based learning journey challenge questions for authentication in online examination using the PBAF approach.
- Evaluate usability of image-based and activity-based learning journey questions.

3   Profile Based Authentication

The PBAF is a knowledge-based authentication approach [8], which utilizes challenge questions and login-identifier and password features. Login-identifier and password based authentication is used for the initial login to access the learning resources, whereas challenge questions authenticates online examinees. The authors designed and evaluated different types of challenges questions: pre-defined text-based questions, image-based questions, and activity-based learning journey questions.

Figure 1(a) shows the PBAF approach, which utilizes pre-defined text-based and image-based questions for authentication. Students are required to record answers to pre-defined questions. Answers to questions are stored into individual's profile. Challenge questions are extracted from individual's profile during authentication process. Challenge and profile questions are the same entities used in the learning and authentication contexts as shown in Fig. 1(a).

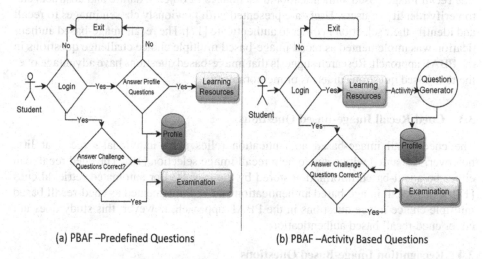

(a) PBAF –Predefined Questions   (b) PBAF –Activity Based Questions

Fig. 1. Profile based authentication design

Figure 1(b) shows the PBAF approach, which utilizes non-invasive programmatically generated activity-based learning journey questions. In typical online course, the traditional learning activities are a combination of lessons, assignments, forum discussion and quizzes etc. Student interaction with the learning activities trigger creation of challenge questions in the background and stored in the profile. As shown in Fig. 1(b), question generator creates activity-based learning journey questions and stored in a student profile. Challenge questions are extracted from individual's profile for authentication in online examination process. Different types of challenge questions are described below:

3.1 Text-Based Questions

The text-based challenge question is a widely used question type implemented by a number of email service providers for authentication purposes [15]. Questions are based on individual's personal and professional information. The text-based questions are further classified into fixed and open type questions [11]. The fixed-type questions are presented to users from a pool of pre-defined questions. The open-type text questions are users' driven and users have full control over choosing question's description and answer. Answers to text-based questions are received in free text form. The text-based challenge questions faces a number of challenges such as memorability, clarity, syntactic variation, which may cause security and usability issues [16].

3.2 Recall Image- Based Questions

The recall image-based authentication uses images of objects, nature and abstracts etc. to verify identity of users. Users are presented with previously chosen images to recall and identify their selection in order to authenticate [17]. The recall image-based authentication was implemented as recall image-based multiple choice challenge questions in the PBAF approach. Research suggests that image-based questions have advantage over the text-based questions in terms of memorability.

3.3 Cued-Recall Image-Based Questions

The cued recall image-based authentication relies upon individual's recall ability, however, it is aided with a cue to help recall image selection [18]. The cued recall can either be a text-based information stored by the user [19] or automated retrieval cues [17]. Cued-recall image-based authentication can be implemented as cued-recall based multiple choice image questions in the PBAF approach, however, this study does not cover cued-recall based authentication.

3.4 Recognition Image-Based Questions

The recognition image-based authentication relies upon individual's recognition ability and authenticate on the basis if an individual has seen or chosen a image before [18]. The correct image is presented with a set of distraction images and user is challenged to recognize a previously viewed or selected image. The recognition based authentication was implemented as recognition based multiple choice questions in the PBAF approach.

3.5 Activity-Based Learning Journey Questions

The activity-based questions are generated programmatically based on individual's learning activity during the learning process [20]. In traditional online courses, learning is a set of pre-defined activities including lessons, forums, quizzes, assignments, chatting activities to name a few. Learners are anticipated to perform multiple learning activities during the learning process. The question generator creates activity-based questions, which is trigged on a student's interaction with a learning activity. The activity-based learning journey challenge questions is an innovative approach to collect information about a student and utilize it for authentication. Characteristics of activity-based learning journey questions are:

– **Security:** Answers to activity-based learning journey questions should be difficult to guess.
– **Usability:** Activity-based learning journey questions should be easy to recall with better usability.
– **Non-Invasiveness:** Unlike traditional challenge questions, where users are required to register answers at the outset, the activity-based learning journey questions are created in the background without interrupting users for registration of answers.
– **Adaptability:** The activity-based questions are short lived and status of automatically created questions are checked and refreshed instantly.

4   Research Methodology

This study was organized to evaluate image-based and activity-based learning journey questions, in a 6 week online learning course involving online students. The description of online course, question generator and usability results is presented below.

– **Online Course:** For the purpose of this study a 6 week "PHP and MySQL" course was developed and instructed online using MOODLE platform. Students were required to choose an image of their choice from multiple-choice images during the learning process. Their selection was recorded in their profiles for authentication. A questions generator was developed and integrated in the PBAF method to create activity-based questions and their answers based on individual's learning activity, which is described below.
– **Question Generator:** To improve usability and security of authentication system in online learning, we used non-invasive activity-based learning journey questions generated in the background on student's interaction with the learning activities. The question generator algorithm was employed to create questions and add them to the student's profile as shown in Fig. 1(b). Questions were created on student's interaction with: forum, discussion, adding a post in forum, lessons, resources and quiz.

Individual student's learning activities were logged and stored into the database. Question generator extracted and correlated logged activities fields with pre-defined question statements according to their semantics. As a result, meaningful and contextual activity-based challenge questions were created and stored into individual student's profile. Each activity-based learning journey challenge question was embedded with distracting multiple choice options including the correct answer.

Table 1 column 1 shows activity based learning journey questions created during the online course. The course was embedded with 5 forums, multiple discussions, 5 lessons, and more than 30 learning resources. In the questions shown in Table 1, original activities in the 6 week "PHP & MySQL" course are replaced with Forum, Lesson, Discussion and Examination for summarizing the results.

Table 1. Authentication result of activity-based challenge questions

Activity-based challenge question	Expired	Matched N (%)	Unmatched N (%)	Response time (sec)
Which of the following is correct for you starting discussion in (Forum)?	0	3(100 %)	0(0 %)	30
Which of the following is correct for your posting in (Forum)	0	1(100 %)	0(0 %)	52
Which of the following is your post?	0	6(100 %)	0(0 %)	23.67
Which of the following is correct for your access permissions to (Examination)	0	6(86 %)	1(14 %)	8.62
Which of the following is correct for your visit to learning resources	23	154(82 %)	33(18 %)	13.51
Which of the following is correct for your access permissions to (Lesson)	1	24(89 %)	3(11 %)	7.58
Which of the following is correct for your starting a (Lesson)	3	5(50 %)	5(50 %)	13.1
Which of the following is correct for your visiting Lesson	3	6(55 %)	5(45 %)	15.06
Which of the following is correct for your visit to (Discussion)	0	5(56 %)	4(44 %)	14.85
Which of the following is correct for your visit to (Forum)	0	3(33 %)	6(67 %)	.89
Sub total		**213(79 %)**	**57(21 %)**	
Activity date				
Which of the following dates have you completed (Examination)	0	2(29 %)	5(71 %)	6.62
Which of the following dates have you posted in (Forum)	0	(100 %)	0(0 %)	52
Which of the following dates have you completed (Lesson)	0	1(25 %)	3(75 %)	7.08
Which of the following dates have you started (Lesson)	3	7(47 %)	8(53 %)	14.51
Which of the following dates have you visited (Discussion)	0	10(29 %)	25(71 %)	13.68
Which of the following dates have you visited (Forum)	0	6(27 %)	16(73 %)	9.86
Sub total		**27(32 %)**	**57(68 %)**	
Grand total		**240(68 %)**	**114(32 %)**	

5   Usability Results

A total of 83 students participated in the initial registration phase. All 83 students submitted answers to at least 3 image-based questions. Of the total 83 students,

72 performed at least one learning activity and the question generator created and stored activity-based learning journey questions in their profiles.

5.1   Efficiency

The efficiency of questions was measured on student response time to questions. The activity-based learning questions were created in the background by question generator during the learning process and response time was not needed. The response time for both activity-based and image-based questions were recorded during the authentication process. An independent sample t-test was performed to compare the mean response time of activity-based and image-based questions. There was no significant difference in the response time of image-based (M = 12.41, N = 18, SD = 6.04) and activity-based questions (M = 18.25, N = 16, SD = 14.51) conditions t (32) = -1.563, p = 0.128 (p > 0.05).

Efficiency of Activity-Based Questions. Table 1 shows activity-based learning journey questions answered during the authentication process. A total of 3464 activity-based questions were generated during the 6 week course. Access to learning was performed recurrently and students were encouraged to participate in learning and examination activities. The activity-based questions were short lived. If a student performed a learning activity multiple times, any correlated questions generated previously were de-activated and new questions created with up to date information. It was aimed to record and present the most recent activity-based questions during the authentication process for better memorability and to avoid ambiguity. Unlike pre-defined text and image-based questions, activity-based learning journey questions increased the efficiency by generating questions in the background without interrupting students for recording answers. The comparison of response-time between image-based questions and "0" response for all activity-based questions show a significant difference (p < 0.01).

Efficiency of Image-Based Questions. Table 2 shows results of recall image-based questions recorded during the authentication process. The participants were asked to select their choice from 5 multiple choice image options. Data in column 1 show image question type and column 4 shows the response time. The mean response time of image-based questions was recorded as 12.42 s. There was no significant difference in the response time between image-based questions and activity-based learning journey questions (p > 0.01) during the authentication process.

5.2   Accuracy

The accuracy was measured on the number of matched and unmatched answers to challenge questions during the authentication process. Of all students, 58 participated in at least one weekly quiz and returned answers to a total of 1347 challenge questions. The accuracy results are described below. There was no significant difference in the accuracy of activity-based and image-based questions (p > 0.05).

Table 2. Authentication results of image-based questions

Image type	Matched N (%)	Unmatched N (%)	Response time (sec)
Books	60(77 %)	18(23 %)	16.62
Pen	45(70 %)	19(30 %)	18.36
Education	56(82 %)	12(18 %)	18.00
Science	21(58 %)	15(42 %)	11.54
Online learning	28(70 %)	12(30 %)	11.80
Network	25(74 %)	9(26 %)	11.91
Exam	11(61 %)	7(39 %)	7.96
Scenery	15(79 %)	4(21 %)	8.45
Fish	14(78 %)	4(22 %)	7.80
Peace sign	9(75 %)	3(25 %)	22.58
Flower	11(92 %)	1(8 %)	22.58
Bear	7(58 %)	5(42 %)	22.64
Lion	6(67 %)	3(33 %)	8.11
Tiger	5(56 %)	4(44 %)	8.11
Wolf	8(89 %)	1(11 %)	8.11
Parrot	5(71 %)	2(29 %)	6.24
Humming bird	4(57 %)	3(43 %)	6.24
Eagle	6(86 %)	1(14 %)	6.24
Total	**336(73 %)**	**123(27 %)**	**12.42**

Accuracy of Activity Based Questions. For better accuracy, we implemented multiple choice answers to activity-based learning journey questions during the authentication process. Results of learning activity based questions from authentication process are presented in Table 1 with the question statement under column 1, and the number of multiple choice options in column 2. The number of activity questions disabled or expired during before being presented to students are shown in column 3. The number of matched, unmatched answers and response time are shown in columns 4, 5 and 6. A total of 354 learning activity based questions were presented for authentication with 240 (68 %) accuracy. The activity questions were analyzed into two categories i.e. activity-based and activity date questions. There was a significant difference in the number matched answers of activity-based (M = 75.10, N = 10, SD = 24.47) and activity-date based questions (M = 42, N = 6, SD = 29.10) conditions t (14) = 2.38,

$p < 0.01$. Students were presented with multiple choice answers, however 114 (32 %) of the total activity-based questions was incorrect and penalized.

Accuracy of Image-Based Questions. Table 2 shows summary of authentication of image-based questions submitted during the weekly quizzes. Results of the image-based questions show 336 (73 %) matched answers during authentication. Each question was presented with 5 multiple choice answers for student to recall their previous selection which was registered during the learning process. However, students were unable to recall matched answer to 123 (27 %) questions and penalized for memorability. Unlike free text answers, multiple choice questions address any issues related with spelling mistakes, spaces, case variation or syntactic variations. This shows that memorability is a common problem with both pre-defined text-based and image-based questions, when students are required to record answers to a large number of questions.

6   Conclusion

Online examination is a high stake process and therefore secure and usable approaches are important for remote authentication. The usability of challenge questions have been an ongoing issue reported by many studies. In this study, we implemented activity-based learning journey questions with predefined image-based questions for authentication.

The use of activity-based questions significantly increased the efficiency by eliminating the process of recording answers to challenge questions. Unlike activity-based questions, students were required to register their answers to image-based questions in an additional step during the learning process. There was no significant difference in the response time between image-based and activity-based learning journey questions. The findings show no significant difference in the accuracy of image-based and activity-based learning journey questions.

The initial usability findings are encouraging and future work will be carried out to analyze the security of activity-based learning journey questions against authentication attacks.

References

1. Karaman, S.: Examining the effects of flexible online exams on students' engagement in e-learning. Educ. Res. Rev. **6**(3), 259–264 (2011)
2. Agency, Q.A.: Code of practice for the assurance of academic quality and standards in higher education. Assessment of Students, Second edition (2006)
3. Harmon, O.R., Lambrinos, J., Buffolino, J.: Assessment design and cheating risk in online instruction. Online J. Distance Learn. Adm. **13**(3) (2010)
4. Grijalva, T.C.: Academic honesty and online courses. Department of Economics, Weber State University (2006)
5. Whitley, B.E.: Factors associated with cheating among college students: a review. Res. High. Educ. **39**(3), 235–274 (1998)
6. Mccabe, D.L., Treviño, L.K., Butterfield, K.D.: Cheating in academic institutions: a decade of research. Ethics Behav. **11**(3), 219–232 (2001)

7. Lanier, M.M.: Academic integrity and distance learning∗. J. Crim. Justice Educ. **17**(2), 244–261 (2006)
8. Ullah, A., Xiao, H., Lilley, M.: Profile based student authentication in online examination. In: International Conference on Information Society 2012, IEEE, London, UK (2012)
9. Ullah, A., Xiao, H., Barker, T., Lilley, M.: Evaluating security and usability of profile based challenge questions authentication in online examinations. J. Internet Serv. Appl. **5**(1), 2 (2014)
10. Ullah, A., Xiao, H., Barker, T., Lilley, M.: Graphical and text based challenge questions for secure and usable authentication in online examinations. In: The 9th International Conference for Internet Technology and Secured Transactions (ICITST) 2014, IEEE, London, UK (2014)
11. Just, M.: Designing secure yet usable credential recovery systems with challenge questions. In: CHI 2003 Workshop on Human-Computer Interaction and Security Systems 2003, Citeseer, Florada, USA (2003)
12. Just, M., Aspinall, D.: Personal choice and challenge questions: a security and usability assessment. In: Proceedings of the 5th Symposium on Usable Privacy and Security 2009, ACM, CA, USA (2009)
13. Schechter, S., Brush, A.J.B., Egelman, S.: It's no secret. Measuring the security and reliability of authentication via 'secret' questions. In: 30th IEEE Symposium on Security and Privacy 2009, IEEE (2009)
14. Ullah, A., Xiao, H., Lilley, M., Barker, T.: Usability of profile based student authentication and traffic light system in online examination. In: The 7th International Conference for Internet Technology and Secured Transactions (ICITST), IEEE, London, UK (2012)
15. Just, M., Aspinall, D.: Challenging challenge questions. In: Socio-Economic Strand 2009, Oxford University, UK (2009)
16. Griffith, V., Jakobsson, M.: Messin' with texas deriving mother's maiden names using public records. In: Ioannidis, J., Keromytis, A.D., Yung, M. (eds.) ACNS 2005. LNCS, vol. 3531, pp. 91–103. Springer, Heidelberg (2005)
17. Wiedenbeck, S., Waters, J., Birget, J.-C., Brodskiy, A., Memon, N.: Authentication using graphical passwords: effects of tolerance and image choice. In: Proceedings of the 2005 Symposium on Usable Privacy and Security 2005, ACM (2005)
18. Hayashi, E., Hong, J., Christin, N.: Security through a different kind of obscurity: evaluating distortion in graphical authentication schemes. In: Proceedings of the SIGCHI Conference on Human Factors in Computing Systems 2011, ACM (2011)
19. Rabkin, A.: Personal knowledge questions for fallback authentication: security questions in the era of facebook. In: SOUPS 2008: Proceedings of the 4th Symposium on Usable Privacy and Security 2008, 23, ACM, New York, NY, USA (2008)
20. Babic, A., Xiong, H., Yao, D., Iftode, L.: Building robust authentication systems with activity-based personal questions. In: Proceedings of the 2nd ACM Workshop on Assurable and Usable Security Configuration 2009, ACM (2009)

Cybersecurity

Adjustable Fusion to Support Cyber Security Operators

François-Xavier Aguessy[1]([✉]), Olivier Bettan[1], Romuald Dobigny[2],
Claire Laudy[2], Gaëlle Lortal[2], and David Faure[2]

[1] Cyber Security Lab, SiX/Theresis, Thales Solutions de Securité and Services,
Campus Polytechnique, 1 Avenue Augustin Fresnel, 91767 Palaiseau Cedex, France
francois-xavier.aguessy@thalesgroup.com
[2] Analysis and Reasoning in Complex Systems Lab., Thales Research and Technology,
Campus Polytechnique, 1 Avenue Augustin Fresnel, 91767 Palaiseau Cedex, France

Abstract. Cyber security operators use Security Information and Event Management systems to process and summarize the huge amount of heterogeneous logs and alerts. However, these systems do not give to the operator a concise view of the attack status or context, a mandatory feature to understand and remediate properly a threat. Moreover, the number of alerts to analyze for a single information system is high, and thus requires to be split into several levels of responsibility distributed among several operators. This layered security monitoring implies a decision problem as well as an automation problem tackled in this paper with the support of an attack graph-based feature. An attack graph is a risk assessment model that accurately describes, in a concise way, the threats on an information system. In this article, we describe how an attack graph can be used for pattern searching and fusion algorithms, in order to add context to the alerts. We also present recommendations for designing future interactive application based on adjustable fusion and a risk assessment model, for cyber security monitoring.

1 Introduction

As information systems are getting ever more complex, they produce large amount of heterogeneous logs and alerts that operators working in Information Security Operations Center (SOC) cannot process without smart aggregation. They thus need to use Security Information and Event Management (SIEM) systems that collect, aggregate, normalize, correlate and report the events generated in an information system. SIEM solutions provide a dynamic view of the security events in a system, but they do not give to operators a concise view of the attack status and context, with knowledge of possible future, which may be necessary to understand and remediate properly a cyber security threat.

Security operators have a huge number of alerts to deal with for a single information system and thus this process has been split into several levels of responsibility shared among several operators. We are facing here a collaborative decision problem and not solely an automation problem. In these approaches at use in SOCs, responsibility involvement, collaboration and awareness of each stakeholder is crucial to ensure the quality of a shared decision making.

Some risk assessment models such as attack graphs allow an operator to understand the threats targeting an information system. An attack graph is a risk analysis model

T. Tryfonas and I. Askoxylakis (Eds.): HAS 2015, LNCS 9190, pp. 143–153, 2015.
DOI: 10.1007/978-3-319-20376-8_13

regrouping all the paths an attacker may follow in an information system. It is composed of nodes, representing the hosts that can be exploited by an attacker. Nodes are linked together with edges, representing the attacks that can be done between these hosts. Contrary to the outputs of SIEM (alerts on ongoing attacks), these threat models represent attacks that are likely to happen, with their context of occurrence. However, it gives a static view of the system with no easy way to know which part of the information system is currently under attack. There is thus a strong need to combine both approaches, in order to take advantages of dynamicity and correctness out of SIEM systems, and of contextual and concise view out of risk assessment models. As the risk assessment models are based on big graphs, and the SIEM events are in some ways a pattern of such graphs, graph fusion and query algorithms can be used to find the patterns that have been detected in the whole graph. We aim at studying in this article, recommendations for designing future interactive application based on adjustable fusion and a risk assessment model, for cyber security monitoring.

This paper is organized as follows: in Sect. 2, we describe the state of the art of the technologies involved: SIEM, responsibility transfer, graph-based risk assessment models and pattern-matching and fusion algorithms. Section 3 presents the graph model used for pattern matching. Section 4 integrates the human aspects of this decision problem, by introducing graph fusion. Section 5 concludes and put this work into perspective.

2   State of the Art

2.1   Security Information and Event Management (SIEM) Systems

Several correlation methods can be used in Security Information and Event Management systems, to reduce the number of alerts and correlate them. They can be regrouped in 3 categories [1]:

- **Similarity-based methods** [2, 3]: aggregating the alerts by using their similarities on attributes or time,
- **Sequential-based methods** [4, 5]: alerts are regrouped, according to a model (pre/post conditions),
- **Case-based methods** [6, 7]: research of specific patterns following scenarios defined in expert rules.

Products using alert correlation are generally one main component of SIEM, which also collect and report security events, related to these alerts. Most of these tools (open source [8, 9] or commercial [10–13]), often used by SOCs operators, first reduce and cluster the alerts, then implement a rule-based correlation approach, using an expert rules correlation engine. This is a quite simple but efficient process. However, detection capabilities of pattern-based SIEM tools are optimal for known and well characterized threats.

2.2   Responsibility Transfer and Collaborative Work

SIEM approaches at works in SOCs propose a segmentation of threats management by human operators into 3 levels: (1) security tickets creation due to alerts raised by security devices and first qualification; (2) Assessment of security incident resulting from alerts correlation and possible remediation proposal; (3) Incident investigation and technical escalation [14].

Figure 1 represents the common escalation process and responsibility transfer in a SOC, which follows the start of an incident (generally with an alert issued by the SIEM), until the incident is closed.

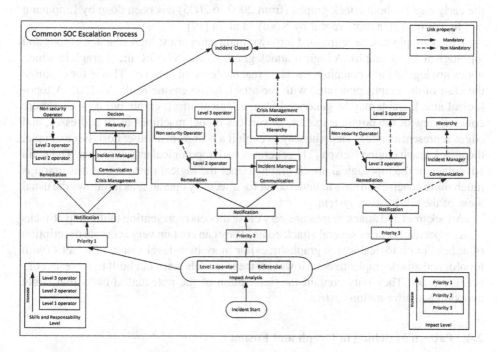

Fig. 1. Common SOC escalation process

2.3 Graph-Based Models for Cyber Security

Attack trees are a well-known multi-step attack model which is very important since it is one of the first graphical models to have been proposed for security assessment. The notion of attack tree was introduced by Bruce Schneier [15]. In his article, the attack trees are defined informally as a tree with AND/OR nodes which describe exactly the possible or required steps to do an attack and arcs modeling dependencies between these steps. The goal of the attack is located in the root of the tree and the basic actions used to achieve this goal are leaf nodes. Attack trees were formalized by Mauw et al. [16].

The main limitation of attack trees is that they only describe one main attack. To respond this limitation, attack graphs have been created. An attack graph is a model that regroups all the steps that an attacker may follow in an information system during an attack from both outside or inside the local network. It has been first introduced by Phillips and Swiler [17]. This formalism has been widely used ever since, thus many heterogeneous models are now behind the name attack graph. Generally, vertices (also called nodes in the literature) represent opportunities in an information system or actions that can be done by an attacker, and edges (also called arcs in the literature) represent the dependency relations between the opportunities and/or actions. An attack graph can be built using information about the potential exploits that can be carried out on a network or using existing vulnerabilities databases. A summary of the state of the art on the early papers about attack graphs (from 2002 to 2005) has been done by Lippmann and Ingols in [18]; a more recent by Kordy et al. in [19].

Attack graphs can be regrouped into two main categories: logical attack graphs and topological attack graphs. A logical attack graph is an AND/OR direct graph in which nodes are logical facts containing what is reachable by an attacker. This is for example the case of the graphs generated with the attack graph engine MulVAL [20]. A topological attack graph may be generated from a logical attack graph, but it gives a more concise view of the possible attacks, as vertices model machines or IP addresses, and edges represent an attack step: the way to exploit a host from another host. For example, the attack graph engine Netspa [21] generates such topological attack graphs. The main advantage of the topological attack graphs rather the logical ones, is that this graph is much more concise and easy to understand for a security operator, as it follows the usual view of the information system.

Attack trees and attack graphs are very close models representing multi-step at-tacks with respectively one or several attack goals. They can contain very accurate description of attacks (with logical attack graphs/trees) or more high-level vision of attacks (with topological attack graphs/trees). However, these models were not built to represent on-going attacks. They only contain the description of the potential at-tacks that could happen in an information system.

2.4 Pattern Matching in Graph and Fusion

High-Level Information Fusion. Soft data fusion is an ever growing trend in the information fusion community. More and more tracks dedicated to soft information are organized within the International Conference on Information Fusion over the years and numerous authors stress the need for soft data management and fusion. For instance, in the detection of people and complex activities, the use of soft information sources is critical. The authors of [22] describe a 5 year program involving several academic actors that aim at addressing major stakes of soft data fusion. It includes the development of a framework as well as evaluation methods.

In addition, many authors relate about new issues raised by soft data fusion. Among them [23] and [24] quote natural language processing, transformation of data into comprehensive and semantic data structures, soft data association and graph matching. As the automation of soft data fusion is a very challenging issue, due to, e.g., error estimation, normalization and context extraction for information interpretation, the authors propose a mixed approach that embeds the participation of a human analyst to the fusion process.

We previously developed a framework based on graph structures, graph algorithm and similarity measures for soft data fusion managing inconsistencies (InSyTo Synthesis v1 [25, 26]). The use case presented in [27] dealt with the management of an information network containing descriptions of entities (companies, universities…) that collaborate through several media such as research project, scientific papers and so on. The InSyTo Synthesis framework was used to enable non-redundant information addition to the information network, as well as graph based information query.

Information Query in Graphs. The graph fusion algorithm relies on the search for matches between sub-graphs and more precisely for a maximal matching subgraph. The idea is to find the largest subgraph of a first graph that cannot be distinguished from a subgraph of second graph. Maximal subgraph matching is used in order to determine, where to add information in an information graph, and which parts of two information graphs are redundant and should thus be fused rather than be repeated twice in the graph resulting from the fusion.

The decision problem of whether two graphs match is well studied and is in NP [28]. The problem of finding matching subgraphs, known as the subgraph isomorphism problem, is known to be NP-complete and difficult to solve in parallel. This problem is well studied and have led to a lot of algorithms, among which several have been parallelized [29, 30]. The InSyTo Synthesis fusion algorithm relies on subgraph isomorphism and maximum subgraph isomorphism algorithms. Both those algorithms must solve highly combinatory problems, on which the execution time may become too long to satisfy user requirements. To manage this problem, the InSyTo Synthesis subgraph isomorphism algorithm is partially parallelized.

3   Attack Model and Alerts Pattern Matching

The goal of the process we describe in this article is to help security operators to identify the attacks that are currently happening in a model of their information system, while taking into account human computer interaction, in order to improve the decision process in Security Information and Event Management systems.

As seen in the state of the art, on one hand, some SIEM tools gather and regroup alerts, but are not sufficient to give the context needed by an operator to properly understand and treat them. On the other hand, some models of the information system represent the attacks that can happen, but they give a static view of the system with no easy way to know which part of the information system is currently under attack. Such models are represented by a graph of the information system, in which fusion and query algorithms can be used.

3.1   Information Representation of the Attack Model

Topological Attack Graph. The model on which we will base our pattern matching and fusion processes is a topological attack graph, which describes all the attacks that are possible in an information system. This choice has been led by the ability of such a model to contain an accurate description of the attacks, while keeping a concise view, easy to understand for a security operator, as it is based on the topological representation of an information system. This graph is constituted of vertices, representing hosts, and edges, representing potential attacks. Each edge is associated with a set of metadata describing, for example, which vulnerability is exploited on this path, the probes that are related to this path, and the log message that may be provided, if such path is actually followed.

Alerts. The alerts that are issued by security probes (such as SIEM, Host or Network Intrusion Detection System (IDS), firewalls...) are parsed, in order to extract meaning from the log message (probe, source host, destination host, vulnerability exploited...). Such alerts can be units (e.g. IDS alerts) or multiples (e.g. SIEM logs that describe multi-steps attack). A security operator may receive numerous alerts in a small time interval. Unit alerts that are received in a short interval or multiple alerts already correlated are part of one main attack scenario and constitutes an attack pattern. The security operator wants to match this pattern in the whole graph, to know the reals attacks that are currently happening, and what can happen next.

A Graph Based Information Representation. We use Basic Conceptual Graphs [31] to represent information. Basic Conceptual Graphs are bipartite graphs containing concept and relation nodes. Figure 2 gives an example of a conceptual graph. The rectangular boxes represent concept nodes and the ovals represent relation nodes.

Graphical form

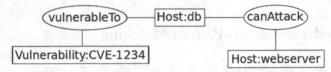

Linear form
vulnerableTo([Host: db@db], [Vulnerability: CVE-1234 @CVE-1234]),
canAttack([Host:webServer@webServer], [Host: db@db]).

Fig. 2. Conceptual graph example

The concepts represent the *things* or entities that exist. For instance, in Fig. 2, the concept Host:webserver represents an instance of a Host object whose name is webserver. The relation nodes indicate the relations that hold between the different concepts of a situation.

The types of concepts are organized into a hierarchy. Therefore, a specialization/ generalization relation may be defined between several graphs [26]. This relation is used within the query function. Answers to a query graph are sub-graphs of the data graph that are more specific than the query graph. This would allow to use this approach with hierarchical attack graphs.

3.2   Graph-Based Information Query

The query algorithm relies on a generic sub graph matching algorithm, which itself uses specific fusion strategies [25]. The graph matching component is in charge of the structural consistency between the query and information graphs. The fusion strategy part is made of compatibility functions over elements of the graphs. They enable the customization of the generic algorithm according to the context in which it is used. Within the query function, we use a *subsomption* strategy and a whole-structure conservation mode.

Query Algorithm. The inputs of the query function are two graphs. The information graph is a big network (the topological attack graph), while the query graph is a relatively small one (the alerts pattern). Our approach to parallelize the graph matching process is to split up the subgraph matching process. A first phase manages the node to node comparisons of the query and data graphs. A second step is in charge of preserving the structure of the graphs. This process has been described more deeply in [25].

Graph Structure Preservation. Once the candidate answers to each subgraph of the query are processed, all the combinations of answer subgraphs are provided, preserving the original structure of the data graph. The candidate answer subgraphs are assembled one with another, if and only if their association respects the structural constraints of the initial data graph. The connectivity between the relations through the concept nodes is checked.

Queries in Topological Attack Graphs. This query algorithm applies to finding alert patterns in topological attack graphs stored in Basic Conceptual Graphs. The topological attack graph stands in for the information graph, as it is the big graph, in which all the knowledge of the information system (topology, vulnerabilities, possible attacks…) is stored. The alert patterns stand in for the query graph, as they represent a smaller graph, subgraph of the information graph. This algorithm outputs the position in the topological attack graph of the detected patterns.

4   Human Computer Interaction in SIEM

4.1   Human Computer Interaction Drawbacks

SOC and SIEM technologies have several drawbacks in terms of HCI. The 1st level (security ticket creation) is tedious and repetitive work, which doesn't enable global situation awareness; The 2nd level (assessment of security incident) generates alert transmission on the different levels of SOC slowing down the logs analysis processes; As for the 3rd level (incident investigation and technical escalation), the added value from cyber security operators is at the crossing of the three levels and in the incident context conceptualization. Visual analytics techniques supporting cyber security monitoring suffer from lack of interactivity and visualization overload despite recent works [32] and are often not structured advisedly. The approach proposed here will fuse the information and then present less information to the operators but more synthetized thanks to the fusion process. This will enable the operators to better understand the situation and take a better decision even facing large/complex attacks.

Moreover, to support the operators in their analyses and decisions, we propose to study responsibility sharing and awareness between the operators at different level [33] to propose design recommendations for a future interactive application based on adjustable fusion and increasing the collaboration between the operators to increase their global understanding and efficiency.

4.2 Operator Dependent Fusion Strategies

The InSyTo Synthesis platform encompasses a generic graph based fusion algorithm that is used for the three functions (information fusion, information synthesis and information query). The usage of the algorithm (parameters and launch mode) determines the function that is realized. The fusion algorithm is made of two interrelated components (see Fig. 3). The first component is a generic subgraph matching algorithm, which itself relies on the use of fusion strategies. The graph matching component takes care of the overall structures of the initial and fused observations. It is in charge of the structural consistency of the fused information, regarding the structures of the initial observations, within the fusion process.

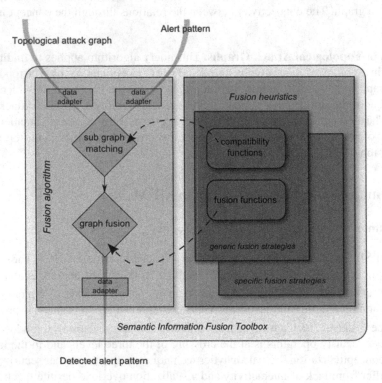

Fig. 3. Fusion architecture

The fusion strategy part is made of similarity, compatibility and functions over elements of the graphs to be fused. They enable the customization of the generic fusion algorithm according to the context in which it is used. The context encompasses the application domain, the semantics of the information items and user preferences.

The fusion strategies enable to manage the discrepancies that may be observed in observations of the same situation by different sources.

5 Conclusion and Perspectives

We presented in this article the status of current approaches at use in Information Security Operations Center, where security operators based their analysis on results of Security Information and Event Management systems. As these operators have a huge number of alerts to treat, this process has been split into several levels of responsibility distributed among several operators, which cause a collaborative decision problem. To improve the decision, we proposed a process using pattern matching and information fusion algorithms, reasoning on topological attack graphs. This process, allowed taking advantages of dynamicity and correctness out of SIEM systems, and of contextual and concise view out of risk assessment models. The adjustable fusion process could be refined to propose solutions enabling to avoid bystander effect, social loafing or group think in collaborative decision making [34]. We assume that to structure the types of interaction with the system(s) following the Sheridan and Verplank model [35] would enable operators to adapt the correlation process to their situation awareness and ground truth modeling needs.

References

1. Salah, S., Maciá-Fernández, G., Díaz-Verdejo, J.E.: A model-based survey of alert correlation techniques. Comput. Netw. **57**(5), 1289–1317 (2013)
2. Zhuang, X., Xiao, D., Liu, X., Zhang, Y.: Applying data fusion in collaborative alerts correlation. In: International Symposium on Computer Science and Computational Technology, ISCSCT 2008, vol. 2, pp. 124–127, IEEE (2008)
3. Ahmadinejad, S.H., Jalili, S.: Alert correlation using correlation probability estimation and time windows. In: International Conference on Computer Technology and Development, ICCTD 2009, vol. 2, pp. 170–175. IEEE, November 2009
4. Zhaowen, L., Shan, L., Yan, M.: Real-time intrusion alert correlation system based on prerequisites and consequence. In: 2010 6th International Conference on Wireless Communications Networking and Mobile Computing (WiCOM), pp. 1–5. IEEE, September 2010
5. Roschke, S., Cheng, F., Meinel, C.: A new alert correlation algorithm based on attack graph. In: Herrero, Á., Corchado, E. (eds.) CISIS 2011. LNCS, vol. 6694, pp. 58–67. Springer, Heidelberg (2011)
6. Cuppens, F., Ortalo, R.: LAMBDA: a language to model a database for detection of attacks. In: Debar, H., Mé, L., Wu, S.F. (eds.) RAID 2000. LNCS, vol. 1907, pp. 197–216. Springer, Heidelberg (2000)

7. Katipally, R., Gasior, W., Cui, X., Yang, L.: Multistage attack detection system for network administrators using data mining. In: Proceedings of the Sixth Annual Workshop on Cyber Security and Information Intelligence Research, p. 51. ACM, April 2010
8. OSSIM, AlienVault. http://communities.alienvault.com/
9. OSSEC, Trend Micro. http://www.ossec.net/
10. QRadar. http://www-03.ibm.com/software/products/en/category/security-intelligence
11. ArcSight ETRM Platform, HP. http://www.hpenterprisesecurity.com
12. RSA Envision. http://www.emc.com/security/rsa-critical-incident-response-solution.htm#!solution_description
13. Splunk. http://splunk.com
14. Kelley, D., Moritz, R.: Best practices for building a security operations center. In: Information Systems Security, pp. 27–32, January-February 2006
15. Schneier, B.: Attack trees. Dr. Dobb's J. **24**(12), 21–29 (1999)
16. Mauw, S., Oostdijk, M.: Foundations of attack trees. In: Won, D.H., Kim, S. (eds.) ICISC 2005. LNCS, vol. 3935, pp. 186–198. Springer, Heidelberg (2006)
17. Phillips, C., Swiler, L.P.: A graph-based system for network-vulnerability analysis. In: Proceedings of the 1998 Workshop on New Security Paradigms, pp. 71–79. ACM, January 1998
18. Lippmann, R.P., Ingols, K.W.: An annotated review of past papers on attack graphs. Project report, no. PR-IA-1, Massachusetts Inst Of Tech, Lexington Lincoln Lab (2005)
19. Kordy, B., Piètre-Cambacédès, L., Schweitzer, P.: DAG-based attack and defense modeling: don't miss the forest for the attack trees. Comput. Sci. Rev. **13**, 1–38 (2014)
20. Ou, X., Govindavajhala, S., Appel, A.W.: MulVAL: a logic-based network security analyzer. In: USENIX Security, August 2005
21. Artz, M.L.: Netspa: a network security planning architecture. Doctoral dissertation, Massachusetts Institute of Technology (2002)
22. Llinas, J., Nagi, R., Hall, D., Lavery, J.: A multi-disciplinary university research initiative in hard and soft information fusion: overview, research strategies and initial results. In: 2010 13th Conference on Information Fusion (FUSION), pp. 1–7. IEEE, July 2010
23. Gross, G.A., Nagi, R., Sambhoos, K., Schlegel, D.R., Shapiro, S.C., Tauer, G.: Towards hard soft data fusion: processing architecture and implementation for the joint fusion and analysis of hard and soft intelligence data. In: 2012 15th International Conference on Information Fusion (FUSION), pp. 955–962. IEEE, July 2012
24. Gross, G.A., Khopkar, S., Nagi, R., Sambhoos, K.: Data association and graph analytical processing of hard and soft intelligence data. In: 2013 16th International Conference on Information Fusion (FUSION), pp. 404–411. IEEE, July 2013
25. Laudy, C.: Semantic knowledge representations for soft data fusion. INTECH Open Access Publisher (2011)
26. Fossier, S., Laudy, C., Pichon, F.: Managing uncertainty in conceptual graph-based soft information fusion. In: 2013 16th International Conference on Information Fusion (FUSION), pp. 930–937. IEEE, July 2013
27. Laudy, C., Deparis, E., Lortal, G., Mattioli, J.: Multi-granular fusion for social data analysis for a decision and intelligence application. In: 2013 16th International Conference on Information Fusion (FUSION), pp. 1849–1855. IEEE, July 2013
28. McKay, B.D.: Practical graph isomorphism. Congressus Numerantium, Department of Computer Science, Vanderbilt University (1981)
29. Plantenga, T.: Inexact subgraph isomorphism in MapReduce. J. Parallel Distrib. Comput. **73**(2), 164–175 (2013)

30. Zhao, Z., Wang, G., Butt, A.R., Khan, M., Kumar, V.A., Marathe, M.V.: Sahad: subgraph analysis in massive networks using hadoop. In: 2012 IEEE 26th International Parallel & Distributed Processing Symposium (IPDPS), pp. 390–401. IEEE, May 2012
31. Chein, M., Mugnier, M.L.: Graph-based Knowledge Representation: Computational Foundations of Conceptual Graphs. Springer Science & Business Media, London (2008)
32. McKenna, S., Mazur, D., Agutter, J., Meyer, M.: Design activity framework for visualization design. In: Proceedings of the IEEE VIS Conference, Paris (2014)
33. Montferrat, P., Lortal, G., Faure, D., Coppin, G.: Intention de transfert de responsabilité pour le travail coopératif. In: Association pour la Recherche Cognitive (ARCo 2009), Rouen, France, Décembre (2009)
34. Montferrat, P., Faure, D., Lortal, G.: The 'Responsibility Cube' in maritime surveillance domain. In: Proceedings of COGIS – Cognitive Systems with Interactive Sensors- (SEE, IET eds.), 6 pages (2009). ISBN: 2-912328-55-1
35. Sheridan, T.B., Verplank, W.: Human and Computer Control of Undersea Teleoperators. Man-Machine Systems Laboratory, Department of Mechanical Engineering, MIT, Cambridge, MA (1978)

The Effects of Awareness Programs on Information Security in Banks: The Roles of Protection Motivation and Monitoring

Stefan Bauer[✉] and Edward W.N. Bernroider

Vienna University of Economics and Business, Vienna, Austria
{Stefan.Bauer,Edward.Bernroider}@wu.ac.at

Abstract. Our aim is to understand how information security awareness (ISA) programs affect the intention of employees for compliant information security behavior. We draw on Protection Motivation Theory (PMT) to uncover indirect influences of ISA programs, and seek to identify the extent to which intention translates into actual compliance is contingent on monitoring. Based on partial least squares structural equation modeling analysis of 183 survey responses consisting of German bank employees, we find strong empirical evidence for the importance of ISA programs, protection motivation and monitoring. While ISA programs effectively change how employees cope with and assess security threats, only coping appraisal is an important condition for the positive behavioral effects of such programs to occur. However, ISA programs may cause a false sense of security, as vulnerability perceptions are reduced by consuming ISA programs but not affecting intentions for compliant security behavior. Perceived monitoring strengthens this confirmed intention-behavior link.

Keywords: Information security awareness programs · Protection Motivation Theory · Employee security behavior · PLS-SEM · Moderation effect

1 Introduction

Banks' information systems are threatened by a huge variety of risks that arise from employees using information technology in their daily work. Actually, bank industry reports highlight the problematic situation by presenting a total number of 45.050 operational loss events with an average gross loss size of € 285.277 reported by 60 international banking groups [23]. Incidents associated with the interaction of employees and information systems occur because of a toxic combination of reasons, often related to employees' non-compliance with banks' information security policy (ISP) [24]. Especially for banks, much is at risk, because an information security breach can lead to enormous reputational and operational damages [10].

To mitigate these risks, banks have implemented employee centric information security awareness (ISA) programs to actively protect their information assets [5]. An increased awareness concerning information security risks and threats is by many considered as the most cost-effective control of an organization [11]. ISA programs

© Springer International Publishing Switzerland 2015
T. Tryfonas and I. Askoxylakis (Eds.): HAS 2015, LNCS 9190, pp. 154–164, 2015.
DOI: 10.1007/978-3-319-20376-8_14

make employees sensitive to foster security of organizations' information systems and be aware of information security risks [8]. Actual topics for ISA programs are, among others, phishing attacks, social engineering, passwords security, secure internet use and clear screen policy [5].

In general, Protection Motivation Theory (PMT) is used to discover motivational influences on the intention for a compliant security behavior [17, 28]. Until now, scientific research has largely neglected analyzing the effects of ISA programs on employees' protection motivation and its subsequent effects on the individual intention to comply with the ISP. We seek to fill this gap and also expect that the variables of PMT will act as mediators governing the relationship between the perception of the ISA programs and the individual's intention to comply with the ISP. Additionally, we assume that employees actually behave in a more desirable way when they know that their actions are monitored by the bank. Previous research on monitoring confirmed that vulnerability or severity may affect individual attitudes toward monitoring [35]. Hence, we also aim at unraveling the influence on monitoring on the actual behavioral outcomes of these behavioral intentions in the ISP context of our study.

The paper has five sections. The next section provides theoretical foundations of ISA programs and PMT, develops the research hypotheses and the research model. Next, the research methodology is presented followed by the evaluation of the measurement and structural models. Then, we briefly discuss the main findings and finally conclude the paper with a short summary and directions for further research.

2 Research Background and Hypotheses

A recent literature review on behavioral information security research highlights the emphasis of prior research on four major theories, namely Theory of Planned Behavior, General Deterrence Theory, Technology Acceptance Model and the PMT [20]. The PMT addresses the determination of fear appeals and how individuals cope with the danger brought about by information security risks and threats [17, 28]. PMT has been considered as one the most powerful theories explaining individuals' intentions to engage in compliant actions [9, 20]. In the context of information security compliance, prior studies reported positive effects of all constructs of PMT on self-reported behavioral intentions [20, 21, 30, 36]. Our research aim is to extend these studies by focusing on the evaluation of the impact of ISA programs on employees' protection motivation, which should in turn impact the intention to comply, thereby conceptualizing protection motivation as mediator. Figure 1 visualizes the research model including all hypotheses, which will be developed in the next sub-sections.

2.1 The Role of Protection Motivation Theory

PMT has been repeatedly examined and discussed in the extant behavioral information security literature [14, 15, 17, 21, 30, 34, 36]. The original theory builds upon threat and coping appraisal. Threat appraisal consists of the constructs perceived vulnerability and perceived severity of an event [30]. Perceived vulnerability is defined as an individual's

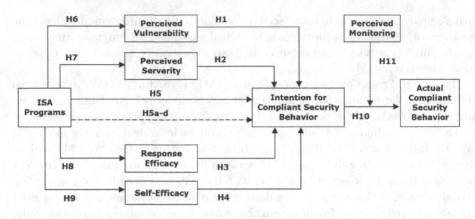

Fig. 1. Research model and hypotheses

perception of the probability of an information security incident, which in our context is caused by behavioral non-compliance with the ISP [17]. In contrast, perceived severity reflects the impact of an information security incident caused by non-compliance with the ISP [17, 31]. Previous research has shown mixed results concerning significant effects of perceived vulnerability and perceived severity on intention for compliant security behavior [15, 17, 25, 30]. Nonetheless, meta studies showed significant low positive effects [9, 20], hence we assume similar outcomes.

Response efficacy and self-efficacy together constitute coping appraisal, which has a significant impact on behavioral intentions according to meta-studies on PMT [9, 22]. Response efficacy is the expectancy of the employee that the threat or risk can be mitigated by conducting the ISP compliant security behavior [20], while self-efficacy is the belief that one is able to conduct the requested behavior for compliance. In particular, self-efficacy has a positive effect on behavioral intention for a compliant security behavior [17, 25, 30]. In terms of, response efficacy previous research provides mixed results with no or marginally significant impacts [18, 25, 31] and positive impacts on compliant security behavior [17]. To conclude, we propose the following:

H1: Perceived vulnerability has a positive effect on the intention for compliant security behavior.
H2: Perceived severity has a positive effect on the intention for compliant security behavior.
H3: Response efficacy has a positive effect on the intention for complaint security behavior.
H4: Self-efficacy has a positive effect on the intention for compliant security behavior.

2.2   The Effects of ISA Programs on Employees' Protection Motivation

The aim of ISA programs is to increase employees' ISA concerning current information security threats and risks by delivering the content of the ISP to banks' employees [5, 33].

In practice, ISA programs vary from bank to bank and different methods are used to make their employees more aware [4, 5]. ISA programs can be structured as intense and coordinated campaigns or simply consist of several isolated initiatives [5, 19]. An increased ISA through such programs can lead to improvements of employees' security compliance behavior [8]. Hence, we generally assume that ISA programs positively affect the intention for compliant security behavior [3]. More specifically, we posit that ISA programs have positive direct and indirect effects on the intention for compliant security behavior. The indirect effects should be delivered via the PMT constructs as mediators. We therefore suggest:

H5 (direct effects): ISA programs have a positive effect on the intention for compliant security behavior.
H5a–d (indirect effects): The positive effects of ISA programs on the intention for compliant security behavior are mediated by perceived vulnerability (H5a), by perceived severity (H5b), by response efficacy (H5c), and by self-efficacy (H5d).

ISA programs usually highlight current information systems risks and threats, such as those related to phishing or other social engineering attacks [5]. Consequently, employees should benefit from getting a realistic picture of threat scenarios. Thus, we assume that ISA programs increase employees' perceptions on vulnerabilities and threat severity. Moreover, employees' response efficacy and self-efficacy should benefit from ISA programs, because employees usually also receive more knowledge about rules and work practices and information on how to conduct compliant security behavior [5]. We assume that employees' ISA is an important precondition for employees' protection motivation, hence we propose:

H6: ISA programs have a positive effect on perceived vulnerability.
H7: ISA programs have a positive effect on perceived severity.
H8: ISA programs have a positive effect on response efficacy.
H9: ISA programs have a positive effect on self-efficacy.

2.3 The Role of Perceived Monitoring

Behavioral theories basing on self-reported data often examine the relationship between behavioral intent and actual behavior [20]. The correlation of these two constructs is assumed in the Theory of Planned Behavior as well as in PMT [20]. Hence, a variety of studies have already confirmed the significance of this relationship in behavioral information security context [25, 30, 31]. But recent research calls for more research on the behavioral contingencies of intention, i.e., the variables which possibly moderate the effects of intention on actual behavior [20]. Especially in the banking context, money is data in the information systems and banks need to monitor how employees are acting [5]. We assume that the employees' perception of monitoring will enhance his or her actual compliant security behavior. Hence, we conclude:

H10: The intention for compliant security behavior has a positive effect on actual compliant security behavior.
H11: Perceived monitoring has a positive moderation effect on the positive relationship between intention and actual complaint security behavior.

3   Research Methodology

A positivistic research approach was applied to test the developed research hypotheses with a quantitative survey. All constructs of our research model were adopted from supporting empirical research in the context of behavioral information security [7, 16, 17, 31]. The questionnaire was pre-tested and afterwards improved according to pre-testers' comments.

Finally, we utilized a crowdsourcing platform to contact bank employees from German banks. The platform has a user base of 70,000 active members from all regions in Germany, which were all invited to participate. The respondents first had to qualify as valid target persons before they were invited to assess the questionnaire. This multi-stage selection process finally led to 183 valid responses from bank employees working in Germany and allowed for covering a range of different banks which differ in the frequency and quality of their ISA programs. A recent study suggested that respondents from crowdsourcing platforms have advantages over other sampling procedures commonly used in behavioral survey research. While their response behavior seems to be equal to traditional participants pools, they, e.g., offer more diversity in particular in terms of work experience when compared to student samples [6]. However, our sample seems to be biased towards younger male professionals. It consists of 135 men and 48 women, and the majority of the respondents is below 30 years old. 85 % of the respondents have between one and ten years work experience in the banking sector.

The collected data was analyzed by conducting a partial least squares structural equation modeling (PLS-SEM) analysis [12] with SmartPLS [27]. We carefully considered all quality and validity criteria following current recommendations [12, 13, 29].

4   Validation of the Measurement Model

The measurement model was tested with all quality and validity criteria required by contemporary recommendations [12, 13, 29]. Table 1 summarizes the goodness-of-fit criteria. First, all relevant values of Cronbach's α and composite reliability are above the critical value (0.70), which is evidence for internal consistency reliability of the results. Second, all assessed loadings exhibit above the required value of 0.70, hence indicator reliability is adequate. Third, regarding convergent validity, the recommended threshold of 0.50 for the criteria AVE was exceeded by all values, hence more than the half of the variance of the indicators is explained by the constructs [12]. Overall, all considered quality and validity criteria meet the contemporary recommendations.

Table 1. Measurement model validity and reliability (all constructs are reflective)

Latent var.	Indicators	Loadings	Cronbach's α	Composite rel.	AVE
Perceived vulnerability	PV1	0.88	0.85	0.91	0.77
	PV2	0.86			
	PV3	0.88			
Perceived severity	PS1	0.90	0.85	0.91	0.76
	PS2	0.83			
	PS3	0.88			
Response efficacy	RE1	0.93	0.81	0.91	0.84
	RE2	0.91			
Self-efficacy	SE1	0.89	0.86	0.91	0.77
	SE2	0.92			
	SE3	0.83			
ISA program	ISAP1	0.83	0.70	0.83	0.63
	ISAP2	0.81			
	ISAP3	0.73			
Intention for compliant sec. behavior	ICSB1	0.85	0.79	0.88	0.71
	ICSB2	0.84			
	ICSB3	0.83			
Perceived monitoring	PM1	0.85	0.79	0.87	0.70
	PM2	0.77			
	PM3	0.88			
Actual compliant sec. behavior	AP1	0.85	0.73	0.84	0.64
	AP2	0.83			
	AP3	0.72			

5   Evaluation of the Structural Model

We firstly conducted a PLS-SEM analysis to test the direct effects of PMT's latent constructs and examine the proposed hypotheses. As Fig. 2 illustrates, the research models' predictive accuracy for the variables intention for compliant security behavior and actual compliant security behavior seems to be acceptable, because the values of R^2 are high compared with the results of prior research [20, 30] and recommendations from scholarly research [12]. In contrast, R^2 values of perceived vulnerability and perceived severity are low. Furthermore, the achieved level of R^2 for response efficacy

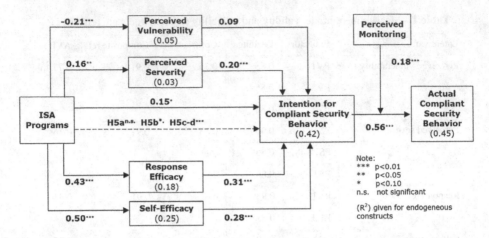

Fig. 2. Empirical results

and self-efficacy is adequate and indicates that ISA is an important precondition for the constructs. It is also necessary to consider the effect sizes (f^2) to discuss the strength of the direct effects on the paths between the latent constructs.

Table 2. Verdict on structural relationships of the research model

Hypotheses	Path coefficient	T-values	f^2	f^2 effect
(H1): Perceived vulnerability → Intention for CSB	0.09	1.23	0.01	No effect
(H2): Perceived severity → Intention for CSB	0.20***	2.62	0.05	Weak
(H3): Response efficacy → Intention for CSB	0.31***	4.02	0.11	Weak
(H4): Self-efficacy → Intention for CSB	0.28***	3.67	0.09	Weak
(H5): ISA programs → Intention for CSB	0.15*	1.95	0.03	Weak
(H6): ISA programs → Perceived vulnerability	−0.21***	2.89	0.05	Weak
(H7): ISA programs → Perceived severity	0.16**	2.25	0.03	Weak
(H8): ISA programs → Response efficacy	0.43***	6.02	0.23	Moderate
(H9): ISA programs → Self-efficacy	0.50***	8.28	0.32	Moderate
(H10): Intention for CSB → Actual CSB	0.56***	8.29	0.45	Strong
(H11): Perceived monitoring moderates INT-actual CSB	0.18***	3.11	0.10	Weak

*$p < 0.10$, **$p < 0.05$, ***$p < 0.01$
f^2 effect sizes: no effect (<0.02); weak (0.02–0.14), moderate (0.15–0.34); strong (above 0.34)

Next, bootstrapping with 5,000 subsamples was conducted to calculate t-statistics and further to evaluate the significance of the path coefficients [12]. Table 2 illustrates path coefficients, t-values and f^2 effect sizes, which were used to quantify the size of an effect of an endogenous on an exogenous factor [12].

Finally, we conducted the mediation analysis. Contemporary mediation analysis suggests firstly focusing on the significance of the indirect variable (IV) for predicting the mediators, which is the case for all four PMT constructs. Secondly, the mediators should affect the dependent variable (DV), which is not the case for perceived vulnerability. Thirdly, the direct path between these variables (IV->DV) needs to be assessed. When removing the mediator, the path coefficient on this direct path should increase and be significant [2]. The later condition holds for our remaining three mediation hypotheses (H5b: $p < .10$, H5c–d: $p < .01$). Finally, the Sobel test [32] confirmed these significant mediation effects after performing bootstrapping with replacement (H5b: $p < .10$, H5c–d: $p < .01$).

6   Discussion of the Results

Overall, our findings confirm the import roles of protection motivation and monitoring in establishing ISA programs that affect the employees' intentions for compliant security behavior. While we can also confirm that ISA programs have a positive weak direct effect on the intention for compliant security behavior, thereby supporting hypothesis H5, three constructs of protection motivation and especially coping appraisal act as a mediators allowing for indirect effects. We will discuss these results now in more detail.

In terms of coping appraisal, we detected moderate positive effects of ISA programs on response efficacy and self-efficacy, thereby supporting hypotheses H8 and H9. The results therefore confirm that coping appraisal is effectively improved by ISA programs. This can be explained by the common use of ISA programs to provide guidelines for employees on how to act and also information about the effectiveness of the actions to comply with the ISP [5]. In addition, both coping appraisals are important variables in terms of mediating the effects of ISA programs on the intention to comply, thereby supporting hypotheses H5c and H5d. This means that improved response efficacy and self-efficacy are conditions which increase the positive effects of ISP programs on the intention for compliant security behavior. Subsequently, both constructs of coping appraisal have weak positive effects on the intention for a compliant security behavior, thereby supporting H3 and H4. This finding corresponds with [17, 21] and contradicts prior research [30]. Our results clearly indicate that employees, which belief that they can mitigate information security risks with their compliant behavior, have a higher intention to act according to the ISP.

With regard to threat appraisal, our results indicate that ISA programs have a weak positive effect on perceived severity, hence hypothesis H7 is supported. In fact, the ISA programs may utilize frightening fear-based communication as well as information to clarify the potential impacts, and therefore successfully highlight the possible negative impact of an information security threat [19]. However, contrary to our expectations, ISA programs have negative effects on the other threat appraisals construct, perceived vulnerability, thereby contradicting hypothesis H6. We therefore assume that employees' consummation of an ISA programs help employees to deal with information security threats and risks, and, consequently, this leads to a decrease of the perceived probability of a security incident. This is also potentially dangerous and may lead to a false sense of security as employees may underestimate the possibility that their information system could be threatened [1]. Further, perceived vulnerability has no direct effect on the intention for a compliant security behavior, thereby not supporting H1. Previous results showed positive effects [17, 30]. An explanation may refer to other environmental or contextual factors to explain this result [16, 24, 33]. Besides, perceived severity has a significant positive effect on intention, thereby supporting H2. While this result supports our theorization, it adds empirical evidence to mixed results reported in literature in terms of positive or negative effects of perceived severity on intention [17, 30]. It terms of mediating effects of ISA programs on the intention to comply, threat appraisals are not as important as coping appraisals. Only hypothesis H5b is weakly supported, while hypothesis H5a is rejected. It seems that ISA programs are more successful in terms of offering coping actions and relatively less effective it terms of actually increasing awareness about threats and risks. Employees may often miss connecting ISP content with the likelihood of a real danger [5]. We need to recommend that future research should explore these relationships in more detail.

Finally, we confirm that perceived monitoring positively moderates the positive effects of intention to actual compliant security behavior, therefore supporting hypotheses H10 and H11. Our data analysis confirms a partial positive moderation effect of organizational monitoring on the intention-behavior link. However, we can assume that also other contextual factors influence this relationship [16, 24, 33] and future research should address further contingencies.

The findings have also several implications for practice. First, ISA programs are currently well designed to increase employees' coping appraisal in terms of both, response efficacy and self-efficacy. This means that they are already effective in convincing employees about the value of the behavior and about how to behave, respectively. Second, in terms of threat appraisals, ISA programs seem to have adverse effects on perceived vulnerability based on our sample. In other words, ISA programs seem to lower the perception of the probability of an information security threat, maybe due to the fact that employees tend to protect themselves better after consuming ISA programs. We still recommend that ISA programs should communicate more the occurrence of real threats from media or inside the company and the concept of residual risks in order to increase the perceptions of vulnerability [26]. Nonetheless, the findings indicate that ISA programs eventually increase the intention for compliant security behavior. Third, ISA programs should communicate that employees are monitored, which strengthens the relationship between intention and actual compliant information security behavior.

7 Conclusion

Our study points to important theoretical implications with regard to PMT as prior literature has largely neglected to investigate the role of ISA programs and organizational monitoring to ultimately improve information security behavior. Our main findings illustrate that ISA programs affect employees' coping appraisals in terms of response and self-efficacy. Both variables are also mediators adding to the positive direct effects of ISA programs on the intention for compliant security behavior. Similarly, ISA programs have positive effects on employees' perceived severity, which positively affects the intention to comply with the ISP. However, ISA programs may have adverse effects on the perceived vulnerability possibly signaling a false sense of security. Especially these initial findings merit more attention in future research. Finally, perceived organizational monitoring is important as it partially positively moderates the well-established intention to actual behavior connection.

References

1. Albrechtsen, E., Hovden, J.: The information security digital divide between information security managers and users. Comput. Secur. 28(6), 476–490 (2009)
2. Baron, R.M., Kenny, D.A.: The moderator-mediator variable distinction in social psychological research: conceptual, strategic, and statistical considerations. J. Pers. Soc. Psychol. 51(6), 1173–1182 (1986)
3. Bauer, S., Bernroider, E.W.N.: IT operational risk awareness building in banking companies: a preliminary research design highlighting the importance of risk cultures and control systems. In: Janczewski, L. (ed.) Proceedings of the International Conference on Information Resource Management 2013 (Conf-IRM 2013), Natal, pp. 1–4 (2013)
4. Bauer, S., Bernroider, E.W.N.: IT operational risk management practices in austrian banks: preliminary results from exploratory case study. In: Nunes, M.B. (ed.) Proceedings of the International Conference Information Systems 2013, pp. 30–38. IADIS Press, Lissabon (2013)
5. Bauer, S., Bernroider, E.W.N., Chudzikowski, K.: End user information security awareness programs for improving information security in banking organizations: preliminary results from an exploratory study. In: AIS SIGSEC Workshop on Information Security & Privacy (WISP 2013), Milano (2013)
6. Behrend, T.S., Sharek, D.J., Meade, A.W., et al.: The viability of crowdsourcing for survey research. Behav. Res. Methods 43(3), 800–813 (2011)
7. D'arcy, J., Hovav, A.: Does one size fit all? Examining the differential effects of is security countermeasures. J. Bus. Ethics 89(1), 59–71 (2008)
8. Eminağaoğlu, M., Uçar, E., Eren, Ş.: The positive outcomes of information security awareness training in companies – a case study. Inf. Secur. Tech. Rep. 14(4), 223–229 (2009)
9. Floyd, D.L., Prentice-Dunn, S., Rogers, R.W.: A meta-analysis of research on protection motivation theory. J. Appl. Soc. Psychol. 30, 407–429 (2000)
10. Goldstein, J., Chernobai, A., Benaroch, M.: An event study analysis of the economic impact of it operational risk and its subcategories. J. Assoc. Inf. Syst. 12, 606–631 (2011)
11. Hagen, J.M., Albrechtsen, E., Hovden, J.: Implementation and effectiveness of organizational information security measures. Inf. Manag. Comput. Secur. 16, 377–397 (2008)
12. Hair, J.F., Hult, G.T.M., Ringle, C.M., et al.: A Primer on Partial Least Squares Structural Equation Modeling (PLS-SEM). Sage, Thousand Oaks (2013)
13. Hair, J.F., Sarstedt, M., Ringle, C.M., et al.: An assessment of the use of partial least squares structural equation modeling in marketing research. J. Acad. Mark. Sci. 40, 414–433 (2011)
14. Herath, T., Rao, H.R.: Encouraging information security behaviors in organizations: role of penalties, pressures and perceived effectiveness. Decis. Support Syst. 47, 154–165 (2009)

15. Herath, T., Rao, H.R.: Protection motivation and deterrence: a framework for security policy compliance in organisations. Eur. J. Inf. Syst. **18**, 106–125 (2009)
16. Hu, Q., Dinev, T., Hart, P., et al.: Managing employee compliance with information security policies: the critical role of top management and organizational culture. Decis. Sci. **43**, 615–659 (2012)
17. Ifinedo, P.: Understanding information systems security policy compliance: an integration of the theory of planned behavior and the protection motivation theory. Comput. Secur. **31**, 83–95 (2012)
18. Johnston, A.C., Warkentin, M.: Fear appeals and information security behaviors: an empirical study. MIS Q. **34**, 549–566 (2010)
19. Kajzer, M., D'arcy, J., Crowell, C.R., et al.: An exploratory investigation of message-person congruence in information security awareness campaigns. Comput. Secur. **43**, 64–76 (2014)
20. Lebek, B., Uffen, J., Neumann, M., et al.: Information security awareness and behavior: a theory-based literature review. Manag. Res. Rev. **37**, 1049–1092 (2014)
21. Meso, P., Ding, Y., Xu, S.: Applying protection motivation theory to information security training for college students. J. Inf. Priv. Secur. **9**, 47–67 (2013)
22. Milne, S., Orbell, P.S., Orbell, S.: Prediction and intervention in health-related behavior: a meta-analytic review of protection motivation theory. J. Appl. Soc. Psychol. **30**, 106–143 (2000)
23. Orx: ORX report on operational risk loss data. In: Operational Riskdata eXchange Association (2014)
24. Padayachee, K.: Taxonomy of compliant information security behavior. Comput. Secur. **31**, 673–680 (2012)
25. Pahnila, S., Siponen, M., Mahmood, M.A.: Employees' behavior towards is security policy compliance. In: Proceedings of the 40th Annual Hawaii International Conference on System Sciences (HICSS 2007). IEEE, Hawaii (2007)
26. Puhakainen, P., Siponen, M.: Improving employees' compliance through information systems security training: an action research study. MIS Q. **34**, 757–778 (2010)
27. Ringle, C., Wende, S., Will, A.: SmartPLS 2.0 (beta). In: Hamburg Uo (ed.) (2005)
28. Rogers, R.W.: A protection motivation theory of fear appeals and attitude change. J. Psychol. **91**, 93–114 (1975)
29. Sarstedt, M., Ringle, C.M., Hair, J.F.: PLS-SEM: indeed a silver bullet. J. Mark. Theory Pract. **19**, 139–152 (2011)
30. Siponen, M., Mahmood, M.A., Pahnila, S.: Employees' adherence to information security policies: an exploratory field study. Inf. Manag. **51**, 217–224 (2014)
31. Siponen, M., Pahnila, S., Mahmood, M.A.: Compliance with information security policies an empirical investigation. IEEE Comput. **43**(2), 64–71 (2010)
32. Sobel, M.E.: Asymptotic confidence intervals for indirect effects in structural equation models. In: Leinhardt, S. (ed.) Sociological Methodology, pp. 290–312. American Sociological Association, Washington DC (1982)
33. Tsohou, A., Karyda, M., Kokolakis, S., et al.: Managing the introduction of information security awareness programmes in organisations. Eur. J. Inf. Syst. **24**(1), 38–58 (2013)
34. Vance, A., Siponen, M., Pahnila, S.: Motivating IS security compliance: insights from habit and protection motivation theory. Inf. Manag. **49**, 190–198 (2012)
35. Workman, M.: A field study of corporate employee monitoring: attitudes, absenteeism, and the moderating influences of procedural justice perceptions. Inf. Organ. **19**, 218–232 (2009)
36. Workman, M., Bommer, W.H., Straub, D.: Security lapses and the omission of information security measures: a threat control model and empirical test. Comput. Hum. Behav. **24**, 2799–2816 (2008)

Analysis of Human Awareness of Security and Privacy Threats in Smart Environments

Luca Caviglione[1], Jean-François Lalande[2,3], Wojciech Mazurczyk[4],
and Steffen Wendzel[5]($\boxtimes$)

[1] Institute of Intelligent Systems for Automation (ISSIA),
National Research Council of Italy (CNR), 16149 Genova, Italy
luca.caviglione@ge.issia.cnr.it
[2] Inria, University Rennes 1, Supélec, CNRS,
IRISA UMR 6074, 35065 Rennes, France
[3] INSA Centre Val de Loire, University Orléans,
LIFO EA 4022, 18020 Bourges, France
jean-francois.lalande@insa-cvl.fr
[4] Institute of Telecommunications, Warsaw University of Technology,
00-665 Warsaw, Poland
wmazurczyk@tele.pw.edu.pl
[5] Fraunhofer Institute for Communication,
Information Processing and Ergonomics (FKIE), 53113 Bonn, Germany
steffen.wendzel@fkie.fraunhofer.de

Abstract. Smart environments integrate Information and Communication Technologies (ICT) into devices, vehicles, buildings and cities to offer an increased quality of life, energy efficiency and economical sustainability. In this perspective, the individual has a core role and so has networking, which enables such entities to cooperate. However, the huge amount of sensitive data, social aspects and the mixed set of protocols offer many opportunities to inject hazards, exfiltrate information, mass profiling of citizens, or produce a new wave of attacks. This work reviews the major risks arising from the usage of ICT-techniques for smart environments, with emphasis on networking. Its main contribution is to explain the role of different stakeholders for causing a lack of security and to envision future threats by considering human aspects.

Keywords: Privacy · Security · Steganography · Smart buildings · Human aspects

1 Introduction

Smart buildings are an elementary component of smart environments, which aim at improving the comfort of individuals and their lifestyle. In essence, they integrate *Information and Communication Technologies* (ICT) into devices, vehicles and buildings to provide a higher quality of life, a reduced environmental footprint and economical benefits. Pushed to the limit, such basic blocks can be

© Springer International Publishing Switzerland 2015
T. Tryfonas and I. Askoxylakis (Eds.): HAS 2015, LNCS 9190, pp. 165–177, 2015.
DOI: 10.1007/978-3-319-20376-8_15

arranged to produce large-scale deployments known as smart cities. Smart environments are the result of a large interdisciplinary effort, ranging from civil engineering to cloud computing. However, in this work we focus on networking/devices, since they provide many important features such as: (*i*) the ability of collecting information from the surrounding environment, (*ii*) the possibility of sending remotely commands and feedback, also in a real-time fashion, (*iii*) the availability of an infrastructure to handle the resulting amount of data. Prime examples are, among the others: wireless loops used to gather information from sensors, *Radio Frequency Identification* (RFID) deployed to monitor the status of a physical area, and the *Internet of Things* (IoT) paradigm to access and control devices or assets like locks, light and household appliances [23].

Alas, smart technologies are tightly coupled with individuals, especially in terms of their lifestyles, bad habits and sensitive data. Therefore, all the information gathered, exchanged and stored within smart environments can lead to severe issues in terms of security and privacy. For instance, detailed personal information can be used for mass profiling or social engineering attacks. Moreover, misuse of devices, bad habits and poor understanding of handled technology can lead to severe security breaches. For example, smartphones are often used to control different parts of smart environments (e.g., buildings) and worms or infected applications could attack the discovered appliances of the user's environment.

In this perspective, this paper analyzes the most relevant security and privacy threats of users in smart environments. Given the example of smart building security, we highlight the practical background which leads to a lack of security functionality and awareness at the side of vendors, integrators and operators. The main contributions of this paper are the following: the systematic review of hazards rooted within the most relevant smart paradigms; an assessment of emerging threats arising by the mix of ICT technologies and human aspects; the discussion of possible countermeasures to mitigate identified security issues. We point out that this paper serves as an introductory work for the HAS session on *Human Aspects of Information Security, Privacy and Trust for Smart Buildings*.

The remainder of the paper is structured as follows: Sect. 2 describes the problem space generated by the smart paradigm. Section 3 deals with human aspects of insecurity of smart buildings, Sect. 4 concentrates on smartphones, and Sect. 5 reviews vehicles. Section 6 proposes a role-based perspective on threats related to smart environments and Sect. 7 gives our future vision of identified threats and possible countermeasures. Section 8 concludes the paper.

2   Description of the Problem Space

Smart environment is an umbrella term comprising different kinds of devices or specific deployments. As today, the most relevant areas of smart things are:

– **Smart Buildings:** they collate a mix of smart devices as to produce an integrated environment. For such a complex deployment, proper middleware in charge of offering a coherent access is usually adopted, as well as proper computing facilities to store user data, process control directives and provide optimizations, especially in the field of energy management. Thus, this scenario can be used to exploit data hiding, for instance to covertly orchestrate a botnet.

- **Smart Devices:** they are quickly becoming widespread and one of the core blocks to pursue the vision of a more "human-centric" environment. Common examples of smart devices are gaming consoles, set-top-boxes, light bulbs and household appliances. These devices can be used to infer habits, even political views, for instance by evaluating the shows watched on the TV. Moreover, the availability of full-featured TCP/IP stacks can be exploited to produce new types of botnets in order to e.g. amplify spam campaigns. It must be emphasized that smart devices will not be investigated in details in this paper due to space limitations and their technical heterogeneity.
- **Smart Phones:** are the most popular tools used to interact with other devices, and can be used to remotely control buildings and vehicles. In addition, they are the preferred platform to connect to the Internet and to communicate using heterogeneous networks (e.g., cellular or WiFi). They store a huge source of sensitive details such as messages and contacts and can be paired with smart watches which increases their potential to collect personal data. As a result, they are one of the preferred targets for data exfiltration of users, while additionally empowering phishing, social phishing, cyber bullying and social engineering [4].
- **Smart Vehicles:** modern automotives offer features to geolocate vehicles, mainly through the *Global Positioning System* (GPS), and to plan routes. Such features are not only used by individuals, since they are at the basis of fleet management and intelligent/smart transportation services. Also, modern vehicles can remotely send telemetry data as to prevent fault and guarantee proper service levels, e.g., for goods delivery. This allows massive user profiling, which leads to understand habits to conduct physical attacks.

The resulting problem space is very composite and needs a thorough understanding of all the technical components used, both to evaluate the degree of (in)security and to engineer proper countermeasures and mitigation techniques. To this aim, functional entities needing an investigation are: (*i*) wireless networks (e.g., the IEEE 802.11) as well as the core protocols used to exchange data or grant human interaction (e.g., HTTP); (*ii*) elaborate a proper taxonomy/ranking to understand where the related weaknesses impact more (e.g., physical security vs. cybersecurity); (*iii*) understand how sensitive data can be used also jointly with those available on *Online Social Networks* (OSNs) as a method to produce a new wave of attacks; (*iv*) understand why standard detection methods can be defeated by the complexity and diversity of smart environments.

3 Smart Buildings

Smart buildings are automated buildings, i.e., those comprising *Building Automation Systems* (BAS) and inter-connected with the IoT. The importance of

BAS for today's societies increases steadily due to various reasons. For instance, being enriched with more features, buildings can perform an additional number of routine tasks such as energy saving and in the context of an aging society, smart buildings ensure that elders can stay longer in their homes before being forced to move to a nursing home.

Various vulnerabilities in the available standards of communication protocols used in BAS are known. Most of these communication protocols, e.g., EIB/KNX, LON or BACnet, were designed many years ago with very limited focus on IT security [11,12]. Improved standards for the most-widely used BAS protocols are already proposed or under development, however, the application of these enhanced protocols in practice and the integration into products is currently not present. Moreover, the integration of newer protocols into legacy BAS environments is hardly feasible and thus, novel solutions like *traffic normalization* must be applied which protect legacy systems [25]. From a human-oriented perspective, the major attacks which can be performed on buildings are:

- **Surveillance**: as shown in [20,26], it is technically feasible to perform surveillance of events in buildings, e.g., caused by inhabitants or employees. Therefore, passive and active attacks are known: the attacker either exploits side channels or directly requests sensor values from Internet-connected BAS. An attacker can, for instance, use surveillance to monitor the behavior of inhabitants or employees.
- **Remote Control**: while surveillance relies on sensor values and actuator states in a smart building, a remote control is feasible, too. Therefore, actuators are used to perform actions, triggered by the attacker. For instance, to break into a building, a thief can send commands to window actuators/door actuators and can attack the physical access control system. In worst case, remote control attacks influence the safety of inhabitants and people working in a building.
- **Physical Exploitation**: being a form of remote control, an attacker can at least indirectly get advantage of exploiting the BAS of other households. For illustration, we use the example of a house with two parties A and B, each possessing its own flat and own BAS. Imagine party A leaves his flat, which is underneath the flat of B, for winter holidays while party B is staying at home. Since the ceiling of A's flat is the ground floor of B's flat, B can attack the BAS of A to maximize the heating level in A's flat. As a result, the temperature of B's flat is also heated a little what saves heating costs for B while increasing the costs for A.
- **Availability**: the functioning of a building is essential for today's organizations. Hence, causing a *Denial of Service* (DoS) attack, e.g., by simple misconfiguration, can affect all areas of building automation, such as physical access control or fire alarm systems, and is thus not only harmful for enterprise processes but for the safety of people.
- **Smart Building Botnets**: when surveillance or remote control is not only performed for a single household or industrial building, but for a larger number of buildings, novel scenarios emerge. So-called *smart building botnets* can

perform mass surveillance and mass remote control [27]. For instance, a local oil distributor may rise his sales by slightly increasing the nightly heating levels of his customer's households. Such large-scale attacks potentially influence the privacy, safety, and living of inhabitants and employees in whole regions.

4   Smart Phones

For years, smartphones have been one of the most important tools to communicate and store personal data. Recently, the advent of frameworks for managing home appliances, monitoring the health of the owner and handling payments, led to an important paradigm shift. In essence, smartphones are the preferred dashboard to access smart homes, and interact with appliances or vehicles. In addition, the security is under the responsibility of the user, since he/she is in charge of managing the administration and installation of the applications, as well as of undertaking security decisions. Yet, there is not any guarantee about his/her level of technical knowledge, which makes the human an effective vector of attack. As a consequence, smartphones are prone to different attacks in terms of human aspects, specifically:

- **Data exfiltration**: capturing user's personal data is one of the primary goals of attackers [8]. After collecting the data, for instance via phishing, the malware uploads it to a remote server. Thus, personal or business information is not only stolen but also stored in a place inaccessible for the user.
- **Exploitation of acquired resources**: a classical secondary goal consists of exploiting the controlled smartphone [8]. For example, it can be used as: a client of a botnet network, to send premium-rate SMS, or to participate in computations for mining bitcoins. From the user perspective, it disturbs the normal behavior of the smartphone and can result in additional cost. As other smart entities can be controlled by an application on the user's smartphone, compromising the smartphone can also give a fresh starting point to attack other smart entities on the same network.
- **Surveillance**: a malware can try to access user's localization and report these data to the attacker. Using the collected positions, more complex attacks can succeed to infer the identity of the user [10].
- **Battery drain**: a severe fragility of smartphones is the intrinsic power limitation due to the usage of battery. Hence, its malicious depletion can be at the basis of a new kind of DoS attack, where the device is made unusable [17]. Possible mechanisms range from the injection of energy wasting code within a malware or a stimulation of the device via its air interfaces. In any case, this attack may isolate the victim, making communications with the rest of the world infeasible. This kind of hazard is also effective for the case of sensors or nodes of an IoT deployment and the victim could have his/her safety framework compromised.
- **Information hiding**: as a consequence of a full implementation of the TCP/IP protocol stack, and the diffusion of BAS over IP solutions, modern smartphones run several applications using a very mixed set of protocols.

The latter can be exploited for information hiding purposes. In essence, multimedia data and network traffic can be used as legitimately appearing carriers by information hiding techniques to make a third-party observer unaware of the resulting flow. This technique can be also used for mass-profiling [28] or for empowering malware exfiltrating data [18].

5   Smart Vehicles

The most useful scenario envisaged for smart vehicles concerns *Vehicular Ad-hoc Networks* (VANETs), which offer features such as, road safety, route planning, entertainment, tolling, traffic management and support for intelligent transportation. In such a deployment, humans should be not endangered by vehicles as a vehicle's misbehavior can lead to severe injuries and safety hazards[1,2]. In addition, the cooperative nature of VANETs puts the network in a central and critical role. Therefore, networking technologies used in vehicles must be protected against malicious activities, which are very effective [6,13]. Their main scopes are to propagate incorrect information about events on the road, to gain sensitive information, and to disrupt the network infrastructure to prevent users accessing the service [14]. Among the others, the most relevant attacks in terms of human aspects are:

- **Injecting bogus information**: an attacker deliberately injects false information into the network to produce arbitrary situations along a route [1]. As an example, a node sending false information to benefit from a reduction of traffic along a common path. This can be done via false information reporting traffic jams, road accidents, and blocked routes as to suggest alternative ways. The most popular methods to achieve such goals are: intentionally creating or modifying existing frames, repeating previously captured data (replay attack), and misleading vehicle's sensors (illusion attack).
- **Sybil attack**: it is based on spoofing the identity of nodes to flood the network with incorrect information [29]. Typically, the attacker produces multiple copies of false data to appear as legitimate. Then, such false data can be used to induce the same reactions previously explained.
- **Wormhole attacks**: it creates a tunnel between two attackers' vehicles as a way to inject false information and disrupt the vehicular network [1]. The wormhole attack can be especially dangerous since it makes routing tables incoherent, thus causing the unavailability of the service for humans.
- **Routing protocols attacks**: vehicular networks use a mixed amount of broadcast and multi-hop traffic, e.g., to deliver data to isolated nodes.

---

[1] Def Con 21 talk by C. Miller and C. Valasekentitled entitled "Adventures in Automotive Networks and Control Units" https://www.defcon.org/html/defcon-21/dc-21-speakers.html#Miller.

[2] Def Con 18 talk by M. Metzger entitled "Letting the Air Out of Tire Pressure Monitoring Systems" https://www.defcon.org/images/defcon-18/dc-18-presentations/Metzger/DEFCON-18-Metzger-Letting-Air-Out.pdf.

In this case, the injection of bogus routing information can cause the routing protocols to misbehave [16, 24]. This may lead to the extension of packets' routes, the creation of routing loops, or the redirection of the traffic to an unreal node (blackhole attacks) or towards the attacker (greyhole attacks).

- **Man in the middle attacks**: there are no significant differences between Man in the middle attacks in VANETs and in typical wired networks. These attacks impact the authenticity of transmitted information which may threaten the privacy and identity of users.
- **DDoS attacks**: two main techniques are utilized to perform DoS attacks [29]. First, by disrupting the frequencies utilized for wireless communication, the attacker produces a jam in a given frequency range. This is quite easy to implement and its effectiveness mainly depends on the transmitting power of the jamming device. Second, by sending large amounts of network traffic by an authorized host, the attacker generates network messages that are valid but with high volumes/rates thus causing congestion, latency and intermittent connectivity. In both cases, the vehicle is unable to send/receive any information and the driver could potentially miss an important announcement, e.g. on the accident nearby or the worsening of weather conditions.
- **GPS spoofing**: it is based on sending a "louder" GPS signal to hide the legitimate one [29]. Current protection methods are mainly based on monitoring the power expected by a legitimate GPS satellite. This attack may lead to a car accident or to driving a vehicle in an abandoned area.

6   Human Awareness of Smart Environment's Threats: A Role-Based Perspective

When comparing human aspects of ICT-related topics with those in smart environments, a clear difference can be recognized. In ICT-related areas, a strong development of security features is achieved. Thus, vendors integrate security into their products and customers clearly demand for such features. In smart environments, especially the classic ones – such as factory automation – there is a clear lack of security, which we mainly illustrate in this section by reviewing the point of view of the different actors in the case of BAS. Most of these views were obtained owing to personal conversation with the different stakeholders.

Vendors. Vendors do not integrate security into their automation equipment as they lack know-how. They focus on engineering aspects and product quality is rather measured in longevity of components instead of in terms of security. When security features are integrated, these are in many cases implemented from scratch. For instance, a number of German BAS vendors promote their BAS network components explicitly with the "feature" that instead of buying a network stack from a country abroad, they have one competent engineer who implemented the stack himself. A one-person implementation of a network stack, such as BACnet, including its complex features is hardly feasible in a secure way by a single engineer.

Customers. On the other hand, the customers lack security awareness as well. Awareness-raising processes are currently taking place on a regional, national, and international scale. For instance, the 28th German *GLT Anwendertagung* – a leading event for professional customers – organized a security session on BAS in 2014. However, the effect of these awareness raising processes is small. For this reason, possessing still no (or very limited) awareness for security threats, customers do not demand security features from *vendors*, which, in turn, see the implementation of additional security features as costly.

Operators. Operators of smart buildings are usually janitors without any know-how on the IT security of their BAS. Even if the operators received additional education on BAS (e.g., certificates on building management), these courses lack any security features. The perspective of an operator is to ensure the functioning of a BAS, including its *safe* operation, for instance an intact fire alarm system, but security aspects are considered an additional overhead.

Additionally, *vendors* provide no tools to monitor or configure the security of BAS components and thus, even if *operators* would possess knowledge on IT security, they could not apply it in practice. In particular, as smart environments are in most cases networked environments, operators require *cyber situational awareness* [9], for example the awareness of any kind of suspicious activity taking place in cyberspace. In various cases, such as larger or inter-connected BAS, the number of events cannot be processed by human operators without any support. To this end, research came up with visualization approaches, which, for instance, present information in such a way that events with higher entropy are easier to spot. However, in practice, these tools are not available and if available are used for spotting misconfiguration problems or malfunctioning equipment instead of detecting cyber security-related attacks.

Project Deployment. Construction of a BAS suffers from non-optimized information exchange of the parties involved in the design, construction, and operation process of a building [21], which includes the planning, integration, and operation of a BAS. Moreover, know-how about the operation must be managed, including to consider its potential loss if operators leave the organization—a problem that is even more important for other critical smart areas such as operator centers for naval vessels or railways [3].

Table 1. Summary of human awareness from a role-based perspective for each "component" of smart environment.

Smart "component"	Vendors	Customers	Operators	Deployment
Buildings	Low	Low	Low	Low
Vehicles	Medium	Low	Low	Low
Phones	High	Medium	High	Medium
Devices	Medium	Low	Low	Low

This analysis is particularly pessimistic for BAS. Other smart components considered in this paper have made better security efforts. We summarize human awareness from a security perspective for each "component" of the smart environment in Table 1. Smartphones have received better attention than vehicles or devices. They benefit from two effects: customers ask for more security because of the increasing connectivity with OSNs; vendors can integrate adapted security technologies that have been matured for GNU/Linux operating systems, especially since Android has taken the lead in the market.

7 Future Vision on Threats and Countermeasures

Today, a number of the attacks presented in previous sections, e.g., smart building botnets, should rather be considered technically feasible than a real-world threat. However, given the linked risks for individuals and communities and the lack of awareness of the involved roles, the hurdles for attackers are considered not higher than for other ICT attacks. For this reason and since smart things of each type quickly gain more widespread, authors who discussed the particular attacks conclude the importance of a rapid countermeasure development as potential attacks are known before emerging on a larger scale in practice (e.g. [27]).

7.1 Future Threats

The potential of attacks can be considered larger if already known attacks from other areas of IT security are getting adapted to smart things. For instance, *watering hole attacks* [15] can be adapted to smart buildings/smart phones. Consider a community that is living in the same building. If an attacker wishes to access the BAS it is enough for her to infect only one inhabitant's smartphone which she uses to control the smart building and eventually other habitants will be infected. This scenario becomes even more significant as some hotels announced to enable smartphone-based hotel room access for guests.

In this perspective, smartphones will definitely be one of the preferred playgrounds to exploit threats. Especially, this is due to the complexity of their security policies, which discourages users to analyze and take adequate decisions. In addition, smartphones possess authentication tools that become of high interest for attackers.

One of the examples of how future mobile malware can covertly exfiltrate user's sensitive data is envisioned in [5]. The proposed steganographic method takes advantage of the built-in Siri service which has been offered for iPhone/iPad as a native service from iOS5 in 2011. Siri allows interacting with the iOS-based device using voice commands. To offload the device, the translation of voice inputs to text is performed remotely in a server farm operated by Apple. To this aim, the iPhone/iPad samples the voice, sends it to a remote facility, and waits for a response containing the recognized text, a similarity score and a time stamp. This characteristic feature can be exploited by an attacker which could produce ad-hoc voice patterns to manipulate the throughput and encode a secret into its shape. In future, a similar approach can be applied to all services relying on a massive conversation between the user's device and similar services in the cloud like GoogleVoice for Android OS or Cortana for Windows Phone.

For other smart devices, the potential of attack is dramatically increasing. For example, the Rapid7 company published in 2013 a security report about several critical vulnerabilities of the UPnP library [19]. These vulnerabilities affect billions of devices, for example Smart TVs, and gives opportunities to build attacks and gain root shells on these devices.

Lastly, because smart devices typically reside inside smart buildings, a compromised device will help an attacker to attack smart buildings. The attacker can try to capture data, infer residents habits, such as food products ordered online (smart fridge) and TV shows watched (smart TV). This can significantly impact privacy and enable the production of a new wave of extremely precise (and effective) social engineering attacks.

7.2 Future Countermeasures

A number of futuristic protection approaches for smart things are imaginable. For smart vehicles, the used protocols should include validation algorithms as it is clear that there, many potential opportunities arise for an attacker to inject malicious information. As used protocols should react in a real-time fashion, the added security should be lightweight and distributed between participants in order to give robust results. These solutions, reviewed in [7], can be based on reliable cryptographic key distribution and has been already actively studied for example for ad-hoc networks. With such tools, the privacy of users should be guaranteed. Also, they can be based on the reputation systems already deployed for peer-to-peer architectures.

A mean for smart buildings could be to introduce multilevel security [26]. Such an approach could, for instance, prevent that devices in a storage room could read sensor values from the management floor of an organizational building.

For the attack vectors discussed for smartphones, the industry is currently working on *Trusted Execution Environments* (TEE) that would introduce a secured trusted space of execution while the regular operating system remains untrusted. This way, vendors would be able to split their applications and protect the critical parts into the smartphone's TEE [2]. Moreover, malware detection is one of the hot topics for researchers in mobile security. Nevertheless, current anti-malware products are easily defeated by transformation techniques of the malware's code [22]. Thus, these aspects remain to be addressed.

8   Conclusion

This paper discussed the human-related security and privacy aspects of smart environments. We highlighted the resulting consequences for humans when various attacks on smart buildings, smart phones, and smart vehicles are performed, also by emphasizing the role of inter-connected things populating smart cities. Furthermore, by discussing the example of smart buildings, we conclude that awareness for smart things is a multifaceted problem. Vendors, customers, and operators as well as awareness for the deployment process of smart things must be considered. We pointed out that research efforts have already been started from smartphones but remain very limited for vehicles, devices and especially for buildings.

We also conclude that a variety of attacks will be possible in a near future. Therefore, we underline the importance of a rapid development of proper and effective countermeasures. Possible countermeasures have to be inspired by the efforts achieved in other fields like peer-to-peer, ad-hoc networks and regular computers. The customer's comprehensiveness of these future security measures is a central requirement in order to be effective. This is a prime research task both for the academia and the industry in order to improve the security of smart environments.

References

1. Al-kahtani, M.: Survey on security attacks in vehicular ad hoc networks (VANETs). In: 2012 6th International Conference on Signal Processing and Communication Systems (ICSPCS), pp. 1–9, December 2012
2. Arfaoui, G., Gharout, S., Traoré, J.: Trusted execution environments: a look under the hood. In: The International Workshop on Trusted Platforms for Mobile and Cloud Computing, pp. 259–266. IEEE Computer Society, Oxford, April 2014
3. Bronkhorst, A., Post, W., te Brake, G.: From human factors to HSI and beyond: design of operations centers and control rooms. In: 9th Future Security - Security Research Conference, pp. 140–146. MEV Verlag, September 2014
4. Caviglione, L., Coccoli, M.: Privacy problems with web 2.0. Comput. Fraud Secur. **2011**(10), 16–19 (2011)
5. Caviglione, L., Mazurczyk, W.: Understanding information hiding in iOS. IEEE Comput. Mag. **48**(1), 62–65 (2015)
6. Checkoway, S., McCoy, D., Kantor, B., et al.: Comprehensive experimental analyses of automotive attack surfaces. In: Proceedings of the 20th USENIX Conference on Security, SEC 2011, pp. 6. USENIX Association, Berkeley (2011)
7. Engoulou, R.G., Bellache, M., Pierre, S., Quintero, A.: VANET security surveys. Comput. Commun. **44**, 1–13 (2014)
8. Felt, A.P., Finifter, M., Chin, E., Hanna, S., Wagner, D.: A survey of mobile malware in the wild. In: 1st ACM Workshop on Security and Privacy in Smartphones and Mobile Devices, p. 3. ACM Press, New York, October 2011
9. Franke, U., Brynielsson, J.: Cyber situational awareness - a systematic review of the literature. Comput. Sec. **46**, 18–31 (2014)
10. Gambs, S., Killijian, M.O., Nunez del Prado Cortez, M.: De-anonymization attack on geolocated data. In: 2013 12th IEEE International Conference on Trust, Security and Privacy in Computing and Communications (TrustCom), pp. 789–797 (2013)

11. Granzer, W., Kastner, W., Neugschwandtner, G., Praus, F.: Security in networked building automation systems. In: 2006 IEEE International Workshop on Factory Communication Systems, pp. 283–292 (2006)
12. Granzer, W., Praus, F., Kastner, W.: Security in building automation systems. IEEE Trans. Indus. Electron. **57**(11), 3622–3630 (2010)
13. Koscher, K., Czeskis, A., Roesner, F., Patel, S., Kohno, T., Checkoway, S., McCoy, D., Kantor, B., Anderson, D., Shacham, H., Savage, S.: Experimental security analysis of a modern automobile. In: 2010 IEEE Symposium on Security and Privacy (S&P), pp. 447–462, May 2010
14. Lipiński, B., Mazurczyk, W., Szczypiorski, K., Śmietanka, P.: Towards effective security framework for vehicular ad-hoc networks. In: Proceedings of 5th International Conference on Networking and Information Technology (ICNIT 2014) (2014)
15. Lowe, M.: Defending against cyber-criminals targeting business websites. Netw. Sec. **2014**(8), 11–13 (2014)
16. Chen, L., Hongbo Tang, J.W.: Analysis of VANET security based on routing protocol information. In: Proceedings 4th International Conference Intelligent Control and Information Processing (2013)
17. Martin, T., Hsiao, M., Ha, D.S., Krishnaswami, J.: Denial-of-service attacks on battery-powered mobile computers. In: Proceedings of the Second IEEE Annual Conference on Pervasive Computing and Communications, PerCom 2004, pp. 309–318. IEEE (2004)
18. Mazurczyk, W., Caviglione, L.: Steganography in modern smartphones and mitigation techniques. IEEE Commun. Surv. Tutor. **PP**(99), 1 (2014)
19. Moore, H.: Security flaws in universal plug and play. Technical report, January, Rapid7 (2013). https://community.rapid7.com/docs/DOC-2150
20. Mundt, T., Kruger, F., Wollenberg, T.: Who refuses to wash hands? privacy issues in modern house installation networks. In: Proceedings 7th International Conference Broadband, Wireless Computing, Communication and Applications, pp. 271–277, November 2012
21. Nöldgen, M., Bach, A., Heinz, T.: Integration of resilience engineering in the transdisciplinary building design process. In: Proceedings 9th Future Security - Security Research Conference, pp. 125–132. MEV Verlag, September 2014
22. Rastogi, V., Chen, Y., Jiang, X.: Evaluating android anti-malware against transformation attacks. In: 8th ACM SIGSAC Symposium on Information, Computer and Communications Security, pp. 329–334. ACM Press, Hangzhou (2013)
23. Snoonian, D.: Smart buildings. IEEE Spectr. **40**(8), 18–23 (2003)
24. Biswas, S., Jelena Misic, V.M.: Performance analysis of black hole attack in vanet. In: Proceedings of 31st Interenational Conference Distributed Computing Systems (2011)
25. Szlósarczyk, S., Wendzel, S., Meier, M., Schubet, F., Kaur, J.: Towards suppressing attacks on and improving resilience of building automation systems - an approach exemplified using BACnet. In: Proceedings Sicherheit 2014, GI, pp. 407–418 (2014)
26. Wendzel, S., Kahler, B., Rist, T.: Covert channels and their prevention in building automation protocols - a prototype exemplified using BACnet. In: Proceedings 2nd Workshop on Security of Systems and Software Resiliency, pp. 731–736. IEEE (2012)
27. Wendzel, S., Zwanger, V., Meier, M., Szlósarczyk, S.: Envisioning smart building botnets. In: Proceedings Sicherheit 2014, LNI, GI, March 2014, vol. 228, pp. 319–329 (2014)

28. Wendzel, S., Mazurczyk, W., Caviglione, L., Meier, M.: Hidden and uncontrolled-
on the emergence of network steganographic threats. In: Reimer, H., Pohlmann,
N., Schneider, W. (eds.) ISSE 2014 Securing Electronic Business Processes, pp.
123–133. Springer, Wiesbaden (2014)
29. Zeadally, S., Hunt, R., Chen, Y.S., Irwin, A., Hassan, A.: Vehicular ad hoc networks (VANETS): status, results, and challenges. Telecommun. Syst. 50(4), 217–
241 (2012)

A Probabilistic Analysis Framework
for Malicious Insider Threats

Taolue Chen[1], Florian Kammüller[1], Ibrahim Nemli[2],
and Christian W. Probst[2($\boxtimes$)]

[1] Middlesex University London, London, UK
{t.chen, F.Kammueller}@mdx.ac.uk
[2] Technical University Denmark, Kongens Lyngby, Denmark
ibrahimnemli@msn.com, cwpr@dtu.dk

Abstract. Malicious insider threats are difficult to detect and to mitigate. Many approaches for explaining behaviour exist, but there is little
work to relate them to formal approaches to insider threat detection.
In this work we present a general formal framework to perform analysis
for malicious insider threats, based on probabilistic modelling, verification, and synthesis techniques. The framework first identifies insiders'
intention to perform an inside attack, using Bayesian networks, and in
a second phase computes the probability of success for an inside attack
by this actor, using probabilistic model checking.

1 Introduction

Cyber security considers attacks on organisations from cyber space [5]. While
many organisations are well protected against technical attacks, combinations
of technical attacks with human factors can be devastating. This integration of
human factors and security is important, and extends security to organisational
issues and society. This combination has almost replaced the classical "security sciences", since it is now apparent that in almost all aspects of security
the human factor is crucial. However, it is an open challenge how to integrate
human behaviour into the design and verification of (secure) systems. A common problem for security analysts is to detect attacks by insiders. Here, more
than anywhere, human behaviour needs to be taken into account when designing
security systems and monitoring information systems.

In this paper, we present a framework that leverages probabilistic modelling
and verification techniques for the analysis of insider threats. As we have shown
in previous work [2], insider threat analysis requires the combination of a macro-
level view and a micro-level view akin to sociological techniques. This is needed
in order to integrate human factors into the context of an infrastructure, like

Part of the research leading to these results has received funding from the European Union Seventh Framework Programme (FP7/2007–2013) under grant agreement no. 318003 (TRE$_S$PASS). T. Chen is partially supported by an oversea grant
from the State Key Laboratory of Novel Software Technology, Nanjing University.

T. Tryfonas and I. Askoxylakis (Eds.): HAS 2015, LNCS 9190, pp. 178–189, 2015.
DOI: 10.1007/978-3-319-20376-8_16

the physical environment of a company and its IT network. We use Bayesian networks to probabilistically model the human disposition for the micro-level analysis to estimate when an actor becomes an insider. Additionally, on the macro-level we use Markov Decision Processes (MDPs) to model actions of an insider within an organisation's infrastructure (physical and logical). This two-fold framework provides a tool for the security analyst to *quantitatively* estimate the actual risk of insider threats by an employee of a company at a given moment.

The micro and macro level are represented in our framework as an intentional analysis and a behavioural analysis. The *intentional analysis* (see Sect. 5) analyses the degree of the intention, in terms of probability, for an employee to be an insider attacker. Once an employee *intends* to be an insider attacker, the *behavioural analysis* (see Sect. 6) identifies the probability of success, using Probabilistic Model Checking (PMC) to support our analysis. To the best of our knowledge, this is the first quantitative framework to provide a comprehensive analysis of malicious insider threats.

Before presenting this framework, we discuss related work followed by an introduction of the basic concepts of insider threats and probabilistic modelling techniques in Sect. 3.

2   Related Work

We base our work on existing taxonomies of insiders [3,9]. In previous work [2], we used Higher Order Logic (HOL) to model insider threats accommodating the view of the insider's disposition based on these taxonomies, and insider patterns based on real case studies [3]. This logical modelling of insider patterns revealed that HOL allows modelling the human factor with its psychological disposition, the company's infrastructure including policies, and use theorem proving to prove that certain behaviours lead to policy violations, i.e., insider attacks. However, the need of a company's security services to quantitatively estimate the risk of an insider attack needs a more detailed analysis like the probabilistic one we present here. The Insider threat patterns provided by CERT [3] use System Dynamics models, which can expres dependencies but do not support probabilities quantifying these dependencies nor any of the probabilistic analysis that we propose here. Axelrad et al. [1] have used Bayesian networks for modelling insider threats, and we are currently investigating how their work relates to our first phase. In earlier work [8], we have used EXASyM [10] to model and analyse attacks based on the infrastructure of a company expressed as a graph in the acKlaim calculus and using the PRISM model checker. There, attacks are based on the probabilities of actors' movements in the infrastructure corresponding to a random walk. Here, we embed this previous analysis tool to provide the tooling for the second part of our framework, but significantly extended to Markov Decision Processes (as opposed to merely Markov Chains) as used in [8].

3   Preliminaries

The behavioural and psychological aspects of actors are related to their personal profile in many ways. These can be seen as the antecedents or key initial factors to understanding an individual's propensity to perform an attack. Nurse *et al.* [9] have identified eight elements that may be especially useful in modelling and analysing this aspect of insider threats. These are the precipitating events (catalyst), an individual's general personality characteristics, historical behaviour, concrete psychological state in a situation, attitudes towards work, skill set, opportunity, and lastly, motivation to attack. All of these values are hard to measure, but if present, can be used to compute probabilities of the occurrence and success of actions.

We represent these probabilities in *Bayesian networks* (BNs) [6], which correspond to the micro level view of our framework. To construct these in general, one has to collect many possible observations that may be relevant to the problem and determine what subset of those observations is worthwhile to model, and then organise the observations into variables having mutually exclusive and collectively exhaustive states [4].

BNs are a graphical model that encodes a probabilistic relationship among variables of interests. In general, a BN for a set of variables $\mathcal{X} = \{X_1, \cdots, X_n\}$ is a tuple (S, P) where S is a *directed acyclic graph* (DAG) that encodes the set of conditional independence assertions on variables in $\mathcal{X}$, and P is a set of local probability distributions associated with each variable. These two components together define a joint probability distribution for $\mathcal{X}$. The nodes in S are in one-to-one correspondence with the variables in $\mathcal{X}$. We usually use X_i to denote both the variable and its corresponding node, and $Pa(X)$ to denote the set of parents of the node X in S as well as the variables corresponding to those parents. In S, the absence of edges between two nodes (variables) encodes conditional independencies (of the two variables). In particular, given the structure S, the joint probability distribution for $\mathcal{X}$ is given by

$$p(x_1, \cdots, x_n) = \prod_{i=1}^{n} p(x_i \mid pa_i)$$

where pa_i denotes the parents of node X_i in S, and P are the distributions corresponding to the term $p(\cdot|\cdot)$.

On the macro level, we use Markov Decision Processes (MDPs) to identify potentially successful insider threats:

Definition 1 (MDP). *A Markov Decision Process* $\mathcal{M} = (S, s_0, A, \mathbf{P}, AP, L)$, *where*

- *S is a set of states with $s_0 \in S$ being the initial state;*
- *A is a set of actions;*
- *$\mathbf{P} : S \times A \times S \rightarrow [0,1]$ is the transition probability function such that for all states $s \in S$ and actions $a \in A$, $\sum_{t \in S} \mathbf{P}(s, a, t) \in \{0, 1\}$.*
- *AP is a set of atomic propositions;*
- *$L : S \rightarrow 2^{AP}$ is the labelling function.*

For any state $s \in S$ and action a, if $\sum_{t \in S} \mathbf{P}(s, a, t) = 1$, then we say the action a is enabled in s.

4   Framework

The overall aim of our analysis is to estimate the probability that an employee of an organisation (conceived as the insider) launches a successful insider attack. We emphasise that, in this work, we only address *intentional, malicious* insider threats, meaning that the insider consciously acts as an attacker. In contrast, the analysis of *accidental* insider threats – where the insider might be social engineered by a malicious outsider – is not addressed and is left as future work. Overall, our framework consists of two components:

- The intentional analysis provides a quantitative measure for the risk that a particular employee may reach the tipping point and turn into a malicious insider; and
- The behavioural analysis estimates where an insider could successfully launch an attack in a company's infrastructure. This is influenced by the personal characteristics of the attacker, for example, the attacker's skill to break a lock or succeed in social engineering the secretary.

Our framework is quantitative in terms of probabilities, which depend on various factors, typically including a *personal profile* and a *type of insider threats*. A *personal profile* comprises a number of factors influencing the person's behaviour; the profile does not describe the behaviour, it is a prediction of likely behaviour, based for example on tests, profiles, and observed behaviour:

- Individuals' personality characteristics. The personnel department will often be able to provide an estimation via some "characteristics test" commonly used in psychology;
- Psychological state;
- Attitude towards work: should be easily evaluated, and formalised as a variable in the interval $[0, 1]$; or
- Skill set: for instance whether one can break a locker, whether one has good knowledge of CCTV, etc.

The personal profile will be used for both the intentional analysis and the behavioural analysis below. We also note that the personal profile is *time-dependent* and should be updated regularly as some attributes might become invalidated, jeopardising the precision of the analysis.

The CERT Guide [3] identifies three main types of insider threats, fraud, theft of intellectual property, and sabotage. Evidently, these types influence both steps of our analysis; for instance, fraud and theft require different skills, and so the probability of success differs.

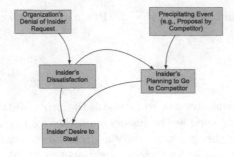

Fig. 1. Example for system dynamics model for entitled independent [3].

5   Intentional Analysis

In this section, we provide the first component of our framework, *i.e.*, the intentional analysis of potential insider threats. The main aim is to have an estimation on the *degree* that an employee of an organisation intends to launch an insider attack. Formally, this is expressed as the *probability* that an employee decides to become an insider attacker. At this stage we do *not* address whether finally the attack is accomplished or not; this is the main subject of the behavioural analysis.

The main part of the analysis is based on Bayesian networks. Modelling using BNs is widely considered as an art, and requires sufficient domain-specific knowledge. However, for insider threats there exist collections of so called *patterns* [3], which turn out to facilitate our modelling significantly. In particular, the *System Dynamics* modelling method is exploited. In this methodology abstract variables define a taxonomy of insider threat cases. Graphically, these variables are presented in square boxes. A *solid* arrow from a box containing variable a to one containing variable b indicates that an increase of a implies an increase of b. A *dashed* arrow represents the inverse relationship, *i.e.*, an increase of a implies a *decrease* of b. An example pattern for "entitled independent" is given in Fig. 1.

The system dynamics, which only gives a high-level, qualitative description, still yields a useful starting point of the intentional analysis. Essentially, we substantially extend the system dynamics by introducing a *quantitative* description, which is considerably more precise and useful. Note that the causalities, quantification, or qualification are encoded as a Bayesian network. In light of this, a crucial step of our methodology is to translate the system dynamics to BN.

The BN has the same graph structure as the system dynamics model, which we assume to be acyclic.[1] In general, for each node in the system dynamics, we introduce a random variable. We usually have the following cases:

---

[1] We note that in practice, occasionally the cycles exist, which we abstract to their strongly connected component as a single node, thus obtaining a proper DAG. We might be able to use Markov logic network to directly encode a system dynamic with cycles, but this is left as the future work for simplicity.

1. For *events* that might happen or not, the corresponding random variable is governed by the *Bernoulli distribution*, i.e., a random variable which takes value 1 with success probability p and value 0 with failure probability $q = 1 - p$; A typical case of this kind is the precipitating event in Fig. 1;
2. For quantities over a finite domain, for instance, the psychological state which might take values from happy, depressed, disgruntled, angry, stressed, as well as the type of motivation which might take values from financial, political revenge, fun, competitive-advantage, power, peer-recognition, we usually introduce discrete random variables with corresponding outcomes as the domain of the quantity under consideration;
3. For quantities of continuous nature, for instance, dissatisfaction in Fig. 1, in principle, we can introduce a continuous random variable, say the *degree* of dissatisfaction, as a value in $[0, 1]$. In practice, we usually apply discretisation to $[0, 1]$ to have a partition of $[0, 1]$.

As the next step, we must specify the conditional probabilities among the introduced random variables. It is worth noting that the concrete probabilities are difficult to obtain; however, this is not the main concern of the current paper which solely aims to establish the basic framework.

We emphasise that such a model should be *parameterised*, for example with the type of threat. The reason is that for different threat types, the introduced random variables should vary, and probably more importantly, the conditional probabilities differ.

Once the BN is established, the next step is to analyse it. In general, we abstract the degree of intention as a value Int $\in [0, 1]$, and the analysis computes the probability that the degree of intention falling into interval I exceeds θ, i.e., $\Pr[\text{Int} \in I] \geq \theta$. This is a typical task of *prediction*. Another kind of analysis is *explanation*, for instance, the analyst might be interested in knowing, once the degree of intention Int $\geq \theta$, what is the most likely cause?

5.1   Example

To illustrate the intentional analysis framework, let's consider the case study of *Entitled Independent* depicted in Fig. 1.

The events "organisation denial of insider request" and "precipitating event" are of type (1), and thus are governed by the Bernoulli distribution. For instance we have that $\Pr(\text{precipitating event} = 1) = 0.1$ meaning that with probability 0.1, the employer receives a job offer from a different company. The "insider's dissatisfaction" is of type (3), and thus we consider the *degree* of dissatisfaction $\beta \in [0, 1]$ and introduce a probabilistic density function (pdf) f_β to specify the distribution of β. However for computation efficiency, we usually prefer to stay in the discrete model, so we could partition $[0, 1]$ into $[0, 0, 1), [0.1, 0.2), \cdots$ and specify the probabilities $p_1, \cdots, p_{10}$. The intuition is that, say, "the probability that the dissatisfaction degree being from 0.5 to 0.6 is p_5".

Alternatively, we can define "low", "mediate", "high" for the dissatisfaction degree, which could correspond to $[0, 0, 3), [0.3, 0.7), [0, 7, 1]$ respectively.

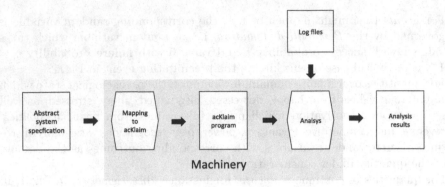

Fig. 2. Workflow of the behavioural analysis framework [8]

This is also the case for "Insider's desire to steal", and "Insider's planning to go to competitor", which practically takes value from "yes", "no", "not sure".

As the next step, we need to specify the conditional probability. For the most interesting case regarding an insider's desire to steal, this could simplistically be formulated as a table, where X denotes "Insider's dissatisfaction", and Y denotes "Insider's planning to go to competitor".

X	Y	Steal (H)	Steal (M)	Steal (L)
High	Yes	0.6	0.3	0.1
High	Not sure	0.2	0.3	0.5
High	No	0.0	0.1	0.9
⋮	⋮	⋮	⋮	⋮

6 Behavioural Analysis

In this section, we provide the second component of our framework, i.e., the behavioural analysis of insider threats. Given the infrastructure of the organisation and a personal profile, this analysis estimates the probability of successful insider attacks. Here the infrastructure of the organisation may refer to the physical locations relevant to the insider threats, their access control policies, etc.

Figure 2 illustrates the workflow, which consists of the following four main steps:

- Step 1: Model the infrastructure in the *abstract system specification*;
- Step 2: Map the abstract system specification to the *acKlaim process calculus* and generate the *transition system*;

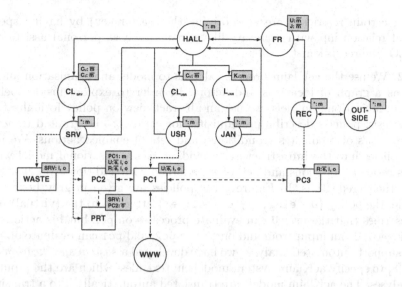

Fig. 3. A simple example system and its representation as a graph including actors, networks, locations, and policies in acKlaim [10]

- Step 3: Translate the *transition system* into *Markov decision processes* by annotating the transitions with probabilities; and
- Step 4: Perform behavioural analysis by verification of the Markov decision process.

We now elaborate these steps in details.

Step 1. The abstract system model is specified as a collection of mathematical constructs that is used to create an abstraction of a real-world system. This abstraction makes it possible to model physical localities, interconnected computers, actors that can move around in the physical localities, and data that can be carried by actors or left at both computers or localities. On top of this there is a fine-grained access control mechanism that limits the mobility of actors, and protects sensitive data. Figure 3 shows an example of a physical model and its representation in acKlaim [10].

It should be noted that in the abstract system, there is no means for modelling dynamic behaviours of actors, but only means of specifying what the initial structure of the system looks like – a static representation of the system model. The dynamic behaviour of the model is supported when the model is mapped to acKlaim in which the semantics of acKlaim uses the abstract system to evaluate the effects of actors movement.

We note further that the location might be *physical* or *logical*. Physical locations such as HALL in Fig. 3 are self-explained. In contrast, logical locations provide a valuable means to model human aspects of insider threat. For instance, it is useful to capture the "secretary" by-pass. Indeed, it is well recognised that a typical scenario of insider threats is that the attacker obtains privilege (e.g., entering certain restricted areas, obtaining the master key) by having special personal relationship with secretary-like persons such as personal assistant of the CEO, the receptionist.

Step 2. We use the acKlaim process calculus to model an organisation and its actors as a graph of locations and actors. In order to explore insider behaviour in organisational models, we use an abstract view on policy formalisations and analysis: policies describe prerequisites for actions to be granted to actors given by pairs of predicates (conditions) and sets of enabled actions. We integrate policies into the infrastructure, providing an organisational model where policies reside at locations and actors are adorned with additional predicates to specify their credentials. In Figure 3, the policies are given in grey boxes. For example, the policy {U: elog, i, o; pc1: e;} attached to the (virtual) node pc2 describes that the user U can evaluate processes on pc2 but his actions are being logged, U can input from and output to pc2, and pc1 can evaluate on pc2.

To support automated analysis, we have developed a *system specification language* [8] to specify acKlaim system models in text files, which are the input for the analyses. The acKlaim models are translated automatically into a transition system [8, Sect. 3.5].

Step 3. Once the transition system is generated, we augment it to obtain a Markov decision process.

Definition 2 (TS). *A transition system is a tuple* $(S, s_0, \rightarrow)$ *where S is a set of states with $s_0 \in S$ being the initial state, and $\rightarrow \subseteq S \times S$ is a transition relation.*

We note that each *state* of the TS denotes a location in Step 1. We identify a subset of *terminal* states $F \subseteq S$. Intuitively, these terminal states denote the places where the insider attack is actually happening. In the framework, we consider the following probabilities:

- For each state (being physical or logical), there is an *entering probability* specifying the probability for an actor (insider) to access that location by any means. In practice, this depends on various different factors, including the access control policy the organisation adopted and the personal profile. Formally, the entering probability is defined as $p_e : S \setminus F \rightarrow [0, 1]$ where F is the set of terminal states. Evidently, p_e must satisfy some constraints. In the simplest case, if the actor is allowed to enter by the access control policy, the entering probability $p_e = 1$. However, even if access is not granted by the access privilege, there is still a certain probability to enter (e.g., by breaking the lock of the door which depends on the skill set of the person under consideration).
- For each terminal state, there is a *successful probability* specifying the probability that an actor manages to accomplish the attack after entering the terminal location, formally defined by $p_s : F \rightarrow [0, 1]$.
- For each state, we also consider the probability of being caught, i.e., when the insider attempts to perform the attack. We consider the four combinations (1) successful attack, undetected; (2) successful attack, detected; (3) failed

attack, undetected; (4) and failed attack, detected. Formally, we define two functions $p_c : S \to [0, 1]$ specifying the probability of being detected in each state. Intuitively, these probabilities depend on, for instance, the presence of surveillance.

By assuming that the event of being successful and the event of being caught are independent (which is a reasonable assumption in practice), one can derive the probabilities for the aforementioned combinations of events.

As before, the model is parameterised. These parameters are used to model various factors which would impact the probabilities $p_e(\cdot)$, $p_s(\cdot)$, and $p_c(\cdot)$ introduced above substantially. A typical case is the daytime vs night mode; breaking in during night time might be easier, so the entering probability must be higher. However, at night, some server might be shut down, so the success probability might be lower if one wants to download a confidential file from the internal server. Moreover, the model should be parameterized with personal profiles to account for attacker skills.

With these probabilities at hand, given the TS $(S, s_0, \to)$ obtained from the previous step, we can define an MDP $\mathcal{M} = (S', s_0', A, \mathbf{P}, AP, L)$ as follows:

- The state space of the MDP $\mathcal{M}$, $S' = (S \cup \{\mathsf{succ}, \mathsf{fail}\}) \times \{\checkmark, \times\}$; and the initial state $s_0' = (s_0, \checkmark)$.
- $A = \{e_{s,t} \mid (s, t) \subseteq \to\} \cup \{\mathsf{commit}\}$;
- For each state of the form $(s, \star)$ where s is *not* a terminal state and $\star \in \{\checkmark, \times\}$, we introduce an action $e_{s,t}$ for each edge (s, t) in the TS. We define the resulting probability distribution $\mathbf{P}(s, e_{s,t}, \cdot)$, written $\mu_{s,t}$ by:

$$\begin{aligned}
\mu_{s,t}(t, \checkmark) &= p_e(t) \cdot (1 - p_c(t)) \\
\mu_{s,t}(t, \times) &= p_e(t) \cdot p_c(t) \\
\mu_{s,t}(\mathsf{fail}, \checkmark) &= (1 - p_e(t)) \cdot (1 - p_c(t)) \\
\mu_{s,t}(\mathsf{fail}, \times) &= (1 - p_e(t)) \cdot \ p_c(t)
\end{aligned}$$

- For each terminal state s, there is only one action commit enabled at s, and we define the resulting distribution $\mathbf{P}(s, \mathsf{commit}, \cdot)$, written μ_{commit}, by:

$$\begin{aligned}
\mu_{\mathsf{commit}}(\mathsf{succ}, \checkmark) &= p_s(s) \cdot (1 - p_c(t)) \\
\mu_{\mathsf{commit}}(\mathsf{succ}, \times) &= p_s(s) \cdot p_c(t)) \\
\mu_{\mathsf{commit}}(\mathsf{fail}, \checkmark) &= 1 - p_s(s) \cdot (1 - p_c(t)) \\
\mu_{\mathsf{commit}}(\mathsf{fail}, \times) &= 1 - p_s(s) \cdot \cdot p_c(t)
\end{aligned}$$

- $(\mathsf{succ}, \star)$ and $(\mathsf{fail}, \star)$ for $\star \in \{\checkmark, \times\}$ are *absorbing* states whose transitions do not affect the analysis. We hence omit the definition here.

Intuitively, the $\checkmark$ means that the insider is *not* caught, while the $\times$ denotes that the insider is caught; succ denotes success of the insider, while fail denotes failure. We remark that the definitions of atomic propositions and labelling functions depend on the properties one wants to analyse. We postpone their definitions to the next step.

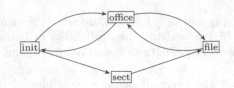

Fig. 4. Transition system.

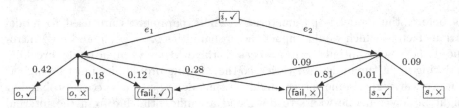

Fig. 5. The fragment of MDP for state init; i, o, s abbreviate init, office, sect respectively.

Example 1. We give a (simplified) example to illustrate the construction of MDPs, The transition system is depicted in Fig. 4. From the init state, the insider could go to the office and from there to the file state, or go to the sect state (bribes the secretary) and from there to the file state as well. For clarity, we only depict the MDP corresponding to the state $(init, \checkmark)$. For this state, there are two enabled actions $e_{init,office}$ (denoted by e_1 in Fig. 5) and $e_{init,sect}$ (denoted by e_2 in Fig. 5).

Step 4. For the last step, we analyse the obtained MDPs by standard probabilistic model checking techniques. The number of interest is the maximum probability that the insider steals a confidential file without being caught. Note that the insider has different strategies, for instance, selecting where to go from a physical location, or trying to social engineer other actors. The insider's goal is to maximise the success probability, whereas from the organisation's perspective, a worst-case scenario should be considered.

Such a problem boils down to the problem of computing the maximum probability to reach the state (succ, $\checkmark$). Formally, one can introduce AP={Succ, NCaught} and a labelling function $L(\text{succ}, \checkmark) = \{Succ, NCaught\}$. The logical formula

$$\mathbf{P}^{\max \, =?}[\Diamond(Succ \wedge NCaught)]$$

and the probabilistic model checker PRISM is able to return the maximum probability, as well as the corresponding strategy of the insider to achieve this probability. By such an analysis, the organisation can identify the potential weakness of the infrastructure, and carry out necessary security improvement.

7 Conclusion

Insider threats are hard to capture in a systematic way. Extending on our earlier work on representing insiders and behaviour with Higher Order Logic, we have outlined a framework for identifying malicious insider threats in system models using probabilistic model checking. Using System Dynamics, this approach captures the behaviour of insiders, and models both their intent or risk of turning malicious as well as the risk of an insider action succeeding.

In future work we plan to investigate the relation to attacker profiles, budgets [7], and skill sets, threats posed by collaborating insiders, and especially the threat posed by accidental insider threats.

References

1. Axelrad, E.T., Sticha, P.J., Brdiczka, O., Shen, J.: A bayesian network model for predicting insider threats. In: 2013 IEEE Security and Privacy Workshops, pp. 82–89. IEEE Computer Society, Los Alamitos (2013)
2. Boender, J., Ivanova, M.G., Kammüller, F., Primiero, G.: Modeling human behaviour with higher order logic: Insider threats. In: STAST 2014. IEEE (2014). co-located with CSF'14 in the Vienna Summer of Logic
3. Cappelli, D.M., Moore, A.P., Trzeciak, R.F.: The CERT Guide to Insider Threats: How to Prevent, Detect, and Respond to Information Technology Crimes (Theft, Sabotage, Fraud). SEI Series in Software Engineering, 1st edn. Addison-Wesley Professional, Boston (2012)
4. Heckerman, D.: A tutorial on learning with bayesian networks. In: Jordan, M. (ed.) Learning in Graphical Models. MIT Press, Cambridge (1999)
5. Kissel, R.: Glossary of key information security terms. Technical report NISTIR 7298 Revision 2, National Institute of Standards and Technology (2013)
6. Koller, D., Friedman, N.: Probabilistic Graphical Models - Principles and Techniques. MIT Press, Cambridge (2009)
7. Lenin, A., Buldas, A.: Limiting adversarial budget in quantitative security assessment. In: Poovendran, R., Saad, W. (eds.) GameSec 2014. LNCS, vol. 8840, pp. 155–174. Springer, Heidelberg (2014)
8. Nemli, I.: Using acklaim and prism to model and analyse insider threats. Master's thesis, DTU Copenhagen (2015). http://www2.imm.dtu.dk/pubdb/views/edoc_download.php/6864/pdf
9. Nurse, J.R.C., Buckley, O., Legg, P.A., Goldsmith, M., Creese, S., Wright, G.R.T., Whitty, M.: Understanding insider threat: a framework for characterising attacks. In: WRIT 2014. IEEE (2014)
10. Probst, C.W., Hansen, R.R.: An extensible analysable system model. Inf. Secur. Tech. Rep. 13(4), 235–246 (2008)

KYPO: A Tool for Collaborative Study
of Cyberattacks in Safe Cloud Environment

Zdenek Eichler, Radek Ošlejšek$^{(\boxtimes)}$, and Dalibor Toth

Faculty of Informatics, Masaryk University, 602 00 Brno, Czech Republic
{xeichler,oslejsek,xtoth2}@fi.muni.cz

Abstract. This paper introduces the KYPO – a cloud-based virtual environment faithfully simulating real networks and enabling users to study cyber attacks as well as to train users in isolated and controlled environment. Particularly, the paper focuses on the user environment and visualizations, providing views and interactions improving the understanding of processes emerged during experiments. Web user interface of the KYPO system supports several collaboration modes enabling the participants to experiment and replay different types of security related tasks.

Keywords: Human-Computer interaction · Collaboration · KYPO · Cyber security

1 Introduction

Cyber attacks become more and more sophisticated and frequent. Internet users face cyber attacks on everyday basis in the form of phishing e-mails, infected attachments or intrusion attempts. A viable option to study attacks and to train users is the simulation of cyber threats in isolated, controlled, scalable and flexible cloud-based environment enabling participants to experience and replay various scenarios in order to understand the impact of the attack on users and devices involved in the infrastructure.

There are many testbed solutions intended to support cyber security-related simulations and training programs in various manners. Some of them, namely DETER [2] and TWISC [3], employ the generic and publicly available *Emulab/Netbed* [13] infrastructure solution, which provides them with basic functionality for virtual appliances' deployment, flexible network topologies configuration, various network characteristics emulation, etc.

In contrast, several security-related testbeds require their own infrastructure solution to be established, which cannot be used for other purposes. For example, ViSe [1], LVC [11], and V-NetLab [8] testbeds employ the VMware virtualization, while the hypervisor-based security testbed [4] requires a KVM-based infrastructure. All these cases require to purchase and establish a dedicated infrastructure, which brings both strengths and weaknesses by itself – while the full control over the infrastructure can lead to easier deployment of testbed's features, it also leads to high initial costs and limited growth-flexibility. The flexibility and scalability

© Springer International Publishing Switzerland 2015
T. Tryfonas and I. Askoxylakis (Eds.): HAS 2015, LNCS 9190, pp. 190–199, 2015.
DOI: 10.1007/978-3-319-20376-8_17

of this lowest layer represent the key factors for possibility to create as many computer networks as needed for specific exercise scenario from the perspective of collaboration.

As another perspective can be considered integrated user environment for specific user roles and use cases. The main goal is to provide access to specific device or computer in testbed. Next important functionality is based on special visualization approaches and analytical tools, usually narrowly focused on particular aspects of network monitoring and utilized by network administrators or security analysts. The level of user interfaces (UI) differs from project to project according to its main purpose, but the majority provides only basic administration of virtual networks and users operate via traditional ways, typically SSH connections to every machine.

Next section describes the KYPO platform, which is used for management of environments for cyber security scenarios described in the paper. Third chapter briefly presents visualizations used by exercise participants for better imagination and understanding. Following chapters discuss collaboration cases of training programs, which are used in KYPO scenarios and provides user experience evaluation.

2   KYPO Architecture

KYPO testbed platform depicted in Fig. 1 provides the environment for modeling and running virtual computer networks. These networks serve as isolated environments for controlled analysis of various cyber attacks as well as for cyber security training programs [7].

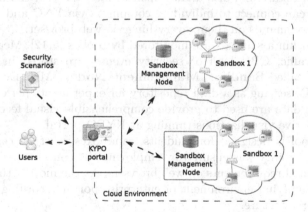

Fig. 1. KYPO Architecture

Security Scenarios are employed in the whole life-cycle of cyber experiments or training programs. They represent a basic document describing the plan and necessary details similarly to screenplays in movie production. Its well-structured JSON format encodes participant roles (e.g. attacker versus defender), their goals, detail instructions, roles of network nodes (e.g. mobile phone of attacker versus server to be compromised), network topology, characteristics of network links and nodes, etc. KYPO provides several predefined templates covering various security interests and domains like DDoS attack simulation, phishing, or simple hacking game. An example of a simple security scenario focused on DDoS attack simulation can be found in [6].

Network-related data encoded in a scenario are used by administrator who is responsible for the preparation of concrete training session. The scenario is uploaded to the administration interface of **KYPO portal**, which mediates access to the KYPO infrastructure for both administrators and participants. The network-related data are processed by the KYPO virtualization subsystem, which automatically allocates so called sandboxes.

Sandbox represents isolated computer network where users can safely perform their tasks. Network infrastructure of sandboxes is fully virtualized. Both nodes and links are build on top of a cloud managed by OpenNebula [9]. This approach provides scalable and flexible solution. Sandboxes can be allocated on demand and accessed remotely without the necessity to maintain hardware devices for each individual security experiment. The abstract network layers simulated by the cloud are transparent for running applications which are hardly able to detect the fact that they are not running on a physical network. The illusion of a real hard-wired network is therefore nearly perfect for both running software and users.

Once a sandbox is allocated in the cloud it can be accessed by authorized participants via KYPO portal. The portal provides users with instructions, various views on network state and also allows them to interact with the network. For example, users can connect to individual computers via VNC and then launch programs and commands on them, everything via web browser.

Activities within a sandbox are monitored by probes [5,12]. Measured data, e.g. network traffic, CPU load or security events, are stored in a database deployed in so called **Sandbox Management Node**, SMN. Every sandbox has its own SMN serving as a data repository for experiments performed in the sandbox. These data are used to provide comprehensible visual feedback to the users via interactive visualizations running at KYPO portal.

Since our tool is designed for students, sandboxes must be easy remotely accessible. Accessibility was ensured by employing the concept of Web applications with minimal requirements on web browsers. As the most fitting approach was chosen an unifying environment of enterprise portal according to its component based architecture.

3   Visualizations

The system provides various visualizations developed specially for educational purposes, where tutor defines which visualizations should be accessible, depending on particular scenario. All visualizations are interactive and follow the Shneiderman's visualization mantra [10]: *Overview first, zoom and filter, then*

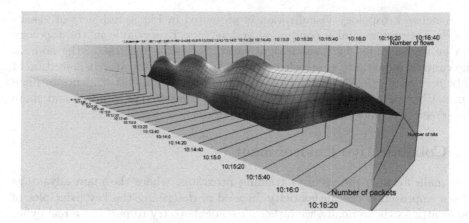

Fig. 2. 3D sequences radar chart

details-on-demand. One of provided visualization developed for education is a 3D sequenced radar chart, which visually compares multiple variables in time. The visualization is implemented in WebGL in order to deliver accelerated visualization in Web environment. The surface of the solid figure (Fig. 2) is a result of the composition of ordinary radar charts along a time scale.

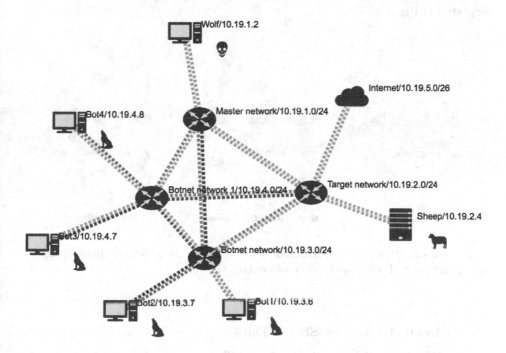

Fig. 3. Visualization of network topology

A network topology visualization is presented in Fig. 3. Subjects of visualization are routers, links, computers and servers. Every node in the topology can be accompanied by a small sign, which represents the role of the node in the running scenario (e.g. attacker or victim). Supported is also visualization of data flow on particular links. This visualization also enables students to open e.g. a VNC (remote access) connection to the computer in sandbox and share the screen of remote computer with other students or lecturer.

4   Collaborative Environment

Our main focus is the security training programs, where the main advantage of our approach is the authenticity. Instead of describing the key principles of cyber attacks theoretically, we rather let students to try to perform a real cyber attacks or let them e.g. to become victims of a phishing attack, all in safe virtual environment. The system provides easy to use user environment, where a lecturer is able to easily define a huge amount of attributes which will be measured in the network during cyber experiments and then presented to students either in real-time or after the experiment.

Security scenarios can significantly differ in the way how the users collaborate. There can be many sandboxes and many training programs prepared or running in KYPO at the same time. In what follows, we discuss collaboration modes of students involved in the same training session. These modes are schematically suggested in Fig. 4.

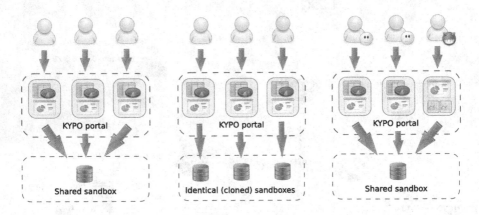

Fig. 4. Collaboration modes: Individual views on shared data (left), individual sandboxes (middle) and role-based collaboration (right)

4.1   Individual Views on Shared Data

Imagine DDoS security scenario. It aims to illustrate principles and impacts of several variants of distributed denial-of-service attacks. The attack is driven by the lecturer who runs appropriate commands in particular sandbox. The state of the sandbox is monitored, measured and recorded in the database running on the Sandbox management node. The DDoS attack can be performed online during the training session or in advance.

Students, each of them sitting at his or her own computer, share the sandbox and the measured data. They have typically the same set of visualizations at their disposal. In the case of DDoS scenario, the most useful are the visualization of network topology emphasizing computer roles (attacker, bots, sheep) together with the utilization of links, as shown in Fig. 3, and also analytical tools like 3D sequence radar chart depicted in Fig. 2, which shows detailed link parameters on a single selected line. Although the visualizations are common for all the students involved in the training session they provide individual views on shared data. Students can focus on different links or return back in time without affecting the views of other students.

4.2   Individual Sandboxes

Imagine a different scenario, where the users should try to compromise a computer. In this case, every participant should have its own private sandbox, in order to handle the attack on its own. Thanks to the cloud-based infrastructure of KYPO it is easy for the lecturer to allocate many identical sandboxes for individual users on demand. The sandboxes have the same network topology, network parameters, software running on nodes, and other aspects. Events and developments of the scenario caused by users in their sandbox are measured and stored inside this sandbox. Therefore, the KYPO is able to provide per-user data after the training session.

4.3   Role-Based Collaboration

Also mixed approach is supported, where students share particular sandbox and every student has it's own role in the scenario, operating different computers. A typical example are so called "capture the flag" games, where groups of participants have access to different vulnerable computers and the goal is to compromise computers of the other groups. Another popular variant of this game defines a group of defenders protecting a vulnerable network and a group of attackers trying to compromise the network. In both the cases, students must cooperate within their groups although they are sitting at their own computers.

Security scenarios of KYPO system enables to define arbitrary roles. They also define which computer is accessible by which role. During the preparation of a training session, the lecturer of the session assigns roles to individual user accounts. The access to the computers inside the sandbox is protected by authentication. Therefore, during the session the KYPO portal provides users with the authentication data with respect to their role and the level achieved in the game.

4.4   Face-to-face Collaboration

Another use case, instead of the above mentioned remote collaboration, is a face-to-face collaboration. Remote collaboration through web portal enables collaboration of participants through network disregarding the geographic location. On the contrary, local face-to-face collaboration enables participants to collaborate during discussion. For this purpose, we are using the Leap Motion device, which helps participants to interactively collaborate when sharing the same computer without e.g. exchanging a mouse. The Leap Motion controller is a small USB device which captures movements of a hand performed above the device. The software recognizes particular gestures, which are then send to our visualizations. Currently, all visualizations described in Sect. 3 can be controlled by the device.

5   Evaluation

Our system was already presented at several cyber security workshops and conferences. Online demo at NOMS 2014 conference was focused on a DDoS scenario simulated in KYPO platform [6]. More complex variant of the attack with 40 virtual machines divided into 6 sub-networks was demonstrated during the tutorial named *Cybernetic Proving Ground: a Cloud-based Security Research Testbed*[1] attached to AIMS 2014 conference. The UI was used for the overview over the network topology traffic during the simulation and for replays of the whole scenario during the presentation for workshop members (Fig. 5).

The second part of the AIMS tutorial was focused on a hands-on training session prepared in a form of game. The main goal was to compromise a server in a company network and to abuse it as an attacker in a DDoS attack. All 20 participants had heir own sandbox with prepared environment (several machines for this scenario) and several tasks to reach the goal (win the game). This game was successfully repeated at FIRST/TF-CSIRT Technical Colloquium[2] in 2015 with 25 involved participants.

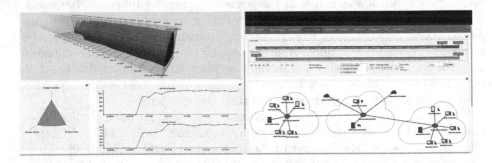

Fig. 5. Screen shot of the KYPO portal during the hands-on training (dual display mode)

---

[1] http://www.aims-conference.org/2014/labs.html.
[2] https://www.first.org/events/colloquia/laspalmas2015.

During these workshops, no significant issues were detected. Unfortunately, no formal qualitative or quantitative feedback was collected. The formal evaluation of the KYPO system was therefore conduced on 10 university students of FI MU[3]. This preliminary evaluation brings promising results, as discussed in what follows.

5.1   Evaluation Process

At the beginning, subjects were asked to evaluate their knowledge about hacking (infiltration to the system) and DDoS attack. Then, subjects logged in to the system and every three or two students shared a sandbox. Instructions were provided to subjects in a form of a level based game very similar to that presented at the AIMS and TF/CSIRT Technical Colloquium, which led the students through the scenario. The goal was to compromise target system and then run DDoS attack from the compromised system. Every subject had its own computer and they were able to collaborate by sharing the screen of the attacker's computer through our web portal (VNC) and view various visualizations described in Sect. 3. When all subjects finished the game, the subjects were asked to the same questions again (same as before the course).

5.2   Results

The subjects evaluated their knowledge about DDoS and hacking on five-point Lickert scale (1 for *I don't know nothing about that*, 5 for *I'm able to perform such an attack*). The difference between before and after the course showed increased knowledge in all subjects. Comparison of DDoS knowledge and hacking knowledge is depicted in Fig. 6. Subjects also evaluated the course itself, also on five-point Lickert scale (1 for *Strongly Disagree*, 5 for *Strongly Agree*) on following statements (mode is a value that appears most often):

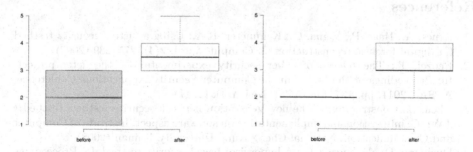

Fig. 6. Tukey boxplot displaying knowledge before and after the course: DDoS (left) and hacking (right)

---

[3] http://www.fi.muni.cz.

- I enjoyed the course. (mode = 4)
- I learned something new. (mode = 4)
- I enjoyed the ability to perform real attack in safe and collaborative environment. (mode = 5)

6 Conclusion

In this paper we have presented a cloud-based research testbed for the simulation and visualization of network attacks, focused on education and practical exercise. Chosen web-based portal technology presents a flexible and scalable solution which allows users to collaborate through various interconnected visualizations in provided web portal satisfying the requirements of broader range of training programs. Usability of our solution was verified by practical demonstrations focused on DDoS attacks and a "hacking game".

Practical evaluation and subsequent survey indicate that the proposed collaborative virtual environment equipped with user friendly interactions could be beneficial for efficient understanding of security threats as well as for the safe forensic analysis of suspicious code or devices. Our next work is therefore aimed to enhancing collaborative tactics supported by smart and intuitive interactions and visualizations.

Acknowledgments. This work has been supported by the project "Cybernetic Proving Ground" (VG20132015103) funded by the Ministry of the Interior of the Czech Republic. We appreciate the access to computing facilities *(a)* owned by parties and projects contributing to the National Grid Infrastructure MetaCentrum, provided under the program "Projects of Large Infrastructure for Research, Development, and Innovations" (LM2010005), and *(b)* provided under the programme Center CERIT Scientific Cloud, part of the Operational Program Research and Development for Innovations, reg. no. CZ. 1.05/3.2.00/08.0144.

References

1. Arnes, A., Haas, P., Vigna, G., Kemmerer, R.A.: Using a virtual security testbed for digital forensic reconstruction. J. Comput. Virol. **2**(4), 275–289 (2007)
2. Benzel, T.: The science of cyber security experimentation: the deter project. In: Proceedings of the 27th Annual Computer Security Applications Conference, ACSAC 2011, pp. 137–148. ACM, New York (2011)
3. Chen, L.: Construction of the new generation network security testbed-Testbed@ TWISC: integration and implementation on software aspect. Institute of Computer and Communication, National Cheng Kung University, Tainan (2008)
4. Duchamp, D., de Angelis, G.: A hypervisor based security testbed. In: Proceedings of the DETER Community Workshop on Cyber Security Experimentation and Test on DETER Community Workshop on Cyber Security Experimentation and Test 2007, DETER, Berkeley. USENIX Association (2007)
5. Hofstede, R., Celeda, P., Trammell, B., Drago, I., Sadre, R., Sperotto, A., Pras, A.: Flow monitoring explained: from packet capture to data analysis with Netflow and IPFIX. IEEE Commun. Surv. Tutor. **16**(4), 2037–2064 (2014)

6. Jirsík, T., Husák, M., Čeleda, P., Eichler, Z.: Cloud-based security research testbed: a DDoS use case. In: Lutfiyya, H., Cholda, P. (eds.) Proceedings of the Network Operations and Management Symposium (NOMS 2014). IEEE Xplore Digital Library, Krakow (2014)
7. Kouřil, D., Rebok, T., Jirsík, T., Čegan, J., Drašar, M., Vizváry, M., Vykopal, J.: Cloud-based testbed for simulation of cyber attacks. In: Lutfiyya, H., Cholda, P. (eds.) Proceedings of the Network Operations and Management Symposium (NOMS 2014). IEEE Xplore Digital Library, Krakow (2014)
8. Krishna, K., Sun, W., Rana, P., Li, T., Sekar, R.: V-NetLab: a cost-effective platform to support course projects in computer security. In: Proceedings of 9th Colloquium for Information Systems Security Education (2005)
9. Milojicic, D., Llorente, I.M., Montero, R.S.: OpenNebula: a cloud management tool. IEEE Internet Comput. 15(2), 11–14 (2011)
10. Shneiderman, B.: The eyes have it: a task by data type taxonomy for information visualizations. In: Proceedings of the 1996 IEEE Symposium on Visual Languages, VL 1996, pp. 336–343. IEEE Computer Society, Washington (1996)
11. Van Leeuwen, B., Urias, V., Eldridge, J., Villamarin, C., Olsberg, R.: Performing cyber security analysis using a live, virtual, and constructive (LVC) testbed. In: Military Communications Conference 2010 - MILCOM 2010, pp. 1806–1811 (2010)
12. Velan, P., Krejčí, R.: Flow information storage assessment using IPFIXcol. In: Sadre, R., Novotný, J., Čeleda, P., Waldburger, M., Stiller, B. (eds.) AIMS 2012. LNCS, vol. 7279, pp. 155–158. Springer, Heidelberg (2012)
13. White, B., Lepreau, J., Stoller, L., Ricci, R., Guruprasad, S., Newbold, M., Hibler, M., Barb, C., Joglekar, A.: An integrated experimental environment for distributed systems and networks. In: OSDI02, pp. 255–270, ACM, Boston, December 2002

Factors Contributing to Performance for Cyber Security Forensic Analysis

Shelby Hopkins, Andrew Wilson, Austin Silva,
and Chris Forsythe[✉]

Sandia National Laboratories, Albuquerque, NM, USA
shopkinl@trinity.edu,
{atwilso,aussilv,jcforsy}@sandia.gov

Abstract. Previously, the current authors (Hopkins et al. 2015) described research in which subjects provided a tool that facilitated their construction of a narrative account of events performed better in conducting cyber security forensic analysis. The narrative tool offered several distinct features. In the current paper, an analysis is reported that considered which features of the tool contributed to superior performance. This analysis revealed two features that accounted for a statistically significant portion of the variance in performance. The first feature provided a mechanism for subjects to identify suspected perpetrators of the crimes and their motives. The second feature involved the ability to create an annotated visuospatial diagram of clues regarding the crimes and their relationships to one another. Based on these results, guidance may be provided for the development of software tools meant to aid cyber security professionals in conducting forensic analysis.

Keywords: Cyber security · Forensic analysis · Decision making · Narratives

1 Introduction

On a weekly basis, reports appear in the media describing a data breach, denial of service or other cyber crimes involving major corporations, governments or military organizations. As those who perpetrate cyber crimes become increasingly sophisticated, there is a growing gap in the number of available cyber security analysts and the demand for their services (Burning Glass 2014). Solutions are needed to enhance the effectiveness of current cyber security analysts while accelerating training of those entering the field.

Within many organizations, cyber security analysts conduct activities comparable to criminal forensic analysis. The analysts piece together clues to understand a series of events, including the likely perpetrator and their objectives and capabilities. The current researchers have experimentally demonstrated that mechanisms facilitating and encouraging construction of a narrative account of events produced superior performance in a cyber forensic analysis task (Hopkins et al. 2015). Research is reported here that considered which features of a narrative representation of events accounted for superior outcomes.

T. Tryfonas and I. Askoxylakis (Eds.): HAS 2015, LNCS 9190, pp. 200–206, 2015.
DOI: 10.1007/978-3-319-20376-8_18

2 Methods

2.1 Subjects

Subjects consisted of 26 employees of Sandia National Laboratories who responded to a company-wide announcement soliciting volunteers to participate in a research study concerning criminal forensic analysis.

2.2 Materials

A scenario was composed based on publicized reports of cyber crimes. The scenario involved a fictitious pharmaceutical manufacturer and subjects were given the pretense that they had been asked to investigate a series of suspicious events at this company. The scenario involved three separate crimes committed by three distinct entities operating independently of one another and with different motives and objectives. The first scenario involved a Hacktivist group intent on proving the pharmaceutical company was involved in controversial activities (i.e., biological weapons research). In the second scenario, a criminal organization committed bank fraud with funds stolen from accounts used by the company. The third scenario consisted of intellectual property theft by an employee of the company (i.e., Insider).

For each crime, a collection of clues were created that realistically, would be available to a corporate security officer conducting a forensic analysis. There were a total of 16 legitimate clues with the Hacktivist thread being the more complex having 8 clues, and the Criminal and Insider threads being somewhat simpler with 4 clues each. There were eight additional clues that served as "red herrings" and had nothing to do with the three crimes. Laminated cards presented a one sentence description of the clues and the associated date the event was noted. Two cyber forensic analysts reviewed each scenario and verified that the storyline and clues were plausible and representative of the types of crimes a cyber forensic analyst might actually encounter.

2.3 Procedure

Subjects were randomly assigned to either a Narrative or Association condition.

Narrative Condition. Subjects were provided 24 laminated cards with magnetic backings on which the clues and associated dates were printed. Subjects were asked to work at a 57" × 46" magnetic whiteboard. Subjects arranged the clues by affixing them to the whiteboard, and used dry erase markers (black, blue, green and red) to draw links between clues and boundaries encircling groups of clues, as well as make notes and other markings. As shown in Fig. 1, features were provided to facilitate and encourage subjects to construct a narrative. Narrative features included 5 Criminal Entity Cards with labeled spaces for subjects to use dry erase markers to denote the identity of the entities, "What trying to do?" and "Why trying to do it?," and a timeline spanning a period encompassing the dates associated with the clues. The upper right corner of the board was labeled "Red Herrings" to encourage subjects to segregate legitimate and red herring clues and subjects were given 12 annotation cards on which to make notes,

8 context cards to identify contexts, and circular magnets to use as tags with 5 different colors (white, blue, green, yellow, and red) and 6 magnets in each color (total of 30 magnets). The board also had a vertical axis labeled, "Criminal Entities," and a horizontal axis for the timeline with months of the year denoted as tick marks. Once subjects had indicated they understood the assignment, they were given a box with the clues arranged in a random order and allowed 25 min to conduct their analysis. At the conclusion of the test session, a photograph was taken of the diagram created by the subject for subsequent data analysis.

Association Condition. The Association condition provided the same visuospatial elements as the Narrative condition, but without features to facilitate construction of a narrative. The same laminated cards with clues were provided and work was completed at the whiteboard. However, subjects were only provided with dry erase markers and the colored circular magnets. Subjects were instructed that the goal of this task was to identify clues that were related to one another and then, signify any relationships between the groupings of clues using the dry erase markers or colored magnets. Figure 2 shows the diagram created by one of these subjects.

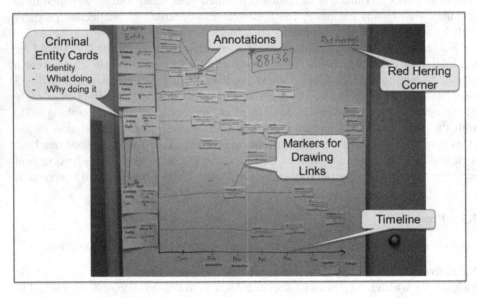

Fig. 1. Example of the whiteboard configuration and features provided to subjects in the narrative condition. Magnetic markers that could be used as tags are not shown here (Color figure online).

Following the forensic analysis, subjects were asked to depict their interpretation of the events using the software tool PlotWeaver (See Fig. 3). PlotWeaver provides an XML-based graphical interface for creating pictorial representations of events. In diagraming stories, PlotWeaver allows entities and interactions between entities to be identified as a time-dependent series of events. Subjects were provided a brief tutorial

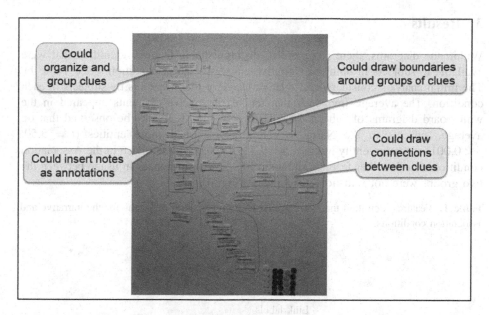

Fig. 2. Example of diagrams created by subjects in the association condition (Color figure online).

on how to use the key features of PlotWeaver. Once the experimenter had verified that subjects understood these features, subjects were given 25 min to create their Plot-Weaver interpretation of events. During this time, whiteboard diagrams created by subjects were available and could be referenced at any time.

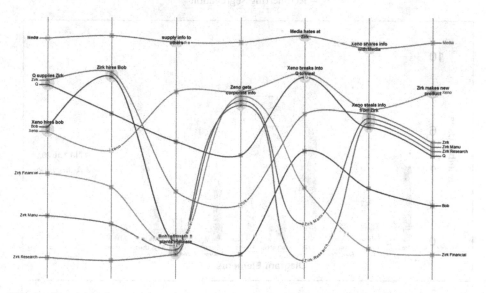

Fig. 3. Example of a PlotWeaver diagram illustrating the subject's interpretation of events within the scenario.

3 Results

Within the diagrams, there were twelve distinguishable features identified that were available to subjects in both the Narrative and Association conditions (See Table 1). The initial analysis considered the relative usage of these features by subjects in each condition. The average frequency that ten of the twelve elements appeared in the whiteboard diagrams of subjects is presented in Fig. 3. It may be observed that on average, subjects in the Narrative condition identified more entities ($t = 5.50$; $p < 0.001$) and more entity motives ($t = 7.48$; $p < 0.001$) than those in the Association condition. For the other features shown in Fig. 3, the differences in usage between the two groups were not statistically significant (Fig. 4).

Table 1. Features identified that were available in constructing diagrams for the narrative and association conditions.

– Group
– Group label
– Group annotation
– Links
– Link labels
– Entities
– Entity motives
– Tag categories
– Tags used
– Questions
– Chronological order
– Red herring segregation

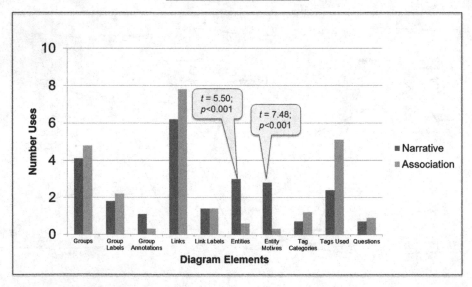

Fig. 4. Average frequency different elements appeared in the whiteboard diagrams of subjects in the narrative and association conditions.

Diagrams were analyzed to identify if subjects had arranged clues in a chronological order. This involved any grouping of three or more clues in which the clues were arranged either vertically or horizontally from earlier to later dates. Groupings may or may not have aligned with the timeline provided in the Narrative condition. It was found that subjects in the Narrative condition were more likely to use chronological orderings of clues ($t = 3.99$; $p < 0.001$).

To determine if subjects had segregated red herring clues from other clues, arrangements of one or more clues were identified where there was no connection made to any of the other clues in the diagram (e.g., no lines were drawn linking clues to other clues or providing the boundary for a group of clues). It was found that subjects in the Narrative condition were more likely to segregate clues that were unassociated with the other clues (i.e., red herrings) ($t = 3.16$; $p < 0.001$).

Groups were compared with regard to how many different types of features and the total number of elements used in the diagrams. It was found that the subjects in the narrative condition used more different types of elements than those in the Association condition ($t = 3.27$; $p < 0.01$). However, when the total number of elements appearing in diagrams was considered (e.g., each arrow connecting clues and each circular magnet was counted as a separate element), the groups did not significantly differ. On average, subjects in the narrative condition used 27.1 distinct elements in their diagrams and subjects in the Association condition used 25.8 elements.

From an analysis of the PlotWeaver storylines constructed by subjects to depict their interpretation of events, it was found that subjects in the Narrative condition used more clues within storylines (Hopkins et al. 2015). Furthermore, while subjects in the Narrative condition included more of the legitimate clues in their plots, both groups included approximately the same number of red herring clues. Thus, subjects in the Narrative condition, developed richer storylines while being no more susceptible to the red herrings. Using each of the twelve features analyzed for the whiteboard diagrams, a stepwise regression was calculated to identify which features accounted for the superior performance of the subjects in the Narrative condition. When the number of clues included in the plots was considered, the resulting model was statistically significant ($F = 6.55$; $p < 0.01$) with three factors (Group Annotations, Entities and Entity Motives) accounting for 60 % of the variance in performance ($R^2 = 60.2$, R^2 adjusted $= 51.0$). Similarly, when the number of legitimate clues included in the plots was analyzed, the resulting model was statistically significant ($F = 4.55$; $p < 0.05$) with the same three factors accounting for 51 % of the variance in performance ($R^2 = 51.2$, R^2 adjusted $= 39.9$).

4 Conclusion

Subjects provided with features to facilitate and encourage their construction of a narrative account of events used these features. In particular, they used the entity cards to identify suspected perpetrators of the cyber crimes and their respective motives, while organizing events within a chronological order. The diagrams constructed by subjects in the Association condition that incorporated comparable visuospatial features, but without the narrative components, included an equivalent overall number of elements. However, the elements were used in a less diverse manner and were less likely to incorporate the features of a narrative. Furthermore, subjects in the Narrative condition performed better with regard to their accurately inferring the nature of the crimes committed, while being no more susceptible to clues that were red herrings.

Further analysis revealed two diagram features that accounted for the performance of the subjects in the narrative condition. First, subjects that focused more on identifying suspected perpetrators and their motives did better than those that devoted less of their analysis to these factors. This suggests that forensic analysts benefit from artifacts that facilitate their ability to discern who may have committed a crime and why they may have done so. Second, subjects that arranged clues in groups and annotated those groups did better than subjects who did not do so. This result may be attributed to the annotations providing memory support in allowing subjects to remember associations and inferences regarding the clues. The scenario used in the current study was complex and somewhat ambiguous. The ability to use annotations may have provided valuable memory support in coping with this complexity.

It is not surprising that the consideration of entities and their respective motives was a primary predictor of performance in the current study. This finding is consistent with event indexing models of narrative comprehension in that entities are considered to be a primary dimension along which stories are organized (Zwaan and Radvansky 1998). Furthermore, entity intentions is a second dimension within this model. It is surprising that the ordering of clues chronologically was not a factor, given that time is also a factor within the event indexing model. The current study did not provide features allowing subjects to organize clues with regard to spatial considerations. It was noted that several subjects did consider spatial factors separating the clues involving outside entities from those involving entities within the fictional corporation and distinguishing different domains from one another (e.g., manufacturing and financial). It is suggested that further benefits may be derived from providing features that facilitate the ability to make spatial distinctions and incorporate these distinctions into the overall representation.

Acknowledgements. Sandia National Laboratories is a multi-program laboratory managed and operated by Sandia Corporation, a wholly owned subsidiary of Lockheed Martin Corporation, for the U.S. Department of Energy's National Nuclear Security Administration under contract DE-AC04-94AL85000. (SAND2014-2123 C)

References

Burning Glass: Job market intelligence: report on the growth of cyber security jobs (2014). http://www.burning-glass.com/media/4187/Burning%20Glass%20Report%20on%20Cybersecurity%20Jobs.pdf

Hopkins, S.E., Silva, A., Wilson, A., Forsythe, C.: Facilitation of forensic analysis using a narrative template. In: Proceedings of the Applied Human Factors and Ergonomics Conference, Las Vegas, NV (2015)

Zwaan, R.A., Radvansky, G.A.: Situation models in language comprehension and memory. Psychol. Bull. **123**(2), 162–185 (1998)

Towards a Successful Exercise Implementation –
A Case Study of Exercise Methodologies

Georgios Makrodimitris(✉) and Christos Douligeris(✉)

Department of Informatics, University of Piraeus,
80, Karaoli & Dimitriou St., 185 34 Piraeus, Greece
{geomakro, cdoulig}@unipi.gr

Abstract. The entire world faces various threats, with a significantly increasing rate. These threats are associated with international terrorism, natural catastrophes, power cuts due to cyber-attacks etc. Without doubt there is a need that an industrial or critical infrastructure should be prepared to face such threats. There exist several methodologies which give guidelines on how to organize and implement an exercise to address these threats at various time instances. After a short description of some of these methodologies, this paper investigates whether they are compliant with the standard ISO. Also, this paper proposes appropriate changes in order for these methodologies to be compliant with the standard and, thus, to become more effective.

Keywords: Exercises · Methodologies · Training · Critical infrastructure · Tabletop exercise · Operational exercise · Functional exercise · Exercise roles · Exercise life-cycle · Evaluation

1 Introduction

Nowadays, the vulnerability of modern industrial and critical infrastructures is an issue that concerns the worldwide public. The annual report from the European Union Agency for Network and Information Security (ENISA), "ENISA Threat Landscape report for 2014" [3], which focuses on the reports analysis from a large number of security labs, concludes that the threats in 2014 have undergone significant developments. The majority of the threats and their trends in the area of cyber physical systems, mobile computing, cloud computing, trust infrastructure, big data, Internet of things/interconnected devices/smart environments and in the area of network virtualization and software defined networking (SDN) have seen a significant increase.

Laurent F. Carrel wrote in his book, [1], on the practice of crisis management that it is necessary to organize and implement exercises systematically:

"Education and training are central tools in order to be prepared for crises. The focus is on being mentally prepared for critical situations. By means of systematic further education, knowledge and experience of individuals, staff or bodies of a crisis concerning the behavior in a crisis, are maintained and improved. During crises, such behavior pays off in many ways, in particular when right from the start a smoothly running organisation, efficient management procedures and institutions are available."

© Springer International Publishing Switzerland 2015
T. Tryfonas and I. Askoxylakis (Eds.): HAS 2015, LNCS 9190, pp. 207–218, 2015.
DOI: 10.1007/978-3-319-20376-8_19

As it is understood, the need for training, good preparation and evaluation to address such situations is obvious and vital. In order for someone to gain knowledge coming out of training, appropriate exercises should be implemented in these industrial and critical infrastructures. The successful implementation of such exercises depends on an accurate planning. For this reason, the generic as well as the major steps of the implementation of an exercise should be setup carefully in order for the objectives of an exercise to be achieved.

Many governmental and private organizations have developed methodologies for the exercises' implementation. Such methodologies are described in the International Organization for Standardization's (I.S.O.) standard 22398 [6], the Federal Crisis Management Training (HERMES) [4, 5], the Guide of the Swedish Civil Contingencies Agency (MSB) [7, 8], and the Good Practice Guide on National Exercises of ENISA [2].

This paper focuses on the analysis and comparison of these methodologies, which are the most popular and well marketed, by presenting their characteristics and requirements. Based on the outcome of this comparison, this paper will provide some questions related to the requirements and specifications, which an infrastructure should be compliant with in order to participate in an exercise, and suggestions for further work.

2   State of the Art

Exercises are the adjunct treatment to defend and protect infrastructures from cyber-attacks. For the planning of such exercises, many organizations have developed methodologies in order to give generic instructions which will lead to a successful exercise implementation.

The exercise life-cycle is similar in all the methodologies, consisting of four phases – the differentiations in the various methodologies relate to how they are named. For the purpose of this paper, the life-cycle of a methodology consists of four phases:

- *Pre-planning phase:* the organizer identifies the need and the objectives of an exercise.
- *Planning phase:* the organizer staffs the planning team and recruits participants.
- *Conducting phase:* the exercise takes place.
- *Evaluating phase:* the evaluation of the exercise is performed.

It is suggested that an exercise should not be implemented only once. The organization which carried out the exercise should take into account the results and the outcomes of the evaluation in order to plan a better exercise in the future. So, the exercise life-cycle can be captured in a spiral scheme as shown in Fig. 1.

In addition, a cartography of the available Information Technology (IT) systems should also be performed first, if an organization wishes to implement an exercise. Based on this cartography, the organizer could then proceed with the first phase of an exercise, in which the need and the set up of the objectives of the exercise will be identified.

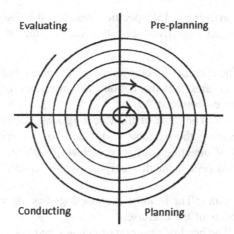

Fig. 1. Exercise life-cycle

During the planning phase, the organizer recruits staff to form the exercise planning team and the participants in the exercise. This means that the organizer should assign responsibilities and tasks to the appropriate personnel, leading to the creation of roles that are necessary for a successful implementation of the exercise.

In the following sections, the essential parts of the most popular exercise methodologies are analyzed and compared.

2.1 Hermes

Hermes OEx is a French methodology to organize exercises, where OEx means "Organisation d' Exercices". Using Hermes, one can define the results, the procedure of how the results will be achieved and the roles of the participants. The activities and the results which are produced using this method are generic. The major characteristic of Hermes is that it is oriented towards results. The results are set up based on the objectives of the project. Hermes helps the exercise organizer not to implement activities which are not related with the project. The results lead to the appropriate processes and roles.

Hermes uses the definition of "tailoring", [4], which reflects that the project modifies the Hermes OEx. Someone can use this method in order to organize either large and complex exercises or short and simple ones. Tailoring helps the irrelevant results not to be produced and the whole effort to be put into achieving the objectives.

Using the term tailoring, Hermes:

- wipes out the irrelevant activities, results, roles and decision points,
- controls the remaining activities, results and roles in order to achieve the project objectives, and
- adds additional, if they are required and deemed necessary, activities, results and roles.

For the organization of an exercise, [5], specific roles should be assigned to assist in the achievement of the project objectives. For this reason, the proposed roles are as follows:

- *Exercise director:* The exercise director guides all the areas that need to be managed in an exercise and ensures that the actions and reactions of the entire exercise management staff are coordinated.
- *Head of directing staff:* The head of the directing staff stages the exercise and is responsible for executing the exercise script and for incorporating the exercise incidents. The head of directing staff works closely with the head of the contact office. The best suited person for this purpose is the scenario and exercise script officer.
- *Head of exercise logistics:* The head of exercise logistics manages and coordinates all the logistical aspects of the exercise.
- *Head of observers:* The head of observers manages and coordinates the observers and prepares the content of any debriefing immediately after the exercise.
- *Head of the contact office:* The head of the contact office manages and coordinates the members of the contact office and ensures that the enquiries and requests of exercise participants are dealt with quickly and competently. The head of the contact office works closely with the head of directing staff when the goal is to develop unprepared dilemmas and exercise incidents and to confront the exercise participants with them.
- *Exercise participants:* They are the members of the organizations, staffs or function holders of the staff who participate in the exercise.

In the guidelines of Hermes, the term "results" is used to describe the outcomes. These outcomes are related directly to the exercise by governing its objectives, such as the preliminary concept of the exercise and the detailed exercise concept.

2.2   MSB

The Swedish Civil Contingencies Agency's MSB (Myndigheten för Samhällsskydd och Beredskap) has as its major objective to increase the security in systems which are crucial and implicitly connected with normal life. If these systems are attacked, then the impact on the society will be large. In order to keep and improve the security of those systems, it is necessary for all the industrial and critical infrastructures to test and evaluate them. These tests can be implemented through the exercises. The exercises based on MSB could be categorized in strategic and operational, based on the goal that a specific infrastructure would like to achieve, [7].

MSB gives guidelines on how to structure and evaluate an exercise, on good crisis management and on procedures for good decision-making. One objective of this methodology is that the implementation and the impact of the measures, which the infrastructure has adopted, should be evaluated and made clear if the infrastructure is ready to face emergencies and crises. Another objective of this methodology is to evaluate whether the goals which have been set up have been achieved totally, partially or not at all.

MSB evaluates whether certain goals have been achieved and shows the benefits and the outcomes of the exercise. Using the evaluation, MSB compares the observations with the outcomes and the goals. Based on the description of the objectives, a report is generated which captures if they are close to reality based on the outcomes of the exercise, [8].

In order for the MSB exercise methodology to be implemented successfully, its tasks should be distributed in different roles. The generic groups of roles are the participants, the exercise management and the evaluator. These roles should understand and be trained very well on the tasks they are responsible for and they have to know the distinction between the roles and their tasks.

The various tasks assigned to participants, exercise management and evaluators should be explained thoroughly in order to create a mutual understanding among the three groups for their respective assignments. These distinctions can be summarized on the following points:

1. It should be clear what someone can earn by participating in an exercise and what will be the outcomes after the exercise implementation.
2. The participants of the exercise should be recruited as soon as possible in order to be informed and well-trained based on their needs. The outcomes will show where it is necessary to improve the exercise team.
3. The exercise should be initiated on a position of shared knowledge and information.
4. The evaluation process should be clear.
5. The importance and the necessity of conducting an exercise and why these specific objectives have been chosen should be shown.
6. The working environment during the exercise should be well-structured in order for the participants to be able to cooperate and exchange information effectively.

The outcomes can be carried out by certain objectives, [8], which could be discrete or combined as follows:

- Investigative (exploratory)
- Needs-oriented (diagnostic)
- Process-oriented
- Results/outcome - oriented.

2.3   ENISA's Good Practice Guide

The European Commission and the Member States have realized that the exercises can play a significant role in increasing the resilience of public e-Communications networks. The authorities that manage industrial and critical infrastructures should be aware of their weaknesses and vulnerabilities by participating in exercises. For this reason, the European Union Agency of Network and Information Security (ENISA) has created and published a good practice guide for the organization and implementation of an exercise, which can be assumed that it is a methodology [2].

Based on this guide, the organization of an exercise is related to the exercise life-cycle. When someone desires to organize an exercise based on this methodology, he should set up the needs and the resources. Based on these, he can decide the type of the exercise which he can prepare, and he has to choose a high-level scenario and identify the participants.

The major value of implementing an exercise is that someone can increase the resilience of the infrastructure. There are different types of exercises depending on the complexity, the size, the examining procedures and the scenario. For the planning and organizing of the exercise, the organizer should:

- Define the measures and processes which will be tested by drilling a specific function, or by developing a business contingency plan.
- Set which the target group will be.
- Identify the resources available for planning and for conducting the exercise.
- Set up the degree of commitment that can be expected from the participants.
- Take into account any available previous experience from other exercises on the side of both the organizers and the participants.

The most important thing in order to organize an exercise is to identify the need of planning it. Using the exercise, someone can measure and evaluate the processes which the infrastructure follows when an incident happens. The organizers should focus on measures which need evaluation, review, improvement and training.

In the case of sectorial exercises or cross-sectorial exercises, the organizer should try to convince the participants to cooperate and coordinate among them focusing on testing the cooperation and showing any existing interdependencies. An organizer can focus on measures such as the common situational awareness of the participants, the needed collaboration (internally and externally) to address the problem, the coordination of resources, the logistics and support capabilities, etc.

Another significant goal for organizing an exercise is to create a high-level scenario which addresses the achievement of the objectives. There are two reasons for choosing the appropriate scenario:

- It helps the organizer to recruit the most appropriate participants to assist in creating a suitable scenario upon the objectives.
- It helps the organizers to have a plan of the exercise before they recruit the planners.

Based on the ENISA's guide, [2], there are many different types of roles during the exercise. The major roles which an infrastructure should have are the following:

- *Organizer:* The organizer is the organization that drives the process of exercise organization.
- *Planner:* The planners are organizations or individuals who participate in the planning of the exercise.
- *Participant* (also Participating Organization, or Participating Stakeholder): A participant is an organization or individual who will play a certain role during the execution of the exercise
- *Exercise Director, Moderator* or *Leadership Team:* A person or team that directs the exercise. The responsibilities include setting up and dismantling the exercise environment, starting and ending the exercise, acting as the central point of contact for questions and problems which arise in the course of the exercise, facilitating tabletop exercises, managing the scenario, etc.

- *Monitor* or *Facilitator:* The roles of monitors and facilitators are related and overlapping.
- *Observer:* Observers are individuals or organizations who are invited to observe the exercise, without participating or monitoring performance.
- *Evaluator:* Evaluators are the individuals involved in the process of evaluating the exercise.

After the implementation of the exercise, the organizer should evaluate the whole process based on the feedback of the participants. This feedback can include recommendations for a better planning and organization of future exercises. Based on the ENISA's guide, this is the most important thing for the planning of the future exercise, as the outcomes of the evaluation are being taking into account by the organizers.

2.4   Overview – Comparison with ISO 22398

As stated in the ISO 22398 standard *"This International Standard describes the procedures necessary for planning, implementing, managing, evaluating, reporting and improving exercises, and the testing designs to assess the readiness of an organization to perform the mission"*. This standard gives the guidelines for organizing and implementing a successful exercise, [6].

The top management is responsible for organizing and implementing the exercise. The exercise should be planned based on its objectives. Also, the information and resources necessary to organize and conduct the exercise should be known in detail. In addition, the need analysis of the exercise should be included in the plan. The documentation of the exercise should describe how the exercise will be supported, how the organizer will recruit participants for the planning, and which are the necessary resources and budget. Also, any other element that can help to make clear and transparent to everyone the planning of the exercise could be added to the documentation.

Based on the standard, the size and the nature of the infrastructure set up the scope and the objectives of the exercise. Moreover, the secondary elements of the exercise, such as the complexity, the functionality and others, depend on the infrastructure type.

The standard states that there should be an *exercise manager, a monitor,* an *evaluator* and *participants*. Each of these roles has different responsibilities based on the tasks they need to perform. The exercise manager manages the exercise efficiently. The monitor and the evaluator measure the implementation of the exercise and the participants take part in the implementation.

At the end, the standard refers that there should be outcomes from the implementation, which the organizer will take into account for the better planning of a future exercise. These outcomes will be collected through the evaluation of the performance of the exercise project team, the ability of the exercise team to implement the exercise and the feedback of all the types of the participants, such as of top management, interested parties, exercise participants and exercise project team members.

Based on Table 1, it is obvious that the good practice guide of ENISA is compliant with the ISO 22398 in the area of the roles and in the area of the outcomes. The other methodologies should be reviewed and updated based on the needs and the requirements of the standard.

Table 1. Comparison based on the roles and the outcomes of each exercise methodology

		ISO 22398	HERMES	MSB	ENISA
OBJECTIVES	The organizer sets up them		√	√	√
ROLES	Exercise manager		√	√	√
	Exercise team		√	√	√
	Observer				√
	Evaluator		√	√	√
	Participants		√	√	√
OUTCOMES	evaluation of the performance of the exercise project team				√
	the ability of the exercise team to implement the exercise		√	√	√
	and the feedback of all the types of the participants		√	√	√

3 Process Comparison

The core element of an exercise is the conducting phase. The suitable and appropriate choice of staff, scenario and participants and the well-defined objectives of the exercise are necessary for a successful operational process. In this section, we present an analysis of the process which each methodology follows for the conducting phase.

3.1 The Conducting Phase of HERMES

The exercise using the Hermes methodology is separated into the following five phases: initialization, preliminary analysis, concept, realization, introduction and finalization [4]. In the initialization phase, a starting point is defined through a connection between the planning level and the operational level of the exercise. In the preliminary phase a decision is taken about the type of the exercise. In the concept phase, why this approach has been chosen should become clear and transparent and the exercise should be evaluated. In the realization phase, all the data and the documents for the implementation are prepared for the participants. In the introduction phase, the exercise is conducted, and evaluated and the report is drafted. In the finalisation phase, the organizer concludes the exercise in an orderly manner.

3.2 The Conducting Phase of MSB

In the MSB methodology, there are four phases for the operational level of the exercise. These phases are the *plan phase*, the *do phase*, *the check phase* and the *act phase* [7].

In the plan phase, the policies, goals, processes and routines are established. In the do phase, the policies, measures, processes and routines are implemented and enforced. In the check phase, the monitoring and auditing are performed by assessing, measuring and reporting. In the act phase, improvements to the exercise elements are realized.

In more detail, the check phase consists of eight stages. The outcomes of these stages are the input to the act phase. The stages are:

1. Appoint a head of evaluation.
2. Plan and organize the evaluation in collaboration with exercise management.
3. Formulate the evaluation questions and the basis for the subsequent analysis.
4. Train the evaluators.
5. Observe the exercise and conduct a direct feedback session.
6. Analyze collected material and compile evaluation report.
7. Present and disseminate evaluation findings.
8. Utilize lessons learned and begin planning the next exercise.

3.3   The Conducting Phase of ENISA's Guide

In the good practice guide of ENISA, there is a distinction of the types of exercises into Discussion-based Exercises and Operations-based Exercises, [2]. This distinction is made based on the exercise tenor.

In Discussion-based exercises, the participants do not have any active participation. They only discuss the scenario and the procedures and test the decision-making. This type of exercises includes seminars, workshops, tabletop exercises, or games.

On the other hand, the Operations-based exercises test the procedures and check whether the staff is prepared to react and follow them. In this type of exercises, the participants are involved and active. Also, this type gives the opportunity for cooperation between the participants, who may be coming from different infrastructures.

The type of the exercise reflects on its size. If someone chooses the Discussion-based exercise, the size will not be as large as if the Operations-based exercise is chosen. If the size of the exercise is large, there exists the ability to test more procedures inside the infrastructure. The disadvantage of a large exercise is that the organizer should be ensured that the scenario covers all the objectives of the exercise, [2].

3.4   Comparison with ISO 22398

The ISO standard 22398 provides guidelines on the operational process of the exercise [6]. These guidelines are summarized below:

- communicating the pertinent parts of the exercise program to interested parties, and informing them periodically for the progress,
- coordinating and scheduling exercise projects and other activities relevant to the exercise program,
- ensuring the selection of exercise project teams whose members have the necessary competence,

- providing necessary resources to the exercise project teams,
- conducting exercises in accordance with the exercise program and within the agreed upon time frame,
- recording exercise activities and managing and maintaining documents, and,
- completing after action reviews and following up on lessons learned and recommendations for improvement.

Based on these guidelines, this paper provides a comparison between the studied methodologies and the standard. As it is illustrated in Table 2, all the methodologies are compliant with the ISO standard.

Table 2. Comparison based on the operational process of each exercise methodology

ISO 22398	HERMES	MSB	ENISA
communicating the pertinent parts of the exercise program	√	√	√
coordinating and scheduling exercise projects and other activities relevant to the exercise program	√	√	√
ensuring the selection of exercise project teams	√	√	√
providing necessary resources to the exercise project teams	√	√	√
conducting exercises in accordance with the exercise program and within the agreed upon time frame	√	√	√
recording exercise activities and managing and maintaining documents	√	√	√
completing after action reviews and following up on lessons learned and recommendations for improvement	√	√	√

In addition, the standard provides guidelines about the type of the exercise. The organizer of the exercise should take into account the scope and the objectives of the exercise and then he should be able determine the exercise type [6]. The proposed types of exercise are summarized below:

- *Alert* exercise: tests the organization by alerting the involved participants and by getting them to arrive at the designated place within a certain time.
- *Start* exercise: tests how fast the emergency management organization can be activated and can start the carrying out of their tasks.
- *Staff* exercise: increases the ability to work with internal processes, staff and information routines in order to create a common operational picture and suggests decisions.

- *Decision* exercise: used to exercise the decision making process within an organization.
- *Management* exercise: a combination of the alert exercise, the start exercise, the staff exercise, the decision exercise and the system exercise.
- *Cooperation* exercise: coordinates the cooperation between the various management.
- *Crisis management* exercise: simulates crisis conditions and tests the crisis management plan.
- *Strategic exercise:* refers to comprehensive exercise activities at the strategic level.

In Table 3, a comparison between the studied methodologies and the standard are provided.

Based on Table 3, one can see that none of the studied methodologies is compliant with the ISO 22398 in the operational process. Each methodology provides different types of exercises to be implemented. At this point, someone can raise an argument and could say that the methodologies may have included the non-covered types in the other types. In order for the methodologies to be compliant with the standard, each methodology should be reviewed and updated based on the guidelines of the standard.

Table 3. Comparison based on the provided exercise types of each methodology

ISO 22398	HERMES	MSB	ENISA
Alert exercise		√	
Start exercise	√	√	√
Staff exercise	√	√	√
Decision exercise	√		
Management exercise			√
Cooperation exercise			√
Crisis management exercise	√	√	√
Strategic exercise	√	√	√

4 Recommendations – Future Work

The industrial and critical infrastructures are organizations and facilities of major importance for the whole world. A failure on their functionality or an attack on these infrastructures is crucial and of high importance. The exercises are the mechanism with which someone can test the reaction and the procedures of an infrastructure.

In this paper, the currently used methodologies were presented and they were compared with the guidelines of the standard ISO 22398. It was observed that the studied methodologies should be reviewed and updated based on the needs, requirements and guidelines set by the standard.

Another point which was concluded as a result of this study is that the methodologies and the standard should set up restrictions and requirements as far as the participants are concerned. Only MSB requires that the participating infrastructure should implement and adopt a risk assessment and security policy, but even for MSB it is not obligatory [7]. The evaluated infrastructure should implement a risk assessment and adopt and implemented a security policy. Without this restriction, it is not clear how the procedures and the measures can be tested.

Acknowledgement. The publication of this paper has been partly supported by the University of Piraeus Research Center.

References

1. Carrel, L.F.: Leadership in Krisen. Ein Handbuch für die Praxis, Bern, p. 23 (2004)
2. ENISA Report: Good practice guide on national exercises - enhancing the resilience of public communications networks. http://www.enisa.europa.eu/activities/Resilience-and-CIIP/cyber-crisis-cooperation/cce/cyber_exercises/national-exercise-good-practice-guide (2009). Accessed 30 Jan 2015
3. ENISA Report: ENISA threat landscape 2014. http://www.enisa.europa.eu/activities/risk-management/evolving-threatenvironment/enisa-threat-landscape/enisa-threat-landscape-2014 (2015). Accessed 30 Jan 2015
4. HERMES OEx: Guidelines for the organisation of exercises. www.hermesoex.ch (2004). Accessed 30 Jan 2015
5. HERMES: Management and execution of projects in information and communication technologies. www.bbl.admin.ch/bundespublikationen (2004). Accessed 30 Jan 2015
6. ISO/IEC: 22398 Societal security — guidelines for exercises and testing. http://www.iso.org
7. MSB: Guide to Increased Security in Industrial Control Systems (2010). ISBN: 978-91-7383-089-8
8. MSB: Handbook – Evaluation of Exercises (2011). ISBN 978-91-7383-127-7

CYSM: An Innovative Physical/Cyber Security Management System for Ports

Spyridon Papastergiou[1(✉)], Nineta Polemi[1(✉)], and Athanasios Karantjias[2]

[1] Department of Informatics, University of Pireaus, Karaoli and Dimitriou 80,
18534 Pireaus, Greece
{paps,dpolemi}@unipi.gr

[2] Information Management Department, SingularLogic S.A., Al. Panagouli and Siniosoglou St.,
14234 Nea Ionia, Athens, Greece
tkarantjias@singularlogic.eu

Abstract. The goal of the paper is to describe the main results of a European research project, namely CYSM, (The authors serve as technical managers of the CYSM project.) which is oriented to address the security and safety requirements of the commercial ports' Critical Information Infrastructures (CII). It aims to introduce an integrated security management system (for port operators) enabling asset modelling, risk analysis, anticipation/management of attacks, as well as stakeholders' collaboration. The proposed system helps port to identify, assess and treat their security and safety problems in an efficient, harmonized and unified manner.

Keywords: Security · Safety · Port's risk assessment

1 Introduction

Ports support a number of business processes that are complex, diverse and involve various external entities (e.g. maritime companies, ministries, banks, other Critical Information Infrastructures -CII-). These operations rely not only upon the physical infrastructures of the ports (e.g. terminals, gates, storage houses) but more substantially upon their ICT infrastructure (e.g. networks, telecom/ICT systems, data, users). The resilience of their infrastructure to complex, persistent and fierce attacks is a primary requirement to guarantee their business continuity.

The adopted ports' security management approaches are ineffective in addressing and treating physical and cyber risks, imposing the need for a holistic and unified approach to secure their dual nature [11]. Usually, a contributory analysis of the inherent risks takes an inordinate amount of operational effort, considering the complexity of the underlying infrastructure and the fact that the security and safety requirements are evolving rapidly. Therefore, it is essential to have a comprehensive and integral approach that facilitates and optimizes the proactive risk identification and treatment of the ports' ICT and physical related risks and threats from an integrated perspective. A holistic methodology for managing security and safety risks could help ports to check their compliance with existing legal, regulatory and standardization regime (e.g. ISO27001

© Springer International Publishing Switzerland 2015
T. Tryfonas and I. Askoxylakis (Eds.): HAS 2015, LNCS 9190, pp. 219–230, 2015.
DOI: 10.1007/978-3-319-20376-8_20

[3], ISO 28005 [5, 6], ISPS code [1, 2]), to detect possible violations and gaps and finally to adapt new regulations and directives.

The authors of this paper share the view (of the European Project CYSM [12]) that the evaluation and mitigation of the cyber and physical risks should not rely only upon highly personalized experience and expertise. It should be an inherently rational and collaborative process that engages corporate personnel with different roles, responsibilities and technical capabilities (e.g. administrators, security officers, maintenance personnel, security guards etc.) and external users, utilising diverse perspectives, knowledge and experiences in order to produce and provide well-defined, acceptable and reliable proofs and information that facilitate the identification and evaluation of potential threats and weaknesses and the estimation of the ports' infrastructure resilience.

Toward this direction, the paper contributes to the effective protection of the ICT and physical ports' infrastructure, by proposing an innovative, evolutionary and sophisticated Collaborative Cyber/Physical Security Management (CYSM) system that helps ports to assess their facilities and revise their risks mitigation plans. This system provides the opportunity to better understand, interpret and finally deal with their security and safety related risks. The paper outlines results from the CYSM project [12] and it is structured as follows: Sect. 2, provides a desk-research analysis and assessment of the available risk management approaches and the existing legal and regulatory framework related to ports' CIIs. Section 3, provides a brief overview of the capabilities and the supported functionality of the proposed Collaborative Cyber/Physical Security Management System, CYSM. The paper concludes with Sect. 4, outlining the most innovative features of CYSM and draws conclusions and directions for further research.

2 Ports' Security and Risk Management Approaches

The main goal of risk management is to protect business assets and minimize costs in case of failures and thus it represents a core duty of successful corporate governance. Hence, risk management describes a key tool for the security within organizations and it is essentially based on the experience and knowledge of best practice methods. These methods consist of an estimation of the risk situation based on the business process models and the infrastructure within the organization. In this context, these models support the identification of potential risks and the development of appropriate protective measures. The major focus lies on companies and the identification, analysis and evaluation of threats to the respective corporate values.

The outcome of a risk analysis is in most cases a list of risks or threats to a system, together with the corresponding probabilities. International standards in the field of risk management are used to support the identification of these risks or threats as well as to assess their respective probabilities. These standards range from general considerations and guidelines for risk management processes (e.g. [14–16]) to specific guidelines for the IT sector (e.g. [4, 17–20]) all the way to highly specific frameworks as, for example, in the maritime sector (e.g. [1, 2, 21]). Most of these standards specify framework conditions for the risk management process, but rarely go into systematic, homeomorphic risk analysis methods; making a direct comparison of the results difficult. Furthermore the above-mentioned efforts are not sector-specific; as a result they are too generic and difficult to in the complex maritime sector.

In principle, selecting an appropriate method and tool for risk evaluation proves to be complicated. In recent years, a number of methods, algorithms (OCTAVE [22, 23], EBIOS [24], MEHARI [25], CORAS [26], NIST [27], ISAMM [28], STORM-RM [30]) and tools (CRAMM [29], S-PORT [10, 31]) have been evolved from research, specially designed to protect the ICT infrastructure and related systems without holistically covering the dual nature (physical and cyber) of the ports CII.

In contrary to the aforementioned general and ICT-specific guidelines for risk management, the International Ship and Port Facility Security (ISPS) Code [1, 2] (as well as the respective EU regulation [21]) defines a set of measures to enhance the security of port facilities and ships, putting emphasis on the physical facilities and the organizational aspects of security not covering sufficiently the cyber facilities and ports' ICT assets. Additionally, a number of risk management methodologies and tools [32, 33] exist, compliant with ISPS but not with the cyber related security standards (e.g. ISO27001, 27005).

3 CYSM Risk Assessment System

This section introduces the collaborative cyber/physical security management, system, CYSM for identifying, classifying, assessing and mitigating risks associated with ports' CII raised by security and safety incidents. This approach has been developed based on a number of customized and specialized self-management functions that aim to optimize, merge and enhance the existing approaches identified in the previous Section. The Section provides an in-depth analysis of the CYSM system, presenting the supported functionality and the adopted processes.

3.1 CYSM Goals and Services

The CYSM system [8, 9] - is an innovative, scalable Risk Assessment Toolkit, which facilitates the ports' security team to efficiently identify, assess and treat their security and safety incidents involving all port operators and users. The toolkit adopts and implements a bouquet of flexible and configurable self-driven functions and procedures [7] which constitute the conceptual pillars for building a solution that assists ports to improve their current cyber and physical level and:

- incorporates a conformance approach that checks and defines the compliance of the ports against the requirements, rules and obligations imposed by a set of security management standards (ISO 27001, ISPS) and the relative security and safety legal and regulatory framework;
- implements a collaborative, multi-attribute, group-decision making algorithm that collects the diverse security-related knowledge located in the ports and the results (e.g. threats, vulnerabilities metrics, prioritization of countermeasures) produced by the automated and semi-automated risk assessment routines and processes in order

to: (i) determine the value of the information assets; (ii) identify the applicable threats and vulnerabilities that exist (or could exist); (iii) identify the existing controls and their effect of the identified risks; (iv) determine the potential consequences; and (v) prioritize the derived risks and ranks them against the risk evaluation criteria set in the context establishment.

- integrates a security policy growing mechanism that provides a flexible way for creating and updating customized security policies and procedures;
- implements a social, collaborative working environment, which facilitates and encourages the ports to jointly work and cooperate, by exchanging ideas and information pertaining to security and safety issues and by allowing them to reach targeted solutions in a collaborative and time effective manner.

The aforementioned elements are combined in an effective and efficient manner to develop the automated routines and workflows that comprise and construct the meaningful CYSM Security Assessment Services [8, 9] i.e. Cyber Risk Assessment Services (CRAS), Physical Risk Assessment Services (PRAS) and the Security Framework Service (SFS). These services are fully customizable depending on the ports' security profile (like the enterprise size, the interdependencies with other IT systems, the services offered, the number of administrators and the security and safety awareness level), covering various aspects such as complexity, automation, terminology, simplification and understanding.

3.2   CYSM System Components

In order for CYSM to meet its objectives, it integrates a set of primary components (Fig. 1). From a conceptual perspective, the main components are the following:

- Community Portal: this area is accessible by all users of the involved ports and comprises of:
  - *Collaboration* suite: encapsulates a set of specialized Web2.0 elements (e.g. blogs, forums) suitable for e-collaborate, collecting and sharing knowledge. These elements enable ports to work together in building open working groups, providing diverse opinions, thoughts and contributions and sharing information, experience and expertise.
  - *e-Library*: acts as the knowledge source of all ports' physical and cyber related information (e.g. European legal and regulatory framework, security related standards, specifications, methodologies and frameworks).
- Port Private Portal: this area provides the appropriate functionality that enables the users to assess and improve the security and safety level of their port's infrastructure. Actually, this area executes the risk assessment processes and routines integrated in the system and consist of the following modules offering the corresponding services:
  - Port *collaboration* suite: encourages and facilitates members of each port to closely cooperate and exchange information and ideas during the risk assessments.
  - Port *e-Library*: is an inventory of confidential announcements, security and safety policies and procedures, guidelines etc.

- *Administration* module: allows customizing of the risk assessment's parameters (e.g. threats, vulnerabilities, controls).
- *Management* module: allows the initiation of a risk assessment.
- *Risk Assessment* module: gives the opportunity to the ports to identify and measure their threats, their vulnerabilities and possible impacts.
- *Security Policy* Reporting module: facilitates the formulation of customized security and safety-related policies and procedures.
- *Risk Assessment Results* module: allows the review of the risk assessment results and the formulation of a mitigation plan.

Fig. 1. Collaborative Cyber/Physical Security Management (CYSM) System

The above services are provided through customized intuitive and interactive Web Interfaces (including interactive screens, online forms, Dynamic Questionnaires) to represent the scenarios and steps as well as the information and content (e.g. requirements, rules, obligations, and recommendations of the standardization framework and regime) required by the supported risk self-assessment routines and functions, presented in the previous Section.

3.3 Showcase Scenario

The scope of this Section is to describe a use case in order to illustrate the functionality of the CYSM system. The scenario involves a commercial port, Piraeus Port Authority (PPA) that supports a number of business operations including the transport and accommodation of people, freight, natural gas, oil, cargoes and manufactured goods. For this reason, PPA manages and operates multiple and dispersed cyber (e.g. computer center) and physical (e.g. facilities for handling all types of cargoes) facilities. According to the scenario, the Port Security Officer (PSO) of the PPA utilizes the CYSM System in order to identify, evaluate and manage the cyber and physical risks associated with the Cruising Facility of the port and to formulate a mitigation plan. The CYSM system guides and directs the PSO via dynamic, interactive and evolutionary interfaces to perform the evaluation process. This process can be divided into the following (5) five sub-processes:

A. *Customization Phase*

Initially, the PSO, authenticates himself (using his credentials) into the CYSM system. Upon approval the PSO gains access to the Community Portal and directed to the PPA Private Portal where he accesses the Administration module (Fig. 2). This module allows the PSO to set various boundaries and constraints, i.e.:

- select standards that will be used to perform the risk assessment (e.g. ISPS, ISO27001, both);
- define the correlation between the controls that can be applied from a port and the requirements imposed by the standards;
- customize the fundamental elements and parameters of the risk assessment procedure (e.g. the scales related to the likelihood of occurrence of the threats, the exploitation level of the vulnerabilities etc.);
- generate the list of threats possible for the port assessed;
- categorise the list of vulnerabilities;
- list the controls that are deployed or can be applied from the port in order to mitigate the risks and deal with their identified threats and weaknesses;
- define the correlation among controls, vulnerabilities and threats;
- classify ports' assets into categories and sub-categories based upon their nature (physical, cyber);

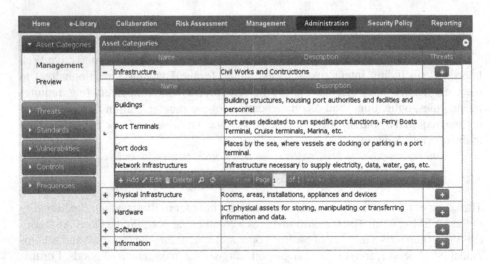

Fig. 2. Administration module

The PSO generates and updates the above mentioned information taking into consideration the literature, the port's particularities, the adopted technological solutions, the knowledge gained from the daily operation of the port, online repositories available from industry/standardization bodies, national governments etc.

B. Risk Assessment Initiation Phase

After the successful customization of the system, the PSO accesses the Management module (Fig. 3) where he is able to initiate a risk assessment. For the definition of a new assessment, the PSO should specify: (i) the basic information (e.g. name, the start and end date and a short description); (ii) the boundaries of the risk assessment (the physical or ICT port facility that will be assessed); (iii) the departments that will be involved and the role and weight of each department to the risk procedure; and finally (iv) the standards or the areas of the standards (ISO27001 and ISPS code) against which the defined area will be evaluated.

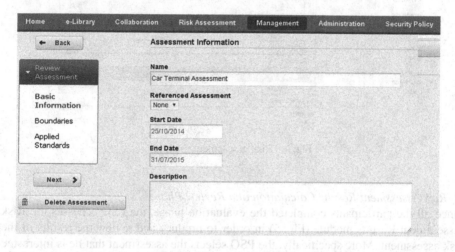

Fig. 3. Management module

C. Evaluation Phase

Having initiated the risk assessment, all members (participants) of the ports' departments, invited to participate in the risk assessment process, login to the CYSM system using their accounts and access the Risk Assessment module (Fig. 4) of the PPA Private Portal. In this module, a list of available assessments appears and the participants select the assessment related to the evaluation of the Cruising Facility (this selection serves as example) in order to complete the following steps:

i.   *Assets Identification:* define the assets comprise the Cruising Facility and categorize them in the main categories (e.g. Infrastructure, Physical Infrastructure, Hardware, Software, Information) and sub-categories (e.g. terminals, docks, servers) defined in the Administration module.

ii. *Impact Assessment:* determine the value of each asset to the organization. In particular, they should define what are the consequences (e.g. financial losses, damage to the reputation, legal consequences) of the loss of integrity, confidentiality and availability of each asset.

iii. *Control Identification:* define the controls applied to each asset.
iv. *Threat Assessment:* estimate the likelihood of occurrence of a predefined list of threats to each asset.

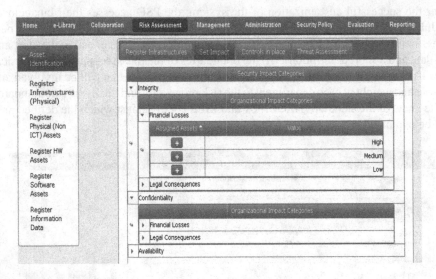

Fig. 4. Risk assessment module

D. Risk Assessment Results Calculation and Review Phase

Once all the participants completed the evaluation phase, the PSO accesses the Risk Assessment Results module (Fig. 5) in order to produce and review the results of the risk assessment. More specifically, the PSO selects the assessment that he is interested in and forces the system to calculate the potential risks associated with the Cruising Facility taking into consideration the answers of the participant completed the evaluation. Now, the PSO is able to review the produced results based on which he can select and prioritize the countermeasures that should be adopted by the PPA in order to handle and mitigate the identified risks. In this way, the PSO can formulate an effective and efficient risk mitigation plan.

E. Security Policy Reporting Phase

Finally, the PSO accesses the Security Policy Reporting module (Fig. 6) in order to formulate the security and safety policies required by the existing regulatory regime (ISO27001 and ISPS code). These policies can be exported in various formats (e.g. pdf, txt, jpg).

CYSM enables the ports to address their specific requirements, identify their specific threats that their assets may face, and meet their business goals by generating targeted security policies. The nature of the CYSM system is associated with a high degree of

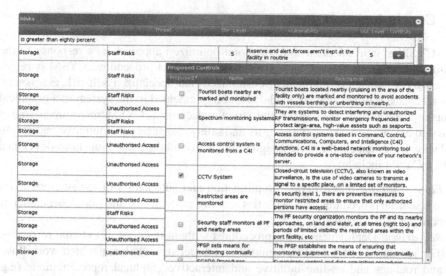

Fig. 5. Risk assessment results module

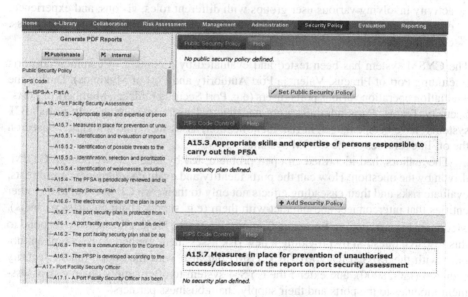

Fig. 6. Security policy reporting module

innovation since it implements new upgrading security and safety self-management functions and processes for the evaluation and mitigation of the risks and threats associated to the ports' infrastructure.

4   Conclusions

The CYSM system adopts a simplified and optimized approach as a response to the traditional time-consuming, not holistic risk assessment procedures. CYSM is represented by a number of automated, customized and specialized self-risk assessment processes and routines that are modeled and implemented in the system in a graphical manner using visualization tools and structured content. CYSM offers open source "easy-to use" tools enabling the security and safety management in intuitive and graphical way. In a Nutshell, the basic design principles of all the related functions developed within CYSM include:

- *Easy to use for non-experts.* Simplification and automation of the supported risk assessment procedures and activities making possible for the ports' personnel to conduct self-assessments.
- *Self-driven.* Deployment of the procedures without the need of external resources. The personnel of the ports are guided and directed through automated work-flows and routines and on-line intuitive and interactive graphical representations (e.g. dynamic questionnaires) to use the provided functionality.
- *Collaborative.* The risk assessment process is treated as a participatory challenge and activity involving various user groups with different roles, visions, and experience, expertise and business expectations, aiming at raising the security awareness, consciousness and responsibility.

The CYSM system has been tested and evaluated by a number of commercial ports (including Port of Piraeus, Valencia Port Authority and Port of Mykonos). During the evaluation operation various ports' users (e.g. Port Security Officers, Members of Ports' Security Teams, Ports administrators and internal users interacting with ports' ICT systems) have been engaged in risk identification, assessment and mitigation based on the on-line services of the CYSM system.

The authors, had identified an open problem, led by their involvement in CYSM, driven by the question: How can the ports identify and evaluate interdependent threats, evaluate risks and their cascading effects not only to their own CII but also to the other entities that interconnect and interact with them (e.g. supply chain business partners). Medusa[1] [13] is a running European Commission (E.C.) Project that aims to respond to this research question by providing a new risk assessment methodology compliant not only with the ISPS, ISO27001 (as CYSM) but also with the supply chain security standard (ISO28000), and extend the CYSM system to offer supply chain risk assessment modules to the ports and their supply chain business partners.

Acknowledgments. The authors are grateful to the E.C. Programme "Prevention, Preparedness and Consequence Management of Terrorism and other Security related Risks for the Period 2007-2013" for their support in funding the CYSM and MEDUSA projects. The authors also thank all CYSM partners (Port Institute for Studies and Co-Operation in the Valencian Region – FEPORTS, Singular Logic, Electrical, Electronics and Telecommunication Engineering and

---

[1] The authors serve as Project managers in this E.C. project.

Naval Architecture Department (DITEN) - University of Genoa (UNIGE), University of Piraeus Research Centre, Piraeus Port Authority (PPA), Fundacion Valencia Port (VPF)) and Medusa parners (University of Piraeus Research Centre, Singular Logic, University of Cyprus (UCY), EUROPHAR EEIG, Austrian Institute of Technology) for their contributions.

References

1. International Maritime Organisation: International Ship and Port Facility Security Code, London, UK (2004)
2. International Standardization Organization: Ships and marine technology – Maritime port facility security assessments and security plan development, Geneva, Switzerland (2007)
3. International Standardization Organization: ISO 27001: Information Security Management System Requirements, Geneva, Switzerland (2013)
4. International Standardization Organization: ISO 27005: Information security risk management, Geneva, Switzerland (2011)
5. International Standardization Organization: ISO 28000: Specification for security management systems for the supply chain, Geneva, Switzerland (2007)
6. International Standardization Organization: ISO 28001: Security management systems for the supply chain – Best practices for implementing supply chain security, assessments and plans – Requirements and guidance, Geneva, Switzerland (2007)
7. Makrodimitris, G., Polemi, N., Douligeris, C.: Security risk assessment challenges in port information technology systems. In: Sideridis, A.B., Yialouris, C.P., Kardasiadou, Z., Zorkadis, V. (eds.) E-Democracy 2013. CCIS, vol. 441, pp. 24–36. Springer, Heidelberg (2014)
8. Papastergiou, S., Polemi, N.: Harmonizing commercial port security practices & procedures in mediterranean basin. SSMDE: Secure and Sustainable Maritime Digital Environment. IISA 2014, pp. 292–297. Springer, Heidelberg (2014)
9. Karantjias, A., Polemi, N., Papastergiou, S.: Advanced security management system for critical infrastructures. IISA 2014. 43(1), pp. 136–158. Springer, Heidelberg (2014)
10. Polemi, D., Ntouskas, T., Georgakakis, E., Douligeris, C., Theoharidou, M., Gritzalis, D.: S-Port: collaborative security management of port information systems. In: Proceedings of the 4th International Conference on Information, Intelligence, Systems and Applications (IISA-2013). IEEE Press, Greece, July 2013
11. ENISA report: Cyber security aspects in the maritime sector. ENISA (2011). http://www.enisa.europa.eu/activities/Resilience-and-CIIP/critical-infrastructure-and-services/dependencies-of-maritime-transport-to-icts
12. CYSM European Commission: Programme prevention, preparedness and consequence management of terrorism. CIPS (2012). http://www.cysm.eu/index.php/en/
13. MEDUSA: Multi-order dependency approaches for managing cascading effects in ports' global supply chain and their integration in risk assesment frameworks. European Commission, Programme Prevention, Preparedness and Consequence Management of Terrorism, CIPS (2014). http://athina.cs.unipi.gr/medusa/
14. International Standardization Organization: ISO 31000: Risk Management – Principles and Guidelines, Geneva, Switzerland (2009)
15. International Standardization Organization: ISO 31010: Risk management – Risk assessment techniques, Geneva, Switzerland (2009)
16. Austrian Standards Institute: ONR 49000: Risikomanagement für Organisationen und Systeme: Begriffe und Grundlagen. Wien, Österreich (2004)

17. International Standardization Organization: ISO 20000: information technology service management. Geneva, Switzerland (2005)
18. Bundesamt für Sicherheit in der Informationstechnik. IT-Grundschutz Kataloge (2013). https://www.bsi.bund.de/DE/Themen/ITGrundschutz/itgrundschutz_node.html
19. The Stationery Office (TSO): Continual service improvement. ITIL V3 (2007)
20. Common Criteria Working Group: Common methodology for information technology security evaluation - evaluation methodology. CCMB-2007-09-004 (2007). http://www.commoncriteriaportal.org
21. European, Commission: Regulation (EC) No 725/2004 of the European parliament and of the council of 31 March 2004 on enhancing ship and port facility security. Off. J. Eur. Union L 129(6), 6–91 (2004)
22. Alberts, C.J., Dorofee, A.: Managing Information Security Risks: The Octave Approach. Addison-Wesley Longman Publishing Co., Inc., Boston (2002)
23. Alberts, C., Dorofee, A.: Operationally critical threat, asset, and vulnerability evaluation (Octave) method implementation guide, v2.0. Software Engineering Institute, Carnegie Mellon University (2001). http://www.cert.org/octave/
24. Expression of needs and identification of security objectives PREMIER MINISTRE Secrétariat général de la défense nationale Direction centrale de la sécurité des systèmes d'information Sous-direction des opérations Bureau conseil. www.ssi.gouv.fr
25. Clusif Methods Commission: MEHARI V3 risk analysis guide (2004)
26. EU Project Nr. IST-2000-25031: CORAS - risk assessment of security critical systems (2003). http://www2.nr.no/coras/
27. Stoneburner, G., Goguen, A., Feringa, A.: Special publication 800-30: risk management guide for information technology systems. Technical report, National Institute of Standards and Technology, Gaithersburg (2002)
28. Information Security Assessment & Monitoring Method (ISAMM). http://www.telindus.com
29. Insight Consulting: CRAMM User Guide, Issue 5.1, United Kingdom (2005)
30. Ntouskas, T., Polemi, N.: STORM-RM: collaborative and multicriteria risk management methodology. Int. J. Multicriteria Decis. Mak. 2(2), 159–177 (2012)
31. Ntouskas, T., Polemi, N.: Collaborative security management services for port information systems. DCNET/ICE-B/OPTICS, pp. 305–308 (2012)
32. Balmat, J.-F., Lafont, F., Maifret, R., Pessel, N.: MAritime RISk Assessment (MARISA), a fuzzy approach to define an individual ship risk factor. Ocean Eng. 36(15), 1278–1286 (2009). doi:10.1016/j.oceaneng.2009.07.003
33. SAFESEANET, a European platform for maritime data exchange between member states' maritime authorities, is a network/internet solution based on the concept of a distributed database. http://ec.europa.eu/idabc/en/document/2282/5926.html

Factors that Influence Information Security Behavior: An Australian Web-Based Study

Malcolm Pattinson[1]([✉]), Marcus Butavicius[2], Kathryn Parsons[2], Agata McCormac[2], and Dragana Calic[2]

[1] Adelaide Business School, The University of Adelaide, Adelaide, SA, Australia
malcolm.pattinson@adelaide.edu.au
[2] Defence Science and Technology Organisation, Edinburgh, SA, Australia
{marcus.butavicius,kathryn.parsons,agata.mccormac,
dragana.calic}@dsto.defence.gov.au

Abstract. Information Security professionals have been attempting to convince senior management for many years that humans represent a major risk to the security of an organization's computer systems and the information that these systems process. This major threat relates to the behavior of employees whilst they are using a computer at work. This paper examines the non-malicious computer-based behavior and how it is influenced by a mixture of individual, organizational and interventional factors. The specific factors reported herein include an employee's age; education level; ability to control impulsivity; familiarity with computers; and personality. This research utilized the Qualtrics online web-based survey software to develop and distribute a questionnaire that resulted in 500 valid responses. The major conclusions of this research are that an employee's accidental-naive behavior is likely to be less risky if they are more conscientious; older; more agreeable; less impulsive; more open; and, surprisingly, less familiar with computers.

Keywords: Information security (InfoSec) · Information risk · Human aspects of cyber security (HACS) · Behavioral information security · Risk management

1 Introduction

Chief Information Officers (CIOs), Chief Information Security Officers (CISOs) and other C-suite executives are, these days, quite convinced that humans represent a major threat to the security of an organization's computer systems and the information that these systems store and process. This realization relates to the behavior of employees whilst they are "operating" a computer which can range between accidental-naïve incidents to deliberate-malicious actions. The research described in this paper was specifically focused on the accidental-naive (and therefore not deliberate-malicious) behavior of employees. For example, such behavior includes the opening of unsolicited email attachments or the inadvertent sharing of passwords with others by writing them on post-it notes and sticking them to their computer monitor. Therefore, if organizations could minimize this type of behavior, that increases the risk of an information security incident,

© Springer International Publishing Switzerland 2015
T. Tryfonas and I. Askoxylakis (Eds.): HAS 2015, LNCS 9190, pp. 231–241, 2015.
DOI: 10.1007/978-3-319-20376-8_21

the organization's information assets would be more secure. So, how can this be achieved? Before this question can be addressed it is necessary to establish why employees unknowingly behave badly when they use a computer. Individuals may not be aware of the consequences of certain behaviors, they may also have limited knowledge of computers, or their attitude towards their employer or computers may influence their subsequent behavior. In other words, what variables are associated with poor accidental-naïve behavior by computer users? If the most significant of these factors can be identified, whether they are individual, organizational or interventional factors, information security professionals will be better placed to design and implement information security interventions that will mitigate this type of behavior. In turn, this will raise the level of information security within their organizations.

This research examines the impact that a selection of factors had on the self-reported accidental-naïve behavior of employees. These factors include their age; the highest level of education that they completed; their ability to control impulsivity; their familiarity with computers; and their personality traits.

1.1 Literature Review

An extensive literature review into the factors that affect information security behavior was conducted by Abraham [1] in 2011. Although Abraham reported a healthy amount of research in this area, most of these studies related to the type of user behavior that impacts on "compliance with security policies". That is, deliberate and possibly malicious behavior. For example, Pahnila et al. [2] examined how the attitudes towards compliance, normative beliefs and habits influence the intention to comply with organizational policies. Abraham [1] reported no evidence of research that was concerned with accidental-naïve behavior, as in this current research. In addition, many of these studies focussed on factors such as attitudes, beliefs and self-efficacy. Very few involved the factors that were examined in this current study such as the ability to control impulsivity and familiarity with computers. For example, a study conducted by D'Arcy et al. [3] examined the behavior of insider computer users, specifically focussing on "intentional insider misuse" and how certain controls and practices deter such deliberate actions. In contrast, Anderson et al. [4], examined the behavioral intentions of "home" computer users. They focused on the impact of factors such as attitude, self-efficacy, subjective norms and psychological ownership.

Since 2011, although there has been an escalation in information security behavioral research, there is still a dearth of research pertaining to factors that affect the accidental-naïve behavior of organisational computer users. Notwithstanding this situation, a relevant study by Vance et al. [5] examined the influence of factors such as perceived security, rewards and vulnerability on employee intention to comply with information system security policies. Also, relevant to this current study, due to the fact that it involved the use of personality traits, was a recent study conducted by Kajzer et al. [6] that examined the effectiveness of different types of information security awareness messages. Messages in this context included newsletters, email, face-to-face instruction, screensavers, signage, seminars, training and education events.

1.2   Aim of this Paper

The aim of this paper is twofold. The first aim is to report on a web-based survey that elicited information from anonymous Australian working adults for the purpose of testing the following two types of hypotheses.

General Hypotheses. A number of studies have been conducted that examined similar factors in regard to various types of behavior in a variety of domains including information technology use (It is beyond the scope of this paper to provide a literature review that is more extensive than Sect. 1.1 above). The following hypotheses relate to self-reported information security behavior and the extent to which it is risky.

H1:   *Age is positively associated with self-reported behavior.*
H2:   *Level of education completed is positively associated with self-reported behavior.*
H3:   *Ability to control impulsivity is positively associated with self-reported behavior.*
H4:   *Familiarity with computers is positively associated with self-reported behavior.*

Exploratory Hypotheses. These hypotheses are exploratory because there is no evidence of previous research regarding the traditional five personality traits and how they impact accidental-naive behavior of computer users.

H5a: *Openness is associated with self-reported behavior.*
H5b: *Concientiousness is associated with self-reported behavior.*
H5c: *Extraversion is associated with self-reported behavior.*
H5d: *Agreeableness is associated with self-reported behavior.*
H5e: *Emotional stability is associated with self-reported behavior.*

The second aim of this paper is to report on the data analysis and how the results can be interpreted in order to improve this type of behavior. This, in turn, will potentially provide a greater level of information security within the respective employee organizations.

The structure of this paper is as follows. The next section provides an explanation of the web-based survey instrument, its validity and how information was collected. Following this, the results are presented and discussed, limitations are conceded and conclusions are expressed.

2   Method

This research utilized the Qualtrics web-based survey software to develop an online survey questionnaire. This questionnaire was distributed to selected respondents who were registered with Qualtrics as people who were interested in responding to questionnaires for a fee. This 'panel' of respondents was selected because they qualified as "Working Australian Adults". These respondents received an email from Qualtrics that contained a clickable link which directed them to the questionnaire. Respondents were excluded if they did not use a computer at work and they were filtered out if their responses appeared to be too "mechanical", that is, not thought out (known as content non-responsivity). A total of 500 responses were considered valid for analysis with SPSS software. The questionnaire took an average of 30 min to complete.

The following data was collected via the questionnaire:

Self-Reported Behavior. Participants were asked to rate each of 21 behaviors on a 5-point rating scale ranging from "Strongly disagree" to "Strongly agree". Three questions were posed for each of seven focus areas that were gleaned from information security standards and guidelines [7–9] and via interviews with senior management and certified information security auditors (CISAs). These focus areas are:

- Password Management
- Email Use
- Internet Use
- Social Networking Site Use
- Mobile Computing
- Information Handling and
- Incident Reporting.

Approximately half of the items were expressed in negative terms and questions were presented in a random order of focus area. Each participant recorded 21 scores between 1 and 5. Scores were aggregated after adjusting for reversed questions. Consequently, the higher a participant's aggregated score, the better behaved the participant was likely to be.

Age. Participants were asked to indicate their age within one of six ranges, namely, "20 or under", "21–30", "31–40", "41–50", "51–60" and "61 or over".

Level of Education Completed. Participants were asked to indicate the highest level of education they completed on the 5-point scale, "Did not graduate from high school", "Year 12 or equivalent", "Some post-secondary", "Bachelor degree" and "Post-graduate degree".

Familiarity with Computers. On a 5-point Likert scale participants were asked to indicate how often they engage in each of 13 different computer activities (Refer Table 1 below) using the question: *How frequently do you engage in the following computer activities using any type of computer or portable device?* Scales were assigned scores as follows: "Daily" = 4, "Weekly" = 3, "Monthly" = 2, "Less than Monthly" = 1 and "Never" = zero. The 13 scores were aggregated to represent a participant's familiarity with computers. In other words, the higher the aggregated score, the more familiar a participant was considered to be with computers.

Personality Traits. This survey used an abbreviated version of the Big Five Inventory (BFI) personality test [10], namely, the Ten-Item Personality Inventory (TIPI) developed by Gosling *et al.* [11]. This measure consists of 10 items each using 7-point ratings (Disagree strongly = 1 to Agree strongly = 7). Two items represent each personality trait, namely, Agreeableness, Conscientiousness, Extraversion, Openness and Emotional stability. A measure for each trait is calculated as the sum of the scores for the two relevant items. This abbreviated method of measuring personality traits was considered adequate and appropriate for an exploratory study of this nature because it consumed much less time to complete than longer versions of the BFI.

Table 1. Percentage of participants (N = 500) who engage in various computer activities (the basis for assessing familiarity with computers).

	Daily	Weekly	Monthly	< Monthly	Never
Email	95%	5%	0%	0%	0%
Seeking information	81%	17%	1%	1%	0%
Word processing and spreadsheets	56%	26%	8%	8%	2%
Gaming	29%	25%	9%	13%	23%
On-line purchases	11%	31%	33%	20%	5%
On-line banking	24%	55%	9%	4%	8%
Internet gambling	4%	7%	4%	10%	75%
Read blogs, on-line forums and communities	24%	25%	16%	21%	14%
Contribute to blogs, on-line forums and communities	12%	17%	13%	22%	36%
Video chat (e.g. Skype)	10%	18%	16%	21%	35%
Internet dating (e.g. Oasis, RSVP)	5%	3%	4%	5%	83%
Access news/weather web sites	52%	29%	8%	7%	5%
Peer to peer sharing (e.g. BitTorrents)	11%	14%	12%	13%	51%

Ability to Control Impulsivity. A participant's ability to control impulsivity was measured by utilizing Frederick's [12] cognitive reflection test. This test consists of three mathematically-simple questions for which intuitive answers are not correct [13]. Each correct answer earns a score of 1, therefore a participant can score between zero (none correct) and three (all correct). Participants who do well in this test tend to be more patient in decisions, that is, they are assumed to be less impulsive in their decision-making.

2.1 Validation

This research was primarily interested in how individual factors influenced self-reported accidental-naive behavior of participants and to a lesser extent how the composite model of independent variables predicted this behavior. Consequently, Standard Multiple Regression was used to analyse the data.

Sample Size. This study, which comprised nine independent variables and one dependent variable, used a sample size of 500 participants. According to Green [14], a minimum sample size for such a study can be calculated as the sum of the number of independent variables plus 104. Consequently, the sample size of this study is not only far greater than 113 but also satisfies the Miles and Shevlin [15] recommended sample size of 200, when using up to 20 predictors that have a medium effect (i.e. how well they predict self-reported behavior).

Multicollinearity. Table 2 below shows the Pearson correlation coefficients (r) and descriptive statistics for all 10 variables in the model. The correlations between each of the independent variables are all less than 0.7, which is considered acceptable according to Cohen [16]. The correlations between the independent variables and the dependent variable, self-reported behavior, are mostly greater than 0.3. This is also considered acceptable, particularly since the Tolerance values are all greater than 0.10 and the VIF (Variance Inflation Factor) values are well below 10. Hence it is reasonable to assume that multi-collinearity has not been violated [16, 17].

Table 2. Descriptive statistics and variable intercorrelations

	Mean	SD	Tolerance	VIF	1	2	3	4	5	6	7	8	9	10
1. Self-reported behaviour	84.53	13.09			1.00									
2. Age	3.39	1.35	0.83	1.20	0.31	1.00								
3. Level of education completed	3.27	1.11	0.95	1.06	-0.06	-0.13	1.00							
4. Ability to control impulsivity	0.79	1.00	0.95	1.05	0.14	0.00	0.13	1.00						
5. Familiarity with computers	28.79	7.97	0.83	1.20	-0.24	-0.33	0.17	0.05	1.00					
6. Openness	5.06	1.08	0.71	1.40	0.34	0.11	0.00	-0.04	-0.01	1.00				
7. Conscientiousness	5.61	1.11	0.64	1.56	0.55	0.21	-0.02	0.07	-0.21	0.44	1.00			
8. Extroversion	4.21	1.33	0.81	1.24	0.15	0.12	-0.01	-0.08	-0.30	0.36	0.25	1.00		
9. Agreeableness	5.02	1.05	0.82	1.22	0.37	0.20	0.01	0.00	-0.13	0.26	0.35	0.06	1.00	
10. Emotional stability	4.94	1.21	0.73	1.37	0.32	0.18	0.02	0.09	-0.03	0.31	0.43	0.30	0.28	1.00

3   Results and Discussion

This paper reports on exploratory research that empirically tested the effect of various factors on the self-reported behavior of employees. These factors are not intended to entirely predict a participant's self-reported behaviour because there are many other individual, organizational and interventional factors that have this same potential. In this study 'self-reported behavior' relates to accidental-naïve behavior of employees whilst they are using a computer. Standard multiple regression analyses were conducted to investigate the impact of nine factors on self-reported behavior. A summary of these results is shown in Fig. 1 below.

The strength of the relationships between the independent variables and the dependent variable are shown in the model together with the amount of variance (39 %) in self-reported behavior that is accounted for by the independent variables combined (R^2). The dependent variable, self-reported behavior, was represented by 21 items. The Cronbach Alpha reliability coefficient for these items was 0.918. Since this is greater than the recommended value of 0.7 [18], construct reliability is assured. Note that the higher the score a participant gets for self-reported accidental-naive behavior, the better (that is, less risky) their behavior is assumed to be.

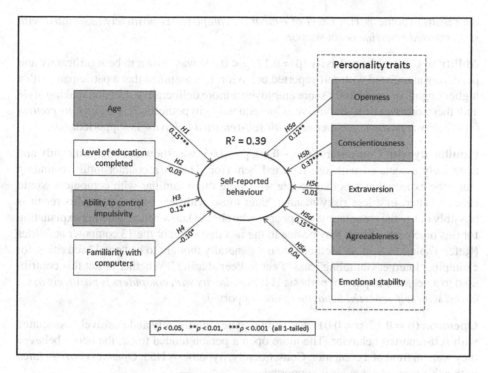

Fig. 1. Regression model

The independent variable Conscientiousness (37 %) makes the strongest individual contribution towards explaining the self-reported behavior of participants. Other predictor variables that contributed to a lesser extent in explaining self-reported behavior, in order of effect, were Age (15 %), Agreeableness (15 %), Ability to control impulsivity (12 %), Openness (12 %) and Familiarity with computers (10 %). The relationships between each of the independent variables and the dependent variable, self-reported behavior, are discussed in more detail below.

Age ($\beta = 0$.15, $p < 0.001$) was shown to be significantly and positively associated with self-reported behavior, accounting for 15 % of the variance. This result suggests that the younger an employees is, the more likely he or she may behave in a risky manner. This result is in concert with D'Arcy and Greene's [19] study that tested the relationship between Age and Compliance with information security policies and found that "older employees are more likely to comply" [19]. Consequently, hypothesis H1: *Age is positively associated with self-reported behavior* is supported.

Level of Education Completed ($\beta = -0$.03) was found not to be significantly associated with self-reported behavior. This result is counter-intuitive since the expectation was that people with a higher education would be more aware of the consequences of serious security breaches and would therefore behave better. Whether or not this contributed to the result, hypothesis H2: *Level of education completed is positively associated with self-reported behavior* is not supported.

Ability to Control Impulsivity (β = 0.12, p < 0.01) was shown to be significantly and positively associated with self-reported behavior. It is assumed that a participant with a higher cognitive impulsivity score employed a more deliberative decision making style and therefore was less impulsive. Consequently, hypothesis H3: *Ability to control impulsivity is positively associated with self-reported behavior* is supported.

Familiarity with Computers (β = −0.10, p < 0.05) was shown to be significantly and negatively associated with self-reported behavior. This is a counter-intuitive finding since the expectation was that people who were more familiar with computers would behave better, in a less risky manner, than those with less experience. This result is possibly due to the complacency of people who should know better. Another explanation for this unexpected result may be due to the fact that some of the 13 computer activities (Refer Table 1 in Sect. 2: Method) are not generally thought to be "good" activities, for example, "Internet Gambling" and "Peer to Peer sharing". Whether or not this contributed to a negative impact, hypothesis H4: *Familiarity with computers is positively associated with self-reported behavior* is not supported.

Openness (β = 0.12, p < 0.01) was shown to be significantly and positively associated with self-reported behavior. The more open a person tended to be, the better behaved they were in front of a computer. Consequently, hypothesis H5a: *Openness is associated with self-reported behavior* is supported.

Conscientiousness (β = 0.37, p < 0.001) was found to be significantly and positively associated with self-reported behavior. This result suggests that the more conscientious a person is, the more likely he or she will behave in a less risky manner. This personality trait was the highest contributor of all the independent variables, accounting for 37 % of the variance. Consequently, hypothesis H5b: *Conscientiousness is associated with self-reported behavior* is supported.

Extraversion (β = −0.01) was shown not to be significantly associated with self-reported behavior. Consequently, hypothesis H5c: *Extraversion is associated with self-reported behavior* is not supported.

Agreeableness (β = 0.15, p < 0.01) was shown to be significantly and positively associated with self-reported behavior. The more agreeable a person is, the more likely he or she will behave better, that is, in a less risky manner. Consequently, hypothesis H5d: *Agreeableness is associated with self-reported behavior* is supported.

Emotional Stability (β = −0.04) was shown not to be significantly associated with self-reported behavior and therefore hypothesis H5e: *Emotional stability is associated with self-reported behavior* is not supported.

Table 3 below summarizes these results.

Table 3. Results of the multiple regression

Variable	Beta coefficient	t-value	Sig.	Results
Age	0.15***	3.82	0.000	H1 supported
Level of education completed	-0.03	-0.85	0.395	H2 not supported
Ability to control impulsivity	0.12**	3.43	0.001	H3 supported
Familiarity with computers	-0.10*	-2.54	0.012	H4 not supported
Openness	0.12**	2.86	0.004	H5a supported
Conscientiousness	0.37***	8.45	0.000	H5b supported
Extroversion	-0.01	-0.35	0.729	H5c not supported
Agreeableness	0.15***	3.94	0.000	H5d supported
Emotional stability	0.04	0.99	0.322	H5e not supported

* $p < 0.05$,   ** $p < 0.01$,   *** $p < 0.001$ (all 1-tailed)

4   Limitations and Future Directions

This research reports on the accidental-naïve behavior of employees whilst they are using a computer. In this study this was measured by self-report, i.e., by asking each employee a series of questions about how they <u>do</u> behave, and how they <u>would</u> behave, when using a computer.

Although there are good reasons to be cautious of self-reported behavior, Workman's [20] study of social engineering found a correlation of 0.89 between self-reported behavior and objective measures of behavior (measured via the propensity to respond to a phishing email). In addition, approximately 80 % of the variance in behavior could be explained by self-report, and hence, the value of self-reported behavior should not be discounted. Furthermore, Spector [21] argued that self-report studies should not be dismissed as being an inferior methodology, and instead, they can provide valuable data as an initial test of hypotheses.

The nature of any self-report study that focuses on an employee's behavior is that their responses may be influenced by the social desirability bias [22]. When asked to respond to questions about how they use a computer as part of their job role, employees may feel the need to respond in a manner that is not truthful. Rather, they may provide the answer they believe their management or peers would find acceptable. The study questionnaire described in this paper minimizes the likelihood of social desirability bias because the design of the questionnaire refrained from asking survey participants to provide their name or the name of their employer. Notwithstanding this anonymity, they were also given additional assurances in the survey itself, as well as in the distribution email, of confidentiality and anonymity. Future research by the authors will seek to validate this self-report approach with alternative techniques.

5 Conclusion

This paper addresses the "future directions that Behavioral Information Security researchers should explore" [23] by examining how a small selection of individual, organizational and interventional factors influence an employee's accidental-naïve behavior relating to their use of computers and the protection of information at their place of work.

The major conclusions of this exploratory investigation are that an employee's accidental-naive behavior is likely to be less risky if the employee is more conscientious; older; more agreeable; less impulsive; more open; and surprisingly, less familiar with computers.

These findings, albeit preliminary, may motivate some managers to attempt to minimize the accidental-naive behavior of employees by addressing some of these factors directly. For example, to counteract low employee conscientiousness and low agreeableness, they could offer an incentive, like a bonus, to all staff if the number of information security incidents is less than, say, in the previous year. In regard to addressing the tendency of employees to be impulsive, management could introduce specialized training that encourages employees to think before they act in situations such as receiving rogue emails with malicious embedded links.

Finally, future research relating to improving computer-based behavior, particularly the accidental-naïve type, is needed to empirically test a variety of management interventions to ascertain which are the most effective and cost-efficient.

Acknowledgements. This project is supported by a Premier's Research and Industry Fund grant provided by the South Australian Government Department of Further Education, Employment, Science and Technology.

References

1. Abraham, S.: Information security behaviour: factors and research directions. In: AMCIS 2011 Proceedings - All Submissions, Paper 462 (2011)
2. Pahnila, S., Siponen, M., Mahmood, A.: Employees' behavior towards IS security policy compliance. In: 40th Annual Hawaii International Conference on System Sciences (HICSS 2007). IEEE, Hawaii (2007)
3. D'Arcy, J., Hovav, A., Galletta, D.: User awareness of security countermeasures and its impact on information systems misuse: a deterrence approach. Inf. Syst. Res. **20**(1), 79–98 (2009)
4. Anderson, C., Agarwal, R.: Practicing safe computing: a multimethod empirical examination of home computer user security behavioral intentions. MIS Q. **34**(3), 613–643 (2010)
5. Vance, A., Siponen, M., Pahnila, S.: Motivating IS security compliance: insights from habit and protection motivation theory. Inf. Manag. **49**(3), 190–198 (2012)
6. Kajzer, M., et al.: An exploratory investigation of message-person congruence in information security awareness campaigns. Comput. Secur. **43**, 64–76 (2014)
7. AS/NZS_ISO/IEC_27002: Information Technology - Security Techniques - Code of practice for Information security management. Standards Australia/Standards New Zealand (2006)

8. NIST_SP800_100: Information Security Handbook: A Guide for Managers. National Institute of Standards and Technology, MD (2006)
9. COBIT5: A Business Framework for the Governance and Management of Enterprise IT. ISACA, IL (2012)
10. John, O.P., Donahue, E.M., Kentle, R.L.: The Big Five Inventory—Versions 4a and 54. University of California, Institute of Personality and Social Research, Berkeley (1991)
11. Gosling, S.D., Rentfrow, P.J., Swann Jr., W.B.: A very brief measure of the Big-Five personality domains. J. Res. Pers. **37**(6), 504–528 (2003)
12. Frederick, S.: Cognitive reflection and decision making. J. Econ. Perspect. **19**(4), 25–42 (2005)
13. Welsh, M., Burns, N., Delfabbro, P.: The cognitive reflection test: how much more than numerical ability? In: Proceedings of the 35th Annual Conference of the Cognitive Science Society (2013)
14. Green, S.B.: How many subjects does it take to do a regression analysis. Multivar. Behav. Res. **26**, 499–510 (1991)
15. Miles, J., Shevlin, M.: Applying Regression and Correlation: A Guide for Students and Researchers. SAGE Publications, London (2001)
16. Cohen, J.W.: Statistical Power Analysis for the Behavioral Sciences, 2 ed. Lawrence Erlbaum Associates, New Jersey (1988)
17. Pallant, J.: SPSS Survival Manual: A Step-by-Step Guide to Data Analysis using SPSS for Windows, 3 ed. Allen & Unwin, NSW (2007)
18. Nunnally, J., Bernstein, I.: Psychological Theory. McGraw-Hill, New York (1994)
19. D'Arcy, J., Greene, G.: Security culture and the employment relationship as drivers of employees' security compliance. Inf. Manage. Comput. Secur. **22**(5), 474–489 (2014)
20. Workman, M.: Gaining access with social engineering: an empirical study of the threat. Inf. Syst. Secur. **16**(6), 315–331 (2007)
21. Spector, P.E.: Using self-report questionnaires in OB research: a comment on the use of a controversial method. J. Organ. Behav. **15**(5), 385–392 (1994)
22. Edwards, A.L.: The relationship between the judged desirability of a trait and the probability that the trait will be endorsed. J. Appl. Psychol. **37**(2), 90–93 (1953)
23. Crossler, R.E., et al.: Future directions for behavioral information security research. Comput. Secur. **32**, 90–101 (2013)

Pervasive Monitoring as an Insider Threat

An Adapted Model

Dana Polatin-Reuben[✉]

Centre for Doctoral Training in Cyber Security, University of Oxford, Oxford, UK
dana.polatin-reuben@cs.ox.ac.uk

Abstract. Revelations that the United States' National Security Agency implemented a global surveillance programme with the help of its allies have drawn increased attention to pervasive monitoring activities in general. With the Internet Engineering Task Force characterising pervasive monitoring as an advanced persistent threat, the possibility of modelling pervasive monitoring as a threat activity has been raised. This paper proposes that pervasive monitoring can be considered an insider threat, with private or state actors using legitimate network functions and credentials to exfiltrate the data of governments, corporations, and end-users. The insider threat model put forth by Nurse *et al.* is examined and adapted with the help of pervasive monitoring case studies.

Keywords: Pervasive monitoring · Insider threat · Threat framework · Surveillance

1 Introduction

Following revelations that the signals intelligence agencies of five anglophone countries – the United States, the United Kingdom, Canada, Australia and New Zealand – co-ordinated with each other and with telecommunications firms to implement a global mass surveillance programme, pervasive monitoring has increasingly come to be seen as an advanced persistent threat to the integrity of the internet. This view has been vocally espoused by the technical community, spearheaded by the Internet Engineering Task Force (IETF), which in May 2014 released an Internet Best Current Practice memo characterising pervasive monitoring as 'a technical attack that should be mitigated in the design of IETF protocols, where possible' [1].

Within this memo, the IETF define pervasive monitoring as follows:

> Pervasive Monitoring (PM) is widespread (and often covert) surveillance through intrusive gathering of protocol artefacts, including application content, or protocol metadata such as headers. Active or passive wiretaps and traffic analysis, (e.g., correlation, timing or measuring packet sizes), or subverting the cryptographic keys used to secure protocols can also be used as part of pervasive monitoring. PM is distinguished by being indiscriminate and very large scale, rather than by introducing new types of technical compromise [1].

By explicitly defining pervasive monitoring as an attack, the IETF have opened up the possibility of using threat modelling to better understand the motivations behind and

© Springer International Publishing Switzerland 2015
T. Tryfonas and I. Askoxylakis (Eds.): HAS 2015, LNCS 9190, pp. 242–251, 2015.
DOI: 10.1007/978-3-319-20376-8_22

attack trees for pervasive monitoring. The creation of threat models to better understand network threats is a common research technique in both the academic community and the private sector [2, 3]. Given that pervasive monitoring has only recently been identified as an advanced persistent threat, existing threat models may prove useful in determining the attack characteristics which pervasive monitoring shares with other threats, as well as in what ways it differs from existing threats.

In this respect, insider threat research is a promising avenue for eliciting a better understanding of pervasive monitoring as a threat. In Cappelli *et al.*'s comprehensive guide to insider threats, malicious insider threats are defined:

> A malicious insider threat is a current employee, contractor, or business partner who has or had authorized access to an organization's network, system, or data and intentionally exceeded or misused that access in a manner that negatively affected the confidentiality, integrity, or availability of the organization's information or information systems [4].

While this definition implies that the malicious insider is a person enacting harm upon an organisation, it is sufficiently broad to cover the case of pervasive monitoring, wherein a service provider or trusted third party with authorised access exploits a network in order to exfiltrate the data of governments, corporations, and end-users.

This paper seeks to establish the utility of characterising pervasive monitoring as an insider threat. The insider threat model recently proposed by Nurse *et al.* will be examined and expanded to cover pervasive monitoring, using case studies gleaned from news articles. Finally, the possibility of adapting other threat models or creating a new model specific to pervasive monitoring will also be explored.

2 Background: The Nurse *et al.* Model of Insider Threat

Detailed in May 2014, the insider threat model developed by Nurse *et al.* is a comprehensive framework examining 'which insiders attack, why they attack, the human factors that lead to accidental threats, how one's background may impact likelihood of attack, what behaviour may be exhibited before or during an attack, what the common attack vectors and steps within an attack are, and what assets and vulnerabilities are typically targeted' [5]. The framework uses the traditional conception of an insider as being an individual taking detrimental action against an organisation.

Figure 1 shows the model, which is divided broadly into four sections: *Catalyst*, *Actor Characteristics*, *Attack Characteristics*, and *Organisation Characteristics*. The first section, *Catalyst*, contains the *Precipitating event* which compels the actor to become an insider threat. Taken together with elements within *Actor Characteristics* depicting the actor's personality, work attitude, motivation and opportunity, the *Catalyst* section contributes an understanding of the actor's propensity to conduct an attack.

Actor Characteristics is a detailed overview of information about the insider. An insider's *Psychological state* at the time of an attack is influenced by their *Personality characteristics*, a category which uses a number of established psychological metrics. [6–8] These two categories together both influence the behaviour of the insider, which comprises *Observed physical behaviour* such as physical threats to colleagues as well as *Observed cyber behaviour* such as disabling security software in order to download

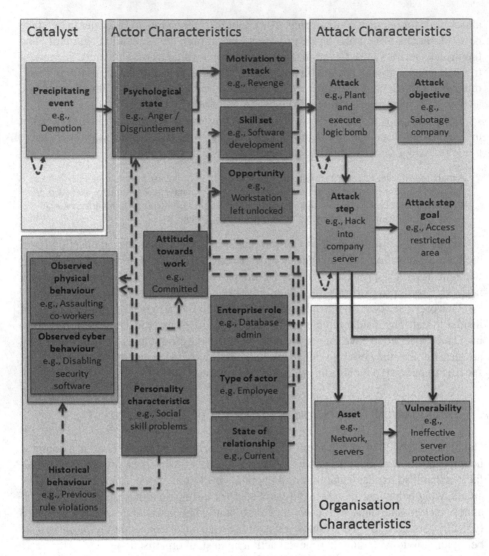

Fig. 1. Nurse *et al.* model of insider threat

files. *Historical behaviour* also influences the range of behaviours which can be observed prior to an attack by an insider, as past patterns of behaviour are strong determinants of future action.

An actor's *Attitude towards work* can contribute to their *Motivation to attack*; for instance, a dedicated employee passed over for a promotion may have incentive to attack. This, combined with the actor's *Skill set* and *Opportunity* for initiating an attack, is an immediate contributor to the launch of an attack. The *Skill set* of the actor can be directly related to their *Enterprise role* or job held within the enterprise, or it may be external to their role. An actor's *Opportunity* to attack is influenced by the *Type of actor* they are, such as whether they are a direct employee or contractor, as well as the *State of relationship* the actor has with the enterprise, with actors who are temporary, serving notice or no longer working for the enterprise posing the greatest threat.

Attack Characteristics examines the anatomy of attacks launched by insiders, with the actual *Attack* being influenced by the motivation, skills, and opportunity of the actor. The *Attack objective* indicates what the actor hopes to achieve by launching a particular attack, such as sabotaging the enterprise or exfiltrating sensitive data. To achieve this objective, the actor undertakes a series of *Attack steps* with particular *Attack step goals*. This section of the model draws from the well-established concepts of attack trees and intrusion kill chains [9, 10].

Finally, the Nurse *et al.* model examines *Organisation Characteristics* of enterprises which experience insider attacks. This section takes into account commonly-targeted *Assets*, such as networks, as well as *Vulnerabilities* like disabled antivirus software.

3   Pervasive Monitoring as an Insider Threat

Given that the Nurse *et al.* model devotes significant attention to the psychological state of what is presumed to be an individual acting as an insider, it is initially hard to draw a comparison with the case of pervasive monitoring, in which an organisation perpetrates an attack on a government, another organisation or end-users of a service. However, the definition of a malicious insider posed by Cappelli *et al.* includes as insider threats 'a current employee, contractor, or business partner' [5]. As the latter two actors can be organisations rather than individuals, this raises the possibility that the definition of an insider threat, and hence the model proposed by Nurse *et al.*, can be expanded to cover cases where an organisation has initiated an attack.

To characterise pervasive monitoring by an organisation upon another organisation or individual as an insider threat, equally significant attention should be paid to the characteristics of the offending organisation. Instead of psychological metrics, political, cultural, or organisational metrics should be used to characterise the actor organisation [11, 12].

Within this adapted model, the four broad categories are largely the same, although *Organisation Characteristics* has been renamed to *Victim Characteristics* to reflect the fact that the victims of pervasive monitoring could be either organisations or end-users. As in the Nurse *et al.* model, the *Catalyst* category is comprised of a *Precipitating event*. In the case of pervasive monitoring, this event is likely to be political or economic rather than personal. For instance, in most of the pervasive monitoring case studies examined, the *Precipitating event* was the September 11 terrorist attacks, which also caused other precipitating events such as the conflict in Afghanistan.

The most modified section of the adapted model is the *Actor Characteristics* section, as extraneous categories pertaining only to individual actors were removed. These include *Observed physical behaviour* and *State of relationship*. Additionally, the titles for a number of categories have changed to reflect that organisations rather than individuals are being considered, including *State of organisational culture*, *Organisational characteristics*, and *Attitude towards mission/work* (Fig. 2).

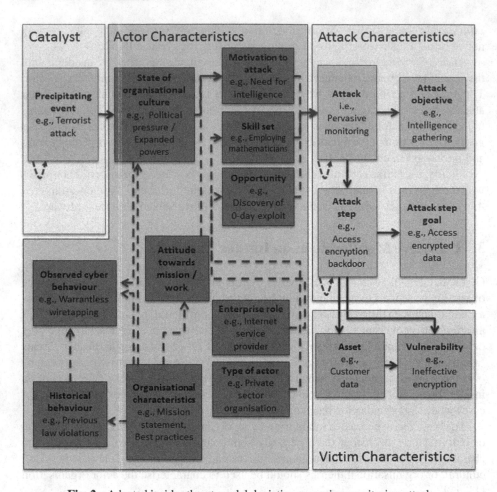

Fig. 2. Adapted insider threat model depicting pervasive monitoring attack

The *State of organisational culture* reflects the current operational realities affecting the working culture within an organisation, such as increased pressure to fulfill a mission. This in turn is influenced by *Organisational characteristics*, which comprises the mission statement, values, and best practices of the organisation actor. Both of these categories together influence *Observed cyber behaviour*, which in the case of pervasive monitoring could include conditions within a provider's terms of service or known cyber activities of the organisation, such as the undertaking of signals intelligence work.

Historical behaviour is a particularly important category for predicting the likelihood of a pervasive monitoring attack, as private-sector firms or government agencies with a track record of previous law violations are more likely to hold an *Attitude towards mission/work* which disregards the applicability of legal standards to their own organisation. This can particularly be seen in the following section, in which three of the five case studies examined had the same perpetrator.

The *Type of actor* category indicates the type of organisation perpetrating an attack, such as a government agency or private sector organisation. The actor's *Enterprise role* reflects the relationship between the actor organisation and the victims of its pervasive monitoring attack. Common examples include intelligence agencies, internet service providers or telecommunications companies.

While the *Motivation to attack* and *Opportunity* categories are largely unchanged, the *Skill set* category has been changed to reflect the talent employed by the organisation. For example, the National Security Agency (NSA) employs a high number of mathematicians, which has enabled them to break commonly-used internet encryption protocols [13].

The *Attack Characteristics* section has remained largely unchanged, with the exception of the *Attack* category, which has been specified to be a pervasive monitoring attack. Likewise, the *Victim Characteristics* section, apart from its name, also remains unchanged, although the type of *Assets* being targeted and the *Vulnerabilites* used to exploit them are different in that end-user data is frequently targeted in a pervasive monitoring attack.

It is worth noting that in the context of a pervasive monitoring attack, the end-users of an entire network or service can be considered victims. This is because pervasive monitoring is often conducted by a service provider, network operator, or trusted third party such as a government agency, with the intent of exploiting the network or service under their control to target the data of their end-users. In the case of a state-initiated pervasive monitoring attack, the scale of the network or infrastructure under state control has implications for the end-users of the entire internet.

4   Case Studies in Pervasive Monitoring

The following case studies, which were gleaned from news reports, were used to adapt the Nurse *et al.* insider threat model to cover cases of pervasive monitoring attacks. They are listed in chronological order of the time of discovery.

4.1   National Security Agency Stellar Wind Programme

On 16 December 2005, the *New York Times* published an article detailing a programme code-named Stellar Wind undertaken by the NSA months after the September 11 terrorist attacks [14]. The NSA colluded with prominent telecommunications firms, such as Verizon, AT&T, and BellSouth, to pervasively monitor the telephone calls and emails of 'tens of millions of Americans' without a warrant [15]. Initially thought to only affect international calls and emails, the programme was later revealed to be far more expansive than the Bush administration had acknowledged.

Stellar Wind shares its *Precipitating event*, the September 11 terrorist attacks, with three other case studies examined for this model, although it arguably was the most directly influenced as its authorisation occurred closest to the attacks and was not muddied by conflicts in Iraq and Afghanistan. However, the *State of organisational culture* within the NSA already predisposed it to pervasive monitoring: in December

2000, a secret document entitled *Transition 2001* detailed the NSA's desire to 'master and operate in the global net of tomorrow' by '[living] on the network' [16].

4.2 National Security Agency Prism Programme

In an echo of the Stellar Wind controversy, the *Guardian* published details of a NSA programme code-named Prism on 7 June 2013 [17]. In operation since 2007, Prism allowed the NSA to collect a wealth of both metadata and communication content directly from the servers of major internet firms, such as Google, Facebook, and Apple. Unlike the Stellar Wind programme which relied on direct collusion with telecommunications firms, Prism seemed to have gained its access without the knowledge or consent of the target firms.

Within the context of the model, Stellar Wind is a clear predecessor to Prism, falling under the categories of *Historical behaviour* and *Observed cyber behaviour*. Given that the NSA is the perpetrator in three of the five examined case studies, its *Organisational characteristics* as a non-transparent signals intelligence agency are worth noting. Also worth noting is that a fourth case study also involves a non-transparent signals intelligence agency.

4.3 Government Communications Headquarters Tempora Programme

Also revealed by the *Guardian* in June 2013 was the existence of the Tempora programme, designed by the Government Communications Headquarters (GCHQ) to create a temporary internet buffer which the agency and its strategic partners, such as the NSA, could analyse for intelligence [18]. GCHQ intercepted data on over 200 fibre-optic cables, some of which were outside of its official jurisdiction. The exfiltrated data, which potentially reached 21 petabytes per day, could then be stored and sifted by intelligence agencies. Bulk data was stored for up to three days, with metadata being kept for up to thirty days.

In this instance, sufficient information was given to list the *Attack steps* and *Attack step goals* of the Tempora pervasive monitoring attack, which can be seen below (Fig. 3).

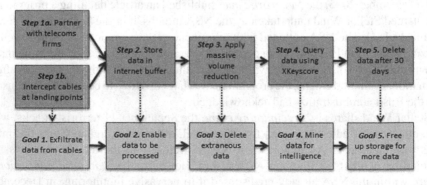

Fig. 3. Attack steps and goals for Tempora programme

4.4   Google Email Scanning

On 27 February 2014, Bloomberg revealed a lawsuit against Google over the company's use of an algorithm to scan the private email messages of its users in order to display relevant advertisements [19]. The court case alleges that in 2010, Google began to intercept and scan emails within its 'delivery pipeline' rather than its storage servers, so that relevant data could be scanned before the receipt of a message. In response to the lawsuit, Google changed its terms of service to reflect its scanning practices, stating that '[our] automated systems analyze your content (including emails) to provide you personally relevant product features' [20].

While the *Type of actor* in this case study is different from the other four – a private-sector firm rather than a government agency – Google's practices are hardly unique among internet service providers. The *Motivation to attack* was for financial gain, with the *Asset* of customer data being exploited via the *Vulnerability* of ineffective privacy protections.

4.5   National Security Agency Somalget and Mystic Programmes

The Intercept revealed the existence of two mobile telephone data collection programmes, Somalget and Mystic, on 19 May 2014 [21]. While the Mystic programme was more widely deployed, it merely gathered the metadata of mobile phone calls, such as the time and destination of calls. But Somalget, which was deployed in two countries, was able to collect and store the content of every mobile phone call made or received within these countries. *The Intercept* named one of these countries as the Bahamas, with the assertion that Somalget was being deployed there to monitor drug traffickers. The identity of the second country was redacted at the request of the United States government. However, WikiLeaks issued a statement on 23 May 2014 identifying the second country as Afghanistan [22].

By the time of these revelations, a clear precedent of *Historical behaviour* and *Observed cyber behaviour* had been set within the NSA. This is a reflection of the NSA's *Attitude towards mission/work*, which privileges the technological superiority of the NSA and its mandate to execute its mission above other considerations such as civil rights. Additionally, while the *Precipitating event* differs between the two countries monitored, the *Motivation to attack* is the same – in both instances, a need for actionable intelligence motivated the launch of a pervasive monitoring attack.

5   Conclusions and Future Work

This is a first attempt to model pervasive monitoring as an attack using an existing insider threat framework. By expanding the definition of an insider to include organisations which operate or control services and networks, and by accepting that end-users can also be victims, pervasive monitoring can be seen as an insider threat and modelled accordingly. Using an insider threat framework particularly gives insight into the motivating factors within an organisation which contribute to the launch of a pervasive monitoring attack.

Characterising pervasive monitoring as an insider threat could be of particular interest to the technical community, especially members of the IETF, the Internet Architecture Board (IAB), and other organisations overseeing the continued development and improvement of internet architecture such as network protocols. Those working on digital privacy issues in the wake of the Snowden revelations may also find the adapted model useful for informing their own understanding of the attack characteristics of pervasive monitoring.

Future work could involve refining and verifying this model using further case studies in pervasive monitoring. In particular, additional work could be done with case studies involving corporate actors as well as state actors outside of the Five Eyes consortium, such as the Russian Federation and the People's Republic of China, both of which have active pervasive monitoring programmes [23, 24]. Additionally, other threat frameworks, such as models depicting a man-in-the-middle attack, could be examined for their applicability to the case of pervasive monitoring. It is also possible that pervasive monitoring may warrant its own threat category, in which case a new model specifically depicting pervasive monitoring can be developed.

Acknowledgments. The Nurse *et al.* model was adapted with the permission of the authors of the original model.

References

1. Farrel, S., Tschofenig, H.: Pervasive Monitoring is an Attack, (RFC 7258) Internet Engineering Task Force, May 2014. https://tools.ietf.org/html/rfc7258 (2014). Accessed 18 Feb 2015
2. Hasan, R., Myagmar, S., Lee, A.J., Yurcik, W.: Toward a threat model for storage systems. In: Proceedings of the 2005 ACM Workshop on Storage Security and Survivability, pp. 94–102. ACM, New York (2005)
3. Johansson, J.M.: Network threat modeling. In: Proceedings of the Twelfth IEEE International Workshops on Enabling Technologies: Infrastructure for Collaborative Enterprises. IEEE, New York, 9–11 June 2003
4. Cappelli, D., Moore, A., Trzeciak, R.: The CERT Guide to Insider Threats: How to Prevent, Detect, and Respond to Information Technology Crimes (Theft, Sabotage, Fraud). Pearson Education Inc, New Jersey (2012)
5. Nurse, J.R.C., Buckley, O., Legg, P.A., Goldsmith, M., Creese, S., Wright, G.R.T., Whitty, M.: Understanding insider threat: a framework for characterising attacks. In: Workshop on Research for Insider Threat (WRIT), in Conjunction with the IEEE Symposium on Security and Privacy (SP). IEEE, New York, 18 May 2014
6. Marcus, B., Schuler, H.: Antecedents of counterproductive behavior at work: a general perspective. J. Appl. Psychol. **89**(4), 647–660 (2004)
7. Wiggins, J.S.: The Five Factor Model of Personality: Theoretical Perspectives. Guildford Press, New York (1996)
8. Paulhus, D.L., Williams, K.M.: The dark triad of personality: Narcissism, Machiavellianism, and psychopathy. J. Res. Pers. **36**(6), 556–563 (2002)
9. Schneier, B.: Attack trees. Dr. Dobbs J. **24**(12), 21–29 (1999)

10. Hutchins, E.M., Cloppert, M.J., Amin, R.M.: Intelligence-driven computer network defense informed by analysis of adversary campaigns and intrusion kill chains. Leading Issues Inf. Warfare Secur. Res. 1(1), 80 (2011)
11. ARMA International: Generally Accepted Recordkeeping Principles®. http://www.arma.org/docs/sharepoint-roadshow/the-principles_executive-summaries_final.doc (2012). Accessed 18 Feb 2015
12. The World Bank: Worldwide Governance Indicators. http://data.worldbank.org/data-catalog/worldwide-governance-indicators (2014). Accessed 18 Feb 2015
13. Ball, J., Borger, J., Greenwald, G.: Revealed: How US and UK Spy Agencies Defeat Internet Privacy and Security, The Guardian. http://www.theguardian.com/world/2013/sep/05/nsa-gchq-encryption-codes-security (2013). Accessed 18 Feb 2015
14. Risen, J., Lichtblau, E.: Bush Lets U.S. Spy on Callers Without Courts, The New York Times, 16 December 2005. http://www.nytimes.com/2005/12/16/politics/16program.html?pagewanted=all&_r=0 (2005). Accessed 18 Feb 2015
15. Cauley, L.: NSA has Massive Database of Americans' Phone Calls, USA Today, 11 May 2006. http://usatoday30.usatoday.com/news/washington/2006-05-10-nsa_x.htm (2006). Accessed 18 Feb 2015
16. National Security Agency/Central Security Service: Transition 2001, December 2000. https://www.eff.org/document/nsa-transition-2001 (2000). Accessed 18 Feb 2015
17. Greenwald, G., MacAskill, E.: NSA Prism Program Taps in to User Data of Apple, Google and Others, The Guardian, 7 June 2013. http://www.theguardian.com/world/2013/jun/06/us-tech-giants-nsa-data (2013). Accessed 18 Feb 2015
18. MacAskill, E., Borger, J., Hopkins, N., Davies, N., Ball, J.: GCHQ Taps Fibre-Optic Cables for Secret Access to World's Communications, The Guardian, 21 June 2013. http://www.theguardian.com/uk/2013/jun/21/gchq-cables-secret-world-communications-nsa (2013). Accessed 18 Feb 2015
19. Rosenblatt, J.: Google Fights E-Mail Privacy Group Suit it Calls Too Big, Bloomberg Business, 28 February 2014. http://www.bloomberg.com/news/articles/2014-02-27/google-fights-e-mail-privacy-group-suit-it-calls-too-big (2014). Accessed 18 Feb 2015
20. Google Inc.: Google Terms of Service (archive), 14 April 2014. http://www.google.com/intl/en/policies/terms/archive/20131111-20140414/ (2014). Accessed 18 Feb 2015
21. Devereaux, R., Greenwald, G., Poitras, L.: Data Pirates of the Caribbean: The NSA Is Recording Every Cell Phone Call in the Bahamas, The Intercept, 19 May 2014. https://firstlook.org/theintercept/2014/05/19/data-pirates-caribbean-nsa-recording-every-cell-phone-call-bahamas/ (2014). Accessed 18 Feb 2015
22. Assange, J.: WikiLeaks Statement on the Mass Recording of Afghan Telephone Calls by the NSA, WikiLeaks, 23 May 2014. https://wikileaks.org/WikiLeaks-statement-on-the-mass.html (2014). Accessed 18 Feb 2015
23. Soldatov, A., Borogan, I.: Russia's Surveillance State, World Policy Journal, Fall 2013. http://www.worldpolicy.org/journal/fall2013/Russia-surveillance (2013). Accessed 18 Feb 2015
24. Walton, G.: China's Golden Shield: Corporations and the Development of Surveillance Technology in the People's Republic of China. International Centre for Human Rights and Democratic Development, Montreal (2001)

Identifying Blind Spots in IS Security Risk Management Processes Using Qualitative Model Analysis

Christian Sillaber[✉] and Ruth Breu

University of Innsbruck, Innsbruck, Austria
`{christian.sillaber,ruth.breu}@uibk.ac.at`

Abstract. The present paper examines quality aspects of models created by stakeholders to identify blind spots in information systems security risk management (ISSRM) processes via a multi-method research study at the organizational level. Stakeholders were interviewed to gain an understanding of their awareness of business processes, models of the information system (IS), and related security requirements in the context of an ongoing ISSRM process. During several modeling sessions, stakeholders were asked to model various aspects of the IS under investigation in the form of component, activity and business process diagrams. We then analyzed the created models qualitatively and linked identified inconsistencies to security issues omitted during the ISSRM process (blind spots). The findings indicate that various quality aspects of models created by stakeholders that describe either the IS or related business processes can contribute to an improved ISSRM process, better alignment to the business environment and improved elicitation of security requirements. Following current research that considers users as the most important resource in ISSRM, this study highlights the importance of using and analyzing model diagrams from appropriate stakeholders at the right time during the ISSRM process to identify potential blind spots and avoid unclarity, that might be introduced by verbal communication. The research provides risk managers with a process for identifying blind spots to improve results and reduce overhead.

Keywords: Information systems security risk management · Stakeholder created models · Risk management process improvement

1 Introduction

As several studies have shown that most incidents related to IS security can be traced back to internal stakeholders (e.g. [1, 2]), IS security literature moved from portraying users as the weakest link in IS security (e.g. [3, 4]) to viewing them as the solution to multiple IS security issues in recent years (e.g. [5, 6]).

To answer calls for more empirical research in this area (e.g. [6–10]) the present paper investigates how models created by stakeholders during IS security risk analysis phases of the ISSRM process can be utilized to identify potential blind spots. The term blind spot is used in the context of this paper to denote any quality issue during the ISSRM analysis phase that might be due to omitted or miss- prioritized components,

© Springer International Publishing Switzerland 2015
T. Tryfonas and I. Askoxylakis (Eds.): HAS 2015, LNCS 9190, pp. 252–259, 2015.
DOI: 10.1007/978-3-319-20376-8_23

overlooked security requirements, wrong assumptions about security properties and similar problems.

Based on the premise that, besides focusing on the participation of stakeholders as mere subjects of IS security policies, it is worthwhile to investigate already available artifacts, such as IS Security documentation, in ISSRM processes, the present paper's research question asks how these artifacts can bring value during analysis phases of the ISSRM process. User participation in IS development and its influence on IS success has been extensively researched and it has been repeatedly argued that the information exchange and knowledge transfer resulting from such participation is the single most important effect [11].

The objective of this paper is to examine the utilization of models created by stakeholders in analysis phases of the IS security risk management processes and to examine how their quality impacts the ISSRM process. In doing so, this paper answers calls for empirical research on user participation in IS security risk management processes [12] and validates the findings in a case study at the organizational level.

The remainder of this paper is organized as follows. First, related work on user participation in ISSRM settings is briefly presented. Next, the study's multi- method research design is outlined, followed by the description of the exploratory study that examined model quality and its contribution to the ISSRM process. Finally, the paper concludes with a discussion of the implications of the study, limitations, and suggestions for future research.

2 Related Work

It has been repeatedly shown that the majority of incidents related to IS security can be traced back to internal stakeholders (e.g. [1, 2, 13]). IS security literature has been continuously moving from portraying users as the weakest link in IS security (e.g. [3, 4]) to viewing them as the solution to multiple IS security issues in recent years (e.g. [5, 6]). However, literature is still lacking empirical studies that examine more closely how users' participation positively impacts IS security risk management processes that go beyond users being viewed as "mere" executors of IS security policies.

Following a synthesis of theories explaining user participation in IS security contexts, Spears et al. [6] define user participation in IS security risk management as the set of behaviors, activities, and assignments undertaken by business users during IS risk assessment and the design and implementation of IS security controls that is expected to add value to security risk management. While the value of stakeholder participation in general is backed by manifold studies, these approaches often reduce stakeholders to mere executors of business security requirements and their derived controls.

IS security risk management is the continuous process to identify and assess risk and to apply methods to reduce risks to an acceptable extent. Recent research has increasingly focused on human factors influencing the outcome of ISSRM processes, including behavioral theories [14] describing the entire ISSRM process or focusing on selected areas including security awareness [15, 16], security behavior [17], communication [18] and the impact of audits [19] and standardization efforts [20]. In [21], the link between stakeholder knowledge on business processes and potential contributions to the ISSRM process were investigated as part of the same research project.

By focusing on the assessment (i.e. analysis) phase, we re-conceptualize the success outcomes, actors, activities and hypothesized links between outcomes and activities to fit the concepts under investigation in the present paper, as suggested in [15]. Therefore, the present paper examines the link between static artifacts i.e. IS security models and activities and the value they add to the ISRM process.

3   Analyzing Blind Spots in Models Created During ISSRM Processes

As this research was conducted as part of an ongoing research project at the organizational level, a mixed-method approach was chosen based on the premise that separate and dissimilar data sets from different settings would provide a richer picture and thus compensate for the fact that experimentations in IS risk management processes are difficult to conduct [22, 23]. We relied on a combination of data collection (models) and interviews with participants of the ongoing organizational IS security risk management process. Refer to [21] for an in-depth description of the research design.

3.1   Exploratory Study

During a several months lasting IS security and risk management process at the organizational level, an exploratory study was conducted to investigate the utilization of models created by stakeholders in ISSRM processes. The organization under investigation is one branch ($\approx$100 employees) of a multinational engineering company, focusing on the development of distributed information systems within a highly regulated domain. Interview partners included employees at the project management level with a university degree in computer science or related areas. Multiple interviews with domain experts from the organization were conducted over a timespan of several months. Five semi-structured inter- views were conducted with five informants including three product managers, one deputy chief information security manager and one technological executive. This convenience sample included three employees with a degree in computer science and one with a specialization in IS security.

Interview partners were repeatedly asked to draw models of various aspects of the IS under investigation. These models included component diagrams, activity diagrams and business processes related to the IS. While the research results regarding models related to business processes are presented in [21], component diagrams and associated system models will be at the focus of interest in the remainder of this paper. Models created by the stakeholders were converted to UML compatible models (component diagrams and class diagrams) to enable further comparison and analysis.

3.2   Data Collection and Measurement Setting

We devised the measurement setting as shown in Fig. 1 to perform the investigation. The four step process was executed for each component of the IS under investigation:

- **Step 1: Stakeholder interview:** In this step, we asked stakeholders to describe the component under investigation and its security properties.
- **Step 2: Stakeholder created models:** In this step, we asked stakeholders to model the component under investigation.
- **Step 3: Creation of models for comparison:** Using the information gathered in step 1 and the model produced in step 2, we digitally created a sanitized model to remove ambiguity.
- **Step 4: Identification of blind spots:** We compared the models from step 3 and identified blind spots (i.e. differences in the models) in both the component model as well as the security requirements elicited by identifying differences in the models.

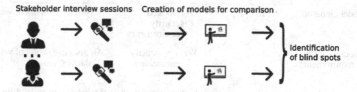

Fig. 1. Overview of the measurement setting (Icons made by Freepik from flaticon.com licensed under CC BY 3.0.).

Content Validity: We made an effort to ensure that the tasks were clearly understood by the participating stakeholders and that they responded to questions that we intended to ask. The entire process was conducted verbally and clarifications were provided by the researchers if needed. All stakeholders that participated in the study could access any organizational knowledge source that is normally available to them (internal documentation, internal wiki, etc.). They could draft their models on paper and/or a whiteboard.

Setting: We conducted each modeling session at the premises of the organization under investigation and told stakeholders to view the researchers as risk managers conducting an IS security risk analysis. With each stakeholder, we went through all components of the IS under investigation. All stakeholders were promised anonymity and the organization was promised confidentiality regarding specific security risk related results and the architecture of their IS.

Model Creation: Based on the input received from stakeholders during the sessions, models were sanitized and digitally recreated. All participants were IS professionals and were product managers or senior developers. Despite the small sample size of 9 stakeholders, we are confident that we provide a reasonably adequate representation of the target population, as we are not interested in perceived effects (requiring a broad sample size) but rather objectively measurable influence in IS security risk management, which would not be gather-able in a broad fashion. A discussion of further limitations and future evaluation in a broader study is presented in the next section.

3.3 Analysis

The descriptive results are provided in Table 1. We identified in total four types of potential blind spots. To analyze the resulting models and elicited security requirements in terms of quantity and quality, we validated whether the elicited security requirements had an understandable description and were linked to at least one component of the IS. Then we compared both the security requirements and the models created by each stakeholder against the models created for the same component by the other stakeholders.

Table 1. Model issues and identified blind spots in the ISSRM process.

Issue in model	# Identified	Blind spot found	Example
Omitted model element	18	Overlooked security requirements	A system component was omitted
Omitted association (to security requirement)	14	Wrong security requirements chosen	An insecure protocol was used for data exchange
Differently modeled components	7	Components with unclear security requirements	Stakeholders had a different understanding of several components of the IS and their security requirements
Omitted association (to component)	3	Missing stakeholder awareness	Several stakeholders did not select security requirements, contradicting organizational policies

As a result, we were able to identify several security requirements that were either not reflected in the IS under investigation or contradicted organizational policies. Furthermore, we were able to identify several components that were currently not aligned with organizational security requirements.

While most stakeholders were able to model the components correctly and elicit the correct security requirements for them (and vice versa), the majority of identified blind spots, as shown in Table 1 were overlooked security requirements. The second largest number of blind spots were omitted associations from either components to security requirements or vice versa. Examples for this category include valid components not linked to valid security requirements or valid security requirements linked to valid (but wrong) components.

By comparing the identified blind spots to the results of the ongoing ISSRM process, we found that all security issues identified during the ISSRM process were also identified by using our approach. A majority of blind spots (27/42) was identified after interviewing only two stakeholders and all blind spots were identified after interviewing four stakeholders - which lead to quicker results than the ISSRM process which required 9 interviews each.

4 Discussion

The present paper examined blind spots in IS security risk management processes using qualitative model analysis. In a mixed-method research study we assessed the models created by stakeholders during an ongoing IS security risk management process and used these models to identify potential blind spots.

Investigation of omitted model elements was found to improve the security risk management process by identifying security issues faster. Thus, qualitatively analyzing models created by stakeholders was found to add value to an organization's IS security risk management process.

4.1 Research Contribution and Implications for Practice

In extension to existing research on user participation in IS security risk management, the present study examined how artifacts created by stakeholders can improve the IS security risk analysis process. We found evidence that the analysis of models created by the stakeholders involved in the IS security risk management process contributes to the overall performance. This study contributes towards the growing body of knowledge on user behavior and stakeholder contribution to the IS security risk management process.

The results of the present study suggest that the IS security risk managers can and should utilize artifacts produced by stakeholders participating in IS security risk management processes. The findings of our study suggest that there is a benefit from making high quality documentation of the security of the IS available to all IS stakeholders (improving awareness). In particular, it seems to be desirable to properly document the security attributes of each component.

Finally, study findings suggest that active user participation in the IS security risk management process is highly desirable and that this participation can lead to a better fit of IS security risk analysis results to the business needs.

4.2 Study Limitations and Future Work

Several limitations of the study need to be acknowledged. First, the process of model creation was subjective and might depends on the stakeholder's ability to recreate the IS under investigation and might contain subjective errors.

A second limitation of the study is that it was conducted within the relatively low population of one organization. This limitation is applicable to all surveys with an in-depth focus on a problem from industry, where objective experimentation or broad surveys are not possible. To limit the threat to generalizability of the findings, we minimized the number of industry-specific components in the investigation and made sure that the IS security risk analysis process did not require industry-specific knowledge.

A third limitation of the present study stems from the fact that the modeling process was conducted in individual settings. Due to organizational constraints at the organization under investigation, it was not possible to conduct extensive group interviews or group modeling sessions. We tried to mitigate this by allowing stakeholders to access any organizational knowledge source (also contact other stakeholders) to gather information.

To improve the generalizability of this research in the future, we plan to apply the proposed research model at other organizations and compare against an objective ISSRM conducted by independent auditors, to remove subjective bias. Furthermore, we seek to refine the process model to include formalized methods of comparing stakeholder created models.

5 Conclusion

We analyzed models created by stakeholders as part of an ongoing IS security risk management process and compared them against models from other stakeholders and reference models (if available). We identified differences in the models and linked them to potential security issues. We identified several patterns and quality issues in models that correlate to blind spots in the ongoing ISSRM process.

The present study provides evidence that models created by stakeholders in ISSRM processes can be utilized to identify and remove potential blind spots and eliminate risks during early stages of the ISSRM process. IS security risk managers can utilize the results of the present study to identify potential blind spots quickly and efficiently prioritize efforts in ISSRM processes without sacrificing quality of the results.

Acknowledgements. This work was supported by the Austrian Federal Ministry of. Economy (BMWFW), QE LaB - Living Models for Open Systems (FFG 822740).

References

1. Ernst and Young's, Into the cloud, out of the fog; Global Information Security Survey, Young, Ernst. Technical report, November 2011
2. Subashini, S., Kavitha, V.: A survey on security issues in service delivery models of cloud computing. J. Netw. Comput. Appl. **34**(1), 1–11 (2011)
3. Wade, J.: The weak link in IT security. Risk Manag. **51**(7), 32–37 (2004)
4. Siponen, M.T.: Critical analysis of different approaches to minimizing user-related faults in information systems security: implications for research and practice. Inf. Manag. Comput. Secur. **8**(5), 197–209 (2000)
5. Stanton, J., Stam, K., Mastrangelo, P., Jolton, J.: Behavioral information security. In: Human-Computer Interaction and Management Information Systems: Foundations, p. 262. M.E. Sharpe, New York (2006)
6. Spears, J., Barki, H.: User participation in information systems security risk management. MIS Q. **34**(3), 503–522 (2010)
7. Vance, A.: Neutralizaiton: new insights into the problem of employee information systems security. MIS Q. **34**(3), 487–502 (2010)
8. Benbasat, I.: An empirical study of rationality-based beliefs in information systems security. MIS Q. **34**(3), 523–548 (2010)
9. Puhakainen, P., Siponen, M.: Improving employees' compliance through information systems security training: an action research study. MIS Q. **34**(4), 757–778 (2010)
10. Siponen, M., Oinas-Kukkonen, H.: A review of information security issues and respective research contributions. ACM Sigmis Database **38**(1), 60–80 (2007)

11. Locke, E.A., Alavi, M., Wagner III, J.A.: Participation in decision making: an information exchange perspective. Res. Pers. Hum. Resour. Manag.: A Res. Ann. **15**, 293–332 (1997)
12. Markus, M.L., Mao, J.-Y.: Participation in development and implementation- updating an old, tired concept for today's IS contexts. J. Assoc. Inf. Syst. **5**(11), 14 (2004)
13. CSI, CSI Computer Crime & Security Survey, Computer Security Institute. Technical report (2008)
14. Alavi, R., Islam, S., Mouratidis, H.: A conceptual framework to analyze human factors of information security management system (ISMS) in organizations. In: Tryfonas, T., Askoxylakis, I. (eds.) HAS 2014. LNCS, vol. 8533, pp. 297–305. Springer, Heidelberg (2014)
15. Spears, J.L., Barki, H.: User participation in information systems security risk management. MIS Q. **34**(3), 503–522 (2010)
16. Mejias, R.: An integrative model of information security awareness for assessing information systems security risk. In: 2012 45th Hawaii International Conference on System Science (HICSS), pp. 3258–3267 (2012)
17. Guo, K.H., Yuan, Y., Archer, N.P., Connelly, C.E.: Understanding nonmali- cious security violations in the workplace: a composite behavior model. J. Manag. Inf. Syst. **28**(2), 203–236 (2011)
18. Heath, R.L., O'Hair, H.D.: Handbook of Risk and Crisis Communication. Routledge, London (2010)
19. Steinbart, P.J., Raschke, R.L., Gal, G., Dilla, W.N.: The relationship between internal audit and information security: an exploratory investigation. Int. J. Account. Inf. Syst., Research Symposium on Information Integrity and Information Systems Assurance **13**(3), 228–243 (2011)
20. Peltier, T.R.: Information Security Policies, Procedures, and Standards: guidelines for effective information security management. CRC Press, Abingdon (2013)
21. Sillaber, C. Breu, R.: Using business process model awareness to improve stakeholder participation in information systems security risk management processes. In: Conference on Wirtschaftsinformatik (2015, in press)
22. Kohlbacher, F.: "The Use of Qualitative Content Analysis in Case Study Research", Forum Qual. Soc. Res. **7**, 31 (2006)
23. Verendel, V.: Quantified security is a weak hypothesis. In: Proceedings of the 2009 workshop on New security paradigms workshop - NSPW 2009, p. 37 (2009)

Privacy and Security in the Brave New World: The Use of Multiple Mental Models

Sandra Spickard Prettyman[1], Susanne Furman[2(✉)], Mary Theofanos[2],
and Brian Stanton[2]

[1] Culture Catalyst, 113 N Democratic St., Tecumseh, MI 49286, USA
`Sspretty50@icloud.com`
[2] National Institute of Standards and Technology, 100 Bureau Drive,
Gaithersburg, MD 20899, USA
`{Susanne.Furman,Mary.Theofanos,Brian.Stanton}@nist.gov`

Abstract. We live in a world where the flow of electronic information and communication has become a ubiquitous part of our everyday life. While our lives are enhanced in many ways, we also experience a myriad of challenges especially to our privacy and security. Survey data shows that the majority of people are 'very concerned' about privacy and security but that they don't always act in ways to protect their privacy. Our goal was to explore how participants understand and experience privacy and security as they engage in online activities. To that end we used a qualitative approach to understand the participants' mental models of online privacy and security. The data from our 40 interviews show that users have multiple mental models that guide their understanding of and experience with privacy and security. These mental models not only operate simultaneously but are rarely fully formed and often contradict each other.

Keywords: Mental models · Online privacy and security · Qualitative approach

1 Introduction

Today there is no such thing as privacy. It looks like privacy and it feels like privacy, but there is no such thing as privacy. I look at what the government could do if they wanted to, so there is no such thing as privacy. (*Patience, Female, Age: 40 to 49*).

We live in a world where the flow of electronic information and communication has become a ubiquitous part of everyday life and embedded in our interactions in and expectations of the world. This technology enhances our lives in many ways, but also comes with its share of challenges especially to our privacy and security. These challenges have become more complex as the devices we use to access and utilize information and communication systems have become more mobile, varied, and used more frequently. With the shift to doing more of our banking, shopping, and communicating with intricately linked and networked systems comes an increased concern about the privacy exposure and security of our personal information. Often these concerns are misunderstood or ignored. In this context, cybersecurity training and education are imperative if end-users are going to navigate the online environment safely and effectively. However,

© Springer International Publishing Switzerland 2015
T. Tryfonas and I. Askoxylakis (Eds.): HAS 2015, LNCS 9190, pp. 260–270, 2015.
DOI: 10.1007/978-3-319-20376-8_24

in order to design effective cybersecurity training and education, we must understand how people think about and experience online privacy and security in their everyday lives. Many researchers in computer and online privacy today argue we need continued research to gain a better understanding of end-user beliefs about, experiences with, and desires for mechanisms to protect privacy and security [1–4].

This study presents findings from a qualitative inquiry into people's understanding of and experiences with online and computer privacy and security. Our goal was to explore how participants understand and experience privacy and security as they engage in online and computer actions and activities in their everyday lives and to determine if a mental model helps them navigate these interactions. Participants in the study articulated a belief that they were living in what we call a Brave New World, one in which privacy is a thing of the past and security is a "blanket with holes in it" (*Patience, Female, Age: 40 to 49*). In this brave new world, people do not draw on a single mental model, rather they use multiple mental models, often at the same time, that are often only partially- (or ill-) formed. Understanding these models and how people utilize them can help us develop and design better approaches to education about cybersecurity for all users.

2 Background: Mental Models, Privacy, and Security

"A mental model is a simplified internal concept of how something works in the real world" (p. 1) [5]. We use mental models to help us decide the best course of action in given or unfamiliar situations. Since the 1990's, mental models have been used to try to understand human-computer interaction, and more recently have been used to explore cybersecurity and risk communication. Camp presents five different mental models that can be used in risk communication to users: physical security, medical infections, criminal behavior, economics failure, and warfare [6]. Subsequent research built on Camp's work found sharp differences in the mental models used by experts and non-experts as they considered security risks [7]. Wash describes two major categories of "folk models" utilized by non-expert participants, finding four models within each category of malicious software and malicious computer users [4]. What links all of this work is that we must first grasp how users understand and experience online and computer privacy and security in order to help protect individuals and institutions.

Privacy is a concept that is highly contextual and often contested, with little agreement in the literature regarding how to define it [3, 8]. Brandeis and Warren asserted that privacy is the right to be left alone, which has influenced privacy legislation in the United States for most of the 20th century [9]. More recent definitions of privacy recognize that a person's privacy depends on the extent to which others have access to information about them [10] or about the degree to which we have control over information about ourselves and our environments [11]. The one constant in the privacy debate is that surveys show the majority of people are 'very concerned' about their privacy [12]. Yet empirical evidence suggests that there is a significant discrepancy between privacy principles and privacy practices [3]. While people articulate a concern for their online privacy, they do not always act in ways to protect it.

This discrepancy may result because users generally view privacy as a social concern and security as a technical concern—something that can be deployed for the purposes of protecting privacy. Dourish and Anderson define security as "the state of being free from danger" (p. 322) [1]. They frame online privacy and security as "collective information practices - the ways in which we collectively share, withhold, manage information and interpret these acts and deploy them in everyday social interactions (p. 335)." In this study, we situate privacy and security as collective information practices.

As researchers, we come at this work from very different disciplines, both academic (i.e., engineering, psychology, sociology, computer science) and methodological (i.e., both quantitative and qualitative); something which we believe helps us "to bridge intellectual traditions" [13] and provide a more holistic understanding of the issues under investigation. The National Research Council (NRC) has argued for more research to be conducted using an interdisciplinary approach [14]. This work responds to that call and seeks to broaden the scope of work found in usability and cybersecurity.

3   Methodological Approach

Given the exploratory and descriptive nature of this work we chose to use a qualitative approach for the study. Our research questions for the study were the following:

1. How do participants describe their experiences with online privacy and/or security?
2. What, if any, perceptions do participants have regarding online privacy and/or security?
3. How, if at all, do participants use mental models as they think about privacy and/or security in the online environment?

We conducted semi-structured interviews with 40 participants and used a recursive analytic process as we worked to make sense of the data. The semi-structured interviews provided us with similar data across the interview participants, allowed for flexibility and the ability to follow participants' leads during the interviews; and provided for structures for coding and analysis and helped us develop analytic accounts rooted in the data. We were interested in how users understand and experience online privacy and security. We were not interested in what larger numbers could tell us statistically, but rather as Schoeman advocates, in the rich and detailed data that our participants could provide [10]. Our goal is to tell the story of online and computer privacy and security from the perspectives and through the words of our participants.

3.1   Sites/Participants

Researchers from the National Institute of Standards and Technology (NIST) recruited participants in the Washington, DC metropolitan area using email and in central Pennsylvania via an advertisement in a local newspaper asking for participation in a NIST study about people's perceptions of online and computer security. They were told that they would participate in a one-hour interview and compensated $50 for their participation with requirements of having an active email address and being 21 years of age or older. Our goal was to have participants from different backgrounds (age, gender, geographic location, employment) and who had a wide range of and experiences with computers.

We interviewed a total of 40 participants for the study, 27 from the metropolitan Washington DC area and 13 from central Pennsylvania giving us a sample from urban, rural, and suburban settings. Throughout this paper, we use pseudonyms when referring to participant statements. There were 21 women and 19 men who ranged in age from 21 to 79. All but two participants had some college education and six held advanced degrees; only one of the participants worked in the technology industry (but not in the realm of privacy and security). Participants were asked to evaluate their level of computer knowledge: 12 (30 %) reported little knowledge; 24 (60 %) reported moderate knowledge; 4 (10 %) reported expert knowledge.

3.2 Data Collection and Analysis

Data collection occurred from January to March 2011. The semi-structured interview protocol included: demographic questions; information about online activities, behaviors, and knowledge; familiarity with security terms and icons; and beliefs and perceptions about computer and online privacy and security. The protocol was designed to elicit data about participants' beliefs, perceptions, and behaviors related to online privacy and security. Once all interviews were completed, a NIST researcher in the project transcribed them, along with any field notes related to them. Initially, quantitative analysis was conducted on the data collected from the interviews [12].

Subsequently, we conducted qualitative data analysis with multiple readings of the full data set by all researchers in the project, followed by individual and group coding sessions. The group constructed and operationalized an initial a priori code list that was based on the literature and on our own knowledge as researchers in the field. We used an iterative process of: working with a subset of four interviews each to determine inter-coder reliability; discussing codes, definitions, and issues using them; refining our use of codes until we reached agreement; operationalizing emergent codes and solidifying our understanding of our new code list. At least two researchers coded each of the remaining interviews. The goal was to insure that the use of codes and their application to segments of text was consistent amongst the researchers; "the more coders (using the same codebook) agree on the coding of a text, the more we can consider the codebook a reliable instrument (i.e., one that facilitates inter-coder reliability)" (p. 310) [16].

4 Results

Previous research argues that a mental model guides people's behavior related to online and computer privacy and security [6, 7, 17]. While different mental models are described in the literature, the implicit understanding is that people use one as they work to make sense of and make decisions about online privacy and security. Our data shows that there are multiple mental models that operate, often simultaneously as users experience privacy and security in this brave new world. These mental models are rarely fully formed, but rather only partially formed, and they often contradict each other. In the sections below, we describe the ways in which participants draw on a variety of multiple mental models as they discuss their understandings of privacy and security.

4.1   Living in the Brave New World: The Need for Multiple Mental Models

In 1965, Gordon Moore conjectured that the number of transistors that could fit on a square inch of silicon would double every year, leading to exponential shifts in our devices and their capabilities [17]. "[T]he impact of "Moore's Law" has led users and consumers to come to expect a continuous stream of faster, better, and cheaper high-technology products" [18]. The pace, types, and consequences of interaction have all changed—leading to a Brave New World where participants attempt to navigate, often without adequate tools or training. A world where a single mental model may limit their ability to adapt to change but where the use of multiple mental models may help users cope in this rapidly changing technological landscape. As Lewis *(Male, Age: 50 to 59)* explained, "Things have moved so fast. There is so much information out there about everyone…I trust if my credit card or bank info is stolen that my bank will take over."

4.2   Life in the Brave New World and a Desire for the 'Good Old Days'

Many participants talked about the world today as if it were a very different place than it had been. A world many of them would like to opt out of, but believe they do not have the ability to do so, and where their experiences with privacy and security lead them to long for the 'good old days' where they felt safer and more comfortable. As Cindy *(Female, Age: 20 to 29)* explained, "…it [Facebook[1]] is like the Hotel California – you can check out but you can never leave. Once they have your email address and your name – you are out there forever.…Our information is all over the place. I would prefer to go back to paper mailing and close out all of my [online] accounts."

Tiffany *(Female, Age: 20 to 29)* said: "My friends make fun of me and call me an old person. I know people say things about how people can just open your mail, but I feel safer. I feel vulnerable when I have to enter my bank routing number and checking number somewhere online. It gives me piece of mind when I write a check and I put it in the envelope and send it off. The comfort comes just from that." Edgar *(Male, Age: 40 to 49)* explained: "I don't pay bills online. I don't trust it – I feel like I have no control if some-thing happens. I would rather call and pay it over the phone. I feel like that is more secure than having all that information situated on the Internet where all these things get done automatically." Kendall *(Female, Age: 20 to 29)* explained: "I don't pay bills online. I feel it is much better to put it in the mail and I feel the mail is pretty secure. I know that people can get viruses and I don't know how much of that is stored on the computer. I feel safer and they don't have access to my information." Norma *(Female, Age: 40 to 49)* said:

---

[1] Disclaimer: Any mention of commercial products is for information only; such identification is not intended to imply recommendation or endorsement by the National Institute of Standards and Technology, nor is it intended to imply that these entities, materials, or equipment are necessarily the best for the purpose.

"I think computers can be dangerous because it gives the information out so quickly. It is not like word of mouth or spreading something to a neighbor or coworkers even. If it is something on a computer then everyone can see it within a second. There is no privacy at all." Murray (*Male, Age: 40 to 49*) explained: "For me, the disadvantage [social networking] is that we have become an impersonal society. For me, I want to hear your voice. People don't even have the courtesy to pick up the phone anymore."

Interestingly, not only the older but also the younger participants wanted to return to the good old days, back to what they perceived as a simpler, safer time. Most lacked a fully formed mental model to guide their thinking about online privacy and security and this may have led them to believe things were better and safer in the past. Without this fully formed mental model they often felt uncomfortable and unsafe.

A few participants did talk about the brave new world as the norm: "Well, it is 2011 and I am 24 – so I never thought about that – the other way was before my time [speaking of online bill paying]." (*Rod, Male, Age: 21 to 29*); "I don't know why we instant message (IM) – sometimes I will IM a friend who lives 10 min away and I don't know why I just don't talk to him. And he likes to talk that way more than he does on the phone." (*Jessie, Female, Age: 40 to 49*); "I licked an envelope the other day and I thought wow this is odd." (*Michelle, Female, Age: 40 to 49*).

For Rod, Jessie, and Michelle, new technologies were part of how the world works, something they did not even think about as they engaged in their daily activities. While they are accepted, most participants are still suspect of new technologies and their relationship to privacy and security. For example, Rod noted that "it is very hard to protect your privacy with Facebook" and that he has "an apocalyptic sense of the future" where "it is this giant database of people."

4.3 There is no Privacy in the Brave New World

Like Patience (*Female, Age: 40 to 49*), whose words begin this paper, many of our participants believed that privacy is something in the past and no longer exists in the interconnected, technologically advanced world of today. Some noted how as soon as you connect (online implied) you have lost privacy, and many discussed how government, businesses, and the general public (including hackers) can (and do) access and store personal information, leading to a loss of privacy and a lack of security.

Doug explained (*Male, Age: 50 to 59*): "You put your name out there and it is already compounded, you can't stop it. Any information you put out there is no longer personal. There is no privacy, you are being watched everywhere." Geoff (*Male, Age: 50 to 59*) said: "The minute you let your guard down then your privacy is gone…but I don't think there's that much privacy in our society anyway. If people want to find things out they will." Mia explained (*Female, Age: 30 to 39*): "When the revolution comes – we are all going to be screwed because we are all in their databases." And Scot (*Male, Age: 60+*) said: "If you go on the network for any reason – privacy is almost eliminated. The network is open to the entire world."

Many of our participants still engaged in some behaviors to protect their privacy even after articulating how and why they thought privacy did not exist in the cyberworld. Patience (*Female, Age: 40 to 49*) delineated a host of precautions she takes to provide security and protect her privacy: strong passwords, signs of secure websites, and the use of a firewall. She said: "It makes me totally paranoid when I see these shows where the guy is sitting there with an open router and picking up everything the person is doing. My cousin is sitting on an open network and I try to explain to him that 'dude it is like walking down the street totally naked'."

Actively engaging in practices to feel more secure and protect their privacy was true for many of those who questioned online privacy and security, representing just one of the ways in which participants had mixed experiences with, beliefs about, and behaviors toward online privacy and security.

Many of the participants who talked about the lack of privacy in the cyber world drew on a Fatalistic Model, noting that "If someone wants to get into my account they are going to get into my account" (*Lewis, Male, Age: 50 to 59*), or that "I guess I am resigned to data mining for marketing" (*Michelle, Female, Age: 40 to 49*). This sense of resignation was present in many of our interviews, and participants often noted how they had become immune to the worry about privacy and security. Viseau et al. found similar results where "participants' privacy perceptions seem to be associated with an attitude of resignation and even of total disregard for the whole subject of privacy" [3]. For example, Hank (*Male, Age: 20 to 29*) talked about "being desensitized to it, I know bad things can happen." Later, he talked about 'background noise' as he discussed security. For Hank, as for many other participants, it did not matter what they did, their privacy and security were going to be compromised in the online environment and it was out of their hands.

Often participants discussed this fatalistic view and then a bit later in the interview presented an Optimistic Model, where they described how everything was fine since nothing bad had happened to date. This cognitive bias of normalcy [19] grew out of a particular innocence about online environments and the potential consequences which Swanson et al., [2] call a "nothing to hide, nothing to fear" attitude.

Hank (*Male, Age: 20 to 29*) is one example. His previous comment about background noise was followed by: "I know that the risk exists and my security can be compromised and my information can be stolen. But I don't hear it happening often to my peers. I haven't heard horror stories of anyone getting my email." Similarly, Tiffany (*Female, Age: 20 to 29*) noted: "Because nothing has happened on my home computer I feel safe. I almost feel it is contingent on nothing happening."

Swanson et al., found similar results. They describe how their participants "trust that others would not victimize them, and believe that something bad is unlikely" [2]. They argue their participants were "naïve" and "guided by a false sense of security" something we also see in our data (p. 45).

It was not unusual for participants to present both a fatalistic and an optimistic perspective, demonstrating a lack of consistency in their understandings of and experiences with sharing and managing their information online. Both perspectives represent "a short-term vision of individual interests and preferences rather than a broader societal perspective" about online privacy and security (p.106) [3].

4.4   Online Privacy and Security: Multiple Mental Models

Participants often drew one mental model and in the next sentence articulating a different one as they describe their experiences with managing their information. Sometimes, a participant utilized three or four different mental models over the course of an interview, often when describing the same thing. Occasionally these mental models would be used in the answer to just one interview question.

For example, at the end of his interview Hank (*Male, Age: 20 to 29*) was asked if he had any other thoughts or comments. He first answered by noting that no matter what he does it would not make much difference, and that if "it [something bad] is going to happen it is going to happen." He began by articulating the idea of not having control, of the online environment being in control. Two sentences later he presents a different idea, and within the space of a few minutes has laid out multiple mental models. "I have this perception that the Internet is less wild…there is less uncharted territory now. You can get confirmation from other people by going to forums that fifty thousand people use and go to trusted websites like Amazon, Google, and Facebook, and Twitter. I go to sites I have established relationships with and have reputations. I feel like unless you are looking for pirated software or going on foreign websites that they are more dangerous. And when I don't go to websites I know, I will do research when something sounds too generic or doesn't sound right. I am a borderline creepy 'Googler'."

Hank initially presented an image of the Internet as a wild place where no matter what he does that things can happen—he is not in control. But then he quickly goes on to describe the Internet as "less wild" with "less uncharted territory" than before. His words evoke the "Wild West" where there was often lawlessness and no control. However, now this wild world has been tamed; you know where to go and who you can trust with your information.

Hank drew on a Reputation Model as he talked about "trusted websites" that he has "established relationships with and have reputations." Like Hank, many of our participants generally limited online transactions to "vendors that we have had a relationship with" (*Mark, Male, Age: 50 to 59*). "I usually shop at places that I have heard of, reputable sites" (*Kendall, Female, Age: 20 to 29*), or "I just try to buy from certain places, like a brand, based on their reputation" (*Coco, Female, Age: 30 to 39*).

When participants used a Reputation Model it was to refer to specific places or brands that they already had developed a relationship with in the physical world. While Hank and other participants considered "reputation" as an indicator of safety, they did not (perhaps could not) describe how or why reputation provided greater security. This is another example of naïve users trusting sites, often based on "feeling" or "a sense" that they have.

Perhaps most interesting is that previously Hank talked about how taking security measures was useless since "it is out of my hands" using a Fatalistic Model to reinforce the lack of control. Yet in this final statement he notes that he is a "borderline creepy 'Googler'" who does research "when something sounds too generic or doesn't sound right" where he draws on a Verification Model when he needs to take action before he decides whether to share or withhold information.

Many participants demonstrated this back and forth in their thinking about online privacy and security. For example, Patience (*Female, Age: 40 to 49*) initially argued, "there is no privacy" today, but also said she is "very keenly aware of the problems that can come around." Later, she discussed how she has a firewall to protect herself, but later noted how "a lot of times I leave my credit card up there, I need to be a bit better with my password, I just use a generic password" and that she gets very frustrated with sites that "give me too many blocks, then I'm going to be turned off." Participants seem to 'flip-flop' in their understanding of risk and their decisions about sharing, withholding, and managing their information online.

At another point in his interview, Hank specifically drew a distinction between at home versus at work security where security is not his responsibility and is relegated to someone else. "I assume my security at work is better because we have a whole group at work that does that. I feel safer at work and it is their job to protect that." Other participants said it was the responsibility of their bank or the website they used. We refer to this as a Not My Job Model, where participants believe the responsibility to provide security and protect privacy rests with someone else. Often, participants used this idea when speaking of banks. Rod (*Male, Age: 20 to 29*) explained: "The bank, it is their job, so they better be doing it." and John (*Male, Age: 50 to 59*) "I am looking for big time security. I rely on the banking sites to take care of that security." When participants relied on others to protect their privacy or provide security, they engaged in a form of "off-loading risk" and "transferring responsibility" to others and failed to see the ways in which such behavior might be risky [2].

Many participants, like John above (or Patience earlier), said they wanted "big time security" but did little or nothing to protect their security. In addition, participants, including Hank, drew on a model of Little Value, where they articulated how they did not think they had anything that others would want. Mia (*Female, Age: 30 to 39*) captures this model well in statements she makes. "I don't know why anyone would want any of my information. There is nothing in my background that anyone would want to steal. I am the most boring person on the planet and I have no money."

This model does not recognize the potential dangers out there or the reasons that others may want to access their information. Similarly in a study by Swanson et al., found that participants "operated under a perception that the things they might reveal would be of limited value to other parties" [2] or in the study by Viseau et al., where participants saw themselves as "simply not interesting enough to justify paranoia about privacy" (p. 105) [3].

Many of our participants used multiple mental models as they spoke of their experiences with sharing, withholding, and managing their information in the cyberworld. Like Hank, their models were often only partially formed, contradictory, and based on misinformation or faulty assumptions linked to real world rather than the online environments.

4.5   A Notable Exception: The 'Expert'

While we noted very few fully formed mental models that guided people's behavior as they talked about their experiences, there was one notable exception. Baldwin (*Male, Age: 30 to 39*) discussed online shopping and banking in the following way: "I have a fatalistic approach and I understand the system is fundamentally not perfect. I am not worried that someone is going to go through my trash and get my credit card number. It is much more likely that somebody will break into the credit card processor's computer and get a million accounts including mine. I still use a credit card even though it can be compromised and I consider it a necessary evil. So it is a tradeoff and the price that I pay for the convenience of having a bank account."

Baldwin realized there are tradeoffs and that the online system is flawed. He talked about the greater likelihood that his credit card will be stolen online. He acknowledged the ways the government and banks work to insure this does not happen. Later he actually used the words 'mental model' to explain how he deals with privacy and security as compared to his friends. "I have developed a mental model—when people buy a car they know they are not just going to pay for the car and it requires maintenance. I see a real lack of knowledge that people assume they buy a computer and it has Windows on it and that is all they have to do." Here, he drew on a Maintenance Model where you need to take care of your computer in order to insure security, just like you need to take care of your car.

5   Conclusions

Through their stories shared by participants in this study, we paint a picture of what privacy and security look like from their perspectives. This picture presents the landscape in what participants see as a brave new world, a world that is constantly shifting and changing, a world where "I am probably two weeks behind those who are out there to try and break into computers, forever two weeks behind" (*Edgar, Male, Age: 40 to 49*).

Mental models utilized by our participants include: Brave New World, Fatalistic, Little Value, Maintenance, Not My Job, Optimistic, Reputation, and Verification. Almost all participants drew on some notion of Brave New World, and of all the models we identified this seems to be the most common. But there was not one overarching mental model to guide them. Instead, they often drew on bits and pieces of multiple partially- or ill-formed mental models that represented their 'naïve' understandings of the cyberworld and its risks.

Viseau et al., argue that "individuals approach privacy from the context of their own actual practices, associating it with their individual experiences and concerns..." (p. 106) [3]. In order to develop successful online privacy and security educational initiatives, we must understand the varied and contextualized ways in which participants engage in collective information practices. "Talking about the need to maintain privacy and provide security, however, frames these concepts as stable and uniform features of the world, independent of the particular social and cultural circumstances in which individuals find themselves at particular moments" (p. 335) [1]. Online and computer privacy and security were not stable but rather fluid concepts, and dependent on the context and type of interaction. This assumption of an overarching and stable understanding of privacy and security may be why "at best, the privacy 'movement' is failing to meet its objectives, and that, at worst, it is misguided" (pp. 105-106) [3].

Many efforts to improve user understandings of cybersecurity focus on the moment when information is released into cyberspace, and not when users are sitting in front of the computer or interacting with it [3]. This may be one reason that users adopt a Fatalistic Model—one reason why they believe that whatever they do it will not matter and that their actions only impact them and not a broader community.

Education and training aimed at preparing better cyber-citizens in this brave new world must: (1) recognize the fragmented, fluid, and often naïve understandings of users; (2) draw on analogies that users currently hold; (3) focus on how we share, withhold, and manage information and the social actions they are aimed at accomplishing; and (4) help users see privacy and security as more than just the moment when data is released. In addition, our data suggest that it is important to position online privacy and security as a communal issue, one that is larger than just the individual, in order to help users develop "more socially sound privacy practices" [3].

References

1. Dourish, P., Anderson, K.: Collective information practice: Exploring privacy and security as social and cultural phenomena. Hum.-Comput. Interact. **21**, 319–342 (2006)
2. Swanson, C., Urner, R., Lank, E.: Naïve security in a Wi-Fi world. Trust Manage. **4**, 32–47 (2010)
3. Viseau, A., Clement, A., Aspinall, J.: Situating privacy online: Complex perceptions and everyday practices. Inf. Commun. Soc. **7**, 92–114 (2004)
4. Wash, R.: Folk models of home computer security. In: Proceedings of the Sixth Symposium on Usable Privacy and Security, p. 1–16. ACM, Redmond (2010)
5. Asgharpour, P., Liu, D., Camp, L.J.: Mental models of computer security risks. In: WOODSTOCK 1997, El Paso TX (1997)
6. Camp, L.J.: Mental models of privacy and security. SSRN (2006). http://ssrn.com/abstract=922735 or http://dx.doi.org/10.2139/ssrn.922735
7. Asgharpour, F., Liu, D., Camp, L.J.: Mental models of computer security risks. In: Work Shop on the Economics of Information Security (2007)
8. Sheehan, K.B.: Toward a typology of Internet users and online privacy concerns. Inf. Soc. **18**(1), 21–32 (2002)
9. Brandeis, L., Warren, S.: The right to privacy. Harvard Law Rev. **4**, 193 (1890)
10. Schoeman, F.: Philosophical Dimensions of Privacy. Cambridge Press, Cambridge (1984)
11. Hoffman, L.: Computers and Privacy in the Next Decade. Academic Press, New York (1980)
12. Furman, S., Theofanos, M.F., Choong, Y.Y., Stanton, B.: Basing cybersecurity training on user perceptions. IEEE Secur. Priv. **10**(2), 40–49 (2012)
13. Charmaz, K.: Constructing grounded theory: a practical guide through quantitative analysis. SAGE, Thousand Oaks (2006)
14. National Research Council: Toward better usability, security, and privacy of information technology. National Academies Press, Washington DC (2010)
15. Dourish, P., Grinter, R.E., de la Flor, J.D., Joseph, M.: Security in the wild: userstrategies for managing security as an everyday, practical problem. Pers. Ubiquit. Comput. **8**(6), 391–401 (2004)
16. Hruschka, D.J., Schwartz, D., John, D.C.S., Picone-Decaro, E., Jenkins, R.A., Carey, J.W.: Reliability in coding open-ended data: Lessons learned from HIV behavioral behavioral research. Field Methods **16**, 307–331 (2004)
17. Stokes, J.: Understanding Moore's Law. ars technica. Accessed on 09 Sep 2014, 27 Sep 2008
18. Schaller, B.: The Origin, Nature, and Implications of "Moore's Law". Research Microsoft.com. Accessed on 22 Aug 2011, (26 Sep 1996)
19. Hutton, D.: Lessons unlearnt: the (human) nature of disaster management, emergency management. In: Eksioglu, B. (ed.) Operations Management. InTech, Rijeka (2012). ISBN: 978-95307-989-9, doi:10.5772/35019. http://www.books/emergency-management/lessons-unlearnt-the-human-nature-of-disaster-management

Usable Trust: Grasping Trust Dynamics for Online Security as a Service

Shenja van der Graaf[1]([⊠]), Wim Vanobberghen[1], Michalis Kanakakis[2], and Costas Kalogiros[2]

[1] iMinds-SMIT Vrije Universiteit Brussel, Pleinlaan 9, 1050 Brussels, Belgium
shenja.vandergraaf@iminds.be, wim.vanobberghen@vub.ac.be
[2] AUEB, Athens, Greece
{kanakakis,ckalog}@aueb.gr

Abstract. This paper aims to unravel the intricacies of the mechanisms of trust vis-à-vis ICTs and the contextual logic guiding user deployment and experience, necessitating a view of trust in the digital realm as a dynamic process. Trust models tend to highlight 'well-placed trust' in their focus on drawing out (sub)components of (perceived) trustworthiness as attributes of the trusted system or party from the trustor's stance. However, less attention has been given to the trustworthy attributes, or behavior of the trusted actor. Therefore, this paper sets out to explore this linkage between ICTs and different trust-related user experiences guided by different sets of trustor attributes. In order to explore the conceptual dynamics, a two-step approach is deployed. On the basis of empirical data attention is drawn to trust levels and user segments. Preliminary insights are yielded into the trustors' segmentation validity and trust estimation accuracy by performing a small-scale experiment in the context of a fictitious online security service.

Keywords: Design · ICT · Trust drivers · Segmentation · Trustor attributes · Security

1 Introduction

Understanding why people trust and how that trust shapes social relations, has been a central interest in various scholarly domains. Social conceptualizations of trust tend to be associated with terms such as honesty, integrity and reliability; or, the extent people have 'faith in others'. Long-standing academic traditions have aimed to provide insights into various aspects underpinning the conceptualization and nature of trust – e.g., as the foundation for interpersonal relationships and cooperation, and as the basis for stability in social institutions and markets. However, robust and systematic results into who and why people trust cannot be easily distilled (cf. 'conceptual confusion' [1]. Looking at conceptualizations of trust, among others, psychologists have stressed the role of personality, economists highlighted rational choice, and sociologists have focused on social structures. Consistent trust typologies accompanied by a set of trust constructs are, therefore, not evident.

© Springer International Publishing Switzerland 2015
T. Tryfonas and I. Askoxylakis (Eds.): HAS 2015, LNCS 9190, pp. 271–283, 2015.
DOI: 10.1007/978-3-319-20376-8_25

Moreover, investigation into trust aspects in the context of Information and Communication Technologies (ICTs) which are considered to be an important factor in the adoption of new technical solutions, is arguably, even less consistent. The reason for this is that although trust research has received sufficient attention, studies tend to readily assume that trust is intrinsically beneficial dismissing dependencies such as the context or situation at a given moment in time [2]. Therefore, in order to better understand people and their trust perceptions and appetite towards digital technologies, particularly, Internet-based applications and platforms, this exploratory paper sets out to yield insight into the dynamics of trust and trustworthiness. It will draw particular attention to trust conceptualizations associated with well-placed trust and user attributes.

In its approach, the paper aims to unravel the intricacies of the mechanisms of trust vis-à-vis ICTs and the contextual logic guiding deployment and the user experience, necessitating a view of trust in the digital realm as a dynamic process. Renewed attention is needed to make the networked conditions apparent that underpin user practices, together with a reassessment of the dynamic and open-ended flow of experiences that guides these practices. In other words, the parameters of the 'fabric of trust' are approached as embedded (user-centric and networked-centric) relationships underpinning a usable and secure ICT design process (cf. [3]). The reason for this is that trust in ICTs such as the Internet and Internet-based applications can be seen to erode. While in the early days, trust was one of the drivers that led to a self-reinforcing cycle of (largely beneficial) socio-economic activity facilitating distribution, sharing and collaboration, the situation is different today. Concerns and reduced trust in sensitive data and assets being treated properly can be detected (globally) such as increased criminal activity is affecting more citizens; business models are becoming less transparent, including 'hidden' business roles such as information aggregators and brokers, profilers and networks; an increasing asymmetry of information and control between users and businesses and governments exists; and, privacy is increasingly difficult to maintain, thanks to social networks, super-cookies, location-sensitive services, data aggregation and profiling, and so forth.

In this context, studies have shown that if users trust the ICT system too much (i.e. assume it is more trustworthy than is actually the case), they are exposing themselves to risks and may suffer harm which can also reduce their level of trust in any system in the future. If users trust the system too little (i.e. assume it is less trustworthy than is actually the case), they are failing to benefit from using the system in high-value applications. While such an imbalance - between the level of trust and the level of trustworthiness of services and applications – needs to be tackled and, at minimum, reduced usability issues (that underpin trust related decisions) tend to be overlooked or do not go easily hand-in-hand with trust attributes [2].

Against this backdrop, we give a high-level description for analyzing and understanding the current/experienced trust level of individual users towards online ICT systems and results from a small-scale experiment in the context of Distributed Attack Detection and Visualization (DADV). Our aim is to capture the aforementioned aspects and to reflect on appearing trust tendencies. In doing so, our study adopts a two-step approach deploying survey research to deliver evidence-based conclusions.

2   In ICTs We Trust...

ICTs such as the Internet are said to have historically coevolved with the public who uses them, as well as with the larger economy of inscription. Put aptly by [4], who has provided ample evidence about media and ICT more broadly, they can be defined "as socially realized structures of communication, where structures include both techno-logical forms and their associated protocols, and where communication is a cultural practice, a ritualized collocation of different people on the same mental map, sharing or engaged with popular ontologies of representation" (2006:7). In its ability to connect people across time and space, the power of online (often referred to by Web 2.0 [5]) is rooted in facilitating a range of easily accessible and scalable channels through which interactions can occur. It includes systems that support one-to-one, one-to-many, and many-to-many interactions. Many of these kinds of interactions opened up a myriad of new possibilities for online connections, supporting the generation of 'digital spaces' for people to gather, participate and create, and users to form (e.g. performative inno-vation, networked publics).

Designing for trust in mediated spaces and interactions has, therefore, become under renewed scrutiny. Understanding the development, maintenance, and enhancement of online trust is of great importance to those involved in the successful design and imple-mentation of digital applications and services. The reason for this is the general belief that trust is central to adoption [6]. Much attention has been given to related elements such as maximizing perceived trustworthiness in e-government services [7] and e-commerce [8], trust cultures [9], and communicating trustworthiness in designing Web sites [10].

In the huge volume of trust research that is available, we have sought to focus on several studies that recognized the need for models of trust and credibility in technology-mediated interactions, particularly, those that aimed to be not-domain specific and tech-nology-independent [1, 2, 7]. These models can be said to offer guidance for researchers across disciplines examining a range of technologies and contexts, thereby highlighting multiple subcomponents, arguably, associated with antecedents (i.e. preconditions of trust), processes of trust building (e.g., interdependence), the context of shaping trust-building (e.g., social relations, regulation), decision-making processes in trust (e.g., rational choice, routine, habitual), implications and uses of trust (e.g., interpersonal entrepreneurial relations, moralistic trust), and lack of trust, distrust, mistrust and repair (e.g., risks, over-trust, trust violations) [11, 12, 14].

What trust models tend to have in common are a categorization by trust referent, and which typically tend to be the characteristics of the trustee (e.g. morality, caring, honesty, willingness to be vulnerable to another). In other words, such models have tended to highlight 'well-placed trust' in their focus on drawing out (sub)components of (perceived) trustworthiness as attributes of the trusted system or party from the trustor's stance, while less attention has been given to the trustworthy attributes, or behavior of the trusted actor [2, 13]. Therefore, we have sought to explore this linkage between ICTs and different trust-related user experiences guided by different sets of trustor attributes.

3 Two-Step Approach

In order to explore the conceptual dynamics underpinning trust-related user experiences and sets of trustor attributes, a two-step approach was deployed. The first step consisted of survey and interview research where respondents were derived from members of the public, the business community, and governmental institutions (February and March 2013, n = 203). Based on a thorough literature review focusing on generic trust models in the design of ICTs supporting (mediated) transactions, the exploratory survey was developed to draw out several key aspects associated with trust in this context. In particular, antecedents, processes of trust building, the context of shaping trust-building, decision-making processes in trust, implications and uses of trust, and lack of trust, distrust, mistrust and repair [1, 2, 7, 11, 15].[1] The purpose was to learn about the combined underpinnings of relevant trust drivers independent from specific technologies and domains. While the first step served mainly to learn about combined constructs in trust-related experiences and attributes, the second step was to conduct a 'segment-specific' analysis so as to learn about different types of subjective trust-related user experiences and attributes in this context. Examining the results of the (end user) survey (n = 90) linkages between different sets of trustor attributes could be associated with trust-related concepts of (1) *Trust stance*: the tendency of people to trust other people across a wide range of situations and persons; (2) *Trust beliefs* in general professionals; (3) *Institution-based trust*; (4) *General trust* sense levels in online applications and services; (5) *ICT-domain specific* sense of trust levels; (6) *Trust-related seeking behavior*; (7) *Trust-related competences*; and, (8) *Perceived importance of trustworthiness design elements*. And, which underpin the segmentation of trust-related user experiences on trustor attributes, thereby, arguably, supporting the estimation of a user's trust level of the ICT system.

4 Results

4.1 Analyzing Trust Levels

It is our aim to assess the relative importance of the trust-related concepts from the literature towards predicting the actual trust in (a set of) online technologies/services, that is, online stores, social networks, professional online networks, online governmental services, online banking, online health services, and online review sites. These trust levels should be considered as general and a priori trust levels towards a particular set of technologies/services, hence, not towards any specific application or on the basis of a concrete experience.[2] We performed the following analysis and present briefly their results.

---

[1] These constructs were operationalized with using five-point rating scales open questions, checklist questions, and ranking questions.

[2] For instance, we asked in general about trust in online stores and not specifically about trust in individual stores such as Amazon. Users without first hand experience could leave the question unanswered; hence they were not forced to express their opinion.

First, the average trust level vis-à-vis several online technologies was explored. Roughly, we can define three clusters of online technologies based on these trust levels: (1) a cluster containing online banking, online governmental services and online stores with high range trust levels and substantial differences in levels of trust between these three technologies; (2) a cluster with midrange levels of trust containing professional online networks and online health services; and, (3) a cluster with somewhat lower trust level containing social network sites and review sites.

Next, pairwise T-tests were conducted to investigate differences in trust level scores between the various online technologies (see Table 1). These results indicate that a few exceptions, notwithstanding average trust levels, do differ significantly when comparing the various online technologies, and which indicates that various set of technologies are not trusted equally.

Table 1. Pairwised t-tests on trust levels

	Mean 1	Mean 2	Std. Dev. 1	Std. Dev. 2	N	t	Sig. (2-tailed)
Online stores - Social networks	2.09	2.68	.690	1.061	127	-6.436	.000***
Online stores - Professional online networks	2.09	2.31	.678	.916	123	-2.575	.011*
Online stores - Online governmental services	2.10	1.88	.671	.816	129	3.009	.003**
Online stores - Online banking	2.08	1.72	.678	.835	130	5.132	.000***
Online stores - Online health services	2.12	2.40	.671	1.137	100	-2.480	.015*
Online stores - Online review sites	2.13	2.75	.667	.734	122	-7.363	.000***
Social networks - Professional online networks	2.69	2.32	1.049	.933	121	4.781	.000***
Social networks - Online governmental services	2.71	1.90	1.074	.828	126	7.996	.000***
Social networks - Online banking	2.70	1.72	1.083	.845	126	9.843	.000***
Social networks - Online health services	2.64	2.38	1.030	1.144	100	1.922	.058
Social networks - Online review sites	2.76	2.76	1.063	.736	119	.081	.936
Professional online networks - Online governmental services	2.32	1.88	.926	.795	123	5.598	.000***
Professional online networks - Online banking	2.34	1.70	.924	.789	122	6.566	.000***
Professional online networks - Online health services	2.35	2.40	.962	1.142	99	-.449	.654
Professional online networks - Online review sites	2.38	2.72	.905	.738	118	-3.660	.000***
Online governmental services - Online banking	1.91	1.73	.818	.837	128	2.234	.027*
Online governmental services - Online health services	1.92	2.38	.837	1.144	100	-4.912	.000***
Online governmental services - Online review sites	1.91	2.74	.793	.736	122	-8.122	.000***
Online banking - Online health services	1.68	2.40	.750	1.137	100	-6.888	.000***
Online banking - Online review sites	1.76	2.75	.844	.734	122	-10.648	.000***
Online health services - Online review sites	2.42	2.73	1.139	.754	98	-2.400	.018*

*= sig.on .05 level, **= sig. on .01 level and ***=sig. on .001 level

Furthermore, in order to investigate the transferability of trust over the various technology domains, a correlation analysis was conducted (see Table 2).

Table 2. Trust levels correlations matrix

Correlations Matrix						
	Online stores	Social networks	Professional	Online governmental	Online banking	Online health
Online stores	1					
Social networks	.364**	1				
Professional online networks	.325**	.649**	1			
Online governmental services	.407**	.308**	.498**	1		
Online banking	.476**	.354**	.239**	.447**	1	
Online health services	.307**	.229*	.445**	.591**	.447**	1
Online review sites	.136	.251**	.263**	-.083	.169	.095
** Correlation is significant at the 0.01 level (2-tailed).						
* Correlation is significant at the 0.05 level (2-tailed).						

The results indicate that all correlations are positive. This suggests that higher trust levels for one type of online technology seem to go hand-in-hand with higher trust levels for other types and which is a prerequisite for trust being transferable. In terms of strength of the correlations, we observe a high number of high strength/significant correlations between different trust domains. In particular, social and professional network sites do correlate rather high (r = .649) and as such seems to be distinct from online governmental services, online banking, online health services. Online review sites do correlate moderately with social and professional network sites while seemingly being uncorrelated to the other technologies. From these exploratory findings, we may carefully assume that although a couple of technologies seem distinct from others, trust is - to a certain extent - transferable from one particular technology/service to another.

Next, we looked into what trust-related concepts can be predictive towards these trust levels. In order to assess the internal validity of various scales, factor-analyses were conducted for each of the trust concepts measured on a scale level. Based on these results following trust constructs proofed to show sufficient to excellent internal validity to construct scales: Trust stance (2 item scale, α = .79); Structural assurance (3 tem scale, α = .66); Trust related seeking behavior (5 item scale, α = .86); and, Trust related competences (4 item scale, α = .88).

The results highlight that trust levels vary over different technologies/services. For example, significant predictors for online banking services includes trust stance (β = .291), the design elements 'works well technically' (β = .231) and 'displays seals of approval (β = .239) and trust related seeking behavior (β = −.256). The regression model for online banking has on explained variance of 21,2 %. These results indicate the importance for online banking services to work well technically and to display seals of approval. Trust related seeking behavior can also be seen in this context as an indication of low trust. Finally, a high predisposition to trust (trust stance) helps in building trust towards online banking services.

Diverging sets of trust drivers can be identified for each type of digital technology/ service, suggesting the need for a more tailored approach when designing trustworthy applications. However, despite these differences some clear patterns and communalities over the different sets of technologies could be identified. For example, the results suggest that for online technologies, such as governmental services and online banking (that emanate from the public sector or from private sectors where there is a rather strong regulation in place and people also have a strong physical interaction with) trust stance,[3] is the driving factor.

If the main interactions with technologies are of a public nature, and tend to occur in the online realm and depending on the goodwill of the other party or other people in the community (such as online stores, social networks and online review sites), structural assurance,[4] seems to be the driving factor. In only a few cases, displaying a seal of approval is crucial to elicit trust (particularly, for online health services). Other design elements like 'works well technically' and 'easiness to use' seem in certain contexts to facilitate eliciting trust. Furthermore, previously experienced harms can impact trust substantially. Interestingly, it is not so much the type of harm (bullying, fraud etc.) as it is the context (for instance, health-related) wherein the harms are experienced that is predictive towards future trust. As trust is to a certain extent transferable towards other

---

[3] Or, or the general tendency people have trust in others.

[4] Or, the belief that someone thinks that structures such as regulation and safeguards exist that are important to successfully complete an action.

domains (such as from health to online stores), impactful harms experienced in one domain may significantly lower trust levels over several other domains. Health is a domain wherein harms are likely to be experienced as impactful.

4.2 Analyzing User Segments

For segmentation purposes, a K-means clustering was performed and an Anova analysis was conducted to test for each item whether statistical significance differences could be retrieved between the uncovered trust-related user experience segments. Some iterative clustering and testing led us to a four segments solution to best explain differences in trust-related user experiences. These segments can be represented by the following terms: High trust (HT), Ambivalent (A) trust, Highly active trust seeking (HATS) and Medium active trust seeking (MATS). They differ on a number of aspects (see below), however, based on our analyses, three major concepts are sufficient to explain their core differences. The three underpinning concepts are 'trust stance' (e.g., 'I usually trust a person until there is a reason not to'), 'motivation to engage in trust-related seeking behavior' (e.g., 'I look for guarantees regarding confidentiality of the information that I provide') and 'trust-related competences' (e.g., 'I'm able to understand my rights and duties as described by the terms of the application provider'). They could be measured on 3, 7 and 4 item-scale with a reliability coefficient of .69, .89 and .87 respectively (Table 3).

Table 3. Segmentation results for the three underpinning concepts

	Total (n = 90)	HT (n = 24)	HATS (n = 28)	MATS (n = 18)	A (n = 20)	Anova	
	Mean	Mean	Mean	Mean	Mean	F	Sig.
Trust stance	3,22	3,85	3,15	2,86	3,50	7,260	,000
Trust related seeking behaviour	3,52	3,14	4,27	3,34	3,01	4,383	,000
Trust related competences	2,44	2,71	2,42	2,94	1,44	2,361	,000

The user experience for each of the segments can be characterized as follows:

- The "HT" segment shows a high level trust stance. This means an overall high trust level for the various online applications (e.g. social networks and online banking), accompanied by only few trust seeking behaviors (e.g. checking trust seals), even though the competences are present to cognitively assess the trustworthiness of online applications and services;
- The "HATS" segment displays a high level of trust seeking beyond the mere scanning of trustworthiness cues. It also suggests that individuals are informed about procedures in case of harms and misuse. It points to the capacity of certain competence level that facilitate the assessment of trustworthiness and to the possession, at least, of a minimal understanding of the rules and procedures to look for in case of complaints and misuse. Varied trust stance and trust levels could be observed, including medium to low stance/trust levels;

- The "MATS" segment displays similar characteristics as the 'High Active'. The difference is that the trust seeking behavior is not so apparent. Although drivers for trust seeking behavior (e.g. a low trust stance) and competences to assess trustworthiness can be observed, people's motivation may not be absent to look for trustworthiness cues.
- The "A" trust segment seems to highlight a clear perceived inability to assess the trustworthiness of online applications and services and which may be explained by the personal competence level. Hence, only few active trust seeking behaviors can be observed, yet do not equal low trust levels per se. Trust seems to be derived from either the general trust stance or basic heuristics, such as 'public organizations are more trustworthy than commercial companies'. The "Ambivalent" nature of this user experience might be explained by a failure to cognitively assess the trustworthiness and a certain need to trust in order to avoid, or to lower the omnipresence of cautious and other negative feelings, and which is a so-called 'forced trust' (that is, trust without trustworthiness evidence and with a possible presence of cautious feelings). These findings point to understanding trustworthiness indicators based on the experience of others (referrals), as the main source of 'trustworthiness information' that is accessible for this cluster, and underlying the outcome of the trustworthiness assessment.

The user experience for the "HT" segment can be characterized by a high level trust stance. This means an overall high trust level for the various online applications, such as social networks and online banking, accompanied by only few trust seeking behaviors, such as checking trust seals, even though the competences are present to cognitively assess the trustworthiness of online applications and services.

For the "HATS" segment, the user experience can be highlighted in terms of a high level of trust seeking behavior beyond the mere scanning of trustworthiness cues. It also suggests that individuals are informed about procedures in case of harms and misuse. It points to the capacity of certain competence level that facilitate the assessment of trustworthiness and to possess, at least, a minimal understanding of the rules and procedures to look for in case of complaints and misuse. Varied trust stance and trust levels could be observed including medium to low trust stance/trust levels.

For the "MATS" segment, the user experience is similar to the "Highly active" one, yet, here, trust seeking behavior is not so apparent. Thus, while drivers for trust seeking behavior, such as a low trust stance, are present as well as competences to assess trustworthiness, people's motivation may be absent to look for trustworthiness cues.

The "A" trust segment seems to highlight a clear perceived inability to assess the trustworthiness of online applications and services and which may be explained by the personal competence level. Hence, only few active trust seeking behaviors can be observed, yet do not equal low trust levels per se. Trust seems to be derived from either the general trust stance or basic heuristics, such as 'public organizations are more trustworthy than commercial companies'. It seems that the "Ambivalent" nature of this user experience can be explained by a failure to cognitively assess the trustworthiness and a certain need to trust in order to avoid, or to lower the omnipresence of cautious and other negative feelings, and which is a so-called 'forced trust' (that is, trust without trustworthiness evidence and with a possible presence of cautious feelings). These findings point to understanding trustworthiness indicators based on the experience of others (referrals), as the main source of 'trustworthiness information' that is accessible for this cluster, and underlying the outcome of the trustworthiness assessment.

By segmenting trust user experiences we are able to pinpoint different sets of trust drivers, competences, attitudes and behaviors. This suggests that (computational) trust models may benefit from including trustor's attributes as model parameters. In this view, and as a next step, we can envision that a user without previous first-hand experience with any system, completes a short intake questionnaire before interacting with the system. That intake questionnaire could serve to (1) to assign a particular user to any of the four clusters of trust related user experiences, and (2) to help initiate and, at a later stage, validate the model by calculating initial trust values.

In the next section, therefore, we outline some preliminary findings of a small-scale experiment of a Distributed Attack Detection and Visualization (DADV) system.

4.3   Validating Results

In order to indicate how different sets of trustor's attributes (trust stance, motivation to engage in trust seeking behavior and competences) may relate or impact different model parameters during a trust estimation phase, an experiment was conducted in October 2014. Participants were asked to test and evaluate an online security service of a fictitious provider providing a service, called DADV, to detect virtual attacks on devices connected to the Internet, such as personal computers. The experiment was performed for two versions of the online service; on the one hand, a service where administrators are responsible for detecting and mitigating attacks, on the other hands, an automated service where all tasks are performed by sophisticated tools (Table 4)

Table 4. Segmentation results for experiment participants (n = 27)

	Total (n = 27)	HT (n = 5)	HATS (n = 4)	MATS (n = 10)	A (n = 8)	Anova	
	Mean	Mean	Mean	Mean	Mean	F	Sig.
Trust stance	2,65	3,40	2,63	2,30	2,63	4,519	,012
Trust related seeking behaviour	2,16	2,06	2,82	1,89	2,25	6,879	,002
Trust related competences	3,53	3,80	4,13	3.58	3.58	3,067	,048

In order to assess whether the four segmentation solution could be deployed, additional empirical research was carried out. For this purpose the survey was dispersed using several Living Lab panels in September 2014 (n = 89). The same analytical steps were followed as above. While some minor variations between the two exploratory analyses could be detected, the dominant drivers that seem to characterize users in each segment appear to be relatively constant. Thus, the findings seem to correspond to the previous ones indicating that the three underpinning users' attributes appear as statistically significant difference. More specifically, we observe that the combined aggregate factor of 'competences' and 'seeking behavior' is again higher for the HATS segment. This finding justifies our approach to correlate higher values of this factor with a more accurate estimation. Furthermore, it is confirmed that a high level of 'trust stance' results to trustworthiness overestimation (misplaced trust) and vice versa (presence of over-cautious users). From those who filled out the intake survey, 27 individuals participated in the second phase of the evaluation (the actual experiment). And which took place on two consecutive days (separate Vanilla and OPTET TTM evaluations), lasting for about 90 min on October 8 and 9, 2014.

In order to validate the trust initialization participants were asked to report their initial trust towards the system before having any other evidence for its performance. To do so, each participant engaged with the DADV system, separately for each version during two different days, starting with the administrated and then with the automated one. After logging in to the online website (and before any attack was performed), they were given the opportunity to access the 'about page' and familiarize themselves with the activated version. This webpage provided general information of the system function-ality and a high-level description of its expected trustworthiness. Furthermore, users who had noticed and clicked on a distinguishable hyperlink were redirected to a more detailed webpage, which explicitly mentioned each system's actual trustworthiness in terms of the metric under interest. In this way we could validate the effects of 'seeking motivation' on the initial trust level of each segment (Figs. 1 and 2).

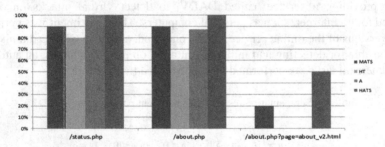

Fig. 1. Percentage of users in cluster that visited the webpages of the administrated DADV at least once. MATS depicts medium-active trust seeking, HT depicts High Trust, A depicts Ambivalent, and HATS depicts highly-active trust seeking.

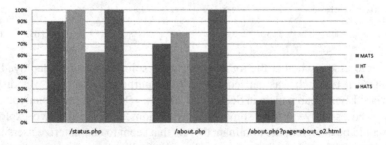

Fig. 2. Percentage of users in cluster that visited the webpages of the automated-enabled DADV at least once.

Afterwards, they observed the service performance for a sequence of 10 attacks that were identical for both DADV cases. During each attack, they could navigate to the 'health statistics page', which was providing a holistic view of the system status. At the end of each attack a message was appearing indicating whether the provider succeeded in preventing any network host from being attacked, or not. These pop-up messages also contained a link to a questionnaire where users were asked to indicate their current trust level that the provider would prevent future attacks from compromised honeypots to their computers.

We observed that the segment HATS achieved the highest percentages in all six webpages of interest (we excluded the Home page because it has been loading and was periodically refreshed automatically). Furthermore, the 'A' segment achieved the lowest percentage in 5 out of 6 webpages. The other two segments had different behavior during the two days.

Table 5 depicts the trust level of the users after the first day of the experiment, where the administrated DADV succeeded in protecting the users' infrastructure 6 out of 10 times. We observed that some members of the HT segment were the only ones to feel extremely secure. Note that the HT mean value for the Trust stance concept in is the highest among all segments. In general, most participants of the other segments were either moderately or very secure.

Table 5. Answers to the Question "To what extent did you feel protected using the DADV service?" (Day 1) (N = 27).

	Slightly	Moderatedly	Very much	Extremely	Total
MATS	7.4 %	14.8 %	14.8 %	0 %	37 %
HT	0 %	3.7 %	11,1 %	3.7 %	18.5 %
A	3.7 %	18.5 %	7.4 %	0 %	29.6 %
HATS	0 %	7.4 %	7.4 %	0 %	14.8 %
Total	11 %	44 %	41 %	4 %	100 %

Table 6 presents the effect on users' trust of having more timely information about on-going attacks. Note that the only segment whose members would not prefer to receive such notifications is the 'A' one, which has the lowest mean value for the Trust-related competences concept. In general, most participants seem to perceive such a feature positively, in particular the Highly-active trust seeking ones who have the highest mean value for the Trust-related competences concept.

The participants were also asked to indicate the extension to which they felt protected using the DADV service. Note that for none of the following graphs significance tests could be performed as most cells had expected count less than 5, and which, as stated in D2.3 makes a large scale experiment rather valuable. Also, when asking the respondents about a possible change in trust level vis-à-vis receiving real-time alerts about attacks, some 45 % of the respondents indicated that it may likely change (m = 3.78, SE = .154, SD = .801). Lastly, the findings have shown that the respondents (N = 24) seemed to prefer the automated-enabled version (8.3 % preferred Day 1 versus 91.7 % that preferred Day 2, m = 1.92, SE = .058, SD = .282). When they were asked to justify their choice, most participants stated that automated-enabled version managed in preventing more compromised sensors from attacking their infrastructure than the administrated one.

Table 6. Answers to the Question "Would your level of trust in the service to protect your infrastructure change if you were to receive real-time alerts of attacks?" (Day 1) (N = 27).

	Slightly	Moderatedly	Very much	Extremely	Total
MATS	0 %	7.4 %	25,9 %	3.7 %	37 %
HT	0 %	14.8 %	3.7 %	0 %	18.5 %
A	3.7 %	7.4 %	7.4 %	11.1 %	29.6 %
HATS	0 %	3.7 %	7.4 %	3.7 %	14.8 %
Total	3.7 %	33.3 %	44.4 %	18.5 %	100 %

Finally, we noticed that a very accurate initial trust value for the HT and HATS segments could be estimated, while the relative error for the A and MATS segments is 10 % and 20 %, respectively. With regard to the trust dynamics, the (computational) models are aligned with the expected user reactions for most segments; namely trust should not decrease after a success and should not increase after a failure. The only exception is for the 'MATS' segment, which appears to constantly increase with the number of trials. This can be attributed to the error in estimating that particular initial value; in such cases the system may result in negative values for one or both update coefficients. We also observe a close estimate of the average trust of the HATS and Ambivalent segments, while for the rest segments the relative error is less than 15 %.

5   Conclusions

In this paper the conceptual dynamics underpinning trust-related user experiences and sets of trustor attributes have been explored. From the segmentation research presented, we conclude that our analysis seems valid and results to the capacity to steadily detect dominant drivers that affect the subjective nature of trust. Based on these findings we derived the expected users behavior, considering also the technical factors that determine system performance. To this end, trust was explicitly formulated as a function of both aforementioned aspects, while shaping the expected behaviors of each segment. However, we did not always manage to closely estimate the actual trust values. We observed that only a small subset of them is adequate so that to estimate trust with great accuracy, while also shaping the actual user's reactions.

Concerning our future work, we aim to perform a large scale experiment with respect to the number and profile of participants and the number of trials observed from each individual. We also aim to validate the user segmentation not only in terms of comparison with other related studies (as the methodology followed here), but also based on their actual attributes and behavior (e.g., pages visited, duration of visit). The reason for this is that there is always the possibility of users not being truthful when answering the questionnaire or competent enough to understand the questions, thereby highlighting and reflecting findings concerning the lifecycle of trust.

References

1. McKnight, H., Chervany, N.: Trust and distrust definitions: one bite at a time. In: Falcone, R., Singh, M., Tan, Y.H. (eds.) Trust in Cyber-Societies: Integrating the Human and Artificial Perspectives, pp. 27–54. Springer, Berlin (2001)
2. Riegelsberger, J., Sasse, M.A., McCarthy, J.D.: The mechanics of trust: a framework for research and design. Int. J. Hum. Comput. Stud. **62**(3), 381–422 (2005)
3. van der Graaf, S.: Imaginaries of ownership; the logic of participation in the moral economy of 3D software design. Telematics Inform. Spec. Issue Ethics Inf. Soc. **32**(2), 400–408 (2015). Elsevier
4. Gitelman, L.: Always Already New: Media, History and the Data of Culture. MIT Press, Cambridge (2006)
5. O'Reilly, T.: What is web 2.0. http://www.oreillynet.com/pub/a/oreilly/tim/news/2005/09/30/what-is-web-20.html (2005). Accessed 4 Sept 2014
6. Lacohée, H., Cofta, P., Phippen, A., Furnell, S.: Understanding Public Perceptions: Trust and Engagement in ICT-Mediated Services. International Engineering Consortium, Chicago (2008)
7. Tan, Y.-H., Thoen, W.: Toward a generic model of trust for electronic commerce. Int. J. Electron. Commer. **5**(2), 61–74 (2001)
8. Cheshire, C.: Online trust, trustworthiness, or assurance? Dædalus J. Am. Acad. Arts Sci. **4**, 49–58 (2011)
9. Karvonen, K., Cardholm, L., Karlsson, S.: Cultures of trust: a cross-cultural study on the formation of trust in an electronic environment. In: Proceedings of the Fifth Nordic Workshop on Secure IT Systems, NordSec (2000)
10. Nielsen, J. (n.d.): Trust or bust: communicating trustworthiness in web design. http://www.nngroup.com/articles/trust-or-bust-communicating-trustworthiness-in-web-design/. Accessed 15 Feb 2015
11. Lyon, F., Möllering, G., Saunders, M.N.K. (eds.): Handbook of Research Methods on Trust. Edward Elgar, Cheltenham (2012)
12. Li, F., Kowski, D.P., van Moorsel, A., Smith, C.: Holistic framework for trust in online transactions. Int. J. Manag. Rev. **14**, 85–103 (2012)
13. Möllering, G.: Trust: Reason, Routine, Reflexivity. Elsevier Ltd., Oxford (2006)
14. Sztompka, P.: Trust: A Sociological Theory. Cambridge University Press, Cambridge (1999)
15. Barbalet, J.N.: A characterization of trust, and its consequences. Theor. Soc. **38**(4), 367–382 (2009)

Privacy, Security and User Behaviour

Exploring the Adoption of Physical Security Controls in Smartphones

Nasser O. Alshammari[1,2(✉)], Alexios Mylonas[1,3], Mohamed Sedky[1],
Justin Champion[1], and Carolin Bauer[1]

[1] Staffordshire University, Beaconside, Stafford, ST18 0AD, UK
nasser.alshammari@research.staffs.ac.uk,
{alexios.mylonas,m.h.sedky,j.j.champion,c.i.bauer}@staffs.ac.uk,
nashamri@ju.edu.sa, amylonas@aueb.gr
[2] College of Information and Computer Science, Aljouf University, Sakaka Saudi Arabia
[3] Information Security and Critical Infrastructure Protection Research Laboratory,
Department of Informatics, Athens University of Economics and Business,
76 Patission Ave., GR10434 Athens, Greece

Abstract. The proliferation of smartphones has changed our life due to the enhanced connectivity, increased storage capacity and innovative functionality they offer. Their increased popularity has drawn the attention of attackers, thus, nowadays their users are exposed to many security and privacy threats. The fact that smartphones store significant data (e.g. personal, business, government, etc.) in combination with their mobility, increase the impact of unauthorized physical access to smartphones. However, past research has revealed that this is not clearly understood by smartphone users, as they disregard the available security controls. In this context, this paper explores the attitudes and perceptions towards security controls that protect smartphone user's data from unauthorized physical access. We conducted a survey to measure their adoption and the reasons behind users' selections. Our results, suggest that nowadays users are more concerned about their physical security, but still reveal that a considerable portion of our sample is prone to unauthorized physical access.

Keywords: User acceptance of security policies and technologies · Smartphone · Security control · Authentication · Anti-Theft · Biometrics

1 Introduction

Smartphones as multi-purpose and ubiquitous devices have managed to change the users' everyday life. Users carry smartphones throughout the day in different, and often insecure locations, accessing a plethora of heterogeneous data. Usually, the same device is used for both personal and business purposes [19, 22] thus smartphones store and/or have access to important data, which must be protected from unauthorized access.

At the same time, smartphone users tend to forget their devices in public places [5] and, as a study from Symantec suggests, device finders tend to try to access sensitive data that are stored in a lost device, e.g. personal data (e.g. social media accounts) and

© Springer International Publishing Switzerland 2015
T. Tryfonas and I. Askoxylakis (Eds.): HAS 2015, LNCS 9190, pp. 287–298, 2015.
DOI: 10.1007/978-3-319-20376-8_26

business data (e.g. corporate human resource files) [8]. As such, the risk of unauthorized physical access to user's data (in a permanent or temporal device loss) is significant, both for individuals and organizations. Moreover, nowadays the request for more security controls against device theft has been implemented by smartphone vendors reducing the number of device theft [4] and unauthorized access to smartphone data. However, this protection is rendered useless unless the respective security controls (such as encryption, remote wipe, etc.) are activated in the device.

In this context, we conducted a user survey in order to explore the attitudes and perceptions towards security controls that protect against unauthorized physical access to the device data (hereinafter referred to as unauthorized physical access). Our study focuses on Android and iOS, which currently hold 95 % of the smartphone market share [6]. Our results, suggest that nowadays users are more concerned about their physical security, but still reveal that a considerable portion of our sample is prone to unauthorized physical access.

The paper is organized as follows. Section 2 presents related work and Sect. 3 provides the methodology of our work. Section 4 presents our results. Finally, Sect. 5 includes a discussion of the results and concludes the paper.

2 Background

2.1 Adversary Model and Assumptions

In this work, we assume the following adversary model. The malicious attacker has gained temporary (i.e. the device owner has not had his device stolen or lost) or permanent access to the smartphone. We assume that the attacker has the knowledge, skills and hardware in order to access device data either with a logical or a physical acquisition. An attacker, however, can access user data remotely (e.g. malicious applications that violate user privacy [20]), but this falls outside the scope of this paper. Finally, we assume average users, i.e. not technically and security savvy ones.

2.2 Related Work

Smartphone users can authenticate and access their device with traditional passwords (PINs (Personal Identification Number) or alphanumeric strings). Unfortunately, users prefer usability, thus choosing memorable passwords that are easy to recall [12], but easy to recover with dictionary attacks [15]. The proliferation of smartphones made other authentication mechanisms popular, e.g. graphical passwords and biometrics (e.g. facial recognition, fingerprint reader).

Graphical passwords are vulnerable to 'traditional' password attacks (e.g. shoulder surfing [21, 25] and brute force attacks [13]), as well as attacks that are unique to graphical passwords due to traces and oily residues left on the screen (i.e. smudge attacks [9–11]. Andriotis et al. [9, 10] focused on human factors that might affect the choice of graphical passwords on a smartphone (such as sub-patterns and starting points), which in combination with smudge attacks can be used to infer the graphical passwords. Finally, in [23] the authors studied the effect of pattern layout on the strength of graphical passwords.

Biometrics as a means of authentication was introduced in the fourth version of Android, with the use of the smartphone's camera for face recognition. However, this security control is not popular, as it can be bypassed with a photograph of the device owner. Modern and more expensive smartphones offer fingerprint readers to provide user authentication to the device. Although, the use of this security control is convenient, it has already been proven to be vulnerable to various attacks [7].

Smartphone vendors have introduced several security controls against device theft to increase post-theft data control, such as Find My iPhone of iCloud and Android Device Manager (ADM) of Google Play. Other third party apps offer similar functionalities such as Prey, Theftie, Avast Anti-Theft and Norton Mobile Security.

All these anti-theft apps support locating a smartphone on a map, playing a sound on a smartphone to help finding it, locking and tracking a smartphone, as well as remotely wiping the data on a stolen or lost smartphone. Remote wiping mechanisms allow owners to remotely delete sensitive data by sending a wipe command to the lost devices through the Internet or SMS [24]. Although, the majority of these anti-theft apps require the smartphone to be online, Find My iPhone suspends all credit and debit cards in Passbook for Apple Pay immediately, even if the iPhone is offline. Some anti-theft apps allow the user to wipe confidential files by sending a special SMS, such as Avast Anti-Theft and Norton Mobile Security.

With iOS 7 (released Q3 of 2013) and later, Find My iPhone is activated by default and includes a feature called Activation Lock, which is turned on automatically. Activation Lock makes it harder for anyone to use or sell an iPhone if it is lost or stolen. This is true, as an Apple ID and password are required before anyone can turn off Find My iPhone, sign out of iCloud or erase and reactivate the smartphone. On the other side, Android Device Manager (released Q4 of 2013) is part of Google's system application suite for all Android devices (version 2.2 and newer). Unlike, other Android third-party applications, where permissions are granted manually by users during installation, ADM can be manually enabled via the user's Google account.

In the user study that was conducted in Q4 of 2011 [19] it was found that smartphone users in the UK and Greece do not use available security controls that can protect smartphone data from unauthorized physical access, namely device locking, remote device locator, encryption and remote data wipe. Moreover, the analysis in [18] revealed that even security savvy users did not protect their data from unauthorized physical access. Moreover, the authors in [16] also studied in Q4 of 2013 the adoption of device locking, as well as the reasons for (not) using this control. Also, their results suggest that less than half of the sample used device locking and that the participants underestimated the time that they spend to unlock their device.

Chin et al. [14] carried out a user study to gain insights into user perceptions of smartphone security, in Q4 of 2011 and Q1 of 2012. Their study shows that both Android and iPhone participants seem equally concerned about phone loss and damage. Kraus et al. [17] examined how privacy and security knowledge and global information privacy concern of a user, influence mobile protection behavior. They found that low knowledge and low global information privacy concern can serve as predictors for not using the protection methods, whereas high knowledge and high concern can serve as predictors for the usage of the evaluated protection methods.

3 Methodology

To explore the adoption of physical security controls in smartphones we conducted a survey with an online questionnaire. The survey took place from November 2014 to January 2015 and targeted smartphone users who are based in the United Kingdom. The questionnaire was distributed via word of mouth, social media, and groups and societies in West Midlands. Before launching the survey we completed a pilot survey in the lab with 6 participants in order to validate the questionnaire.

The survey starts by asking the participants demographic questions (c.f. Appendix). Then, users are asked whether they use a locking mechanism (e.g. password, biometric) in their device. According to their responses, the participants are asked for the reasons why they do so, as well as the type of locking mechanism that they use. Next, the sample is asked if they use a password for an individual application on their device and according to their responses, the reasons why they do so. The last part of the survey asks users whether they have had their device stolen. Also, the participants are asked whether they use any anti-theft mechanism (such as remote data wipe, remote device locator, encryption, etc., c.f. Appendix) and the reason for doing so. The questionnaire uses open ended questions to collect from the participants the reasons why they use a security control or not. The participants directly expressed their reasons either directly, e.g. "the control is not useful to me", or indirectly "to protect my stuff from people who want to snoop me".

We collected data from 208 survey participants. After the removal of participants who were not Android or iOS users and/or any incomplete questionnaires or data that failed our data validation, we ended up with 192 participants. Among them, 48 % used Android, ~65 % were male and 82 % were aged [18–35] ($min_{age} = 18$ $max_{age} = 67$). Regarding their IT skills the respondents classified themselves: (a) 11 % non-technically savvy ('moderate' IT), (b) 42 % with good IT skills, and (c) 47 % technically savvy ('excellent' IT). Finally, 17 % of the participants had their device stolen.

The next section presents our findings from descriptive and inferential statistics (χ^2 tests and φ coefficient). We compare our common results with the UK sample, which was collected in [19] and is referred to as *UK2011* sample. It is worth noting that compared to *UK2011* [19], the users have more options with regards to locking their devices, and the threat of unauthorized physical access is more well-known [4, 5, 8].

4 Results

4.1 Results Regarding Device Locking

An early finding in our analysis is that currently smartphone users, lock their device more frequently (76 %) than in the past (compared to the ~61 % in the UK sample in [19], c.f. Fig. 1). The results revealed that 40 % of the participants used application passwords, which is a considerable amount of participants if one considers that this is a third-party app that the user has to find and install on his own.

More specifically, the analysis revealed that 67 % of the Android participants and 84 % iOS participants lock their device. As summarized in Fig. 1, while PIN is the most

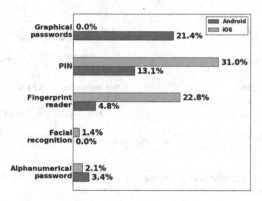

Fig. 1. Distribution of device lock mechanisms in Android and iOS users

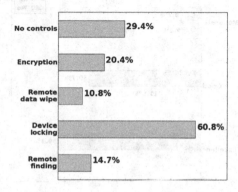

Fig. 2. Adoption of security controls by the *UK2011* sample in [19]

popular authentication mechanism in our sample, a considerable number of our participants used patterns and fingerprints for their authentication.

Our results suggest that in Android, patterns or graphical passwords are popular and user friendly alternatives to PINs, whereas fewer participants used fingerprint readers for their authentication and none used facial recognition (Fig. 1). On the other hand, the results suggest that iOS users opt for PIN and fingerprint readers. It is worth noting that, currently, fingerprint readers are only provided by expensive smartphones and, as a result, the popularity of this control might increase in the future, when the cost of the devices drops.

When the participants were asked about the reasons for using the abovementioned controls, they attributed security and privacy as the main reason (79 % of the sample) for using a particular device locking control. The rest of the reasons that were identified were: ease of use (41 %), organization policy (3 %) and default settings (8 %). Moreover, our results suggest that the participants who use the fingerprint reader, selected the control because of its ease of use ($\chi^2 = 16.452$, p = 0.00005, $\varphi = 0.337$). We did not find any statistically significant correlation between the rest of the reasons and device locking controls.

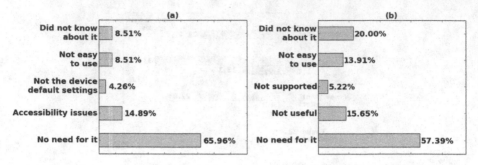

Fig. 3. (**a**) Reasons the participants do not use device locking (**b**) Reasons the participants do not use application password.

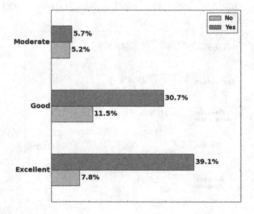

Fig. 4. Adoption of device lock versus the IT skills of the participants

Figure 3 depicts the reasons[1] the participants are not using the device locking and application passwords. In both cases the participants claimed that the security controls were not needed. In addition, as Fig. 3b suggests, currently a considerable amount of our participants are not aware of application passwords, which is somewhat expected as this control is only available as a third-party application.

Our analysis revealed that almost one third of the participants who had their device stolen (10 out of 32) did not lock their device, leaving their device and its data exposed to unauthorized access. Among them, 5 participants had both device locking and application passwords disabled.

Finally, as in [19] the analysis revealed that the IT skills of the participants affect the adoption of security controls. In this survey, as depicted in Fig. 4, the technical savvy participants tend to lock their device. However, we did not find such finding for application password.

---

[1] The reasons are self-explanatory, except for "Accessibility" that refers to any impairment that prevents the participant from using the control.

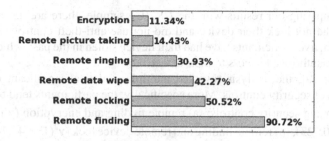

Fig. 5. Distribution of anti-theft security controls in the sample

4.2 Results Regarding Anti-theft Controls

The analysis revealed that 51 % of the sample used an anti-theft control. Our analysis suggests that remote finding the device was the security control that was mostly used by the participants, followed by remote locking and remote data wiping. Considerably less participants reported the use of encryption and remote picture taking. The afore-mentioned are summarized in Fig. 5. Also, the results reveal that the participants who use remote picture taking are more likely to be Android users ($\chi^2 = 8.402$, $p = 0.04$, $\varphi = 0.209$). We did not find any other statistically significant correlation between the adoption of the anti-theft controls and the participants' operating system, or their IT skills and the adoption of anti-theft controls.

It is worth noting that the analysis revealed the same misconception about encryption that was found in [19], stemming from the fact that in iOS the device is encrypted when the user enables device lock [3]. Specifically, in this work, we found 45 iOS participants who were using a PIN out of which 43 of them (96 %) reported that they are not using encryption. Similarly, 33 iOS survey participants used the fingerprint reader and 31 of them (94 %) did not know that they were using encryption.

When asked about the reasons of using anti-theft controls, again the majority of respondents identified security and privacy as their main reason (85 %), followed by default settings (11 %) and organization policy (4 %). Also, as Fig. 6 suggests, lack of knowledge about the existence of anti-theft controls was the main reason why the respondents ignored them.

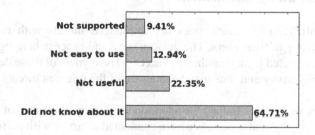

Fig. 6. Reasons the participants do not use ant-theft controls

When comparing our results with the *UK2011* sample, there are less participants (17 %) who did not lock their device and did not use anti-theft controls (c.f. Fig. 2). Amongst them, five participants have had their device stolen in the past, which increases their risk of unauthorized access to their device.

As in [18, 19], the analysis revealed multiple statistical significant correlations between pairs of security controls. More specifically, the participants tend to have disabled the following security controls: (a) remote finding and encryption ($\chi^2(1) = 9.550$, $p = 0.02$, $\varphi = 0.223$), (b) remote finding and remote device lock ($\chi^2(1) = 42.148$, $p < 001$, $\varphi = 0.469$), (c) remote ringing and remote locking ($\chi^2(1) = 62.520$, $p < 0.001$, $\varphi = 0.571$), (d) remote finding and remote picture taking ($\chi^2(1) = 17.847$, $p < 0.001$, $\varphi = 0.305$), (e) remote finding and remote wiping ($\chi^2(1) = 36.992$, $p < 0.001$, $\varphi = 0.439$), (f) remote wiping and remote locking ($\chi^2(1) = 62.273$, $p < 0.001$, $\varphi = 0.570$), (g) remote ringing and remote finding ($\chi^2(1) = 37.008$, $p < 0.001$, $\varphi = 0.439$), and (h) device ringing and device wiping ($\chi^2(1) = 57.202$, $p < 0.001$, $\varphi = 0.546$).

The analysis also revealed statistically significant correlations regarding the use of the controls, namely: (a) participants who encrypt their device are more likely to use remote device locator ($\chi^2(1) = 9.550$, $p = 0.02$, $\varphi = 0.223$), (b) participants who unlock their device with their fingerprint are more likely to use remote device locator ($\chi^2(1) = 7.476$, $p = 0.06$, $\varphi = 0.197$), (c) participants who enable remote locking tend to enable remote finding ($\chi^2(1) = 42.148$, $p < 001$, $\varphi = 0.469$), (d) participants tend to enable remote locking and remote ringing together ($\chi^2(1) = 62.520$, $p < 0.001$, $\varphi = 0.571$), (e) participants tend to enable remote locking and remote wiping together ($\chi^2(1) = 62.273$, $p < 0.001$, $\varphi = 0.570$), (f) participants who enable remote picture taking tend to enable remote finding ($\chi^2(1) = 17.847$, $p < 0.001$, $\varphi = 0.305$), (f) participants who enable remote wiping tend to use remote finding ($\chi^2(1) = 36.992$, $p < 0.001$, $\varphi = 0.439$), (g) participants who enable remote ringing tend use remote finding ($\chi^2(1) = 37.008$, $p < 0.001$, $\varphi = 0.439$), and (h) participants tend to enable device ringing and device wiping together ($\chi^2(1) = 57.202$, $p < 0.001$, $\varphi = 0.546$).

5   Discussion and Conclusions

The commercialization of smartphones has introduced threats with regards to the security and privacy of their users. The devices store and process heterogeneous data, which must be protected from unauthorized access. The owners of these devices are not necessary security savvy and thus may be unaware of the relevant threats and countermeasures.

In this paper, we have examined the adoption of security controls that protect users from unauthorized physical access. We have conducted a survey with participants from the United Kingdom in order to explore the use of security controls, as well as the reasons for (not) using device locking (such as PINs, graphical passwords, and fingerprint readers) and anti-theft controls (such as remote wipe and remote finding the device, etc.). Our findings suggest that, compared to surveys that preceded ours [16, 18, 19], smartphone users tend to use the available controls more frequently, which is particularly true for device locking controls.

One of the reasons for this is that nowadays smartphones offer controls that are easier to use, which - as our results suggest - gradually replace PINs and passwords (e.g. graphical passwords in Android and fingerprint readers in iOS). Another reason is that users have been trained to authenticate with passwords, e.g. before they access their computer/laptop or online services (e.g. social media) and, as a result, they are aware about device unlocking. However, as our results suggest, this does not hold for application passwords and the anti-theft controls, since a main reason behind not using these controls is users' unawareness of their existence.

The demographics of our sample introduce limitations to our work. Thus, it might be the case, that our findings are biased towards the demographics of our sample. Moreover, our survey used an online questionnaire, thus, it relies on self-reported data. However, we consider that our results give considerable insights regarding the attitudes and perceptions towards physical security controls. This holds true, as our results are validated from the common security findings of the most recent related survey [16], which studied the use of device locking and the reasons for (not) using this control. More specifically, in [16] participants also attributed security and privacy as the main reason for using the security control. Similarly to our results, the main reason for not using device locking was user perception that the control is not needed.

PIN is still the most popular device locking control as it has been revealed in this work, as well as in [16, 19]. However, in our work we found that other controls are getting more popular, such as the graphical passwords and the fingerprint readers. We consider that the latter will gain more popularity in the near future as the cost of the devices that are offering them decreases. This holds true, as we found that the participants who were using fingerprint readers identified ease of use as a reason for its selection. The fingerprint reader seamlessly authenticates the user and does not interrupt her from fulfilling tasks, especially when a task might last less time than the authentication attempt (e.g. in the case that the user needs to check the calendar and has to first enter a PIN/ password). This is an important factor if one considers the amount of time that users spend in order to unlock into their devices [16].

Our results, as in [18, 19] reveal occasions in which users disable or enable together the controls that allow the user to remotely control her device (e.g. lock it, wipe it, find it, etc.). One obvious reason for this is that they are managed by the same software/ configuration interface. Finally, as in [18, 19], this work revealed iOS users who had encryption enabled by default without knowing it. This is a security feature that could be adopted by Android to protect its user base, especially if one consider the low adoption of encryption by Android respondents.

As future work, we plan to repeat this user survey to examine if the attitudes and perceptions of smartphone users with regards to physical security controls will significantly change.

Acknowledgement. Nasser O. Alshammari receives funding from the Ministry of Education in Saudi Arabia.

Appendix

Questionnaire

Q1: What is your gender? *Only one choice of* {Male, Female}

Q2: What is your age? *(Open-ended question)*

Q3: How good are you with computers in general? *Only one choice of* {Excellent, Good, Moderate}

Q4: What is your smartphone operating system? *Only one choice of* {Android, Apple iOS, Windows Phone, Blackberry, I do not know, Other}

Q5: Do you use a mechanism on your smartphone to lock/protect it? *Only one choice of* {Yes, No}

Q5a: What type of locking mechanism do you use on your smartphone? *(Only shown if Q5 answer is "Yes", Multiple choices of* {Numerical password (PIN), Alphanumerical password (characters and/or numbers), Graphical password (patterns), Fingerprint readers, Facial recognition, Other}

Q5b: Why do you use this locking mechanism? *(Only shown if Q5 answer is "Yes")* *(Open-ended question)*

Q5c: Why you chose not to use a locking mechanism? *(Only shown if Q5 answer is "No") (Open-ended question)*

Q6: Do you use passwords for individual applications on your smartphone? *Only one choice of* {Yes, No}

Q6a: Why you use a password for applications on your smartphone? *(Only shown if Q6 answer is "Yes") (Open-ended question)*

Q6b: Why you chose not to use a password for applications on your smartphone? *(Only shown if Q6 answer is "No") (Open-ended question)*

Q7: Have you ever had your smartphone stolen? *Only one choice of* {Yes, No}

Q8: Do you use any anti-theft mechanisms on your smartphone? *Only one choice of* {Yes, No}

Q8a: What type of anti-theft mechanisms do you have? *(Only shown if Q8 answer is "Yes", Multiple choices of* {Remotely wipe data, Remotely find the device location, File encryption, Remotely take pictures using the smartphone camera, Remotely lock the smartphone, Remotely ring the smartphone, Other}

Q8b: Why you do have anti-theft mechanisms? *(Only shown if Q8 answer is "Yes") (Open-ended question)*

Q8c: Why you chose not to have anti-theft mechanisms? *(Only shown if Q8 answer is "No") (Open-ended question).*

References

1. App Lock. http://www.domobile.com
2. iApp Lock. http://iapplock.thinkyeah.com/
3. Apple: iOS Security Guide. Technical report, October 2014
4. London Smartphone Theft Drops. http://www.theguardian.com/technology/2015/feb/11/london-smartphone-theft-drops-after-kill-switch-introduction-iphones/

5. Phone Theft In America. https://www.lookout.com/resources/reports/phone-theft-in-america/
6. Sales of Smartphones Grew 20 Percent in Third Quarter of 2014. http://www.gartner.com/newsroom/id/2944819
7. Spoofing Fingerprints. https://srlabs.de/spoofing-fingerprints
8. Symantec Smartphone Honey Stick Project. http://www.symantec.com/connect/blogs/introducing-symantec-smartphone-honey-stick-project
9. Andriotis, P., Tryfonas, T., Oikonomou, G.: Complexity metrics and user strength perceptions of the pattern-lock graphical authentication method. In: Tryfonas, T., Askoxylakis, I. (eds.) HAS 2014. LNCS, vol. 8533, pp. 115–126. Springer, Heidelberg (2014)
10. Andriotis, P., Tryfonas, T., Oikonomou, G., Yildiz, C.: A pilot study on the security of pattern screen-lock methods and soft side channel attacks. In: Proceedings of the Sixth ACM Conference on Security and Privacy in Wireless and Mobile Networks - WiSec 2013, Association for Computing Machinery, pp. 1–6. ACM, New York (2013)
11. Aviv, A.J., Gibson, K., Mossop, E., Blaze, M., Smith, J.M.: Smudge attacks on smartphone touch screens. WOOT **10**, 1–7 (2010)
12. Bonneau, J.: The science of guessing: analyzing an anonymized corpus of 70 millionpasswords. In: 2012 IEEE Symposium on Security and Privacy, pp. 538–552. Instituteof Electrical & Electronics Engineers (IEEE) (2012). http://ieeexplore.ieee.org/xpls/abs_all.jsp?arnumber=6234435
13. Botelho, B.A.P., Nakamura, E.T., Uto, N.: Implementation of tools for brute forcing touch inputted passwords. In: 2012 International Conference for Internet Technology and Secured Transactions, pp. 807–808. IEEE, New Yok (2012)
14. Chin, E., Felt, A.P., Sekar, V., Wagner, D.: Measuring user confidence in smartphone security and privacy. In: Proceedings of the Eighth Symposium on Usable Privacy and Security - SOUPS 2012. Association for Computing Machinery (ACM), New York (2012)
15. Ding, Y., Horster, P.: Undetectable on-line password guessing attacks. SIGOPS Oper. Syst. Rev. **29**(4), 77–86 (1995)
16. Harbach, M., von Zezschwitz, E., Fichtner, A., De Luca, A., Smith, M.: It's a hard lock life: a field study of smartphone (un) locking behavior and risk perception. In: Symposium on Usable Privacy and Security (SOUPS), pp. 9–11 (2014)
17. Kraus, L., Wechsung, I., Möller, S.: A comparison of privacy and security knowledge and privacy concern as influencing factors for mobile protection behavior. In: Workshop on Privacy Personas and Segmentation (PPS) (2014)
18. Mylonas, A., Gritzalis, D., Tsoumas, B., Apostolopoulos, T.: A Qualitative metrics vector for the awareness of smartphone security users. In: Furnell, S., Lambrinoudakis, C., Lopez, J. (eds.) International Conference on Trust, Privacy & Security in Digital Business (LNCS), pp. 173–184. Springer, Heidelberg (2013)
19. Mylonas, A., Kastania, A., Gritzalis, D.: Delegate the smartphone user? security awareness in smartphone platforms. Comput. Secur. **34**, 47–66 (2013)
20. Mylonas, A., Theoharidou, M., Gritzalis, D.: Assessing privacy risks in android: a user-centric approach. In: Bauer, T., Großmann, J., Seehusen, F., Stølen, K., Wendland, M.-F. (eds.) RISK 2013. LNCS, vol. 8418, pp. 21–37. Springer, Heidelberg (2014)
21. Tari, F., Ozok, A.A., Holden, S.H.: A comparison of perceived and real shoulder-surfing risks between alphanumeric and graphical passwords. In: Proceedings of the Second Symposium on Usable Privacy and Security - SOUPS 2006, pp. 56–66. Association for Computing Machinery (ACM) (2006)

22. Theoharidou, M., Mylonas, A., Gritzalis, D.: A risk assessment method for smartphones. In: Gritzalis, D., Furnell, S., Theoharidou, M. (eds.) SEC 2012. IFIP AICT, vol. 376, pp. 443–456. Springer, Heidelberg (2012)

23. Uellenbeck, S., Dürmuth, M., Wolf, C., Holz, T.: Quantifying the security of graphical passwords. In: Proceedings of the 2013 ACM SIGSAC Conference on Computer & Communications Security - CCS 2013, pp. 161–172. ACM (2013)

24. Yu, X., Wang, Z., Sun, K., Zhu, W.T., Gao, N., Jing, J.: Remotely wiping sensitive data on stolen smartphones. In: Proceedings of the 9th ACM Symposium on Information Computer and Communications Security - ASIA CCS 2014, pp. 537–542. ACM (2014)

25. Zakaria, N.H., Griffiths, D., Brostoff, S., Yan, J.: Shoulder surfing defence for recall-based graphical passwords. In: Proceedings of the Seventh Symposium on Usable Privacy and Security - SOUPS 2011, ACM (2011)

What 4,500+ People Can Tell You – Employees' Attitudes Toward Organizational Password Policy Do Matter

Yee-Yin Choong[✉] and Mary Theofanos

National Institute of Standards and Technology, 100 Bureau Drive,
Gaithersburg, MD 20899, USA
{yee-yin.choong,mary.theofanos}@nist.gov

Abstract. Organizations establish policies on how employees should generate, maintain, and use passwords to authenticate and gain access to the organization's information systems. This paper focuses on employees' attitudes towards organizational password policies and examines the impacts on their work-related password activities that have security implications. We conducted a large-scale survey (4,573 respondents) to investigate the relationships between the organizational password policies and employees' password behaviors. The key finding of this study is that employees' attitudes toward the rationale behind cybersecurity policies are statistically significant with their password behaviors and experiences. Positive attitudes are related to more secure behaviors such as choosing stronger passwords and writing down passwords less often, less frustration with authentication procedures, and better understanding and respecting the significance to protect passwords and system security. We propose future research to promote positive employees' attitudes toward organizational security policy that could facilitate the balance between security and usability.

Keywords: Password behavior · Organizational password policy · Cybersecurity · Perception · Attitudes · Usability

1 Introduction

Passwords are the most widely used authentication mechanism for controlling employees' access to organizational information systems within public (e.g., government) and private sectors (e.g., corporations). To protect data integrity and system security, organizations often establish enterprise-specific password policies dictating how employees should manage their organizational passwords, including: password composition requirements on length and character usage, password expiration, password reuse policy (e.g., unique password for each system, can't reuse the past 10 same/similar passwords), and password storage requirements (e.g. can't write down, can't share with others). Those password policies are intended to ensure good password behaviors from the employees.

Often times, the stringent nature of those organizational password policies imposes humanly-impossible challenges for employees to be fully compliant, especially with

© Springer International Publishing Switzerland 2015
T. Tryfonas and I. Askoxylakis (Eds.): HAS 2015, LNCS 9190, pp. 299–310, 2015.
DOI: 10.1007/978-3-319-20376-8_27

multiple passwords as there are fundamental limitations on human cognition, e.g., difficulty in generating complex passwords, limited memory span, memory decay, recognition vs. recall, and memory interferences [e.g., 1–4]. However, policy makers may not be fully informed of how many passwords an average employee must use to access their organization's information systems on a daily basis and how this could lead to errors and affect productivity. Policy makers may not be aware that the overly complex password policies only make it more difficult for employees to follow the directives. These demands on managing multiple passwords often impose high cognitive load on users and may indirectly weaken overall security as users are forced to act in insecure manners with respect to their passwords such as reusing password across multiple accounts, e.g., [3, 5, 6] or writing down passwords, e.g., [7, 8].

Research in the security and usability community in the past has provided invaluable insight on users' password behaviors. However, most of those studies are on non-work related accounts such as personal emails, websites, social media or school accounts. Questions regarding security activities and practices in the workplace such as employees' attitudes toward strict password policies, amount of time and effort employees spend on generating passwords, employees' authentication experiences and activities, and potential relationships among those questions have remained unanswered.

Research has shown that attitudes can guide, influence, shape, or predict behaviors as summarized by Kraus [9]. Employees' positivity is associated with positive attitudes and behaviors and may combat negative reactions to organization-wise changes or policy viewed as unfavorable [10]. In this study, we focus on investigating employees' password behaviors across three stages in the end-user password management lifecycle, namely, generation, maintenance, and authentication [11]. We examine employees' attitudes and experiences with respect to organizational policies in order to inform the development of effective password policies that take both security and usability into considerations. This research explores the relationships between the organizational password policy and employees' password and security activities to answer questions such as: are there possible associations amongst employees' attitudes toward password requirements of length and complexity and employees' password generation strategies or employees' propensity to store and "write down" passwords or how much employees experience login problems?

2 Methodology

We designed an on-line survey to collect data on employees' password management behaviors and their attitudes toward computer security and policy with respect to their work accounts and not personal or social accounts by sampling the United States (US) government workers. This paper focuses on the data collected from employees of the Bureaus of the US Department of Commerce (DOC). The survey was sent out via email to DOC employees asking for voluntary participation. The employees were informed that their responses would be collected anonymously to reduce possible social desirability bias and to encourage more honest responses [12].

The survey consists of nineteen questions related to password management and computer security and six demographic questions. The complete survey and detail results are documented in the NIST internal report – NISTIR7991 [13]. On average, it took those who elected to take the survey about fifteen minutes to complete. A total of 4,573 DOC employees completed the survey.

3 Results and Discussion

3.1 Attitudes Toward Password Policy and Requirements

In general, employees thought that their bureaus have clearly communicated the password policy (*very clear* – 53.8 %, *somewhat clear* – 33.1 %). Although "using the same password for different accounts" is prohibited in most bureaus' policies, more than 50 % respondents admitted that they have done that (*always* – 17.9 %, *more than half of my accounts* – 19.8 %, *about half of my accounts* – 18.9 %).

The majority of employees viewed the organizational password requirements as *burdensome*: *too long* (56.9 %) and *too complex* (50.7 %), as shown in Table 1. While most bureaus require password lifespan be shorter than 90 days, employees felt that their work-related passwords change too frequently as over 70 % of the respondents preferred that a password stays valid for longer than 90.

Table 1. Employees' attitudes toward password requirements

Question	Scale	Count	%
Password length requirement	Too long	2604	56.9 %
	About right	1644	36.0 %
	Too short	41	0.9 %
	No opinion	285	6.2 %
Password complexity requirement	Too complex	2318	50.7 %
	About right	2017	44.1 %
	Too simple	25	0.6 %
	No opinion	213	4.6 %
Preferred password lifespan	30 days or less	61	1.3 %
	31-60 days	263	5.8 %
	61-90 days	857	18.7 %
	91-120 days	831	18.2 %
	121-180 days	792	17.3 %
	181 days or more	1602	35.0 %
	No opinion	167	3.7 %

Although the bureaus have done a good job in communicating the password policies to their employees, these policies undermine employees' main concerns to be productive at their jobs. It results in usability issues and behaviors that may decrease security. The organizational password requirements have become more and more stringent over the past decade, i.e., long passwords, complex composition rules, and frequent change cycles, and have imposed burdens on the end-users. Many respondents expressed their frustration toward the requirements. One stated, *"Sometimes it's[sic] taken me 20 min to change a password to one that meets the requirements and isn't too far off from my other ones (so I can remember it!)."* Another one stated, *"I understand that for 'security' reasons it is good to change a password - but seriously are we all expected to magically remember 12 different passwords, most of which are 10 cha- recters[sic] long, and can't look like a word (I agree with the reason for the complexity - it just hard on the user)."* Yet another respondent echoed, *"The requirements have gotten so complex and the valid timeframe has shortened that that[sic] I often need to write down my passwords."* Some respondent wrote, *"Security has become so complex, it's interfering with being able to do a job efficiently."*

3.2 Importance of Employees' Attitudes Toward Password Requirements

While over 50 % of the respondents viewed the length and complexity requirements as *burdensome* (i.e. *too long, too complex*), there were still a good number of respondents who were quite receptive to those requirements (36 % chose *about right* for password length and 44 % chose *about right* for password complexity). It is of great interest to investigate whether these two divergent views hold any relationships to employees' password and security behaviors.

We categorize responses based on respondents' attitudes toward the password requirements: the *burdensome* group respondents view the length requirement as *too long* or view the complexity requirement as *too complex*; the *about right* group respondents view the length requirement as *about right* or view the complexity requirement as *about right*. We compare differences in responses from this categori- zation to examine their relationships with the employees' attitudes. Before performing any statistical analyses, we carefully examined the demographic characteristics of the respondents based on these divergent views to make sure that the demographic dis- tributions are relatively consistent and comparable (see *Appendix*). As those survey responses are either nominal or ordinal data, we used a nonparametric statistical method, namely, Mann-Whitney Independent Samples U test, for comparisons between independent samples. The level of all tests for statistical significance is set to 0.05. It should be noted that any significant differences only show the existence of relationships between attitudes and users' security behaviors and experiences and do not provide the direction of causality.

3.2.1 Password Generation Considerations

The two most important considerations for the DOC respondents while generating passwords are *Easy to remember* (81.0 %) and *Compliant* (58.3 %), and the least is *Strong* (31.3 %) [12]. We investigate whether there are differences in those consider- ations between the *burdensome* group and the *about right* group, for employees' attitudes toward password length requirement and complexity requirement. All com- parisons are statistically significant ($p < 0.05$).

To demonstrate those differences, we examine the responses of *"very important"* on those password generation considerations. We plot the data from those three considerations against the two divergent views toward the length and complexity requirements (Fig. 1) for the frequently used passwords. The trends for the occasionally used passwords are similar.

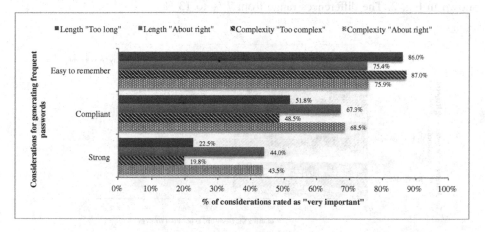

Fig. 1. Password generation considerations with respect to attitudes toward requirements

While *Easy to remember* is still the most important consideration during password generation for both groups, significantly more respondents who find the password requirements *burdensome* rate it as *"very important"* compared to those who find the requirements *about right*. For example, for the length requirement, 86.0 % of the *burdensome* group view *Easy to remember* as a very important password generation consideration while 75.4 % of the *about right* group rate it as very important. The attitudes toward the complexity requirement follow the same trend for the *Easy to remember* consideration with 11 % difference between the two groups.

Interestingly, it is the opposite for *Compliant* and *Strong* considerations. The difference between the *burdensome* respondents and the *about right* respondents is about 15 % for consideration of being *Compliant* for frequently used passwords, i.e. significantly more respondents who find the requirements *about right* rate *Compliant* as *"very important"*; whereas for *Strong* consideration, the percentage of the *burdensome* respondents rate *Strong* as *"very important"* is much lower (about half) than the percentage of the *about right* respondents.

3.2.2 Password Generation Strategies

Reusing passwords and modifying from existing passwords are often viewed as insecure user practices, e.g., [14, 15]. However, the top three password strategies used for generating frequently used passwords are: *Minor change* (67.8 %), *Existing password* (43.5 %), and *Recycle old passwords* (38.2 %) [12]. This indicates that employees are trying to minimize their effort in generating passwords by utilizing characters from existing passwords partially or fully, or they have difficulties in generating a completely different new password each time when a password generation event is triggered (e.g., old password expired, new account setup, password compromised).

When comparing between the *burdensome* group and the *about right* group, there are significant differences on all comparisons of those top three password generation strategies ($p < 0.05$). The *burdensome* group tend to use those strategies to generate their frequently used passwords more often compared to the *about right* group as shown in Fig. 2. The differences range from 7 % to 13 %.

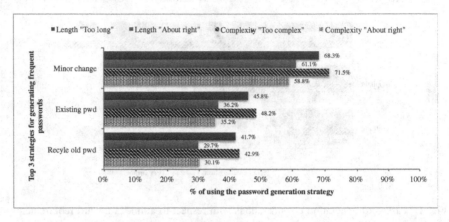

Fig. 2. Top 3 password generation strategies with respect to attitudes toward requirements

3.2.3 Storing or "Writing Down" Passwords

While it is a common practice in organizations to prohibit or discourage employees from storing their work-related passwords in any forms such as writing on paper or saving electronically in files or devices, it has been proven that solely relying on memorization is humanly impossible when users have to juggle multiple passwords at the same time. From this survey, the primary methods for tracking frequently used passwords are memorization (69.0 %), writing down on paper (64.4 %) (either disguised, locked, or in plain view), and saving electronically in files (28.8 %) (unencrypted or encrypted) [12]. However, if we look at various storing methods together (paper, file, electronic device, or password manager), a much higher percentage of the respondents (84.5 %) reported using at least one of those password storing methods for their frequently used passwords.

When we examine closely the relationship between employees' attitudes toward password requirements and their password tracking methods by comparing the two groups *burdensome* and *about right*, we find all comparisons statistically significant ($p < 0.05$). When employees think the passwords requirements are *burdensome*, they use memorization less, write on paper more, and store in files more, compared to respondents who think the requirements are *about right* (Fig. 3).

This phenomenon is even more pronounced when we examine the data further by looking at only the method of writing passwords on paper in plain view, e.g., on a sticky note next to a computer or on a desk. In Fig. 4, it shows that there is about a

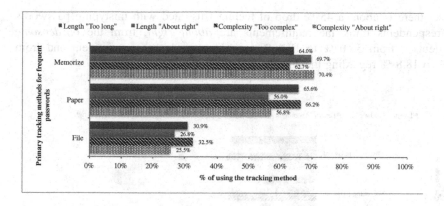

Fig. 3. Primary tracking methods with respect to attitude toward password requirements

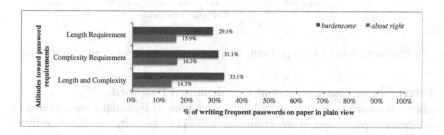

Fig. 4. Passwords on paper in plain view with respect to attitudes toward requirements

50 % drop of writing on paper in plain view when respondents think the requirements are *about right*, compared to *burdensome* respondents – from 29.1 % to 15.9 % regarding the length requirement and from 31.1 % to 16.3 % regarding the complexity requirement. When we further narrow it down to the two extreme cases, i.e., respondents who chose both *about right* and respondents who chose both *too long* and *too complex* on the requirements, the difference is even more – from 33.1 % to 14.3 %.

3.2.4   Experience with Login Problems

People reported the top three login problems experienced at work in the past six months as: mistyping password, forgetting password, and getting error messages while changing a password [12]. When respondents view the password requirements as *about right*, they are less likely to perceive *a lot* of frustration with the login problems. All comparisons for the top three login problems between the two groups *burdensome* and *about right* are statistically significant ($p < 0.05$).

To demonstrate those differences, we examine the responses of "*a lot*" of frustration on the top three login problems. It shows a significant finding that the percentage of the *burdensome* group experiencing a lot of login problems is about twice as much of the percentage of the *about right* group across all three login problems (Fig. 5). For example, there is about a 45 % drop of feeling frustrated with mistyping passwords when respondents think the requirements are *about right*, from the *burdensome* respondents – from 33.0 % to 18.4 % regarding the length requirement and from 34.4 % to 18.8 % regarding the complexity requirement.

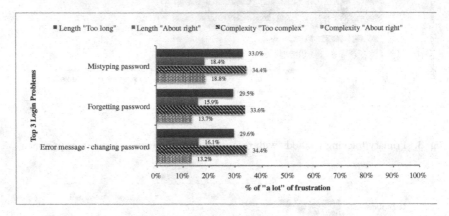

Fig. 5. Frustration with top 3 login problems with respect to attitudes toward requirements

3.2.5 Perception on Consequences of Compromised Passwords

We asked an open-ended question on people's perception of potential consequences if their work-related passwords were compromised. The majority of the free-form responses are related to the severity of the consequences, for example, "*None. My work is not sensitive.*" (classified as *None*), "*Minor consequences. Most data backed up in multiple ways.*" (classified as *Minor*), or "*Major, system compromise, violation of government trust.*" (classified as *Major*). We are surprised that a large percentage (35 % total: 6.8 % – *Don't know*, 22.8 % – *None*, and 5.3 % – *Minor*) of the responses did not perceive major consequences (only 9.9 % mentioned *Major* consequences) from potential compromises of the work-related passwords [12]. About 11 % of the responses mentioned that the consequences would depend on the sensitivity of the accounts compromised.

Upon further examination of the data, we discover an important relationship between the perceived severity of consequences from compromised passwords and the employees' attitudes toward the password requirements as shown in Fig. 6. While the perception of *Minor* consequences and *Don't know* are about the same across different groups, it is clear that the *about right* respondents are much less likely to answer *None* consequences (-14 % difference for length requirement, and -17.4 % difference for complexity requirement, both comparisons are statistically significant, $p < 0.05$) and they are more likely to perceive *Major* consequences (+7.1 % difference for length requirement, and +7.8 % difference for complexity requirement, both comparisons are statistically significant, $p < 0.05$) if their work-related passwords were compromised.

Another interesting finding is that the *about right* group is more likely to gauge the consequences depending on the types of accounts that the passwords might be compromised (+6.7 % for length requirement, and +6.6 % for complexity requirement, both comparisons are statistically significant $p < 0.05$).

Further analysis of the two extreme cases: respondents choosing both *about right* for the length and complexity requirements and respondents stating both as too *burdensome*, i.e. "too long" and "too complex," we find the same trends with even bigger differences (Fig. 6). For example, the both *about right* group is 21.3 % less likely to perceive *None* consequences, 10.5 % more likely to perceive *Major* consequences, and 8.1 % more likely to gauge consequences depending on accounts.

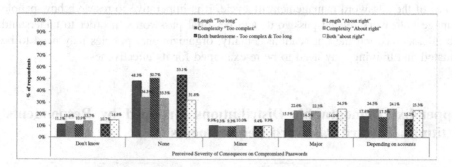

Fig. 6. Perceived severity of consequences with respect to attitudes toward requirements

4 Conclusions

The findings of this study on how people manage their work-related passwords show that the cognitive demands to comply with organizational password policies (e.g. length, composition rules, change frequency, reuse policy) and to maintain multiple passwords have pushed to the limits of human cognition. The DOC employees felt that the organizational policies require too long and too complex passwords, and the passwords have to be changed too often. As a result, in order to perform their jobs effectively, they have to employ coping mechanisms such as generating *easy to remember*, less *strong* passwords, reusing existing passwords, and "*writing down*" their passwords.

The key finding of this study is that employees' attitudes toward the rationale behind cybersecurity policies are statistically significant with their behaviors and experiences. When employees hold positive attitudes toward the password requirements, they tend to employ more secure behaviors and have more positive experiences throughout the three stages in password management lifecycle.

Compared to employees with negative attitudes toward the password requirements, positive employees, when generating passwords, indicate that *easy to remember* is less important, and *compliant* and *strong* become more important considerations. And, positive employees tend to reuse passwords less often. When maintaining their work passwords, positive employees are more likely to memorize passwords and "*write down*" passwords less often. Employees with positive attitudes perceive less frustration with login procedures and have better understanding and respecting to the significance of the need to protect passwords and system security.

While this survey was conducted with US federal employees, the findings are applicable to all organizations with formal password policies and security procedures for employees in the workplace. Currently, the security community is working toward long-term solutions for the password challenges, e.g., [16]. We will continue to perform research on the factors in promoting positive employees' attitudes toward cybersecurity in general and passwords in particular. It is also of great interest to investigate the direction of causality, i.e., if it's the positive attitudes that lead to better behaviors and experiences, or if it's the better behaviors and experiences that form the positive attitudes. We need to understand users' cognitive processes during the three stages of the password management lifecycle. It is imperative to research how people manage both work-related passwords and personal passwords in order to understand the interactions and the implications. Finally, organizational policies may need to be updated and training may need to be re-examined for its effectiveness.

Appendix: Demographic Distributions Grouped by Respondents' Attitudes Toward Password Requirements

Demographics		Attitudes toward length requirement		Attitudes toward complexity requirement	
		About right	Too long	About right	Too complex
Age	<= 25	4.5 %	2.9 %	3.6 %	3.5 %
	26–35	21.2 %	20.2 %	20.2 %	20.9 %
	36–45	22.6 %	23.2 %	22.4 %	23.4 %
	46–55	28.2 %	31.1 %	30.0 %	29.8 %
	56–65	19.2 %	17.9 %	19.1 %	18.3 %
	>= 66	2.6 %	2.2 %	2.9 %	1.8 %
	(not specified)	1.6 %	2.4 %	1.8 %	2.3 %
Gender	Male	57.6 %	57.8 %	57.4 %	58.0 %
	Female	39.1 %	38.8 %	39.6 %	38.4 %
	(not specified)	3.3 %	3.4 %	3.0 %	3.7 %
Education	High school	8.8 %	5.8 %	8.7 %	5.5 %
	Associate	5.2 %	5.3 %	5.4 %	5.0 %
	Bachelor	35.4 %	34.6 %	34.1 %	35.6 %
	Master	32.8 %	31.1 %	32.3 %	31.4 %
	Doctorate	12.8 %	16.9 %	14.6 %	15.9 %
	Professional degree	2.2 %	2.8 %	1.9 %	3.1 %
	(not specified)	2.8 %	3.6 %	3.1 %	3.4 %

(Continued)

(Continued)

Demographics		Attitudes toward length requirement		Attitudes toward complexity requirement	
		About right	Too long	About right	Too complex
Computer skill (self reported)	Novice	0.4 %	0.5 %	0.6 %	0.4 %
	Average	27.4 %	29.3 %	28.2 %	29.2 %
	Advanced	50.7 %	51.1 %	50.8 %	50.7 %
	Expert	21.1 %	18.7 %	20.1 %	19.2 %
	(not specified)	0.3 %	0.3 %	0.3 %	0.4 %
Federal service length (years)	< 1	6.1 %	5.3 %	6.5 %	4.7 %
	1–3	15.5 %	11.9 %	13.8 %	13.1 %
	4–5	7.8 %	7.9 %	7.9 %	7.7 %
	6–10	14.4 %	15.5 %	14.5 %	15.3 %
	11–14	11.5 %	11.1 %	10.2 %	12.1 %
	15–20	10.6 %	11.8 %	10.5 %	12.1 %
	> 20	33.7 %	35.9 %	36.1 %	34.5 %
	(not specified)	0.4 %	0.5 %	0.4 %	0.6 %
Job levels	Executive	1.6 %	2.1 %	1.5 %	2.2 %
	Manager	10.1 %	10.0 %	9.1 %	10.6 %
	Supervisor	13.1 %	14.1 %	12.5 %	15.0 %
	Team lead	10.9 %	12.1 %	10.9 %	12.1 %
	Non-supervisor	64.0 %	61.0 %	65.6 %	59.3 %
	(not specified)	0.3 %	0.8 %	0.4 %	0.8 %

References

1. Sasse, M.A., Brostoff, B., Weirich, D.: Transforming the 'weakest link' — a human/computer interaction approach to usable and effective security. BT Technol. J. **19**(3), 122–131 (2001)
2. Vu, K.P.L., Bhargav, A., Proctor, R.W.: Imposing password restrictions for multiple accounts: Impact on generation and recall of passwords. In: Proceedings of the Human Factors and Ergonomics Society Annual Meeting 47(11), 1331–1335 (2003)
3. Brown, A.S., Bracken, E., Zoccoli, S., Douglas, K.: Generating and remembering passwords. Appl. Cogn. Psychol. **18**(6), 641–651 (2004)
4. Vu, K.L., Proctor, R.W., Bhargav-Spantzel, A., Tai, B., Cook, J., Schultz, E.E.: Improving password security and memorability to protect personal and organizational information. Int. J. Hum Comput Stud. **65**, 744–757 (2007)
5. Florêncio, D., Herley, C.: A Large-Scale Study of Web Password Habits. In: Proceedings of the 16th International Conference on World Wide Web 2007, pp. 657–666 (2007)

6. Das, A., Bonneau, J., Caesar, M., Borisov, N., Wang, X.: The tangled web of password reuse. In: Proceedings of NDSS (2014)
7. Inglesant, P.G., Sasse, M.A.: The true cost of unusable password policies: password use in the wild. In: Proceedings of the SIGCHI Conference on Human Factors in Computing Systems, pp. 383–392. ACM (2010)
8. Grawemeyer, B., Johnson, H.: Using and managing multiple passwords: a week to a view. Interact. Comput. 23(3), 256–267 (2011)
9. Kraus, S.J.: Attitudes and the prediction of behavior: a meta-analysis of the empirical literature. Pers. Soc. Psychol. Bull. 21(1), 58–75 (1995)
10. Avey, J.B., Wernsing, T.S., Luthans, F.: Can positive employees help positive organizational change? Impact of psychological capital and emotions on relevant attitudes and behaviors. J. Appl. Behav. Sci. 44(1), 48–70 (2008)
11. Choong, Y.-Y.: A cognitive-behavioral framework of user password management lifecycle. In: Tryfonas, T., Askoxylakis, I. (eds.) HAS 2014. LNCS, vol. 8533, pp. 127–137. Springer, Heidelberg (2014)
12. Ong, A.D., Weiss, D.J.: The impact of anonymity on responses to sensitive questions. J. Appl. Soc. Psychol. 30(8), 1691–1708 (2000)
13. Choong, Y.-Y., Theofanos, M., Liu, H.-K.: United States Federal Employees' Password Management Behaviors – a Department of Commerce Case Study. NISTIR 7991, National Institute of Standards and Technology, Gaithersburg, US (2014)
14. Ives, B., Walsh, K.R., Schneider, H.: The domino effect of password reuse. Commun. ACM 47(4), 75–78 (2004)
15. WEBROOT.com: New Webroot Survey Reveals Poor Password Practices that May Put Consumers' Identities At Risk (2010). http://www.webroot.com/us/en/company/press-room/releases/protect-your-computer-from-hackers. Accessed on 20 Jan 2015
16. National Strategy for Trusted Identities in Cyberspace. The White House, Washington, DC, US (2014). http://www.whitehouse.gov/sites/default/files/rss_viewer/NSTICstrategy_041511.pdf. Accessed on 08 Jan 2015

An Investigation of the Factors that Predict an Internet User's Perception of Anonymity on the Web

Shruti Devaraj, Myrtede Alfred[(✉)], Kapil Chalil Madathil,
and Anand K. Gramopadhye

Clemson University, Clemson, SC, USA
malfred@g.clemson.edu

Abstract. The growth of the Internet as a means of communication has sparked a need for researchers to investigate the issues surrounding different social behaviors associated with Internet use. Of particular interest is the importance of a user's perception of anonymity. The independent variables for the study were demographic information, social networking habits and prior negative experience. The dependent variable for this study was perception of online anonymity. Data for this analysis were taken from the Pew Research Center's Internet & American Life Project's July 2013 Pew Internet Anonymity Survey. A binomial logistic regression analysis was performed to predict perception of anonymity on the Web. Results indicated that gender, income level, education level, social networking habits and compromised identity are significant in predicting one's perception of anonymity on the web. Age and prior negative experience were not significant predictors. Differences in technological proficiency and access to the web are two factors believed to have contributed to these results, particularly those related to demographics. The findings from this research could be used to help target demographics with the education and support needed to protect their identity on the web. This study also offers insight about who are more likely to attempt to use the web anonymously and will help further identify the patterns of behavior associated with anonymous web use. This paper calls for further studies to analyze to what extent do the opinions and experiences of friends and relatives impact an individual's perception of anonymity.

1 Introduction

According to Lin et al. (2000), the number of internet users has increased more than tenfold in the past decade alone. One of the major concerns of this growth is the idea of anonymity of the user, both technically and socially. Technical anonymity refers to the removal from the internet of all meaningful identifying information about users, including their names, addresses, genders or other identifying information. Social anonymity refers to the perception of others and/or an individual as unidentifiable because of the lack of cues creating an identity; examples include the use of pseudonyms or multiple email addresses such as a personal one and a professional one. In this case the information disclosed in each varies, creating a form of anonymity. A non-essential email address for social websites, for example, offers more protection from

T. Tryfonas and I. Askoxylakis (Eds.): HAS 2015, LNCS 9190, pp. 311–322, 2015.
DOI: 10.1007/978-3-319-20376-8_28

privacy invasions than if a business or personal email address is used, and even though a person is not completely anonymous in this social context, he/she may *perceive* himself or herself to be so to others (Traynor 2005). No matter the type or the reason for it, anonymity means that a person cannot be identified based on the dimensions of legal name, location, pseudonyms that can be linked to the name or location, or pseudonyms that cannot be linked to specific identity information but that can provide other clues to identity, revealing patterns of behavior, membership in a social group or information, items or skills that indicate personal characteristics (Marx 1999).

Research suggests that people camouflage or hide their identity primarily to maintain their privacy (Ackerman et al. 1999), an increasing concern of internet users. According to a 2004 study conducted by the USC Annenberg School of Communication-Center for the Digital Future, 88.2 % of internet users were concerned about the privacy of their personal information. However, recent literature (Wismer et al. 2012; Fraune et al. 2013) suggests that anonymous behaviors for achieving this privacy and security have various benefits and limitations. For example, they can remove inhibitions, resulting in acts of kindness or generosity, on the one hand, or abuse and misbehavior on the other. Researchers have also suggested that people use anonymity as a "layer of protection" to counter the effects of discussing unpopular and/or taboo topics. Anonymity can also become a mask, representing an online persona different from the one exhibited offline in an attempt to maintain privacy. These masks typically include incorrect information such as the false age or false information about gender (Chen and Rea 2004), the former being especially relevant in cases of children providing incorrect ages to access restricted sites (Lehman 2000).

Past research also has explored the methods used to remain anonymous on the web, with using proxy servers and anonymous names and pseudonyms, and clearing cookies and browser history, being some of the more common techniques (Turner et al. 2003, Berendt 2005). Using a proxy server allows internet users to hide their internet protocol (IP) address by essentially using the IP address of the proxy as a "middle man" (Clark et al. 2007). Cloning IP addresses, another common technique used to mask a user's identity, allows for accessing a particular website through a different IP address, usually a fake one. The use of pseudonyms, such as screen names, allows users to keep their real names private, and clearing cookies and browser history helps to prevent online activity from being tracked.

While previous studies suggest that attitudes about particular online communities or sites, technical knowledge and privacy preferences help explain the motivation for seeking anonymity, there is limited research on how gender, age, education, income level, prior experiences on the web and use of social networking sites influence perceptions of anonymity. To address this need, this research developed a model that helps predict an internet users' perception of anonymity on the web by considering the following:

1. How do demographic characteristics influence perceptions of anonymity?

One such characteristic of particular interest is gender, as past research has found differences in computer and internet skills between men and women (Chalil Madathil et al. 2013). Men tend to be more frequent users of the internet than women and are also more likely to experiment with and tweak features on the web. In addition, men are more aware of privacy settings and the use of cookies and options such as history and incognito windows, as well as loopholes on the web (Bimber 2000, Gefen et al. 1997). Research has also shown that men exhibit better online skills, in particular the ability to locate content online, than women (Hargittai and Shafer 2006). Thus, this research hypothesizes that men are more likely to believe they can maintain anonymity while using the internet than women.

2. How do prior negative experiences on the web influence perceptions of anonymity?

Research indicates that people are affected by such negative experiences as the loss of personal information and compromised identities. As a result, they tend to be cautious when placed in similar situations again (Holt and Crocker 2000; Sweeney et al. 2008). For example, a study discussed by Sweeney and colleagues (2008) found that respondents who had their identity stolen in a simulated scenario were more willing to change their behavior as a result of this negative experience. Considering these results, it is hypothesized that people who have had prior negative experiences on the web are more likely to believe that it is not possible to use the web anonymously.

3. How likely are the users of social networking sites to believe that it is possible for someone to use the internet completely anonymously?

Over the past decade, social networking sites, online portals allowing users to create profiles and build a personal network by connecting to other users, have grown from a niche activity into a phenomenon that engages millions of internet users (Subrahmanyam et al. 2008, Abhayankar 2011). Currently, this figure is closer to 2 billion users, with Facebook alone accounting for 1.1 billion active social media users (Number of worldwide social network users). Studies have indicated that these sites, as well as discussion boards (Chalil Madathil et al. 2013), are increasingly being used to share information and news (Bakshy et al. 2012). Users of such sites have increased access to information about anonymity and ways of using the web anonymously (Boyd and Ellison, 2007). Thus, it is hypothesized that users of social networking sites are more likely to believe that it is possible to use the internet anonymously.

To investigate these issues and factors that predict users' perception of anonymity on the internet, this study used a logistic regression model.

2   Method

Data Source. Data for this analysis were taken from the Pew Research Center's Internet & American Life Project's July 2013 Pew Internet Anonymity Survey (Pew Research Internet Project 2013), a survey of adults in the United States conducted by Princeton Survey Research Associates International on anonymity on the internet. These telephone interviews were conducted in English by Princeton Data Source from July 11 to July 14, 2013. This survey data consisted of responses from 1002 participants. The data were subsequently weighted to correct known demographic discrepancies (Pew Research Internet Project 2013). The subsample used in this study included only the respondents who answered "Yes" to the question, *"Do you use the Internet, at least occasionally?"* The definition of internet for this survey was someone who uses the internet, sends/receives emails or accesses the internet on a mobile device at least occasionally. The demographic information of the sample used in the analysis is shown in Table 1 along with the participants' anonymity perception.

Table 1. Anonymity perceptions based on demographics

Individual characteristics respondents (Weighted N = 1002)	Can anonymity be achieved?	
	No (%)	Yes (%)
Age		
18–34	32.9	40.0
35–49	27.3	23.8
50–64	28.0	25.5
65+	11.6	10.6
Education		
High school or less	30.1	37.9
Post high school but < 4 year college degree	34.6	35.7
4- year college degree and above	35.3	26.3
Race		
White	80.1	69.3
African American	9.7	15.4
Others	10.1	15.3
Gender		
Male	44.3	55.1
Female	55.6	44.8
Income level		
< $30,000	26.9	34.9
$30,000 to < $50,000	18.7	22.7
$50,000 to < $75,000	19.5	12.7
> $75,000	34.9	29.6

*percentages may not add to 100 % due to exclusion of *"I don't know"* responses

Independent Variables. The independent variables in this study included demographic characteristics, social networking habits, loss of personal information and compromised identity. The demographic variables included age, education, race, gender and income level. In this analysis, age was coded as a continuous variable and gender as a dichotomous variable (1 = Male and 2 = Female) while race was coded into three categories (1 = White, 2 = African American and 3 = Others) as was educational level (1 = High school or less, 2 = Post high school but less than a four-year college degree, 3 = 4 year-college degree and above). Finally, income level was coded as a 1 = <$30,000; 2 = $30,000 to <$50,000; 3 = $50,000 to <$75,000; 4 = $75,000 and above. The use of social networking sites was analyzed based on the question *"Do you ever use the internet to use a social networking site like Facebook, LinkedIn or Google*

Plus?," with the respondents answering "Yes," "No," "Don't know" or "Refused." Because the last two response categories received no responses, they were not included in the analysis.

Prior negative experiences were evaluated by the question *"Have you ever had personal information stolen such as your social security number, your credit card or bank account information?"* Coded as a dichotomous variable, respondents' answered either "Yes" or "No," with a 1 being recorded for the former and a 2 for the latter. Compromised identity was assessed by *"Have you ever had an email or social networking account of yours compromised or taken over without your permission by someone else?"* Similar to prior negative experiences, this variable was also considered as a dichotomous one, with a yes response being coded as 1 and a no as a 2.

Dependent Variable. User perception of anonymity on the internet was measured with the question, *"Considering everything you know and have heard about the internet, do you think it is possible for someone to use the internet completely anonymously – so that none of their online activities can be easily traced back to them?,"* with respondents answering either "Yes," "No," "Don't know" or "Refused." Only the responses of "Yes" and "No" were included in this study, meaning that the two categories of dependent variables included respondents who perceive that it is possible for someone to use the internet anonymously and those who do not.

Analysis. A binomial logistic regression analysis was conducted using SPSS 21.0 to predict perception of anonymity on the web. The three logistic regression models were developed to assess the characteristics associated with perceptions of anonymity. These models included the demographic variables of gender, age, education, race and income level as well as a variable measuring the use of social networking sites such as Facebook, LinkedIn and Google Plus. In addition, the variables measuring negative prior experiences, such as the loss of personal information and compromised identity, were also included in the analysis. Fit indices, pseudo R-squared, effect size estimates, logistic regression coefficients and their significance, corresponding odds ratios and confidence intervals were calculated for all three models.

3   Results

Table 2 shows the results of the logistic regression, including the logistic regression coefficients, their corresponding standard errors, their odds ratios and the confidence intervals for these odds ratios. The results indicated that all predictors except age and loss of personal information were significant in predicting an internet user's perception of anonymity. The model yielded a Chi-square value of 162.28 and 12 degrees of freedom.

The results indicated that gender was a significant factor, with men being more likely to believe that they can maintain anonymity while using the web than women. Specifically, the probability of men perceiving that it is possible to remain anonymous was 0.46. Figure 1 shows the mean predicted value of perception of online anonymity for gender.

Table 2. Estimated coefficients of the binomial logistic regression model

Predictor		Model 3				Δχ2
		B	SE	OR	95 % CI for OR	
Intercept		-1.04	0.24	0.35	-1.5,-0.57	19.39
Gender						
	Male	0.50	0.08	1.65	0.33,0.67	32.69
	Female	0ᵃ				
Age		0.01	0.01	1.00	-0.00,0.01	2.28
Income level						
	<$30,000	0.18	0.12	1.19	-0.06,0.42	2.19
	$30,000 to < $50,000	0.26	0.12	1.29	0.01,0.51	4.21
	$50,000 to < $75,000	-0.32	0.13	0.72	-0.58,-0.04	5.34
	> $75,000	0ᵃ				
Race						
	White	-0.59	0.13	0.55	-0.85,-0.32	18.66
	African American	0.00	0.17	1.00	-0.34,0.34	0.00
	Others	0ᵃ				
Educational level						
	High school or less	0.47	0.12	1.6	0.23,0.71	15.01
	Post high school but less than 4-year college	0.267	0.11	1.31	0.05,0.48	5.82
	4-year college degree and above	0ᵃ				
Use of social networking sites						
	Yes	0.24	0.11	1.27	0.03,0.45	5.02
	No	0ᵃ				
Loss of personal information						
	Yes	-0.15	0.14	0.86	-0.42,0.12	1.13
	No	0ᵃ				
Compromised identity						
	Yes	0.64	0.11	1.89	0.44,0.85	33.5
	No	0ᵃ				
Chi-square		162.28				
Df		12				
-2log likelihood		2903.63				
Sample size		2434				

Note. *p < 0.05; ᵃreference category

Race was also found to be a significant factor, with people who are White being less likely to perceive that the internet can be used anonymously than those of another race. The probability of people who perceive that it is possible to use the web

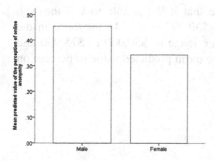

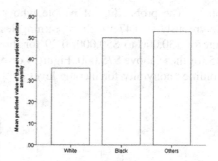

Fig. 1. Mean predicted value of perception of online anonymity for gender.

Fig. 2. Mean predicted value of perception of online anonymity for race.

anonymously is 0.38 for whites, 0.51 for African Americans and 0.53 for others. Figure 2 displays the mean predicted value of perception of online anonymity for race.

Another predictor of perception about anonymous use of the internet was educational level. Individuals with an educational level of high school or less were more likely to perceive that the internet can be used completely anonymously than those with a four-year college degree and higher. Similarly, people with an educational level of post high school but less than a four-year college degree were more likely to perceive that it is possible to use the web anonymously than those with an education level of four-year college degree or higher. The mean predicted value of perception of anonymity for high school or less is 0.48, post high school but less than a four-year college degree is 0.39 and an educational level of four-year college degree or higher is 0.33. Figure 3 shows the mean predicted value of perception of anonymity for the different education levels.

Income level was also a predictor of the perception of anonymity, with the analysis indicating that people with an income between \$50,000 and \$75,000 were least likely to perceive that the web can be used anonymously, while those with an income level below \$30,000 were most likely to perceive that it is possible to use the web anony-

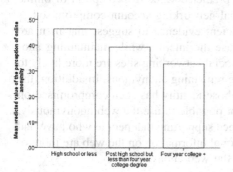

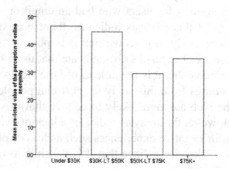

Fig. 3. Mean predicted value of perception of online anonymity for education level.

Fig. 4. Mean predicted value of perception of online anonymity for income level.

mously. The probability of people who perceive that it is possible to use the web anonymously is 0.47 for those earning less than $30,000/year, 0.45 for those in the range of $30,000 to $50,000, 0.29 for those in the range of $50,000 to $75,000 and 0.35 for those above $75,000. Figure 4 displays the mean predicted value of perception of online anonymity for income level.

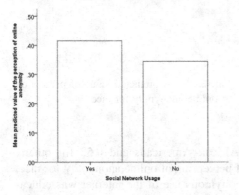 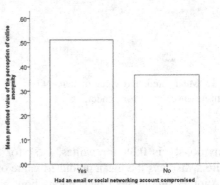

Fig. 5. Mean predicted value of perception of online anonymity for social network usage.

Fig. 6. Mean predicted value of perception of online anonymity for users who had an email or social networking account compromised.

Another variable impacting the perception of anonymity on the web was social network habits. People who use such social networking sites as Facebook, LinkedIn and Google Plus were more likely to perceive that it is possible to use the internet anonymously than those who do not. The probability of people perceiving that it is possible to use the web anonymously was 0.41 for those who use social networks and 0.35 for those who do not. Figure 5 shows the mean predicted value of perception of online anonymity for social network usage.

Compromised identity was another predictor of how users perceive anonymity on the internet, with the results indicating that those who have had an email or social networking account compromised were more likely to perceive that the internet can be used anonymously. Figure 6 shows the mean predicted value of perception of online anonymity for users who had an email or social networking account compromised.

As this analysis indicates, there was sufficient evidence to suggest that men are more likely to perceive that it is possible to use the internet while maintaining anonymity. The results also indicate that users of social networking sites are more likely to perceive that it is possible to use the web while remaining anonymous. In addition, the findings from this study suggest that people whose identity has been compromised on the web are more likely to believe that it is not possible to use the web anonymously. However the analysis indicates a lack of evidence supporting that people who have had prior negative experiences such as loss of personal information on the web are more or less likely to believe that it is possible to use the web anonymously.

4 Discussion

Anonymous use of the internet has become an important issue over the past few years, in part because the increase in its capabilities has transformed its use. The ease of information access coupled with the ready availability of personal data have made it easy and tempting for interested parties (individuals, businesses and governments) to intrude into people's privacy in unprecedented ways (Rezgui et al. 2003). This desire to maintain privacy has been one of the primary reasons people attempt to use the web anonymously (Rezgui et. al. 2002). To explore this phenomenon, this study explored the factors that predict an internet user's perception of anonymity.

One of the important findings from this analysis is that men were more likely than women to perceive that the internet can be used anonymously. This result seems consistent with previous studies that found that men are more aware of the function- alities of the web and are more prone to tweak or experiment with them. (Hargittai et al. 2006) Conversely, because women are less familiar with the capabilities of the web, they are less likely to believe that they can use the web anonymously.

Race was also a significant factor. Whites, on average, were less likely to believe that anonymity on the web could be achieved, perhaps because of the "digital divide" purported to exist between Whites and minorities in the US. It has been observed that demographic groups with greater access to the Internet were the same groups (Whites, men, city-dwellers) with greater access to education and income, among other resources (DiMaggio and Hargittai 2001). DiMaggio & Hargittai proposed a finer distinction in the inequality in technology use than just those who have it and those who do not (2001). They point to differences in the equipment users have, the level of freedom they have when using the web (home versus work or public location), their skill level, the amount of support they receive and their purpose for using the internet. Because of these differences, it is possible that Whites, due to better equipment, greater autonomy, more proficiency and/or more support, have had more opportunities to explore anonymity on the web.

This analysis also found that education level was a significant factor, with those having less education being more likely to perceive that the internet can be used anonymously than people with more education. One explanation for this result is that while less educated individuals are not as technologically proficient, they may also be less aware of the various methods by which an internet user can be tracked and identified, an explanation supported by past research which has found higher educa- tional levels correlate to better understanding of the technological aspects of the web (Porter and Donthu 2006; Chalil Madathil et al. 2013).

Similar to education level, income level was also a significant predictor, exhibiting the greatest deviation in the means between the highest (.47) and lowest (.29) groups. Individuals in the lower income brackets, those earning less than $50,000 per year, were more likely to believe they could surf the web anonymously. This finding could perhaps be due to a correlation between the level of education and income, as individuals with more education typically earn more than those with less—and those with a higher level of education are typically more knowledgeable about the capabilities of the web.

This analysis also showed that the use of social networking sites was an important predictor. This result can be associated with the fact that people interact and communicate extensively on such sites. Since information and messages are frequently being shared on such platforms, people are more likely to learn about ways to mask their identity on the web. Past research indicates that 8.7 % of Facebook users are fake profiles (CNET 2012), suggesting that social anonymity is practiced on these sites, perhaps explaining why social networking usage is a predictor of perceptions of anonymity on the web.

In addition, people whose email or social networking account had been compromised are also more likely to perceive that the internet can be used anonymously. However, the loss of personal information was not a significant predictor of the perception of anonymity.

5 Implications

This study investigated the factors that predict an internet user's perception of anonymity and found that gender, race, education and income level were all significant predictors. The findings concerning demographic differences in anonymity perceptions and the related disparities in technological proficiency could be used to help target demographics with the education and support needed to protect their identity on the web. Findings from this research also offer insight about who are more likely to attempt to use the web anonymously and will help further identify the patterns of behavior associated with anonymous web use. The study can also be extended to understand what applications or services demand anonymous use and educate users about its implications.

Current literature indicates that the experiences and opinions of friends and relatives play a major role in the perception of anonymity on the web. However, as these users were not investigated in this study, further analysis is required to determine how these relationships influence the perception of anonymity (Kang et al. 2013). Further research is also needed to explore the difference between technical and social anonymity and how users embrace anonymity in these situations. Findings from the study suggest that individuals more proficient in the use of the internet are more likely to believe they can use the web anonymously, but it would be interesting to determine if this is actually the case or if their perceptions represent false confidence. Since the Internet now plays a key role in everyday life, it is critical to understand the role and need for anonymity on the web, in particular if and when such use of the internet should be advocated.

References

Abhyankar, A.: Social Networking Sites. Samvad, SIBM (2011)

Ackeman, M.S., Cranor, L.F., Reagle, J.: Privacy in E-Commerce: Examining User Scenarios and Privacy Preferences. In: Proceedings of 1st ACM Conference on Electronic Commerce, pp. 1–8 (1999)

Bakshy, E, Rosenn, I., Marlow, C., Adamic, L.: The role of social networks in information diffusion. In: WWW 2012 – Session: Information Diffusion in Social Networks (2012)

Berendt, B.: Privacy In E-Commerce: Stated Preferences Vs Actual Behavior. Commun. ACM **48**(4), 101–106 (2005)

Bimber, B.: Measuring the gender gap on the internet. Soc. Sci. Q. **81**(3), 868–876 (2000)

Boyd, D.M., Ellison, N.B.: Social networking sites: definition, history and scholarship. J. Comput. Mediated Inf. **13**(1), 210–230 (2007)

Chalil Madathil, K., Greenstein, JUST, Nines, DAM, Juan, K., Gramopadhye, O.K.: An investigation of the informational needs of Ovarian cancer patients and their supporters. In: Proceedings of the Human Factors and Ergonomics Society's International Annual Meeting, San Diego, CA, September 2013

Chen, K., Rea, A.: Protecting personal information online: a survey of user privacy concerns and control techniques. J. Comput. Inf. Syst. **44**(4), 85–92 (2004)

Clark, J., Van Borscht, P.C., Adams, C.: Usability of anonymous web browsing: an examination of tor interfaces and deploy ability. In: Proceedings of the 3rd Symposium on Usable Privacy and Security, pp. 41–51. ACM, July 2007

DiMaggio, P., Hargittai, E.: From the 'digital divide'to 'digital inequality': studying internet use as penetration increases. Princeton University Center for Arts and Cultural Policy Studies, Working Paper Series number, 15 (2001)

Fraune, M., Juang, K., Greenstein, J.S., Chalil Madathil, K., Koikkara, R.: Employing user-created pictures to enhance the recall of system-generated mnemonic phrases and security of Passwords. In: Proceedings of the Human Factors and Ergonomics Society's International Annual Meeting, San Diego, CA (2013)

Gefen, D., Straub, D.: Gender differences in the perception and use of e-mail: an acceptance of the technology acceptance model. MIS Q. /December **21**, 389–400 (1997)

Hargittai, E., Shafer, S.: Differences In Actual And Perceived Online Skills: The Role Of Gender. Social Science Quarterly **87**(2), 432–448 (2006)

Holt, D.T., Crocker, M.: Prior negative experiences: their impacts on computer training outcomes. Comput. Educ. **35**(4), 295–308 (2000)

Protalinski, E.: Facebook: 8.7 percent are fake users [Web blog post] (2012). http://www.cnet.com

Kang, R., Brown, S., Kiesler, S.: Why do people seek anonymity on the internet? informing policy and design. CHI 2013, April 27–May 2 2013

Lehman, D.: Protecting kids' privacy is costly, Computer World, April, p. 97 (2007)

Lin, J.C., Lu, H.: Towards an understanding of the behavioral intention to use a web site. Int. J. Inf. Manage. **20**(3), 197–208 (2000)

Marx, G.T.: what's in a name? some reflections on the sociology of anonymity. Inf. Soc. **15**(2), 99–112 (1999)

Pew Research Internet Project (2013). http://www.pewinternet.org/datasets/july-2013-anonymity-omnibus/

Porter, C.E., Donthu, N.: Using the technology acceptance model to explain how attitudes determine internet usage: the role of perceeived access barriers and demographics. J. Bus. Res. **59**(9), 999–1007 (2006)

Rezgui, A., Bouguettaya, A., Eltoweissy, M.Y.: Privacy on the web: facts, challenges and solutions. IEEE Secur. Priv. **1**(6), 40–49 (2003)

Rezgui, A., Ouzzani, M., Bouguettaya, A., Medjahed, B.: Preserving privacy in web services ACM 1-58113-593-9/02/001 (2002)

Subrahmanyam, K., Reich, S.M., Waechter, N., Espinoza, G.: Online and offline social networks: use of social networking sites by emerging adults. J. Appl. Dev. Psychol. **29**, 420–433 (2008)

Sweeney, J.C., Soutar, G.N., Mazzoral, T.: Factors influencing word of mouth effectiveness: receiver perspectives. Eur. J. Mark. **42**(3/4), 344–364 (2008)

Traynor, M.: Anonymity and the internet. Comput. Internet Lawyer **22**, 2 (2005)

Turner, E., Dasgupta, S.: Privacy on the web: an examination of user concerns, technology and implications for business organizations and organization. Inf. Syst. Manage. **20**(1), 8–19 (2003)

USC Annenberg School of Communication-Center for the Digital Future, Surveying the digital future-year four. http://www.digitalcenter.org/downloads/DigitalFutureReport-Year4-2004.pdf

Wismer, A., Chalil Madathil, K., Koikkara, R., Juang, K., Greenstein, J.S.: Evaluating the usability of CAPTCHAs on a mobile device with voice and touch input. In: Proceedings of the Human Factors and Ergonomics Society 56th Annual Meeting, Boston, MA (2012)

Do Graphical Cues Effectively Inform Users?

A Socio-Technical Security Study in Accessing Wifi Networks

Ana Ferreira[1,2], Jean-Louis Huynen[1,2]([✉]), Vincent Koenig[1,2],
Gabriele Lenzini[2], and Salvador Rivas[1]

[1] Institute of Cognitive Science and Assessment, University of Luxembourg,
Luxembourg, Luxembourg
[2] Interdisciplinary Centre for Security Reliability and Trust,
University of Luxembourg, Luxembourg, Luxembourg
jean-louis.huynen@uni.lu

Abstract. We study whether the padlock and the signal strength bars, two visual cues shown in network managers, convey their intended messages. Since users often choose insecure networks when they should not, finding the answer is not obvious; in our study we clarify whether the problem lies in uninformative and ambiguous cues or in the user who, despite understanding the cues, chooses otherwise. This paper describes experiments and comments the results that bring evidence to our study.

1 Introduction

In [1] we studied the human-computer interactions in hypothetical situations where users select one out of several hotspots offering access to Wi-Fi networks. Motivated to discover *where* security can fail, we highlighted the points in the user-interaction protocol where users opt for an open (insecure) network even for tasks that require security, and despite the presence of visual indicators (called *cues*) reminding the insecurity of the choice. However, to improve the security of those interactions one should rather understand *why* users decide insecurely when they should not and whether users consider or not in their decision making, the message carried by the security cues.

This paper's goal is to answer this *"why"* question, and clarify why Wi-Fi users select a certain network instead of others. There is little research on this question in relation to the security and to the understanding of symbols that network managers rely on. The closest is the research done by Jeske *et al.* who argue that the padlock and signal strength unintentionally nudge people to insecure choices [2]; however they do not explain *why* this happens: are these visual cues unclear and misleading the users? Are they ambiguous and leading users to ignore them? Or are they clear in their messages, but are users choosing insecurely for other reasons extraneous to the cues?

This research is supported by FNR Luxembourg, project I2R-APS-PFN-11STAS.

T. Tryfonas and I. Askoxylakis (Eds.): HAS 2015, LNCS 9190, pp. 323–334, 2015.
DOI: 10.1007/978-3-319-20376-8_29

These three questions motivate the present paper. Generally speaking, we could think that users and interfaces are engaged into a sort of *visual conversation* and so it is legitimate to expect it to follow the same principles that rule a constructive and clear conversation. P. Grice, who studied this topic in the philosophy of language, calls them *cooperative conversation* and lists those principles as follows [3]: *quantity* (state what is informative, no more and no less than that); *quality* (don't state what is false, don't state what lacks evidence); *relation* (be relevant); *manner* (avoid obscurity, ambiguity, verbosity, and be orderly).

To clarify whether cues are "cooperative" in the sense given above leads to an interesting approach to answer "*why* do users choose insecurely?" in the presence of cues. The approach consists of separating what can be explained in regard to "ineffective" cues from what instead is about an informed choice by the user.

Contribution. The paper describes the particular scenario where a user chooses a Wi-Fi network. We question whether the common visual cues employed in this task —the padlock and the bars that indicate the signal strength— succeed in communicating their intended message, and we contribute to understanding why. This study builds on observed behaviour of about 1000 participants.

Other authors have studied related questions. As noted earlier, Jeske *et al.* [2] observe that convenience-oriented students *behave* as if the padlock is a barrier to secure choices. They have however not investigated *why* users behave this way. Several key questions thus remain unanswered: does a user *behave* so because they *misunderstand* the padlock or rather because they overlook the padlock due to accompanying factors that force different meanings?

The difference between behaving and understanding is key for us. A user may (a) understand but ignore the cues, and this is after all an *informed* decision. Or they can (b) understand a different message and so take a *misinformed* decision, or they can (c) ignore completely the cue so prefer an *uninformed* decision.

Case (a) suggests that the cue works fine. But (b) suggests that the cue fails and needs a revision, whereas case (c) the cue is irrelevant, and thus useless. Moreover, in (a) one can still decide insecurely, as well as one can still behave securely in (b) or (c). But, in any of those situations, what nudges the user's behaviour should not only be searched for in the cue itself, but also in other factors, such as in the presence of other indicators, which influence a cue's message, or in the task a user is performing, or in the user.

Therefore, this work's main research questions are the following: Are the padlock and the signal strength and their relative importance responsible for a user's *informed*, *misinformed*, or *uninformed* decision? Which cues are the most influential in causing that difference, if any? Are the user's background and different Wi-fi scenarios also affecting the user's behaviour?

2   Methods

To distinguish the situations where people take *informed*, *misinformed*, and *uninformed* decisions, we need to compare people's understanding of the Wi-Fi networks' properties and visual cues relative to the choices they make. Therefore, we conduct a study where we ask participants the following: first, to read the description of a specific scenario setting, a given context and a specific task to perform; second, to choose between different Wi-Fi networks to achieve the task; third, to answer questions about the meaning of the visual cues they encountered; and finally, to answer questions about their knowledge regarding Wi-Fi networks.

What we investigate is whether the choice of a Wi-Fi network depends on the properties of the Wi-Fi network itself and on the specific task to be undertaken. Thus, more precisely, the *dependent variable* we investigate is the participants' Wi-Fi choice, a dichotomous (i.e., 0/1, wrong/right) variable. As main *independent variables* we choose the presence/absence of the padlock sign (🔒) —supposed to indicate *secure communication*, technically the presence of encryption— and the presence of one of the two signal strength sign 📶 or ⌄)—supposed to indicate *quality of connectivity*, technically the strength of the received Wi-Fi signal. These are in fact the properties of Wi-Fi networks typically communicated to the user. In our study we thus display one of the four possible combinations: '⌄', '⌄ 🔒', '📶', or '📶 🔒'. In the remainder of this document, for sake of conciseness, we use the terms "Encryption" for *secure communication* and "QoS" for *good connectivity*.

"Encryption" (i.e., *secure communication*) and "QoS" (i.e., *good connectivity*) represent also the two meaning dimensions that we assess from our participants in relation to how they understand the cues. We measure how much the participants think a cue means "Encryption" or "QoS", and this is driven by the task a user is involved in; we consider four tasks designed to evoke a need for "Encryption" and "QoS" through context description.

Additional *independent variables* that we consider to be important factors to control for are the following: the order of the Wi-Fi network names; speed of appearance over time, i.e., how quickly or slowly the network is listed by the network manager; and the participant's social and personal background, i.e., tech-savvy *vs* non-tech-savvy users. Moreover, to ensure that participants do not avoid encrypted networks because they do not have a password, we provide a password to half of the sample, aleatorily.

To investigate those factors, while maximizing internal validity, we chose an in-between subject study design. Participants were presented only one scenario to avoid security priming of one scenario on the others. The study was conducted on-line: the flow of the study design comprised a socio-demographic questionnaire; the description of a scenario with instructions to select a Wi-Fi network from a given list; several rounds of network selections; an assessment of the meaning participants have for the given cues; and a follow-up questionnaire to assess further attitudes and beliefs about ICT security (e.g., misconceptions and beliefs regarding Wi-Fi networks). In each scenario, we describe for the participant a character they implicitly inhabit and ask him/her what network s/he would select given the context and task to be accomplished. Participants were assigned to respond to 1 scenario out of 4 possible ones; thus the probability of assignment was of .25. Each scenario differed in terms of the requirements the Wi-Fi network should have to complete the task (i.e., combination of 'Encryption"

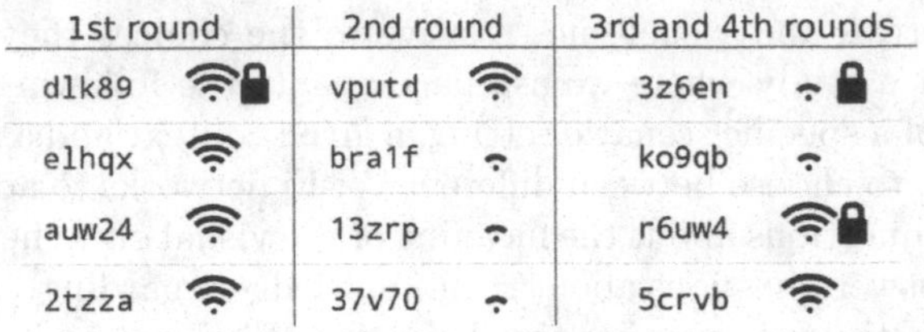

1st round		2nd round		3rd and 4th rounds	
d1k89	🛜🔒	vputd	🛜	3z6en	🛜🔒
elhqx	🛜	bra1f	🛜	ko9qb	🛜
auw24	🛜	13zrp	🛜	r6uw4	🛜🔒
2tzza	🛜	37v70	🛜	5crvb	🛜

Fig. 1. Rounds of choices.

and "QoS"). Participants had five rounds of choices; each round presented a list of 4 Wi-Fi networks, ordered randomly, each displaying a randomly generated name, a signal strength indicator (🛜 or ⌐), with or without a padlock sign (🔒). Figure 1 shows the Wi-Fi networks for the four rounds. To test for consistency we added a fifth round, not shown in the figure: it is one of the presented 4 rounds, randomly chosen. Due to space limitations, in this manuscript we focus and describe only the results associated with the third round of network choices. Either, we have no space to present and discuss how the delay, and/or the timing, of the listing of network names affects the Wi-Fi network choices; and also how the sequential order of the Wi-Fi networks makes a difference. This is left as future work.

To assess whether users associate the right intended meaning to the cues ("Encryption" for the padlock, and "QoS" for the signal strength bar) we ask the participants to express their understanding using a 4-points Likert scale (Not at all, Partially, Mostly, Completely) the extent to which they agree that each of the 2 visual cues (🔒 and 🛜) corroborate in meaning with 4 words related to "Encryption" (confidential, protected, encrypted, and private), and 4 related to "QoS" (good signal strength, high-bandwidth, high-speed, and fast).

As mentioned above, we complement the study with additional attitude and belief questions regarding the participants' use of Wi-Fi networks. For instance we ask such things as their thoughts about whether the padlock sign 🔒 means "locked out", and whether they tend to make choices out of convenience. To be clear, our *convenience* variable is a composite of three questions (Cronbach's $\alpha = 0.76$) and is used as such in our analyses. Additional questions are used to measure ICT skills: these are split into 2 separate variables, *stated ICT skills* (s.ICT) reflecting the participants' stated ICT skills, and *measured ICT skills* (m.ICT) reflecting how well the participants answered the technical questions. We collected a host of other variables thought to be associated with the Wi-Fi network choice; for the sake of space we ought to omit these results as well.

Choosing the Tool for our On-line Survey. We aimed to have a large number of participants and among a population larger than the one we could reach if we had run our experiment within our University quarters. Therefore, we opted for Amazon Mechanical Turk (mturk), a market place for on-line work which however offers readily available and substantially large samples of participants. The use of mturk as a tool for social experiments is debated; we are aware of it and of mturk's potential limitations (e.g., [4]) that can harm internal validity. For this reason we took several countermeasures to maximise as much as we could the quality in the collected data. We implemented a great amount of quality checks to detect that participants provide answers simply by clicking randomly. Namely, we implemented attention checks, for instance we added choices like: "I answer randomly and I should not be paid: Yes or No"; we repeated questions several times and we presented them with different wording; we measured the time participants took to answer each question to test unusually fast answering which can potentially indicate a low quality data; we also prevented a participant from participating more than once.

On the positive side, however, mturk allows us to recruit participants world-widely, and in the specific case of the US (and we admitted only participants from this country, see later in this paragraph) it is thought to be better representative of the general population than those commonly recruited via university settings [5]. Moreover, evidence suggests that self-reported behaviours gathered with mturk are comparable to observed behaviours in laboratory studies [6]. To make our analyses and interpretation of our results easier, we choose to recruit only participants located in the US, where the majority of mturk workers do not use the tool as their primary source of income. We ran the study by batch of 100 participants at different times of the day, during workdays and week-ends. Following the guide edited by a community [7] of mturk workers, we took great care to guarantee workers' rights of information and privacy, and we paid USD 0.90 for an average of 5 min of participation. We collect their age, gender, how comfortable they feel with ICT and their occupation. Occupation categories are organized following the US Bureau of labor statistic's classification major groups [8]. Optionally, participants can communicate ethnicity related information that follow the US census' interviewing manual guidelines [9].

The Pilot Study. Another issue, not related to mturk, but yet could potentially challenge the reliability of the data and the internal validity of the study is whether the participants in fact understand correctly what they are presented. In particular, because in theory there is an infinite number of scenarios we could have used to convey and illicit a need for certain Wi-Fi network properties, we had to take special care to pilot test several possible scenarios to identify the ones we ultimately used in our study. For instance, to evoke a task that does not need secure communications or good connectivity, we can ask the participants to picture themselves waiting at a bus stop (no time pressure) searching for a Wi-Fi network to browse the Internet (no need for security), but this scenario could be understood differently by men and women. To guarantee unambiguity in understanding the scenarios, we ran a pilot study using the same tools and settings as the main study that aimed at finding the most intelligible and less biased scenarios. We built 3 different "vignettes" [10], or candidates, for each scenario, and asked 156 participants to rate how much the task mentioned in the vignettes should comply with several properties. There were 6 properties related to "secure communications" (confidential, protected, encrypted, secret, masked, and private), and 6 related to the "good connectivity" (good signal strength,

Table 1. Chosen vignettes to convey the need for "Encryption" or "QoS" and their limitations.

Scenario	Intended meaning		Displayed text	Limitations
	Encryp.	QoS		
S0-0	0	0	I am sitting in a coffee shop with some friends. As they want to go for dinner later, I use my smartphone to check for a good restaurant. Unfortunately, there is no 3G/4G network available, so I have to use an available Wi-Fi network instead.	QoS is not significantly perceived as needed or not needed, males significantly perceive it as not-needed.
S0-1	0	1	I am a graphic designer intending to show my latest work to some of my friends. Since the 3G/4G connection is failing to retrieve the files, which are rather big, I decide to try an available Wi-Fi network to get some connectivity.	No limitation.
S1-0	1	0	I am waiting at a bus stop and I need to verify whether the check I deposited yesterday has been cleared. I need to use the bank's application on my smartphone to check the bank account's balance, but unfortunately there is no 3G/4G. I thus decide to try an available Wi-Fi network to get some connectivity.	QoS significantly tends to be perceived as needed whereas we intend to convey the converse meaning.
S1-1	1	1	I am a government official staying at an hotel. I scheduled an international online meeting. I planned to use the hotel's Wi-Fi network but the hotels Wi-Fi proved unreliable when I called my family earlier to test the connection. There is no 3G/4G network, so I decide to go somewhere else to find an available Wi-Fi network.	No limitation.

Table 2. Sociodemographics profile by scenario.

	S0-0	S0-1	S1-0	S1-1	Total
Gender: Female	41 %	43.4 %	36.1 %	41.2 %	40.4 %
Gender: Male	59 %	56.6 %	63.9 %	58.8 %	59.6 %
Highest ed: High-School	47 %	41 %	42.9 %	40.8 %	42.9 %
Highest ed: Bachelor Degree	41.7 %	48 %	46.4 %	44.6 %	45.2 %
Highest ed: Master Degree	7.9 %	8.2 %	8.7 %	12 %	9.2 %
Comfortable in IT: Not at all	3 %	6.2 %	2.8 %	3.9 %	4 %
Comfortable in IT: Not Very	18.8 %	13.7 %	16.7 %	18.5 %	16.9 %
Comfortable in IT: Somewhat	55.3 %	58.2 %	59.5 %	57.5 %	57.6 %
Comfortable in IT: Very	22.9 %	21.9 %	21 %	20.2 %	21.5 %
Total counts	266	256	252	233	1007

high-bandwidth, high-speed, first-class, responsive, and fast). We analysed the results of the pilot study with the R statistical software [11] and performed Wilcoxon rank tests [12] to discriminate the vignettes with the best psychometrical discrimination while checking for gender, age, and other social background variable effects. Table 1 shows for each scenario: the technical property that it intends to convey ("Encryption" or "QoS"), the selected vignette, and the limitations we need to be aware of when using it.

In summary, we model the dichotomous outcome (dependent variable) using Logistic Regression [13]: we estimate the conditional probability of choosing the target response option "clicking on the network with a 🔒 and a 📶" net of important independent variables. Our statistical modelling approach is relatively straightforward: firstly, we investigate the effect of the password because we expect it to be an important and significant control; we in fact find evidence of this and thus include it in all subsequent models. Secondly, we investigate the question of whether participants make an informed decision relative to each scenario, and then whether the participants' answers reflect, in a consistent way, their expressed choice relative to the meaning they attribute to the 🔒 and 📶 cues. Finally, we investigate whether the respondents' choices vary significantly by several basic socio-demographic variables.

3   Results

A total of 1090 participants took part in our study. Of these 83 failed the post-hoc data quality and integrity checks, and we remained with 1007 consistent cases. As shown in Table 2 and Fig. 2, our sample is rather balanced with regard to gender. The age distribution has a wide range (56 years). Table 3 shows the frequency of clicks (counts) and percentages for the round under investigation in this manuscript, the 3rd. Only 7 participants chose a network with a 📶; since this gives a too low variability, we excluded those 7 cases and proceeded with our statistical analysis on the 1000 remaining cases that display a 📶.

Varying "Encryption" and "QoS" (independent variables) in order to measure WiFi selection outcomes (dependent variable) may give biased results, because choosing or avoiding network selections marked with a 🔒 can occur as an effect of our independent variables or as an effect of simply having a password available or not. In order to control this potential bias, we provided half of the sample with a password. Performing a logistic regression allows to determine if the password is a significant predictor of the outcome "clicking on the network with a 🔒" and to what extent it is an effect based on our independent variables. With a password, odds of clicking on the target are 2.1 times higher (exponentiated coefficient (expcoeff) = 2.1 with $p < 0.001$). Tested in each scenario, the password effect is significant in S0-0 (expcoeff = 3.22, $p < 0.001$), and S0-1 (expcoeff = 4.7, $p < 0.001$). As the scenarios evoke the need for "Encryption" and/or for "QoS", we first analyze if the scenario is a predictor of the outcome i.e. "clicking on the network with a 🔒" while adjusting for password. If people understand the meaning of the cues correctly, using S0-0as intercept: S0-1 ("QoS" needed)should not increase the odds of clicking on

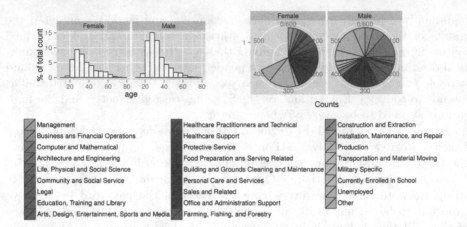

Fig. 2. Age and Occupation distribution for Males and Females

Table 3. Counts and frequencies for the third round of the study.

	counts	frequencies
?	5	0.5 %
📶	688	68.3 %
? 🔒	2	0.2 %
📶 🔒	312	31 %

Table 4. Trimmed results of the logistic regression of network selection on password + scenario. (S0-0 reference category)

Password	S0-1	S1-0	S1-1
p	< 0.001	< 0.01	< 0.01	< 0.001
expcoeff	2.2	2.0	1.9	4.2

the target, and S1-0 ("Encryption" needed)and S1-1should increase the odds in the same proportion. The results shown in Table 4 prove that scenarios S0-0and S1-1increase the odds in the same proportion and that S1-1nearly increases the odds twice as much. To investigate this result further and to determine if the participants took an "informed" decision, we consider the meaning the respondents associated with their responses. That is to say, we include an interaction term (*meaning × scenario*) and checked the resulting model fit statistics (LR test). Table 5 shows that while the main effects of the meaning dimensions are by large significant, with the exception of the encryption for the 📶 symbol, the LR tests show lack of improvement in model fit by including the interaction terms. This suggests that the effects of the meaning dimensions do not vary significantly per scenario.

Then we turn our attention to the socio-demographic effects. Age has a significant effect (p < .001) as increasing age by 1 multiplies the odds of clicking on the target by expcoeff = 1.026. Having good measured IT skills multiplies the odds of clicking on the target by expcoeff = 1.389 (p < 0.05). Convenience-driven participants are expcoeff = 0.104 (p < 0.001) times less likely of clicking on the target. Interactions of convenience with the scenarios are not significant.

Table 5. Exponentiated coefficients of the logistic regressions for the main effect of "Encryption" and "QoS" while controlling for password and scenario. LR tests compare models with and without interaction terms.

Cue	Dimension	Main effect		LR Tests
		expcoeff	p	p
🔒	Encryption	0.823	< 0.01	NS
	QoS	0.727	< 0.001	NS
📶	Encryption	0.860	NS	< 0.05
	QoS	0.826	< 0.01	NS

Table 6. Logistic regression results. Tests are perfmormed between the current model and the previous one. AIC is evaluated as well. (* < .05; ** < .01; *** < .001)

Variables	Step 1	Step 2	Step 3	Step 4	Model fit	
					LR Tests	AIC
Password	2.2 ***	2.4 ***	2.4 ***	2.4 ***	-	1171.88
S0-1	2.0 **	NS	NS	NS	-	1171.88
S1-0	1.9 **	1.8 *	1.8 *	1.8 *	-	1171.88
S1-1	4.2 ***	4.5 ***	4.6 ***	4.7 ***	-	1171.88
Convenience	-	0.10 ***	0.11 ***	0.11 ***	< 0.001	1000.87
m.ICT			Not significant, not added.			
🔒 = Enc.			Not significant, not added.			
🔒 = QoS	-	-	0.91 **	0.91 **	< 0.01	993.25
📶 = Enc.			Not significant, not added.			
📶 = QoS			Not significant, not added.			
age	-	-	-	1.0 **	< 0.01	986.72
gender			Not significant, not added.			
occupation			Not significant, not added.			
s.ICT			Not significant, not added.			
Ethicity			Not significant, not added.			
n = 1000						986.72

Gender, occupation, ethnicity and stated ICT skills don't have significant effects. To investigate the predictive power of the independent variables in our model, we conducted a series of logistical regressions in a stepwise fashion. We start with an adjusted model that includes password and scenario, then we add: the convenience, the measured ICT skills, the meaning dimensions, and the socio-demographic variables. Results are presented in Table 6 and discussed in the section below.

4 Discussion

Previous research shows that the 🔒 can act as a barrier for the user to choose a secure network [2]. This suggests that users are taking a "misinformed" decision, misunderstanding the meaning of that cue. This is actually the case because Table 6 shows that when 🔒 is misunderstood as meaning "QoS", users are less likely to choose the encrypted network.

Our results support that ⚡ is the cue that interferes the most with the other cues. That is to say, we were unable to perform any substantive statistical analysis on this particular issue because only 7 participants out of 1007 chose a network with a ⚡: participants avoided the ⚡ sign without any regard for the other cues it was associated with or any other contextual factors. We can't discuss further the weight of its meaning in the decision without statistical evidences, but as participants massively rated ⚡ as being the least related to "QoS" we can infer that they took "informed" decisions.

Table 6 lists the results of our regression modelling approach and shows the effect of adding other factors one by one. "Convenience" is the *most powerful predictor* of Wi-Fi network selection. We find that being convenience-driven lowers the probability of choosing the encrypted network by 89 %. In fact, when we include "Convenience" in our model, it cancels-out the effect of scenario S0-1 ("QoS" needed); this effect suggests that the choices made for that scenario are explained by the convenience factor rather than the scenario itself.

"Scenario" is the *second most powerful predictor*. For instance, in the final model (Step 4), participants are 4.7 times more likely to choose the encrypted network in S1-1 ("Encryption" and "QoS" needed) than in the S0-0scenario, which is the reference point. But the results also reveal an unexpected behaviour: participants are, almost equally, more likely to choose the encrypted network in both S0-1 ("QoS" needed) and S1-0 ("Encryption" needed). In S1-0 ("Encryption" needed), we can interpret that the participants seek for "Encryption" (still "QoS" can interfere because of the limitations, see Table 1), but in S0-1 ("QoS" needed)only the need for "QoS" can foster the choice of the encrypted network. Furthermore, still relatively to S0-0, change in odds in S1-1are more than double than those for S1-0 ("Encryption" needed)– this difference suggests that participants confuse "QoS" and "Encryption"; and that needing "QoS" contribute to the choice of the encrypted network. Finally, we already observed that the introduction of "Convenience" in Step 2 cancels out the effect of S0-1 ("QoS" needed), but this inclusion has a limited effect on S1-1and S1-0 ("Encryption" needed). This suggests that the choice of an encrypted network that is only nudged by the need of "QoS" is fragile; the same choice performed in a scenario needing "Encryption" is stronger. That is to say, even convenience-driven people tend to adopt secure behavior when the situation calls for it.

We cannot say definitively whether or not the participants' understanding of the meaning of the cues is the cause of the discrepancies we observe in Step 1's odds of choosing the secure network for S1-0 ("Encryption" needed)and S1-1. As shown in Table 6 this is an important factor, but Table 5 shows that it does not interact with the scenario and therefore it is not the cause of those discrepancies.

The *third most powerful predictor* is the "Possession of a Password": participants with a password are 2.4 times more likely to choose the encrypted network (see final step in model). But the effect interacts with the scenario: in a scenario needing "Encryption" participants tend to choose the encrypted network, ignoring whether they have a password or not; but when the scenario does not require

"Encryption" it appears that they do not look for an encrypted network, unless we provide them with a password.

The ICT skills that we asked our participants about did not result in significant effects as shown in Table 6. Furthermore, we found evidence that knowing what a cue means in terms of the dimensions we asked about, has very little impact on the participant' decisions. Thus, taking "informed" decisions does not foster a secure behavior and computer literacy seems to play little role in the decision process. The last significant factor is age, but its effect ends up being nonsignificant.

5   Conclusion

This paper explains *why* people choose Wi-Fi networks, and it does so by investigating how the cues (🔒, ⚡ and 📶) displayed by Wi-Fi network managers affect Wi-Fi network selection. Using a sample of 1000 participants, collected through the Amazon mechanical turk, we analyzed through a series of logistic regressions the relative importance of the various factors associated with the participant's choice of Wi-Fi network.

We shed light on whether users understand and use the padlock and the signal strength visual cues to decide which Wi-Fi network to connect to: they blankly avoid the networks displaying ⚡ because they understand that it is a sign of bad connectivity, but the decision is more subtle when 📶 🔒 and 📶 are competing. The choice of a network displaying a 🔒 is subject to more influences: users who are not convenience-driven tend to pick an encrypted network if they are provided a password or if the task undertaken calls for "QoS"; when needing "Encryption", all users tend to choose encrypted networks. But our analysis shows that the meaning our participants attribute to the cues and other socio-demographic variables do not explain why our participants choose encrypted networks when the task asks for "QoS", or even "Encryption". These results suggest that beliefs and circumstances (i.e., context) are the real motivators behind our participants' choices, and that even if they that take ill-informed decisions regarding the meaning of the cues, they take "informed" decisions with regard to other factors.

In future work, we will seek to confirm our findings reported in this manuscript relative to the other rounds of data collected in our study. We will further investigate how the expressed beliefs of our participants regarding Wi-Fi networks affect their network choices. Moreover, we will investigate more closely the socio-demographic profiles of those who we have been identified as being convenience-driven.

References

1. Ferreira, A., Huynen, J.L., Koenig, V., Lenzini, G.: Socio-technical security analysis of wireless hotspots. In: Tryfonas, T., Askoxylakis, I. (eds.) HAS 2014. LNCS, vol. 8533, pp. 306–317. Springer, Heidelberg (2014)

2. Jeske, D., Coventry, L., Briggs, P.: Decision justifications for wireless network selection. In: 2014 Workshop on Socio-Technical Aspects in Security and Trust (STAST), pp. 1–7, July 2014
3. Grice, P.: Studies in the Way of Words. Harvard University Press, Cambridge (1989)
4. Rand, D.G.: The promise of Mechanical Turk: how online labor markets can help theorists run behavioral experiments. J. Theor. Biol. **299**, 172–179 (2012)
5. Paolacci, G., Chandler, J., Ipeirotis, P.: Running experiments on amazon Mechanical Turk. Judgm. Decis. Mak. **5**(5), 411–419 (2010)
6. Crump, M.J.C., McDonnell, J.V., Gureckis, T.M.: Evaluating Amazon's Mechanical Turk as a tool for experimental behavioral research. PLoS One **8**(3), e57410 (2013)
7. We are dynamo turker community: guidelines for academic requesters. http://wearedynamo.org/
8. Bureau, U.S., Statistics, L.: Standard Occupational Classification and Coding Structure, pp. 1–7. Health, San Francisco (2010)
9. U.S. department of the census: current population survey interviewing manual, June 2013
10. Finch, J.: The vignette technique in survey research. Sociology **21**(1), 105–114 (1987)
11. R Development Core Team: R: A Language and Environment for Statistical Computing. R Foundation for Statistical Computing, Vienna (2008). http://cran.rproject.org/doc/FAQ/R-FAQ.html#Citing-R
12. Wilcoxon, F.: Individual comparisons by ranking methods. Biom. Bull. **1**(6), 80–83 (1945)
13. McCullagh, P.: Generalized Linear Models. Chapman and Hall, New York (1989)

Usable-Security Evaluation

Yasser M. Hausawi[1]([✉]) and William H. Allen[2]

[1] Institute of Public Administration, Jeddah, Saudi Arabia
hawsawiy@ipa.edu.sa
[2] Florida Institute of Technology, Melbourne, FL, USA
wallen@fit.edu

Abstract. Developing software products which align security and usability to make a synergistic relationship between security and usability is an engineering process that starts from the first phase of the Software Development Life-Cycle (SDLC), and continues through the rest of the phases: design, construction, and testing. However, a summative evaluation of such a process must be done after the software product is completely developed with careful attention to measuring the alignment between security and usability (i.e.: usable-security), and integrating such alignment properly within the SDLC. Therefore, this paper proposes a usable-security measuring matrix that provides a summative evaluation of the whole process of applying usable-security on software products.

Keywords: Security · Usability · Human computer interaction · HCI · HCI-SEC · Usable security · Quality attributes evaluation

1 Introduction

As a result of the increased adoption of a user-centered approach to improve human-computer interaction and increasing concerns regarding computer-related privacy and security issues, researchers and scientists have proposed many design techniques that incorporate usable-security [11,15]. Those techniques are used to build software systems that seek to balance usability and security. However, if we take a careful look at the currently available software systems, we often find that quality attributes, such as security and usability, are applied and evaluated separately [3,10,20].

Therefore, the vast majority of those systems are built and deployed without giving proper attention to evaluating the state of integrating the quality attributes, such as usable-security. It is very important to be sure that software systems are usable and secure enough [15,19], so that people can rely on such systems and interact with them as if interacting with actual human beings. People ought to be able to use and deal with systems with hands-on ease, as this helps in a better cooperation between the people and the systems [9,10]. Also, people must be able to trust that the systems are secure enough against

T. Tryfonas and I. Askoxylakis (Eds.): HAS 2015, LNCS 9190, pp. 335–346, 2015.
DOI: 10.1007/978-3-319-20376-8_30

any malicious penetration behavior that may cause any intentional undesired change or update during the human-computer interaction [2,22].

Unfortunately, without careful consideration of the balance between usability and security, a system can be designed so that those properties will actually work against each other and cannot be aligned and evaluated together as one joint concept [1,16,25]. One approach that has proven successful combines usability and security with the goal of improving the performance and quality of computer systems [8]. Therefore, we adopted the approach of bridging usability and security attributes together as one combined attribute: usable-security. One way to achieve that goal is using models and frameworks that help in assessing software usability, security, and usable-security requirements based on formative evaluation approach [10,13,20]. Assessing usable-security helps in predicting to which level software systems could be simultaneously usable and secure [13]. This work proposes a summative usable-security evaluation matrix based on the usable-security assessment models and frameworks. The matrix represents a solid component of a large scale ongoing research project for designing a Usable-Security Engineering Framework (USEF) for enhancing software development when balancing security and usability is an important matter.

Section 2 presents background on how important usability and security are to software systems and Sect. 3 introduces a proposed mathematical-based evaluation model to help determining the levels of usability and security quality attributes. Section 4 introduces a proposed matrix to evaluate usable-security of software systems. The last section is a conclusion about applying the matrix.

2   Background

Despite the success of most of the available systems in making human life even easier, they need continual evaluation and enhancement to make sure that such systems meet the usability and security requirements and standards [4,17].

2.1   Usability

One usability concern is that software systems must be effective. For example, when airline companies use automatic speech recognition systems for phone reservations, those systems can only be considered effective if they are able to convert a traveler's speech into a textual representation that can be then processed as accurately as a textual request. Another usability concern is that the systems must be efficient enough to save processing time for both users and business owners. However, there are many examples where the extended time of the sound representation process negatively impacts the speed of the automatic speech recognition systems' ability to access customers' information. Consequently, lack of effectiveness and efficiency creates unsatisfied customers and owners of such software systems [4].

2.2   Security

Security is also another important aspect to be evaluated and enhanced continually [17]. For instance, NLP approach is used in voice biometric authentication and access control management applications [5]. The voice representation techniques that are used in voice authentication systems must maintain confidentiality to prevent access to the representation techniques, which could lead to the penetration of authentication systems. Voice authentication systems can also be used against the important security goal of integrity by allowing unauthorized alterations to representation techniques that lead to a misleading or improper representation process. Human-Computer Interaction software systems must guarantee the availability of any application for legitimate users at any time according to the availability requirements specifications. For example, when biometrics systems are used for authentication, it must be available during all access permission requests to resources. Once the biometric authentication is not available, no access control will be activated.

Based on the above justifications on how important are both usability and security to any software system, Sects. 3 and 4 propose an evaluation methodology and a matrix to help in the evaluation of software systems.

3   Usability-Security Measuring and Evaluation

In order to develop a useful evaluation methodology, developers should have appropriate measuring techniques before the evaluation process begins. Access to suitable metrics gives developers the ability to predict the evaluation's outcome. However, usable-security is difficult to measure, consequently, it is difficult to evaluate as well [7,11]. Therefore, this work proposes new measuring and evaluation techniques based on OWASP [20] and SAULTA [10]. The evaluation technique serves as extended research work for the Assessment Framework for Usable-Security (AFUS) [13]. The following subsections describe methods for measuring and evaluating usability and security. In order to provide evaluation consistency, all the attributes and their properties are evaluated according to Table 2 after processing their measurements according to Table 1.

3.1   Usability Evaluation

The term usability is defined by the International Standard Organization (ISO) as the range in which a product can be operated by legitimate users to satisfactorily perform specific tasks in an effective, efficient, and specified way [26]. Some others add accuracy, memorability, and learnability as secondary usability factors [16]. This paper focuses only on the three factors of the ISO definition.

In order to evaluate the targeted usability level on any developed software system during the evaluation phase, the application state (level) of each of the usability properties (efficiency, effectiveness, and satisfaction) must be focused on, as well as providing a method to determine a measurable way to evaluate these properties on software systems. The following evaluation equations are adapted from Bevan and Macleod's concepts [6,18].

338   Y.M. Hausawi and W.H. Allen

Table 1. Usability and Security Attributes and their Properties' Measuring Guidance, where the listed measuring statuses: HA, MA, SA, and NA represent High Achieved, Mostly Achieved, Some Achieved, and Not Achieved; respectively. α and β represent Usability and Security, respectively.

	Measuring Status				
	HA	MA	Achieved	SA	NA
EF1	$EF1 \geq 0.9$	$0.7 \leq EF1 < 0.9$	$0.6 \leq EF1 < 0.7$	$0.3 \leq EF1 < 0.6$	$EF1 < 0.3$
EF2	$EF2 < 1.0$	$EF2 = 1.0$	$1.0 < EF2 \leq 1.2$	$1.2 < EF2 < 1.5$	$EF2 \geq 1.5$
SA1	$SA1 \geq 0.9$	$0.7 \leq SA1 < 0.9$	$0.6 \leq SA1 < 0.7$	$0.3 \leq SA1 < 0.6$	$SA1 < 0.3$
α	$\alpha \geq 0.9$	$0.7 \leq \alpha < 0.9$	$0.6 \leq \alpha < 0.7$	$0.3 \leq \alpha < 0.6$	$\alpha < 0.3$
CO1	$CO1 \geq 0.99$	$0.95 \leq CO1 < 0.99$	$0.90 \leq CO1 < 0.95$	$0.80 \leq CO1 < 0.90$	$CO1 < 0.80$
IN1	$IN1 \geq 0.99$	$0.95 \leq IN1 < 0.99$	$0.90 \leq IN1 < 0.95$	$0.80 \leq IN1 < 0.90$	$IN1 < 0.80$
AV1	$AV1 \geq 0.99$	$0.95 \leq AV1 < 0.99$	$0.90 \leq AV1 < 0.95$	$0.80 \leq AV1 < 0.90$	$AV1 < 0.80$
β	$\beta \geq 0.9$	$0.7 \leq \beta < 0.9$	$0.6 \leq \beta < 0.7$	$0.3 \leq \beta < 0.6$	$\beta < 0.3$

Table 2. Usability and Security Attributes and their Properties' Evaluation Guidance, where the listed measuring statuses: HA, MA, SA, and NA represent High Achieved, Mostly Achieved, Some Achieved, and Not Achieved; respectively.

	Evaluation				
Measuring Status	HA	MA	Achieved	SA	NA
Evaluation Value	9	7	6	3	1

Effectiveness. Systems can only be considered as effective if their users are able to achieve their goal of operating such systems. The effectiveness property can be measured based on a goal-centered view by counting the number of successful tasks that legitimate users perform [12]. For example, a software systems is effective if it allows users to successfully create their passwords, login using their previously created passwords, or provide their biometric traits. Equation 1 can be used to evaluate the effectiveness for software systems, where n represents the total number of accepted tasks that legitimate users perform, R represents the result of each performed task's trial (either "failure" or "success"), *EF1* represents the system effectiveness rate.

$$EF1 = \frac{1}{n} \sum_{i=1}^{n} \delta(R[i]) \tag{1}$$

$$Where \qquad \delta(\theta) \text{ is defined as: } \delta(\theta) = \begin{cases} 0 & \text{if } \theta = \text{failure} \\ 1 & \text{if } \theta = \text{success} \end{cases}$$

According to Table 1, if the result of system effectiveness rate, $EF1 \geq 0.9$, this means that the software system is highly effective. On the other hand, if the result of $EF1 < 0.3$, this means that the system is ineffective and may need further enhancement. After measuring the effectiveness, it is evaluated according to Table 2, because this provides the consistency among all of the usability properties.

Efficiency. Efficient systems must complete a specific task or process to reach a particular goal within an acceptable amount of time. The efficiency property is important because both the vendors and the users will not rely on a system that takes too long a time to perform a specific task (for instance: authentication). The measurement used to evaluate the efficiency is the amount of time that is consumed for achieving a particular goal or to complete a particular task. Equation 2 depicts the evaluation, where n represents number of trails to perform a particular task, β represents the standard average amount of time to finish such task, and T represents the amount of time to perform the task on each trial.

$$EF2 = \frac{\frac{1}{n}\sum_{i=1}^{n} T[i]}{\beta} \qquad (2)$$

According to Table 1, if the result of system efficiency rate, $EF2$, is less than 1, this means that the software system is highly efficient. In contrast, if the resultant value of $EF2$ is greater than or equal to 1.50, this means that the software system is inefficient because the average amount of time consumed to perform that task is too far beneath the standard average, β. After measuring the efficiency, it is evaluated according to Table 2, because this provides the consistency among all of the usability properties.

Satisfaction. For a system to be satisfactory, both the vendors and the users must be happy with the system. This is determined by the willingness of both vendors and users to rely on and reuse the system. It is important to be aware that the satisfaction is compellingly affected by the vendors' and the users' mood [16]. It is most likely to be perceived as satisfactory if it is both simultaneously effective and efficient. Evaluating the satisfaction property is a challenging task due to the difficulty of having accurate measurement tools. However, the best way to evaluate satisfaction is via questionnaires such as in SUMI [18] and the SUS [23] surveys, or interviews [16]. Therefore, satisfaction is evaluated through involving HCI-SEC principles that are related to user-centered approach [27] that focus on the ease of use, the degree of happiness, and the degree of confusion. Based on the results of the given survey, user satisfaction, $SA1$, is measured according to Table 1. After measuring user satisfaction based on the above degree of satisfaction via surveys, it is evaluated according to Table 2, because this provides the consistency among all of the usability properties.

Evaluating the above standard usability properties leads to an overall usability evaluation through summing the evaluations of the three properties (effectiveness, efficiency, and user satisfaction) as in Eq. 3, where α represents the usability:

$$\alpha = \frac{EF1 + EF2 + SA1}{3} \qquad (3)$$

Equation 3 provides the α measure shown in Table 1. Consequently, same as evaluating the usability properties, overall usability of software systems is evaluated based on Table 2, because this provides the evaluation consistency among three quality attributes under investigation (usability, security, and usable-security).

3.2 Security Evaluation

The term "security" is identified in many ways. Essentially, system security is a set of methods and techniques used to prevent weaknesses from being exploited by applying three security goals: confidentiality, integrity, and availability [21]. Software systems have vulnerabilities that need to be discovered and closed, or at least protected from being imposed. Therefore, to reach an acceptable level of security, the three security properties must be applied and achieved. The following analyzes the importance of the security properties, how they are applied on the systems, and how they are measurably evaluated.

Confidentiality. Confidentiality is a goal of all secure systems. Confidentiality is defined as the ability to grant access only to authorized users. If unauthorized users gain access to computer systems, confidential information may be accessed and then used against the systems' vendors or users. To measure software systems' confidentiality, Eqs. 4, 5 and 6 are applied where n represents the total number of access trials, α represents an individual access trial (either "false access" or "true access"), TAR represents true access rate, FAR represents false access rate, and $CO1$ represents system confidentiality evaluation value.

$$CO1 = TAR \tag{4}$$

$$TAR = \frac{\sum_{i=1}^{n} \delta(\alpha[i])}{n} \tag{5}$$

$$Where \qquad \delta(\theta) \text{ is defined as: } \delta(\theta) = \begin{cases} 1 & \text{if } \theta = \text{true access} \\ 0 & \text{if } \theta = \text{false access} \end{cases}$$

and

$$FAR = 1 - TAR \tag{6}$$

According to Table 1, if the result of system confidentiality rate, $CO1$, is greater than or equal to 0.99, this means that the system is highly confidential. In contrast, if the resulted value of $CO1$ is less than or equal to 0.80, this means that the system failed to provide confidentiality because access was granted for too many unauthorized users. After measuring confidentiality, it is evaluated according to Table 2, because this provides the consistency among all of the security properties.

Integrity. Integrity means that for the authorized users, the system does not allow them to perform tasks in an improper way, and protects the data from any unauthorized alteration. As having usable-security evaluation for software systems is the goal of this paper, the integrity property must be correctly applied to make such systems secure. This property is achieved by enabling systems to create auto-backup and auto-check using proper techniques and tools like hashing, the process of comparing backup files with the same files on the system. Equation 7 depicts the integrity calculation on software systems, where n represents the total number of selected files for hashing, $IN1$ represents the integrity evaluation result.

$$IN1 = \frac{1}{n} \sum_{i=1}^{n} \delta\left(\frac{systemfile[i]}{backupfile[i]}\right) \tag{7}$$

$$Where \qquad \delta(\theta) \text{ is defined as: } \delta(\theta) = \begin{cases} 1 & \text{if } \theta = 1 \\ 0 & \text{if } \theta \neq 1 \end{cases}$$

According to Table 1, if the result of system integrity, *IN1*, is greater than or equals to 0.99, this means that the system is provides integrity, because the result of the hashing (comparing be-tween the system and the backup files) indicates that there were not any unauthorized alterations of system files. In contrast, if the resulted value of *IN1* is less than 0.80, this means that the system did not provide integrity because a critical alternation occurred. After measuring integrity, it is evaluated according to Table 2, because this provides the consistency among all of the security properties.

Availability. Availability is a security factor where the system's services and contents, or data, must be available at any time an authorized user needs to access them. It is measured based upon the number of success services or data access requests a system receives. Equation 8 shows the availability calculation, where n represents the total number of access trials, α represents an individual access trial (either "available" or "unavailable"), and *AV1* represents availability rate.

$$AV1 = \frac{1}{n} \sum_{i=1}^{n} \delta(\alpha[i]) \tag{8}$$

$$Where \qquad \delta(\theta) \text{ is defined as: } \delta(\theta) = \begin{cases} 1 & \text{if } \theta \text{ is available} \\ 0 & \text{if } \theta \text{ is unavailable} \end{cases}$$

According to Table 1, if the result of system availability evaluation, *AV1*, is greater than or equal to 0.99, this means that the software system is highly available, because it is accessible to its authorized users whenever needed. In contrast, if the resulted value of *AV1* is less than 0.80, this means that the system was not available because more than 20 % of the requests were not serviced. After measuring availability, it is evaluated according to the unified numerical evaluation values of Table 2, because this provides the consistency among all of the security properties.

Evaluating the above standard security properties leads to an overall security evaluation through summing the evaluations of the three properties (confidentiality, integrity, an availability) divided by 3. Equation 9 illustrates the calculation, where β represents the security:

$$\beta = \frac{CO1 + IN1 + AV1}{3} \tag{9}$$

The outcome of the above calculation provides one of the measuring statuses of Table 1. Consequently, same as evaluating the security properties, overall security of software systems is evaluated based on Table 2, because this provides the evaluation consistency among three quality attributes under investigation.

4   Usable-Security Evaluation Matrix

Analysis and measurement studies of usability and security properties on systems produced detailed understanding of the nature and structure of systems' usable-security. Based on the previous section, a usable-security evaluation matrix can be constructed that can be used as a guidance to achieve the overall goal of this paper, which is evaluation and enhancement for software systems to be both more usable and secure enough (see Fig. 1). The matrix shown in Fig. 1 is a proposed method for evaluating usable-security of software systems. Systems' usable-security can be evaluated by using Eqs. 3 and 9 that evaluate the systems' usability (effectiveness, efficiency, and satisfactory), and security (confidentiality, integrity, and availability). The results are then used in Eq. 10, where α represents the overall usability evaluation, β represents overall security evaluation, γ represents the matrix score, which is the usable-security evaluation.

$$\gamma = (\alpha \times \beta) - |\alpha - \beta| \tag{10}$$

The highest measuring evaluation category in the matrix is when the system attains a score of at least 0.81 as displayed in Fig. 2. This means that the system has applied and achieved the highest level of all of the six usability and security properties. Such a system is considered as usable and secure not only because it achieved the usability and security goals, but because it bridged both usability and security together with careful consideration to the HCI/user-centered approach from the begining of the development process.

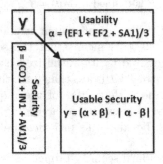

Fig. 1. The Usable-Security Evaluation Matrix: The evaluation process consists of two components: formative mathematical-based modeling that evaluates the security and usability properties, and a summative matrix that evaluates the Usable-Security based on the results of the formative modeling.

On the other hand, the lowest measuring evaluation category in the matrix is when a software system scores at most 0.01 as shown in Fig. 2, which means that the system has not achieved any beneficial values of the usability and security attributes. Such a system is considered neither usable nor secure not only because it does not achieve the usability and security goals, but because it does not bridge

γ	Highly Usable	Mostly Usable	Usable	Some Usable	Not Usable
Highly Secure	0.81	0.43	0.24	-0.33	-0.71
Mostly Secure	0.43	0.49	0.32	-0.19	-0.53
Secure	0.24	0.32	0.36	-0.12	-0.44
Some Secure	-0.33	-0.19	-0.12	0.09	-0.17
Not Secure	-0.71	-0.53	-0.44	-0.17	0.01

Fig. 2. Usability and Security Measuring Values: The measuring values and categories of the Security and usability attributes are used to evaluate Usable-Security

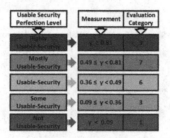

Usable Security Perfection Level	Measurement	Evaluation Category
Highly Usable-Security	$\gamma \geq 0.81$	9
Mostly Usable-Security	$0.49 \leq \gamma < 0.81$	7
Usable-Security	$0.36 \leq \gamma < 0.49$	6
Some Usable-Security	$0.09 \leq \gamma < 0.36$	3
Not Usable-Security	$\gamma < 0.09$	1

Fig. 3. Final usable-security evaluation and categorization guidance

usability and security as well. In addition, such a low score for a system indicates that its developers might have not considered the HCI/user-centered approach from the begining of the development process.

Walking through the whole evaluation process, a final usable-security evaluation is reached as one of five perfection levels: high usable-security when $\gamma \geq 0.81$, mostly usable-security when $0.49 \leq \gamma < 0.81$, usable-security when $0.36 \leq \gamma < 0.49$, some usable-security when $0.09 \leq \gamma < 0.36$, and not usable-security when $\gamma < 0.09$. Overall, a numerical categorization is given to each perfection level as follows: high usable-security is categorized as 9, mostly usable-security is categorized as 7, usable-security is categorized as 6, some usable-security is categorized as 3, and not usable-security is categorized as 1. Figure 3 presents the final usable-security evaluation and categorization guidance.

5   Case Study: Authentication Approaches

In order to show the advantage of using the usable-security evaluation matrix, this section presents the results of assessing the usability levels of an experiment that compares two authentication approaches. The Choice-Based Authentication Approach (CBAA) and the Traditional-Based Authentication Approach (TBAA) are described in detail in [14]). The experiment used 30 different scenarios for each approach and the results from the experiment are described below.

For the security values, we used one value (mostly secure: 0.7) for all the thirty scenarios of the TBAA, with expected entropy between 2^{26} and 2^{27}. As the assumed security value is considered as the security level that can be achieved when the NIST SP 800 Series is used as a foundation security policy [24]. However, security level of the CBAA has been increased because of the increased complexity for adversaries by displaying multiple authentication methods during the login process as explained in [14], where the expected entropy is between 2^{64} and 2^{65}, in addition to biometrics. Hence, we anticipated that the CBAA security should at least be better than the TBAA by 0.1. Therefore, we used a unified security value for all the thirty scenarios of the CBAA as (mostly secure: 0.8). Figure 4 displays the two sets of the scenarios.

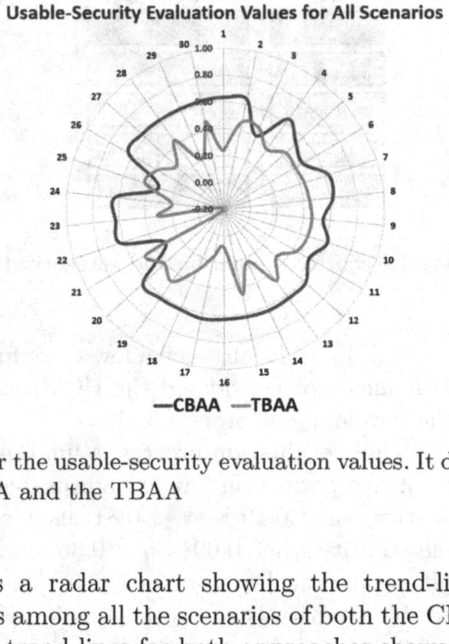

Fig. 4. Radar chart for the usable-security evaluation values. It displays usable-security coverage by the CBAA and the TBAA

Figure 4 displays a radar chart showing the trend-lines from evaluating usable-security levels among all the scenarios of both the CBAA and the TBAA. A comparison of the trend-lines for both approaches shows that the CBAA provided a better balance of usable-security than the TBAA. Moreover, it indicates that the usable-security evaluation results are more stable in the CBAA than the TBAA. In addition, the figure shows the usable-security coverage for both approaches and indicates that the CBAA occupies a wider domain than the TBAA.

Following the guidelines in Fig. 3, the results in Fig. 4 for the CBAA show that scenarios 21 and 25 achieved the "some usable-security" level (0.31 and 0.32, respectively), scenarios 3 and 6 provide the "usable-security" level of 0.40 and 0.48, respectively, while the rest of the 26 scenarios reached the "mostly usable-security" level (i.e.: the values are greater than or equal to 0.49, and less than 0.81). As a result, the overall usable-security evaluation value for the CBAA is 0.58, which is at the "mostly usable-security" level.

On the other hand, the TBAA scenarios displayed on Fig. 4 show that the scenarios 16 and 22 only achieve the "not usable-security" level (0.09 and −0.19, respectively). Moreover, 10 scenarios reached the "some usable-security" level, and only 18 scenarios provided the "usable-security" level. Consequently, the overall usable-security evaluation value for the TBAA is 0.35, which is the "some usable-security" level.

6   Conclusion

It is important that developers are able to evaluate usability, security, and usable-security software quality attributes that were specified within a system's requirements and were properly designed, correctly constructed, accurately evaluated, and appropriately deployed. However, existing methodologies for applying the above attributes do not assure the development of systems that can meet the necessary high quality standards for usability and security. The integration of such attributes becomes more important than just applying each attribute individually. The work presented in this paper goes beyond the application of attributes' integration, as it proposes an evaluation methodology to test the alignment of those attributes. Moreover, the proposed evaluation matrix is flexible enough to be used to modify the attributes' measures. It can also be extended to evaluate other quality attributes.

Acknowledgment. The authors would like to thank the Institute of Public Administration (IPA) in Saudi Arabia for their support of this work.

References

1. Adams, A., Sasse, M.A.: Users are not the enemy. Commun. ACM **42**(12), 40–46 (1999)
2. Alkussayer, A., Allen, W.H.: The ISDF framework: integrating security patterns and best practices. In: Park, J.H., Zhan, J., Lee, C., Wang, G., Kim, T., Yeo, S.-S. (eds.) ISA 2009. CCIS, vol. 36, pp. 17–28. Springer, Heidelberg (2009)
3. Alkussayer, A., Allen, W.H.: A scenario-based framework for the security evaluation of software architecture. In: 3rd IEEE International Conference on ICCSIT, vol. 5, pp. 687–695. IEEE (2010)
4. Atallah, M.J., McDonough, C.J., Raskin, V., Nirenburg, S.: Natural language processing for information assurance and security: an overview and implementations. In: Proceedings of the 2000 Workshop on New Security Paradigms, pp. 51–65. ACM (2001)
5. Benson, G., Re, S.R.: System and method for device registration and authentication, 8 June 2012, uS Patent App. 13/492,126
6. Bevan, N., Macleod, M.: Usability measurement in context. Behav. Inf. Tech. **13**(1–2), 132–145 (1994)
7. Cranor, L.F., Garfinkel, S.: Guest editors' introduction: secure or usable? IEEE Secur. Priv. **2**(5), 16–18 (2004)

8. DeWitt, A.J., Kuljis, J.: Is usable security an oxymoron? Interactions **13**(3), 41–44 (2006)
9. Ferre, X.: Integration of usability techniques into the software development process. In: International Conference on Software Engineering (Bridging the Gaps Between Software Engineering and Human-Computer Interaction), pp. 28–35 (2003)
10. Folmer, E., van Gurp, J., Bosch, J.: Scenario-based assessment of software architecture usability. In: ICSE Workshop on SE-HCI, Citeseer, pp. 61–68 (2003)
11. Garfinkel, S.: Design principles and patterns for computer systems that are simultaneously secure and usable. Ph.D. thesis, Massachusetts Institute of Technology (2005)
12. Hamilton, S., Chervany, N.L.: Evaluating information system effectiveness-part i: comparing evaluation approaches. MIS Q. **5**, 55–69 (1981)
13. Hausawi, Y.M., Allen, W.H.: An assessment framework for usable-security based on decision science. In: Tryfonas, T., Askoxylakis, I. (eds.) HAS 2014. LNCS, vol. 8533, pp. 33–44. Springer, Heidelberg (2014)
14. Hausawi, Y.M., Allen, W.H., Bahr, G.S.: Choice-based authentication: a usable-security approach. In: Stephanidis, C., Antona, M. (eds.) UAHCI 2014, Part I. LNCS, vol. 8513, pp. 114–124. Springer, Heidelberg (2014)
15. Hausawi, Y.M., Mayron, L.M.: Towards usable and secure natural language processing systems. In: Stephanidis, C. (ed.) HCII 2013, Part I. CCIS, vol. 373, pp. 109–113. Springer, Heidelberg (2013)
16. Kainda, R., Flechais, I., Roscoe, A.: Security and usability: analysis and evaluation. In: ARES 2010 International Conference on Availability, Reliability, and Security, pp. 275–282. IEEE (2010)
17. Kim, H.-C., Liu, D., Kim, H.-W.: Inherent usability problems in interactive voice response systems. In: Jacko, J.A. (ed.) Human-Computer Interaction, Part IV, HCII 2011. LNCS, vol. 6764, pp. 476–483. Springer, Heidelberg (2011)
18. Kirakowski, J., Corbett, M.: Sumi: the software usability measurement inventory. Br. J. Educ. Technol. **24**(3), 210–212 (1993)
19. Mayron, L.M., Hausawi, Y., Bahr, G.S.: Secure, usable biometric authentication systems. In: Stephanidis, C., Antona, M. (eds.) UAHCI 2013, Part I. LNCS, vol. 8009, pp. 195–204. Springer, Heidelberg (2013)
20. OWASP: risk rating methodology (2013)
21. Pfleeger, C.P., Pfleeger, S.L.: Security in Computing. Prentice Hall PTR, Upper Saddle river (2006)
22. Simpson, S.: Fundamental Practices for Secure Software Development: A Guide to the Most Effective Secure Development Practices in Use Today (2011)
23. Tullis, T., Albert, W.: Measuring the User Experience: Collecting, Analyzing, and Presenting Usability Metrics. Morgan Kaufmann, San Francisco (2013)
24. Weiß, S., Weissmann, O., Dressler, F.: A comprehensive and comparative metric for information security. In: Proceedings of IFIP International Conference on Telecommunication Systems, Modeling and Analysis (ICTSM 2005), pp. 1–10 (2005)
25. Whitten, A.: Making security usable. Ph.D. thesis, Princeton University (2004)
26. Good, M., Spine, T.M., Whiteside, J., George, P.: User-derived impact analysis as a tool for usability engineering. In: ACM SIGCHI Bulletin, vol. 17, pp. 241–246. ACM (1986)
27. Gutmann, P., Grigg, I.: Security usability. IEEE Secur. Priv. **3**(4), 56–58 (2005)

Reminding Users of their Privacy at the Point of Interaction: The Effect of Privacy Salience on Disclosure Behaviour

Thomas Hughes-Roberts[✉]

Nottingham Trent University, Computing and Technology, Nottingham, UK
thomas.hughesroberts@ntu.ac.uk

Abstract. Privacy is a well-documented issued for users of social networks were observable behaviour does not appear to match stated levels of concern. Given that the User Interface (UI) is the environment with which users react to, it would appear to be ideally placed to address the potential causes of poor privacy. This paper looks at the use of the Theory of Planned Behaviour and its Behavioral Attitude aspect to examine how users could be reminded or informed of the behavioral consequences of information disclosure. A series of "Privacy Lights" are presented that aim to highlight the potential sensitivity of data items. An experiment explores the effect of these lights on participants who are asked to register to a new social network by answering a series of questions of varying sensitivity. Exposure to the lights in the treatment group resulted in significantly less disclosure than the control suggesting that simple UI additions can be utilized to address the privacy problem.

Keywords: Privacy · Social networks · Human computer interaction (HCI) · Theory of planned behaviour

1 Introduction

Privacy is a well-documented problem for users of social networks. The privacy paradox describes how stated levels of concern for personal privacy does not match observable behaviour within the network [1]. Behavioral psychology describes behaviour as a reaction to environmental stimulus [2]. Given that the User Interface (UI) of a social network can be considered the environment with which users react, the question is raised: how could the UI be designed to encourage more protective privacy behaviour? Theories of behavioral change such as the Theory of Planned Behaviour (TPB) [3] could provide a solution for guiding the design of UI's as they describe the influential factors of individual action. Indeed, a user based approach may be required given that privacy is highly individual and fluid [4] making the UI ideally placed to address the privacy issue as it is the point of interaction.

This paper will outline the potential causes of poor privacy behaviour and propose how the TPB can be used to define solutions to the problems caused. The Personal Attitude (PA) feature in this model and its influence over intention is used as the basis

© Springer International Publishing Switzerland 2015
T. Tryfonas and I. Askoxylakis (Eds.): HAS 2015, LNCS 9190, pp. 347–356, 2015.
DOI: 10.1007/978-3-319-20376-8_31

to design a UI element aimed at informing or reminding users of their personal privacy needs at the point of interaction. An experiment is proposed to explore the effect of this UI addition where users register to a new social network by answering a series of questions. The amount of questions answered is compared to a control group for difference. Which questions answered in terms of sensitivity is also examined against the control group to determine if privacy is taken into consideration.

2   Literature Review

The causes of poor privacy behaviour are wide ranging and varied. The system itself could be designed to be persuasive, encouraging disclosure of information or not make privacy protection mechanisms obvious enough for users [5, 6]. For example, there may be a lack of privacy salient information embedded into the environment to inform and aid the user [7]. This is coupled with the role the user themselves may play as there level of technical skill or lack of privacy awareness could have an impact [8, 9]. Furthermore, the behaviour of one's peers and social circle could impact on the decision to disclose certain pieces of information [10] as users give in to peer pressure.

However, users do state a desire for privacy that is not apparent from behaviour; a phenomenon known as the privacy paradox [11]. It has been suggested that privacy suffers from a secondary goal problem, that the idea of privacy and the user's perception of it are not considered when in pursuit of some other goal [12]. Furthermore, Social Networks could potentially be a persuasive technology, encouraging users to behave in a way that they may not normally do [13]. The question is therefore raised: what would happen if the software was designed to remind users of their personal privacy preferences during interaction?

Indeed, the User Interface (UI) would be ideally placed to address the aforementioned potential causes of poor privacy behaviour; either by reminding users of their privacy or by informing and raising their awareness of privacy issues. The addition of privacy salient information to the UI aimed at achieving this could play an important role in promoting more protective privacy behaviour. However, what this salient information should look like and the role it could play in the UI is unclear.

The Theory of Planned Behaviour (TPB) (Fig. 1) could present a means of defining and informing such content. This presents three aspects of salience that influence an individual's intention and behaviour [3], which include their personal attitude, their subjective norms and their perceived control.

This paper proposes that UI elements could be designed based on each of these salient aspects that aim to promote more protective privacy behaviour. Indeed, it has been suggested that there lacks a critical focus on the role of the UI in addressing privacy issues [14].

Behavioral attitude suggests that an individual's awareness and perceptions of the consequences of an action inform their intention. This fits well with the more user centric causes outlined earlier and is the primary focus for this paper.

Subjective norms suggest that intention is influenced by one's peers and perceived social pressures again this covers the previously outlined causes. A UI could inform

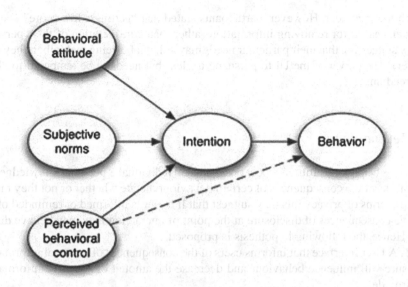

Fig. 1. The Theory of Planned Behaviour [3]

users of good behaviour that is going on around them and promote privacy rather than disclosure.

Finally, an individual's perceived control in terms of how easy certain behaviour is to perform influences both intention and action. A UI could be designed to make privacy protection easier and more accessible for example (results from this experiment are outlined in a separate paper and an overview given here in Sect. 2.1).

Each of these salient properties has been used as the basis for an experimental treatment aimed at encouraging more protective privacy behaviour. This paper focuses on the behavioral attitude treatment which sought to inform and/or remind users of the potential consequences of disclosure.

Utilizing the UI is not without precedence in exploring influencing factors on privacy behaviour and the paradox described previously. Research has found that the presence of counter-arguments displayed as messages during interaction has found that users' privacy opinions are swayed, particularly among those users who have a low level of online knowledge [15].

2.1 Perceived Control Experiment

A similar paper from the same experiment examined the role of perceived control [16]. Participants were given the opportunity to review and edit their data in a privacy focused context. Following submission of their data, a UI with privacy oriented elements added allowed this review where participants could delete data items without the goal of account creation being as clear. A dynamic privacy score rated the amount of questions answered and their sensitivity which increased when items were deleted. Participants did disclose significantly less information than a control group after reviewing their data through the treatment. However, participants stated that "getting a low score" was the dominant reason for removing information rather than consideration of their personal privacy suggesting that their particular needs may still not be being met (albeit they may be safer). The power of the UI to persuade is clear but needs to be tempered to allow user freedom.

3   Methodology

The TPB's behavioral attitude aspect posits that an individual's personal knowledge and perceptions of the consequences of certain behaviour dictate whether or not they intend to act. In terms of privacy this may suggest that if a user is informed or reminded of the negative consequences of disclosure at the point of interaction they may behave differently. Hence, the following hypothesis is proposed:

H1. A User Interface that informs users of the consequences of personal information disclosure will influence behaviour and decrease the amount of sensitive information they provide.

3.1   Control Group

In order to test this hypothesis an experiment was devised that asked participants to register to a new social network service for their University (in this case Nottingham Trent). Participants were asked a variety of questions, the answers to which would form their profile on the network and put them in contact with like-minded peers. Figure 2 illustrates the main page of the experiment.

The design of the front page (and subsequent pages) draws inspiration from Facebook in order to promote the ecological validity of the experiment [17]. The majority of the questions asked of the participant appear on the second page (a "profile builder"). These questions vary in sensitivity and are based and adapted from similar work [18]. In total, participants view 33 questions over the course of the experiment spread across two web pages, a third page asked for privacy settings to be applied. Inputs varied for

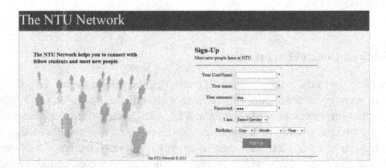

Fig. 2.   Experiment home page

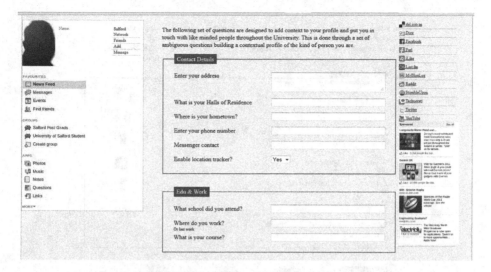

Fig. 3. Profile builder page

the questions ranging from text boxes to check boxes and drop-down menus; the aim of which being to test if this held an impact on their decision to answer. An example of the profile builder screen can be seen in Fig. 3.

The number of questions answered was measured in a database for comparison with a treatment group based on influencing a participant's personal attitude.

3.2 Treatment Design

The treatment is designed to either remind participants of their privacy preferences or to inform them such that they can make a decision at the point of interaction. To that end a UI metaphor derived from a traffic light system sought to classify the information requested in the questions according to their potential risk. An illustration of this addition to the UI is shown in Fig. 4.

A green light indicates that that particular question carries light risk and disclosure would generally be acceptable but may result in low level consequences: for example, social embarrassment. A yellow light indicates that caution should be exercised and that disclosure may not result in serious ramifications but could affect, for example, employment prospects. Finally, a red light indicates that there could potentially be serious consequences from disclosure: for example, breaking the law.

It is important to note that these are not intended to be clear cut classifications of sensitivity but are intended to only allow participants to take into consideration their personal privacy preferences during interaction.

The amount of questions answered is compared to the control and assessed for difference. Furthermore, the location of disclosure (i.e. within the defined sensitivity categories) within each group is also compared to the control in order to assess the potential influence of the treatment: has disclosure been significantly less in the defined higher sensitive areas as might be expected?

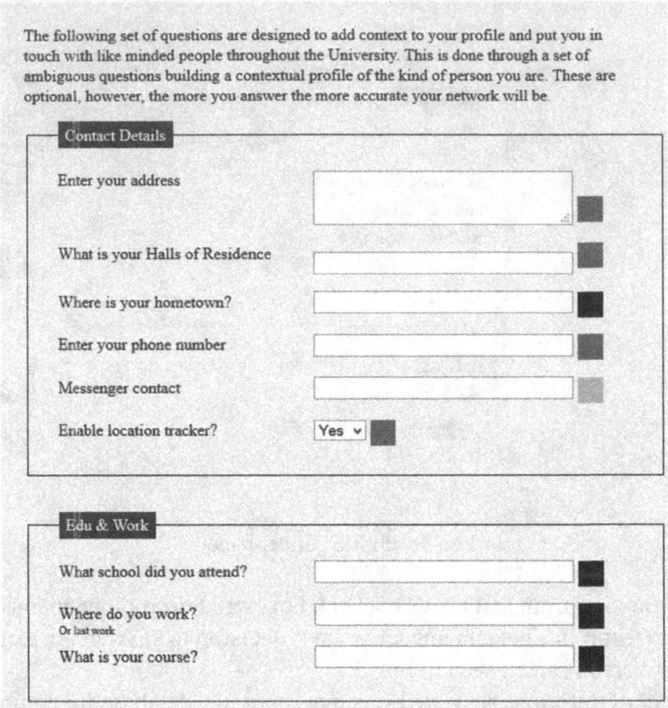

The following set of questions are designed to add context to your profile and put you in touch with like minded people throughout the University. This is done through a set of ambiguous questions building a contextual profile of the kind of person you are. These are optional, however, the more you answer the more accurate your network will be.

Contact Details

Enter your address

What is your Halls of Residence

Where is your hometown?

Enter your phone number

Messenger contact

Enable location tracker?   Yes ⌄

Edu & Work

What school did you attend?

Where do you work?
Or last work

What is your course?

Fig. 4. Privacy traffic lights

A short exit-survey follows the experiment aiming to assess the degree to which participants felt the treatment was useful and what the general perceptions are of it. This consists of specifying a level of agreement with the following statements:

1. I found the privacy information helpful.
2. The privacy information helped to select what to fill in.
3. I believe the privacy information would be beneficial in the long run.
4. I acted differently due to its presence.

Furthermore, a selection of participants took part in a focus group to further assess the motivation behind behaviour within the experiment.

3.3   Sample

In total, 43 participants were recruited to take part in the experiment and were randomly assigned to either the control or a treatment group. This resulted in 20 participants (16 male and 4 female) in the control group compared to 23 in the treatment group (17 male and 6 female). These participants were recruited from Nottingham Trent University's Information Systems course and completed the experiment within a scheduled lab session – they were asked if they would like to sign-up to a new social network.

The sample is pre-dominantly male and from what could be considered a technical background and as such may not be considered representative of a social network population.

4   Results

A summary of the total amount of disclosure for the experiment is illustrated in Table 1. This shows the percentage amount of questions answered as a whole (note, PA indicates the personal attitude treatment).

Table 1.   Disclosure summary

Group	Number of participants	Total % of questions answered
Control	20	82 %
PA	23	66 %

The reduction in answered questions stands 16 % which is a statistically significant reduction in the total amount of questions answered with a p-value of < 0.0001 (Mann Whitney U). This would therefore suggest that the earlier stated hypothesis is true as participants within the treatment group disclosed significantly less than the control. A breakdown of the location of disclosure (illustrated in Table 2) would also seem to support this assumption.

Table 2.   Spread of Disclosure

Group	% of "Green" questions answered	% of "Yellow" questions answered	% of "Red" questions answered
Control	83 %	82 %	81 %
PA	81 % (p = .523)	66 % (p < .0001)	51 % (p < .0001)

Disclosure was decreased in the higher sensitivity (as defined by the treatment) when compared to the control as the yellow and red category was reduced with statistical significance as summarized in Table 2.

This would certainly seem to suggest that participants took their privacy needs into consideration and were less likely to disclose data of a higher sensitivity. However, it is not clear if participants are being informed, reminded or persuaded by the treatment design. Table 3 illustrates the responses to the exit-survey statements that aimed to explore this point in greater detail and shall be referred to during the discussion section following.

Table 3. Exit survey responses

Statement	Agreed	Neutral	Disagreed
I found the privacy information helpful	75 %	19 %	6 %
The privacy information helped me answer	63 %	25 %	12 %
I believe the privacy information would be beneficial in the long-run	81 %	19 %	0 %
I acted differently due to the privacy information	75 %	25 %	0 %

5   Discussion

Results from the experiment suggest that participants demonstrated a greater degree of thought during interaction where the treatment interface was present demonstrated by the reduction in answers to questions with a higher degree of sensitivity. From the exit-survey 75 % of participants found the extra information useful and the same amount felt that they did indeed behave differently. The effect is therefore acknowledged by participants and the majority appeared to have found the presence favorable. Post-experiment, in the focus group, a participant stated: *they* (the lights) *did highlight ones that could cause problems, like address*. The intended effect of the treatment would therefore seem to have been achieved with privacy concerns clearly highlighted and put into focus during the interaction.

However, for some participants it appeared to have the effect of reminding them rather than informing: *I could see why* (the ratings were in placed) *but I made up my own mind* and *I made decisions based on my own common sense*. This would suggest that reminding participants at the point of interaction will enable them to think about their own personal privacy needs. It may also be that participants are unwilling to admit to the potentially persuasive effects of the treatment and wish to still have ownership of their behaviour. Indeed, wider research has found that individuals tend to downplay the effect of the persuasive communication over themselves [19].

Despite their being a potential subconscious effect on participants that further work should address, the general consensus from participants appeared to be a positive perception of the UI addition (from the exit-survey). Indeed, one participant stated in the focus group: *it made me think twice about the information I put on Facebook*. It therefore would seem to have provided participants with a gentle nudge to think about their privacy without being too intrusive. "Privacy nudges" have been proposed in wider research [20] and work within this paper provides some data regarding their usability and look.

This is apparent positive experience is unlike the perceived control (PC) treatment [16]. This PC treatment exhibited less disclosure than the PA design described in this paper; however, perceived usefulness was also less. The PC treatment was designed to place the interaction squarely into a privacy focused one which participants may have felt took their ownership of their behaviour away. For example, a dynamic "P-Score" encouraged the removal of information, making the goal of interaction to get a lower score rather than enact appropriate desired behaviour. This would suggest that salient privacy information needs to be subtle enough to allow participant to maintain their ownership of behaviour and still feel like their needs are being met. Such persuasiveness may be described as a suggestion rather than a direction [21].

6   Conclusions and Further Work

This paper has presented an example of privacy salient information (informed by the Theory of Planned Behaviour) in the form of a UI element and examined its potential effect on end-users. Findings suggest that a privacy suggestion can play a role in encouraging more protective privacy behaviour. Such designs could be added to existing user interfaces through the use of browser extension or existing system API's. This would allow for a more longitudinal study to take place examining if behaviour change is a long lasting alteration to habit. This would also examine if privacy salient nudges are enabling users to enact their privacy needs when privacy is taken into account with varying goals of system use. As there may be a danger that such UI elements are also persuading users to be more private than they perhaps need to be which may cause adverse social affects. It is unclear from this experiment what the effect would be if the goals of system use are user derived; here, the goal was defined by the experiment (to sign-up); however, what would the effect be if used with users live streams or post-account creation where the goals are perhaps more personal?

Future work could also incorporate eye-tracking software to gauge the extent to which each individual light is looked at or is the effect observed a cumulative one based on the presence of the lights as whole; i.e. how much focus is placed on each individual form elements, how much to surrounding content and how much consideration takes place?

There is evidence here, however, that simple additions to a UI can produce more protective privacy behaviour within the context defined in this experiment. More work is required to understand the driving psychology behind the observed effects and how the UI elements can be further used to address the privacy problem with longer lasting effects.

References

1. Barnes, S.B.: A privacy paradox: social networking in the united states. First Monday, **11**(9) (2006)
2. Breakwell, G.M.: Research Methods in Psychology. Sage Publications Ltd., Oxford (2006)
3. Ajzen, I.: The Theory of Planned Behaviour. Organ. Behav. Hum. Decis. Process. **50**, 179–211 (1991)
4. Rosenblum, D.: What anyone can know: the privacy risks of social networking. IEEE Secur. Priv. **5**(3), 40–49 (2007)

5. Fogg, B.J., Iizawa, D.: Online persuasion in facebook and mixi: a cross-cultural comparison. In: Oinas-Kukkonen, H., Hasle, P., Harjumaa, M., Segerståhl, K., Øhrstrøm, P. (eds.) PERSUASIVE 2008. LNCS, vol. 5033, pp. 35–46. Springer, Heidelberg (2008)
6. Livingstone, S.: Taking risky opportunities in youthful content creation: teenagers' use of social networking sites for intimacy, privacy and self-expression. New Media Soc. **10**(3), 393–411 (2008)
7. Houghton, D.J., Joinson, A.: Privacy, social network sites, and social relations. J. Technol. Hum. Serv. **28**(1–2), 74–94 (2010)
8. Kolter, J., Pernul, G.: Generating user-understandable privacy preferences. In: International Conference on Availability, Reliability and Security, pp. 299–306 (2009)
9. Miller, R.E., Salmona, M., Melton, J.: Students and social networking site: a model of inappropriate posting. In: Proceedings of the Southern Association for Information Systems Conference, Atlanta (2011)
10. Strater, K., Richter, H.: Examing privacy and disclosure in a social networking community. In: Symposium on Usable Privacy and Security, pp. 157–158 (2007)
11. Acquisti, A., Gross, R.: Imagined communities: awareness, information sharing, and privacy on the Facebook. In: Danezis, G., Golle, P. (eds.) PET 2006. LNCS, vol. 4258, pp. 36–58. Springer, Heidelberg (2006)
12. Bonneau, J., Anderson, J., Church, L.: Privacy suites: shared privacy for social networks. In: 5th Symposium on Usable Privacy and Security (2009)
13. Fogg, B.J.: The behaviour grid: 35 ways behaviour can change. In: PERSUASIVE 2009, Clairemont, California (2009)
14. Masiello, B.: Deconstructing the privacy experience. IEEE Secur. Priv. **7**(4), 68–70 (2009)
15. Baek, Y.M.: Solving the privacy paradox: a counter-argument experimental approach. Comput. Hum. Behav. **38**, 33–42 (2014)
16. Hughes-Roberts, T.: Privacy as a secondary goal problem: an experiment examining control. In: HAISA 2014, Plymouth, pp. 69–79 (2014)
17. Lew, L., et al.: Of course I wouldn't do that in real life: advancing the arguments for increasing realism in HCI experiments. In: Computer Human Interaction (2011)
18. Brandimarte, M., Acquisti, A., Loewenstien, G.: Misplaced confidences: privacy and the control paradox. In: Workshop on the Economics of Information Security, Harvard (2012)
19. Debatin, B., et al.: Facebook and online privacy: attitudes, behaviors, and unintended consequences. J. Comput.-Mediated Commun. **15**(1), 83–108 (2009)
20. Wang, Y., et al.: Privacy nudges for social media: an exploratory Facebook study. In: Proceedings of the 22nd international conference on World Wide Web companion, International World Wide Web Conferences Steering Committee (2013)
21. Fogg, B.J.: Persuasive Technology: Using Computers to Change What We Think and Do, Grudin, J., Nielsen, J., Card, S.K (eds.). Morgan Kaufmann, San Francisco (2003)

Profit-Maximizing Trustworthiness Level of Composite Systems

Costas Kalogiros[1(✉)], Michalis Kanakakis[1], Shenja van der Graaf[2], and Wim Vanobberghen[2]

[1] Athens University of Economics and Business,
76, Patission Str., Athens, Greece
{ckalog, kanakakis}@aueb.gr
[2] iMinds-SMIT, Vrije Universiteit Brussel,
Pleinlaan 9, 1050 Brussels, Belgium
shenja.vandergraaf@iminds.be, wim.vanobberghen@vub.ac.be

Abstract. Service providers face the ever-increasing problem of meeting customer expectations while maximizing profits. This optimal balance is very important for delivering better service quality to users and keeping costs under control through efficient resource allocation. In this paper we suggest optimal strategies for managing system trustworthiness in two different contexts. In the first one the provider has limited information about the users' trustworthiness preferences, which have to be satisfied on every transaction. In the second context, the provider knows what the effect of possible outcomes on customer's trust level and, given that the customer will perform a certain number of transactions, would like to know whether the system trustworthiness should be managed at any point in time in order to meet customer's expectations in a cost-effective way. The optimality of the proposed strategies is demonstrated via both analytical techniques and simulations.

Keywords: Trustworthiness management · Trust management · Optimal strategies · Trust · Trust computational model · Run-time · Composite systems · Economics of security

1 Introduction

Most user interactions on the Internet, e.g., checking email correspondence, sharing thoughts with online friends, buying from digital stores, watching movies online usually involve more than one provider, even though this is not directly observable by the average end-user. Retail providers of ICT (Information and Communications Technology) services, for example, are increasingly relying on cloud computing providers for computational, storage and networking services.

It is expected, however, that the outsourcing trend will not diminish in the future. Recent initiatives, such as smart transportation systems, ambient-assisted living, etc., follow the paradigm of Service-Oriented Architectures in which application components are orchestrated to provide services to other components over a network. Each of those components can belong to different providers, and in most cases, supply is under competition.

© Springer International Publishing Switzerland 2015
T. Tryfonas and I. Askoxylakis (Eds.): HAS 2015, LNCS 9190, pp. 357–368, 2015.
DOI: 10.1007/978-3-319-20376-8_32

While the popularity of cloud computing is mostly attributed to reduced average cost, elasticity and reliability stemming from economies of scope and scale, the increased interdependencies and the inability to control all operational aspects increase the complexity for providers of composite services to meet security and other trustworthiness objectives. A system's trustworthiness can be assessed with several metrics, such as mean availability, mean response time, minimum encryption, etc. For a detailed analysis of trustworthiness metrics, including security ones, the interested reader is redirected to [1]. We should note that a trustworthiness metric can be objectively measured, in the sense that two separate entities can agree on a single formula and given the same (or a sufficiently large) set of run-time observations/evidences they would eventually reach the same outcome.

This paper focuses at the production phase of such composite systems and, more specifically, how retail providers should meet customer expectations while maximizing profits. This optimal balance is very important for delivering better service quality to users, increasing market share by gaining users' trust, mitigating adverse effects and keeping costs under control through efficient resource allocation. However, achieving this balance is not an easy task for the following reasons. The retail provider has no perfect information about the actual trustworthiness of each individual component/ service instance and the customer expectations are usually unknown.

The provider could compare the trustworthiness of candidate components by querying a marketplace that carries detailed trustworthiness certificates, such as the ones described in [2]. Furthermore, the provider could offer SLA's (Service Level Agreements) where the exact security/trustworthiness levels are described as a set of metrics and their respective target values. Then we could assume that the user would not trust the provider again in the future if any threshold value was not met. In this paper, however, we will assume that the retail provider does not want to offer SLAs.

More specifically in Sect. 2 we assume that the provider is paid for each successful transaction only and has some information about the distribution of users' trustworthiness preferences. Its purpose is to maximize the expected profits by finding the component to replace a failed one. While the authors of [3] suggest a Genetic Algorithm for selecting the components of a system so that a function of cost and an aggregate metric of trustworthiness is maximized, they ignore user's expectations.

In Sect. 3 we will assume that the user will interact with the provider's system several times and the number of transactions is known in advance (i.e., is the only term of the contract). For example, a bank manager that wants to process all saving accounts (e.g., calculate interests etc.) at the end of the day and enters into a monthly contract with a cloud computing provider. Whenever the cloud provider believes that the customer's trust is lower than a certain threshold the former could make the necessary changes to system in order to regain customer's trust after a few transactions. The optimal changes that should take place at any point in time are based on the finite-stage dynamic programming model of [4], which has been adapted so that changes are restricted by the available components (instead of assuming that trustworthiness is a continuous function of effort which is more suitable for services offered by humans). In order to estimate the current user's trust level we employ a trust computational model that has been described and validated in [5]. Finally, we conclude the paper with summary and possible future extensions in Sect. 4.

2 Managing System Trustworthiness for Individual Transactions

2.1 The Model

We assume that whenever the system during a particular transaction fails to meet user expectations regarding response time (e.g., a deadline specified in SLA or system performance exceeds user's patience) then the user has the ability to cancel the transaction and pay nothing to the provider. Otherwise, she pays r units to the provider. The exact user patience is unknown to the provider. Suppose, however, that the provider knows that user's patience T is exponentially distributed with mean $1/\beta$, so that $P(T \geq t) = e^{-\beta t}$.

The provider is interested in maximizing her expected profit from each transaction. She is able to monitor the behaviour of all system components at run-time and thus can identify when a particular component is unavailable; the adverse behaviour we are focusing on this section. Let system s perform functions $1, \ldots, f$ and assume that l components are capable of performing function m ($m \leq f$). These components, depending on the context, can be machines running software instances, networking assets (e.g., routers), as well as, individuals (such as personnel performing a task) and their equipment. Each candidate component $g \leq l$ has known trustworthiness metrics and cost c_g, which is paid to the suppliers only for successfully completed transactions. This information can be retrieved from a marketplace of alternative subsystems or supplied by the provider itself.

Furthermore, we denote with $a_g \geq 0$ the probability that the component g will be functioning after being installed. The mean delay of component g to produce the required output is D_g, which is assumed to be exponentially distributed with parameter λ_g, while D_g, D_h are independent $\forall g \neq h$. The fixed time that is needed for integrating any new component to the system and checking its availability is denoted with $d > 0$; there is always the possibility that the newly deployed component is found unavailable after being installed and another component has to be deployed.

At t_0 a transaction starts and assume that the provider checks every z time periods (e.g., seconds) whether all components are in healthy condition, or unavailable due to an attack, or failure. Suppose also that at t_{n-1} all components were running but at the next inspection time (t_n), and before the transaction in question has been concluded or the user patience is exhausted, the provider finds component k to be unavailable. Her options would be to either replace it with a new one or do nothing (if for example the expected transaction revenues don't recover the expected costs).

We have the following theorem:

Theorem 1. The provider should try candidate components in the order $1, 2, \ldots, l$ provided that $W_1 \geq W_2 \geq \ldots \geq W_l \geq 0$, where $W_g = \dfrac{(r - c_g) u_g \frac{\lambda_g}{\lambda_g + \beta} e^{-\beta d}}{1 - (1 - a_g) e^{-\beta d}}$.

Proof. If the provider selected component g and given that at time t_n the user's patience was not exhausted, then the probability that the both the component integration and the transaction will be successfully completed is given by:

$$Pr[D_g = \min\{D_g, T\}|T > d] = Pr[D_g = \min\{D_g, T\}\&T > d]/Pr[T > d] \quad (1)$$

Given that at time t_n the user's patience is not exhausted, then the probability that the user will still be waiting for the outcome after d time units is given by:

$$Pr(T > t_n + d|T > t_n) = P(T > d) = e^{-\beta d} \quad (2)$$

Furthermore $D_1, D_2, \ldots, D_l$ and T are independent exponentially distributed random variables with rate parameters $\lambda_1, \lambda_2, \ldots, \lambda_l$, and β respectively, the $\min\{D_g, T\}$ is also an exponentially distributed random variable with rate parameter $\lambda_g + \beta$. Thus

$$Pr(D_g = \min\{D_g, T\}|T > t_n + d) = \lambda_g/(\lambda_g + \beta) \quad (3)$$

Substituting Eqs. (2, 3) into Eq. (1) results in

$$Pr[D_g = \min\{D_g, T\}\&T > t_n + d] = \frac{\lambda_g}{\lambda_g + \beta} e^{-\beta d}$$

The provider should replace component k with g instead of h if the following inequality holds:

$$(r - c_g)a_g \frac{\lambda_g}{\lambda_g + \beta} e^{-\beta d} + (r - c_h)(1 - a_g)a_h \frac{\lambda_h}{\lambda_h + \beta} e^{-2\beta d}$$

$$\geq (r - c_h)a_j \frac{\lambda_h}{\lambda_h + \beta} e^{-\beta d} + (r - c_g)(1 - a_h)a_g \frac{\lambda_g}{\lambda_g + \beta} e^{-2\beta d}$$

where $a_g \frac{\lambda_g}{\lambda_g + \beta} e^{-\beta d}$ is the probability that the component g is found to be available (after d time units) and produced its output before the user's patience had been exhausted. With simple algebra transformations and rearrangements we have the following inequality:

$$(r - c_g)a_g \frac{\lambda_g}{\lambda_g + \beta} e^{-\beta d}[1 - (1 - a_h)e^{-\beta d}] \geq (r - c_h)a_h \frac{\lambda_h}{\lambda_h + \beta} e^{-\beta d}[1 - (1 - a_g)e^{-\beta d}]$$

$$(4)$$

Since $\beta > 0$, $d > 0$ we have that $e^{\beta d} > 1$ and given that $a_h > 0$ it follows that $a_h > 1 - e^{\beta d} \Leftrightarrow e^{\beta d} - 1 + a_h > 0$.

Furthermore, $e^{-\beta d} > 0$ and we have that $e^{-\beta d}(e^{\beta d} - 1 + a_h) > 0 \Leftrightarrow 1 - e^{-\beta d} + a_h e^{-\beta d} > 0 \Leftrightarrow 1 - (1 - a_h)e^{-\beta d} > 0$. Similarly, we have that $1 - (1 - a_g)e^{-\beta d} > 0$ and thus we can divide each term of Eq. (4) with $[1 - (1 - a_h)e^{-\beta d}]$ $[1 - (1 - a_g)e^{-\beta d}]$, getting the following inequality:

$$\frac{(r-c_g)a_g\frac{\lambda_g}{\lambda_g+\beta}e^{-\beta d}}{1-(1-a_g)e^{-\beta d}} \geq \frac{(r-c_h)a_h\frac{\lambda_h}{\lambda_h+\beta}e^{-\beta d}}{1-(1-a_h)e^{-\beta d}} \Leftrightarrow W_g \geq W_h$$

Again, the expected transaction revenues should cover the expected costs and thus $W_g \geq W_h \geq 0.\blacksquare$

2.2 Evaluation

In this section we will compare the cost-effectiveness of the optimal strategies to other simpler strategies, using simulations. The rest strategies are: 'Least Cost Component', 'Highest Mean Availability Component', 'Least Mean Response Time Component' and 'Random Selection'.

We created a discrete-time simulator where one transaction is processed each time and the initial system (composed of a single component) has a certain probability of failing/becoming unavailable. Each experiment consisted of 10 candidate components, 10,000 transactions for each strategy, with fixed revenue (150 monetary units), and integration delay d (100 time units). Furthermore, each experiment is performed for 10 possible user-acceptable durations, from 100,000 down to 100 time units.

For each transaction, costs and mean response times are drawn from a uniform distribution and assigned to each candidate component (in [1, revenue] and [200, 2000] respectively). Furthermore, the mean availabilities for both initial and candidate components are selected from a uniform distribution in [0.7, 1]. Finally, the user patience is selected from an exponential distribution based on the experiment's parameter.

The provider monitors periodically the system in order to be able to manage trustworthiness; each poll can be seen as a Bernoulli experiment. Whenever the system is found unavailable, a replacement takes place using one of the supported strategies. We assume that when a component is found unavailable then it remains unavailable, so in an extreme scenario the transaction fails because none of the components can handle the request. If the selected component is available then the transaction will fail if only its response time is larger than the remaining user's patience/deadline.

In Fig. 1 the provider's average profit for each strategy in case of unknown user patience is presented. As expected, the proposed strategy achieves the highest average profit, followed by the strategy 'Least Cost Component'. Furthermore, when users are patient the 'Least Mean Response Time Component' reaches significantly lower profits than the previous two, but for more critical systems this strategy scores higher than the 'Least Cost Component' one. The 'Random Selection' and 'Highest Mean Availability Component' strategies achieve consistently lower profits. Similar trends are obtained for different parameter values.

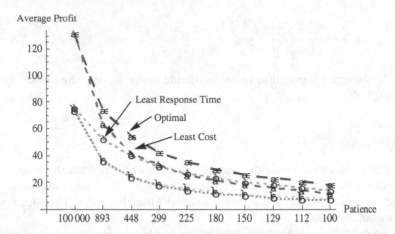

Fig. 1. The average profit for each strategy in case of unknown user patience

3 Managing System Trustworthiness for a Set of Transactions Based on Estimated User's Trust Level

In this section we will describe an approach for allowing a provider of composite system to minimize the total expected cost of meeting the expectations of a certain customer. We will first describe the trust computational model that is used for translating the subjective user expectations into objective trustworthiness targets.

3.1 A Personalized Trust Computational Model

The trust computational model distinguishes between four different types of users, whose differences could be explained by three major techno-socio-economic factors: (a) "trust stance" (e.g., "I usually trust a person until there is a reason not to"), (b) "motivation to engage in trust-related seeking behaviour" (e.g., "I look for guarantees regarding confidentiality of the information that I provide") and (c) "trust-related competences" (e.g., "I'm able to understand my rights and duties as described by the terms of the application provider"). More specifically, each user is clustered to one of the four identified segments, namely "High Trust" (HT), "Highly Active Trust Seeking" (HATS), "Medium Active Trust Seeking" (MATS) and "Ambivalent" (A), which were found to have statistically significant differences. The personal attributes of users in each segment, affect not only their initial trust level, but also the way that this value is updated based on the experienced system outcomes.

We now proceed with a formal definition of the computational model. Suppose that for each system s there is a non-empty set H_s of trustworthiness factors for which any trustor i is interested in and let w_j be its trustworthiness value for factor j. Examples of trustworthiness metrics include availability, successful completion of transaction, etc. For each factor j the consumer has a personal opinion on how likely it is that the system will behave as expected. In other words every user has a subjective estimation of the probability that the system will be available, will store transaction results, etc. This subjective opinion is called trust level and we formulate it by means of a Beta pdf. In a mathematical formulation, the trust level of a user i for metric j after n transactions, where k were successful, is given by:

$$\tau_i^j(n) = \frac{\alpha_0 + \alpha * k}{\alpha_0 + \alpha * k + \beta_0 + \beta * (n - k)} \tag{5}$$

More specifically, α_0 is a measure of the trustor's confidence that the system will fulfil its objectives, β_0 is a measure of the trustor's belief that the system will not meet its expectations while α, β are the two parameters that correspond to the effect of each system's success or failure respectively on trust level. In the availability metric for example, n would represent the number of attempts and k those were the system was responding (even if the output was incorrect, intercepted by an eavesdropper, etc.).

In [5], we describe and validate our approach for estimating those parameter values for each segment and consequently computing the trust levels. Notice that if $a = \beta$, then we have the classic Beta pdf whose mean value is known to converge to the average trustworthiness level after a sufficiently high number of transactions. According to our analysis this property appears only for the "HATS" segment, which means that these users have an accurate estimation of trustworthiness. On the contrary, users in "HT" segment, whose attributes result into trustworthiness overestimation, place greater importance on a success compared to a failure (meaning that $a > \beta$), while those in "MATS" and "A" segments underestimate the trustworthiness level $(a < \beta)$.

3.2 The Dynamic Programming Model

Suppose that the provider offers a single service plan to all interested buyers, which allows them to place a fixed number of n transactions for an upfront payment p_s, or unit price $p = p_s/n$. All candidate customers, being rational entities, will investigate whether they should engage with that provider, or not (the interested reader is redirected to [5] for a detailed decision criterion). If multiple providers exist in the market then obviously each customer would select the one that maximizes her expected net benefit. First-time buyers will have not experienced any system outcome before and thus their initial trust metrics $(\tau_i^j(0))$ would depend on their personality (e.g., predisposition) and any information that they can find in service description, or from their peers. For simplicity, in the following we will assume that a single binary trust metric j is important for the system only and thus the overall trust at any time is given by $\tau_i = \tau_i^j$.

Let us assume that a certain customer i has found this service plan to be beneficial. After making the upfront payment, the customer answers a questionnaire that helps the provider to identify the trustor's segment. This would allow the provider to use the trust computational model to compute the initial trust metrics. This value could be considered as a safe, minimum target for the overall trust (or respective trust metric in the general case) after n transactions in order for the trustor to renew the business relationship. The rationale is that *ceteris paribus* the user's decision would be positive if its trust level after n transactions will not have decreased.

The next step would be to compute k, the minimum number of successes necessary for reaching the initial trust level. Again, the complexity of this step can be significantly reduced by relying on the mechanics of the trust computational model. More specifically the minimum number of successes can be computed by solving the following equation for k:

$$\tau_i(0) = \frac{\alpha_0 + \alpha * K}{\alpha_0 + \alpha * K + \beta_0 + \beta * (n - K)} \Leftrightarrow K = \frac{\tau(\alpha_0 + \beta_0 + \beta n)}{\alpha - \tau(\alpha + \beta)} \tag{6}$$

The last step is to create a contingency plan for reaching the initial trust level in the most cost effective way, or abandon serving the customer as early as possible. This contingency plan would suggest to the provider the optimal level of system trustworthiness at any possible situation. A situation is characterized by the tuple (number of successful transactions still necessary, number of transactions remaining). Obviously, such a contingency plan requires that the provider is able to make the necessary changes to system trustworthiness between two consecutive transactions. For example, in case of a composite system the provider could replace a component with another one and obtain the target trustworthiness value. In case of a monolithic system the trustworthiness could be affected by a different configuration. We should note that usually different system compositions, or configurations, entail a change in provider's costs. Furthermore, we would expect that increasing a component's trustworthiness is costly for its developer, e.g., a component's cost in the market equilibrium is an increasing function of trustworthiness.

Thus, the provider has received p_s monetary units in advance and knows the conditions for securing that revenue stream in the future. Suppose that the provider can query an online application marketplace and find information about the trustworthiness t_m and cost c_m of any component m that is compatible with the rest system. At the beginning or at state (k, n) she has 2 main options:

1. Serve the customer and hope that will be trustworthy enough for getting an extra amount p_s for the next set of transactions.
2. Keep the money and do nothing.

Depending on the trustworthiness level $t_s\widehat{(k, n)}$ of the system s chosen at state (k, n) there are two cases:

- With probability $t_s\widehat{(k, n)}$ we go to state $(k - 1, n - 1)$
- With probability $1 - t_s\widehat{(k, n)}$ we go to state $(k, n - 1)$

The same options are valid at any later state apart from the following situations:

- (k^-, n^+) where $k^- \leq 0$, $n^+ > 0$ and the provider has no incentive to keep placing effort, since effort is costly and would not further increase its future revenues.
- $(k^+, 0)$ where $k^+ \geq 0$ and the provider will have exhausted the number of attempts before satisfying the customer.

Thus, the run-time provider's problem can be phrased as "what is the most cost-effective trustworthiness level for the next transaction given the total number of transactions remaining and the minimum number of successes required to meet the customer's expectations?".

Such a problem can be solved by employing a finite-stage dynamic programming model, like the one described in [4]. This contingency plan can be produced proactively and be used by the provider to take any corrective actions deemed necessary at run-time. Note that the contingency plan suggests a trustworthiness level for the overall system. In the case of a composite service for example, the provider would have to replace a subcomponent with another one (or add a new) so that that the overall system meets the new security level. This is not a trivial task, but the provider could rely on tools that allow estimating the end-to-end trustworthiness of a particular system composition, like the [6].

Similar to [4], let $V_n(k)$ be the minimal expected cost incurred when the provider is at state (k, n), which refers to the path on the tree shown in Fig. 2 below with the minimum total remaining expected cost. Then the provider's maximum expected profit π^* is given by $\pi^* = 2p_s - V_n(k)$. The first term represents the maximum revenues that the provider can receive in this 2-period setting, while the latter includes both the operating costs, as well as, any missed opportunities.

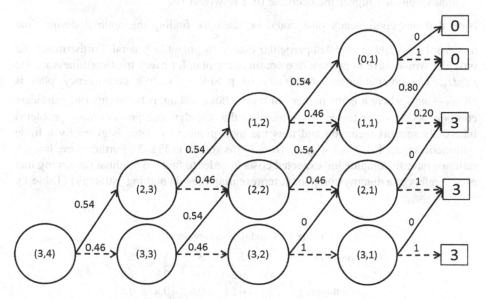

Fig. 2. An example of the contingency plan

Furthermore, assume that:

- $V_0(x) = p_s$, where $x > 0$, which means that the provider misses the opportunity to renew the contract with the customer, and
- $V_y(x) = 0$, where $x \leq 0$ and $y \geq 0$, which means that there is no "penalty" when the minimum number of successful transactions is met.

Then, the Bellman optimality equation for this problem can be written as

$$V_n(k) = \min_{p_s \geq c \geq 0} \left\{ c + t_s\widehat{(k, n)} \, V_{n-1}(k-1) + \left(1 - t_s\widehat{(k, n)}\right) V_{n-1}(k) \right\}$$

where $c = \sum_m c_m$ is the total cost and we would expect that the provider considers
system compositions/configurations whose total cost does not exceed the retail price.

This dynamic programming model is equivalent to the one studied in [4]; the only difference being that there is no SLA between the two parties and thus the penalty refers to the missed opportunity for receiving another upfront payment. Since the upfront payment p_s is fixed, the condition $V_0(x+2) - V_0(x+1) \geq V_0(x+1) - V_0(x)$ is still satisfied and the optimal policy that was found is still valid. Thus, in general, the contingency plan would instruct the provider to do the following:

1. Increase the TW the closer we get to contract's end and the minimum number of successful transactions was not reached. Furthermore, the higher the number of pending successful transactions the higher the increase of TW would be.
2. Decrease the TW as the number of pending transactions to reach a certain number of successful transactions increases. Furthermore, the higher the number of pending transactions the higher the decrease of TW would be.

Note that this contingency plan could be used for finding the optimal design-time trustworthiness $t_s\widehat{(k, n)}$ for that particular user, or segment in general. Furthermore, the provider would have to prepare one contingency plan for every trustworthiness metric $j \in H_s$. The computational complexity of producing such a contingency plan is $O(\frac{n(n+1)}{2} |m|)$, where n is the number of transactions and $|m|$ is the number of candidate components. In order to see this remember that the dynamic programming problems inherently support recursion and thus the total number of states is given by a finite arithmetic series, $1 + 2 + 3 + \ldots + (n+1)$ (as shown in Fig. 2). Furthermore, in each state we have to compute $|m|$ expected costs in order to find the minimal (assuming that $m = 1$ refers to a dummy component representing the "do nothing" strategy) (Table 1).

Table 1. Candidate components

Component m	1	2	3	4	5
Cost c_m	0	0.3	0.4	0.8	1.9
Trustworthiness t_m	0	0.54	0.6	0.8	0.85

3.3   An Example

Suppose for simplicity that the provider can manage system trustworthiness (security) by replacing one component with another from the marketplace, while the rest components are proprietary. The following table presents the cost c_m per transaction and the trustworthiness t_m of each candidate component (again we focus on a single trustworthiness metric), where $m = 1$ refers to a dummy component representing the "do nothing" strategy.

Furthermore let us assume that the offered service plan covers 4 transactions for an upfront payment of 3 monetary units; thus $n = 4$ and $p_s = 3$. If the customer, upon registration, had answered a questionnaire for revealing the trustor segment and it was found that she belongs to the "High Trust" segment, then her initial trust level would be $\tau_i(0) = \frac{\alpha_0}{\alpha_0+\beta_0} = \frac{2.2144}{2.2144+0.7106} = 0.7571$. Thus, in order for her trust level after 3 transactions to be >=0.7571 the provider would have to succeed in at least $\lceil k \rceil = \lceil 2.35424 \rceil = 3$ transactions, where k is given by Eq. (6) or more specifically:

$$\frac{2.2144 + 0.9583 * k}{2.2144 + 0.9583 * k + 0.7106 + 0.4399 * (4 - k)} = 0.7571 \Leftrightarrow k = 2.35424$$

Figure 2 presents the contingency plan that would be produced in this example. Solid lines represent the trustworthiness of the optimal component that should be selected, while the dashed line gives the transition probability to a state where the remaining number of successful transactions remains the same. Rectangles denote a final state and any missed revenues. Note that during the first two transactions the provider should employ $m = 2$. Furthermore, at state $(1, 1)$ the provider would maximize its expected profits by using $m = 4$ that has increased trustworthiness and cost. Finally, note that whenever the provider realizes that, either the minimum number of successful transactions cannot be met, or it has already been achieved, then the optimal component is $m = 1$ (doing so reduces costs without affecting future revenues).

The maximum expected profit is $\pi^* = 2 * 3 - V_4(3) = 6 - 2.72028 = 3.277972$. To see why this problem is not trivial, let us examine the following two extreme cases. The first option of the provider would be to place no effort at all. In that case the provider's expected profit during the two phases would be $\dot{\pi} = 2 * 3 - V_0(3) = 6 - 3 = 3$ (the upfront payment of the first phase, only). The other strategy would be to employ the most trustworthy component so that the customer will have observed the maximum number of successes and the probability of renewing the contract is maximized. However, c_5 is so high that the total expected cost is higher than the missed opportunities from further revenues; more specifically $\dot{\pi} = 2 * 3 - V_0(-1) = 6 - 3.99009 = 2.00991$.

4 Conclusions and Future Work

In this paper we have provided strategies of trustworthiness management that, under certain assumptions, maximise the provider's expected profits in presence of uncertainty regarding customers' trustworthiness expectations. While in the first model we have assumed that the user's patience is exponentially distributed, in the second model we have relied on knowledge about the effect of trustors' properties on the trust dynamics. In the latter case we help service providers in producing an optimal contingency plan proactively and which allows them to keep the users' trust level high enough so that their profits are maximized.

In the future, we plan to extend the dynamic programming model in order to support contingency plans for systems that are not segment-specific. In this way, a provider will be able to manage a single system for all of its customers.

Acknowledgements. This work was supported by the EU-funded project OPTET (grant no. 317631).

References

1. Mohammadi, N.G., Paulus, S., Bishr, M., Metzger, A., Könnecke, H., Hartenstein, S., Weyer, T., Pohl, K.: Trustworthiness attributes and metrics for engineering trusted internet-based software systems. In: Helfert, M., Desprez, F., Ferguson, D., Leymann, F. (eds.) CLOSER 2013. CCIS, vol. 453, pp. 19–35. Springer, Heidelberg (2014)
2. Di Cerbo, F., Bisson, P., Hartman, A., Keller, S., Meland, P.H., Moffie, M., Mohammadi, N. G., Paulus, S., Short, S.: Towards trustworthiness assurance in the cloud. In: Felici, M. (ed.) CSP EU FORUM 2013. CCIS, vol. 182, pp. 3–15. Springer, Heidelberg (2013)
3. Elshaafi, H., et al.: Trustworthiness monitoring and prediction of composite services. In: 2012 IEEE Symposium on Computers and Communications (ISCC). IEEE (2012)
4. Derman, C., et al.: Optimal system allocations with penalty costs. Manag. Sci. 23(4), 399–403 (1976)
5. Kanakakis, M., et al.: Towards Market Efficiency Using a Personalised Trust Computational Model. Telecommunications Policy (Under Review)
6. Mohammadi, N.G., et al.: Trustworthiness Evaluation of Socio-Technical-Systems using Computational and Risk Assessment Approaches, CAiSE Forum (2015, To appear)

Re-designing Permission Requirements to Encourage BYOD Policy Adherence

Lotus Lee[✉] and Jeremiah D. Still[✉]

San José State University, San Jose, CA, USA
{lotus.lee,jeremiah.still}@sjsu.edu

Abstract. Many corporations and organizations support a Bring Your Own Device (BYOD) policy, which allows employees to use their personal smartphones for work-related purposes. Access to proprietary company data and information from an employee's smartphone raises serious privacy and security concerns. Companies are vulnerable to data breaches if employees are unable to discern which applications are safe to install. Situating privacy requirements ought to encourage safer application install decisions and decrease risker ones. This study examines the use of context-relevant warning messages, which alert employees to be cautious when the company's BYOD policy may be violated. We also explore the impact of presenting permission requirements before and after making the install decision. We provide evidence that the presence of warnings, despite the timing of when they were presented, facilitated a lower number of risky installations. In situations when it was safe to install an application, warning messages presented before the install decision drastically encouraged installations compared to when there were no warnings. Interestingly, the opposite pattern was found when warning messages were presented after the decision. Overall, better privacy and security decisions will be made if permission requirements are displayed with relevant warning messages. In addition, safe installations will be encouraged through the placement of these meaningful warnings on the description page of a mobile application before a user has decided to install it.

Keywords: Decision-making · Interface design · Mobile security · Privacy · Trust · User experience

1 Introduction

Smartphones allow users to easily access and share valuable and sensitive data digitally (e.g., banking, intellectual property). This access is supported by a plethora of mobile applications (app) available for download from several official app stores (e.g., Apple's App Store, Android's Google Play). Apps are popular because they are perceived as useful (Mylonas et al. 2013). Unfortunately, approximately one-third of Android apps are over privileged (Felt, Chin, Hanna, Song and Wagner, 2011). In some cases over privileged apps threaten the security of sensitive data. When making a selection, users rely on information that is readily available on the description page of the mobile app. Ratings, reviews, cost, and number of downloads become some of the main criteria

© Springer International Publishing Switzerland 2015
T. Tryfonas and I. Askoxylakis (Eds.): HAS 2015, LNCS 9190, pp. 369–378, 2015.
DOI: 10.1007/978-3-319-20376-8_33

used to make an install decision (Felt et al. 2012; Kelley et al. 2012; Kelley et al. 2013). Rarely do users consider company and personal privacy violations when installing an app. Mylonas et al. (2013) found that privacy was ranked near the bottom of the app decision criteria. Most smartphone users are unaware of the severity of the risks associated with an app installation because they rely on an external entity for protection (i.e., the app store) (Mylonas et al. 2013). Part of the reason is because the majority of smartphone users are not security experts (Mylonas et al. 2013). Users are not equipped with the right mental models to understand how their actions impact their privacy. Privacy self-management is also not considered to be their primary task (Pfleeger and Caputo, 2012). However, an important part of the app store experience requires users to consent to a certain level of data access that may involve detrimental consequences like identity theft. Several studies have demonstrated that there are inherent vulnerabilities with consent-based permission systems unbeknownst to smartphone users (Balebako et al. 2014; Barrera et al. 2010; Felt et al. 2011). Attempts to incorporate warning messages have failed as users will act on privacy related information even if they do not fully comprehend its meaning (Felt et al. 2012).

A growing concern in the field of mobile security within the enterprise space is that the majority of smartphone users do not exhibit the ability to maintain their privacy to avoid increased risk for themselves or associated organizations (Solove, 2013). There are several factors that come into play when examining the behaviors that dictate a smartphone user's absence of privacy self-management. Users will dismiss or overlook privacy related information due to technical jargon or becoming habituated to their prevalence (Felt et al. 2012). Over time, smartphone users have been trained to ignore privacy policies, warning messages, consent dialogs, and permission request screens (Bohme and Kopsell, 2010; Chia et al. 2012; Kelley et al. 2012). Although risk communication could help facilitate a heightened awareness of the potential dangers associated with installing mobile apps, the consent-based permission systems ought to be improved in a way that naturally encourages users to make informed decisions through more direct communication. Altering risky user behavior can be accomplished by communicating how the harm can personally relate back to users and their associated organizations' Bring Your Own Device (BYOD) policies (Pfleeger and Caputo, 2012).

Users are simply not provided with the proper information needed to flag privacy concerns. The task of maintaining awareness of personal and professional risk on a smartphone is becoming increasingly difficult. Therefore, the use of contextual warning messages may help to convey relevant privacy and security information that transparently and effectively connect risk with permission requirements. As a caveat, attention and comprehension to privacy information on a smartphone is significantly different than when using a desktop computer. 50 % of users take no more than 8 s to read consent dialogs on websites (Bohme, 2010). Therefore, the mobility and form factor of a smartphone requires immediate recognition of privacy relevant information that will prompt users at the appropriate time when making a decision to install an app. They cannot be overloaded with too much information that distracts them from moving forward or it will be ignored. Several studies have experimented with the timing and presentation of privacy information to motivate securer behavior and prevent risk in other contexts (Akhawe and Felt, 2013; Egelman et al. 2009; Kelley et al. 2013). In this study, we seek to explore the impact

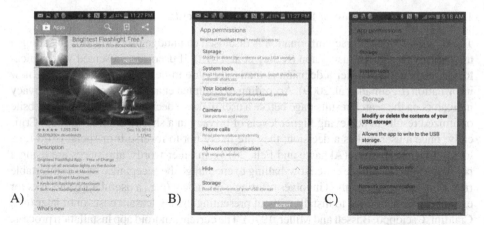

Fig. 1. Current Android mobile application screens

that warning messages and the temporal location of when permission requirements are presented have on the discernment of identifying risky and safe apps.

1.1   Relevant Warning Messages

Routinely experiencing the same standard warning messages may be misinterpreted overtime as trustworthy because of its sheer familiarity (Bohme and Kopsell, 2010). Similarly, default settings or Calls to Actions (CTAs) have an underlying influence on the user's privacy decisions without him being aware of it (Solove, 2013). Current defaults do not provide the appropriate framing necessary for users to proceed with caution. According to Jou, Shanteau and Harris (1996), "framing is a form of manipulating the salience or accessibility of different aspects of information" (p. 9). We propose that warning messages should be dynamic to the security needs of a particular context and be recognizable by the user. Figure 1 provides an example of an Android mobile app screen. As displayed in screen B, the interface provides a list of permission requirements without any visual indication to communicate risk or give warning that these items could potentially violate the user's privacy. Users are required to read through the information to interpret the risk and make their decisions accordingly without any visual support. Choe et al. (2013) found that the representation of privacy related information in a visual way could influence decision making, specifically with the use of color and symbols that resonate with common cultural experiences. Red has been used in privacy contexts to indicate conflicts between current settings and previous selections (Egelman et al. 2009). We explored the addition of warnings by highlighting risky permission requirements in red text, as well as placing a red stop sign to increase the likelihood that users will stop and attend to the permission requirements. We did not delineate the level or severity of risk per permission item. The level of risk has to be interpreted by the user. The warning message denotes permission requirements that are in violation of their BYOD policy or personal privacy.

1.2 Temporal Location of Permission Requirements

The timing of when privacy information is disclosed can nudge users towards installing a trustworthy or compromising app (Kelley et al. 2013). If users are presented with indicators of increased risk after a decision is made, they are more likely to disregard the new information (Egelman et al. 2009). According to Egelman et al. (2009), presenting privacy indicators on the search results page before a user makes a decision to proceed to a website optimized results in achieving higher levels of privacy in a shorter amount of time. Critically, once a user makes a decision, they are likely not to reverse it or spend extra time looking for alternatives (Akhawe and Felt, 2013). In other words, app stores are using a popular selling technique called low-balling to encourage the acceptance of uncomfortable risk. This persuasive method involves offering a great deal (e.g., a useful app) and asks for explicit agreement (e.g., to install) without presenting the unpleasant costs until later (c.f., Cialdini, Cacioppo, Bassett and Miller, 1978). The current Android app installation process, shown in Fig. 1, presents privacy requirements only after a user has made the decision to install the app (see screen B). Prior to the install decision, the user is given non-privacy related criteria (see screen A). Once the user has made the install decision by tapping on the Install button, screen B prompts them to "Accept" the required permissions. Please note, that screen C is hidden until the user taps on the individual permission items from screen B to get more details. The main CTAs on the first two screens (A and B) encourage users to install and then accept. There is no distinction on the user interface that explicitly distinguishes the binary choices to "Install" or "Not Install" on screen A, and "Accept" or "Not Accept" on screen B. Users are given permission requirements on screen B only after deciding to install the app on screen A. Kelley et al. (2013) found that users practically glossed over the permission requirements if presented after the install decision in the context of new apps. We propose to move the permission requirements from screen B to screen A to test which location facilitates safer choices and less risky behaviors.

1.3 Experiment Overview

Identifying malicious apps from safe ones is a difficult task, especially when there is no visual or contextual distinction between them. In this experiment, we explore the use of warning messages and the timing of the permission requirements' location relative to the install decision. We hope to encourage more secure decision-making and increase the number of safer app installations by presenting warnings prior to the install decision. This should help users recall their BYOD policy and personal privacy preferences in order to minimize risk and increase attention to the consent-based permission system.

2   Methods

2.1 Participants

The university institutional review board approved all experimental procedures. A total of twenty-two undergraduate volunteers received course credit for a sixty-minute effort. To maintain the counterbalance in our four experimental lists, the data collected from six extra participants were excluded from further analysis. This allowed us to have an equal number of four participants represented across the four lists. The age of participants ranged from 18–35 years old with eight males and eight females. Four participants reported that English was not their first language. At the end of the experiment, participants were asked to fill out a survey regarding their general app usage. Fourteen out of 16 participants use an iPhone as their personal smartphone; the remaining two were Android users. On average, participants stated that they downloaded about one to two apps per month. 13 participants reported that they store private information on their smartphones, but only four reported that they have security or safety concerns with the device. All of the participants have never experienced identity theft in the past. Participants were also given a survey at the end of the experiment to measure their general trust in the hypothetical app store system. The survey is comprised of five negative and seven positive semantic statements (Jian et al. 2000). Overall, participants reported that they trusted the system ($M = 4.99$, $SD = 1$).

2.2 Apparatus

The study was created and run within Paradigm (http://www.paradigmexperiments.com/), an experimental presentation software employed for precise timing and data recording. Participants played Bejeweled (http://www.bejeweled.com) as a distraction task to pass time. The design of the hypothetical app store was modeled after the Android interface with slight modifications to the layout, iconography, and color scheme (see Fig. 2 for examples). In the experimental conditions where permission requirements are presented before the install decision, we introduced a tab-based menu to separate permissions, reviews and screenshots on the description page of the app. Permission requirements are defaulted to the first tab. The trials were created based on 10 real-world app types from the productivity category in the Google Play app store (e.g., calendar, calculator, reader, dictionary, flashlight, notes, reminders). Permission requirements, descriptions, and screenshots were taken directly from the apps. App logos, developer brands, and the name of the apps were customized to avoid confounds tied to familiarity.

2.3 Procedure

Participants were asked to fill out a demographic survey prior to beginning the experiment. They were then told to imagine they have just started employment at a new company and would be presented with a BYOD policy. A scenario was given to them explaining that they are employing an Android smartphone for personal and business purposes. They were prompted to study the hypothetical company's BYOD policy, then asked to play five minutes of Bejeweled. This ensured they were dependent on long-term memory for access to the BYOD policy. They were presented with one of four possible experimental condition blocks, ordered by using Latin square. After each block, participants were asked to reflect on their decision making process and prompted about their experience or familiarity with any of the apps. At the end of the experiment, two surveys regarding their application usage and level of trust with the hypothetical app store were given.

TEMPORAL LOCATION OF PERMISSION REQUIRMENTS

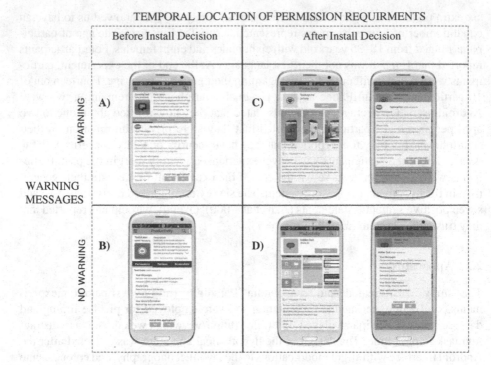

Fig. 2. Examples of the experimental conditions

Figure 2 shows the four experimental conditions stemming from a within-subjects design: Warning Messages 2 (present or absent) X Temporal Location 2 (before or after install decision). The four experimental condition blocks contained 10 trials each. Therefore, there were a total of 40 trials. We labeled the conditions as A, B, C, and D (denoted in Fig. 2). The order of the conditions was counterbalanced across participants: list 1 -ABCD, list 2 - BCDA, list 3 – CDAB, and list 4 - DABC. In each block of 10 trials, participants were asked to determine whether or not they would install the app. We measured the number of correct responses for each condition. 70% of trials were set up to have NO as the correct response, which meant that these apps are considered too risky to install. The NO trials represent risky apps that contain "dangerous" permissions that may store, capture, and share the user's data with remote third parties (Barrera et al. 2010; Mylonas et al. 2014). The permission requirements for these apps violated at least one of the company's BYOD policy given at the beginning of the experiment. The remaining 30 % of the trials was set to YES as the correct response. The YES trials represent apps that have limited access or fewer permission requirements that do not pose as much of a threat to the user. Therefore, users are safe to install these apps even though there may be warning message(s) present.

3   Results

A repeated measures ANOVA was employed to examine Warning Messages 2 (present or absent) X Temporal Location 2 (before or after install decision) on the portions of correct decisions to install. We separated the data according to the NO trials, when the user should not install the app, and YES trials for when the user should install the app.

3.1   Should not Install - Risky App

The analysis revealed that providing warning messages with the permission requirements significantly discouraged users from installing risky apps ($M = .80$, $SEM = .03$) compared with not having a warning message ($M = .61$, $SEM = .05$); $F(1,15) = 7.68$, $p = .014$, $\eta_p^2 = .034$. Unfortunately, users still installed dangerous apps approximately 20 % of the time even with relevant warning messages. The temporal location of permission requirements did not have a statistically significant impact on performance when presented before the install decision ($M = .70$, $SEM = .02$), or after ($M = .72$, $SEM = .05$); $F(1,15) = .15$, $p = .71$, $\eta_p^2 = .01$. Contrary to previous findings (e.g., Kelley et al. 2013), it appears the placement of the privacy information in relation to the install decision is not critical when it comes to identifying risky apps. There was also no statistically significant interaction between warning messages and permissions location $F(1,15) = .15$, $p = .71$, $\eta_p^2 = .01$.

3.2   Should Install - Safe App

The analysis showed no main effect of warning messages. There was no difference when warnings were present ($M = .57$, $SEM = .06$), or when there were no warnings ($M = .59$, $SEM = .06$); $F(1,15) = .09$, $p = .77$, $\eta_p^2 = .01$. However, there was a significant main effect for the temporal location of permission requirements on appropriate app installation; more appropriate decisions were made when the permission requirements were presented before the install decision ($M = .71$, $SEM = .05$) compared to after ($M = .46$, $SEM = .07$); $F(1,15) = 12.73$, $p = .003$, $\eta_p^2 = .46$. However, these findings were qualified by a significant interaction between warning messages and temporal location, $F(1,15) = 9.48$, $p = .01$, $\eta_p^2 = .39$ (see Fig. 3). Paired-samples t-tests were employed to further explain the interaction. When looking at the comparisons between the two temporal locations, warning messages presented before the install decision significantly increased safer installations ($M = .81$, $SEM = .05$) compared to when there were no warnings before the install decision ($M = .60$, $SEM = .07$); $t(15) = 2.43$, $p = .028$. However, when the warning messages were presented after the install decision, the opposite result occurred where warnings actually decreased safer installations ($M = .33$, $SEM = .09$) compared to when there were no warnings ($M = .58$, $SEM = .09$); $t(15) = -2.16$, $p = .048$. This suggests that meaningful warning messages increase trust of safe apps when placed on the description page. Interestingly, placing a warning message after a decision is made to install creates distrust.

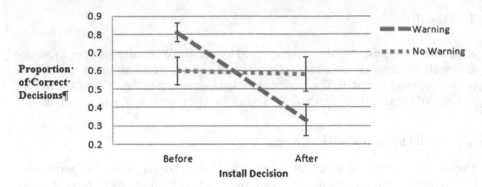

Fig. 3. Displays the interaction between Warning Message (present or absent) X Temporal Location (before or after install decision)

4 Discussion

We need to design secure systems that help users make safer decisions. Traditionally, warning messages do not account for the complexities of human decision-making (Solove, 2013). They assume cyber security expertise and are removed from the use context. We need to make the task of installing safer mobile apps relevant to a decision process and draw the user's limited attention to critical data. Current consent-based permission systems are not designed in a way that connects with users in a meaningful way. Smartphone users have a difficult time trying to identify risk using their current mental models. Further, they do not realize the degree to which they need to manage their privacy or have the ability to keep track of everything on the go (Kelley et al. 2012; Mylonas et al. 2013; Solove, 2013).

In this experiment, we explored the use of warning messages on permission requirements and the timing of when it was presented in relation to the install decision. We anticipated that users will make safer and less risky choices if warning messages are meaningful and presented as part of the decision criteria for selecting the appropriate apps to install. This experiment considered the impact of the manipulations on risky and safe app installation decisions. We found that the presence of warning messages facilitated a lower number of risky apps installations, but did not find temporal location had an impact either before or after the install decision. However, both warning messages and temporal location impacted safe app installations. We speculate that in the conditions with permission requirements presented before the install decision, warning messages were considered a part of the decision criteria, so users can factor in risk at their own discretion. However, in the conditions with permission requirements presented after the install decision, warning messages are unexpected. Therefore, we propose that warning messages given after the install decision are implicitly indicating to the user that the app may not be safe to install.

Yee (2005) explained that security interfaces could be designed in a way that helps bridge the communication between the system and the user in a cohesive and non-intrusive way by embedding the privacy needs of the user into the task at hand. The use of recommendations, such as default button choices that hint at safer paths, can alleviate some of the challenges that make privacy self-management difficult. Although privacy management should be encouraged in the user interface to support better decisions to install safer apps while avoiding malicious ones, we need to remember that it is not a primary task that warrants the user's constant attention (Pfleeger and Caputo, 2012). Privacy self-management poses a serious concern for companies that support BYOD policies because a smartphone user's inclination is to defer privacy and security tasks onto the system; unfortunately, that system is unaware of BYOD policies and other contextual information. It is likely that users assume that the system is providing protection, therefore placement of their trust in app stores seems logical. It is also likely that they do not understand the security risks associated with sharing information. Therefore, authority is simply given to the app without any necessary validation or extra precautionary security measures (Mylonas et al. 2013). Several studies have suggested ways to communicate appropriate trust by highlighting the flaws and vulnerabilities of mobile app systems (Balebako et al. 2014; Barrera et al. 2010; Chia et al. 2012; Felt et al. 2011; Mylonas et al. 2013). We believe increased transparency supports successful risk assessments by conveying extra precautions when consenting access to personal or business data.

Acknowledgment. This research was supported by the Psychology of Design laboratory. We thank Auriana Shokrpour, Dorian Berthoud, Felicia Santiago, Jarad Bell, Michelle Gomez, and Peter McEvoy for their assistance collecting data.

References

Akhawe, D., Felt, A.P.: Alice in Warningland: a large-scale field study of browser security warning effectiveness. In: Usenix Security, pp. 257–272 (2013)

Balebako, R., Marsh, A., Lin, J., Hong, J., Cranor, L.F.: The privacy and security behaviors of smartphone app developers. In: Workshop 2014 Usable Security Experiments (USEC) (2014)

Barrera, D., Kayacik, H.G., van Oorschot, P.C., Somayaji, A.: A methodology for empirical analysis of permission-based security models and its application to android. In: Proceedings of the 17th ACM Conference on Computer and Communications Security, pp. 73–84 (2010)

Bohme, R., Kopsell, S.: Trained to accept? a field experiment on consent dialogs. In: Proceedings of the 28th International Conference on Human Factors in Computing Systems, pp. 2403–2406 (2010)

Chia, P.H., Yamamoto, Y., Asokan, N.: Is this app safe? a large scale study on application permissions and risk signals. In: Proceedings of the 21st International Conference on World Wide Web, pp. 311–320 (2012)

Choe, E.K., Jung, J., Lee, B., Fisher, K.: Nudging people away from privacy-invasive mobile apps through visual framing. In: Kotzé, P., Marsden, G., Lindgaard, G., Wesson, J., Winckler, M. (eds.) INTERACT 2013, Part III. LNCS, vol. 8119, pp. 74–91. Springer, Heidelberg (2013)

Cialdini, R.B., Cacioppo, J.T., Bassett, R., Miller, J.A.: Low-ball procedure for producing compliance: commitment then cost. J. Pers. Soc. Psychol. **36**, 463–476 (1978)

Egelman, S., Tsai, J., Cranor, L.F., Acquisti, A.: Timing is everything?: the effects of timing and placement of online privacy indicators. In: Proceedings of the Conference on Human Factors in Computing Systems, pp. 319–328 (2009)

Felt, A.P., Chin, E., Hanna, S., Song, D., Wagner, D.: Android permissions demystified. In: Proceedings of the 18th on Computers and Communications Security, pp. 627–638 (2011)

Felt, A.P., Ha, E., Egelman, S., Haney, A., Chin, E., Wagner, D.: Android permissions: user attention, comprehension, and behavior. In: Symposium on Usable Privacy and Security, pp. 1–14 (2012)

Jian, J.-Y., Bisantz, A.M., Drury, C.G.: Foundations for an empirically determined scale of trust in automated systems. Int. J. Cogn. Ergon. 4(1), 53–71 (2000)

Jou, J., Shanteau, J., Harris, R.J.: An information processing view of framing effects: the role of causal schemas in decision making. Mem. Cogn. 24, 1–15 (1996)

Kelley, P.G., Consolvo, S., Cranor, L.F., Jung, J., Sadeh, N., Wetherall, D.: A conundrum of permissions: installing application on an android smartphone. In: Conference of Financial Cyptography and Data Security, Workshop on Usable Security, pp. 1–12 (2012)

Kelley, P.G., Cranor, L.F., Sadeh, N.: Privacy as part of the app decision-making process. In: Proceedings of the 2013 ACM Annual Conference on Human Factors in Computing Systems, pp. 3393–3402 (2013)

Mylonas, A., Kastania, A., Gritzalis, D.: Delegate the smartphone user? security awareness in smartphone platforms. J. Comput. Secur. 34, 47–66 (2013)

Mylonas, A., Theoharidou, M., Gritzalis, D.: Assessing privacy risks in Android: a user-centric approach. In: Proceedings of the 1st International Workshop on Risk Assessment and Risk-Driven Testing, pp. 21–37 (2014)

Pfleeger, S.L., Caputo, D.D.: Leveraging behavioral science to mitigate cyber security risk. Comput. Secur. 31(4), 597–611 (2012)

Solove, D.J.: Privacy self-management and the consent dilemma. Harv. Law Rev. 126, 1880–1903 (2013)

Yee, K.P.: Guidelines and strategies for secure interaction design. In: Russell, D. (ed.) Security and Usability: Designing Secure Systems that People can Use, pp. 247–273. O'Reilly Media Inc., Sebastopol (2005)

Real-Time Monitoring of Privacy Abuses and Intrusion Detection in Android System

Shancang Li[1]([✉]), Junhua Chen[2], Theodoros Spyridopoulos[2],
Panagiotis Andriotis[2], Robert Ludwiniak[1], and Gordon Russell[1]

[1] School of Computing, Edinburgh Napier University, Edinburgh, UK
{s.li,r.ludwiniak,g.russell}@napier.ac.uk
[2] Cryptography Group, University of Bristol, Bristol, UK
{th.spyridopoulos,p.andriotis}@bristol.ac.uk

Abstract. In this paper, we investigated the definition of privacy, privacy abuse behaviours, and the privacy abuse in Android systems, which may be very useful for identifying the malicious apps from 'normal' apps. We also investigated the injection technology, service binding, and service proxy in Android system, which are widely used by normal apps to steal privacy information. A real-time monitoring system (app) is developed on Android system to monitor potential privacy data abuse. The app is able to monitor permission requests for all installed apps as well as analyse the potential privacy abuse behaviors.

1   Introduction

Mobile device is becoming a primary platform equipped with powerful sensing, computing, and networking capabilities [1]. The convenience to users and developers has made mobile device a fun and intelligent information-processing terminal. The popularity and advanced functionality of mobile devices eared the attention of hackers and cybercriminals. Android based devices are so widely used that millions applications (apps) have been developed related to daily life. It is reported that the Android is at the highest as greater than 80 % share of the global market in 2014 [2–4]. Meanwhile, the 99 % of mew mobile malware is designed to target Android [5]. As a result, it is very urgent to find a method to evaluate, monitor, and solve the security issues in Android. In Android, most apps are running in a "sandbox" and cannot affect other apps [6]. Therefore, most malicious apps are unable to break the system but they can steal the personal informations of Android device users, which should be treated as private data abuses [7–9]. To identify and manage user data and information is a very crucial and sensitive topic in Android system. Most of private data abuse behaviors could be detected when apps are submitted to official apps market, such as **Play Store**, etc. "Permission system" is the most important part of security system in Android [6]. However, most apps ask for many more permissions than they require. It is very difficult for Android users to manage and understand the app permissions requests. This may causes the personal data is being abused against the users' wishes. Android users are unable to know what an app would

© Springer International Publishing Switzerland 2015
T. Tryfonas and I. Askoxylakis (Eds.): HAS 2015, LNCS 9190, pp. 379–390, 2015.
DOI: 10.1007/978-3-319-20376-8_34

really do. Installing an app takes just a couple clicks to choose whether to allow the required permissions. However in using an app, it is very difficult for users to change the granted permissions [9].

In Android systems, many apps are able to access to sensitive information on the mobile device. Misusing permissions to access these information is a major cause of privacy breaches and data leakage. The Android users are not able to control over the capabilities of apps once the apps have been granted the requested permissions upon installation. This makes it possible for malicious and intrusive apps to abuse the granted permission, data, and resources. This may expose sensitive information to unauthorized apps or code. In recent, a number of serious vulnerabilities have been reported that some malware and adware apps can authorize themselves properly to access the contacts, sms, email, and other sensitive information. Numerous security applications have been developed for most bands of mobile devices; however most of them are not currently targeting actual data, mobile malware attacks. The Android systems have to face the new challenge on user privacy preservation and security protection. In response to the growing threat, mobile device are developing built-in security features. In the meantime, users can protect their data by carefully cutinizing third-part applications, and avoiding suspicious information fishing.

Therefore, a real-time monitoring system is needed to protect users from privacy data abuse. It can help the users to make real decision by real time monitoring permissions according to the behaviors of an app. The system can protect users from privacy abuse before it happens. Actually, a number of security apps can be found in `Play Store`, such as `LBE Privacy Guard`, `Clueful Privacy Advisor`, `PrivacyScanner`, `360 Mobile Safe` etc. [5–11]. These apps are developed to help users know the details of apps when they are running in Android by analysing their permissions, network flows, access, etc. However, it is still difficult to tell user what apps really do. The goal of this paper is to analyse the behaviors and intent of recent types of privacy-invasive.

2   Privacy Abuse in Android System

A basic Android system includes four layers: *application layer, application framework, library & Android runtime*, and *linux kernel* [12,13]. Each app in Android runs in Dalvik virtual machine (DVM) and it is unable to affect other apps because each application runs in their own sandbox. The `AndroidManifext.xml` defines all permissions of an app [1,14].

2.1   Potential Vulnerabilities in Android System

Although the permission system in Android is designed to protect the users information, it is widely reported that many apps are able to steal user data [9]. It isn't strong enough to protect users' privacy and prevent abuse [13], which can tell users the accessibility to privacy for each app, but unable to identify malicious apps from normal apps.

Table 1. List of privacy in android systems

Privacy	Related to
Call history	Privacy
Contact list	Privacy
Sms	Privacy
Sending short message	Identity
Phone number (IMSI)	Identity
IMEI	Identity
GPS location	Privacy & User's physical freedom
Camera	Privacy & Users' life embarrassing fact
WiFi	Network
Bluetooth	Network

2.2 Privacy in Android

The definition of privacy should fit the environment. Privacy data and information are issues for users of all types of electronic device [10]. A running app can access the 'call history', 'contact list', 'sms', 'location', *etc.*, some of these information are sent to developers or specific sites without users knowing about or being able to opt out of the practice. Mobile Android users are more concerned with privacy on their devices and they especially worry about the threat of malicious apps [10], such as `call logs`, `contacts`, `sms`, `phone numbers`, `locations`, etc. Table 1 lists the commonly used privacy information.

2.3 Privacy Abuse Behaviors in Android

It is difficult to define the *privacy abuse behaviour*. In [15] and [16], behaviors such as *"identifier disclosure"*, *"short message service misuse"*, *"spy camera"*, and *"location leakage"* are defined as privacy abuse behaviors. If the identifiers are leaked, the mobile devices could be tracked or sensitive information could be abused. The misusing of `sms` may lead serious problem in some checking system. Similarly, the location leakage can cause tracking or more serious things. The privacy abuse is seriously on Android system. Although many vulnerabilities could be fixed by a system patch but it is not an ultimate solution since the patch may be unable to fix all problems [17]. In this work, we summarized the potential privacy abuse behaviors in Android systems as Table 2.

2.4 Privacy Abuse Detecting

There are three commonly used methods to detect malware apps: *static, dynamic, extra information*, as shown in Table 3. The *static* method statically check the permissions, imported package, instruction (opcode), et al. of apps but

Table 2. List of privacy in android systems

Privacy	Potential privacy abuse behavior
Reading call history	The call history contains information about users' life, work, and network, which is a potential privacy abuse behavior
Reading contact List	Contact list leakage can leave owner of device and it's contact member in a risk state
Reading sms	Sms contains very private information of users. Furthermore, some payment systems are use sms as a second authentication method
Sending short message	Attempting to send a sms by malware app can cause serious results
Reading phone number	The phone number is an identity of users
Reading IMSI number	The international mobile subscriber identity (IMSI) is also an identity of SIM card of users
Reading IMEI number	The international mobile equipment identity (IMEI) is the identity of device
Reading GPS location	The location of user or mobile device is a kind of sensitive information
Using camera	Improper use of camera or photos in mobile device can cause privacy leakage
Using WiFi	Untrust WiFi can cause information leakage
Using bluetooth	Similar to WiFi

cannot analyse apps at runtime. *Dynamic* methods check the runtime behaviors of apps, such as *system calls, etc.* The *extra information* methods use extra information such as *the author of apps, description of apps* to analyse apps for judging whether apps are malware. On the other hand, the `service manager` can be used to detect the privacy abuse behavior, with which the attacker can use the `ptrace` function to inject the specific code to steal privacy information.

2.5 Resist Privacy Abuse

The permissions list and comments can help users make decision as to whether an app might need the permissions. Furthermore, the potential behavior of privacy abuse can be real-timely detected by hooking the `service manager`, which are logged for further analysis to help user to decide to uninstall apps or not. These methods are used to help users to resist the privacy abuse before it happens.

3   Real-Time Monitoring of Privacy Data Abuse System

This section will describe the detailed design of the system, which aims at real-time monitoring the permissions and behaviors of all installed apps to protect

Table 3. List of privacy in android systems

Methods	Advantages	Disadvantages
Static analysis	Stable, don't affect running apps	Cannot real-timely detect potential privacy abuse behaviors
Dynamic analysis	Accurate, can real-timely detect behaviors	May affect running apps
Extra information	Stable, Don't affect running apps	(1) Cannot real-timely detect behaviors of apps; (2) Inaccurate; (3) The extrainformation may be faked

users from privacy abuse. When finding some suspect apps, the system will blocked these apps and send notification to user. All suspect behaviors will be logged for further analysis. With this system, users are able to decide to block a malware behavior. The system contains following four basic tasks: (1) It can list permissions of all installed apps in an Android device; (2) It is able to monitor all predefined suspect behaviors; (3) The system can read/write comments for each apps; (4) The injection module can replace a function in a process of Android, which demonstrates how a fake `ioctl` function replace the original function; (5) A proxy services is implemented that can work as a proxy between applications and original services, which is able to detect potential privacy abuse behaviors.

3.1 Architecture Design

The system contains multiple four modules, including `activity module`, `inject process module`, `online comment service module` and `background service module`. The `background service` contains tow submodules: `service proxy` and `log record`. The `inject process module`, `service proxy module` and `log record` module are the core components. Figure 1 shows the architecture of the system.

3.2 Activity Module

The `activity module` can interact with Android. The system uses activity module to read the permission lists and of each installed app. Similarly, all logs can also be access via the watch log activity. The user can comment each app through reading/writing the logs stored in `log record` module. It can also be online accessed with the `java online comment` service. With the `notify activity`, the system can notify users when suspect privacy behaviors are found.

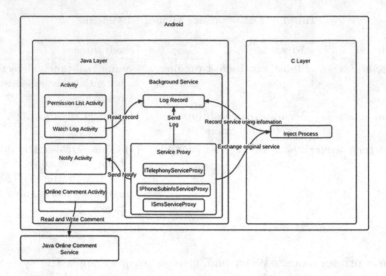

Fig. 1. Structure of real-time privacy abuse monitoring system

3.3 Inject Module

The `inject module` is used to inject third part code into the `service manager` process and replace original function, which contains two submodules: `inject program` and `hook library`. The injection process following steps: (1) `background service` module starts the inject program by forcing target process to load hook library; (2) the inject program edits the memory of target process and replace the address of original function with that of function in hook library; (3) the `service manager` loads functions in the hook library. The `inject module` is also responsible for registering binder service and returning the handle of service. The developed system can analyse and log the request of services from client apps. When `service proxy` module registers service in `service manager`, the system will record the address of binder handle. If need, it can replace the handle of proxy services. Figure 2 shows the injection process in Andriod.

3.4 Background Service Module

It contains two submodules, `log record` and `proxy service`. It first be initialized when the Android device is turned on. The background service module starts the `inject` module and then extracts some original service from `service manager` to create `proxy service`. Then, it sends the binder address of original service to proxy service and registers proxy service in `service manager`. Finally, the `log record` module will be loaded in a new thread.

The `proxy service` can analyse the requests from client apps and the suspect requests is logged in `log record` module. If some suspect behaviors are found, the `proxy service` will call `notify activity` and ask the users make

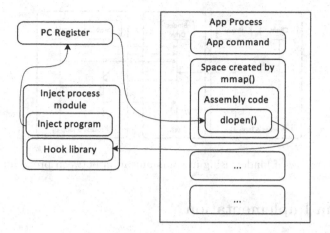

Fig. 2. Injection in an app process

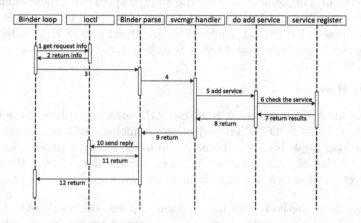

Fig. 3. Find the handle of service in `service manager`

a decision on whether to accept the request. The `log record` module can store and analyse logs received from `proxy service` and `injection module`. When the `activity module` asks for logs, the `log record` module will send a container of logs to `activity module`. Figure 3 shows the registration of service in `service manager`. Figure 4 describes the workflow of using binder in communication between proxy and service.

3.5 Java Online Comment Service Module

This module runs on a remote machine and a simple protocol is used to communicate with the `online comment` activity. The aim of this module is to enable user to online comment an apps.

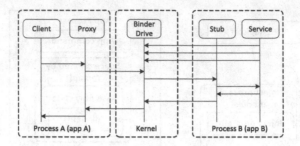

Fig. 4. Workflow of binder using in communication between proxy and service

4   System Implementation

This section addresses the details of implementation of real-time monitoring system. The system is implemented as an app and the app development environment includes Eclipse, Android Development Tools (ADT) plug-in and Android Software Development Kit (SDK). Android Native Development Kit (NDK) is used to develop the `Injection module` that is implemented in C.

4.1   API Hook

The key technology in injection is to use API hook to replace the address in Global offset Table (GOT). The injection technology is used to force target process to load hook library, where the address of target process in GOT is replaced with that of attack process. In this system, we demonstrate the workflow of app injection as shown in Fig. 5. It includes two steps:

- *Injection*, is a method that one process invades the workflow of another process. The *ptrace* function is used to force target process to allocate a space to save the injection assembly code. By doing this, the target process can be forced to load the injected.
- *GOT*, contains actual addresses of functions. By changing the address of target function in GOT of a target app, target process, it is possible to replace a function in an app.

4.2   Hook Functions

After injecting the code and replacing the address in GOT, the target process will load the hooked function instead of original target function. In Android system, the `service manager` is a name system which provides client apps service binder address according to the requested. In this work, it is found that the information of request of service from client apps can be easily fetched through the hooked `ioctl`. Actually, the handle of service can be easily exchanged here. The hooked `ioctl` can record the handle of service that created in `service proxy` module.

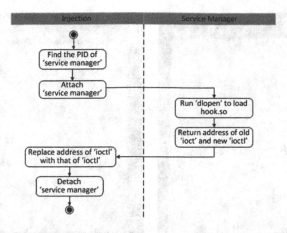

Fig. 5. workflow of injection

The hooked `ioctl` can load the original `ioctl` to send the handle of proxy service to client app. Then, the client apps will use the proxy service instead of the original service.

4.3 Test and Comparison

A `HTC Wildfire S A510e` mobile phone is used to test the developed system, where the Andriod version is 2.3.5. Figure 6(a) shows the list of all installed apps and Fig. 6(b) shows all the permissions of them. The system is able to real-time monitor the suspect privacy abuse behaviors, such as 'read phone number', 'read/write contacts', 'send/receive sms', etc., as defined in Sect. 2. Figure 6(c) shows an example of the logs of privacy abuse of the popular social

Table 4. Comparison with LPG and 360

	Develeoped system	360 mobile safe	LBE privacy guard
Real-time monitoring	Yes	Yes	Yes
Comprehensive protection	No	Yes	No
Injection detection	Yes	No	No
Contact access	Yes	Yes	Yes
SMS reading/writing	No	Yes	Yes
Camera using detection	Yes	No	No
Notification	Yes	No	No
Log	Yes	No	No
Online comment	Yes	No	No
Root needed	Yes	Yes	Yes

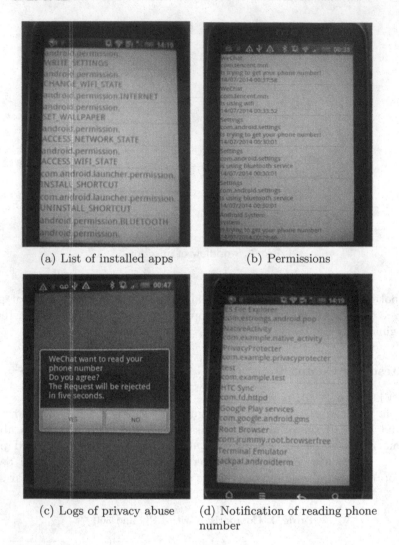

(a) List of installed apps   (b) Permissions

(c) Logs of privacy abuse   (d) Notification of reading phone number

Fig. 6. Developed system over HTC Wildfire S 510e

app: "WeChat", where "WeChat" is trying to read phone number and the system found this suspect behaviors and send notification to the user of the device. Figure 6(d) shows an example of notification when the system found that the app is reading the phone number.

Actually, there are a number of commercial privacy protection apps have been developed and released on Google Play that are able to real-time monitor privacy abuse, such as Clueful Privacy Advisor (CFA), LBE Privacy Guard (LPG), 360 Mobile Safe (360), etc. The 360 is able to monitor privacy data leakage as well as malware detection. In Table 3, we compared our developed system with the two popular commercial apps: LBE Privacy Guard

(LPG) and 360 Mobile Safe (360) in terms of suspect behaviors detection capabilities.

From Table 4 we can see that our developed system are able to detect more suspect behaviors than 360 Mobile Safe LBE Privacy Guard.

5   Conclusion

This paper analyse the potential dangerous behaviours of *apps* and proves that it is possible to real-timely monitor the privacy abuses on Android devices. An app is developed on a rooted HTC A510S Wildfire mobile phone to demonstrate all the technology proposed above.

Acknowledgments. This work was partially supported by the European Unions Prevention of and Fight against Crime Programme "Illegal Use of Internet" - ISEC 2010 Action Grants (HOME/ 2010/ISEC/AG/INT-002).

References

1. Chen, J.: Realtime monitoring of private data abuses in android system. M.Sc. Thesis, University of Bristol, September 2014
2. Ong, J.: Report: android reached record 85% smartphone market share in Q2 (2014). Xiaomi now fifth-largest vendor. http://thenextweb.com/google/2014/07/31/android-reached-record-85-smartphone-market-share-q2-2014-report/ (2014). Accessed 4 August 2014
3. Zhou, Y., Singh, K., Jiang, X.: Owner-centric protection of unstructured data on smartphones. In: Proceedings of the 7th International Conference on Trust and Trustworthy Computing (TRUST 2014), Crete, Greece, June 2014
4. Zhou, W., Wang, Z., Zhou, Y., Jiang, X.: DIVILAR: diversifying intermediate language for anti-repackaging on android platform. In: Proceedings of the 4th ACM Conference on Data and Application Security and Privacy (CODASPY 2014), San Antonio, TX, March 2014
5. Kelly, J.: Report: 97% Of mobile malware is on android. This is the easy way you stay safe. http://www.forbes.com/sites/gordonkelly/2014/03/24/report-97-of-mobile-malware-is-on-android-this-is-the-easy-way-you-stay-safe/ (2014). Accessed 4 August 2014
6. Tang, W., Jin, G., He, J., Jiang, X.: Extending android security enforcement with a security distance model. In: IEEE 2011 International Conference on Internet Technology and Applications (iTAP), pp. 1–4 (2011)
7. Google play: clueful privacy advisor. Available from: https://play.google.com/store/apps/ (2014). Accessed 22 July 2014
8. Google play.: privacy scanner (Antispy) free. Available from: https://play.google.com/store/apps/details?id=net.hobbyapplications.privacyscanner (2014). Accessed 24 July 2014
9. Androids permissions system is broken and google just made it worse. Available from: http://www.howtogeek.com/177904/androids-permissions-system-is-broken-and-google-just-made-it-worse/ (2015). Accessed 15 February 2015

10. Gates, C.S., Chen, J., Li, N., Proctor, R.W.: Effective risk communication for android apps. IEEE Trans. Dependable Secur. Comput. **11**(3), 252–265 (2014)
11. Mobile safe. Available from: https://play.google.com/store/apps/details?id=com. qihoo360.mobilesafe (2014). Accessed 1 September 2014
12. Gargenta, A.: Deep Dive into android IPC binder framework at android builders summit. Available from: http://events.linuxfoundation.org/images/stories/slides/ abs2013_gargentas.pdf (2013). Accessed 26 April 2014
13. Jiang, D., Fu, X., Song, M., Cui, Y: A security assessment method for android applications based on permission model. In: 2012 IEEE 2nd International Conference on Cloud Computing and Intelligent Systems (CCIS), vol. 2, pp. 701–705 (2012)
14. Kuzuno, H., Tonami, S.: Signature generation for sensitive information leakage in android applications. In: 2013 IEEE 29th International Conference on Data Engineering Workshops (ICDEW), pp. 112–119 (2013)
15. Wei, T.E., Jeng, A.B., Lee, H.M., Chen, C.H., Tien, C.W.: Android privacy. In: 2012 IEEE International Conference onIn Machine Learning and Cybernetics (ICMLC), vol. 5, pp. 1830–1837 (2012)
16. Wu, L., Du, X., Fu, X.: Security threats to mobile multimedia applications: camera-based attacks on mobile phones. IEEE Commun. Mag. **52**(3), 80–87 (2014)
17. Cannon, T: Android data stealing vulnerability. Available from: http://thomas cannon.net/blog/2010/11/android-data-stealing-vulnerability/ (2010). Accessed 11 April 2014
18. Jiang, X.: Android 2.3 (Gingerbread) data stealing vulnerability. Available from: http://www.csc.ncsu.edu/faculty/jiang/nexuss.html (2011). Accessed 11 April 2014

Hey, I Have a Problem in the System: Who Can Help Me? An Investigation of Facebook Users Interaction When Facing Privacy Problems

Marilia S. Mendes[1](✉), Elizabeth Furtado[2], Guido Militao[2], and Miguel F. de Castro[3]

[1] Federal University of Ceará (UFC), Russas, CE, Brazil
`marilia.mendes@ufc.br`
[2] University of Fortaleza (Unifor), Fortaleza, CE, Brazil
`{elizabet,militao}@unifor.br`
[3] Federal University of Ceará (UFC), Fortaleza, CE, Brazil
`miguel@great.ufc.br`

Abstract. When users face problems while using social systems, they tend to expose these problems in the own system, by asking their contacts for solutions. The other users, in turn, interact differently with certain types of content. In this study, we conducted an experiment with 52 postings of Facebook users in order to investigate the user interaction regarding postings about system problems. The results show that most users interact by providing help and solutions.

Keywords: Human computer interaction · Facebook · Interaction

1 Introduction

There is a widely known concept in the use of interactive systems which is providing help and documentation. Such concept was proposed by Nielsen [19] on a set of ten usability heuristics. The author's idea was make the system easy to use, thus preventing user errors. However, in case of possible errors, it is necessary to offer help and high quality documentation, making it not very extensive, easy to find and with a focus on user task [19].

The amount of times the user has searched for help, the time it has taken to access it, whether it been useful and whether it has solved their issue are examples of measures used in usability testing [10]. However, online help systems are typically used (if at all) as a last resource [25].

From the increasingly frequent use of social systems (SS) (e.g. Twitter, Facebook, MySpace, LinkedIn etc.), with features such as frequent exchange of messages and spontaneous expression of feelings, Morris et al. [17] observed that people turn to their friends, relatives and colleagues when they have doubts. The authors investigated the reasons why users make questions in SS, and found that 29 % of the questions were related to Technology. Sharoda et al. [24], in turn, analyzed questions made on Twitter and found that 4 % of them were about the own system. Mendes et al. [16] investigated

© Springer International Publishing Switzerland 2015
T. Tryfonas and I. Askoxylakis (Eds.): HAS 2015, LNCS 9190, pp. 391–403, 2015.
DOI: 10.1007/978-3-319-20376-8_35

that, in addition to questions, users praise, criticize, compare and give suggestions in the system being used.

Thus, this study aims to investigate the interaction of users arising from questions and problems about using the system, posted on an SS. More specifically, we aim to investigate the role of users in this case.

The research developed in this study used the context of Facebook Privacy as a case study, once that represents an aspect that has worried many users in SS[1], such that Facebook has recently invested in this resource. We used as data the authorized information of the participants (Facebook users), such as their contacts, postings, likes and comments and we interviewed some users. We used a descriptive and exploratory approach. Descriptive since it has focused on the identification and analysis of users data for determining the results, and exploratory since we needed the data to its characterization.

We analyzed 221 comments obtained from the posting of problems from 52 Facebook users and we carried out the following investigations: (a) analysis of users interaction when facing postings regarding doubts and problems about the use of the system; (b) analysis of the obtained comments and (c) analysis of the usefulness of answers.

This paper is organized as follows: in the next section, we approach concepts and other studies related to this work. In the third section, we describe the investigative studies and results. In the fourth and fifth sections, we present the discussion, conclusions and future work.

2 Background

2.1 Contents and the Interaction in SS

Several studies were performed in SS in order to investigate its posted content, relevance, popularity, credibility, interaction, sharing, recommendation etc. Cvijikj and Michahelles [5] conducted a content analysis of the messages shared on Facebook pages, and their results indicated that products, sales and brands are the three most discussed topics, while requests and suggestions expressing affection and sharing are the most common intentions for participation.

Java et al. [9] conducted a study of users intentions on Twitter and found that the main types of user intentions are: daily chatting, conversations, sharing of information and news reports. Newman et al. [18] investigated why and how people share health information in SS and found that participants used Facebook and online health communities for emotional support, motivation, responsibility and advice regarding weight loss and diabetes control.

In [17], Morris et al. interviewed 624 users of SS in order to investigate what and why people make questions in SS. In this investigation, they questioned about the motivation in asking and answering questions from users. Most users (28.9 %)

---

[1] Dazeinfo. Available in: http://www.dazeinfo.com/2014/09/08/facebook-inc-fb-tops-list-platforms-internet-users-worried-privacy/. Acessed: October 16th, 2014.

answered they asked questions because they rely more on friends than in search engines, and most of the answers (37 %) explaining why they answer the questions was justified by altruism: to try to help, to keep friendship or to improve social life. In this and in other studies reviewed, no investigation was conducted specifically on the interaction of users with respect to problems in the system posted by users while using it.

2.2 Facebook

Facebook[2] is, currently, the biggest online social network, with 1.3 billion active users[3]. Facebook's main purpose is to enable the sharing of contents of the following types: text, links, images or videos. The content is shared on the main Facebook page, which is called "wall" or "News Feed". The contacts of a Facebook user are called "friends". The postings of a user are visible to anyone with permission to view their full profile.

The choice of Facebook as the SS for this investigation was because it allows a greater social interaction among its members[4]. The way a user can interact on Facebook from a content posted are: like, comment and share. This investigation examines two forms of interaction: like and comment.

3 Investigation

3.1 Participants

This research was conducted in the first half of 2014 with 52 participants, undergraduate students of Computer Sciences, 37 men and 15 women, aged 20–26 years old.

3.2 Procedure

We planned to apply this investigation throughout three investigative sessions, as follows: (a) the first meeting aimed to identify privacy issues on Facebook; (b) in the second meeting, we proposed them to post those issues on Facebook, with a due date of one week and; (c) in the third meeting, we discussed the results with them. These steps are better explained below.

(a) Identification of Privacy Issues on Facebook
This step consisted in identifying potential issues which might affect the privacy of users on Facebook. For this step, we conducted an investigation session with all the participants, addressing the theme: Social Systems. At this session, we presented the main features, ways of interaction and the main concerns of use in SS, mainly focusing on privacy issues. We questioned them: *"What would a privacy issue on Facebook be*

---

[2] Available on: https://www.facebook.com.

[3] Available on: http://www.statisticbrain.com/facebook-statistics/.

[4] Available on: http://www.nngroup.com/articles/definition-user-experience/.

to you?". The participants interacted by suggesting what would represent privacy issues to them. This moment was a brainstorm, in which all participants reported problems and stories that happened to them.

From the first session, we identified 10 main privacy issues on Facebook. Such issues focus on features that they did not know how to set up, and we present them as questions in Chart 1.

Chart 1. Privacy issues on Facebook

---

1. Access to personal information, profile, contacts, photos and postings on the wall of users is of public domain (can it be configured and controlled?);

2. Being tagged by friends in photos (can it be configured for authorizing the tagging before it is published, or can a tag be removed?);

3. Being added into discussion groups without permission (can this be configured?);

4. Facebook users can post any content on the wall of friends and strangers (can this be avoided?);

5. Sharing postings with unknown contacts (can this be configured?);

6. Friendship request and comments from strangers (how can this be controlled?);

7. When posting on Facebook via mobile devices, the current location is sent along with the postings (can this be solved?);

8. Hiding postings of users depends on the platform used, so it does not work for mobile devices (can this be solved?);

9. Publication of user profile in marketing actions related to Facebook (can this be controlled?);

10. Blocking friends can be noticed (can this be solved?).

(b) Posting Privacy Issues on Facebook

In the second session, we explained how they should post the problems on Facebook. The aim of this step was to investigate how the contacts of the participants would react to a problem posted by their friends.

In order to contextualize the posting of privacy issues on Facebook, we used the scenarios technique of describing situations in which those problems usually happen. Thus, we defined a scenario for each problem identified. According to Rosson and Carroll [23], a scenario is a story about people running an activity. A scenario should describe the context of use in which a certain problem affects users' privacy.

Therefore, we described ten scenarios. Some of these were stories told by the participants during the brainstorm of problems. We named the scenarios according to their theme. Chart 2 shows the scenarios created to represent the problems of Chart 1.

We presented the scenarios above describing the privacy issues to the participants, and they were free to choose a scenario according to their preferences.

Their activities consisted of:

1. Rewriting the scenario in their own words and posting it on their Facebook wall in the first person, as if it was something that happened to them;
2. Interacting, commenting (responding to contacts) and storing all comments (by using screen shot);

Chart 2. Scenarios (S) for the privacy issues on Facebook

(S1) Only those I want! Maria wants to post photos of her birthday on her Facebook profile so that only her parents, who live in São Paulo, can see what her party was like. Since she is very reserved, she does not want others to see these pictures. She publishes the photos and tries to restrict their view only to her parents.

(S2) Don't tag me! Luana was tagged on a photo on Facebook by her friend but she did not like the picture. So, she would like to prevent others to tag her in pictures.

(S3) How have I joined this group? Today, as I logged onto Facebook, I realized I'm taking part in the "rock group", but how have I got into it since I don't even like rock?

(S4) Not on my wall! Lucia always publishes prayers on her friends' walls, but one of her friends, Claudia, did not like this habit and decided to block Lucia. However, she does not know how to do that.

(S5) But I don't even know this person... The other day I saw a message from Célia telling everyone that her grandmother had died. *"Oh no, how sad!"*, I thought... Then I realized I don't actually know Celia, but certainly one of my friends does. How can I prevent friends of mine from sharing content from their contacts that I don't know?

(S6) Come on, do I know you? Alice is upset because people she has never met in life have come to ask her to add them on Facebook... and, once they have mutual friends, she is afraid not to accept those requests, but she does not want to accept them. How should she proceed in order to limit friend requests?

(S7) Where are you? Joana traveled with her family to a very beautiful place and she wants to post a photo on her profile so her friends can see it. However, for security reasons, she does not want her location to be revealed.

(S8) Is Facebook different on mobiles? Lana spends all day posting on Facebook about every little thing she does. I got tired of so much nonsense and hid her publications so I don't see them anymore. However, when I access Facebook from my mobile I still see those postings because this option (hide messages) doesn't work.

(S9) Poster Girl? Peter got shocked when he saw a picture of his wife published on a website with a notice saying. *"Hey, Peter, a sexy single girl is waiting for you"*. The announcement was from a service that promoted encounters (not only virtually). Peter decided to seek explanations about how the photo of his wife had ended up there.

(S10) I block him, but does he know that? Paulo always publishes advertisements of products he is selling on his friends' timeline. However, one of his friends, Luis, did not like this habit and decided to block Paulo, but he does not know how to do so that Paulo does not find out he has been blocked.

3. Providing us with the following details of their Facebook page: amount of likes and comments of their 10 most recent postings (the latest published).

Collecting the data of item 2 allowed us to analyze the postings made and investigate the interaction from each scenario. Item 3 aimed to calculate the average interaction ("likes" and "comments") of the 10 latest postings of their page before posting the scenario and comparing it to after posting the privacy issue. We requested such data from the participants at the time of application of the activity through a questionnaire. The delivery time was one week.

Given this, we analyzed, from the interaction between Facebook users, the participant who posted the scenario and the other users who interacted from the posting.

Each participant adapted their scenario according to their personality, though without affecting the context of the problem described. The number of participants for each scenario was as follows: S1(6); S2(6); S3(10); S4(4); S5(8); S6(2); S7(4); S8(5); S9(2); S10(5). Chart 3 illustrates an example of a posting related to Scenario 1 adapted by a participant.

Chart 3. Scenario adapted by a participant

> *"Hey guys, how can I set up Facebook so that only my friends would see those who are my relatives? I mean, my mother just added me as her son here, but I want only my friends to be able to see it, got it?"*

(c) Analysis of the Interaction of Contacts When Facing the Posted Scenario

We conducted three analyses to investigate the interaction of contacts when facing the scenario: (A) Analysis of the forms of interaction: "like" and "comment"; (B) Analysis of the obtained comments; and (C) Analysis of the usefulness of answers.

For the first analysis, we calculated, for each participant, an average for the two forms of interaction, "like" and "comment", of their last ten postings before posting the scenario. Then, this average was compared to the average number of "likes" and "comments" obtained from the scenario posted.

For the second analysis, all comments obtained with the 52 posted scenarios were classified according to their main characteristics.

For the third analysis, we observed whether the obtained comments helped solve the problem posted by the participant.

3.3   Results

The results are presented according to the analyses carried out.

(a) Analysis of the Forms of Interaction "Like" and "Comment"

Graph 1 shows the results obtained for the interaction "*like*", and Graph 2 shows the results for the interaction "*comment*". In blue, we show the average of each interaction

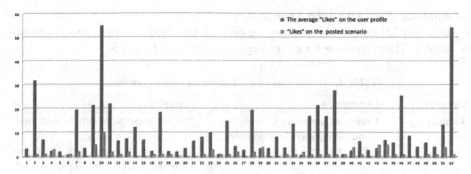

Graph 1. Results of the interaction "*like*" for the scenarios applied

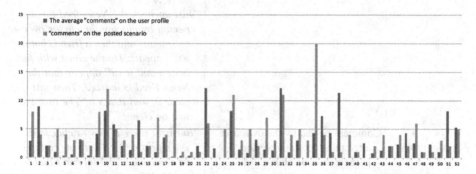

Graph 2. Results of the interaction "*comment*" for the scenarios applied

obtained from the last ten postings of each participant, and in red we show the amounts obtained for the posted scenarios.

From the 52 participants who made the postings, for only 6 (11 %) of them the interaction "like" was greater than the previous average obtained in each profile (Graph 1). One possible reason for this may be the actual concept of the interaction "like". According to Facebook, clicking the like button in a posting is a way of telling a friend you have liked their posting without leaving comments. Once the scenarios posted referred to questions and problems, that concept would not have been appropriate. This has been widely discussed on the Internet, even leading to the suggestion of creating a button called "sympathize"[5], alternative for "like" when facing sad or unpleasant news.

As for the interaction "*comment*" (Graph 2), more than half (67 %) received more comments on the scenario applied than the average of comments of each profile. The feeling of help and the particularity of the scenarios (questions and complaints) provide evidence of the contacts that provided solutions.

---

[5] Available in: http://www.huffingtonpost.com/2013/12/05/facebook-sympathize-button_n_4394451. html. Acess in January 15.

(b) Analysis of the Obtained Comments

We obtained 221 comments, and then we divided them into four categories, as shown in Table 1. The percentage for each category is shown in Graph 3.

Table 1. Description of the categories of the comments

Category	Description	Examples
Solution	Comment intending to help, indicating ways how to solve the problem	*"Go to 'about'> 'Family'> 'edit' and choose 'only friends'…";* *"Go into settings and then just below Privacy there is the "Timeline and marking settings", then you choose one of two options that you have there :)";* *"Just uncheck the News feed for that person by placing the cursor over their name and then a friends button will appear.: Do the same with this button and it will appear that the News Feed is marked. Then just clear it, and that's it! The timeline will be clean!"*
User participation	Comment posted by the own user attempting to stimulate the participation of others	*"But isn't there a way to choose it when posting?"; "but how can that be controlled?"; "but can't that be avoided?"; "Thank you";*
Support	Comments showing support, agreement or even describing a similar problem	*"I also don't know."; "I also have doubts"; "That privacy thing is quite bad, they should improve it."; "I also wanna know, please tell me if you find a solution"; "I don't know how to do this, but it would be nice if I could do that."; "I don't know how to do that, but I'm gonna search it and I'll tell you in a minute"*
Teasing	Response having nothing to do with the question, just teasing the person	*"LOL"; "Try deleting your account"; "That's quite simple, just delete your account"; "Stop having a Facebook account and that will finish! :D"*

As shown in Graph 3, the highest percentage of comments (52 %) is classified as solution, followed by the participation of the user who posted the scenario (21 %), messages of support (19 %) and teasing (8 %).

(c) Analysis of the Usefulness of the Answers

Table 2 shows the amount of answers of the type solution and the number of correct answers, those actually solving the issues of the participants. The average percentage of responses that solved the problem was 19.8 %. Many responses gave solutions that did not solve the problem or signaled a private answer, such as, *"I'll tell you in person/by phone/by e-mail."*

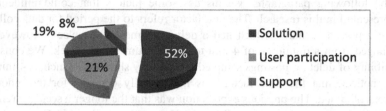

Graph 3. Percentage of the categories of the comments

Table 2. Validation of the problems found by the heuristic evaluation

Scenario	Number of responses classified as solution	Number of responses solving the problem
S1	17	7
S2	13	7
S3	15	0
S4	11	3
S5	16	0
S6	10	1
S7	6	2
S8	6	0
S9	3	0
S10	12	4

4 Discussion

After analyzing the interaction with the scenarios, we conducted a group interview (focus group) with all the 52 participants. At this point, we suggested the participants to investigate their contacts who had interacted with the scenarios, whether by clicking on *like* button or by making a *comment*. The goal was to investigate their motivation to like, to comment or to privately answer the posted scenario.

The answers of the contacts who *liked* the scenario (about why they had *liked* it) were: identification with the problem and support to their friends. Those who *liked* it but did not comment justified they did not know the answer. Those who commented on the scenario said they did it because they felt need to help. Those who left a comment with a wrong answer were sure their answers were correct or justified that the problem had no solution. Those who responded privately had two concerns: either their answers might be incorrect or they did not want to be exposed.

Some of the scenarios posted in this research had actually no solution, such as scenarios S3, S5 and S8. As for S3, Facebook does not provide a warning for addition into groups before the user is added into the group; As for S5, the user cannot block postings of a friend's contact without blocking also the friend's postings. They can either block all postings of a contact or none; and, as for S8, some applications have different settings for mobile phones.

In the following paragraphs, we discuss some factors that could influence the results presented in this research. The first factor refers to the period for data collection regarding a posted scenario, which had a delivery time of one week. However, this period ranged from a minimum of 4 min to a maximum of one week. We considered the possibility of deleting postings sampled after a very short time (such as 4 min), but we then noticed that the time factor was not actually decisive for the amount of interactions obtained. The previous expectation was that the longer a scenario remained available, the more comments it would have. However, as shown in Graph 4, reality was quite different.

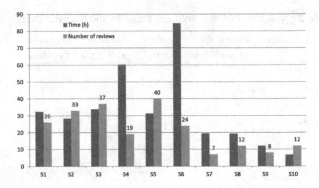

Graph 4. Time and number of comments at the moment of sampling the scenario

Another factor that could influence the results would be the participant's influence on the posted scenarios, which refers to the participant's popularity, with the following question: *Would the participation of users be influenced by the participant's popularity?* Some authors [2, 20] have classified a Facebook user as popular for the amount of friends added into their contacts list. Leitão *et al.* [12] adds the number of comments and likes in postings for classifying a user as popular, besides the freshness (frequency) of their postings and the amount of shared postings. In this investigation, we did not evaluate either the freshness or the amount of shared postings. However, we evaluated the average number of interactions "*like*" and "*comment*" for the previous 10 postings published by each participant, which provided us with the relative popularity of each participant before posting the scenario.

After completing this experiment, Facebook has provided a new functionality that allows users to ask questions about the system[6]. The most popular topic had 2,304 questions and, for each of them, there were around 600 comments, confirming the characteristics of users investigated in these experiments: commenting about the system on the own system.

---

[6] https://www.facebook.com/help/community/?view=top.

5   Final Considerations and Future Work

The objective of this work was not to evaluate privacy on Facebook. This topic was already discussed by a number of authors [1, 3, 4, 6–8, 11, 13, 14, 21, 22, 26–28]. Our goal was to investigate how users interact from problems and questions posted by other users, since this represents a frequent practice in SS.

In this research, we analyzed two main forms of interaction on Facebook: *like* and *comment*. The interaction *like* was not higher regarding scenarios, though the interaction *comment* was, thus representing a greater share of this form of interaction for a scenario. The highest percentage of type of comments obtained was *solution*. Such comments were characterized for containing details of use of the system.

Some studies have already been carried out from the Postings Related to the Use (PRUs) of users in SS. In [24], we investigated a new form of assessment of Usability and User Experience in SS through the PRUs of users while using the system. In [15], we proposed a Evaluation Model of the User Textual Language. We intend to continue this work by studying characteristics of PRUs and how they can be useful in order to obtain user perceptions regarding the system.

References

1. Agosto, D.E.; Abbas, J.: High school seniors' social network and other ICT use preferences and concerns. In: Proceedings of the 73rd ASIS&T Annual Meeting on Navigating Streams in an Information Ecosystem (ASIS&T 2010), Pittsburgh, vol. 47, no. 65, pp. 1–10, October 2010
2. Angeletou, S., Rowe, M., Alani, H.: Modelling and analysis of user behaviour in online communities. In: Aroyo, L., Welty, C., Alani, H., Taylor, J., Bernstein, A., Kagal, L., Noy, N., Blomqvist, E. (eds.) ISWC 2011, Part I. LNCS, vol. 7031, pp. 35–50. Springer, Heidelberg (2011)
3. Bergmann, F.B.; Silveira, M.S.: "Eu vi o que você fez.:. e eu sei quem você é!": uma análise sobre privacidade no Facebook do ponto de vista dos usuários. In: Proceedings of the Symposium on Human Factors in Computing Systems (IHC 2012), Cuiabá, MT, Brazil (2012)
4. Castillo, C., Mendoza, M., Poblete, B.: Information credibility on twitter. In: Proceedings of the 20th International Conference on World Wide Web (WWW 2011), Hyderabad, India, pp. 675–684 (2011)
5. Cvijikj, I.P., Michahelles, F.: Understanding social media marketing: a case study on topics, categories and sentiment on a facebook brand page. In: MindTrek 2011, Tampere, Finland, 28–30 September 2011
6. Fahl, S., Harbach, M., Muders, T., Smith, M., Sander, U.: Helping Johnny 2.0 to encrypt his Facebook conversations. In: Proceedings of the Eighth Symposium on Usable Privacy and Security (SOUPS 2012), Article No. 11, Washington, DC, USA (2012)
7. Faisal, M., Alsumait, A.: Social network privacy and trust concerns. In: Proceedings of the 13th International Conference on Information Integration and Web-based Applications and Services (iiWAS 2011), Ho Chi Minh City, Vietnam, pp. 416–419 (2011)

8. Hanne, M., Silva, C., Almeida, J., Gonçalves, M.: Analysis of vulnerability to Facebook users. In: Proceedings of the 18th Brazilian symposium on Multimedia and the Web (WebMedia 2012), São Paulo-SP, Brazil, pp. 335–342 (2012)
9. Java, A., Finin, T., Song, X., Tseng, B.: Why we Twitter: understanding microblogging usage and communities. In: 9th WEBKDD and 1st SNA-KDD Workshop 2007, San Jose, California, USA (2007)
10. Jeffrey, R., Chisnell, D.: Handbook of Usability Testing: How To Plan, Design, and conduct Effective Tests. Wiley, New York (2008)
11. Lampinen, A., Lehtinen, V., Lehmuskallio, A., Tamminen, S.: We're in it together: interpersonal management of disclosure in social network services. In: Proceedings of the SIGCHI Conference on Human Factors in Computing Systems (CHI 2011), Vancouver, BC, pp. 3217–3226 (2011)
12. Leitão, T., Morgado, C., Cunha, J.C.: Measuring popularity in social network groups. In: Second International Conference on Cloud and Green Computing (CGC), pp. 485–492 (2012)
13. Mao, H., Shuai, X., Kapadia, A.: Loose tweets: an analysis of privacy leaks on twitter. In: Proceedings of the 10th Annual ACM Workshop on Privacy in the Electronic Society (WPES 2011), Chicago, IL, USA, pp. 1–12 (2011)
14. Mazzia, A., Lefevre, K., Adar, E.: The PViz comprehension tool for social network privacy settings. In: Proceedings of the Eighth Symposium on Usable Privacy and Security (SOUPS 2012), Article No. 13, Washington, DC, USA (2012)
15. Mendes, M.S.: MALTU - model for evaluation of interaction in social systems from the users textual language. 200 f. Thesis (Ph.D. in computer science) – Federal University of Ceará (UFC), Fortaleza, CE, Brazil (2015)
16. Mendes, M.S., Furtado, E.S., Castro, M.F.: Do users write about the system in use? an investigation from messages in natural language on Twitter. In: 7th Euro American Association on Telematics and Information Systems (EATIS 2014), Valparaiso, Chile (2014)
17. Morris, M.R., Teevan, J., Panovich, K. What do people ask their social networks and why? a survey study of status message Q&A behavior. In: Proceedings of the CHI 2010, pp. 1739–1748. ACM Press (2010)
18. Newman, M.W., Lauterbach, D., Munson, S.A., Resnick, P., Morris, M.E.: "It's not that I don't have problems, I'm just not putting them on Facebook": challenges and opportunities in using online social networks for health. In: CSCW 2011, Hangzhou, China (2011)
19. Nielsen, J.: Heuristic evaluation. In: Mack, R., Nielsen, J. (eds.) Usability Inspection Methods, pp. 25–62. Wiley, New York (1994)
20. Quercia, D., Lambiotte, R., Stillwell, D., Kosinski, M., Crowcroft, J.: The personality of popular Facebook users. In: Proceedings of the ACM 2012 Conference on Computer Supported Cooperative Work (CSCW 2012), Seattle, Washington, USA, pp. 955–964 (2012)
21. Reynolds, B., Venkatanathan, J., Gonçalves, J., Kostakos, V.: Sharing ephemeral information in online social networks: privacy perceptions and behaviours. In: Campos, P., Graham, N., Jorge, J., Nunes, N., Palanque, P., Winckler, M. (eds.) INTERACT 2011, Part III. LNCS, vol. 6948, pp. 204–215. Springer, Heidelberg (2011)
22. Rodrigues, K.H., Canal, M. C., Xavier R.C., Alencar, T.S., Neris, V.P.A.: Avaliando aspectos de privacidade no Facebook pelas lentes de usabilidade, acessibilidade e fatores emocionais. In Proceedings of the IX Symposium on Human Factors in Computing Systems (IHC 2012), Cuiabá, MT, Brazil (2012)
23. Rosson, M.B., Carroll, J.M.: Scenario-Based Development of Human-Computer Interaction. Morgan Kaufmann Publishers, San Francisco (2002)

24. Sharoda, A., Lichan, H. Chi, E.H.: What is a question? crowdsourcing tweet categorization. In: CHI 2011 (2011)
25. Silveira, M.S., de Souza, C.S., Barbosa, S.D.J. (2003) Um Método da Engenharia Semiótica para a Construção de Sistemas de Ajuda Online. In: Proceedings of the Latin-American Conference on Human-Computer Interaction (CLIHC 2003), Rio de Janeiro, Brazil (2003)
26. Staddon, J., Huffaker, D., Brown, L., Sedley, A.: Are privacy concerns a turn-off?: engagement and privacy in social networks. In: Proceedings of the Eighth Symposium on Usable Privacy and Security (SOUPS 2012), Article No. 10, Washington, DC, USA (2012)
27. Terto, A., Alves, C., Rocha, J., Prates, R. Imagem e privacidade: contradições no Facebook. In: Proceedings of the IX Symposium on Human Factors in Computing Systems (IHC 2012), Cuiabá, MT, Brazil (2012)
28. Wang, N., Xu, H., Grossklags, J.: Third-party apps on Facebook: privacy and the illusion of control. In: Proceedings of the 5th ACM Symposium on Computer Human Interaction for Management of Information Technology (CHIMIT 2011), Boston, MA, USA (2011)

An Extensible Platform for the Forensic Analysis of Social Media Data

Huw Read[1,2(✉)], Konstantinos Xynos[1], Iain Sutherland[1,4], Frode Roarson[1,2],
Panagiotis Andriotis[3], and George Oikonomou[3]

[1] University of South Wales, Pontypridd, CF37 1DL, UK
huw.read@southwales.ac.uk
[2] Noroff University College, 4608 Kristiansand S, Vest Agder, Norway
[3] University of Bristol, Bristol, BS8 1TH, UK
[4] Security Research Institute, Edith Cowan University, Perth, Australia

Abstract. Visualising data is an important part of the forensic analysis process. Many cell phone forensic tools have specialised visualisation components, but are as of yet able to tackle questions concerning the broad spectrum of social media communication sources. Visualisation tools tend to be stove-piped, it is difficult to take information seen in one visualisation tool and obtain a different perspective in another tool. If an interesting relationship is observed, needing to be explored in more depth, the process has to be reiterated by manually generating a subset of the data, converting it into the correct format, and invoking the new application. This paper describes a cloud-based data storage architecture and a set of interactive visualisation tools developed to allow for a more straightforward exploratory analysis. This approach developed in this tool suite is demonstrated using a case study consisting of social media data extracted from two mobile devices.

Keywords: Visualisation · Social media · Digital forensics · Mobile device

1 Introduction

Visualisation is a subject of growing importance to the field of computer forensics, in particular when dealing with large volumes of data from certain sources, such as social media sites. In an age where personal digital communication devices that can house information about our whereabouts, our conversations, or even current emotions are common [1], there are a multitude of ways that this information can be of value to a forensics investigation. Providing varied information on the different facets of an individual's activity [2]. The data sets can be extensive considering some of the new devices providing monitoring of personal fitness or health. It may be possible to query personal digital devices and social media for a wide range of data: What on-line names do they use? What information was sent to their contacts or received from their contacts? Even who had an elevated heart rate? The volume of data is further complicated by the process of trying to identify a conversation traversing multiple communication mechanisms, Facebook, Twitter, WhatsApp, iMessage, email, and SMS across multiple devices.

© Springer International Publishing Switzerland 2015
T. Tryfonas and I. Askoxylakis (Eds.): HAS 2015, LNCS 9190, pp. 404–414, 2015.
DOI: 10.1007/978-3-319-20376-8_36

Existing research has made some progress in addressing this issue [3–6]. However the difficulty currently faced by forensic examiners is that the process involves extensive data sets, is time-consuming and requires a degree of manual processing. There are current tools that are able to visualise aspects of the data as part of a digital forensics investigation. Current visualisation tools provide only limited interactivity and an expert understanding of different visualisation tools, often with different input formats.

This paper presents an architecture that encourages direct interaction with social media data in the visualisations to compliment the exploratory and investigative mindset of an investigator. Social media application data is stored in an abstracted fashion into cloud-based storage and a defined API provides the interface for different visualisation tools to make requests for data. Visualisation tools retrieve data bound by their inherent data types and can send data directly to other visualisation tools depending on the pairing of compatible input/output data types. The key contributions of this work are summarised below:

- We present a visualisation tool framework encouraging data exploration between tools.
- We demonstrate how heterogenous social media data sources can be unified and exploited by investigators.
- We highlight a novel way of recording the visualisation trail to store the thought process of an investigator.

The rest of this paper is arranged as follows. Firstly, related work in the area of cell phone forensics visualisation is considered, secondly the architecture of the platform is described, thirdly a case study is presented to highlight the advantages of the platform, fourthly the outcome of the case study is analysed, finally the conclusions and future work are discussed.

2 Related Work

As stated by Garfinkel [7] forensic visualisations tend to serve two purposes, presentation and discovery. The former specialising in describing what has happened to a courtroom, the latter helping an investigator reach conclusions about some criminal activity. Discovery tools should be [7] data driven, have fixed, predictable, static output and interactive for producing the visualisation. In addition to [7] we should also be seeking to record the data-mining activities the investigator uses in order to retrace through the thought/decision making process (Fig. 1). The visualisations should indeed be repeatable so prosecution and defence can view the same output however a means of visualising how an investigator derived their conclusions would also be beneficial when describing the process to a jury for example.

Social media should be an area of considerable interest to the forensics investigator as it provides an insight into user actions and activities although these need to be interpreted with care [8].

Mutawa [9] has suggested when considering smartphones and social media that these devices are "…a goldmine for forensic investigators" and demonstrated that social

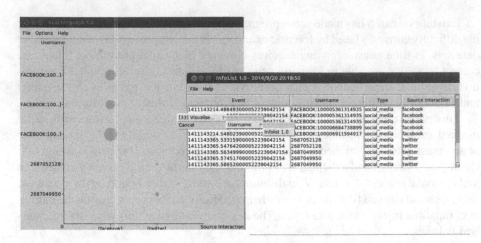

Fig. 1. A scattergraph plot sends a list of usernames from gathered social media data to a listing tool

media activity is retained on a number of cell phones, while recognising that this type of communication takes place across multiple devices [9]. A number of efforts have been made to examine the connections between mobile devices to better understand user activities [3]. Other tools have been applied to the visualization of social media including NodeXL [10] an extension of Microsoft Excel to enable a 'network graph' visualisation of data. There have also been efforts made into visualizing other aspects of social networks [4] and visualising the results. There are therefore existing tools, techniques and solutions of both commercial and open source forensics tools that can be applied to an investigation involving social media data. There are also a number of big data tools that can be used for social media analysis, including those tools used for e-discovery [11–15]. The tool proposed in this paper bridges the gap between these tools providing an extensible social media analysis tool capable of visualisations that are appropriate for forensic analysis.

2.1   Cell Phone Forensics Visualisations

There are existing tools available for forensic visualisation; these can provide some visual representation of the data. How can we visualise cell phone social media communications? Commercial software is already looking at social-based data. However, as can be seen below, commercial applications are not yet able to visualise much social networking information, instead relying on more manual query languages to obtain answers in investigations. Social links tend to be made from more traditional digital communications, emails between individuals, SMS/MMS messages, telephone calls, etc. Open source software tends to follow a more generic approach, towards visualising any structured data rather than anything focusing on a specific niche like cell phone forensics.

The following considers the state of cell phone forensics and how recovered social media data is being incorporated into visualisations.

2.1.1   AccessData MPE+

MPE+ is the mobile phone forensics application from AccessData, producers of FTK and FTK Imager. MPE+ itself specialises in data extraction from mobile phones [16], and has its own visualisation component [17]. It uses SMS, MMS, and call histories to look for relationships, and has a social analysis that looks for relationships via email addresses. Mention is made of an SQL Builder feature, which allows investigators to run custom queries on app data, but nothing specific is mentioned about correlations from social media sources.

2.1.2   Micro Systemation XRY and XAMN

Micro Systemation focuses on the data extraction with XRY and the visualisation with XAMN [18]. XAMN provides a number of different views including timeline, list, connections and geographic. Although XRY provides the means to extract application data, XAMN does not currently visualise social media communications.

2.1.3   CelleBrite UFED Link Analysis

CelleBrite provides presentation and discovery visualisations through the Link Analysis software [19]. Link Analysis provides the means to view commonalities across multiple cell phones in terms of phone calls, SMS, MMS, email, chat and a few others. Social media communications do not presently feature in Link Analysis.

2.1.4   Oxygen Forensics

Oxygen Forensics suite contains several different visualisation tools [20], timeline, web connections & locations, links & stats, but of particular interest is the Social Graph. The Social Graph looks at relationships between device owners and their contacts, i.e. how much time was spent using different communication mechanisms. Metrics include call length, number of messages sent and times of communication [20].

2.1.5   Open Source Software (OSS) Cell Phone Tools

OSS tools tend to concentrate on the extraction of data from the standard sources (call history, SMS, MMS, email [21]) and then on an application-by-application basis (e.g. WhatsApp [22], Skype [23]). Some of the tools generate lists as a visual aid for presentation. There are a number of OSS tools that lend themselves expertly to big-data social network visualisation [24] but are not designed for the type of focus required of the types of digital forensic investigations described in this paper.

To the best of the authors' knowledge no one has addressed the discovery side of visualisation for cell phone forensics in the open source community with a focus on the analysis and correlation of social media activity.

3   Architecture and Implementation

The architecture of the platform discussed in this paper is introduced below, highlighting the different core components of the storage, tool-to-tool data exchange and the audit process of the examiner.

3.1   Cloud Storage

SQlite is a database format found on most cell phones, as it is portable (i.e., store as files) and provides the advantages that come with relational database architectures. Mobile applications on Google's Android and Apple's iOS primarily make use of SQlite.

One of the main issues with these relational databases is the way the information is stored. This is usually in a standard format, as per the SQlite specification, although the actual table and column layouts are bespoke on the needs of the application. This poses a challenge to investigators and any tools they may rely upon. Applications are updated very frequently and it would not take much for a database design to change overnight.

In order to support the tools that have been developed, the database design proposed in [5, Fig. 2] provides a unifying database design for storing social media information. Individual parsers for Twitter and Facebook were created to convert the SQlite information into XML and then these were transformed then into the relevant social media XML format which is inserted into the cloud-based data store. Apache Cassandra was used to store the information and an XML middleware was then used to store and extract information when required by the visualisations.

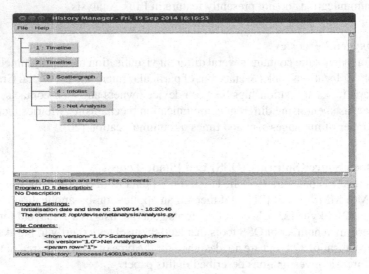

Fig. 2. History Manager records an investigators progress.

```
<?xml version="1.0" encoding="UTF-8" ?>
  <idoc>
      <from version="1.0">Scattergraph</from>
      <to version="1.0">Net Analysis</to>
      <param row="1">
          <object name="From Account Relationship">
              <data type="from_account_relationships">1347865813.632551000052239042154</data>
          </object>
          <object name="To Account Relationship">
              <data type="to_account_relationships">1347865813.632551000052239042154</data>
          </object>
      </param>
  </idoc>
```

Fig. 3. Recording the visualisation progression can reveal much about an investigation when expert testimony is required.

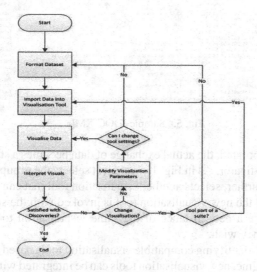

Fig. 4. Rapid visual investigation: Timeline (Top Left) to Scattergraph (Top Right) to InfoList (Bottom).

3.2 Interacting with Different Visualisation Tools

To facilitate data exchange between visualisations, the tools must incorporate the following components:

A configuration file (CDOC) that describes the quantity and type of data it can accept as input. These XML CDOCs are used whenever an investigator selects a subset of data within one visualisation tool. A list is presented to the investigator of other visualisation tools that can accept the subset as input.

An information file (IDOC) that is used to transport the data between tools.

It is an XML file that describes where the relevant data is in the underlying data source that the receiving tool needs to query. The structure stores the source visualisation tool, the destination visualisation tool, the type of information to be visualised, and the identifier of the row entry that stores the information. In the following sample, we can see two tools exchanging information relating to the relationships between social media accounts (Fig. 5).

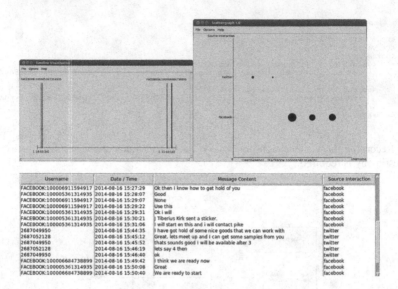

Fig. 5. Sample IDOC XML.

With these incorporated, the actual exchange of data becomes a straightforward task for the forensic investigator. As in Fig. 1, an analyst selects the grouping or pattern they wish to investigate further, selects another visualisation tool that can receive such input from the library, and the new visualisation tool is invoked with the subset. The investigator can even create a new instance of the same visualisation tool (albeit with the reduced dataset) if they wish.

As the process of identifying compatible visualisation tools based on their data-types is performed in real-time, new visualisation tools can be integrated without closing down the entire system and disrupting the investigative process.

3.3   Recording the Thought Process

When a forensic practitioner is using visualisation as a mechanism to discover facts relating to an investigation, the process is typically unidirectional. Large datasets are visualised, groupings of interest are investigated, subsets are extracted for further visualisation until a discovery is made (Fig. 3). With the architecture, we log the exchange that takes place between visualisation tools to let an investigator reinvoke existing visuals at a later date. As mentioned above, each visualisation tool is started with an IDOC XML file that describes the location of the data the tool needs to request data from the cloud data store.

As the investigator moves from one visualisation to another, we store the IDOC files and use a GUI tool called the History Manager (Fig. 2) to visualise the investigator's trail. Any views the investigator had seen previously are stored with the IDOC. The History Manager provides the facility to the investigator to select an existing IDOC and launch the visualisation tool, with the same inputs, and produce the same visual output again. The History Manager simply stores the files and other descriptive information in a hierarchical directory structure, which can easily be stored and recalled for later use or archiving.

4   Case Study

There are a range of potential sources for social media data. Access to corporate servers may be a lengthy legal process leading investigators to consider other possible sources [5, 25]. Therefore the case study detailed in this paper uses data collected directly from the mobile phones.

A simple scenario was developed to test the system between three individuals typifying communication usage across several platforms such as instant messages, voice over IP and different devices. As part of the study the individuals also shared documents using Google drive and email. The simulated criminal activity is the selling of illegally obtained information and software. Much of the discussion between the phone owners take place over Facebook and Twitter; in particular making use of Twitter's direct messaging function and Facebook's Messenger application.

The investigator, as part of his research, wants to look into the social media communications to identify any evidence of nefarious activity. However, it appears the thread of communication occurs over several social media types. In particular the following are found during an investigation of applications found on the cell phones:

- com.twitter.android/db/xxxxxxxxxx.db
- com.facebook.orca/db/threads_db2

These SQLite files contain private messages between the phone owner and others. The investigator begins by ingesting the files of interest into the data store. Once these have been parsed, he opens the Timeline tool to obtain an appreciation of the timescales in the data.

The investigator then tries to look for correlations between the different usernames and social media formats found. To do this he interacts with the Timeline tool (Fig. 4, Top Left) by clicking the background, which initiates a search for other tools in the architecture that can take these visualised data-types as input. The Scattergraph tool is selected, and the dataset is transferred as an IDOC XML file. This is stored in the HistoryManager and can be accessed at a later date if required.

The Scattergraph tool (Fig. 4, Top Right) initially shows the two types it was provided (Date/Time and Usernames). The axes are altered to show the Source Interaction against the Usernames. This highlights how users sent messages via different social media formats. From this visualisation, the investigator now wants to look at the actual messages sent, across all social media types, ordered by time.

The Infolist application (Fig. 4, Bottom) provides a view that lets the investigator see the messages sent in time order. It includes all social media formats from this case study and is not focused purely on one type.

5   Case Study Results and Evaluation

The case study highlights the advantages of the architecture. An investigator is able to easily transition from one tool to another, and rapidly data mine to gain an understanding of what has happened in their investigation. It should be clear from the case study that the emphasis in this paper is on the facilitation of interactivity rather than any perceived novelty of the visualisations themselves.

The investigator has the ability to choose which visualisation tools they want to use when visually mining the data. In this fashion they are able to make discoveries more rapidly as the data mining process is effectively tailored to suit.

By looking for commonalities across social media formats we are able to process the data collectively. Using the right combination of visualisation tools conversation threads across different communication mediums can be aligned and interpreted in a more straightforward fashion than existing mechanisms.

The analysis process in the case study was kept short for brevity. However, true of both a quick triage and a full investigation, the History Manager stores all interactions between visualisation tools. The IDOCs are effectively a log or audit trail of an investigators visualisation thought process.

6   Conclusions

Visualisation of social media is of major importance to computer forensic investigators in an age where personal digital communication occurs over various applications on multiple platforms. Existing tools and techniques for analysis include a range of commercial and open source forensics applications and Big Data visualisation tools. This paper has highlighted the lack of forensics tools that are appropriate for interactively visualising social media from cell phones. This paper describes the testing of an open source platform capable of large scale forensics visualisation. Data is stored in an abstracted fashion into cloud-based storage and a defined API provides the interface for multiple interactive visualisation tools to access the data. Visualisation tools retrieve data and can send data to other tools. This platform supports a forensic investigators analysis by enabling multiple simultaneous interactive visualizations to be generated: While capturing the investigators actions to record and log the process of the investigation. Future work will concentrate on the possibility of integrating other third-party visualisations into the platform, and the exploration of other potential evidence sources in a unified fashion to provide a more holistic view of an investigation.

Acknowledgements. The research leading to these results has received funding from the European Research Council under the European Union's Seventh Framework Programme (FP/ 2007-2013)/ERC Grant Agreement Number: HOME/2010/ISEC/AG/INT-002.

References

1. Samsung Galaxy S5. http://www.samsung.com/global/microsite/galaxys5/features.html
2. Cellebrite: Cellebrite's outlook for the mobile forensics industry 2014. White Paper (2014). http://www.cellebrite.com/collateral/OUTLOOK_FOR_THE_MOBILE_FORENSICS_ INDUSTRY_2014_WP.pdf

3. Catanese S.A., Fiumara, G.: A visual tool for forensic analysis of mobile phone traffic. In: Proceedings of the 2nd ACM workshop on Multimedia in Forensics, Security And Intelligence, pp. 71–76 (2010). ISBN:978-1-4503-0157-2, doi:10.1145/1877972.1877992, http://dl.acm.org/citation.cfm?id=1877992
4. Perer, A., Shneiderman, B.: Balancing systematic and flexible, exploration of social networks. IEEE Trans. Visual. Comput. Graphics 12(5), 693–700 (2006). http://hcil2.cs.umd.edu/trs/2006-25/2006-25.pdf
5. Andriotis, P., Tzermias, Z., Mparmpaki, A., Ioannidis, S., Oikonomou, G.: Multilevel visualization using enhanced social network analysis with smartphone data. Int. J. Digit. Crime Forensics 5, 34–54 (2013)
6. Andriotis, P., Tryfonas, T., Oikonomou, G., Li, S., Tzermias, Z., Xynos, K., Read, H., Prevelakis, V.: On the development of automated forensic analysis methods for mobile devices. In: Holz, T., Ioannidis, S. (eds.) Trust 2014. LNCS, vol. 8564, pp. 212–213. Springer, Heidelberg (2014)
7. Garfinkel, S.L.: Forensics Visualizations with Open Source Tools (2013). http://simson.net/ref/2013/2013-11-05_VizSec.pdf
8. Browning, J.G.: Digging for the digital dirt: discovery and use of evidence from social media sites. SMU Sci Tech L Rev. 14, 465 (2010). http://heinonline.org/HOL/LandingPage?handle=hein.journals/comlrtj14&div=26&id=&page=
9. Al Mutawa, N., Baggili, I., Marrington, A.: Forensic analysis of social networking applications on mobile devices. In: Proceedings of the 2012 Digital Forensic Research Workshop. http://www.dfrws.org/2012/proceedings/DFRWS2012-3.pdf
10. Smith, M. A., Shneiderman, B., Milic-Frayling, N., Mendes Rodrigues, E., Barash, V., Dunne, C., Capone, T., Perer, A., Gleave, E.: Analyzing (social media) networks with NodeXL. In: Proceedings of the Fourth International Conference on Communities and Technologies, pp. 255–264, New York, NY, USA (2009). ISBN:978-1-60558-713-4, doi:10.1145/1556460.1556497, http://hcil2.cs.umd.edu/trs/2009-11/2009-11.pdf
11. Afentis Facebook Forensics Tool. http://www.facebookforensics.com/features.html
12. Forte, D., Power, R.: Electronic discovery: digital forensics and beyond. Comput. Fraud Secur. 2006(4), 8–10 (2006)
13. Ringtail E-discovery Tool. http://www.ftitechnology.com/Products-Services/Software-and-Services/Ringtail/Ringtail.aspx
14. Attenex E-Discovery Software. http://www.ftitechnology.com/Products-Services/Software-and-Services/Attenex.aspx
15. Xera I-conect. http://www.iconect.com/
16. AccessData Mobile Phone Examiner. http://www.accessdata.com/solutions/digital-forensics/mobile-phone-examiner
17. AccessData, Mobile Device data Visualization with MPE+ (2012). https://www.youtube.com/watch?v=bjcLDjju-kU
18. Micro Systemation, XAMN (2014). https://www.msab.com/xry/xamn
19. Cellebrite, UFED Link Analysis (2014). http://www.cellebrite.com/mobile-forensics/products/applications/ufed-link-analysis
20. Oxygen Forensics, Social Graph Tool (2014). http://www.oxygen-forensic.com/en/features/analyst/social-graph
21. ViaForensics, Aflogical OSE (2014). https://viaforensics.com/resources/tools/android-forensics-tool/#aflogical-ose
22. Ztedd, Whatsapp Xtract: Backup messages extractor (2012). http://forum.xda-developers.com/showthread.php?t=1583021
23. Garronski, N.: Skype Xtrator v.0.1.8.8 (2014). http://www.skypextractor.com/

24. Forensics WIKI: Graph and (Social) Network Visualization (2013). http://www.forensicswiki.org/wiki/Tools:Visualization#Graph_and_.28Social.29_Network_Visualization
25. Mulazzani, M., Huber, M., Weippl, E.R.: Social Network forensics: tapping the data pool of social networks. In: Eighth Annual IFIP WG 11.9 International Conference on Digital Forensics (2012). https://www.sba-research.org/wp-content/uploads/publications/social Forensics_preprint.pdf

Opinions or Algorithms: An Investigation of Trust in People Versus Automation in App Store Security

David Schuster[1](✉), Mary L. Still[1], Jeremiah D. Still[1], Ji Jung Lim[2],
Cary S. Feria[1], and Christian P. Rohrer[2]

[1] San José State University, San Jose, CA, USA
{david.schuster,mary.still,jeremiah.still}@sjsu.edu
[2] Intel Security, Santa Clara, CA, USA
diannejlim@gmail.com, christian.p.rohrer@intel.com

Abstract. Mobile application (app) stores are a critical source of information about risk in an uncertain environment. App stores ought to assess and communicate the risk associated with an installation so that users are discouraged from installing risky or harmful apps in app stores. However, only a limited number of studies offer designers information about how to communicate risk effectively. We focused on the user's trust associated with security information stemming from crowd-sourced evaluations compared to those generated from an automated system. Both of these sources of security information are pervasively used to indicate possible risk associated with an app. We investigated whether biases exist for a particular source of information given similar amount of security information being available. We found that participants preferred to install apps rated by automation to those rated by humans despite equivalence in stated risk. Further, we found evidence of a gender difference in trust in automation.

Keywords: Mobile device security · App stores · Trust in automation · Interpersonal trust

1 Introduction

Mobile application (app) usage has become ubiquitous in society, therefore it is increasingly important for users to be able to identity those that pose a security threat. Increases in the number [1] and capabilities of mobile devices have lead to a proliferation of app stores. These stores provide a centralized source for discovering, purchasing, and installing apps [2]. While the security of unknown applications has been long been a concern for desktop computer users, fears could be assuaged by selecting from established brands purchased from brick-and-mortar stores or speaking with those more knowledgeable. Now, app stores provide users with a large number of unknown applications from unfamiliar brands. Further, it may be unclear whether an app's business model is based on gathering personal information or defrauding users. Users must depend on the app stores to protect them from malicious software and to clearly communicate possible risk.

It is not surprising that as the number of available mobile apps increases, so does the prevalence of malware [3, 4]. It appears users are among the last lines of defense in their

© Springer International Publishing Switzerland 2015
T. Tryfonas and I. Askoxylakis (Eds.): HAS 2015, LNCS 9190, pp. 415–425, 2015.
DOI: 10.1007/978-3-319-20376-8_37

own mobile security. They must rely upon information gathered through interactions with app stores to make decisions about the security implications of the apps they download. These interactions with the app store are critical for successful mobile device security.

Unfortunately, app stores may not provide effective and usable communication about the associated installation risks. For example, in their test of apps from the Google Play store, Felt, Chin, Hanna, Song and Wagner [3] found that approximately one-third of Android apps are over-privileged. That is, they present a request for unnecessary permissions (e.g., location data for a flashlight app). Nevertheless, research has shown that users do assume apps are safe and dismiss security warnings [5].

In addition, the typical users of app stores are not security experts, and therefore, most do not know how to interpret security information [6]. The information provided to support their decision to install an app needs to be jargon free and needs to transparently communicate importance. Lin and colleagues [7] suggested, "users have very little support in making good trust decisions regarding what apps to install" (p. 501). It appears they are often making app installation decisions simply based on perceived usefulness [5]. Further, less than 11 % of users in Mylonas and colleagues' study considered the provided reviews, reputation, or security associated with the app. The users who do express concern about security depend on app store community reviews and ratings beyond brand familiarity for establishing trustworthiness before installation. Unfortunately, fellow users, not security experts, generate this content. Despite this, users need a transparent and consistent way to be informed about the variety of possible risk associated with installing a particular app. According to Chia, Yamamoto, and Asokan [8], embedding the Web of Trust service into app store platforms has the potential to better inform users of risk during the app selection decision making process. Web of Trust provides crowd-sourced ratings of web sites as users browse [9]. It appears providing quality information is key to encouraging safe decisions.

In this study, we aimed to inform the presentation of security-relevant information in mobile app stores by comparing two sources of this information: ratings of apps provided by end users and ratings of apps provided by automated methods that evaluate mobile app security.

1.1 User-Generated Versus Automated Security Ratings

App security information can be based on user-generated reviews or automated methods. We focus on the distinction between security information generated using a crowd-sourced method and security information generated using an algorithm. In the former source of information, other users of the technology review and rate applications they use. In the latter source, a software agent examines the app and provides a conclusion about its riskiness in terms of security and privacy.

User-generated ratings provide a mechanism for other users to obtain data about other users' experience with an app. Because users share similar goals, the language they use to describe the costs and benefits of using an app may be easier for others to understand. Further, app store owners need only provide a mechanism for users to rate apps; they do not have to develop and maintain their own ratings and reviews. A limitation of this approach is that it requires a large pool of users to provide ratings with sufficient reliability to be of use. Accumulating a large number of user ratings takes time. In the interim, such as when a given app is new to the store, users must download apps without the benefit of ratings or on the basis of few ratings. The reliability of these ratings is, unfortunately, limited [8].

The benefit of technology-generated ratings, like other forms of automation, is that once an algorithm is developed, providers of an app store can rate apps instantly without delays associated with human input. Technology-generated ratings may work like a virus scanner by looking for suspicious patterns in the app [10] or by comparing the app to known malware. The algorithm may incorporate user feedback and permissions use to assign a trustworthiness metric, as proposed by Kuehnhausen and Frost [11]. In another automated method, software examines the functionality of an app and compares it to the functionally of other known apps [12]. A large difference between the functionality of the app and similar apps could be indicative of over-privilege or malware. Even with these benefits, automated methods share a weakness of user-generated ratings in that they are imperfect. They may miss threats that are present or incorrectly detect threats that are not present (i.e., a false alarm or false positive).

Because both user-generated and technology-generated ratings are used in app stores, and both methods provide imperfect information about the security of apps, an important question is whether users will follow the recommendations of one potentially inaccurate method or another when the warning presented by each is the same. At issue for developers and users is whether people differentially trust people or computers to provide security information.

1.2 Trust in App Selection

Trust in an app store provider has been shown to be a factor in user decisions to install apps [13], but within an app store, questions remain about how users trust security ratings to make decisions about which apps to install.

Trust is "the attitude that an agent will help achieve an individual's goals in a situation characterized by uncertainty and vulnerability" (p. 51) [14]. Trust is adaptive; it allows us to make decisions and accept risk under conditions of uncertainty [15] and it allows us to benefit from the effort and expertise of others [14]. Using the term *agent* broadly, several forms of trust are relevant in app store ratings.

The first of these, interpersonal trust, is trust amongst humans [16]. Interpersonal trust describes an expectancy of one human agent that the communications from another human agent are reliable. Although humans are the source of the information, user-generated security ratings are a form of technology-mediated communication. It is important to note differences between trust in a human providing a rating and trust in a medium used to communicate messages from a human. Patrick [15] suggested that both of these are important, and that trust is more difficult to establish when communication is mediated by technology, which he called a once-removed transaction. This is distinguished from non-removed transactions, which involve direct communication between two people. User-generated ratings within an app store are thus an example of a once-removed transaction where interpersonal trust may be a factor in the decision to install an app.

A second form of trust is one of human trust in technology, or trust in automation. It has been repeatedly shown that people base their trust in automation in large part based on perceptions of the performance of the technology [17, 18]. In general, the reliability of automated aids has a strong affect on people's ability to use it [19]. That is, people tend to trust and use technology more if they perceive it to be reliable [20]. Unfortunately, attributions of technology reliability are not always accurate, especially when users have a limited number of interactions with the technology. This can lead to mis-calibrated trust [21]. When trust is mis-calibrated, people may overtrust, leading to use of a technology beyond its capability, or they may distrust and disuse technology that could be helpful to them [14].

Interpersonal trust (including trust in once-removed transactions) and trust in automation share some similarities (see [14]), but because of important differences between humans and machines, interpersonal trust is affected by different factors than trust in automation [22]. For example, trust in people may be less constrained than trust in automation; a person might be unconditionally trusted across a wide variety of scenarios, but machines are only trusted to do certain tasks [22]. Lewandowsky, Mundy, and Tan [23] found that people felt more responsibility when they believed they were working with automation instead of another person in a simulated pasteurization plant. This suggests that trust is more important for delegation to automation than to a human.

In addition to the qualities of the task and environment, individual differences also affect trust. One such difference is a tendency to trust, a stable trait that also predicts a person's ability to properly calibrate trust [14]. The literature distinguishes between the tendency to trust in other people [16] and the tendency to trust machines [17]. These traits are distinguishable from trust in a particular person, technology, or setting, which may be fluid and change with experience [14].

Gender is another individual difference examined in this literature. Although there is a limited theoretical basis for gender effects in automation trust, gender is commonly collected demographic information that could influence the degree to which a rating method is useful. A study on technology acceptance found that women perceived e-mail as easier to use and more useful than men, but that these differences did not significantly affect e-mail use [25].

In all, the literature suggests that interpersonal trust and trust in automation are separate constructs. Further, we can distinguish between trust in a particular person or tool from a tendency to trust. However, research has not examined whether user-generated or automated methods are trusted more, or used more, at similar levels of uncertainty and risk. To examine this process, we presented users with a series of apps in a simulated app store. Our primary question was whether, when given equivalent alternatives, users would select apps with user-generated ratings or apps with automated ratings. A secondary question was which trust constructs and individual differences predict a decision to rely on user-generated or automated ratings.

2 Method

2.1 Participants

Forty undergraduate students aged 18–22 years (19 female and 21 male; aged 18–22 years; $M = 19$, $SD = 1.27$; two did not report age) participated in the experiment in exchange for course credit. No participants reported having color-deficient vision.

All participants reported owning at least one device (e.g., tablet, phone) that runs apps. Participants reported downloading an average of two apps per month ($M = 2.17$, $SD = 1.70$).

2.2 Materials and Procedure

Participants in this study completed several measures of trust and were presented with simulated situations in which they selected apps in the context of potential risk. First, participants completed a measure of trust in automation [24], a measure of interpersonal trust [16], and a series of demographic questions.

After completing these initial surveys, participants were presented with a simulated app store; this was done on a desktop computer. Participants were given the following instructions, "In this task, you are selecting apps to install on your mobile device. However, apps might have security risks. You will be shown a series of apps, four at a time. For each set of apps, select the safest one. You should always select one of the apps, and you cannot select more than one. To help you decide, security ratings are provided with each app."

Participants were asked to download one app in each trial. During the experiment, participants completed 24 discrete trials. On each trial they were presented with four apps and were to select one of the apps for download. All four apps in a trial belonged to the same category: social media, finance, news, or media player. After making their selection, the next trial was presented.

Of the 24 trials, half were critical trials and half were filler trials. Every trial contained two apps that had user-generated ratings and two apps with automated ratings. On critical trials, two apps, or all four of the apps, were tied for the lowest level of risk according to their ratings. Thus, to select the safest app, participants were forced select between a human and an automated rating.

App safety was indicated by a general security rating with redundant color-coding: "Safe" was displayed in a green font, "Caution" was displayed in orange font, and "Risky" was displayed in red font. Immediately following the security ratings was a verbal description of the threat (see Figs. 1 and 2). Four general types of security threats were used: presence of malware, ability to access and modify account information, perceived breech of privacy, and ability to access and modify phone states (e.g., location services). The apps within one trial had matching threat types (e.g., all might present a perceived privacy breech). An icon and label were used to indicate which ratings were from humans and which were automated. To further differentiate the ratings and preserve a naturalistic element in the study, "human" descriptions were gathered from publically available online comments about existing apps. Automated descriptions reflected generic classes of threats that could be detected using algorithms.

Several measures were taken to reduce the chance of strategic effects in participants and to control the influence of other factors. To reduce strategic effects, 12 filler trials were distributed throughout the 12 critical trials. Those trials contained four apps, as did the critical trials, but the user-generated and automated ratings did not have equivalent safety ratings. This helped disguise our use of a forced-choice paradigm. We were also concerned that specific app icons or names might be more appealing to users and

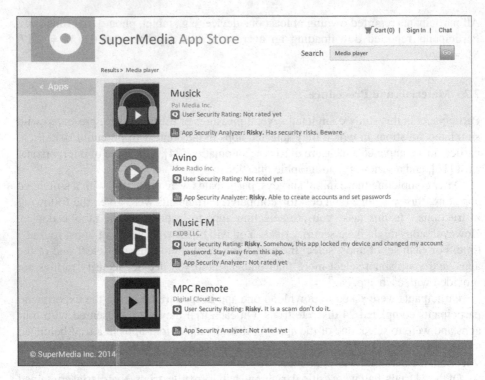

Fig. 1. Example of critical trial with equivalent threat levels (*risky*)

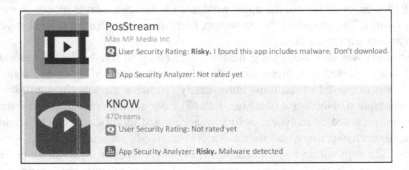

Fig. 2. Detail of one *risky* threat rated by the user-generated method (top) and one generated by the automated method (bottom).

confound the data. For example, if most of the preferred icons and names were associated with human-rated apps, it might appear that users trust those ratings more than automated ratings, when in fact, they merely preferred the icon. To control for this, each icon and name was paired an equal number of times with human and automated ratings. This was manipulated between-subjects; for each icon, half of the participants saw it paired with a user rating, and the remaining half of participants saw it paired with an automated rating. Similarly, stimulus presentation was blocked by app category; for instance, all six social media app trials all six social media app trials were presented one after another. This was done to make the task seem more naturalistic. To control for any order effects created by this blocking technique, we counterbalanced app category order across participants.

After completing the experimental portion of the study, participants completed the checklist for trust between people and automation [26], a self-report survey designed to capture trust in the automated ratings. Participants were instructed as follows: "There are several scales for you to rate intensity of your feeling of trust, or your impression of the computer-generated security ratings in the task you just completed."

3 Results

3.1 Preference for Apps with the Lowest Risk Rating

Our manipulation of app store rating affected user decisions to select apps as we expected. Participants selected the safest app of the four listed the overwhelming majority of the time ($M = .96$, $SD = .05$). This includes performance on all trials, including distractor trials that were discarded before analyses of rating preference, which we describe next.

3.2 Preference for User-Generated Versus Automated Security Ratings

To test our hypothesis that participants would be less willing to trust an automated rating than a human-generated one, we conducted a one-sample t-test to compare the proportion of trials in which participants selected the app with the automated rating to the proportion expected by chance (0.50). This analysis was conducted on critical trials only, those in which the lowest level of security warning was tied between user-generated and automated ratings. When given equivalent human and automated ratings, participants selected apps with automated ratings most of the time ($M = .61$, $SD = .18$), more often than would be expected by chance, $t(39) = 3.77$, $p = .001$.

3.3 Individual Differences and Trust

Although participants tended to trust apps rated by automation in comparison to those rated by humans, there may be individual differences in that trust. To explore relationships among trust constructs, we computed a series of Pearson product-moment correlation coefficients. These included the automation induced complacency scale, a dispositional measure of trust in automation [24]. Higher values on this scale indicate greater trust in automation, in general. The checklist for trust between humans and automation [26] measured self-reported trust in the automated ratings used in the study. Higher values on this measure indicate greater trust in a specific technology. Additionally, we included the measure of interpersonal trust [16], the proportion of critical trial automation-rated apps selected (as described previously), and Pearson point-biserial correlations with gender. The results of this analysis are presented in Table 1.

Table 1. Values of Pearson's r and r_{pb} among trust constructs and individual differences

	M	SD	1	2	3	4
1. Trust in automation	42.38	5.52	–			
2. Interpersonal trust	63.43	5.02	–.054	–		
3. Checklist for trust	52.90	14.82	.544***	.136	–	
4. Automated ratings	0.61	0.18	.082	.178	–.085	–
5. Gender (r_{pb})			–.488**	.090	–.353*	–.077

$N = 40$; $* p < .05$, $** p < .01$, $*** p < .001$

Trust measures revealed a significant positive relationship between dispositional trust in automation and trust in the automated ratings ($p < .001$). Gender was significantly related to trust; females were less trusting of automation than males ($p = .001$) and less trusting of the automated ratings in the study ($p = .026$).

4   Discussion

Previous research suggested users rely on app stores to protect them [5]. Because users remain the last line of defense in their own device security, users need access to information will facilitate better decision-making without requiring expertise in information security (cf. [27]). Trust describes a factor in a users' decision to rely on a source of information given some uncertainty. Our results suggest that users are more likely to trust automated ratings than human-generated ones when both ratings provide seemingly similar levels of risk. This was evident in both users' behavior (i.e., the apps they selected) and in users ratings of trust in the automated rating systems.

The gender differences observed in this study are noteworthy, as females reported less trust in the automated ratings and less trust in automation in general, but we did not observe a similar relationship with preference for automated ratings. Trust is not the only determinant in the decision to use one rating or another, and other factors not measured in this research (e.g., confidence; see [28]) may explain why gender differences in trust did not lead to significant differences in behavior.

Automated ratings are based on imperfect algorithms, and thus they may incorrectly detect threats that are not present or miss threats that are present. However, users may mistakenly believe that the technology-generated ratings are infallible. Thus, if an automated rating states that a particular security problem is present in an app, users may take this as a fact. Over-reliance on automation is a problem of too much trust in automation, a problem that has been demonstrated across domains [14]. At the same time, if a human-generated rating states that a particular security problem is present in an app, users may assume that the human rater could have been mistaken in their assessment of the source of the problem and that the problem might not have been due to the app itself. For instance, if a human rating states that the app changed their account passwords, the user might question whether the account passwords might have been changed by some other process rather than the app and incorrectly attributed to the app. Also, users might think that the problem described in the rating might have occurred only for that one human rater, and not for other people who have used the app. As people may be more likely to leave comments on crowd-sourced review websites when they have had a negative experience than when their experience was uneventful [29], readers might suspect that the negative occurrence is uncommon.

In this study, each app was displayed with either one user-generated rating or one automated rating. The presence of only one human rating is most representative of a new app for which there has not yet been sufficient time on the market to accumulate numerous ratings. The present results suggest that in the absence of multiple human ratings, users will prefer to base their app security decisions on a technology-generated rating. When only a small number of human ratings are available, users are not able to know how common a problem is or even whether to believe that the problem described in the review is a true problem. However, this lack of trust in human ratings might change if the number of human ratings were to increase, as would be representative of an app that had been on the market for a longer time. Users may scale their trust in user-generated ratings depending on the size of the crowd that contributed to it. Future research should investigate whether users become more likely to base their decisions on human ratings, and have increased trust in human ratings, as the number of human ratings, displayed increases.

Acknowledgments. The authors gratefully acknowledge the work of Dorian Berthoud, Jarad Bell, Ashley Cain, Cherrylyn Cawit, Michelle Gomez, Jeremy Koss, Kaitlyn Kuhach, Peter McEvoy, Ashley Palma, Felicia Santiago, and Khoa Tran who assisted with stimuli development, data collection, and data coding.

References

1. Statista: Number of apps available in leading app stores as of July 2014 (2014). http://www.statista.com/statistics/276623/number-of-apps-available-in-leading-app-stores/
2. Cramer, H., Rost, M. Bentley, F., Shamma, D.A.: 2nd workshop on research in the large. using app stores, wide distribution channels and big data in UbiComp research. In: UbiComp, pp. 619–620. ACM, New York (2012)
3. Felt, A.P., Chin, E., Hanna, S., Song, D., Wagner, D.: Android permissions demystified. In: 18th ACM Conference on Computer and Communications Security, pp. 627–638. ACM, New York (2011)
4. Zhou, Y., Wang, Z., Zhou W., Jiang, X.: Hey, you, get off of my market: detecting malicious apps in official and alternative Android markets. In: Proceedings of the 19th Network and Distributed System Security Symposium (2012)
5. Mylonas, A., Kastania, A , Gritzalis, D.: Delegate the smartphone user? security awareness in smartphone platforms. Comput. Secur. **34**, 47–66 (2013)
6. Felt, A.P., Ha, E., Egelman, S., Haney, A., Chin, E., Wagner, D.: Android permissions: user attention, comprehension, and behavior. In: Symposium on Usable Privacy and Security, pp. 3–16. ACM, New York (2012)

424   D. Schuster et al.

7. Lin, J., Amini, S., Hong, J.I., Sadeh, N., Lindqvist, J., Zhang, J.: Expectation and purpose: understanding users' mental models of mobile app privacy through crowdsourcing. In: Proceedings of the 2012 ACM Conference on Ubiquitous Computing, pp. 501–510. ACM, New York (2012)
8. Chia, P.H., Yamamoto, Y., Asokan, N.: Is this app safe? a large scale study on application permissions and risk signals. In: Proceedings of the 21st International Conference on World Wide Web, pp. 311–320 (2012)
9. Web of Trust. https://www.mywot.com/en/aboutus
10. Gilbert, P., Chun, B.-G., Cox, L.P., Jung, J.: Vision: automated security validation of mobile apps at app markets. In: 10th International Workshop on Multiple Classifier Systems, pp. 21–26. ACM, New York (2011)
11. Kuehnhausen, M., Frost, V.S.: Trusting smartphone apps? to install or not to install, that is the question. In: IEEE International Multi-Disciplinary Conference on Cognitive Methods in Situation Awareness and Decision Support, pp. 30-37. IEEE (2013) doi:10.1109/CogSIMA.2013.6523820
12. Sarma, B., Li, N., Gates, C., Potharaju, R., Nita-Rotaru, C., Molloy, I.: Android permissions: a perspective combining risks and benefits. In: Symposium on Access control Models and Technologies, pp. 13–22. ACM, New York (2012)
13. Eling, N., Krasnova, H., Widjaja, T., Buxmann, P.: Will you accept an app? empirical investigation of the decisional calculus behind the adoption of applications on Facebook. In: The 34th International Conference on Information Systems. Association for Information Systems (2013)
14. Lee, J.D., See, K.A.: Trust in automation: designing for appropriate reliance. In: Human Factors, vol. 46, pp. 50–80. HFES, Santa Monica (2004)
15. Patrick, A.: Privacy, trust, agents & users: a review of human-factors issues associated with building trustworthy software agents. Technical report, National Research Council Canada (2002)
16. Rotter, J.B.: A new scale for the measurement of interpersonal trust. J. Pers. **35**, 651–665 (1967)
17. Hancock, P.A., Billings, D.R., Schaefer, K.E., Chen, J.Y., De Visser, E.J., Parasuraman, R.: A meta-analysis of factors affecting trust in human-robot interaction. Hum. Factors: J. Hum. Factors Ergon. Soc. **53**, 517–527 (2011)
18. Muir, B.M., Moray, A.N.: Experimental studies of trust and human intervention in a process control simulation. Ergonomics **39**, 429–460 (1996)
19. Johnson, R.C., Saboe, K.N., Prewett, M.S., Coovert, M.D., Elliott, L.R.: Autonomy and automation reliability in human-robot interaction: a qualitative review. In: Proceedings of the Human Factors and Ergonomics Society Annual Meeting, vol. 53, pp. 1398–1402. Human Factors and Ergonomics Society, Santa Monica, CA (2009)
20. Madhavan, P., Wiegmann, D.A.: Similarities and differences between human–human and human–automation trust: an integrative review. Theor. Issues Ergon. Sci. **8**, 277–301 (2007)
21. Dzindolet, M.T., Peterson, S.A., Pomranky, R.A., Pierce, L.G., Beck, H.P.: The role of trust in automation reliance. Int. J. Hum Comput Stud. **58**, 697–718 (2003)
22. Hoffman, R.R., Bradshaw, J. M., Ford, K.M., Underbrink, A.: Trust in automation. In: IEEE Intelligent Systems (2013)
23. Lewandowsky, S., Mundy, M., Tan, G.: The dynamics of trust: comparing humans to automation. J. Exp. Psychol. Appl. **6**, 104 (2000)
24. Singh, I.L., Molloy, R., Parasuraman, R.: Development and validation of a scale of automation-induced "Complacency". In: Proceedings of the Human Factors and Ergonomics Society Annual Meeting, vol. 36, pp. 22–25. SAGE Publications (1992)

25. Gefen, D., Straub, D.: Gender difference in the perception and use of e-mail: an extension to the technology acceptance model. MIS Q. **21**, 389–400 (1997)
26. Jian, J.-Y., Bisantz, A.M., Drury, C.G.: Foundations for an empirically determined scale of trust in automated systems. J. Cogn. Ergon. **4**, 53–71 (2000)
27. Tam, J., Reeder, R.W., Schechter, S.: I'm allowing what? disclosing the authority applications demand of users as a condition of installation. Technical Report, Microsoft Research (2010). http://research.microsoft.com/apps/pubs/default.aspx?id=131517
28. Parasuraman, R., Riley, V.: Humans and automation: use, misuse, disuse, abuse. Hum. Factors **39**, 230–253 (1997)
29. Hu, N., Pavlou, P.A., Zhang, J.: Can online reviews reveal a product's true quality?: empirical findings and analytical modeling of online word-of-mouth communication. In: Proceedings of the 7th ACM Conference On Electronic Commerce, pp. 324–330. ACM, New York (2006)

SafetyPIN: Secure PIN Entry Through Eye Tracking

Mythreya Seetharama[1], Volker Paelke[2], and Carsten Röcker[3](✉)

[1] Ostwesfalen-Lippe University of Applied Sciences, Lemgo, Germany
[2] Bremen University of Applied Sciences, Bremen, Germany
[3] Ostwestfalen-Lippe University of Applied Sciences
and Fraunhofer IOSB-INA, Lemgo, Germany
carsten.rocker@iosb-ina.fraunhofer.de

Abstract. When a user enters a personal identification number (PIN) into an automated teller machine or a point of sale terminal, there is a risk of some one watching from behind, trying to guess the PIN code. Such shoulder-surfing is a major security threat. In order to overcome this problem different PIN entry methods have been suggested. In this regard, gaze interaction methods are receiving attention in recent years, owing to the lowering cost of eye tracking technology. In this paper, we present SafetyPIN - an eye tracking based PIN entry system - which is aimed at making the PIN entry more secure with the help of an eye tracking device. We discuss the implementation and the initial evaluation of this system.

Keywords: PIN entry · Eye tracking · Security · Usability · Point of sale terminals

1 Introduction

The use of PINs (personal identification numbers) as passwords for authentication is ubiquitous nowadays. This is especially true for banking applications where the combination of a token (e.g. bank card) and the user's secret PIN is commonly used to authenticate transactions. In financial applications PINs are typically four-digit numbers, resulting in 10000 possible numbers. The security of the system relies on the fact that an attacker is unlikely to guess the correct PIN number and that the systems (e.g., Automated Teller Machines) limit the user to few attempts (e.g., 3) for entering the correct PIN. As most applications that use PINs for authentication operate in a public setting a common attack is to try to observe and record a user's PIN entry (shoulder-surfing). These security problems have been recognized for a long time and researchers have proposed a number of different schemes to minimize the risk of PIN entry observation. One such proposed alternate PIN entry method requires the user to input some information, which is derived from a combination of the actual PIN and some additional information displayed by the system, instead of the

© Springer International Publishing Switzerland 2015
T. Tryfonas and I. Askoxylakis (Eds.): HAS 2015, LNCS 9190, pp. 426–435, 2015.
DOI: 10.1007/978-3-319-20376-8_38

PIN itself [1]. Another approach proposes the use of an elaborate hardware to make PIN entry resilient to the observation attacks [2]. However, these methods have not been introduced into practical applications because the users would have to be retrained to use a completely different approach to PIN entry and the significant additional costs involved in the hardware setup.

In the SafetyPIN project our goal is to prevent observation attacks during PIN entry while retaining the same workflow that user's are already familiar with and with minimal additional hardware cost. Our setup can be easily integrated into existing designs of automatic teller machines (ATMs) and point of sale systems. To avoid shoulder-surfing attacks and enable users to enter their PIN without fear of being observed we have developed a system that employs an eye tracking device. With SafetyPIN, users select PIN numbers with their eyes by simply focusing on digits displayed on a screen. Since 0the physical key-press is not used for the PIN entry, no information about the entered digit is given away to the attacker through visual observation. Use of fake keypads are also rendered unnecessary.

The rest of the paper is structured as follows. In Sect. 2, some previous efforts related to preventing shoulder-surfing and use of eye interaction are mentioned. In Sect. 3, conceptual approach behind SafetyPIN is explained. Section 4 details the implementation. In Sect. 5, the initial evaluation and the results are discussed. Section 6 concludes the paper.

2   Related Work

Researchers have been evaluating the user gaze as an interaction method using eye tracking devices. In 1987, Ware et al. [3] evaluated two methods of interacting with the computers using eyes as input: dwell gaze, look and shoot. The dwell gaze method relied on the user looking at the region of interest on the screen for a certain amount of time. In the look and shoot method the user looked at the region of interest and then physically clicked a predefined button on the keypad to activate the region. The dwell gaze method needs more time for activation compared to the look and shoot method, as it needs the dwell time to ensure that spurious activations are avoided. On the other hand, the look and shoot method, though quicker, gives away more information for the potential shoulder-surfer via the button click feedback. Both these methods require calibration to be performed for the individual user.

Kumar et al. [4] evaluated the above two methods for ATM password entry to avoid shoulder-surfing. They used the Tobii 1750 eye tracker and a qwerty alpha numeric keypad for this purpose. The evaluation suggested that these methods are capable of deterring shoulder-surfers while taking comparable time for entering password as compared to conventional keypad. They also suggested that the calibration data for the user can be stored in the ATM card itself so that it need not be performed every time.

De Luca et al. [5], in addition to the methods above, introduced a gaze-gesture method of password entry and compared it with the other two methods. In the gaze-gesture method the user is required to remember a graphical pattern and then input that pattern via gesturing through his/her eyes [6,7]. The advantage of this method is that it requires no calibration as it depends on the relative position of the eye, not the absolute position. However, it suffers on the usability front as the users need many retries to get the pattern right.

Other such efforts can be seen in [8,9]. In SafetyPIN, we have implemented a new activation method called Blinking, along with the other two methods. In this method, unlike the look and shoot, the user looks at the region he/she wants to activate and then instead of pressing a key, blinks his/her eyes to activate the region. This is more secure than the look and shoot, since the feedback given to the shoulder-surfer via the physical pressing of the button is completely avoided. This method is also less error prone compared to the gaze method since the spurious activations are less likely.

3   Conceptual Approach

Our initial prototype runs on a standard Windows PC and uses the Tobii EyeX low-cost eye tracker. The eye tracker consists of a small bar that can be attached to a display screen and could be incorporated into an ATM at a later stage. The sensor bar contains micro-projectors that project distinct patterns of infrared light at the user's eyes. The reflections of these patterns are then recorded by infrared cameras in the sensor bar. Through image processing the user's eyes are detected and the eye movements tracked, which is then used to determine the user's gaze

Fig. 1. 9-digit visual key-pad displayed on the screen, Tobii EyeX eye tracker mounted below the screen

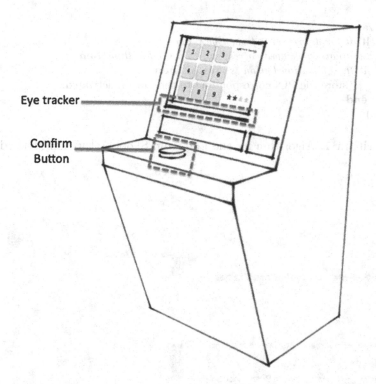

Eye tracker

Confirm
Button

Fig. 2. SafetyPIN hardware components for retrofitting into existing point of sale terminals

point: the point on the screen that the user's view currently focuses on. For the PIN input we display the possible digits on the screen (see Figs. 1 and 2).

From the practical perspective a key advantage of the SafetyPIN approach is that only minimal additional hardware is required which fits easily into existing terminals. Because the sensor bar is small and placed directly below the screen it could be integrated into the screen housing of existing terminals, simplifying the development of new versions with integrated SafetyPIN entry and proving the opportunity to retrofit existing terminals.

4   Implementation

The prototype is aimed at mocking up a typical ATM PIN entry screen and allowing the user to enter the PIN using three different interaction methods: look and shoot, gaze activation and blink activation. The GUI is a 1680 × 720 pixel window with buttons labeled 0–9 along with ',' and '.'. The GUI buttons are 160 × 100 pixels in dimension with a spacing of 50 pixels between them. The user is supposed to enter a predefined sequence of numbers as his PIN. The software then checks for the accuracy and speed of the entered PIN for each of the three entry methods mentioned above. This software has been developed in VC++.

initialization;
while *Wait for data/events from EyeX* **do**
    if *coordinates receieved correspond to a GUI button* **then**
        if *the activation button is pressed* **then**
            store the PIN corresponding to the button activated;
        end
    end
end

Algorithm 1. Algorithm for the Look and Shoot Activation Method

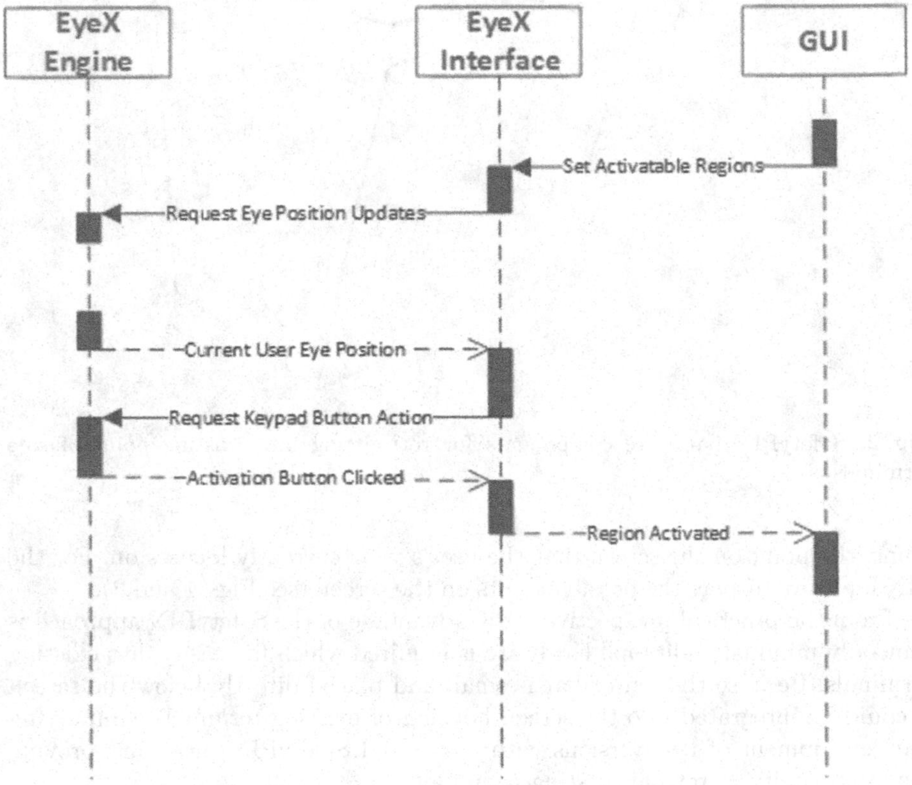

Fig. 3. Sequence diagram for the look and shoot activation method

The Tobii SDK [10] provides drivers for the eye tracking device along with C/C++ library engine which gives API for interfacing with the device. These APIs provide functionalities higher than the raw eye position data from the device. The engine provides two kinds of high level operations. On the one hand the application program can inform the engine about the boundaries of the regions that it wants to get activated on. The engine will then intimate the application program about when the user looks at one the regions specified.

initialization;
while *Wait for data/events from EyeX* **do**

> **if** *coordinates receieved correspond to a GUI button* **then**
>
> > **if** *gaze event notification is received for the current GUI button* **then**
> >
> > > store the PIN corresponding to the button activated;
> >
> > **end**
>
> **end**

end

Algorithm 2. Algorithm for the Gaze Activation Method

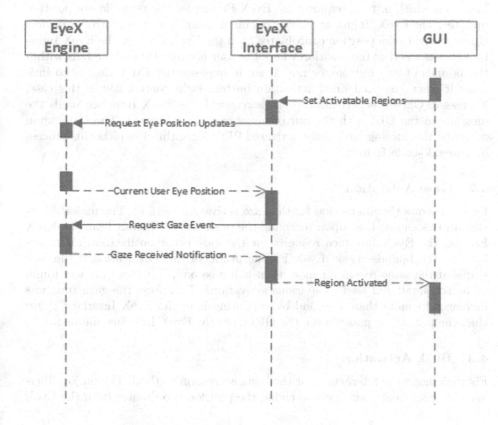

Fig. 4. Sequence diagram for the gaze activation

This scheme relieves the application program from having to poll the incoming raw position data from the device. On the other hand, the application program can register for one of the many events for which it would like to get notifications on. For example, when the user looks at a region for more than half a second a gaze event can be notified and when the device does not see the user's eyes for more than a second an absence event can be notified to the application program depending on whether the application program has registered for the event or not. These notifications are used in our GUI application program.

The three different methods of activation are described below with the help of pseudo-code and sequence diagrams.

4.1 Look and Shoot

The sequence diagram in Fig. 3 shows the three major modules of the software and gives an overview of their interactions. The GUI interacts with the EyeX Engine using an EyeX Interface module. The GUI initializes the windows and button components and sends the coordinates of the buttons to the EyeX Interface, which in turn requests the EyeX Engine for the periodic eye position updates. The EyeX Engine is directly communicating with the controller device. Upon receiving the position coordinates from the EyeX Engine, the EyeX Interface checks whether the position where the user is currently looking falls within the bounds of any buttons or not. If so, it requests the EyeX Engine to intimate it when the predefined activation button, right control key in this case, is pressed. Once this activation event is received, the EyeX Interface sends the message to the GUI with the button number to be activated. The GUI, upon receiving this message stores the activated PIN. Algorithm 1 depicts this process in a pseudo-code fashion.

4.2 Gaze Activation

Figure 4 shows the interaction for the gaze activation method. The major difference in this case is that upon receiving the position coordinates from the EyeX Engine, the EyeX Interface requests for the gaze event notification after performing the bounds check. EyeX Engine produces this notification if the user stares at the same region for more than half a second. But this time was found to be too small and lead to spurious activations. Therefore, the gaze time was increased to more than a second by validating it in the EyeX Interface. After this, the message is passed onto the GUI from the EyeX Interface module.

4.3 Blink Activation

Figure 5 shows the interaction for the blink activation method. The major difference in this case is that upon receiving the position coordinates from the EyeX

```
initialization;
while Wait for data/events from EyeX do
    if coordinates receieved correspond to a GUI button then
        temporarily remember this GUI button;
        if user absence event notification is received then
            if user presence event notification received then
                store the PIN corresponding to the button remembered;
            end
        end
    end
end
```

Algorithm 3. Algorithm for the Blink Activation

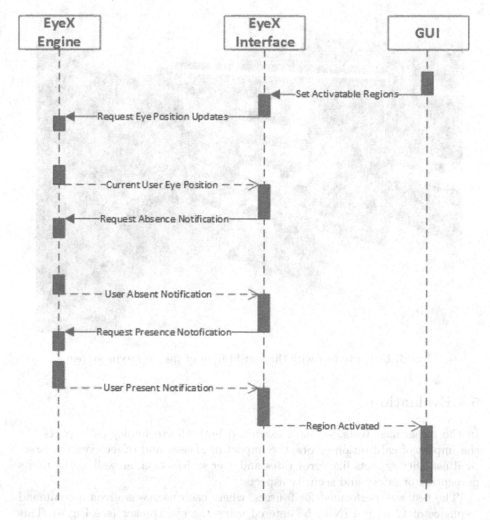

Fig. 5. Sequence diagram for the blink activation

Engine, the EyeX Interface requests for the 'user absence' notification after performing the bounds check and temporarily saving the button number. EyeX Engine produces this notification if the device fails to see the eyes of the user for more than a second. Therefore, if the user closes his eyes for a second, he effectively becomes absent for the device, producing the required notification. Upon receiving this notification, EyeX Interface requests for the 'user presence' notification, effectively waiting for the user to open his eyes again, thus performing a blink operation. Once the user opens his eyes the EyeX Engine sends the required notification and the EyeX Interface sends the component number of the saved button to the GUI.

Fig. 6. Usability test with the user in front of the prototype system

5   Evaluation

In the initial user tests, we have examined both the technological aspects like the impact of calibration errors, the impact of glasses and other eyeware, practical usability aspects like error rates and user satisfaction, as well as the user's perception of safety and security aspects.

The test was performed for 9 users, where each user was given a command sequence of 12 digit PIN to be entered using the eye tracker (see Fig. 6). This test was performed for all three activation methods, four times per activation method. The PIN entered by the user was stored and then compared with the command PIN to find out how many errors occurred. Time taken by the users for the test was also recorded. After the tests were completed, the users were given a questionnaire to collect the feedback from the users regarding how usable and useful did they feel the system was. Their feedback on the safety was also recorded.

Results of these tests have been very encouraging in all the three activation methods. The average error rate was around 5 % and the average time taken was around 1.6 s per a digit entry or around 6.7 s for a typical 4 digit PIN entry. Most of the errors were committed by the users when they did not remember the correct PIN and therefore entered the wrong PIN, rather than activating an unintentional PIN. Users felt that the system was easy to use and that this was a safer way to enter their pin compared to the traditional pin entry method. To draw statistically significant conclusions, we need to perform further tests with larger sample set.

6   Conclusions

In order to protect the users from shoulder-surfing in ATMs while entering the PIN, new methods of entering the PIN are being evaluated. With the eye tracking technology becoming cheaper, eye interaction for PIN entry is emerging as a practical solution. In this paper, we have discussed SafetyPIN, which proposes retrofitting the ATMs with an eye tracking device, so that users can enter their PIN without using the keypad for pin entry. In our prototype, we have implemented and evaluated the system for a PC. In addition to the 'look and shoot' and gaze activation methods, we have introduced a new activation method called blink activation. Initial user evaluations have yielded encouraging results, prompting further work.

References

1. Roth, V., Richter, K., Freidinger, R.: A PIN-entry method resilient against shoulder surfing. In: Proceedings of the ACM conference on Computer and communications security (CCS 2004), New York pp. 236–245 (2004)
2. Sasamoto, H., Christin, N., Hayashi, E.: Undercover: authentication usable in front of prying eyes. In: Proceedings of the SIGCHI Conference on Human Factors in Computing Systems (CHI 2008), Florence, pp. 183–192 (2008)
3. Ware, C., Mikaelian, H.: An evaluation of an eye tracker as a device for computer input. In: Proceedings of CHI 1987, Toronto (1987)
4. Kumar, M., Garfinkel, T., Boneh, D., Winograd, T.: Reducing shoulder-surfing by using gaze-based password entry. In: Proceedings of the 3rd Symposium on Usable Privacy and Security, pp. 13–19. ACM (2007)
5. De Luca, A., Weiss, R., Drewes, H.: Evaluation of eye-gaze interaction methods for security enhanced PIN-entry. In: Proceedings of the 19th Australasian Conference on Computer-human Interaction: Entertaining User Interfaces, pp. 199–202. ACM (2007)
6. Drewes, H., Schmidt, A.: Interacting with the computer using gaze gestures. In: Baranauskas, C., Abascal, J., Barbosa, S.D.J. (eds.) INTERACT 2007. LNCS, vol. 4663, pp. 475–488. Springer, Heidelberg (2007)
7. Drewes, H., De Luca, A., Schmidt, A.: Eye-gaze interaction for mobile phones. In: Proceedings of the 4th International Conference on Mobile Technology, Applications, and Systems and the 1st International Symposium on Computer Human Interaction in Mobile Technology, pp. 364–371. ACM (2007)
8. Forget, A., Chiasson, S., Biddle, R.: Shoulder-surfing resistance with eye-gaze entry in cued-recall graphical passwords. In: Proceedings of the SIGCHI Conference on Human Factors in Computing Systems, pp. 1107–1110. ACM (2010)
9. Dunphy, P., Fitch, A., Olivier, P.: Gaze-contingent passwords at the ATM. In: 4th Conference on Communication by Gaze Interaction (COGAIN), pp. 59–62 (2008)
10. Tobii EyeX SDK for C/C++, Developer's Guide. Tobii Technology (2014)

An Identification of Variables Influencing the Establishment of Information Security Culture

Emad Sherif[1(✉)], Steven Furnell[1,2,3], and Nathan Clarke[1,3]

[1] Computer Centre for Security, Communications and Network Research,
University of Plymouth, Plymouth, UK
{Emad.Sherif,S.Furnell,N.Clarke}@plymouth.ac.uk
[2] Centre for Research in Information and Cyber Security,
Nelson Mandela Metropolitan University, Port Elizabeth, South Africa
[3] Security Research Institute, Edith Cowan University, Perth, Australia

Abstract. A significant volume of security breaches occur as a result of the human aspects and it is consequently important for these to be given attention alongside technical aspects. Many breaches occur due to human error. Researchers have argued that security culture stimulates appropriate employees' security behavior towards adherence and therefore developing a culture of security can contribute in minimizing or avoiding security breaches. Although, research on the concept of security culture has received little attention this paper aims to address the security culture concept, and it's relation to the national culture. Specifically, it is largely hypothesized that cultivating security culture can have a positive effect on employees' security compliance. The purpose of this paper is to identify variables that influence cultivating a security culture. In order to do so, a comprehensive literature review has been conducted. The outcome of the literature analysis has identified potential variables that influence security culture (e.g. top management support, information security behavior, and awareness), and the paper subsequently outlines a framework for modeling security culture that indicates the relationship between these variables.

Keywords: Security culture · National culture · Organizational culture · Security policies · Security compliance · Security behavior

1 Introduction

Recent research shows that as many as 35 % of global of data breaches happen due to a negligent employee 'human factor' (Ponemon Institute, 2013). Unfortunately, the "user error" has been neglected by small, medium and large organizations (Connolly and Lang, 2013). According to Connolly and Lang (2013), many organizations are investing significant money and time into implementing technical security controls in order to protect their assets, whilst ignoring the human element of the problem, which is often the main cause of data breaches. We therefore, argue that establishing an information security culture can assist organizations to eliminate or minimize such breaches. Similarly, Van Niekerk and Von Solms (2010) argued that establishment of

© Springer International Publishing Switzerland 2015
T. Tryfonas and I. Askoxylakis (Eds.): HAS 2015, LNCS 9190, pp. 436–448, 2015.
DOI: 10.1007/978-3-319-20376-8_39

an organizational sub-culture of information security is key to managing the human factor involved in information security. Although, many researchers have been addressing the concept of 'security culture', there are not any clear views on how to create this organizational culture to support security (Ruighaver, et al. 2007). Therefore, Johnson and Goetz (2007) suggested that security executives should address secure culture when they are considering building security into their organizations. According to Da Veiga and Eloff (2010), "some research shows that a security-aware culture will minimize risks to information assets".

In the literature, security culture has been referred to as a mean to control the 'human factor' to enhance security. Therefore, the intended focus of this paper is to analyze twenty-five related studies in order to identify factors and variables that influence security culture. This discussion covers the concepts of organizational, national, and security cultures, and explores the relationship between them along with exploring the relationship between information security compliance and information security culture. This paper also presents the research model design, which leads to combining three models into a conceptual framework.

2   Literature Review and Theoretical Background

Preliminary literature search has been carried out in order to find out and define the research gaps in the area of information security. Suitable publications including peer reviewed journals and conferences were identified, and the main themes emerging from them are outlined in the sub-sections that follow.

2.1   Culture as a Concept

Most social scientists view culture as consisting primarily of the symbolic, ideational, and intangible aspects of human societies (Connolly and Lang, 2013). In terms of a definition of culture, Damen (1987) suggests it to be "learned and shared human patterns or models for living; day-to-day living patterns". These patterns and models pervade all aspects of human social interaction. Culture is mankind's primary adaptive mechanism. The Intercultural Studies Project at the Center for Advanced Research on Language Acquisition at the University of Minnesota has defined culture as "the shared patterns of behaviors and interactions, cognitive constructs, and affective understanding that are learned through a process of socialization. These shared patterns identify the members of a culture group while also distinguishing those of another group" (CARLA, 2014). A simpler definition is "the unwritten rules of the social game" (Hofstede, 1984). In addition, according to Thomson and Von Solms (2004), "A better way to think of culture is to realize that it exists at several 'levels' and those we must understand and manage the deeper levels". And thus, to summaries; culture exists at several levels, and it is about how people perceive, think, feel about their day to day living patterns of behavior. Culture is not inherited, it can be learnt.

2.2 Organizational Culture

Research by Hofstede (1984) has found that organizational cultures distinguish different organizations within the same country or countries. Hofstede's research has shown that organizational cultures differ mainly at the level of practices (symbols, heroes and rituals). Thomson and Von Solms (2004) argued that there is a relationship that exists between the fields of corporate governance, information security and organizational culture. And thus, to summaries; the concept of organizational culture is similar to the concept of culture however it differs at the level of practices (symbols, heroes and rituals). It also refers to shared patterns in employees' behavior in firms, and to the existing relationship between organizational culture and information security. According to Schein (1999), "due to the nature of beliefs and values they cannot be measured accurately, which is why a company culture is often referred to as just the way we do things around here". Furthermore, according to Fagerstrom (2013), a widely accepted way of thinking about company culture is to look at the different levels at which it exists. These levels are; Artifacts: "Artifacts are what can be seen, heard and felt, in an organization", Espoused Values: "How the espoused values are interpreted and implemented depends heavily on the shared tacit assumptions of the employees", Shared Tacit Assumptions: "These are the beliefs, assumptions and values shared and taken for granted by the organization's employees and form the essence of that organization's culture", and Knowledge: "Employees need to have the required knowledge to perform their everyday tasks securely".

2.3 National Culture

Research by Hofstede (1984) and others has shown that national cultures differ in particular at the level of, usually unconscious, values held by a majority of the population. The Hofstede dimensions of national cultures are rooted in our unconscious values, because values are acquired in childhood, national cultures are remarkably stable over time (Hofstede, 1984). Furthermore, according to O'Brien, et al. (2013), a recent study was conducted with regards to national culture that applied Hofstede's framework; Power Distance: "A measure of the equitable distribution of power", Long-term orientation: "Degree of traditions in a specific culture and to what extent these traditions are connected to their past and future", Masculinity/Femininity: "Degree to which social roles are separated on a gender basis", Individualism: "Measure of the balance between tasks over relationships", and Uncertainty Avoidance: "Measure of degree to which cultural members are threatened by uncertain risks". Although the study discusses the important cultural differences between developing and Western countries and how these relate to information security, an area for further research would be to take the step further and investigate how different cultures relate to security compliance (O'Brien, et al., 2013). And thus; the concept of national culture is similar to the concept of culture however it differs at deeper level of unconscious values that held by majority and it affects an organization's business strategies as well as practices in the global environment.

2.4   Information Security Culture

In general and according to Roer (2014), security culture can be defined as "the ideas, customs, and social behavior of a particular people or society, that helps them being free from danger or threat". According to Ross (2011), "no security policies, standards, guidelines or procedures can foresee all of the circumstances in which they are to be interpreted". Therefore, if stakeholders are not grounded in a culture of security, there is potential for improper actions (Ross, 2011). However, according to Malcolmson (2009), "a culture of security is not an end in itself, but a pathway to achieve and maintain other objectives, such as proper use of information". Some aspects of an organization's security culture have evolved as a logical response to security threats, and are espoused by the management of the organization. These manifest themselves in the security practices and policies of the organization, the level of compliance with and understanding of those practices and policies, and the acknowledgement and awareness of security threats to the organization (Malcolmson, 2009). And thus, to summaries; the concept of security culture is similar to the concept of culture with the focus on being free from danger or threat in terms of human and improper actions, however, security culture have evolved as a logical response to security threats, and are espoused by the management of the organization.

3   Research Model Design

This paper is seen as a part of a wider research activity that aims to address security culture. Based on the results of the literature review, we therefore postulated:

- H1: Identifying factors that influence security compliance positively influences the establishment of an information security culture.
- H2: Organizational and national cultures influence the establishment of an information security culture.

3.1   Instrumentation

We used a hypothetical scenario in which items have been adopted from various peer-reviewed sources during the literature review. A main step in developing the models in our study was to make sure that these models were realistic based on the findings of the sources listed in Table 1.

Although, we listed some sources' findings without samples, here are the highlights of the other adopted samples/instruments:

Surveys. Different types of surveys that of relevance have been examined as outlined below. Some of these surveys were conducted by large security companies such as; Symantec, others were conducted by government agencies, whereas, some surveys were conducted by scholars themselves.

- According to Furnell and Clarke (2005), "the DTI Information Security Breaches Survey 2004, which found that 89 % of the teams responsible for security lacked

Table 1. Summary of current proposed variables

Variables	Source
Security compliance; *Security behavior*	Vroom and von Solms (2004)
	Herath and Rao (2009)
	Alfawaz et al. (2010)
	Greene and D'Arcy (2010)
	Gabriel and Furnell (2011)
	Padayachee (2012)
Organisational culture; *Top management support*	Ngo et al. (2005)
	Johnson and Goetz (2007)
	Ruighaver et al. (2007)
	Dojkovski et al. (2007)
Organisational culture; *Top management support & Security policy & Security acceptance & Security awareness*	Thomson and von Solms (2005)
Organizational culture; *Security acceptance*	Furnell and Thomson (2009)
Organizational culture; *Security behavior*	VanNiekerk and VonSolms (2010)
	Da Veiga and Eloff (2010)
Top management support & Security policy & Security awareness	Chipperfield and Furnell (2010)
Top management support & Security behavior	Ashenden (2008)
	Moyano et al. (2011)
Organizational & National cultures; *Security policy & Security acceptance & Security behavior*	Furnell and Rajendran (2012)
Security compliance; *Security acceptance & Security behavior*	Alfawaz et al. (2010)
Security behavior & Security policy & Security awareness	Cheng et al. (2013)
Organizational & National cultures; *Security behavior*	Connolly and Lang (2013)
Top management support & Security awareness	Furnell and Clarke (2005)
	Fagerström (2013)
Organizational culture; *Security policy & Security awareness*	O'Brien et al. (2013)
National culture; *Security behavior*	Flores et al. (2014)

security qualification". Furnell and Clarke (2005) have concluded that an important element in establishing a culture of security is the security awareness and training that is run by teams that should have the appropriate background and skills.

- According to Chipperfield and Furnell (2010), "findings from the survey conducted by European Network and Information Security Agency suggest that only 42 % of organizations compare the level of information security awareness pre and post-programme". Chipperfield and Furnell (2010) have concluded that the security awareness program needs to be shaped to fit individual's roles, their level of interest.

- According to Furnell and Rajendran (2012), "UK's biennial Information Security Breaches Survey series show a significant rise in the proportion of organizations claiming to at least have information security policies". Furnell and Rajendran (2012) have concluded that despite having security policies in place, there are various influence factors within and outside of an organization can have an impact upon an employee, such as; factors that influence compliance behavior.

- According to Padayachee (2012), "the global security survey found that 79 % of participants cite the human factor as the root cause for failure". Padayachee (2012) suggested that identifying and studying the factors that influence compliance behavior contributes in preventing security policy violation intentions.

- According to Connolly and Lang (2013), "recent survey shows that 39 % of security breaches happen due to user error". Connolly and Lang (2013) suggested that understanding of the various variables that influence individual security behavior can have a positive impact towards the cultivation of a security culture.

- According to Flores, et al. (2014), "Global State of Information Security Survey conducted by PWC Advisory Services & Security in 2013 found that 54 % of North American firms conduct background checks of individuals before employing them and have implemented employee security awareness training programs, while 42 % of European firms have implemented the same information security measures". Flores, et al. (2014) has concluded that the effect of behavioral security as a variable on the establishment of security culture differs between Swedish and US organization. Therefore, we argue that national culture influences the establishment of an information security culture.

Questionnaires. Four related sources have been cited as follows:

- According to Furnell and Thomson (2009), from 1007 UK businesses questioned by (Business Enterprise and Regulatory Reform), "it was revealed that 62 % believed the cause of their worst security incident had been internal rather than external". Furnell and Thomson (2009) have found that management can begin cultivating a culture of security firstly by recognizing the current levels of security acceptance.

- According to Herath and Rao (2009), "data was collected using 312 responses from 77 different organizations in Western New York". Herath and Rao (2009) have found that security behaviors can be influenced by both intrinsic and extrinsic motivators, such as; perceived contribution by individual actions and information security policy compliance intentions.

- According to Gabriel and Furnell (2011), "a group of 20 employees & managers working within the technology sector was recruited to participate in a series of security assessments & personality tests". Gabriel and Furnell (2011) suggested that personality test results may possess a predictive value for security behavior.

- Cheng, et al. (2013) presented data that was collected by using a sample of 185 usable questionnaires that were distributed to employees in 10 organizations in Dalian, China; they have found that job satisfaction and security acceptance can positively prevent employees' information security policy violation intentions. And thus, this positively influences employees' security compliance intentions. Therefore, we argue that job satisfaction and acceptance may positively influence employees' behavior toward compliance with an organization's security policies.

3.2   Scenario Design

Additionally, twenty five studies were analyzed in Table 1. However, Table 2 summarizes the candidate variables for modeling information security culture. In the following section we lay the overall framework for modeling information security culture (see Fig. 1) and hypothesize the relationship between cultures and security compliance. Based on the literature review analysis we identified five top candidate variables as follow:

Table 2. Summary of the candidate variables

Variable	No. of times cited/25	Variable ranking
Information security behavior	15	1
Top management support	10	2
Security education & awareness	6	3
Information security policy	5	4
Information security acceptance	4	5

Management. According to Thomson and Von Solms (2004), the corporate information security policy should describe the vision and goals of senior management in relation to information security. Also, Furnell and Clarke (2005) concluded that management of the organization needs to appreciate where their problems lie, and what each awareness or education option could do to help.

Information Security Policy. According to Thomson and Von Solms (2004), the corporate information security policy should describe the vision and goals of senior management in relation to information security. However and with regards to information security policy violations, Cheng, et al. (2013) concluded that the empirical results of their study suggest the importance of deterrence and social pressure factors in preventing security policy violation.

Information Security Awareness. Furnell and Clarke (2005) suggested that management of the organization needs to appreciate where their problems lie, and what each awareness or education option could do to help. Also, Chipperfield and Furnell (2010) concluded that many organizations do not naturally think to check whether awareness is getting through. However and according to Furnell and Clarke (2012), human aspects can have a significant role in ensuring the overall security of systems and data, and effort is needed to help them become part of the solution.

User Acceptance. Furnell and Thomson (2009) argued that cultivating security culture starts by recognizing the current levels of security acceptance. However, Furnell (2010) suggested that getting individual users to a point where they can accept and act upon their security responsibilities can influence the cultivation of a culture of security. However, "the fact that achieving security acceptance is a multi-stage process can of course represent a challenge in its own right" (Furnell, 2010).

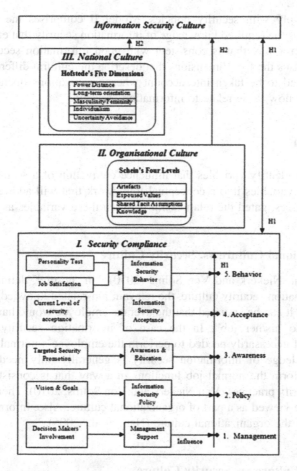

Fig. 1. A conceptual framework for modeling information security culture

Security Behavior. Alfawaz et al. (2010) developed a framework of information security practices that could contribute to information security management by identifying behaviors related to different modes of information security practice. However, Moyano, et al. (2011) developed an integrated framework with which to approach the behavioral study of threats and attacks on information and computer systems in organizations.

3.3 A Conceptual Framework for Modeling Information Security Culture

Figure 1 depicts the proposed variables and factors that influence information security culture.

The concepts are clustered into three models: National & Organizational cultures, and security compliance that form the framework. Model I consists of parent variables and its sub-variables that have been identified with regards to their role in influencing intention to comply with security policies. Model II comprises the organizational culture levels, plus the required knowledge of information security that employees need to do their job in a way that is consistent with good information security practices. Model III comprises the five dimensions that describe the cultural differences between countries that need to be taken into account when organizations operate in a global environment and how these relate to information security.

4   Discussion

We were able to identify variables that influence cultivation of a security culture, by integrating these variables into a conceptual framework that will address the research gap, this study investigated the relationship between these variables as follows:

4.1   Organizational Culture vs. Security Culture

According to Van Niekerk and Von Solms (2010), "in 'normal' definitions of organizational information security culture, the relevant job-related knowledge is generally ignored, because it can be assumed that the average employee would have the required knowledge to do his/her job". In the case of information security, the required knowledge is not necessarily needed to perform the employee's normal job functions. And thus, knowledge of information security is generally only needed when it is necessary to perform the normal job functions in a way that is consistent with good information security practices (Van Niekerk and Von Solms, 2010). Therefore, security culture should be viewed as a part of organizational culture. Also, information security culture is part of the organizational culture (Ngo, et al., 2005).

4.2   National Culture vs. Security Culture

Many researchers view a connection between national culture and employees' as well as organizational culture in terms of compliance (Hofstede, 1984). Also, and according to Gulev (2009), "organizational cultures do emulate national culture characteristics along three finely defined dimensions: knowledge sharing, traditions, and behavior". Flores, Antonsen and Ekstedt (2014) found that national culture should be taken into consideration in future studies in particular when investigating organizations operating in a global environment and understand how it affects behaviors and decision-making. Therefore, with regards to organizational culture vs. security culture; information security aims and objectives need to be aligned with formal organizational culture as well as national culture.

4.3   Security Compliance (Security Behavior) vs. Security Culture

Information security behavior could involve adherence to an organisation's policies, additionally, it can evolve over time as the security culture becomes more established (Da Veiga and Eloff, 2010). Although, researchers argued that security behavior and security compliance influence the establishment of information security culture, the question is what should organizations do to influence individual behavior and improve security compliance (Fagerstrom, 2013). Therefore, this section is divided into two subsections; information security behavior and information security compliance that can be influenced by behavior as outlined below.

Security Behavior. Furnell and Thomson (2009) suggested that organizations need to recognize the level of security culture, and take steps to enhance it. Thus, there is a clear case for promoting security culture within organizations to ensure that the necessary practices become part of the natural employee behavior. For example, according to Da Veiga and Eloff (2010), "Implementing security components impact the interaction of employees with information assets, and employees consequently exhibit certain behavior referred to as security behavior. The objective is to instill security behavior that is conducive to the protection of information assets based on the organization's policies. Such behavior could involve the reporting of security incidents, or adherence to a clear desk policy. In time, this security behavior evolves as the way that things are done in the organization and security culture is therefore established".

Security Compliance. According to Cheng, et al. (2013), information security policy is a written statement that defines the requirements for the organizational security management. It is the employees' responsibility and obligations, sanctions and countermeasures for non-compliance. Even more, Vance, et al. (2012) have discussed that perceived severity positively affects employees' intention to comply with information security policies, as well as, practitioners need to ensure that employees recognize information security threats and the risks. Also, Cheng, et al. (2013) have discussed that perceived certainty of sanctions will be negatively related to employees' information security policy violation intention, as well as, the empirical results of their study suggest the importance of deterrence, social bond and social pressure factors in preventing information security policy violation (influencing compliance/security behavior). Furthermore, O'Brien, et al. (2013) has concluded that the knowledge retained within the people working for an organization are the real assets, balancing the fine line between the end user's demands and the security risks posed is where organizations should focus their efforts. However and according to Ubelacker (2013), "national culture needs to be taken into account, but it is not changeable".

5 Conclusion

In the literature, security culture has been referred to as a mean to control 'human factor' in order to enhance security compliance.

With regard to employee behavior and awareness, Furnell and Thomson (2009) proposed that organizations need to recognize the level of security culture, and take steps to enhance it. And thus, there is a clear case for promoting security culture within organizations to ensure that the necessary practices become part of the natural employee behavior. However, Furnell and Clarke (2005) concluded that security culture also implies that security issues are considered as part of organizational operations, and therefore awareness and understanding of security is fundamental to establishing a successful security culture. Furthermore, cultural change is needed in order to implement and cultivate a newly developed security culture.

This paper is considered as a contribution study to a wider research study that aims to investigate the role of culture in influencing employees' security compliance. However, there are some recognized limitations to be addressed in future research. Firstly, although adopting findings from peer-reviewed sources were used to enhance the trustworthiness of the research, the study at this stage has not used any self-collected data. A second limitation is lack of prior empirical research studies on the topic. The concept of information security culture is new. Finally, this study suggests that there is a relationship between culture's values and security compliance's factors, which raises the question of whether the proposed framework can be analyzed and tested.

Finally, researchers have argued that culture influences employees' behavior and therefore developing a culture of security can contribute in minimizing or avoiding security breaches. It has been hypothesized that cultivating security culture can have a positive effect on employees' security compliance. As such, the proposed framework that will contribute in cultivating an information security culture, along with considering national and organizational cultures as well as security compliance variables within organizations, can be adopted, studied, investigated and tested in future research. Thus, from an information security research point of view, this paper fills an important gap in the literature.

References

Alfawaz, S., Nelson, K.: Information security culture: a behaviour compliance conceptual framework. In: AISC, vol. 105 (2010)

Ashenden, D.: Information Security management: A human challenge?, Information Security Technical report, 13(4), 195–201 (2008). Accessed 16 Sep 2014

CARLA: What is Culture? University of Minnesota (2014). http://www.carla.umn.edu/culture/definitions.html. Accessed 16 Sep 2014

Cheng, L., Li, Y., Li, W., Holm, E., Zhai, Q.: Understanding the violation of IS security policy in organizations: an integrated model based on social control and deterrence theory. Comput. Secur. 2013(39), 447–459 (2013)

Chipperfield, C., Furnell, S.: From security policy to practice: sending the right messages. Comput. Fraud Secur. 2010(3), 13–19 (2010)

Connolly, L. Lang, M.: Information systems security: the role of cultural aspects in organisational settings. In: AIS SIGSEC pre-ICIS Workshop on Information Security and Privacy (WISP) Milan, Italy, 14 December 2013

Veiga, Da, Eloff, J.H.P.: A framework and assessment instrument for information security culture. Comput. Secur. 29(2), 196–207 (2010)

Damen, L.: Culture Learning The Fifth Dimension on the Language Classroom. Addison-Wesley, Reading (1987). http://www.carla.umn.edu/culture/definitions.html. Accessed 22 Aug 2014

Dojkovski, S., Lichtenstein, S., Warren, M.J.: Fostering Information Security Culture in Small and Medium Size Enterprises: An Interpretive Study in Australia, pp. 1560–1571 (2007)

Fagerstrom, A.: Creating, maintaining and managing an information security culture. MSc thesis, Arcada Finland (2013)

Flores, W., Antonsen, E., Ekstedt, M.: Information security knowledge sharing in organizations: investigating the effect of behavioural information security governance and national culture. Comput. Secur. **43**, 90–110 (2014)

Furnell, S.: Jumping security hurdles. Comput. Fraud Secur. **2010**(6), 10–14 (2010)

Furnell, S., Clarke, N.: Organisational security culture: embedding security awareness, education and training. In: Proceedings of the 4th World Conference on Information Security Education (WISE 2005), Moscow, pp. 67–74 (2005)

Furnell, S., Clarke, N.: Power to the people? The evolving recognition of human aspects of security. Comput. Secur. **31**(8), 983–988 (2012)

Furnell, S., Rajendran, A.: Understanding the influences on information security behaviour. Comput. Fraud Secur. **2012**(3), 12–15 (2012)

Furnell, S., Thomson, K.L.: From culture to disobedience: Recognising the varying user acceptance of IT security. Comput. Fraud Secur. **2009**(2), 5–10 (2009)

Gabriel, T., Furnell, S.: Selecting security champions. Comput. Fraud Secur. **2011**(8), 8–12 (2011)

Greene, G., D'Arcy, J.: Assessing the impact of security culture and the employee-organization relationship in IS security compliance. In: Proceedings of the 5th Annual Symposium on Information Assurance, New York, pp. 42–49 (2010)

Gulev, R.: Are national and organizational cultures isomorphic? evidence from a four country comparative study. Managing Glob. Transitions **7**, 259–279 (2009)

Herath, T., Rao, H.R.: Encouraging information security behaviors in organizations: role of penalties, pressures and perceived effectiveness. Decis. Support Syst. **47**(2), 154–165 (2009)

Hofstede, G.: National cultures and corporate cultures. In: Samovar, L.A., Porter, R.E. (eds.) Communication Between Cultures. Wadsworth, Belmont (1984). http://www.carla.umn.edu/culture/definitions.html. Accessed 28 Sep 14

Johnson, M.E., Goetz, E.: Embedding information security into the organization. IEEE Secur. Priv. Mag. **5**(3), 16–24 (2007)

Malcolmson, J.: What is Security Culture? Does it differ in content from general Organisational Culture? IEEE Cody Technology Park, Farnborough, Hants (2009)

Martinez-Moyano, I.J., Conrad, S.H., Andersen, D.F.: Modeling behavioral considerations related to information security. Comput. Secur. **30**(6-7), 397–409 (2011)

Ngo, L., Zhou, W., Warren, M.: Understanding transition towards information security culture change. In: Proceedings of 3rd Australian Information Security Management Conference, pp. 67–73 (2005)

O'Brien, J., Islam, S., Bao, S., Weng, F., Xiong, W., Ma, A.: Information Security Culture: Literature Review. Unpublished Working Paper, University of Melbourne (2013)

Padayachee, K.: Taxonomy of compliant information security behavior. Comput. Secur. **31**(5), 673–680 (2012)

Ponemon Institute: 2013 Cost of Data Breach Study: Global Analysis. Symantec (2013). https://www4.symantec.com/mktginfo/whitepaper/053013_GL_NA_WP_Ponemon-2013-Cost-of-a-Data-Breach-Report_daiNA_cta72382.pdf. Accessed 28 Sep 14

Roer, K.: How to build and maintain security culture (2014) http://roer.com/2014/04/08/build-maintain-security-culture/. Accessed 19 Sep 2014

Ross, S.J.: Creating a Culture of Security. In: ISACA (2011). http://www.isaca.org/Knowledge-Center/Research/ResearchDeliverables/Pages/Creating-a-Culture-of-Security.aspx. Accessed 19 Sep 2014

Ruighaver, A.B., Maynard, S.B., Chang, S.: Organisational security culture: extending the end-user perspective. Comput. Secur. **26**(1), 56–62 (2007)

Thomson, K.-L., von Solms, R.: Information security obedience: a definition. Comput. Secur. **24** (1), 69–75 (2004)

Schein, E.: The Corporate Culture Survival Guide. Jossey-Bass Inc, San Francisco (1999)

Übelacker, S.: Security-aware organisational cultures a starting point for mitigating socio-technical risks socio-technical risk management/motivation. In: RiskKom Workshop INFORMATIK 2013, Koblenz, Germany (2013)

Van Niekerk, J.F., Von Solms, R.: Information security culture: A management perspective. Comput. Secur. **29**(4), 476–486 (2010)

Vance, A., Siponen, M., Pahnila, S.: Motivating IS security compliance: insights from habit and protection motivation theory. Inf. Manag. **49**, 190–198 (2012)

Legal Issues and User Experience
in Ubiquitous Systems
from a Privacy Perspective

Patricia C. de Souza[✉] and Cristiano Maciel

Laboratório de Ambientes Virtuais de Aprendizagem, Instituto de Computação,
Universidade Federal de Mato Grosso, Cuiabá, Brazil
{patriciacs, cmaciel}@ufmt.br

Abstract. Guaranteeing privacy in digital systems is an effort that moves several computing areas such as computer security, cryptography, computer networks, safe protocols, system design and human-computer interaction. One of the hypotheses in our work is that many users of mobile applications are not aware of the risks they run of their data being accessed by intruders, mainly because they do not know what they are exposed to and then, because the terms used in access policies are difficult to understand, too long for a dynamic reading and offer little or no flexibility to allow users to make adjustments according to their preferences. Improving users' experience means verifying if the implementation of new ways of interaction that provide freedom and flexibility in the control of privacy settings as well as access policies for mobile applications has allowed for higher levels of security and reliability on the users' side.

Keywords: Privacy · User experience · Legal aspects · Ubiquitous systems

1 Introduction

Privacy issues have become a growing concern among those who entrust their data to IT systems, especially considering the numerous reports of security flaws in systems that had been considered safe; for example, sensitive data stolen or compromised by hackers and digital espionage scandals.

This is the reason why the trust relationship between a user who wishes to store his sensitive data and a service that offers storing has become more unstable. It can be noticed, in modern society, that the very concept of what is private has undergone transformations and suffered from influences according to the context, be it in the offline world or the online world.

Many studies have focused on human behavior regarding privacy in online social networks [1–3] and in ubiquitous applications [6, 8–10]. Some discussion can also be found on the influence of cultural and emotional issues, on values and awareness concerning confidence and on privacy awareness as a reflection of users' attitudes.

One of the hypotheses in our work is that many users of mobile applications are not aware of the risks they run of their data being accessed by intruders, mainly because they do not know what they are exposed to and then, because the terms used in access policies are difficult to understand, too long for a dynamic reading and offer little or no

© Springer International Publishing Switzerland 2015
T. Tryfonas and I. Askoxylakis (Eds.): HAS 2015, LNCS 9190, pp. 449–460, 2015.
DOI: 10.1007/978-3-319-20376-8_40

flexibility to allow users to make adjustments according to their preferences. In this sense, two support fronts for users of ubiquitous applications can be envisioned: digital education and improving users' experience. The first one involves issues of behavior related to values and knowledge, specific to each individual, learned at home or through formal education. Digital education also involves creating regulations to protect citizens against the use of private information. An example of this is the Marco Civil da Internet (Civil Rights Framework for the Internet) a law passed by the Brazilian federal government. This law establishes principles, guarantees, rights and responsibilities for the use of Internet in Brazil (Lei N° 12.965, 2014).

Improving users' experience means verifying if the implementation of new ways of interaction that provide freedom and flexibility in the control of privacy settings as well as access policies for mobile applications has allowed for higher levels of security and reliability on the users' side. In this case, a study on the process of applications re-designing must be developed along with different types of tests. In this sense, the objective of this research was to analyze issues related to privacy, in regard to legal aspects and user's experience, based on the assessment of design products in mobile Apps.

2 Background

2.1 Privacy

Privacy is a fundamental right guaranteed by the Universal Declaration of Human Rights, which was adopted and proclaimed by the United Nations General Assembly and states in its Article XII that "no one shall be subjected to arbitrary interference with his privacy, family, home or correspondence, nor to attacks upon his honor and reputation. Everyone has the right to the protection of the law against such interference or attacks" [12].

The legal field in Brazil provides specific definitions in different spheres regarding privacy and public life. Reference [13] defines a triad of legal rights without which privacy cannot be guaranteed: (1) the right not to be monitored; (2) the right not to be registered and (3) the right not to be recognized. The author states that any information that is judged irrelevant for a system, should not be required or stored, and this includes photographs as well as unauthorized video and audio recordings. The right not to be recognized is understood as the right not to have photographs, videos or other records published in the media.

According to Durlak in [14] privacy is a human value consisting of four elements he calls rights. Reference [14] divides these rights into two categories. The first category includes three rights that an individual can use to fence off personal information seekers: solitude, anonymity and intimacy. The second category contains those rights an individual can use to control the amount and value of personal information given out: reserve (methods of dissemination controling one's personal information).

Based on the analysis of the definition provided by the Houaiss dictionary for the term *private* [15] "3. that which belongs to an individual in particular; 4. that which is personal and not to be expressed in public; 5. restricted, reserved to the rightful owner; confidential", several situations can be identified where these concepts are abused. The unauthorized use of users' data, the disclosure of their information and third-party publication without the user's consent, or even when the user himself discloses personal information due to unawareness or negligence are examples of situations where the right to privacy is violated. In this sense, privacy is a concept closely linked to the concept of anonymity regarding the wish to remain unidentified or even be noticed.

Reference [14] introduces a classification of the different types of privacy:

• Personal privacy involves the privacy of personal attributes.
• Informational privacy: the protection of unauthorized access to information itself. It includes: personal information, financial information, medical information, information related to transactions over the Internet.
• Institutional privacy: it refers to the custody of organizational private data (marketing strategies, data on sales and products) as well as information on the business itself.

Vianna's concept introduces a vision of greater control regarding data, defining data protection as something essential [13, 16] offers a complementary opinion suggesting that the current society has different views on privacy. Driven by a desire to achieve recognition, members of our society reveal private issues via computational systems. Reference [16] raises the issue of the value of privacy in modern society where he considers that, for some subjects, privacy is an irrelevant concept when people in general give up their private life for the sake of recognition and prominence.

According to [17], the very concept of privacy is changing due to modern life and the advent of technology. Even if people try to keep their life intimate and private, many of their actions are registered, such as credit card payments, online shopping, mobile phone calls and Web searching among others [14, 17].

It can be noticed that the concept of privacy is subjective and can vary among different individuals and cultures. Whatever is acceptable for some people might be considered a violation to privacy for others. Privacy is also determined by the environment, the individual time and confidence awareness, which may or not encourage a person to reveal more or less information.

2.2 Brazilian Efforts Towards Preserving Privacy

The Brazilian Constitution [19], when listing Citizens' Individual and Collective Rights and Responsibilities, states in its 5th Article, Paragraph X, that "intimacy, privacy, honor and the image of people are inviolable, being the right to compensation guaranteed for property or moral damages resulting from their violation".

Still, Brazil has been concerned, along recent years, about the recurrent digital privacy and espionage problems and has consequently taken some initiatives to regulate these issues. The Internet Governance Act (Law n° 12.965, 2014) establishes principles, guarantees, rights and responsibilities for the use of Internet in Brazil. This law comprises three major aspects of Internet use: neutrality, privacy and freedom of expression. The Law states in its 8th Article that "the guarantee of the right to privacy and to freedom of expression in communication is a pre-requisite for the full exercise of the right to internet access…".

There is such a great concern about these issues in Brazil that, in a democratic way, a public debate (http://participacao.mj.gov.br/dadospessoais/) is being carried out on the preparation of a draft for a Data Protection Bill. Any person, not necessarily a Brazilian citizen, can participate with suggestions on the minutes. There is an English version available online (http://participacao.mj.gov.br/dadospessoais/2015/02/texto-do-anteprojeto-disponivel-em-ingles/).

The bill draft on data protection intends to ensure control and transparency for citizens about which data corporations and government are dealing with and how they are dealing with them. It is expected that this regulatory bill will protect citizens in all instances and sectors in which personal data are managed, establish bases for addressing issues related to surveillance and monitoring of the Internet and its applications, be aligned with international standards and, furthermore, according to principles of security and responsibility, provide for eventual user's compensation for damages.

Another initiative was triggered by the Special Commission for Human-Computer Interaction that is linked to the Brazilian Computer Society (SBC). During the IHC 2012 symposium (XI Brazilian Symposium on Human Factors in Computational Systems) a panel entitled "Great HCI Research Challenges in Brazil – Gran DIHC-BR" was put up to receive proposals from the HCI community. According to the report that summarizes the proposals [20], the great challenges that resulted from the panel "represent the HCI community's reflection on the field, likely to inspire and guide the course of HCI research in the country for years to come. We hope that these Great Challenges serve as a guiding principle for the development of projects to produce significant scientific advances, with social and technological applications".

The proposals discussed in the panel were divided into five thematic groups. The G4 - Human Values, considers "Privacy within the Connected World" as one of the challenges, bringing forward issues such as: "What information is collected and what can it, directly or indirectly, expose about the users? How can users be allowed to anticipate the combination of parameters in terms of what information about them is visible and to whom? How can harmonious levels of sociability and privacy be guaranteed?" [21].

The report proposes the discussion and publication of articles within the field and the survey of design products (hardware, software, websites, etc.) that explicitly consider these aspects, among other strategies to deal with this challenge. One of the difficulties and barriers for the success of the mentioned studies is "the difficulty in aligning research and the creation of legal regulations, due to the lack of communication between the academic and the legislative spheres. Those who make laws is not necessarily involved in or knowledgeable about the research studies in the area." In this sense, the discussion proposed in this paper articulates the elements above, comparing concepts and legal regulations with technical aspects related to privacy in mobile applications.

2.3   Related Works

Privacy exposure is critical in ubiquitous and or pervasive systems. This is due to the fact that applications need to capture and share context data from users to be able to take advantage of their features. According to [6], there are growing concerns about the misuse of location data by third parties, which fuels the need for more privacy controls in such services. Reference [5] state that "the pervasive computing paradigm raises the level of the challenge to protect privacy of end-users, mainly due to the fact that devices operating in such an environment will be embedded in the fabric of the everyday life and will exhibit enhanced tracking and profiling capabilities".

In the authors' view, basic characteristics introduced by these systems generate the new Privacy Enhancing Technology (PET), since "appropriate mechanisms that are able to evolve with the needs of the users and interact with them in order to meet their privacy requirements" are necessary. Reference [10] argue that "when sensors capture data about people, and digital systems interpret and respond to that data below the line of user visibility, two fundamental questions arise. First, are current notions of consent relevant in the emerging class of pervasive systems and, secondly, what are the practical consequences of dealing with consent for such environments?".

According [8], we live in a world where people often decide to sacrifice their informational privacy for useful or free services. The author's opinion is that "privacy is a right, but security is a primary state function" since "a loss of privacy can result immediately in a loss of security when data become public or leak". He then adds: "we must ensure that our social norms reflect not only the pleasure we get from visibility to the network, but also the important benefits that protecting privacy will produce for society as a whole. This can't be a matter of regulation, but rather depends on us all taking our responsibilities seriously."

With the emergence of more lenient privacy protection laws, those who develop systems should pay attention to the compliance of legal requirements and users' satisfaction. Reference [7] proposed a technique called Privacy Interface Analysis where "the human factors requirements for effective privacy interface design can be grouped into four categories: (1) comprehension, (2) consciousness, (3) control, and (4) consent". This technique shows how interface design solutions can be used when developing a privacy-enhanced application or service.

Reference [9] conducted an online study aimed at understanding the preferences and practices of LSS users in the US. The authors found that the main motivations for location sharing were to connect and coordinate with one's social and professional circles, to project an interesting image of oneself, and to receive rewards offered for 'checking in.' In this study, there are design suggestions, such as delayed disclosure and conflict detection, to enhance privacy-management capabilities of LSS. They are:

- Delayed disclosure: this usage suggests that it may be possible to mitigate many location-sharing regrets and privacy violations simply by decoupling the time of location broadcast from the time of the decision to share location (e.g., by daily or weekly batching).
- Special handling of purpose-driven sharing. In cases where location disclosures serve an immediate and specific purpose, specialized handling could provide better privacy depending on the purpose. In the way of example, the authors mention recommendations made in situations which might be published later on.
- Conflict detection. Over 20% of research respondents who experienced location-sharing regrets mentioned that the regret was caused by being caught lying.

For example, a user might be cautioned before sharing location if his or her calendar indicates a conflicting event at another location.

Luger and Rodden [10], through a review of multidisciplinary perspectives on consent and technology, offer a set of recommendations to designers as considerations for future systems design: (i) electronic consent mechanisms (ECMs) must cease to be designed around 'moments in time' and allow for negotiation; (ii) systems should enable establishment of user expectations and development of norms; (iii) systems should be sensitive to third-party interactions; and (iv) we should move beyond designing for user control towards designing for user autonomy.

In the analysis of specific studies on privacy in social networks [1–3], it is evident that there is a common concern about understanding human attitudes related to the behavior when faced with privacy issues: security awareness, confidence awareness, the influence of cultural issues, the influence of knowledge about the risks related to a high exposure of private information as well as the necessary skills to maintain protection.

3 Methodology

The issues discussed in this article are part of a research project in an international partnership between France and Brazil[1] in which an architecture that supports the development of ubiquitous applications called Devices, Environments and Social Networks Integration Architecture (DESIA) [18] was proposed. The concepts of the proposed DESIA architecture are detailed in terms of services, requirements and architecture. The main services offered by DESIA are: collection, storage and query of context information; situation inference; user and environment interfaces; and integration with external sources of data. The functional requirements were grouped in seven different categories including Location-related requirements; Privacy; and Security and permissions. Examples of Privacy-related requirements are:

PRIV-01. The architecture must permit setting the user's privacy options.
PRIV-03. The architecture must permit defining rules to obtain third parties' information, considering confidentiality, reputation mechanisms and information classification, for example.
PRIV-05. The system must include documents detailing the Terms of Use and Privacy Policy of the application, which must be available for users and these must be explicitly notified about any alteration.
PRIV-06. The system must provide dynamic solutions aligned with the application features so that users may choose what information they desire to be visible or to be shared in which contexts, so as to safeguard their privacy.

Associated Non-functional requirements are:

[1] Sponsored by Fapemat, Brazil.

NFR-03. The system developers must use techniques according to usability regulations.

NFR-04. The architecture must consider cultural aspects.

NFR-05. The architecture must provide Terms of Use and Privacy Policy according to existing laws in each country.

The efforts committed to this stage of the research, of an exploratory character and qualitative approach, are included in the detailed explanation of these functional and non-functional requirements. They are based on: (1) the analysis of how applications have implemented terms of use and privacy policies; (2) studies related to the study object in the area of HCI; and (3) the study of regulations, considering the need to understand the whole context and the ease of use of the systems. In order to achieve this, concepts on privacy and the legal apparatus in this area in Brazil were analyzed, especially in the Marco Civil da Internet [11] (Brazilian Internet Governance Act) and in the Data Protection Bill.

Aiming to analyze privacy features and settings of the applications, five applications were inspected, along with their terms of use and privacy policies. Based on the survey of the applications' design products, problems and solutions are discussed in order to improve user experience from the perspective of privacy.

The results of this stage will help elaborate guidelines in favor of the quality of user experience in ubiquitous systems from a privacy perspective, being this a future stage in the study.

4 Exploratory Study

The exploratory study involved the analysis of the Terms of Use and Privacy Policy of five randomly chosen applications: Viber (text messaging and phone calls), Waze (community-based GPS), Facebook Messenger (instant messaging). Snapchat (picture-based messaging) and Google Now (intelligent personal assistant). This resulted in a report offering a critical analysis of the privacy problems found and suggestions to improve users' experience.

Among the applications that were analyzed, Snapchat, Viber and Waze do not present the text for the Access Policy and/or Terms of Use in Portuguese, which makes reading difficult and probably leads the user to simply agree having no idea of what is written. Other applications, even though they present a Portuguese version of the Terms of Use, make it clear that, in case of divergence, the English version is the only one that will be considered.

In some cases, the labelling is in Portuguese, but the section's contents are in English. Depending on the users' literacy level, these issues may interfere with the use of the application causing doubts as they go against usability principles such as ease of use, consistency and standardization.

Reference [23] state that in Human-Centered Informatics "it is important to understand people's situated interactions with information, in other to help us understand how to better support them". The authors propose a model with core elements of an anticipation-based information journey, with thinner arrows indicating feedback,

P.C. de Souza and C. Maciel

anticipating demands. Anticipating the demands of interpretation and validation, it is possible to select sources in which they have confidence while also selecting topics (or reinterpreting a question) in order to minimize the interpretation demands.

Moreover, this kind of situation could have been foreseen in legal rules of the countries where the applications are used; in the case of Brazil, the Internet Governance Act should discredit any application that does not make the Terms of Use text available in the country's native language.

In general, the Terms of Use and/or Privacy Policy are long texts to be read on a smartphone's interfaces. In some applications such as Waze and Facebook Messenger the interfaces are offered with a summary data and services that the application can access. However, it can be noticed that these interfaces are purely informative and they do not allow any type of choice on the user's part. Application users are nowadays made hostages considering that in order to use the application the user must accept the Terms of Use and other policies in full.

The installation of the Facebook Messenger application for messaging has recently become mandatory for Facebook users. It is very likely that thousands of Facebook users have not bothered to read the Messenger Terms of Use. Furthermore, when modifying the decoupling of the application to the social network, many users became confused with alterations such as: the request to access the camera or the microphone in the mobile device and published news on the application's permissions on an Android system [22].

In view of this, three items considered problematic in the Terms of Use were chosen to be described:

1. Permission to access the call history in the device, including incoming and outgoing calls. This permission simply creates log files in the device, but other malicious applications can access this information without the user realizing. This kind of permission may challenge security policies, since the creation of log files and the fact that malicious applications may access this information turn the risk of improper use imminent.
2. Permission to access information on the user's contacts, including the frequency with which the user communicates via e-mail or other means of contact. Such an authorization may indicate a breach in security, since as the App scans the user's device looking for other Apps to synchronize information, confidential data might be used without the user's permission. Even when this information is used to improve the user's experience in using the application, the user has no knowledge nor has he consented to this action.
3. Permission to access the user's personal information that is stored on the device, such as contacts' name and data. This means that the company may identify the user and keep a customer database.

Along this short list, two kinds of problem can be identified: first, permission is unrestricted, i.e. the term does not clarify that the application may access the user's whole contact list because it needs this access when the user wants to use a contact to make a call through the App. In this case, the text does not help the user to trust the application. The second problem is that it is difficult to understand the application's real need to access certain data, such as the above-mentioned situations.

Such situations are not only found in Facebook Messenger, but in other applications as well. On the on hand, the user needs the services, agility or convenience the application offers; on the other hand, the application does not help the user to establish an adequate confidence for its use. Even so, there is a concern in the sense that many users simply ignore the risks and terms of use, either because of their need or hurry to use the application or in order to feel part of a social group.

In another application (Viber), privacy policies lead users to understand that their information is protected. Yet, a study carried out on this application by researchers of the UNH Cyber Forensics Research & Education Group at the University of New Haven [24] in the US identified, by testing mobile phones in 2014, that the application sent and stored the users' messages on their servers without encrypting them – including images, pictures, videos, doodles and location. As privacy is linked to data security, the group pointed out, in terms of solution: "Make sure the data is encrypted over a tunnel when it is sent. Also make sure the data is encrypted properly when saved, and authenticated when being accessed".

In order to use the Google Now App, for example, the user needs to authorize the application to collect various personal data. This allows a constant surveillance on the application's part. An interesting design solution in this application is that google makes access to the collected data available to the user so that, in case he does not want this information to be visible, he can simply delete it. In case the user does not want any information to be recorded, he can delete everything and cancel the registration definitely. However, if the user does this, he will not be able to access all the application's features, since the he depends substantially on personal information to be able to act. The Privacy Policy (https://www.google.com/intl/pt-BR/policies/privacy/) is clear concerning the user's collected data, how the company uses this information and how it is protected.

Waze, also Google's, is an application that provides a lot of interaction with/for the user, considering as key features issues involving privacy. It allows the user to share his routes, favorite places, information on accidents and traffic jams, among other data. Accordingly, people may have their personal activities disclosed, also through the integration of social networks. At the same time, the application allows that, in the case the user does not want to share anything, he can just use the GPS in a standard manner. In addition, in order to use the application in all its features, the user should not be bothered by, for example, the sharing of his information on alternative routes, if he did accept and authorize the Terms of Use.

Another interesting solution for these applications, regarding the deletion of users' data, an issue that has been put forward by Internet regulatory laws, is the specification of the maximum latency time that the user data may be stored after canceling the account. Except for cases where the information is part of a lawsuit, the user may be notified when the data has been definitely excluded from the server. Furthermore, applications must be careful not to have user data stored by third-party applications without prior notice, not to cause conflict between Terms of Use and Privacy Policies.

According to Article X in the Internet Governance Act, "the custody and availability of the connection and access logs to Internet applications to which this law refers, as well as that of personal data and the contents of private communications, must meet the preservation of intimacy, private life, honor and image of the directly or indirectly involved parties". According to the law, "the content of private communications will only be made available by means of a court order".

The Draft Bill on Data Protection states in its Article 6 nine principles on the processing of personal data. The following two principles serve as example: "I – Principle of purpose, by which the processing must be made according to legitimate, specific and explicit purposes known to the holder; II – Principle of adequacy, according to which the processing must be compatible with the aimed purposes and with the holder's legitimate expectations according to the processing context". Even though the text is still being discussed, it can be noticed how the existing Terms of Use and/or Privacy Policies will need to be improved, considering that they are usually generalist, superficial and not very explicit about the requirements of use and processing of personal and sensitive data.

In addition, the Draft Bill on Data Protection explicitly deals on the difference between personal data, sensitive data and anonymous data. Once approved, even after alterations, the Data Protection Law may become a landmark in Brazil to safeguard fundamental rights such as freedom, intimacy and privacy of a person.

One possibility, during the design or re-design of applications, viewing to meet privacy regulations, is the mapping between the items in the Terms of Use and the application's features in order align them with the systems requirements.

5   Conclusions

Privacy, as a software requirement, needs to be guaranteed by technical and legal means. Understanding privacy as a social and cultural process, it must be delivered to the user in a simple and clear manner, since he will be continuously interacting with computer systems. Privacy modeling is a challenge in mobile applications, especially those that require location-sharing services.

If on one hand we have a wealth of interesting, useful, free solutions, on the other hand we need to produce terms of use and privacy policies that are clear to users and in agreement with legal regulations. Faced with so many privacy-related challenges, the issue is how to structure users' consent to the use of their data. How can the design of applications favor reliability and provide the user with security. How can terms of use be developed in order to make them more interactive?

Another relevant issue is the fact that many companies make their terms of use so that they can protect themselves against users' misuse and not really thinking about the users. Many of the inspected applications make the user a hostage when he must accept the entire terms of use and allow more access to data than he would need so that he can use the application in all its features.

As much as interactive solutions are required, from the perspective of implementation, it is well known that it is challenging to suggest terms of use where users may choose specific items, since such choices might interfere in the system's features. However, intermediate solutions can be thought of. In addition, warnings can be given out to the user while he is using the application, not only in situations where he is disclosing private information, but also as an educational tool.

Privacy protection involves education, technology and rules. In this sense, the creation of regulations, discussing them and analyzing technological solutions must be done constantly. Certainly, these three fronts must be in harmony, since technology provides services that will result in regulations. Education in turn assumes knowledge and skills so that users may use it in the best possible way in order to, for example, understand and have control over the privacy settings of each application.

Future stages of this research will involve interviewing professionals in the fields of sociology, law and computing. The objective is to deepen knowledge on the concept, and social, legal and technological issues surrounding the understanding of privacy and terms related to the establishment of confidence, the social circle among others. A quantitative research will be carried out with users of X, Y and Z-generation ubiquitous applications, as a follow up to works the group has already started [4]. This research intends to understand the behavior of the three different generations faced with the use of mobile technology as well as analyze how they react to the privacy and security issues. Results will help produce guidelines to enhance use experience in ubiquitous systems from the perspective of privacy.

References

1. Nosko, A., Wood, E., Molema, S.: All about me: Disclosure in online social networking profiles: the case of FACEBOOK. Comput. Hum. Behav. **26**, 406–418 (2010)
2. Fogel, J., Nehmad, E.: Internet social network communities: risk taking, trust, and privacy concerns. Comput. Hum. Behav. **25**, 153–160 (2009)
3. Shin, D.: The effects of trust, security and privacy in social networking: a security-based approach to understand the pattern of adoption. Interact. Comput. **22**, 428–438 (2010)
4. Borges, G., Ribeiro, T., Maciel, C., Souza, P.C.: Who is this guy who liked my picture? privacy control mechanisms on Facebook for Generations X and Y. In: 15th International Conference on Enterprise Information Systems (ICEIS 2013), France, pp. 179–186 (2013)
5. Dritsas, S., Tsaparas, J., Gritzalis, D.: A generic privacy enhancing technology for pervasive computing environments. In: Fischer-Hübner, S., Furnell, S., Lambrinoudakis, C. (eds.) TrustBus 2006. LNCS, vol. 4083, pp. 103–113. Springer, Heidelberg (2006)
6. Bilogrevic, I., Jadliwala, M., Kalkan, K., Hubaux, J.-P., Aad, I.: Privacy in mobile computing for location-sharing-based services. In: Fischer-Hübner, S., Hopper, N. (eds.) PETS 2011. LNCS, vol. 6794, pp. 77–96. Springer, Heidelberg (2011)
7. Patrick, A.S., Kenny, S.: From privacy legislation to interface design: implementing information privacy in human-computer interactions. In: Dingledine, R. (ed.) PET 2003. LNCS, vol. 2760, pp. 107–124. Springer, Heidelberg (2003)
8. O'Hara, K.: Are we getting privacy the wrong way round?. In: Internet Computing, IEEE, vol.17, no. 4, pp. 89–92, July–August 2013
9. Patil, S., Norcie, G., Kapadia, A., Lee, A.J.: Reasons, rewards, regrets: privacy considerations in location sharing as an interactive practice. In: Proceedings of the Eighth Symposium on Usable Privacy and Security (SOUPS 2012). ACM, NY, USA (2012)
10. Luger, E., Rodden, T.: Terms of agreement: rethinking consent for pervasive computing. Interact. Comput. **25**(3), 229–241 (2013)
11. Lei N° 12.965: Marco Civil da Internet (2014). http://www.planalto.gov.br/ccivil_03/_ato2011-2014/2014/lei/l12965.htm

12. ONU: Declaração Universal dos Direitos Humanos. http://portal.mj.gov.br/sedh/ct/legis_intern/ddh_bib_inter_universal.htm
13. Vianna, T.L.: Transparência pública, opacidade privada: o Direito como instrumento de limitação do poder na sociedade de controle. Tese de doutorado, Universidade Federal do Paraná (2006). http://www.midiaindependente.org/media/2008/05/419863.pdf
14. Kizza, J.M.: Ethical and Social Issues in the Information Age, 5th edn. Springer, New York (2013)
15. Houaiss, A.: Dicionário Eletrônico Houaiss da Língua Portuguesa. Objetiva, São Paulo (2012)
16. Sibila, P.: La intimidad como espectáculo, 1st edn. Fondo de Cultura Económica, Buenos Aires (2008). http://cmap.javeriana.edu.co/servlet/SBReadResourceServlet?rid=1J2SK927M-22DBXQG-1TB
17. Jennings, C., Fena, L.: Priv@cidade.com – Como preservar sua intimidade na era da internet. Futura, São Paulo, SP (2000)
18. Maciel, C., Souza, P.C., Viterbo, J., Mendes, F.F., Seghrouchni, A.E.F.: A multi-agent architecture to support ubiquitous aplications in smart environments. In: Fifth International Workshop on Collaborative Agents - Research & Development (CARE) - 13th International Conference on Autonomous Agents and Multiagent Systems (AAMAS 2014), Paris-France (2014)
19. Constituição da República Federativa do Brasil (1998). http://www.planalto.gov.br/ccivil_03/constituicao/constituicao.htm
20. Baranauskas, C., Souza, C.S., Pereira, R. (Orgs.): I GranDIHC-BR - Grandes Desafios de Pesquisa em Interação Humano-Computador no Brasil. Relatório Técnico. Comissão Especial de Interação Humano-Computador (CEIHC) da SBC (2014)
21. Maciel, C., Pereira, V., Hornung, H., Piccolo, L.G.S., Prates, R.O.: Valores humanos. In: Baranauskas, Souza and Pereira (orgs.) I GranDIHC-BR — Grandes Desafios de Pesquisa em Interação Humano-Computador no Brasil. Relatório Técnico. Comissão Especial de Interação Humano Computador (CEIHC) da SBC, pp. 27–30 (2014)
22. Fiorela, S.: The Insidiousness of Facebook Messenger's Android Mobile App Permissions (2013). http://www.huffingtonpost.com/sam-fiorella/the-insidiousness-offace_b_4365645.html
23. Blandford, A., Attfield, S.: Interacting with information. Synth. Lect. Hum.-Centered Inf., Morgan & Claypool **3**, 1–99 (2010)
24. UNHCFREG: Viber security vulnerabilities: do not use Viber until these issues are resolved (2014). http://www.unhcfreg.com/#!Viber-Security-Vulnerabilities-Do-not-use-Viber-until-these-issues-are-resolved/c5rt/BB4208CF-7F0A-4DE1-92A4-529425549683

Security in Social Media and Smart Technologies

Users' Mental Models for Three End-to-End Voting Systems: Helios, Prêt à Voter, and Scantegrity II

Claudia Z. Acemyan[1(✉)], Philip Kortum[1], Michael D. Byrne[1,2], and Dan S. Wallach[2]

[1] Department of Psychology, Rice University, Houston, TX, USA
{claudiaz,pkortum}@rice.edu
[2] Department of Computer Science, Rice University, Houston, TX, USA
{byrne,dwallach}@rice.edu

Abstract. This study sought to understand voter's mental models for three end-to-end (e2e) voting systems: Helios, Prêt à Voter, and Scantegrity II. To study voters' mental models of e2e systems, 16 Houston area voters participated in mock elections that required them to vote first with a paper ballot and then with the three e2e systems. After using each system, subjects were asked to draw their mental model—or how the system works, then describe it to the experimenter, and last complete an interview. We found that most participants think about the systems first and foremost in terms of how-to-vote procedures, rather than detailed, conceptual models that describe all aspects of a system, including how they work. When designing e2e voting systems, the findings from this study can be used by system developers to ensure that voters find the systems easy to use and that the designs align with voters' pre-existing mental models for voting.

Keywords: Mental models · Voting systems · End-to-end voting methods · User centered design

1 Introduction

Problems often arise when system developers expect future system users to have a specific mental model for a system when in fact they will have another [1]. Differences between the two models may lead to users making errors while trying to complete a task, becoming frustrated, taking longer to complete goals, failing to recognize why they have to execute procedures, using the system differently than conceptualized, and avoiding using the system all together despite its advantages. Even with this knowledge, system developers continue to make assumptions—from how future users will think about the system to how they will use it—rather than using empirical data that can be used to optimize principles like usability, learn ability, satisfaction, expectations, and problem solving.

An example of a system type in which many of the developers made assumptions about the users' mental models is end-to-end (e2e) voting systems. E2e voting systems were designed to improve the integrity of elections by ensuring that voters can cast

© Springer International Publishing Switzerland 2015
T. Tryfonas and I. Askoxylakis (Eds.): HAS 2015, LNCS 9190, pp. 463–474, 2015.
DOI: 10.1007/978-3-319-20376-8_41

intended vote selections using a reliable, cryptographically secure system and that these votes will then be counted accurately as cast. The systems also provide a means to audit the system by election officials, voters, and any interested third party. For instance, if a voter wants to make sure their ballot is recorded by the system, many e2e systems give them a way to do this through a website after polls close.

In the process of developing e2e voting systems, voting experts also wanted to enhance voters' awareness of system security, make how the systems work more transparent, increase accuracy by having voters be active participants in the voting process, and either increase voters' trust in the systems that they use or eliminate the need for voters to trust that a system is working as it should. Not only have the system developers defined the operational improvements of each system, but they also presented theoretical frameworks that set their systems apart from non-e2e voting technologies.

By way of example, when the Helios system is described, it is touted as having the property of "unconditional integrity" [2]—meaning the system is accurate and a tally cannot be faked. The developers of Helios thought this was the most important property that a voting system should have, and they also believed it would be important to others, especially voters. Accordingly, the Helios team worked to realize a system that voters could trust because they thought it would be better to trust a reliable, accurate system than potentially corrupt election officials.

While voters are supposed to trust Helios, Prêt à Voter (PaV) was designed in such a way that a person does not have to "trust" the system. Instead, the system "assures a high degree of transparency while preserving the secrecy of the ballot" [3], meaning it provides evidence to the voter, throughout the voting and tallying processes, that proves the system is working as it should. Specifically, voters are issued a receipt that they can use to check online that their ballot was recorded as they cast it. Auditing teams can also check the decryption of votes without ever revealing specific voters' choices. If voters or independent auditors notice that something is wrong, then fraud can be identified.

Scantegrity II "offers a level of integrity not found in conventional voting systems" [4]. To achieve this end, the system has features that allow the voters to check that it is accurate and performing as expected. For example, when a voter makes a ballot selection with a special decoder pen, a unique code is revealed inside the selected bubble. This code, along with the ballot ID, can be recorded on a receipt. Voters can then choose to keep the receipt if they want to later verify that their votes have been cast as intended, all while keeping their actual selections private. Despite the inclusion of all these special features, the voter experience for Scantegrity II was intended to be identical to that of voting with an optical scan bubble ballot, except for the creation of the optional verification receipt.

But do voters who use e2e voting methods associate concepts of increased accuracy, security, and transparency with the systems? All of these system elements require a voter to have at least *some* awareness of them and understand them, even if only at the most basic level. If voters do not, then the assurances and benefits of the systems are potentially lost. To make matters worse, voters might be frustrated with the deviations from voting procedures that they are accustomed to or expect (e.g., casting a ballot by placing it in a ballot box versus scanning it), or perhaps voters might not know what they are doing and/or why (e.g., voters might not understand why PaV requires them to essentially tear their ballot in half, shred the side with candidate names on it, and then scan the half with their selections).

These issues are of concern not only to human factors researchers, but also to voting security experts. Ben Adida pointed out few people recognize that ballot casting assurance (when voters know that their votes were correctly captured) and universal verifiability (in which any observer can verify the correct tally of all votes) are two properties of the Helios voting system [2]. Moreover, Adida hypothesized that a system like Helios is not widely recognized by its users to represent a major improvement over methods currently used in elections. The means to determine how voters think about these e2e voting systems is to gather empirical data. Only then can we know if the gap Adida describes truly exists.

The aim of this project was to understand the mental models that users form after vote casting and vote verifying with the Helios, Prêt à Voter, and Scantegrity II methods. These systems were selected because they are representative of the different types of e2e systems, are widely accepted as viable options by the voting research community, and have been used in elections [5]. Through this research, there was also a desire to determine if these models support the security concepts integral to the e2e systems. Glimpses into the mental models users have for these systems will allow several important questions to be answered: Do voters understand how the systems work? Do voters know why they are doing the actions that are required to cast a ballot or check on it after the election? And do voters find the systems to be more secure, trustworthy, and transparent than other voting methods like the paper ballot? Or do Voters think of e2e systems no differently?

To date, there has not been published research specifically on users' mental models for any voting system. While there has been a very limited effort to study if users understand a specific system feature of an e2e voting system (e.g., why voters must tear their ballot in half when voting with PaV [6]), the exclusive focus of this body of work was on assessing system usability, not on understanding user mental models.

In contrast, there is an extensive, diverse body of work on mental models. A single definition for mental models does not exist, as the term seems to be continually redefined across researchers and projects. Hence, in this paper, a mental model for a voting system is defined using a combination of the previously published definitions [7–9]: a mental model is a user's understanding of what a system does, why the system does what it does, how one can interact with it, the expected responses to specific actions, system perceptions, and the ideas a user associates with the system.

This study aimed to capture participants' mental models through drawings and interviews after using each of the e2e systems in a mock election. In turn, it was hoped that the mental models would reveal what users understood and did not understand about the systems. This information could then be used in future iterations of the e2e systems to decrease voter frustration, discouragement, or inability to act for any reason, while increasing their feelings of trust, security, and accuracy.

2 Research Study

2.1 Methods

Participants. Sixteen participants completed this study. These participants were eligible voters (i.e., 18 years old or older and residents of the United States) who lived in the Houston area. Subjects were recruited through two methods. First, eight participants were Rice University undergraduates recruited through the university's subject pool. Each received credit towards a course requirement for their participation. Second, eight participants were recruited through an online advertisement. These subjects were paid $25 for their time. The mean age was 32 years, with a range from 18 to 65 years. Eight participants were male and eight were female. The mean number of national elections that these participants had previously voted in was 3.1, with a range of 0–12. On average, participants had voted in 4.3 other types of elections, (e.g., local, state, or school), with a range from 0 to 10.

Design. The study was a within-subjects design. Participants voted with each of the following systems: paper bubble ballot, Helios, Prêt à Voter, and Scantegrity II. Even though this study focused on mental models of e2e voting systems, participants were asked to also vote with a paper ballot so they would be able to directly compare the "enhanced" voter verifiable systems to the more traditional, basic method.

So that voters knew for whom they should vote, they were randomly assigned one of two lists of candidates and propositions. Their list was either primarily Republican or it was primarily Democratic. These two lists were the same as those used in previous voting studies conducted at Rice University [5, 10].

The main dependent variable was the mental model formed for each voting system. To capture the mental models, several methods were used. Participants drew on a piece of paper a representation for how they thought the voting system worked. They were also interviewed about their mental model drawing and asked further questions about security features, system accuracy, unnecessary procedures, things that they did not understand about the systems, their preferences, and how the e2e systems compared— especially with respect to security and auditability—to the paper ballot voting system. In addition, basic demographic and background information was collected.

Procedures. The study began by having participants complete an IRB approved informed consent form. The experimenter read to them study instructions and gave the participants a randomly assigned Republican or Democratic slate so they knew how to vote. Subjects then went on to vote with a paper ballot in the mock election. After voting, the participants were asked to draw a representation or picture that described how the voting system worked—from the moment they were handed a ballot until the election outcome had been determined. They were then asked to verbally describe their mental model and answer follow-up questions that included a query about if the system had any security features, if they did anything unnecessary, or if they were unsure of what they were doing at any point while voting. Next they were asked to both vote and verify that they had voted with one of the three e2e voting methods. The order of system presentation was randomly assigned, and all orders were used. Even though vote verification is an optional step not required to vote with the e2e systems, participants were asked to check on their votes to see how they might go about doing this and if they understood the potential advantages. As with the paper ballot, they were then asked to draw their mental model and were interviewed about the system using the same types of questions. With the e2e systems, though, one additional question was included: "Do you think the system is more secure than the paper ballot voting method?" This question was asked to determine if the participants thought that the system was more secure than a non-e2e voting method. The participants repeated this portion of the procedure until they had voted with all the voting methods. Next they completed a final interview that covered topics like system preferences and how the systems differed with respect to accuracy and security. Last, the participants were debriefed, compensated, and thanked for their time.

Materials. The following is a general summary of study materials. For detailed information, refer to our previous paper [5]. The ballot was composed of 21 races and six propositions. These were the same candidates and propositions used in Rice University's previous voting studies. The Helios voting system ran through Helios' website at https://vote.heliosvoting.org during the summer of 2013. The PaV system was developed by consulting published papers and its website [3, 11–13] and through discussions with Peter Ryan, one of the primary developers. The Rice version of Scantegrity II was based on 2009 Takoma Park printed election materials [e.g., 16, 17], published articles about the system [e.g., 3, 16, 18], and in consultation with both Aleks Essex and Richard Carback who were involved with the development and implementation of the system (A. Essex, personal communication, December 14, 2012; R. Carback, personal communication, December 13, 2012).

2.2 Results

A careful review of the participants' drawn mental models led to the realization that almost every single participant represented on their paper only the steps required to vote, either generally, or with respect to the specific system. Out of the 64 ballots cast in this study's mock election, 58 (91 %) showed or listed out the steps a voter had to execute in order to have a ballot cast and counted in an election that would impact election outcomes. See Fig. 1 for a representative example. As for the subjects who did not focus on the how-to-vote procedures, one participant drew a different symbol for each of the voting systems that expressed their impressions of the system. Another participant drew a diagram of the respective ballot and the order in which it should be completed. But these two participants were anomalies. As a whole, when voters were asked to draw their mental model for the voting system that they just used, they expressed the how-to-steps required to cast a vote that would be later counted. As observed by Norman in his review of mental maps [8], the drawings did not highlight every single step, the models were incomplete as they left parts of the system out all together (e.g., verification procedures), and the drawn models were inaccurate at times (e.g., some voters thought Helios included steps to make sure that they were a human voter, versus a computer system).

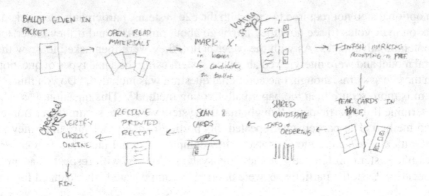

Fig. 1. One example of a drawn mental model for PaV

The mental models produced by hand did not vary a great deal across systems. It was not evident that participants had a deeper or more robust understanding of one system over others, or that participants accurately and fully understood any of the e2e systems. What did change in the mental models associated with each system was the specific steps required to vote, equipment or features unique to a system.

System Security and Accuracy. *Paper Ballots.* Through an examination of both the drawn mental models and the interviews, it was revealed that some participants associated varying degrees of security features with the systems. The listed secure features included a locked ballot box (38 %) that would be tracked through a chain of custody (6 %), manually counting ballots (13 %) because they trusted their neighbors to do the task correctly, automated machine scanning and counting of the ballots (6 %), and/or the fact that a change to the ballot would require physically altering it (6 %). The presence of many of these security concepts, like the chain of custody, highlight that select participants do indeed have a more conceptually complex mental model for paper voting systems as they can explain in detail how the system works beyond rote procedures. However, few participants (6 %) indicated this level of understanding. Overall, it can be inferred from these reported percentages that the majority of participants either associate few security features with paper ballots or did not think they were secure in any sense.

Helios. For Helios, seventy-five percent of the participants recognized that their ballots were encrypted by the system. Many of these subjects associated encryption with keeping their votes secure and/or private. At the same time, about 13 % said they did not really understand what "encryption" meant, but knew it was a security feature. The smart ballot tracker (44 %), voting on a computer (25 %), the ability to audit the ballot (13 %), and/or only being allowed to make one selection per race (6 %) were also mentioned, but at a lower frequency than ballot encryption. While every voter did not present a mental model saturated with features that are proposed to keep elections secure and accurate, it seems that most people did at least realize that there was something different about this system when compared to non-e2e voting methods.

Prêt à Voter. For PaV, the security aspect most often drawn and spoken about was the detachment from the ballot cards and subsequent shredding of the candidates list.

Eighty-eight percent of the participants drew it or mentioned it. Some participants elaborated that this was to keep others from knowing how someone voted. Sixty-three percent of participants expressed that did not really understand why they needed to tear their ballot in half and shred a part of it. Nineteen percent indicated that they did not realize the candidates were randomly ordered for every participant and worried that their ballots could be reconstructed to determine how they voted. Twenty-five percent felt that scanning the ballot cards would help keep an accurate record and count. Seventy-five percent indicated the system issued a printed receipt that could be used to go online to make sure the system counted their vote. Thirty-one percent explained that the verification system showed their actual selections on the ballot card. The take-away for PaV is that some participants recognized the features that kept the system transparent, secure, and accurate, but for the rest of the participants it left them confused and without understanding that the system had potential benefits to voters.

Scantegrity II. Security and accuracy features voters associated with Scantegrity II included the vote selection confirmation sheet (19 %) in which the voters recorded their unique ballot ID (25 %) and codes (69 %), the special marking device used to complete the ballot (44 %), scanning of the ballot (44 %), the storage of the ballots in a locked ballot box (13 %), and/or the booth participants stood in while completing their ballot (25 %). There were points of confusion surrounding Scantegrity II's perceived security features. Thirteen percent did not know why they had to use a special marking device despite a long, block of instructions presented to voters at the top of the ballot. Thirteen percent complained that they could not check their actual votes online, as they were only shown codes. And 6 % said that the ballot did not keep their selections private because anyone could look at it and see which bubbles they filled.

System Security Comparisons. Participants were asked if they thought each e2e system was more secure than the paper voting method. Sixty-nine percent of participants said Helios was more secure. They thought the system was more secure than paper because voting took place on a computer, the ballot was encrypted, and no humans were involved who could make mistakes. As for the 31 % of participants who said Helios was not more secure, they were concerned about hackers, computer glitches, and the fact that they had no idea what the system did with their data.

Sixty-three percent of participants thought PaV was more secure than the paper method. Evidence to support their opinion included automated record keeping and tallying, a candidates list separate from the ballot selections to keep votes anonymous, and online verification. The 38 % of participants who said, "no" cited that the candidates list was in the same order for everyone so votes could be reconstructed, the removal of their candidates list was keeping them from seeing who they voted for when viewing their receipt at home, the system was too complicated, and there was a possibility of hacking since the votes were stored and tallied on a computer.

Half of the participants thought Scantegrity II was more secure than voting with a paper bubble ballot. When using Scantegrity II to vote, a group of participants said there was less chance for human error due to automated ballot scanning and vote tallying. The special marking device and online verification system made it more secure. And one participant did not know what the codes were for, but they made him feel "psychologically secure." The other half of participants did not think Scantegrity II was more secure because of things like not knowing the benefits of the codes or which codes corresponded to which selections.

To summarize the security findings, voters generally recognized security and accuracy features of the system, and these features varied across the four systems. But participants neither thought e2e voting systems were more secure or accurate than the traditional paper ballot—implying there is a gap between the actual integrity of e2e systems and the perceptual integrity of the systems.

Unnecessary Steps and Procedures. Participants were asked if they thought they performed any unnecessary steps or procedures while voting with the systems. This question was asked to determine if there was a procedure or mechanism central to the voting system that they did not understand, or that they felt was superfluous to the core act of voting. The logic was that if they did understand why a novel procedure or feature was implemented, then they would not think it was unnecessary. But if they thought it had no purpose, then it could be inferred that they did not fully or accurately understand how the system worked, or the benefits of it. For Helios, 38 % of participants said there were unnecessary steps, system features, or equipment. Their explanations included being an active participant in the ballot encryption process, being issued a smart ballot tracker, logging into their e-mail account before casting their ballot, and the high number of steps. Seventy-five percent of participants said PaV included unnecessary procedures and components: detaching and shredding the candidates lists from the ballot cards, shredding the candidates lists before being issued a receipt, and the option to verify online. Fifty-six percent of participants felt Scantegrity II had unnecessary elements, which included the codes revealed by the marker, online verification, having to write down so many codes, and the number of steps required to cast a ballot. Many of the cited components across systems were the very features—according to the system developers—that make the systems accurate, transparent, secure, anonymous, and audible. This indicates that the system developers have a different conceptual model for the e2e systems from the actual voters.

Procedural Uncertainty. Participants were asked if they were unsure of what they were doing, or why they were doing it, at any point while using the system to vote or verify their vote. The reason for asking this question was to identify both the aspects of the system that the participants did not understand and the how-to-vote steps that were not clear. Forty-four percent of participants said they were uncertain as to what they were doing while using Helios. Some participants did not know what encryption was and/or were unsure how to encrypt their ballot. Others did not know what to do with their smart ballot tracker, how to print the webpage that showed their smart ballot tracker, or how to cast their completed ballot. Fifty-six percent of subjects said that they were uncertain at some point while using PaV. They did not know if they really should tear their ballot in half and shred a part of it, why they needed to remove this candidates list, of if the page order mattered when they scanned in their ballot cards. The highest uncertainty response rate was for Scantegrity II, with 75 % of participants having said they were unsure. Participants said there were too many directions for the system. They also noted that there were many things they did not know what to do with. Some had trouble operating the single-use scanner, which only required the participant to insert the ballot into it as it then automatically fed the paper through. The majority of these confusion points relate to executing procedures, with the minority dealing with the reason why a step was required to vote or check on their vote.

System Preferences. When asked which of the four methods participants would prefer to use in a real election and why, 38 % preferred Helios. The participants thought Helios was straightforward, fast, secure, familiar since it required the use of computers, and advantageous that it only required voters to figure out how to use one piece of equipment. Yet, there was not evidence to support a difference in proportions of responses across systems, χ^2 (3, N = 16) = 3.5, $p = 0.32$. When asked which of the four methods partic- ipants would least prefer to use in a real election, participants least preferred Scantegrity II, with 38 %. Participants said the system was "annoying," it was hard to read the codes in the bubbles, they could not fix mistakes or change a vote on their ballot once it was marked, the confirmation codes were an annoyance to record and write down correctly, some people knew there should be codes revealed but they could not find them (since they used a pen vs. the special marking device) and hence could not verify their votes online, and they felt that overall the system was confusing. Again, there was no evidence to support a difference in proportions of responses across systems, χ^2 (3, N = 16) = 3.5, $p = 0.32$. The posthoc power analysis revealed the sample size was not large enough to detect effects if they were present, so future research should address this issue.

In many ways, these portions of the participants' mental models, made-up in part by their experiences with them, highlight the best and worse features of all of the systems. Participants want a system that is easy to use, efficient, accurate, and secure. In contrast, subjects wanted to avoid confusing, lengthy procedures, and not knowing how to vote and verify. This alignment is beneficial because it shows that voters recognize strengths in e2e systems like Helios, even if for not for the same reasons the system developers find them to be better.

3 Discussion and Conclusion

The drawn mental models of end-to-end voting systems generated in this study outlined each system's how-to-vote procedures. They did not show any of the inner workings for the systems or explain how they operate. But when interviewed, it became clear that a subset of the participants could describe the presence of system features that made the systems secure, accurate, and transparent—setting them apart from the paper ballot. At the same time, many participants did not view these newer e2e systems as being more secure or accurate than a paper-based voting method. In the mental models, no partici- pant could describe with complete accuracy, or in any detail, how the systems function or why they do what they do. Thus participants have mental models for the e2e voting systems, but they are incomplete, as they do not account for the entire system. In addition, participants' mental models do not significantly change depending on the voting method used and at times are inaccurate.

Perhaps the static nature of e2e mental models is the product of voters relying on a global model for voting in a democratic election, which is then enhanced by the *specific voter's* rote procedures of voting with a specific method. Instead of developing a mental model for how each system works, voters appeared to refer to the larger construct of the voter's voice being heard by going to a polling station to fill out an anonymous ballot, placing it in a secure ballot box, having the votes counted carefully by honest election officials, and then this tally determining the election outcome. They did not describe how the system worked, various system states and responses to user actions, or any of the theories and concepts detailed by the developers in their papers. Embedded within the general voting framework was the "how to cast a ballot" steps for the system at hand. If this theory holds true in future studies, it might also account for inaccuracies expressed in the mental models, such as leaving entire steps out, which make the mental model more generic. It would also explain why voters made errors like trying to cast a vote with PaV and Scantegrity II by placing a ballot in the ballot box, instead of first scanning it [5].

The nature of the mental models found in this study are also likely a product of many participants' only exposure to these e2e systems being this study. The subjects read lengthy instructions telling them how to vote with a method, then they voted with the system by completing a series of steps using the provided equipment. They were never told what was special about the systems, nor did they likely have any conceptual framework for the e2e systems. Therefore, it is unsurprising that the participants could not do anything else but describe what they did to vote and the novel features and procedures that they encountered. Without access to the researchers' concepts behind the systems, there was no way for the participants to articulate these concepts as they were not explicitly apparent during system use.

Importantly, this is *not* a limitation to this study. Voters do not generally get to choose what kind of system they use to vote (except that they may be able to choose to either vote by mail or use the voting method at their designated polling station). As such, voters in real elections would encounter the same predicament as the participants in this test, and they would likely end up with similar mental models for the system they just used. This disconnect must always be considered when forming assumptions about what the voters know about the systems and how they view them.

Future research is required to determine how the participants' mental models can be enhanced or altered to avoid moments of confusion, uncertainty, and negative affect, and in turn make the systems trustworthy and truly transparent. One area for further exploration might be to examine whether the implementation of cues to indicate the presence of a specific security feature, and an inline explanation of why that feature exists, helps voters form a better, more complete model without causing them to slow down. For example, if Helios tells voters not only that their ballot is encrypted, but in a sentence or two why encryption is important, then perhaps users might not feel uncertain about the benefit of encrypting their ballot. Or if Scantegrity II indicated to voters that each code is unique, associated with the selections on their particular ballot (and no other), and used to keep their votes completely private yet trackable, then perhaps voters will recognize their value. In turn, these enhanced mental models might then lead to higher usability scores and better user performance on these systems.

While it would be wonderful to be able to make certain that voters understand a system that they use to vote in order to increase their confidence in the voting method and recognize it as an improvement over other methods, voters should not be required to have a comprehensive, detailed mental model for a system in order to use it successfully. Think about the telephone; almost every person can pick up a landline and dial a phone number. Few people can probably describe the operational nature of the phone system (Kieras and Bovair [17]). Similarly, voters just need to be able to get through the how-to-vote sequence that allows them to easily cast a ballot as they intend. They should not have to understand the system, or think it is accurate and secure, to be able to cast a vote that is counted.

One limitation of this research study on voters' mental models of e2e systems is that there are many sources of potential bias introduced into the models. The mental models presented in this paper are the authors' conceptualization of these participants' mental models [8]. Consequently, the voters' interpretations are directly impacted by the training, background, and approach that was used to study the problem. The models were also impacted by the methods used to collect the models because participants might not be able to fully express their mental model through any singular method. These are limitations that every mental model study faces, yet there is still utility in studying them [17].

Another limitation with the study is the sample size and how the participants were recruited. The sample size is small, and is not fully representative of the population of U.S. voters since half of the subjects were Rice University students. Nevertheless, even the students are real voters, and the collected data offer a glimpse into how people might think about the voting systems.

In conclusion, voters do not have comprehensive, conceptual mental models for any of the tested voting systems, including paper ballots. However, they do have mental models that highlight the steps required to vote in order for their voice to be heard in an election, some unique system-specific features, and principles the general democratic voting process. While this study is not the final word on the matter, it does provide a glimpse into how voters are actually thinking about the systems as opposed to how others expect them to think about e2e voting methods. This research should also serve as a friendly reminder to all system developers to collect data from actual system users, rather than make assumptions about how those users will think about and use the system.

Acknowledgements.   This research has been supported in part by NSF award CNS-1049723. We would also like to thank Molly Ahn for assisting with the study.

References

1. Nielsen, J.: Mental Models. http://www.nngroup.com/articles/mental-models/
2. Adida, B.: Helios: Web-based open-audit voting. In: USENIX Security Symposium, pp. 335–348 (2008)
3. Ryan, P.Y.A., Bismark, D., Heather, J., Schneider, S., Xia, Z.: Prêt à voter: a voter-verifiable voting system. IEEE Trans. Inf. Forensics Secur. **4**, 662–673 (2009)
4. Chaum, D., Essex, A., Carback, R., Clark, J., Popoveniuc, S., Sherman, A., Vora, P.: Scantegrity: End-to-end voter-verifiable optical-scan voting. IEEE Secur. Priv. **6**, 40–46 (2008)

5. Acemyan, C.Z., Kortum, P., Byrne, M.D., Wallach, D.S.: Usability of voter verifiable, end-to-end voting systems: baseline data for Helios, Prêt à Voter, and Scantegrity II. USENIX J. Elect. Technol. Syst. **2**, 26–56 (2014)
6. Winckler, M., Bernhaupt, R., Palanque, P., Lundin, D., Leach, K., Ryan, P., Alberdi, E., Strigini, L.: Assessing the usability of open verifiable e-voting systems: a trial with the system Prêt à voter. In: Proceedings of ICEGOV 2009. pp. 281–296 (2009)
7. Rouse, W.B., Morris, N.M.: On looking into the black box: Prospects and limits in the search for mental models. Psychol. Bull. **100**, 349–363 (1986)
8. Norman, D.A.: Some observationson mental models. In: Gentner, D., Stevens, A.L. (eds.) Mental Models, pp. 7–14. Lawrence Erlbaum Associates, Hillsdale (1983)
9. Rasmussen, J.: On the structure of knowledge: a morphology of mental models in a man-machine system context. Risø National Laboratory, Risø (1979)
10. Byrne, M., Greene, K., Everett, S.: Usability of voting systems: Baseline data for paper, punch cards, and lever machines. In: Proceedings of the SIGCHI Conference on Human Factors in Computing Systems, pp. 171–180, ACM (2007)
11. Lundin, D., Ryan, P.Y.: Human readable paper verification of Prêt à voter. In: Jajodia, S., Lopez, J. (eds.) ESORICS 2008. LNCS, vol. 5283, pp. 379–395. Springer, Heidelberg (2008)
12. Ryan, P.Y., Peacock, T.: A threat analysis of Prêt à voter. In: Chaum, D., Jakobsson, M., Rivest, R.L., Ryan, P.Y., Benaloh, J., Kutylowski, M., Adida, B. (eds.) Towards Trustworthy Elections, New Directions in Electronic Voting. LNCS, vol. 6000, pp. 200–215. Springer, Heidelberg (2010)
13. Ryan, P.Y., Schneider, S.A.: Prêt à voter with re-encryption mixes. In: Gollmann, D., Meier, J., Sabelfeld, A. (eds.) ESORICS 2006. LNCS, vol. 4189, pp. 313–326. Springer, Heidelberg (2006)
14. Carback, R., Chaum, D., Clark, J., Conway, J., Essex, A., Herrnson, P., Mayberry, T., Popoveniuc, S., Rivest, R.L., Shen, E., Sherman, A., Vora, P.L.: Scantegrity II municipal election at Takoma Park: the first E2E binding governmental election with ballot privacy. In: Proceedings of the 19th USENIX Security Symposium (2010)
15. The City of Takoma Park Maryland. http://www.takomaparkmd.gov
16. Sherman, A.T., Carback, R., Chaum, D., Clark, J., Essex, A., Herrnson, P.S., Mayberry, T., Popoveniuc, S., Rivest, R.L., Shen, E., Sinha, B., Vora, P.: Scantegrity mock election at Takoma Park. In: Proceedings of the NIST Workshop on End-to-end Voting Systems, pp. 45–61 (2009)
17. Kieras, D.E., Bovair, S.: The role of a mental model in learning to operate a device. Cogn. Sci. **8**, 255–273 (1984)

Messaging Activity Reconstruction
with Sentiment Polarity Identification

Panagiotis Andriotis[✉] and George Oikonomou

University of Bristol, Merchant Venturers Building, Woodland Road, Clifton,
Bristol BS8 1UB, UK
{p.andriotis,g.oikonomou}@bristol.ac.uk

Abstract. Sentiment Analysis aims to extract information related to
the emotional state of the person that produced a text document and also
describe the sentiment polarity of the short or long message. This kind
of information might be useful to a forensic analyst because it provides
indications about the psychological state of the person under investigation at a given time. In this paper we use machine-learning algorithms to
classify short texts (SMS), which could be found in the internal memory
of a smartphone and extract the mood of the person that sent them. The
basic goal of our method is to achieve low False Positive Rates. Moreover, we present two visualization schemes with the intention to provide
the ability to digital forensic analysts to see graphical representations of
the messaging activity of their suspects and therefore focus on specific
areas of interest reducing their workload.

Keywords: Smartphone · Forensics · Text-mining · Short-text
messages

1 Introduction

This is without a doubt the era of remarkable achievements in the area of mobile
communications. Smartphones dominate the market and people have the choice
to purchase mobile devices from a wide range of manufacturers. Those devices
are primary used for texting, messaging, chatting and connecting to the Internet.
These actions leave traces in the internal memory of the phones, which can be
used as evidence in forensic investigations. The evidence acquisition should be
performed by a specialist, but it does not require very complicated methods, as
stated in [2]. Open source tools can be used to conduct a sound investigation
without any cost, when our target phone is running under the Android operating
system [2]. The major sources of evidence are text, sound and images stored
usually in SQLite databases, in the cache of the device or in emulated and
external storage media.

Considering the examination of textual data, a more traditional approach
is currently used during an investigation, utilising tools like 'grep', 'strings' or
'xxd' to extract information out of text. However, Text Mining and Natural

© Springer International Publishing Switzerland 2015
T. Tryfonas and I. Askoxylakis (Eds.): HAS 2015, LNCS 9190, pp. 475–486, 2015.
DOI: 10.1007/978-3-319-20376-8_42

Language Processing can offer automated solutions and perform various tasks on our evidence, such as text classification. Sentiment Analysis for example is a research area that became very popular nowadays because of the proliferation of social media and the need to handle 'big data' which are available in the Internet. Micro blogging services like Twitter have been used as sources (corpora) of textual information [17]. The similarity between a Twitter post (tweet) and a Short Message Service (SMS) text has been evaluated in [3]. Additionally, Task 2 at the "SemEval-2013: Semantic Evaluation Exercises"[1] competition was dedicated to Sentiment Analysis on Twitter data and a special category included SMS too. The idea was to train classifiers with Twitter data and test their Sentiment Analysis ability on SMS datasets. The concept behind this approach is that, as researchers, we do not have access to large SMS datasets because of privacy and legal issues; hence we can train classifiers using public data which present structural similarities with the short text messages we use in our private communication with other people.

In this paper we propose our methodology to classify SMS (and other short texts such as chatting logs) found in the internal memory of a smartphone considering their emotional polarity. The F-score our classifier achieves approaches the accuracy the current state-of-the-art systems [19] provide, but it needs less computing power. Furthermore, our approach aims to decrease False Positive Rates in order to provide more reliable results during the forensic analysis. Another contribution of this study is the proposal of two different visualization schemes that reconstruct the actual messaging activity of the phone. They focus on the emotional polarity of the exchanged messages and propose novel methods to merge Digital Forensics with Text Mining.

2   Related Work

The basic task for a Sentiment Analysis (or Opinion Mining) algorithm is to separate text documents in two (or three) classes; positive, negative (and neutral). Prior work presents how we can use various lexicons and tokenize documents in order to separate words related to sentiment classes [22]. Another approach to solve the problem of opinion mining is the use of Machine-Learning methods [20]. Naïve Bayes, Support Vector Machines (SVM) and Maximum Entropy are among the most popular algorithms used for sentiment categorization. These algorithms can be amplified by other techniques like lexical normalization [14] or distant supervision [21] to make a more robust classification scheme. Sentiment analysis is a concept, which can be applied to various aspects of our lives. At the past, handcrafted lexicons were utilized to create methods to perform opinion mining on market stocks [8]. Additionally, a holistic approach that used multiple opinion words to review various products was presented in [9]. Other systems are able to provide real-time evaluation of the public sentiment for electoral candidates [23].

---

[1] http://www.cs.york.ac.uk/semeval-2013/ (and its successor on 2014).

Multinomial Naïve Bayes (MNB) and SVM were used in [18] to evaluate the hypothesis that sentiment analysis is easier on short texts than on larger documents. The authors achieved an accuracy of 74.85 % for binary classification and concluded that a unigram feature representation is sufficient for short texts. Sentiment analysis on micro blogs was also the topic of [6]. In [22], Taboada et al. used lexicons and their word valence and concluded that sentiment analysis on blog postings and video games reviews can be robust and accurate. We mentioned previously that Twitter posts are widely used as corpora [17] because they are public. Thus we do not need any special permission to test our algorithms on them. However, automated approaches for Twitter feeds (and micro blogging data in general) might be problematic because the language we are using on such media contains non-standard (elongated or abbreviated) words and unusual vocabulary [15]. Despite these variations, tweets are quite similar to SMS [15] and therefore we can use them to simulate SMS for our research.

Text mining in Digital Forensics was basically used to extract linguistic patterns from emails and perform user-profiling [10]. Other research papers focus on the characteristics that constitute the texting language, which is commonly used in mobile devices and messengers [7]. Despite the fact that we have seen studies aiming to use text mining for various purposes, like text searching optimization [5], there is a limited number of technical papers targeting sentiment analysis on SMS. An interesting study on the public sentiment extracted by SMS content is presented in [24]. A recent sentiment analysis competition (Task 2: SemEval-2013) among academics used Twitter posts to train the contestants' classifiers and a SMS dataset to test the accuracy they could achieve. The best team, which created a complex classifier, reached an accuracy of 0.69. The same concept was applied in [3] but in this context the authors did not train any model for the SMS classification. They were testing a bag-of-words approach and how efficient this simplified method could be to categorize SMS. The algorithm was highly depending on the lexicon that was used and the classification for negative messages was not competitive enough. However, this was the first attempt to use Text Mining in Digital Forensics and the outcome of this work was a system able to produce the 'Sentiment View timeline'.

3   Methodology and Evaluation

In order to provide a framework that will decrease some of the problems occured in previous work (for example the poor classification results for negative messages) we had to decide which is the most efficient classifier for our task. First we trained three classifiers using an open source data mining program called 'Weka' [13]. The software provides a graphical user interface and it can perform numerous machine learning tasks. We trained three different classifiers: Naïve Bayes Multinomial (MNB), the default SVN (Sequential Minimal Optimization: SMO Polykernel) and the Maximum Entropy classifier called 'Logistic'. In order to work with text in Weka we have to utilize the FilteredClassifier module. This module aggregates the classifier functionality but first it uses a filter to pre-process the documents. Our documents (short texts) were transformed to vectors with the unsupervised filter StringToWordVector. In our experiments we filtered the documents using the LovinsStemmer (described in [16]) and the default tokenizer. However, we removed the symbols '()' from the delimiter list to capture any emoticon that is present in the text.

We chose popular datasets to train and test our algorithms. The first corpus we used to train the classifiers came from the Sentiment140 (SENT140) dataset [12] that consists of 1.6 million Twitter feeds (classified as positive, negative and neutral). We noticed that the classification scheme used to distribute tweets contained in the SENT140 set was not very accurate and a lot of short texts were distributed in the wrong class. For this reason, we manually classified a random set of tweets (2280) in three classes: neutral, positive and negative. This set was enriched by previous positive and negative lexicons [3] and created the final training data consisted of approximately 5000 documents. The test dataset consisted of 3075 randomly picked SMS from a SMS Corpus [1], initially used for spam filtering. We manually classified these short texts into three classes (neutral, positive, negative).

The basic assumption we made before we train and evaluate our classifiers is that the forensic analysis should be primarily focused on identifying positive and negative mood trends between entities that exist in the smartphone ecosystem. For this reason, during classification and evaluation, we assumed that there exist two main classes. One superclass contained positive and neutral messages and one class contained negative messages.

Table 1. Correctly and incorrectly classified instances of Twitter feeds

Classifier	Correctly classified	Incorrectly classified
MNB	78.5471 %	21.4529 %
SVM	76.3458 %	23.6542 %
MaxEnt	70.9826 %	29.0174 %

Table 2. Training results using Twitter feeds

Classifier	Class	TP rate	FP rate	Precision	Recall	F-measure	ROC area
MNB	Negative	0.877	0.318	0.756	0.877	0.812	0.849
	Positive	0.682	0.123	0.832	0.682	0.75	0.849
	Weighted avg.	0.785	0.226	0.792	0.785	0.783	0.849
SVM	Negative	0.883	0.371	0.728	0.883	0.798	0.756
	Positive	0.629	0.117	0.827	0.629	0.715	0.756
	Weighted avg.	0.763	0.251	0.775	0.763	0.759	0.756
MaxEnt	Negative	0.83	0.423	0.688	0.83	0.752	0.689
	Positive	0.575	0.164	0.757	0.575	0.653	0.697
	Weighted avg.	0.71	0.301	0.721	0.71	0.706	0.693

We trained the classifiers taken into account the aforementioned assumption. The numbers of correctly and incorrectly classified instances are shown in Table 1 and the results about the classifiers' accuracy are shown at Table 2. The Naïve Bayes classifier (MNB) seems to achieve better accuracy on the training data since more than 78.5 % of the dataset was correctly classified and the weighted ROC area was 0.849. The SVM model also produces satisfying results but the weighted average rates are not very competitive compared to the MNB model. Table 2 suggests that the more appropriate model for our type of documents is the MNB classifier.

Furthermore, we evaluated the classifiers on our SMS dataset. The numbers of correctly and incorrectly classified instances are shown in Table 3 and the results about the classifiers' accuracy are shown in Table 4. We can see that the MNB classifier was able to correctly classify approximately 74.29 % of the dataset. The weighted average of the True Positive Rate (TP) was 0.743 and the False Positive Rate (FP) was 0.358. The other classifiers did not achieve better results on the test set. However, the SVM model seems to perform in a similar manner compared to the MNB model.

A comparison between previous results (presented in [3]) and the outcome of the supervised classifiers shows that the MNB model achieves a better TP Rate on the negative messages. Also the FP Rate is quite low (0.186) suggesting that the NB classifier is better than the bag-of-words approach when we want to classify SMS messages that represent negative emotions. For the SMS with positive emotional fingerprint we had a good TR Rate but the FP Rate was quite

Table 3. Correctly and incorrectly classified instances of the SMS dataset

Classifier	Correctly classified	Incorrectly classified
MNB	74.2878 %	25.7152 %
SVM	72.2367 %	27.7633 %
MaxEnt	61.3134 %	38.6866 %

Table 4. Evaluation results on the SMS dataset

Classifier	Class	TP rate	FP rate	Precision	Recall	F-measure	ROC area
MNB	Negative	0.57	0.186	0.56	0.57	0.565	0.769
	Positive	0.814	0.43	0.821	0.814	0.817	0.769
	Weighted avg.	0.743	0.358	0.744	0.743	0.744	0.769
SVM	Negative	0.58	0.219	0.524	0.58	0.551	0.681
	Positive	0.781	0.42	0.818	0.781	0.799	0.681
	Weighted avg.	0.722	0.361	0.732	0.722	0.726	0.681
MaxEnt	Negative	0.504	0.341	0.38	0.504	0.433	0.581
	Positive	0.658	0.472	0.771	0.658	0.71	0.611
	Weighted avg.	0.613	0.433	0.657	0.613	0.629	0.602

high. We believe that this feature appeared because we assumed that neutral messages belong to the same superclass with positive messages. For this reason we propose our hybrid classifier that will deal with the problem of classifying neutral and positive messages in a better and more accurate way.

Our hybrid approach aims to propose a methodology that will be able to correctly classify as many SMS as possible efficiently and accurately. This means that we intend to reduce the False Positives the MNB classifier produces in order to make our scheme more robust and less error-prone. As stated in Sect. 2, the team that managed to win the SemEval-2013 competition using a Twitter dataset to train a classifier and a SMS dataset to test it, reached an average F-score of approximately 0.69. Also, recent results from experiments that were testing the sentiment polarity of the same SMS dataset (using a simple bag-of-words approach) [3] showed that the task of identifying negative messages was even more difficult (0.49 TP Rate and 0.29 FP Rate on the negative messages). The MNB classifier in our current experiments achieved a better TP Rate on negative messages (0.57 as shown in Table 2) and a low FP Rate (0.186). However, the MNB classifier cannot distinguish positive and neutral messages because it is trained to classify only two major classes (a 'positive' superclass that contains positive and neutral messages and a negative class which contains negative messages).

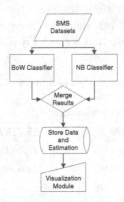

Fig. 1. Hybrid classification methodology

The scheme described in Fig. 1 is a system that merges the advantages of our MNB and the bag-of-words (BoW) classifiers. First, we have to input the SMS database (or any SQLite database that contains information from messaging applications). Android smartphones for example, store this information in the data partition of their internal memory. In more details, the file our system should parse is the mmssms.db SQLite database from the folder /data/com.android.providers.telephony/databases and especially the 'SMS' table which consists of attributes describing who sent the message to whom, which is the actual message, when the transaction happened and other relevant information.

The set of short text messages will then be fed to our two classifiers, the bag-of-words (BoW) and the Naïve Bayes (MNB) schemes for classification. BoW will distribute them in three classes (neutral, positive, negative) and NB will classify the messages in two classes (a positive superclass and a negative). After this phase has been completed the results will be passed to the merging algorithm for the final classification of each message. The algorithm classifies as negative those messages that were predicted as negative by the MNB classifier. Those messages that were predicted as positive by the MNB classifier are crosschecked with the output of the second classifier (BoW). If BoW indicates that the message is negative, our system flags the SMS as neutral. If BoW indicates the message as positive then we classify it as positive and, finally, if BoW indicates the message is neutral, we classify it as neutral. Then, the estimations and the messages are stored in a database which will be the source that will feed the visualization module (we will describe it in Sect. 4) to depict the mood trends among the various entities that exist in the SMS database of the smartphone.

Table 5 presents the evaluation of the classification scheme shown in Fig. 1. The basic feature we should underline is that our approach achieves low FP Rates in the negative and the positive messages (0.186 and 0.164 respectively). Also, approximately 60 % of the whole set will be successfully classified in the appropriate class providing a fairly clear indication of the emotional trends among people on a given time. Finally, our methodology does not require large training steps and the results approximate those that were achieved by very complex classifiers [19] (for instance the F-score on the positive set is 0.679). These setups were heavily based on very detailed data pre-processing steps. The extracted information from our classifier can be visualized using the methods we present at Sect. 4 in order to reconstruct the emotional fingerprint that the exchange of short texts produces.

Table 5. Evaluation results for the hybrid system on the SMS dataset

Class	TP rate	FP rate	F-measure
Positive	0.599	0.164	0.679
Neutral	0.57	0.281	0.615
Negative	0.57	0.186	0.565

4 Visualization Module

In this Section we discuss our concept to visualize the extracted information that depict possible mood alterations and relations between the people interacting with the person that owns the smartphone we analyze. The idea is to create a dynamic graph that reconstructs all the activity stored in a database like the mmssms.db which holds the history for short texts messaging. People that exchanged messages with the person under investigation will represent the nodes of the graph and each message will be the action-edge that connects those entities. In our approach we are using three colours to represent mood trends extracted by the SMS; blue for neutral, green for positive and red for negative messages. For example, if a person A sent a message to a person B (expressing a positive emotion) on a specific time T, then the graph will show two nodes A and B linked with a green arrow starting from A towards B. If another interaction between the two parties takes place again, a new arrow with a new colour will link the two nodes. This time the edge will be shown thicker to underline the fact that these two entities have frequent communication and its colour will imply the emotional fingerprint of the specific interaction.

In addition, the graph will be dynamic, which means that a node will not be shown until the first interaction happens. However, when the interaction takes place, its representative edge can be shown until the final completion of the graph. This attribute will make the graph able to illustrate all interactions that happened in a given time scope. Furthermore, the forensic analyst will be able to see a graphical representation of activities that might affect the mood of persons involved in a case.

We are using the open source tool 'Gephi' [4] to produce the visualizations. This is a platform which accepts various file formats as inputs but we chose to utilize gexf files in our visualization module. We made this decision because gexf format is easy to understand and produce (it is an xml file) and according to the official Gephi documentation provides better functionality. The visualization module we present here is able to produce two types of data graphical representations. The first one is the aforementioned 'dynamic graph view' that reconstructs the SMS activity and it is focused on the expressed emotions via the exchanged messages. The second approach we will present is the 'heat map view'. This type of visualization will provide a convenient and overall view of the predominant mood extracted by exchanged messages between two parties. It is basically a colourful grid which illustrates the emotional fingerprint of the exchanged messages (between two entities) within a month or within a broader period of time.

4.1 Dynamic Graph View

The concept behind the specific visualization scheme is to construct an animated representation of actions between entities that interact in the singular ecosystem defined by the smartphone. Hence, forensic analysts who investigate a case and have seized a smartphone as evidence have the choice to select the time scope of their examination. For this reason the proposed scheme (in order to produce the visualization) requires from the analyst to input the start time (ST) and the end time (ET) of the actions that will be reconstructed. The conceptual design is further discussed at the rest of this subsection.

We assume that our data (and the extracted mood class) are stored in the database described in Fig. 1 and the analyst has set the ST and ET. Thus, each row in our database contains a 'copy' of the rows of the 'SMS' table (located in the original mmssms.db) and also the extracted emotion polarity; -1 for negative, 0 for neutral and 1 for positive. Such a row contains attributes like

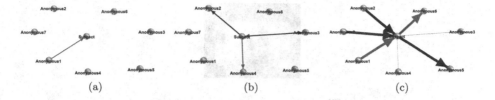

(a)   (b)   (c)

Fig. 2. Messaging activity graphical representation

'address' (the telephone number interacting with the examined phone), 'date'
(a timestamp describing when the transaction happened), 'type' (1: received
and 2: sent), 'body' (the short text) and the extracted 'emotion'. The algorithm
which creates the gexf file requires a double pass from this database. During the
first pass we will query the database to get rows related to the time scope of our
investigation (ST until ET). Furthermore, the first pass will store information (in
a temporary storage area) about the entities that interact with the smartphone.
These entities will be written in the gexf file as the nodes of the graph. If the
algorithm sees a new entity interacting with the phone, the 'date' attribute will
be written in the gexf file as the 'start' attribute of the given node. The 'end'
attribute will always be the ET. During the second pass the algorithm parses
again the database and creates the edges. Each row in the database is a new
edge and the timestamp which describes when the action happened will be the
'start' attribute of the edge. The 'end' attribute again is the ET. If the 'emotion'
attribute is −1, the edge will be coloured red. If the 'emotion' is 0, the edge will
be blue and if it is 1 the edge will be shown as green.

Figure 2 demonstrates how the messaging activity is reconstructed in Gephi
(after our gexf file has been loaded) and it also highlights the mood fingerprints
of the exchanged SMS. For this illustration we replaced messages from an original
mmssms.db with random SMS from our testing dataset (Sect. 3) and we used the
timeline feature of Gephi. We should also underline that we are using Gephi in
this study just to present the concept of the mood and messaging activity reconstruction. Its current version (0.8) is not able to handle multigraphs but, according to the official documentation, the next version (0.9) will be able to present
such complex graphs. However, other tools like GraphViz [11] can produce multi-
graph visualizations and the concept can be easily applied to files supported by
the specific open source project. Figure 2 shows three different screenshots from
the beginning towards the end of the created timeline from Gephi.

4.2   Heat Map View

The second visualization concept we propose in this study is the 'Sentiment
Heat Map view'. This graphical representation of the extracted mood is initially
designed to depict interactions between two entities within a timeframe of a
month. We assume we want to see the mood fingerprints of exchanged messages
existing in the mmssms.db between the person under investigation and someone
found in the smartphone's contact list. Thus, the queries on the database seen

Fig. 3. Sentiment heat map view

in Fig. 1 will return tuples only for those two entities within a period of a month (or so). The output is a coloured grid (heat map) formatted as a calendar. Each day of the calendar is shown as a square on the grid; if the exchanged message emits negative mood it will be shown as a red square. The positive mood is depicted with light green, the neutral mood with dark green and if on a given day there is no message, the square will be coloured black. (We use Matlab in this illustration.)

In Fig. 3 we present the 'heat map view' produced for a hypothetical scenario which shows the extracted mood from messages that were sent FROM the person under investigation TO a person from the smartphone's contact list. For clarity we assume that only one message (or none) was sent each day on a specific month. If more than one message we exchanged, the scheme can be further extended either by calculating the overall sentiment valence of all the exchanged messages during a day or by recursively dissecting each square (that represents a day) in smaller coloured squares.

The visualization can be produced either by using open source tools like Octave (utilising the command 'imagesc(A)') or other commercial tools like Matlab (with the command 'HeatMap(A)'). In both cases A is a matrix that represents the calendar. If we keep the format of A intact and if we change the numbers 1, 2, ..., 31 with other numbers that represent the mood we will be able to see a calendar like the one shown in Fig. 3. Of course, this is a simplified illustration of the concept and it does not include cases where on the same day we had more than one 'sent' messages. However, we can further extend the idea as discussed in the previous paragraph to include these cases in the future.

5   Conclusions and Future Work

In this study we investigated the impact of machine-learning algorithms trained on Twitter posts to classify SMS according to their sentiment polarity. We manually labelled tweets and texts in three categories (neutral, negative, positive) and tested the efficiency of 3 training models (MNB, SVM, MaxEnt). We evaluated the models on the SMS test set and concluded that MNB works better on these short texts and it is faster and more accurate than the other classifiers. Furthermore, we proposed a classification scheme in order to decrease the FP Rate the MNB classifier produced on negative messages. We believe that during a forensic investigation we would be more interested in a method that produces less erroneous estimations. Thus, our scheme is competitive against the current state-of-the-art systems. These systems use complex feature vectors resulting to a costly consumption of memory, time and processing power.

Additionally, we proposed two visualization approaches to provide the opportunity to show a reconstructed animated representation of the messaging activity illustrating the extracted mood fingerprints. The 'dynamic graph view' provides a generic insight to the messaging activity including all the SMS that were sent (and received) from a smartphone. The 'heat map view' is a concise solution that focuses on two specific entities and provides an automated calendar-like projection of emotions that occurred during the period of a month. These two modules are designed to reduce the workload of an analyst but they cannot eventually be used as evidence, because they still remain a construction. However, in this study we bring together two research areas (Natural Language Processing and Digital Forensics) aiming to present methods in order to create automated and accurate representations of evidence existing in smartphones, tablets or wearable devices.

Despite the low FP Rates we achieved on positive and negative SMS in our set, there is still space for improvements, especially on the neutral message classification. Future work will focus on the improvement of our feature selection. We also believe that the input of an SMS subset in the training procedure will provide better F-scores and increase the system's accuracy. Furthermore, the proposed visualization schemata can be extended to cover more that one smartphones which are seized in a specific case. A mapping of the sentiment in a closed environment (for example when forensic analysts examine multiple corporate phones) is also a direction for further work.

References

1. Almeida, T.A., Maria Gomez, J., Yamakami, A.: Contributions to the study of SMS spam filtering: new collection and results. In: DOCENG 2011: Proceedings of the 2011 ACM Symposium on Document Engineering, pp. 259–262, 1515 BROADWAY, New York, NY 10036–9998, USA (2011)
2. Andriotis, P., Oikonomou, G., Tryfonas, T.: Forensic analysis of wireless networking evidence of android smartphones. In: 2012 IEEE International Workshop on Information Forensics and Security (WIFS) pp. 109–114, 345 E 47th St, New York, NY 10017, USA (2012)
3. Andriotis, P., Takasu, A., Tryfonas, T.: Smartphone message sentiment analysis. In: Peterson, G., Shenoi, S. (eds.) Advances in Digital Forensics X. IFIP Advances in Information and Communication Technology, vol. 433, pp. 253–265. Springer, Heidelberg (2014). doi:10.1007/978-3-662-44952-3_17
4. Bastian, M., Heymann, S., Jacomy, M.: Gephi: an open source software for exploring and manipulating networks. In: ICWSM, pp. 361–362 (2009)
5. Beebe, N.L., Clark, J.G.: Digital forensic text string searching: improving information retrieval effectiveness by thematically clustering search results. Digit. Invest. 4(1), S49–S54 (2007)
6. Bermingham, A., Smeaton, A.F.: Classifying sentiment in microblogs: is brevity an advantage? In: Proceedings of the 19th ACM International Conference on Information and Knowledge Management, pp. 1833–1836. ACM (2010)

7. Choudhury, M., Saraf, R., Jain, V., Mukherjee, A., Sarkar, S., Basu, A.: Investigation and modeling of the structure of texting language. Int. J. Doc. Anal. Recogn. **10**(3–4), 157–174 (2007)
8. Das, S.R., Chen, M.Y.: Yahoo! for Amazon: sentiment extraction from small talk on the web. Manage. Sci. **53**(9), 1375–1388 (2007)
9. Ding, X., Liu, B., Yu, P.S.: A holistic lexicon-based approach to opinion mining. In: Proceedings of the 2008 International Conference on Web Search and Data Mining, pp. 231–240. ACM (2008)
10. Estival, D., Gaustad, T., Pham, S.B., Radford, W., Hutchinson, B.: Author profiling for english emails. In: Proceedings of the 10th Conference of the Pacific Association for Computational Linguistics, pp. 263–272 (2007)
11. Gansner, E., North, S.: An open graph visualization system and its applications to software engineering. Softw.-Pract. Experience **30**(11), 1203–1233 (2000)
12. Go, A., Bhayani, R., Huang, L.: Twitter sentiment classification using distant supervision. CS224N Proj. R. **657**, 1–12 (2009)
13. Hall, M., Frank, E., Holmes, G., Pfahringer, B., Reutemann, P., Witten, I.H.: The weka data mining software: an update. ACM SIGKDD Explor. Newsl. **11**(1), 10–18 (2009)
14. Han, B., Cook, P., Baldwin, T.: Lexical normalization for social media text. ACM Trans. Intell. Syst. Tech. **4**(1), 5 (2013)
15. Laboreiro, G., Sarmento, L., Teixeira, J., Oliveira, E.: Tokenizing micro-blogging messages using a text classification approach. In: Proceedings of the Fourth Workshop on Analytics for Noisy Unstructured Text Data, pp. 81–88. ACM (2010)
16. Lovins, J.B.: Development of a Stemming Algorithm. MIT Information Processing Group, Electronic Systems Laboratory, Cambridge (1968)
17. Martinez-Camara, E., Teresa Martin-Valdivia, M., Alfonso Urena-Lopez, L., Montejo-Raez, A.: Sentiment analysis in Twitter. Nat. Lang. Eng. **20**(1), 1–28 (2014)
18. Melville, P., Gryc, W., Lawrence, R.D.: Sentiment analysis of blogs by combining lexical knowledge with text classification. In: KDD-09: 15th ACM SIGKDD Conference on Knowledge Discovery and Data Mining, pp. 1275–1283, 1515 Broadway, New York, NY 10036–9998, USA (2009)
19. Mohammad, S.M., Kiritchenko, S., Zhu, X.: NRC-canada: building the state-of-the-art in sentiment analysis of tweets. In: Proceedings of the Seventh International Workshop on Semantic Evaluation Exercises (SemEval-2013), Atlanta, Georgia, USA, June 2013
20. Pang, B., Lee, L.: Opinion mining and sentiment analysis. Found. Trends Inf. Retrieval **2**(1–2), 1–135 (2008)
21. Suttles, J., Ide, N.: Distant supervision for emotion classification with discrete binary values. In: Gelbukh, A. (ed.) CICLing 2013, Part II. LNCS, vol. 7817, pp. 121–136. Springer, Heidelberg (2013)
22. Taboada, M., Brooke, J., Tofiloski, M., Voll, K., Stede, M.: Lexicon-based methods for sentiment analysis. Comput. Linguist. **37**(2), 267–307 (2011)
23. Wang, H., Can, D., Kazemzadeh, A., Bar, F., Narayanan, S.: A system for real-time twitter sentiment analysis of 2012 US presidential election cycle. In: Proceedings of the ACL 2012 System Demonstrations, pp. 115–120. Association for Computational Linguistics (2012)
24. Wang, Z., Zhai, L., Ma, Y., Li, Y.: Analysis of public sentiment based on SMS content. In: Yuan, Y., Wu, X., Lu, Y. (eds.) ISCTCS 2012. CCIS, vol. 320, pp. 637–643. Springer, Heidelberg (2013)

Televoting: Secure, Overseas Voting

Chris S. Crawford[✉], Naja Mack, Wanda Eugene,
and Juan E. Gilbert

Department of Computer and Information Science and Engineering,
432 Newell Drive, Gainesville, FL 32611, USA
{chrisscrawford,najamac,weugene,juan}@ufl.edu

Abstract. Because many members of the armed services are overseas during elections, they are unable to cast their ballot in person. Although the Uniformed and Overseas Citizens Absentee Voting Act (UOCAVA) gives soldiers located overseas the right to mail in absentee ballots, they are often left uncounted due to issues with shipping. This paper presents Televoting, an approach to Internet voting (E-Voting) modeled after Telemedicine systems that utilizes video communication technology. Televoting attempts to address security issues that have plagued previous E-Voting platforms by producing a paper ballot instead of storing votes on a server. This paper discusses the system design and the voting process users experience when using Televoting.

Keywords: Televoting · E-Voting · Remote voting · Security · Privacy

1 Introduction

Voting is a tenant of Democracy and a fundamental right afforded to every American citizen. While it is the expectation of every voter that their vote will be counted, there are instances when this expectation is not met. Because many members of the armed services are away from their local polling place during election cycles, they are unable to cast their ballot in person. As a result, The Uniformed and Overseas Citizens Absentee Voting Act (UOCAVA) was passed allowing qualified service members to vote by mail. This process allows a state to mail a blank ballot to the UOCAVA voter. After the voter makes selections on the ballot, it can be mailed back to his or her home state to be counted. Although UOCAVA is the law, many service members and overseas voters still do not have their ballots counted due to various circumstances. According to a 2010 survey conducted by the United States Election Assistance Commission, only about 35 % of the ballots sent to UOCAVA voters were returned to the states [1]. Of those returned ballots, almost seven percent were not counted. The reasons for ballot rejection include lack of a post-mark, missed deadlines and irregularities with voter signatures. Because their ballots are often not received or are received and not counted, military and overseas voters are essentially being disenfranchised. While many have considered Internet voting to be the solution to this problem, there are those who worry about its security.

Dr. Barbara Simons, a member of the Board of Advisors of the U.S. Election Assistance Commission, has stated that Internet and electronic voting are much less

T. Tryfonas and I. Askoxylakis (Eds.): HAS 2015, LNCS 9190, pp. 487–494, 2015.
DOI: 10.1007/978-3-319-20376-8_43

secure and reliable than traditional paper ballots, like those currently used by UOCAVA voters. She argues that Internet and electronic voting systems are not secure because many do not print a paper ballot that can be hand counted [2]. Additionally, she explains that these systems are susceptible to both simple and sophisticated, viruses and denial of service, attacks [3]. The first structured analysis of Internet voting in the US was presented by the California Internet Voting Task Force (IVTF) [4]. The idea of Internet voting has been around for well over a decade. Although many issues remain such as security and Internet availability to the general public a structured well thought out Internet voting system could provide a solution to the issues of military overseas absentee voting. Along with security, scalability is often a concern for voting systems with client-server architecture. Evidence of ways to address this has been shown in previous work [5]. In the past the adoption of Internet voting systems was based on the potential benefits they offered over current implementations [6, 7]. This research suggests the development of a process called Televoting that could give military and overseas voters the ability to cast a private ballot that is counted on Election Day. With the use of the Televoting process UOCAVA voters will not need to sign and mail their ballots. This eliminates the possibility of any ballot being rejected due to signature irregularities or problems with the mail. Televoting also addresses security issues raised by Dr. Simons and others. This process is presented as a secure alternative to the problem of mailed ballots and Internet voting in general for uniformed and overseas citizen communities.

2 Related Works

There have been many Internet based voting systems developed worldwide. Many of these systems rely heavily on cryptography to make sure votes are not hacked or altered. The Estonian voting system serves as one of the first Internet voting systems implemented [8]. Currently it has the longest history of development, usage and evaluation. With this systems voters can vote on their computers/smart-card based systems or mobile phones. In the event that voters want to change their selections they also have the option of voting at a polling place later. Although the option of overriding votes is very useful, this system suffers from a vulnerability to malware hijacking the GUI. In this case voters may submit an incorrect vote without knowing. Another Internet based voting system is Helios [9]. Helios was developed mainly for low-coercion elections. Helios allows users to check if their vote has been counted using a web interface. Also it enables user to check if their ballot was changed on the server. Helios takes an interesting approach to Internet voting but is still vulnerable to malware injections during the ballot-casting phase. In the case that votes are tampered with prior to being sent to the server, voters will not be able to detect if their initial selection was changed or not. Remotegrity is another Internet voting solution that was initially developed as an absentee voting system [10]. Remotegrity is an end-to-end voting system that claims to offer voters ballot privacy. Unlike Helios, with Remotegrity ballot manipulation can be detected. After voting, users are able to verify their vote by visiting a website. Although this implementation provides advantages, it still requires users to visit polling stations. The Rijnland Internet Election System (RIES) is another implementation that utilizes the Internet [11]. RIES is amongst one of the largest Internet voting systems in the world. With RIES voters are able to check if their vote has been counted after an election is closed. The RIES system also gives users the ability to vote by regular mail. Despite some benefits, this system allows connections from all computers and assumes each connected client can be trusted.

Although these previous voting systems have made progress in recent years, many issues for Internet voting still exist. Many previous systems rely heavily on cryptography only. Previous research has shown that even with the advancements of modern day cryptography these systems could still be vulnerable to ballot manipulation. This paper presents Televoting, which builds off videoconference technology advancements used in Telemedicine. Televoting gives overseas voters the ability to vote securely and verify their vote with no need of keeping it on a server.

3   Approach

The following sections discuss the Televoting voting process and the system design. Further, current limitations will be discussed along with ways Televoting addresses current issues present in previous E-Voting systems.

Fig. 1. Voter waiting to be connected to poll worker

Fig. 2. Polling station view

Fig. 3. Voter and poll worker

Fig. 4. Voter using Prime III

Fig. 5. Voter view of printer and poll worker

Fig. 6. Poll worker using liveness test on face camera

Fig. 7. Poll worker using liveness test on printer camera

3.1   The Voting Process

Televoting is an in-browser voting system that allows voters to vote and communicate with election officials via a video stream. Voters begin the process of using Televoting by filling out his/her ballot online using Prime III from their web browser [12]. Once the voter is done filing out their ballot, the voter is placed in a queue and the system notifies all connected election officials back in the voter's home precinct. Once the election official is done assisting other voters they can service the next voter in the queue. Once connected, the voter will see and hear the election official assigned to him/her. The election official will verify the voter's identity and vice versa.

When the voter confirms that they are ready to cast their ballot, the election official clicks the print button. This will cause the voter's ballot to print in the same room as the poll worker back in the voter's home precinct. As the ballot prints, the voter can hear and see the ballot being printed in real time via a camera that sits under the printer. As an additional security message the poll worker shows a number that shared between them and the voter. Figures 6 and 7 also show a secret id number ('83' in this case) that can be shared between the poll worker and voter as an additional security measure. The number is shown first in the face camera view and then on the printer view. This approach allows voters to verify that their ballot made it to the correct poll worker. As an additional security method the clock shown in the Fig. 6 provides a liveness test.

A camera connected to the printer will provide visual feedback to the voter allowing them to visually verify that the ballot is correct. In the case that the ballot is incorrect and has been manipulated the voter will notice and notify the poll worker. At that point the poll worker will be able to report the incident and the issue can be addressed. Once the voter confirms the contest selections on the printed ballot, s/he will tell the poll worker the correct ballot was printed and the poll worker presses a button which releases the ballot from the printer into the ballot box and the session ends.

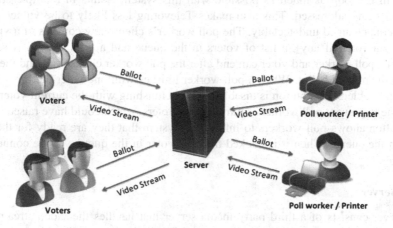

Fig. 8. Televoting system design

3.2   Client

The client side interface was built using html, JavaScript, and ActionScript. The current version of Televoting uses web pages for the voter and poll worker interface. Prior to being connected to the poll worker voters are able to view the poll workers working at the polling station they will be connected to. Figure 1 shows a user waiting to be connected and browsing through the poll workers that are assisting overseas voters. Voters also have the ability to view the polling station from a bird's eye view via an IP camera as shown in Fig. 2. This feed is sent from IP cameras over a server and sent to the voter as shown in Fig. 8. This feature was added so that voters could get a view of the poll workers they will be connected to within the polling station. Other citizens that would like to audit the polling station can also use this same view. In this way Televoting not only presents a way to submit votes but also enables citizens to detect when suspicious activity is happening at a polling station. Seeing the poll worker within their home precinct could also build voter trust regarding the system. These factors greatly influence the addition of IP cameras in the Televoting design. Prior to being connected to the voting official, voters complete their ballot as shown in Fig. 4. When the voter is done no data is sent over until the poll worker is connected. Figure 3 depicts an overseas military voter and a domestic poll worker waiting to be connected. When the poll worker is connected data is sent over and the poll worker has the ability to print the ballot. The voter page includes three video feeds as shown in Fig. 5. One feed shows a video stream of the connected election official and another feed shows the printer that prints the voter's ballot. An additional feed shows the voter a view of both the poll worker and printer. When the voter views the stream with the poll worker's face they will be able to confirm that it matches with the listed poll workers' pictures. This was also a feature aimed at increasing trust and making it easier for voters to detect when the system has been compromised. In the rare case that hackers are able to intercept the video stream and stage a fake polling precinct it would also be necessary to find a poll worker that looks extremely similar to the real voting official. Keeping the human in the loop as much as possible with this system results in multiple security concerns being addressed. This also makes Televoting less likely to be vulnerable to votes being changed undetectably. The poll worker's client view consists of a view of the current voter (if any), a list of voters in the queue and a print button. A session between a poll worker and voter can end after the poll worker clicks print and the voter verifies the printed ballot. When a poll worker finishes with one voter the 'next voter' button is enabled. This button is disabled prior to finishing with the current voter. This was done to prevent poll workers from skipping voters, which could have raised issues. This button allows poll workers to inform the system that they are ready for the next voter in the queue. When it is clicked the next voter in the queue will be connected.

3.3 Server

The server consists of a third party media server that handles the video streams and messages between the poll workers and voters. The logic of the poll worker and voters connections is handled on the server. A connection is triggered when a poll worker selects the next voter button. This causes the server to connect the poll worker with the next voter in the queue. When connected, the server sends the video stream from the printer camera and poll worker camera to the connected client. Also a video stream from the voter web camera is sent to the poll worker. The ballot is sent to the server temporarily. Once the poll worker clicks the print ballot button the ballot is printed and the vote is deleted on the server. Deleting the ballot from the server does not influence the ability to perform a recount. Televoting relies on the printed ballot in the case that a recount is needed. The server also handles the transmission of video streams from IP cameras connected at the polling stations. These cameras use a connection that can be accessed by the public but would not interfere with the private connections between poll workers and voters. A third party media server handles the transmission and encryption of the video streams and ballots. Security concerns that may affect the server side implementation are address in the following section.

3.4 Security Concerns

All Internet based systems are susceptible to cyber attacks. Televoting was developed with security in mind first. To develop an effective Internet based voting system that achieves societal acceptance, security concerns must be a primary focus. One concern with many systems that include client-server architecture is Secure Shell (SSH) vulnerability. A way that attackers may try to attack the server is through scripts that spawn remote commands via SSH variables. If successful in gaining root access this could lead to the system being compromised and ballots being sniffed as they are submitted temporarily. Even though this would not influence voter privacy since ballots are not connected uniquely with voters it could allow attackers to stop processes running on the server. This could result in video streams or ballots not being transmitted between voters and poll workers. Another major concern is that attackers may be able to change votes on the server if the attack is successful. Although this is technically possible voters would be able to detect this change once the ballot is printed. In this case even if an attacker gains access to the server it would be nearly impossible to change the ballot without being detected. To achieve this, attackers would have to set up a extremely sophisticated system that consists of staging a fake poll station and recruiting multiple poll workers that resemble those listed on an official government regulated website. One example of a client-side vulnerability for Internet voting systems, is Cross-site scripting (XSS). XSS allows attackers to execute Java-Script by entering into elements such as input boxes. Not addressing this issue could enable attackers to retrieve information about the election (vote cast, etc.). To address this issue all input boxes within Televoting are sanitize before being passed between pages. This involves making sure no JavaScript was included in the input box. Even though this vulnerability doesn't pose a major risk to Televoting due to how data is handled it was still addressed as a precautionary measure. Man-in-the-middle attacks are also another security concern for Internet based voting systems. These attacks allow hackers to view transmitted data with network sniffers such as Wireshark. Successful man-in-the-middle attacks can also tamper with data as it is being transmitted. As mentioned before, manipulated ballots can be detected with Televoting via the video stream of the printed ballot. Televoting takes an approach that utilizes multiple types of security measures. Along with liveness test, made possible by the video conferencing technology, standard security procedures are applied. To address the issue of man-in-the-middle attacks HTTPs connections are used. As an additional measure multiple certificates are installed on client and server machines. There are two types of clients in Televoting: voter and poll worker. The poll worker and voter have two separate keys. The first key is a public key on the client side. The second key is a private key on the server side. Without a key, other computers will not be able to connect to the server. A second certificate is required for the poll worker computers. This certificate would help insure attackers cannot attempt to stage fake polling stations.

4   Conclusion

Internet voting has gained popularity in many regions but has yet to gain much popularity in the US. This is mainly due to low societal acceptance, and security vulnerabilities that have been exposed in previous implementations. To develop an Internet system that achieves societal acceptance it must first resemble the process that is currently in place. Televoting combines the benefits of the traditional ways of voting with the benefits offered by modern day technology. More work must be done before Televoting can be offered to the general public, but it functions as a feasible option to serve overseas soldiers. Although some limitations still exist such as cost and man power, this system offers our soldiers a fundamental right that they deserve while they are serving their country.

5 Future Work

To further test Televoting, pilot studies are being scheduled on a regional level. Security is a major concern with any Internet voting system. With this in mind input from security experts from around the country are currently being collected. After the first round of testing is complete, work will be done on Televoting's scalability and addressing security concerns such as denial-of-service. It is also important that all users (voters, poll workers) have a good experience with Televoting. To insure this, user studies will be done to investigate Televoting User Experience (UX). Based on these findings the system will be modified to better address expressed user needs and concerns.

References

1. U.S Election Assistance Commission.: Uniformed and overseas citizens absentee voting act survey observations, October 2011. Retrieved from http://www.eac.gov/assets/1/Documents/EAC2010UOCAVAReport_FINAL.pdf
2. Simons, B.: Interview by C Rose [Web Based Recording]. Barbara Simons on her book "broken ballots: Will your vote count?". Barbara Simons, (2012). Retrieved from http://www.charlierose.com/view/interview/12588
3. Simons, B.: Internet voting: an idea whose time has not come [PowerPoint slides] (2012). Retrieved from http://research.microsoft.com/apps/video/default.aspx?id=171182
4. California Internet Voting Task Force (California Secretary of Security, IEEE Transactions on, 4(4):729–744, Dec. 2009. State). A report on the feasibility of internet voting, January 2000. Technical Guidelines Development Committee, editor. http://www.ss.ca.gov/executive/ivote
5. Rössler, T., Leithold, H., Posch, R.: E-voting: a scalable approach using XML and hardware security modules. In: Proceedings of the 2005 IEEE International Conference on e-Technology, e-commerce and e-Service EFF2005 (2005)
6. Voting, Parliamentary Office of Science and Technology, (2001). http://www.parliament.uk/post/pn155.pdf
7. Delaune, S., Kremer, S., Ryan, M.: Verifying properties of electronic-voting protocols. ftp.cs.bham.ac.uk/pub/authors/M.D.Ryan/06-wote.pdf
8. Heiberg, S., Laud, P., Willemson, J.: The application of I-voting for Estonian parliamentary elections of 2011. In: Kiayias, A., Lipmaa, H. (eds.) VoteID 2011. LNCS, vol. 7187, pp. 208–223. Springer, Heidelberg (2012)
9. Adida, B.: Helios: web-based open-audit voting. In: SS2008: Proceedings of the 17th conference on Security Symposium, pp. 335–348. USENIX Association, Berkeley (2008)
10. Carback, R., Chaum, D., Clark, J., Conway, J., Essex, A., Herrnson, P.S., Mayberry, T., Popoveniuc, S., Rivest, R.L., Shen, E., Sherman, A.T., Vora, P.L.: Scantegrity II municipal election at Takoma Park: The first e2e binding governmental election with ballot privacy. In: USENIX Security Symposium, pp. 291–306, USENIX Association (2010)
11. Hubbers, E., Bart, J., Wolter, P.: RIES: Internet voting in action. In: Proceedings of the 29th Annual International Computer Software and Applications Conference. IEEE Computer Society, Edinburgh (2005)
12. Cross, E.V., II, McMillian, Y., Gupta, P., Williams, P., Nobles, K., Gilbert, J.E.: Prime III: A user centered voting system. In: Proceedings of 2007 Conference Human Factors in Computing Systems (CHI), pp. 2351–2356 (2007)

Personalized Voting: The Intersection of Cloud and Mobility

Shaneé Dawkins$^{(\boxtimes)}$ and Sharon Laskowski

National Institute of Standards and Technology, 100 Bureau Drive, Gaithersburg,
MD 20899, USA
{dawkins, sharon.laskowski}@nist.gov

Abstract. Current research and development being conducted by the international Global Public Inclusive Infrastructure Consortium (GPII) is to create technology for cloud-based accessibility. Using this new technology, users of computer systems can create personal profiles that specify how computer applications should be configured to meet their individual needs. National Institute of Standards and Technology researchers have developed a prototype voting support system with enhanced accessibility capabilities based on the cloud-based accessibility work of the GPII, to evaluate the applicability of this new technology in the voting domain. Using this prototype, the Next Generation Voting Platform (NGVP), voters can use a mobile device (e.g. tablet computer) to exchange data with a cloud-based system to download settings in order to configure complex ballot interfaces for marking a blank ballot. The research performed on the NGVP suggests that cloud-based accessibility has the potential to be useful to voters when integrated into mobile ballot-marking systems.

Keywords: Accessibility · Cloud-based accessibility · Help America vote act · HAVA · Human factors · Voting systems · GPII

1 Introduction

Computing systems designed for people with disabilities are continually evolving through the research and development (R&D) of assistive technologies and improved design practices. At the forefront of these R&D endeavors is the creation of cloud-based accessibility technology, led by the international Global Public Inclusive Infrastructure Consortium (GPII) [1]. With cloud-based accessibility, people have the ability to automatically customize an application to their personal needs. This "autopersonalization" can operate on any computer, including mobile computing devices. Therefore, people can have the experience of personalized accessibility on any public computer, including a mobile device, as if it were their own. As the technology for this cloud-based accessibility grows, research is being conducted to evaluate its applicability in various domains [2–5].

Recognizing the importance of reducing barriers to voting for people with disabilities the goal of this research was to perform an evaluation of cloud-based accessibility in the voting domain. GPII has not been extensively evaluated in the civic realm; applying it to the voting domain permits evaluation of public use by a wide

© Springer International Publishing Switzerland 2015
T. Tryfonas and I. Askoxylakis (Eds.): HAS 2015, LNCS 9190, pp. 495–505, 2015.
DOI: 10.1007/978-3-319-20376-8_44

population of people with a range of abilities. The foundation of this next generation voting research is a mobile ballot-marking application prototype, referred to as the Next Generation Voting Platform (NGVP). The application was designed to allow voters to mark a blank ballot using cloud-based accessibility to personalize its presentation. Although discussed here, as the demonstration of cloud-based accessibility in voting was the goal of the project, this paper does not fully delve into the ownership or operation of the GPII cloud, nor into the security concerns that may arise when voters cast their vote at the polling place.

2 Background

2.1 Voting, HAVA, and the VVSG

Voting system technology is continuously evolving, along with the voting process itself. Over the past decade, technology in particular has changed drastically due to the passage of the Help America Vote Act (HAVA), reforming the voting process throughout the nation [6]. Through HAVA, the U.S. Election Assistance Commission (EAC) was formed, in part, to develop technical guidelines for the design and certification of voting systems [7]. Since the creation of the 2005 Voluntary Voting System Guidelines (VVSG), NIST and the EAC have published additional materials to support those guidelines [8]. The VVSG and supplemental reports provide recommendations (e.g., for human factors, accessibility, privacy, security, software) for various voting systems (i.e., electronic and paper-based systems). As voting systems, concepts, and processes evolve to incorporate various technologies (e.g. commercial-off-the-shelf (COTS) hardware), it has become necessary to update the original standards.

The VVSG in use today does not address the usability and accessibility of mobile computing devices, COTS hardware, or cloud-based services. As such, this work may have considerable implications for future standards. Certain aspects of the interface of mobile COTS devices vary greatly from the stationary systems on which the current guidelines were based, particularly in size. Similarly, the interaction using accessibility features local to the computing device differs from those afforded by the use of cloud-based accessibility. While this paper does not make recommendations for new guidelines, it is a building block in the conversation about next generation standards.

2.2 Global Public Inclusive Infrastructure (GPII)

The Global Public Inclusive Infrastructure, or GPII, is a project[1] started in 2010 that aims to simplify the development, delivery, and support of accessible technologies. The GPII infrastructure supports a "secure personalization profile system that allows users' access features to be automatically invoked and set up for them," through the use of

---

[1] GPII is a project created by the Switzerland-based Raising the Floor organization. Raising the Floor is made up of over 100 organizations and individuals whose collective goal is "AccessForAll" – accessibility and digital inclusion for each individual's needs [1].

cloud computing technology. Using the GPII cloud, users will have the ability to automatically configure any computer or information and communication technology (ICT) to comply with the assistive techniques and technologies needed [1].

GPII is a concept that is still in the development stage. The goal of GPII is to ensure that all people, regardless of ability or economic resources, have access to the internet, its information, and services. However, because this concept is scaled for global development and deployment, it requires the coordination of national infrastructures, funding, and operation. In 2011, The European Commission provided funding for the Cloud4All program with the objective of developing key technical components of GPII [1, 9]. As GPII and Cloud4All are still in the early stages of the development process, many unknowns exist pertaining to global and national use. Exploring the use of GPII within the voting domain at this point of its implementation is an opportunity to evaluate its potential civic use; however, to facilitate current exploration in the voting domain, the overarching GPII concepts necessary for the development of the NIST NGVP prototype were simulated.

The GPII concept of a "personalization profile system" allows a user to login to a cloud-based system to access their personal profile. This profile, or "Needs and Preferences set" (N&P set), is stored on the cloud and contains characteristics of a user interface (UI) that are necessary for the user to interact with any system without barriers. Using cloud-based accessibility-enabled computing system, a user can log into their cloud profile and interact with an interface that is automatically adjusted to his or her needs (as specified in that particular user's N&P set). Settings of N&P sets fall under display, control, or content categories, and include visual, auditory, and physical interaction features [10]. This autopersonalization – the customization of the UI based on the user's N&P set – was simulated for the NIST NGVP.

3 Design and Implementation

3.1 Accessible Voting Use Case

There are many variables to consider when formulating use cases for accessible voting with mobile devices. The first of these is the method by which voters will cast, or submit, their ballot (independent from making their ballot selections). Due to unresolved security issues prevalent in internet voting [11], the use cases presented here do not suggest that voters cast their ballots over a network. Rather, the two main methods for casting ballots for this mobile accessible voting use case are via mail-in or in-person at the voter's polling place. For voters who live in jurisdictions that do not support mail-in voting, they can scan their completed ballot (or ballot representation, e.g., a barcode) at the polling place.

The second consideration is the location where the ballot marking will take place. Given the mobility of the voting device, voters could conceivably mark their ballot from anywhere. For the purposes of this project, we consider "anywhere" to be the voter's home, an assisted living facility, a public place (e.g., a library), or a traditional polling place.

The final variable to consider is the ownership of the mobile device. Is the device owned by the voter, an official election entity, or an alternate public or private entity? This has a direct impact on the nature of the accessibility of the device. If the device is privately owned, the accessibility features can be local to the device, configured according to the user's exact needs (potentially eliminating the need for cloud-based accessibility). However, a downloaded blank ballot is required for privately owned devices (since they are not pre-loaded). If the device is owned by an election jurisdiction, cloud-based accessibility would benefit the voter; since the device is shared between many voters, there is a greater need for autopersonalization. In this case, blank ballots can be local to the device (eliminating the need for blank ballots to be downloaded), but voters' N&P sets would need to be downloaded to configure the interface.

A wide range of use cases can be constructed given the aforementioned variables and the personas described in the Background section. The following factors make up the cloud-based accessible voting use case.

1. Voters can mark their ballot in any location.
   (a) Voters must have internet access to download the ballot and to download their accessibility needs from the cloud.
2. The mobile device can have public or private ownership.
   (a) Regardless of public/private ownership, the application will retrieve the voter's accessibility needs from the cloud. For privacy reasons, although it is currently an available option, voters should not be required to electronically save their ballot to an external device, nor to electronically send their ballot for future printing.
   (b) If the device is publicly owned, there must be access to a printer to print the completed ballot or a representation of the completed ballot.
   (c) If the device is privately owned, the voter has the option either to scan the printed completed ballot or a representation of the completed ballot, or to scan an electronic form of the completed ballot at the polling place.
3. Ballot casting is either done via mail-in or in-person at the polling place.[2]
   (a) Voters who cast at the polling place (by scanning a printed paper or an electronic form) must confirm, or verify, the accuracy of their completed ballot prior to casting, via a verification system.[3] Therefore, polling place verification systems must be accessible, implementing cloud-based accessibility in one of two ways. (1) Verification systems at the polling place have the capability to connect to the cloud to download the voters' accessibility needs. This requires a network connection. (2) The ballot (or ballot representation) scanned at the polling place includes UI specifications, based on the voter's GPII N&P set with which the ballot was originally marked. This bypasses the need for a network connection for the verification system.

---

[2] Ideally, for mail-in voting, voters would be able to verify their printed completed ballot prior to mailing. However, no such verification system is in place for mail-in voting.

[3] Alternately, if a voter would like to spoil their completed ballot, they may discard their ballot or ballot representation and complete a new ballot.

(b) For mail-in voting, voters print their completed ballot, then mail it to the elections office. If the mobile device used is owned by the election jurisdiction, there should be an accessible method for the voter to verify the printed ballot prior to mailing (in one of the two methods mentioned in the previous bullet). However, no such verification system exists if the voter is using a privately-owned device, or a device owned by an alternate public entity.

3.2   The Next Generation Voting Platform (NGVP)

Voting Process. The introduction of mobile devices into the voting process presents a multitude of methods for voters to vote and cast their ballots. For voters with disabilities, this adds flexibility to a once static voting process. The majority of voting jurisdictions in the U.S. require voters to complete the entire voting process – sequentially from voter check-in to ballot casting – in centralized polling places. This static process poses a challenge to some voters with disabilities because of the duration of their required physical presence at the polling place. Additionally, many of these polling places have a limited number of accessible voting machines – which are not capable of being fully customized to meet the wide variety of voters' needs.[4]

The use of mobile devices and cloud-based accessibility during the voting process would yield a more flexible experience for voters for various reasons. The most obvious benefit is that the use of mobile devices allows voters to mark their ballot anywhere, reducing the time required to be physically present at the polling place. Another major difference is that voters with disabilities would have the ability to vote on any device and have that device auto-configured to meet their personal needs.

The NGVP has built upon the traditional voting process by incorporating mobile devices and cloud-based accessibility. The complete NGVP voting process can be summarized as follows, with steps one through four anywhere and steps five through eight at the polling place:[5]

1. The voter establishes desired accessibility configuration based on features stored in the cloud.
2. The voter downloads a blank ballot.
3. The voter completes the ballot.
4. The voter generates their completed ballot (or ballot representation) for casting.
5. The voter checks-in with the poll worker at their polling place.
6. The voter scans their ballot (or ballot representation).
7. The voter verifies their ballot.
8. The voter casts their ballot.

Design. The NGVP was implemented based on a design for the use case presented in the Accessible Voting Use Case section. The NGVP is designed to use COTS mobile

---

[4] Some accessible voting systems have the functionality for the voter to modify certain characteristics of the system interface as needed; however, these options are not an extensive list of modifiable characteristics.

[5] For states where mail-in voting is required, or for absentee ballots, steps 5 and 6 are bypassed, and mailing the completed ballot is considered casting for step 8.

devices as electronic ballot marking web-based interfaces in which the voter downloads and marks (completes) a blank ballot anywhere. The verification and casting of the marked ballot occurs separately at their polling place (unless mail-in voting is permitted). Figure 1 illustrates the NGVP design. From any location with internet access, the mobile device accesses the GPII cloud for the UI configuration, and the Ballot cloud to download the blank ballot.[6] After completing the ballot, the voter brings the device, or optionally printed ballot representation, to the polling place. At the polling place, a scanner or code reader captures the ballot selections and transfers them to the ballot verification system. The ballot verification system may retrieve the voter's UI configurations from the GPII cloud or from the scanner/QR code reader (optional; shown as dashed arrow in Fig. 1). Once verified by the voter, the ballot is cast as a part of the verification system or a separate vote tallying system. The next two sections describe the interaction with the GPII cloud.

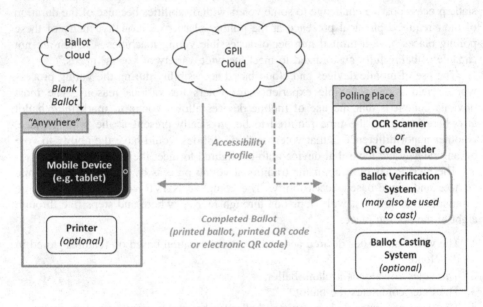

Fig. 1. NGVP design diagram

Ballot Marking and Cloud-Based Accessibility. The nature of voting – its infrequent occurrence and wide range of voter abilities – requires technology that is easy to use and accessible. Therefore, some voting systems employ a universal design – designing all products, buildings and exterior spaces to be usable by all people to the greatest extent possible [12] – enhancing voting system usability and accessibility for many voters. However, a universal design may not be sufficient to allow all citizens of all abilities to vote. The NGVP goes beyond universal design by incorporating cloud-based accessibility into the development of the tablet-based ballot-marking application.

---

[6] The specific blank ballot downloaded corresponds to the voter's address. The NGVP prompts the voter to enter this information after interface settings have been set.

With typical voting systems, a universal design may be achieved by allowing the voter to manually alter characteristics of the ballot interface, such as text size and speech volume. Using cloud-based accessibility – GPII technology – the NGVP provides voters the option to automatically modify the necessary ballot interface characteristics to be more helpful to them.

Thus far, three configurable ballot interface characteristics have been implemented for the NGVP tablet-based prototype: text size, audio volume, and speech rate. The text size feature applies to the visual ballot interface, while the audio volume and speech rate apply to the audio ballot interface. Before the voter loads a ballot, they are presented with a screen to manually adjust these ballot interface settings (see Fig. 2). In the left margin of this screen, below the instructions, are textboxes where the voter can use their existing GPII username and password to login to the GPII cloud to retrieve their N&P set. Once the GPII voter profile information is retrieved, the NGVP interface settings automatically adjust, and the voter will immediately see (or hear) changes to the ballot interface based on the configurations in their N&P set (see Fig. 3). The voter is then able to modify the new settings as needed, or to continue to the ballot with the GPII adjustments. At any point in the following process to mark the ballot, the voter can return to the ballot settings page to adjust the interface.

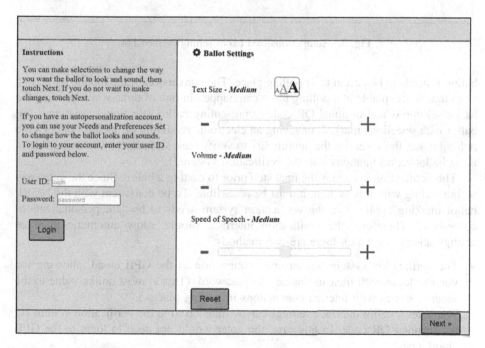

Fig. 2. NGVP default ballot settings screenshot

Ballot Verification and Cloud-Based Accessibility. There are two main stages of the NGVP voting process – marking the ballot "anywhere," and verifying and casting the completed ballot at the polling place (or mail-in). After the voter completes an NGVP

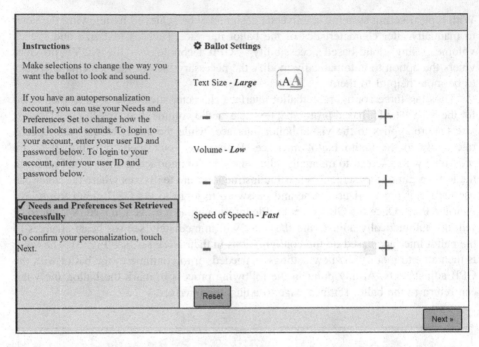

Fig. 3. Autopersonalized ballot settings screenshot

ballot, it needs to be cast at their polling place. The conversion of the mobile ballot to a form that is acceptable at a polling place can happen in one of three ways: printing the ballot selections and optional QR code (representing ballot selections), printing a full ballot with selections marked, or saving an electronic rendering of the QR code. At the polling place, the voter has the opportunity to verify their selections by scanning one of these ballot representations into the verification system.[7]

The verification system is the final step prior to casting a ballot. Since the voter will be interacting with this system, it must be accessible. To be consistent with the NGVP ballot marking application, the verification system needs to be "autopersonalization-compliant." Therefore, the verification interface should allow automatic interface configurations, for which there are two methods:

- The verification system has an open connection to the GPII cloud, allowing the voter to login with their username and password. (This is most unlikely due to the security issues with internet connections in polling places.)
- The voter's ballot interface settings can be transferred to the verification system via the scanned QR code. In this case, the voter would not need to login to the GPII cloud again.

---

[7] Verification and casting (ballot submission) was conceptualized for the NGVP voting process, but outside of the scope of project implementation.

In both of these methods for verification, the system must have an auto-configurable interface.

4 Discussion

4.1 GPII Technical Considerations

As the research and development plans for GPII in the U.S. grow, so too will the potential for GPII to influence the design of new and existing applications.

Infrastructure and Application Design. In order for GPII technology to transition from theory to practice, unanswered development questions need to be addressed.

1. *Where is the cloud?* The GPII, which will eventually be a collaborative initiative of National Public Inclusive Infrastructures (NPII), must be built [1]. For the NPII to be implemented at the federal level, where will the cloud reside? Will it be solely for use for government services, or will it be open to public and private institutions, organizations, and corporations? Who funds, builds, operates, and maintains the NPII?
2. *What type of settings can be configured?* Will developers have the capability to adjust settings [10] at the application level, the system level, or both? In an online ballot-marking tool, the application can control its UI, but perhaps not the browser or system settings.
3. *Are there potential conflicts in the permissions?* There is a permission hierarchy for settings access and use, between the applications and systems on which they run. If a user has multiple profiles on the cloud, one for each level, how is priority assigned?

The responses to these questions may not directly impact the end users, but it will have a bearing on if and how developers will utilize the NPII. In all, although a promising initiative, the practical use of the cloud-based accessibility infrastructure cannot be fully achieved until these unknowns are resolved.

User Accounts. In order to utilize the autopersonalization feature in the NIST prototype, voters can login to the accessibility cloud with their GPII user name and password, possibly leading to the issues of (1) voter inability to recall their GPII credentials, or (2) voters wish to create a new GPII account or profile. Additionally, the NGVP ballot-marking application is not intended to be a portal to the accessibility cloud, but instead, to take advantage of the information stored within it. Therefore, typical account login features such as resetting user passwords or offering challenge questions are not available in the NGVP application. GPII profile initialization and management should be an entirely separate application and process, so as not to cause major interference with the voting process.

Cloud Implications of Hardware and Software Updates. As more organizations and individuals use cloud services [13], general usability issues of cloud access, reliability, and operability arise [14]. Issues include device independence, availability, and consistency. Device independence allows users to access the cloud services from any device at any location. Availability ensures that the user can access the cloud at any time, under any situation. Consistency addresses the fulfillment of user access to all features on all supported devices. These three principles can become major issues if cloud software is updated by the cloud manager (as required), but without proper assurance testing. These access issues may also arise if the user updates their device hardware. Additionally, how would this affect the settings stored in the users' profiles? With an abundance of mobile devices used by voters, as well as a wide and diverse range of assistive technologies, addressing these types of issues are essential to the success of GPII, within and beyond the voting realm.

4.2 Privacy and Trust

The convenience of autopersonalization comes with a cost – storing personal information on the accessibility cloud. In this case, personal information does not include typical personal identifiable information (PII), such as name, birthdate, and social security number, but rather the preferences and settings catered to an individual. In the design of voting systems, the privacy of an individual is a major design attribute [15]. With cloud-based accessibility, voters may be concerned that they, or their disabilities, may be identified based on the information in their profiles.[8]

Because voting systems require access to retrieve a voter's settings, it is conceivable that voters may be uncomfortable storing information about their assistive needs.[9] To clarify, consider a voter with a disability that is not readily visible in public. Any UI adjustment information stored in their profile would be exposed to anyone with access to that information (see previous section on who owns and manages the cloud). For example, a voter with a visual or mild dexterity disability may feel violated if an election official is aware of his or her disability (or feel in danger if this information is disclosed to others) solely based on the interface settings in their GPII account profile. While organizations have been working to address issues of internet related privacy and identity management [16, 17], no one solution has yet gained widespread acceptance.

5 Conclusion

The goal of the NIST project was to examine how cloud-based accessibility could be applied to the voting domain and to investigate how this process might be applied to other domains. In exploring next generation voting processes, cloud-based accessibility was found to have the potential to vastly improve the accessibility of voting system interfaces [18]. Cloud-based accessibility is a promising immediate future research area, one that once important questions are addressed, can have a great impact on elections technology.

---

[8] This is often the case in traditional polling places, where only one voting machine of the many setup is accessible, and is used by very few (often one) voters.

[9] One alternative to username and password is to use voter registration information, which would indeed link the voter needs and preferences to what is typically referred to as PII.

Acknowledgements. This research was conducted by NIST, partially via support from NIDRR under Agreement No. ED-OSE-12-J-0003.

References

1. Global Public Inclusive Infrastructure. http://gpii.net/
2. Lewis, C.: Issues in web presentation for cognitive accessibility. In: Proceedings of the 6th international conference on Universal Access in Human-Computer Interaction: Design for all and EInclusion - Volume Part I (UAHCI'11), Constantine Stephanidis (Ed.), Vol. Part I. pp. 244–248. Springer, Berlin (2011)
3. Cloud4all. http://www.cloud4all.info/
4. Mulfari, D., Celesti, A., Puliafito, A., Villari, M.: How cloud computing can support on-demand assistive services. In: Proceedings of the 10th International Cross-Disciplinary Conference on Web Accessibility (W4A2013). 4 page ACM, New York. Article 27 (2013). http://doi.acm.org/10.1145/2461121.2461140
5. Martínez, J.A., Vanderheiden, G., Treviranus, J.: GPII, CLOUD4All: Auto-Personalization for Universal Accessibility. European Commission, FP7 Project 289016 (2012). http://cloud4all.info/pages/news/detail.aspx?id=6&tipo=2. Retrieved from 2014
6. Help America Vote Act of 2002 (HAVA): Pub. L. No. 107–252, 116 Stat. 1666–1730 (2002), codified at 42 U.S.C. §§15301–15545. http://www.fec.gov/hava/law_ext.txt
7. The U.S. Election Assistance Commission http://www.eac.gov
8. Voluntary Voting System Guidelines (VVSG). http://www.eac.gov/testing_and_certification/voluntary_voting_system_guidelines.aspx. Retrieved from 2014
9. European Union 7th Framework Programme for Research and Technological Development. http://cordis.europa.eu/project/rcn/101353_en.html. Retrieved 2014
10. ISO/IEC 24751-2:2008, Information technology – Individualized adaptability and accessibility in e-learning, education and training – Part 2: "Access for all" personal needs and preferences for digital delivery
11. NISTIR 7770, Security Considerations for Remote Electronic UOCAVA Voting (2011). http://www.nist.gov/itl/vote/upload/NISTIR-7700-feb2011.pdf. Retrieved from 2014
12. Mace, R., Hardie, G., Place, J.: Accessible environments: toward universal design. In: Preiser, W.F.E., Vischer, J., White, E.T. (eds.) Design Intervention: Toward a More Humane Architecture. Van Nostrand Reinhold, New York (1991)
13. Mell, P.M., Grance, T.: NIST SP - 800-145 – The NIST Definition of Cloud Computing. National Institute of Standards & Technology, Gaithersburg (2011)
14. Cloud Services Measurement Initiative Consortium: Service Measurement Index. http://csmic.org/. Retrieved from 2014
15. Vanderheiden, G. et al.: Creating A Global Public Inclusive Infrastructure (CLOUD4ALL & GPII), AEGIS International Conference, December 2011 Brussels, Belgium. (Retrieved 2013 from http://gpii.net/sites/default/files/2011%20AEGIS-Creating%20a%20Global%20Public%20Inclusive%20Infrastructure-Final.doc)
16. Identity, Credential, & Access Management.: http://www.idmanagement.gov/identity-credential-access-management. Retrieved from 2014
17. NSTIC. http://www.nist.gov/nstic/index.html
18. Dawkins, S., Laskowski, S.: Cloud-based Accessibility for Voting Applications. NISTIR 8047 National Institute of Standards and Technology, Gaithersburg (2015)

Hobson's Choice: Security and Privacy Permissions in Android and iOS Devices

John Haggerty[1]([⊠]), Thomas Hughes-Roberts[1], and Robert Hegarty[2]

[1] School of Science and Technology, Nottingham Trent University,
Clifton Campus, Clifton Lane, Nottingham NG11 8NS, UK
{john.haggerty,thomas.hughesroberts}@ntu.ac.uk
[2] School of Computing, Mathematics and Digital Technology,
Manchester Metropolitan University, Chester Street, Manchester M1 5GD, UK
r.hegarty@mmu.ac.uk

Abstract. The use of smartphones and tablet devices has grown rapidly over recent years and the widespread availability of software, often from unknown developers, has led to security and privacy concerns. In order to prevent security compromises, these devices use access control as a means by which a user is able to specify an application's ability to interact with services and data. However, the use of access control as a security countermeasure in this environment is severely limited. For example, once permissions are granted to software, they may share data, such as location or unique identifiers with third persons without informing the user, whether or not the application is itself running. This paper presents the results of a comparative study conducted with computing students at two UK universities that identifies the issues surrounding software access control permissions in Android and iOS operating systems. Through this study, we are able to quantify the impact of security access permissions on mobile device security and privacy, even amongst specialist users.

Keywords: Mobile device security · Access control · Android · iOS

1 Introduction

The use of smartphones and tablet devices has grown rapidly over recent years. The relatively low cost and high power of such devices has made them attractive to consumers, providing them with a truly mobile computing experience. The widespread adoption of mobile devices has resulted in the availability of thousands of applications for their owners. There are two models of software provision in this market; open and closed. In open markets, such as Google Play, application developers are able to distribute their software for a small fee or free of charge with little control by the owners of the store. In closed markets, such as the Apple App store, the distribution of software is more tightly controlled by the market owners. Software from both markets can be downloaded to a device and installed instantly, making it an attractive service for users and automated, dynamic analysis techniques are employed to identify malware.

The widespread availability of software, often from unknown developers, has led to security and privacy concerns. Many black market software stores exist, where malware is crafted into pirated commercial software and provided to end users free of

© Springer International Publishing Switzerland 2015
T. Tryfonas and I. Askoxylakis (Eds.): HAS 2015, LNCS 9190, pp. 506–516, 2015.
DOI: 10.1007/978-3-319-20376-8_45

charge. For example, viruses and Trojan applications can be made readily available by malicious developers through both legitimate and pirate software stores and researchers have demonstrated that it is possible to obfuscate malware from detection techniques (Apvrille and Nigram 2014). This software can compromise the security of the device and the user by sending messages to premium rate services or stealing information, such as logon credentials or passwords (Delac *et al.* 2011). Alternatively, many applications interact with other online services, such as Google, through authentication tokens (Google 2015). These tokens are sometimes sent in plain text, and can therefore be intercepted by a malicious application monitoring data sent from the device or a network to which they belong, to steal these credentials and access private information held elsewhere online.

In order to prevent security and privacy compromises, both Android and iOS devices use access control as a means by which a user is able to specify an application's ability to interact with services and data. For example, in the Android operating system, application data is held in isolated environments within the file system and inter-process communications are controlled through access permissions. The access rights depend upon the software to be used and the services that they require. For example, the BBC iPlayer application requires access to internet services to stream multimedia, phone calls so that the software is notified when the phone rings, and system tools to prevent the device entering sleep mode (Madden 2012). Irrespective of the software and its source, users readily provide applications that they download with a range of permissions within the operating system.

However, the use of access control as a security countermeasure in this environment is severely limited. For example, once permissions are granted to software, they may share data, such as location or unique identifiers with third persons without informing the user, whether or not the application is itself running. The granularity of many requested access rights is too coarse to be useful, for example, the Internet permission provides broad-ranging capabilities without restricting access to specific URLs or domains. In the Android operating system, a user is presented with a list of capabilities, such as network services, location information, access to personal data, etc. upon installation. The user is not able to selectively grant access rights to the application as the only choice is to install the software or not, with all the permissions required by the developers rather than owner of the device. In the iOS operating system, a user will only grant capabilities as they use the software. However, to use the software with the functionality required by the user, they must grant the permissions requested. In both models, the user is presented with Hobson's choice; they are presented with the choice of installing or not installing, or using or not using, the software, with the potential cost to the security and privacy of information if they choose to install or run an application. Permission revocation is not an option unless the software is removed wholesale and users often fail to understand the risk posed by composite permissions. More importantly, the decision to grant permissions is being made by users that are potentially unaware of the security implications of making such a choice.

This paper presents the results of a comparative study conducted with computing students at two UK universities that explores issues surrounding software access control permissions in Android and iOS operating systems. Through this study, we are able to quantify the impact of Android and iOS security access permissions on mobile phone device security and privacy, even amongst specialist users. In particular, the results of this survey identify the permissions that participants are prepared to accept in installing applications from unknown sources. Moreover, it identifies whether these permissions, if wide ranging or inappropriate for the application, are questioned by the user. This paper will therefore quantify the problem of access control in the mobile environment and discuss appropriate countermeasures to mitigate the issue.

This paper is organized as follows. Section 2 discusses related work. Section 3 posits the methodology used for the comparative survey. Section 4 presents the results of the survey and discusses their significance to mobile device security. Finally, we make our conclusions and discuss further work.

2   Related Work

The most common operating systems in the mobile device market are Android and iOS, which combined accounted for over 90 % of smartphones in late 2014 (ID 2015). Both of these operating systems are based on the Linux kernel to provide hardware abstraction; Android builds on Linux whilst iOS is derived from OS X, a variant of BSD UNIX. On top of the kernel are the native libraries, which provide some of the common services for applications and other programs. Running processes rely on virtualization, whereby a virtual machine (VM) runs an application in its own instance. On top of this layer is the application framework, where code running for and on the VM provides service to multiple operations.

Due to the popularity of such devices running this architecture, mobile security and privacy has received much attention. In particular, their widespread use has introduced a range of new threats as well as transposing issues long associated with more traditional computing devices. For example, Delac et al. (2011) present an attacker-centric threat model for mobile devices. This model realizes that the sources of threats to mobile devices are wide and varied, such as through Bluetooth connections, access to the Internet or networks, or USB peripherals. Erturk (2012) identifies the issue of privacy-invasive adware on mobile devices that target open-source platforms such as Android. Frank et al. (2012) suggest that the Android operating system and Internet access through social network services such as Facebook can provide third-party applications with access to user's private data as well as perform sensitive operations such as post online messages or make phone calls. Many of these potential issues do not have to be developed by very experienced software developers engineers or developers. For example, Mylonas et al. (2011) suggest that all smartphone platforms could be used by average developers for attacking privacy or harvesting data without the user's knowledge or consent.

A number of countermeasures to these wide and varied threats have been proposed. For example, Batyuk et al. (2011) posit a scheme whereby applications available via the Android market place are assessed for security vulnerabilities and a report is made available to users. This scheme also reverse-engineers applications to adjust security settings according to the user's requirements. Ghosh et al. (2012) propose a scheme for user privacy based on contextual information analysis to maintain user privacy when using applications that access and share device location and surroundings data.

Luo *et al.* (2013) posit a method for the protection of user data by introducing a secure, enhanced kernel and data-at-rest encryption. In this way, they aim to provide data protection rather than address application privileges. Encryption has since been implemented and deployed in recent versions of the Android and IOS operating systems, with Android employing SELinux to provide Mandatory Access Control. Fazeen and Dantu (2014) propose a model for the identification of Android applications' intentions to identify malware through permission requests.

However, the issue remains that the principal defence strategy employed in both Android and iOS devices is based on the granting of access rights to applications, often obtained from unverified sources. This is compounded by the current practice of only allowing access to an application if, and only if, the user grants all the capabilities presented to them by that software.

Due to the complexity of applications running on powerful mobile devices, we posit that it is difficult for users to determine the implications of the often loosely scoped permissions. This problem is worsened by the security implications of composite permissions; with permissions that seem harmless in isolation, presenting a security risk in combination with other permissions. As mentioned previously the Internet permission is loosely scoped, permitting malicious applications to leak information obtained from other permissions granted by the user, this 'gateway permission' requires much finer grain control. Tighter granularity for key permissions such as Internet access would reduce the ability of malicious applications to breach user privacy. If URL or domain specific permissions were provided, the increase in transparency would enable users to make more informed decisions about the applications they install, and the destination of data leaving their devices.

The above challenges have emerged as consumers shift from a conventional computing environment, using PCs and laptops to a mobile environment in which they use smartphones and tablets. Unfortunately it is not immediately apparent to many users, that mobile devices contain much more sensitive personal information than conventional computing devices. Coupled with this conventional computing environments do not typically require the end user to grant permissions, rather a user agrees to a EULA (often without reading it). Thus, even experienced computer users are not well equipped to deal with the threats to privacy posed by the transition from a conventional to mobile computing environment. A further 'at risk' group are users who have little to no experience of computing devices; this group has stumbled into computing due to the low cost and high availability of smart phones, and may be unaware of the threat computing devices pose to their personal privacy.

While malware is usually found in software from unverified sources, there have been instances of malware in the app stores of both iOS and Android (Porter Felt *et al.* 2011). The user's judgment may be impaired through the false sense of security that using an official app store provides. Both the major app stores deploy automated (e.g. Google Bouncer) and manual vetting of applications, however the purpose of such vetting is to identify malware. These vetting processes do not take account of the user's privacy, with the choice of whether to accept permissions being delegated to the end user. Furthermore, the way in which consent is obtained differs between platforms with some requiring full consent at installation and others during run-time (Porter Felt *et al.* 2012). The question is therefore raised: does the way in which permissions are requested influence the extent of consent and general user consent? Given the prominent role the user plays in managing the security of a personal mobile device, understanding end-user perceptions is vital in designing appropriate solutions.

In the next section, we present the methodology of a survey of computing students at two UK universities that attempts to quantify the security challenges that this model raises.

3   Survey Methodology

The aim of the survey is to begin exploring how users approach permissions on a mobile device by comparing the two prevalent methods of application permission acceptance in iOS and Android devices. Participants are therefore presented with an application's permissions request and asked what their reaction would be: accept or reject. They are then asked to provide an explanation for their choice.

The first part of the survey presents the permission screens as they would within an Android OS. That is, in order to download and install the app they must agree to all the required permissions. The second part of the survey presents the permissions as they would be found within iOS where acceptance is required in increments and based on the task at hand. To that end the participant is presented with a sentence detailing the context of the permissions request; for example, "you wish to make an in-app purchase, the app requires permission to access…"

Table 1 provides an overview of the applications present in the survey, the permissions of which are taken from actual software on the market.

Table 1. Part 1: applications overview

App	From (at time of survey)	Notes
Social network	Facebook	
Messenger	Facebook messenger	
Invasive flashlight	High powered torch	
Less invasive flashlight	LED Torch	Only if rejected invasive flashlight
File store	Dropbox	
Game	Angry birds transformers	
Invasive camera	Google camera	
Less invasive camera	Camera 1080	Only if rejected invasive camera
Banking	HSBC	
Loyalty card	Game rewards	

For each of these applications, the participant is presented with the generic name of the application (e.g. "you wish to download a social networking application") and an accompanying permissions screen, an example of which can be seen in Fig. 1.

The second half of the survey took three of these applications and split their permissions based on a specific usage of the software. Table 2 provides and overview of the applications presented to the respondent and the contextual statements behind the permission request.

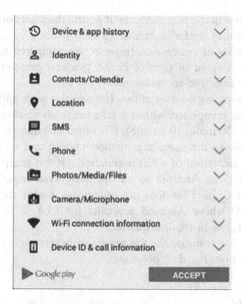

Fig. 1. Example permissions screen

Table 2. Part 2: Apps overview

App	Context	Permissions
App 1 – Social network	Install and launch	Device
		Profile
		Contacts/calendar
		Wi-Fi
	Post a picture on timeline	Photos/media/files
		Camera/microphone
		Location
	Text control over account	SMS
		Phone
App 2 – Game	Install and launch	Profile
		Wi-Fi
		Phone state
	Save game	Photos/media/files
	Make an in-app purchase over SMS	In-app purchases
		SMS
		Phone
	Play-for-free	Location phone state
App 3 – Banking App	Install and launch	Identity phone state
	Find local branch	Location
	Remote check deposit	Camera/microphone
	Transfer to contact	Phone contacts list

Following the review of the two methods of permissions acceptance participants are asked which approach they prefer in managing their privacy.

Responses to each set of permission requests are compared against each other to examine if the greater degree of control in the granular permissions approach does indeed lead to a more selective acceptance.

Participants on computing courses at two Universities were approached to take part in the study which was completed within a scheduled lab session. In total, 60 participants took the survey (50 male, 10 female); it is noted that there is a bias in the sample in terms of gender due to the sampling method chosen and as such this cannot be considered a true representation of a full population. Of this sample, the same number of participants used iOS as Android as an operating system: 45.8 % each with the remainder using other OS's. This does not reflect the market shares in 2014 as suggested by IDC (2015) where Android accounts for 84.4 % of the mobile market compared to iOS's 11.7 % in the last quarter.

The following section summarizes the results from this survey and presents points for further discussion from the data obtained.

4 Survey Results

The breakdown of acceptance for whole permission requirements (part 1 of the instrument) is broken down in Table 3.

Table 3. Whole acceptance summary

App part 1	% Accept
Social network	50 %
Messenger	66.7 %
Invasive flashlight	18.3 %
Less invasive flashlight	61.2 %
File store	71.7 %
Game	48.3 %
Invasive camera	28.3 %
Less Invasive camera	90.7 %
Banking	60 %
Loyalty card	30 %

Interestingly, despite only 50 % of participants stating that they would accept the permissions for the social networking application, 80.7 % of participants admitted to having the social networking app Facebook on their phone (which these permissions were taken from). Furthermore, if this particular response is broken down then the majority of change is from iOS users where 74.1 % would reject the permissions presented them but 85.2 % have the app on their phone. The change is much less pronounced in users of Android where 75 % of participants stated they would accept the permissions with a similar amount (71.4 %) admitting to having the app on their phones. Indeed, it is the Android users who would be more used to this style of permission acceptance.

Perhaps unsurprisingly, there was a large increase in the number of acceptances in the two applications where a less invasive version was offered if the first was rejected. Participants stated that the requests were much more reasonable: "it needs this", "only requires relevant access for the flashlight to function". This would suggest that attention was paid to the permissions requested within the context of the survey and an assessment made as whether or not they are reasonable. However, a number of participants still felt access to the camera was unreasonable: "it would still have access to my camera and microphone, there are other ways of turning on the flashlight". This is despite the flashlight being governed by the same set of permissions as the camera in Android suggesting there is a lack of understanding of the technical aspect of permissions; this is further discussed later in the paper. Furthermore, a number of participants did state that the reason they accepted was "I always do it without thinking" and this was carried through to the survey for a number of example applications.

Results from Table 4 would suggest that participants, when given the opportunity, will be more selective of their acceptable permissions. On each of the above sample scenarios the total amount of complete answers is less than the comparable app in the previous section. For example, 60 % of participants confirmed that they would accept the banking app's permissions when all are required for install compared to only 19.3 % who confirmed that they would accept each of the permissions when given separately. This would espouse the benefits of more granular control over permissions on a mobile device. Indeed, the majority of participants (66.7 %) preferred this style of permission management. However, they would still need to accept all permissions in totality were they to be able to use the software.

Table 4. Part 2: Permissions overview

App	Context	% Accept
App 1 – Social network	Install and launch	66.7 %
	Post a picture on timeline	75 %
	Text control over account	65 %
	Accept to each	40 %
App 2 – Game	Install and Launch	74.1 %
	Save Game	72.4 %
	Make an in-app purchase over SMS	48.3 %
	Play-for-free	52.6 %
	Accept to each	24.6 %
App 3 – Banking app	Install and launch	82.1 %
	Find local branch	89.3 %
	Remote check deposit	29.8 %
	Transfer to contact	61.4 %
	Accept to each	19.3 %

However, the likelihood of acceptance appears to be coupled with understanding. For example, 89.3 % of participants allowed the banking app to access the devices location to find the local branch. Reasons for acceptance appeared to suggest that the request reasonable: "It needs it", "Seems helpful", "Needs to locate you and find the nearest branch". When understanding is lacking the likelihood of response is less. For example, in the same app the permission requires access to a camera to take a picture of check in order to make a remote deposit. Only 29.8 % of participants agreed to this particular access: "Why would it need my camera", "Camera not needed", "I don't think it needs these" etc. This reflects the approach some app developers are taking, by explaining the reason behind permissions in the app market, in order encourage users to install applications with obscure looking permissions.

5 Conclusions and Further Work

Mobile devices and their associated software stores have become a ubiquitous part of society. Users from a wide spectrum of backgrounds frequently interact with the permissions systems employed by app stores during the installation and updating of mobile apps. Mobile devices are much more integrated into our daily lives than fixed computers facilitating a wide variety of tasks (e.g. diary, contacts, navigation, and photography). As a consequence they contain large amounts of personal data. Permissions are requested to enable users to determine what personal data applications have access to.

The findings of the survey illustrate that the respondents are aware of software permissions, however in many instances accept the permissions requested for the majority of applications. It is obvious that a user's decision about whether to install an application or not is governed by more than just their permissions.

Existing usage of a service is likely to increase the chances of an application being installed. The motivation for the user is likely that of acceptance; "the provider already has access to my data, as I'm already a user of the service". Alternatively the reputation of the provider is assessed with the user making a value judgment based on the size/reach/popularity of an application provider and utility of the application. For example many users rejected the generic social network application, yet admitted to having software installed from one of the established social networks.

User understanding plays a large role in the acceptance of application permissions. It was clear from the survey responses that some effort was made by users to understand why permissions are requested. However awareness of the broad granularity of permission is limited. Additionally users demonstrate their lack of understanding of the underlying fundamentals of how some applications work, refusing to install a banking application that required camera access in order to scan/photograph a cheque. This limited understanding identified in the sample group of computer specialists is likely much larger in the general population. At present the user is provided with a list of the functionality each permission provides, rather than the reason that the permission is required, leaving the user to guess why each permission is needed. It would be beneficial if a description of the reason each permission request is being made was presented to the user during the installation process. The description could be derived from the requirements stage of the software development process. However, such additions to the application must not add to the complexity of the interaction or risk being similarly ignored by the user. The question is therefore raised: how can users be made aware of the context of permission requests without adding to the complexity of the system?

In spite of the additional factors considered by users installing applications, and misunderstandings related to the permissions model, a more granular approach to application permissions resulted in users being more selective about the software that they install, i.e. rejecting invasive applications.

We therefore conclude that increased choice, realized through a more granular approach to application permissions provides improvements to user privacy.

Further work is required to determine how users interact with an application permission during a software update. The value judgment made by users is likely to vary when they are prompted to grant permissions for software that they have used frequently for an extended period of time.

References

Apvrille, A., Nigam, R.: Obfuscation in Android malware, and how to fight back. Virus Bull. pp. 1–10 (2014)

Batyuk, L., Herpich, M., Camtepe, S.A., Raddatz, K., Schmidt, A.D., Albayrak, S.: Using static analysis for automatic assessment and mitigation of unwanted and malicious activities within android applications. In: Proceedings of the 6th International Conference on Malicious and Unwanted Software, 18–19 Oct 2011, Fajardo, Puerto Rico, pp. 66–72 (2011)

Delac, G., Silic, M., Krolo, J.: Emerging security threats for mobile platforms. In: Proceedings of MIPRO 2011, 23–27 May 2011, Opatija, Croatia, pp. 1468–1473 (2011)

Erturk, E.: A Case study in open source software security and privacy: android adware. In: Proceedings of the World Congress on Internet Security, 10–12 June 2012, Ontario, Canada, pp. 189–191 (2012)

Fazeen, M., Dantu, R.: Another free app: does it have the right intentions? In: Proceedings of the 12th Annual Conference on Privacy, Security and Trust, 23–24 July 2014, Toronto, Canada, pp. 283–289 (2014)

Frank, M., Dong, B., Porter Felt, A., Song, D.: Mining permission request patterns from android and facebook applications. In: Proceedings of the 12th International Conference on Data Mining, 10–13 Dec 2012, Brussels, Belgium, pp. 870–875 (2012)

Ghosh, D., Joshi, A., Finin, T., Jagtap, P.: Privacy control in smart phones using semantically rich reasoning and context modeling. In: Proceedings of the Symposium on Security and Privacy Workshops, 24–25 May 2012, San Francisco, CA, USA, pp. 82–85 (2012)

Google: Using OAuth 2.0 for server to server applications. https://developers.google.com/accounts/docs/OAuth2ServiceAccount (Accessed on Feb 10, 2015)

IDC (International Data Corporation): Smartphone OS Market Share, Q3 2014. (2015) http://www.idc.com/prodserv/smartphone-os-market-share.jsp (Accessed on Feb 10, 2015)

Madden, D.: BBC internet blog - BBC iPlayer android app update. (2012) http://www.bbc.co.uk/blogs/legacy/bbcinternet/2012/02/bbc_iplayer_android_update.html (Accessed Feb 10, 2015)

Mylonas, A., Dritsas, S., Tsoumas, B., Gritzalis, D.: Smartphone security evaluation the malware attack case. In: Proceedings of the International Conference on Security and Cryptography, 18–21 July 2011, Seville, Spain, pp. 25–36 (2011)

Felt, P.A., Egelman, S., Finifter, M., Akhawe, D., Wagner, D.: How to Ask for Permission. In: Proceedings of HotSec '12, 7 Aug 2012, Bellevue, WA, USA (2012)

Felt, AP., Finifter, M., Chin, E., Hanna, S., Wagner, D.: A survey of mobile malware in the wild. In: Proceedings of the 1st ACM Workshop on Security and Privacy in Smartphones and Mobile Devices, 17–21 Oct 2011, Chicago, IL, USA, pp. 3–14 (2011)

Luo, Y., Gu, D., Li, J.: Toward active and efficient privacy protection for android. In: Proceedings of the International Conference on Information Science and Technology, 23–25 March, 2013, Yangzhou, Jiangsu, China, pp. 925–929 (2013)

Information Presentation: Considering On-line User Confidence for Effective Engagement

Elahe Kani-Zabihi[1]([✉]), Lizzie Coles-Kemp[2], and Martin Helmhout[3]

[1] University of West London, London, UK
elahe.kanizabihi@ntu.ac.uk
[2] Royal Holloway - University of London, London, UK
[3] University of Oxford, Oxford, UK

Abstract. In order to design on-line services that are able to support the end-user in making informed choices about when and how to disclose personal information, a close understanding of the relationship between privacy and confidence is therefore needed. UK citizens accessing on-line services have privacy concerns about sharing personal information with government organizations. The physical distance between service user and service provider (increased by on-line service delivery) can reduce confidence in the management of personal information. A close understanding of the relationship between user confidence and information presentation can suggest new design principles to support them in making informed choices about when and how to disclose personal information. This paper presents the result of three user studies to understand user confidence with relation to graphical information presentation, which led to three distinct types of confidence: Institutional; Technological; and Relationship. The final study represents the impact of using graphical information presentation on users' privacy concern and their confidence in using on-line services. The result indicated service users' privacy concerns decrease when their privacy awareness increase.

1 Introduction

The work presented in this paper is part of a project (2009–2012) entitled Visualisation and Other Methods of Expression (VOME) whose main objective was to develop methods of expressing privacy that enable a wider range of privacy concerns to be articulated and offer a broader variety of privacy protection responses [1, 2, 4, 5]. This project was part of a wider movement [3, 6, 9, 11] focused on gaining a greater understanding of information practices. This paper represents the impact of using graphical information presentation on users' privacy concern and their confidence in using on-line services.

2 Trust and Confidence

In an attempt to learn more about confidence in current literature, we learned confidence is considered to be an aspect of trust. It has long been understood that trust is socially-constructed and multi-faceted. It is also understood that trust in an on-line

© Springer International Publishing Switzerland 2015
T. Tryfonas and I. Askoxylakis (Eds.): HAS 2015, LNCS 9190, pp. 517–525, 2015.
DOI: 10.1007/978-3-319-20376-8_46

service covers many different aspects: Trust in technology and Trust in the institution that delivers the service. Technological trust represents trust by individuals or institutions in technologies, from a reliability and security perspective. When users believe that the system will protect their safety and security then there is a technological trust in that system. Trust can be dependent on: perceptions of technology; trust in the security mechanisms used to secure transactions [7] and confidence in the reliability of the whole system [10]. For example, e-services with restricted access have gained users' confidence [6]. Furthermore, achieving desirable user experience goals is possible by being more responsiveness in communications. In order to build trust, service providers should work on their relationships with service users. Kuriyan et al. [7] reports two types of trust which define relationships: Relational trust and Process-based trust. Relational trust is where trust is being a property of relations between different social actors both institutions and individuals. When there is a good relationship between a user and other actors (other users, service provider and third parties) there is a relational trust between them. Process-based trust involves an incremental "give and take" process. The institutional trust (or confidence) is built inductively through experiences and reputation. Smith [10] reported users' positive experience during their interaction with the e-service had influenced their trust on the institution. The less confidence users say they have the less likely they are to carry out a range of activities and transactions on-line. This has ramifications for on-line engagement and the successful delivery of public services on-line. Creating conditions in which end-users can build up meaningful confidence in a service provider's ability to manage their personal data is important. Quality of data also potentially increases the effectiveness of the services that can be offered. To define confidence, we use Luhmann's [8] definition: "confidence takes place where actions are executed under the assumption expectations will be met". This definition is used because it most accurately reflects the service user attitude under which personal information is disclosed.

3   Background

Our first user study included interviews of 56 participants with varying levels of ICT literacy. The purpose of this study was to observe users' privacy practices and hear their on-line privacy concerns during their interaction with the on-line registration process. The main objective was to gather users' expectations from an on-line service provider. The result obtained from the study has been published [5]. We learned certain level of confidence in management of personal information should exist before one discloses accurate personal data. Participants showed a desire to have a service design that provided spaces and tools through which they could think through personal information disclosure questions. Service users can have low confidence in a service provider's ability to protect their personal information even if those service users trust the overall brand. Wretchedly, contemporary on-line service designs have failed to support users to build their confidence. It was discovered users with privacy concern adopted one of the following strategies: Give false information; Discontinue with registration; Continue with registration, give accurate information but reduce the degree of on-going service engagement. However, the initial study only gave a partial picture as to the dimensions of confidence that affect a citizen's feelings about personal information disclosure in on-line contexts. Further studies were set up to develop a more complete picture.

4   The Digital Intervention

In order to better understand the dimensions of confidence and their relevance to the management of personal information we developed a digital intervention. This was of an on-line registration process which represented a mock-up council, named Your Local Council (YLC). YLC (Fig. 1) offered an on-line smartcard registration service for citizens to use for local public services which adopted the smartcard for delivering the following services: a Library service, a Local Shops discount scheme and Local Transport. The prototype was designed according to a combination of user requirements, HCI and CRM principles obtained from the first user study [5]. We asked participants to engage with YLC website by assuming the role of a citizen and imagine the council to be their 'real' council.

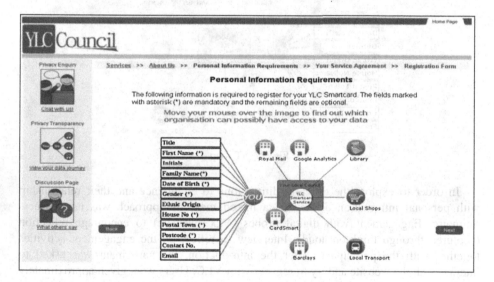

Fig. 1.   YLC - 1st prototype

4.1   The First Prototype

In the second user study, we were interested to know users' opinion of our new graphical information presentation design, which was an interactive data flow map (Fig. 2) named Social Translucence Map (ST map). The map showed what data, in this fictional context, would be needed when eventually the user registers for a particular service and who (local service providers) will have access to what part of their personal information. Users could hover the cursor over the map to receive further information.

After the introduction to smartcard services provided by YLC, users were asked to interact with the website which guides them through a sequential registration process. Every page has the same layout and contains three icons on the left side which provides three probes (left hand panel in Fig. 1). Each probe enables a different kind of communication: interaction with the service provider (privacy enquiry), interaction with other service users (discussion page) and visual representations of information flows to third parties (ST map). The probes are designed to explore how different technological approaches can help to build awareness of the privacy features of the registration process. These probes have been fully described in [5]. The ST map is one of the Privacy Transparency probe which was used by researchers to explore the effect of transparency on both the confidence in a service provider's ability to protect personal information and on the effectiveness of this approach to increase privacy awareness.

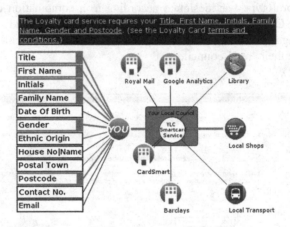

Fig. 2. ST map

In order to explore the different dimensions to confidence and their relationship with personal information disclosure, a mixed methods approach was used: Questionnaire; Engagement with digital probes (YLC website) to encourage reflection (captured through think-out-loud); Interview to reflect on the engagement activities together with the participant. After the introduction, the participant was asked to interact with the website and try to register with YLC. Users were given approximately 5 min to register. Participants who had successfully registered with the website were asked to interact further with the mock-up to accomplish a set of tasks. The aim of these tasks was to explore topics of confidence with participants by using the privacy awareness probes.

Participants. 100 (65 female and 35 male) participants recruited from 8 UK Online Centres (an organization focusing on IT training and supporting the digital inclusion of the UK public) based in London, Guildford, Bracknell, Bradford, Sheffield, and Sunderland (cities in UK). All participants (Internet users at the centre aged between 16 and 65 years old) were recruited by the Centre Manger and offered a shopping voucher as a reward for their contribution to the research. We were interested in the broad spectrum of Internet experience. 85 % of the participants had more than a year's Internet experience. In addition to experienced Internet users with more than five years, we recruited 'non-users' as well. In HCI non-users are regarded as potential users, which refer to people who might in the future engage with the system but are currently inactive users [5]. Not only are "non-users" interesting in the sense that they might potentially be on their way to becoming users but also some of the participants in the initial study indicated that "non-users", for example grandmothers, played a role in influencing on-line behaviours of family members. As a result they are included in this study and their views on confidence and personal information disclosure elicited.

Results. All participants engaged with the technology probes whilst completing the registration tasks. In particular, all participants engaged with the ST map. Almost 93 users felt the registration process was easy to do. However 43 users indicated they needed help in order to complete the task. A comparison between users' general opinion about websites and their specific opinion about the YLC prototype was made with Wilcoxon-pairs signed-ranks analysis ($p < 0.05$): When users interact with the prototype do they feel less concerned about their privacy compared to their general experiences with websites on the Internet? The participants confirm that this is the case. Users feel significantly less concerned when asked for information but also did not really feel that they had to think twice before submitting their information. Although the prototype gave the user no choice other than to follow the steps and deliver the required information (in comparison to opt-out/opt-in) the majority of participants ($n = 68$) perceived that the service provider gave them enough freedom to make decisions about how their information was collected, used and shared. 52 participants were of the opinion that the YLC discloses how information is collected, processed and used. Only 6 users did not agree. In other words, the majority of users perceive that the provider is making them aware of how their personal information is handled. There were also significantly less concern about how the YLC prototype takes care of the safety of their personal information. 48 users disagree that YLC does not care about the safety of their personal information. 73 users think that a website should contain security marks indicating that the website is secure. Although YLC did not contain any security marks only 30 users disagreed that YLC was a secure website. The majority of users ($n = 76$) agrees that YLC uses information after giving consent. YLC makes people feel assured that their information is not used for different reasons. Most users ($n = 66$) agreed that this is the case and appreciate the fact that the prototype was transparent concerning the way information was used. Finally, one of the important questions that supports our research questions is whether users are made aware by the prototype about how their personal information will be used. The highly significant outcome indicates that YLC is performing well (only 13 users disagreed) with regards to making people aware of how their information is used compare to other website in general.

Less-experienced users had difficulties to proceed to 'Registration Form' as they had lack of confidence in various forms. These have been categorised in: Institutional confidence; Technological confidence; and Human relationship confidence.

Institutional Confidence. The reactions to the probes demonstrated that an important method of engendering confidence is service providers' openness. For instance, Sally an experienced Internet user (age of 30–40) stated service provider's "openness" and "honestly" gained her confidence. Richard (age 20–30), was "amazed" by the way information was presented (ST map) and "impressed" by the service provider's disclosure on the process. 92 participants said they trust the service provider as it is an e-government service and they are confident the local council will keep their information confidential.

Technological Confidence. 72 participants had self-confidence in being able to use the technology and also confidence that the service provider has the technology in place to protect personal information. It has long been established that confidence in technology is related to a willingness to disclose personal data. However, this study showed that there are several distinct aspects to the question of technology confidence. It is both a question of feeling confident in being able to use the technology presented to you as part of the service and also a confidence in the technology to keep any disclosed information secure. Even when a participant trusted the service provider's brand and had experience of that brand, they were likely to still look for signs of technological security controls. Designing for confidence requires the interface used for Information Presentation to be clear and easy to understand. Interfaces also need to be designed to support users under time pressure. Service users need to have confidence in using the technology before feeling comfortable about disclosing personal information. Julie (age 40–50) as a non-user was reluctant to register. She had no confidence in using the probes. Rose (age 40–49) a novice Internet user preferred to continue using services off-line. Chris (age 50+) another novice user, felt very "frustrated" as he expected to see a registration form instead of the ST map. It is not only important for the service design to engender confidence in the use of the technology but also to engender confidence in the technological capability for information protection. For example, Antony (age 50+) with less than 1 year experience was looking for security signs on the website. Confidence building is not linear and media reports and publicised breaches that affect users' confidence. Richard is a young-adult who considered himself as an experienced Internet user. In the past Richard has ignored on-line privacy issues and would reveal his personal information whenever he needed a service. He stated: *"I registered with the play station network which had my details and some hackers got in and stole seventy seven million people's details and so that's probably made me a little bit more cautious to the companies and what various companies do to secure data".* Although he has confidence in the service provider, he has lost his confidence in their ability to protect his personal information. This demonstrates that service providers are evaluated on their technical ability to manage personal information. The design of a service needs to reflect and articulate the safety and security mechanisms in place. However, the technical evaluation can be part of the social relationship recommender network that service users often operate within. Reliance on family members to evaluate unknown service providers, particularly for female service users, was also a pattern that could be seen in the results. Pam (50+ years old) an experienced user checks the security mechanisms used on the website and this consists of checking the URL address of the website to see if it is HTTP or HTTPS (HTTP Secure). The most prominent service design features to engender a service user's own confidence could be the visibility of system status and the aesthetic qualities of the interface.

Human Relationship Confidence. Throughout the VOME studies it has been a fairly frequent comment that people seek or use personal recommendations. 70 participants said Feedback from previous users is very important element for them to make their decision about using the service. Some participant such as Carla (age 40–50) an experienced user were in favour of a chat system and said "immediate connection" is an important factor. Others felt having a chat system "for privacy may be a bit excessive" (Stephone, 30–39 years old, experienced user). The evident drawback which participants were mostly concerned about was incapability of the chat system to run through a voice chat as well as text. Jaali (20–29 years old, experienced user) said: "*...you don't know who you're talking to and that bit I didn't like... it could be weird to [chat] with somebody I didn't know, especially about something like privacy issues. It's like, I'm talking about privacy issues, but I don't know who I'm talking to.*" Therefore, the principle of a real-world implementation of face to face communication is important for the effectiveness of service user to service provider communication. In the case of the probe design, the anonymity of the communication and, in some cases, the lack of privacy resulted in little increase to feelings of confidence. The rule of confirmation is also an important principle if the method of communication is accepted.

4.2   The Second Prototype

The prototype (Fig. 3) embedded ST map with the registration page in which a user could choose to reveal less, but losing out on some opportunities. In order to be consistent with the previous study the same research methodology used. Users' behaviours and their interaction with ST map as well as their perceptions of on-line privacy probes were recorded to test and evaluate our research hypotheses. 102 participants (aged between 18 and 60 years old) were recruited through UK Online Centre of which 64 were experienced Internet users with more than 5 years. Participants were equally clustered in two groups: Group One (G1) to interact first with the second version of the prototype - YLC with privacy probes and ST map (privacy features (**PF**)) and then use YLC without PF. Group Two (G2) started with YLC without PF. The null hypothesis was: The order of which website they use does not have effect on their responses.

Data collected were analysed with SPSS and T-test were applied. The result obtained from T-Test ($p > 0.05$) indicates it is likely that the null hypothesis is true and the order of which participants use websites does not have effect on their responses. Therefore, our result reported here considered data gathered from G1 and G2. The result obtained from the interview, observation and questionnaire showed the presentation of privacy information (ST map) had huge impact on users' privacy awareness. 72 participants stated they are now more aware of privacy risks on-line and their attitude towards disclosure will be vigilant. 81 participants said they prefer to use an on-line registration form with ST map. More advanced Internet users said it is "time consuming" and ST map should not be embedded as part of the registration process but as a reference available for users with privacy concern. It was interesting to see 40 participants in G2 were reluctant to register with the YLC registration form without PF. 28 users from this group changed their mind and were more confident to use the service when they were exposed to the graphical information presentation in the YLC

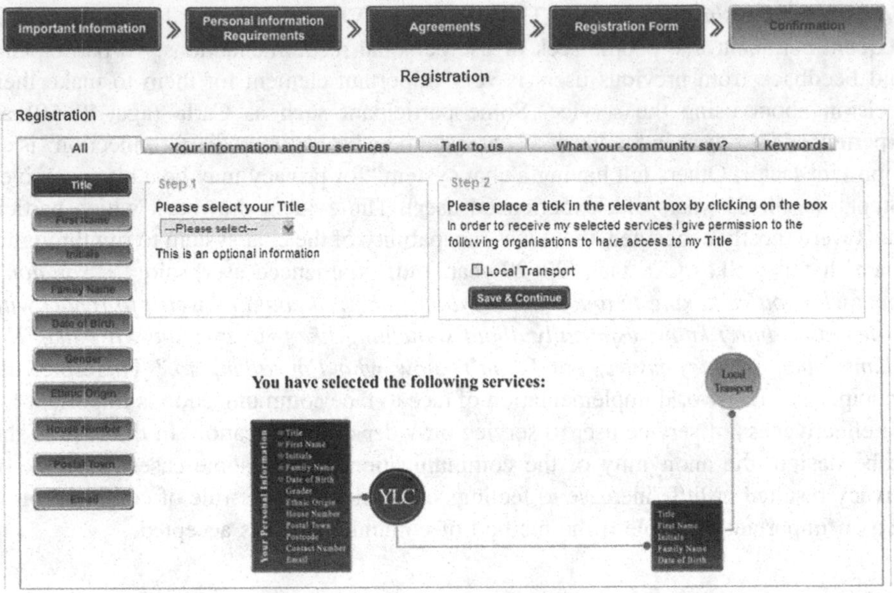

Fig. 3. Registration form with ST map

registration form with PF. All participants were satisfied with the way YLC-with PF deals with personal information. 69 participants agreed that YLC-with PF is concern about the safety and security of their user. However, 90 participants of YLC-without PF thought otherwise. 75 participants were concerned with YLC-without PF to ask them about personal information and only 12 participants were concerned with YLC-with PF. Finally, 81 users agreed YLC-with PF gives them enough freedom to make decisions about how their information is collected, used and shared. This number was much lower for YLC-without PF (n = 48).

Our research to discover more from the final user study is still on-going. Our future publication will report our further findings. Currently, we have learned transparency in privacy information and better presentation increases users' confidence in service providers' ability to protect their privacy. This increases users' privacy awareness which results in more effective engagements with on-line services.

5   Conclusion

How far it is economically interesting for a service provider to support confidence by design will depend on the service and the type of relationship they wish to have with their service users. Clearly, a lack of confidence has data quality and service support implications. This has cost implications for service providers needing to build close relationships with service users in order to deliver an effective service. We tested this by introducing an interactive visual map where the service provider was able to reveal its relationships with other parties and what personal information will flow to those organisations. The result obtained from our user study demonstrated that by interacting with ST map, users were encouraged to explore and gather information. Users were also more aware about what to expect and what the consequences are regarding privacy when they register for the service. Users were in favour of the map and felt more confidence. The interaction with the map also raised some interesting discussion which helped us to see other dimensions in User Confidence. This paper presented this result and discuss three distinct types of confidence: Institutional; Technological; and Relationship. The last user study focused on user confidence and user privacy awareness. Users were asked to interact with a more enhanced graphical information presentation of YLC website. The result indicated information presentation has a considerable impact on users' confidence in using on-line services. Therefore in order to help users to have that 'positive experience' it is important to increase user's privacy awareness though better design and transparent information.

Acknowledgements. We are grateful to all participants who took part in this study. This work as supported by the TSB; EPSRC and ESRC [grant number EP/G00255/X].

References

1. Coles-Kemp, L., Kani-Zabihi, E.: On-line privacy and consent: A dialogue not a monologue. In 21–23 Sep ACM PRESS, Ed. ACM Press, pp. 1–15 (2010)
2. Coles-Kemp, L., Kani-Zabihi, E.: Practice makes perfect: motivating confident on-line privacy protection practices. In: IEEE International Conference on Privacy, Security, Risk and Trust and IEEE Internationa Conference on Social Computing, 9–11 Oct, Anonymous IEEE, pp. 866–871 (2011)
3. Dourish, P., Grinter, R.E., La De Delgado Flor, J.: Security in the wild: user strategies for managing security as an everyday, practical problem. Personal Ubiquitous Comput. **8**, 391–401 (2004)
4. Kani-zabihi, E., Coles-Kemp, L.: Service users' requirements for tools to support effective on-line privacy and consent practices. In: The 15th Nordic Conference in Secure IT Systems (NordSec' 10), 24–30 Oct, LNCS, Ed. ACM Press, pp. 106–120 (2010)
5. Kani-Zabihi, E., Helmhout, M.: Increasing service users' privacy awareness by introducing on-line interactive privacy features. In: Pre-Proceedings of Nordsec 2011 16th Nordic Conference on Secure IT-Systems, Talinn, Estonia, Oct 26–28, 2011, Anonymous, pp. 287–306 (2011)
6. Karahasanovic, A., Brandtzæg, P.B., Vanattenhoven, J., Lievens, B., Nielsen, K.T., Pierson, J.: Ensuring trust, privacy, and etiquette in Web 2.0 Applications, pp. 42–49 (2009)
7. Kuriyan, R., Kitner, K., Watkins, J.: ICTs, development and trust: an overview. Inf. Technol. People **23**, 216–221 (2010)
8. Luhmann, N.: Familiarity, Confidence, Trust: Problems and Alternatives. Trust: Making and Breaking Cooperative Relations, Electronic Edition, pp. 94–107. Department of Sociology, University of Oxford, Oxford (2000)
9. Ofcom Media Literacy Matters.: Online trust and privacy: People's attitude and behaviour (2010)
10. Smith, M.L.: Building institutional trust through e-government trustworthiness cues. Inf. Technol. People **23**, 222–246 (2010)
11. US Federal Trade Commission: Privacy Online: Fair Information Practices in the Electronic Marketplace: A Report to Congress. FTC, Washington, DC (2000) (Retrieved June 6, 2000)

Privacy Principles in Design of Smart Homes Systems in Elderly Care

Ella Kolkowska[✉]

Örebro University School of Business, Örebro, Sweden
ella.kolkowska@oru.se

Abstract. Privacy is considered as a main concern in developing and implementing smart home systems for elderly care (SHSEC). Privacy-by-Design (PbD) can help to ensure privacy in such systems and can support the designers in taking the protection of the privacy into account during the development of such systems. In this paper, we investigate the suitability of the PbD principles (PbDPs) suggested by Cavoukian et al. [1] in the context of SHSEC. This research is conducted as a qualitative case study, where we highlight limitations of existing PbDPs in this context. Based on our findings, we suggest seven additional PbDPs which complement the existing PbDPs and adjust them in the context of SHSEC.

Keywords: Privacy by design · Aging in place · Smart home system · Privacy · Elderly

1 Introduction

A smart home network is a unified combination of people, wireless networks, and other technical devices [2]. By using this technology, a smart home system (SHS) can provide information about activities and the status of different entities in the home environment. Recently, smart home technology has been used to support the independent living of elderly people allowing them to stay at home as long as possible [3, 4]. Using smart home technologies in elderly care is beneficial in many ways. The elderly can live longer independently in their homes where they usually have a richer social life and can maintain established habits. For caregivers, such solutions reduce their workload and for the society, smart home solutions substantially decrease the costs for elderly care since the cost of care at home is almost always a fraction of the cost of residential care [5]. However, to allow the elderly to stay at home, the smart home technologies must ensure the safety of the residents and give caregivers the opportunity to quickly react to any health problem or any emergency in the smart home. This is realized by extended monitoring of the activities of the inhabitants [6], which raise many new privacy concerns [3, 7]. Ensuring privacy of the elderly is thus one of the main concerns in design of smart home systems in elderly care (SHSEC). This is one of the reasons why the EU advocates the principle of privacy-by-design (PbD) [8].

However there are different ways in how PbD is understood and applied in practice because of the different needs and the differences in defining privacy in various contexts

© Springer International Publishing Switzerland 2015
T. Tryfonas and I. Askoxylakis (Eds.): HAS 2015, LNCS 9190, pp. 526–537, 2015.
DOI: 10.1007/978-3-319-20376-8_47

[3, 9]. Kosta et al. [10] argue that applying general ethical guidelines in the context of SHSEC is difficult because of the complexity of this environment and because of the conflicting interests that can arise between the different stakeholders within such environment. It is also recognized that ethical issues such as privacy that can come up in relation to the development and implementation of SHSEC are not sufficiently focused during the development of such systems [11]. Most of today's projects are technically oriented and focus on development and effectiveness of these technologies [7, 12]. Thus development of practical privacy guidelines that can be easily adapted in this context is seen as a real challenge [10]. The aim of this paper is to highlight limitations of existing PbDPs in the context of SHSEC and suggest a set of PbDPs adjusted to this context. A starting point for this research is a set of PbDPs suggested by Cavoukian et al. [1] for the context of personal health monitoring.

The paper is structured as follows. Section 2 contains a discussion about privacy in the context of SHSEC. In Sect. 3 we present our research method. Section 4 reports on our analysis of the case study. In Sect. 5 we present a set of PbDPs applied in this context. Finally the paper ends with conclusions in Sect. 6.

2 Privacy in the Context of SHSEC

New technologies such as SHSs are promoted as a means of retaining autonomy and quality of life for elderly people enabling them to continue to live independently in familiar settings [11]. The decreasing costs of such technologies together with their increased efficiency and portability create almost limitless possibilities to collect, process and communicate physiological and environmental data from the smart home to different stakeholders such as relatives, health care personnel, social workers etc. [13]. The complexity and special characteristics of SHSEC environments raise new privacy issues that are very different from those related to traditional applications and systems [3, 10].

Some scholars [i.e. 14] argue that the elderly people themselves do not worry about privacy and do not experience the monitoring devices in their homes as something disturbing. However, other studies [i.e. 3] show that privacy concerns are one of the biggest barriers to the successful implementation of SHSECs in practice. Nordgren [9] argues that some individuals are concerned about their privacy and some are not, but because we do not know it in advance, privacy has to be protected for everyone [9]. Moreover ensuring privacy of sensitive personal data, such as monitoring data, is regulated by law in most of the countries and therefore, it cannot be ignored. It is also known that most of the people are not capable of protecting their own sensitive information and thus the privacy protection has to be standardized and automatized by PbD [8]. According to Cavoukian et al. [1], PbD is a concept of embedding privacy into the design specifications of technologies. The authors suggest seven PbDPs for the context of personal health monitoring: (1) Proactive, not reactive; preventative, not remedial, (2) Privacy as the default, (3) Privacy embedded into the design, (4) Functionality —positive-sum, not zero-sum, (5) End-to-end lifecycle protection, (6) Visibility and transparency, and (7) Respect for users' privacy. These principles are an adjustment of general OECD

"Guidelines on the Protection of Privacy and Transborder Flows of Personal Data". Nordgren [9] discuss the suitability of the PbDPs suggested by Cavoukian et al. [1] in ensuring privacy of the patients in the context of personal health monitoring and concludes that the principles are supportive in ensuring privacy of the patients in this context. In this paper we study the suitability of these principles in the context of SHSEC.

3   Research Method

This study was conducted in the context of the European project GiraffPlus (http:// www.giraffplus.eu/). GiraffPlus aims at developing a SHS that supports independent living for the elderly who wish to remain in their homes as long as possible. GiraffPlus is a complex system of sensors and a telepresence robot, Giraff, which is used for both monitoring and communication. In this project, special emphasis is put on evaluations and on feedback from both the primary and secondary users. Primary users are the elderly people who will actually be using the GiraffPlus system/services to allow them to live at home. Secondary users are persons who are in direct contact with a primary user. This group is further divided in health care professionals and formal and informal caregivers. Formal caregivers are home care personnel and informal caregivers are close relatives or friends who take care of the primary user.

We have followed the project for a period of three years and focused on under-standing what types of privacy requirements were formulated during the development process, which ones were implemented and why they were implemented. Hence, this makes an interpretative approach suitable [15]. Data was collected during these three years by reviewing the project's deliverables, its working documents and the project's blog. A few interviews were also conducted with developers responsible for test sites in Sweden. The collected data was analysed in four steps. First, we identified privacy requirements. Second, we investigated how the requirements were implemented in the system. The requirements could, for instance, be implemented as a technical mechanism or a guideline or not implemented at all. In the third step we compared the privacy requirements and their implementations with the PbDPs defined by [1]. This was done in order to find which PbDPs were applied and which were ignored. We also studied whether the implementations of privacy requirements were in line with the PbDPs. Finally, we investigated the reasons why some of the PbDPs were not applied. An example chosen from the analysis is presented in Table 1. The limitations of the PbDPs identified in the project were then discussed and finally, based on this discussion, PbDPs adjusted for the context of SHSE were suggested.

4   Compliance with PbD Principles - Analysis of the Case Study

Since GiraffPlus aims to collect, store, process and transfer a considerable amount of personal and medical data, privacy and security issues were often raised during the project and the importance of data security and privacy was emphasized during development of the GiraffPlus system[1]. In the following text we describe how the privacy requirements formulated in the GiraffPlus project and their implementations comply with PbDPs stated as Cavoukian et al. [1].

Table 1. Compliance with PbDPs

Privacy requirement	Implementation	Compliance with PbD	Explanation
GiraffPlus shall allow access to personal data only by authorized personnel and only for legally authorized purposes	An access control system based on passwords. When authorized, the different kinds of users (i.e. health care personnel, therapists, relatives) are able to access all the information about the elderly. Relatives can only access information about their relative, other users, when authorized, can access information about all caretakers	Data limitation (collection limitation principle) which is a key aspect of PbD was not applied	The current implementation was seen as a temporary solution that would be improved in future versions of the system

4.1 Principle 1: Proactive not Reactive; Preventative not Remedial

The first principle emphasizes that respect for privacy should be included before the technology is developed. In the GiraffPlus project the requirements related to privacy were stated and formulated early in the project, before the construction of the GiraffPlus system began, indicating that this principle was followed. The privacy requirements were formulated on a general level, mainly based on the current EU data protection directive 95/46/CE as well as other privacy legislations such as Swedish law for data protection. Compliance with current privacy regulations was emphasized as very important in the project.

However following the documentation of the project we can see that privacy was not in focus when the users' requirements were collected and design principles for the system were formulated[2]. The main goal of the focus groups, questionnaires and workshops was to understand the users' requirements regarding the type of services and parameters to monitor and to study the users' preferences with respect to system design and physical appearance and not their preferences regarding privacy. As it is described

---

[1] D1.3 System Reference Architecture, D2.1 First Prototype of Sensors, Giraff Platform and Network System.
[2] D1.1 Deliverable 1.1 User Requirements and Design Principles Report.

in the documentation[3] the data privacy and security issues emerged during the focus group and the workshop phases. The concerns raised during these phases were related to the continuous monitoring and access to the data, however practical solutions to these concerns were often postponed to the future and the privacy problems were solved when they occurred during or after the deployment of the system. For instance, very soon after the system was deployed at the test sites, it was discovered that informal caregivers could access too much information about their elderly relative (medical data) and also in some cases they could access information about other elderly persons participating in the projects. The problem was eventually taken care of but as one of the developers put it "it took much more time than expected, resulting in a delay in the project"[4].

To conclude, the development of the GiraffPlus system was functionality-driven and not privacy-driven. Privacy requirements were formulated in the beginning of the project, but on a general level. Their implementation was not focused in the early stages of the development process raising sometimes privacy problems that were taken care of after they occurred. This in turn resulted in delays in the project. One of the reasons for this functionality-driven focus was that defining the system's functionality was the main objective of the project. Another reason was that it was important to be able to test a functional prototype of the GiraffPlus system in home settings where it is supposed to support vulnerable elderly people. Lacking functionality could jeopardize the elderly persons' safety and security.

4.2 Principle 2: Privacy as the Default

This principle means that privacy protection is built into the system by default and thus the individual does not need to perform any extra actions to protect his/her privacy when interacting with the system. Some parts of personal data processing are automatically protected in the GiraffPlus system. For instance, transmitted and stored data is encrypted and all access to the system is protected by usernames and passwords. However other privacy requirements cannot be implemented in the GiraffPlus system by default because they are highly individual and changeable in time. For instance, one of the privacy requirements of the GiraffPlus system is: "the GiraffPlus system can be installed with a minimum number of sensors which is decided by the users in accordance with the specific monitoring needs (i.e. the ability of customization)"[5]. Hence, the number of sensors cannot be decided beforehand (for instance as a standard solution), but must be decided every time the system is installed at an elderly person's home. Also, it is impossible to decide beforehand where the sensors can be installed and where not. Usually, the bathroom should be avoided for privacy reasons[6]; however, there are situations when the monitoring of these places (constantly or temporarily) might be justified. For instance, during the GiraffPlus project, relatives requested monitoring of their elderly relative's toilets habits. They wanted to monitor how often and for how long the elderly

---

[3] ibid.
[4] The project's blog.
[5] D1.3 System Reference Architecture.
[6] D1.1 Deliverable 1.1 User Requirements and Design Principles Report.

person visits the toilet. The request was justified by the elderly person's illness. Many such questions were raised in the project indicating the need for personalization of the services and flexibility of the technical implementations. To summarize, some parts of privacy cannot be standardized and built in the technical solution but have to be decided by consulting the elderly person and other stakeholders who take care of that person. The privacy requirements can also change over time and this means that the privacy configurations may need to be changed when the SHSEC is in use. However once the configuration is made the elderly person does not need to perform any extra actions to protect his/her privacy when interacting with the system.

4.3 Principle 3: Privacy Embedded into Design

The third principle says that privacy should be built into the technology. As highlighted in relation to the first principle, privacy and security were emphasized as very important in the context of the GiraffPlus project. Several technical security and privacy safeguards were thus implemented to protect the sensitive personal data during processing, communication and storing. For instance, the technical devices used to build the system, such as sensors, cameras etc. where chosen carefully following the existing security standards and e-health standards relevant for the project[7]. Most of the sensors were provided to the project by the industrial partners i.e. Intellicare and Tunstall. Both these companies provide sensor-technologies that follow the valid standards. Moreover, all the data sent to and stored in the server or kept locally is encrypted with secure and reliable encryption codes[8]. Further, in order to guarantee maximum privacy, a private cloud using existing PaaS open source infrastructure was established[9]. Finally, to ensure the confidentiality of data processed in the system, a two layer approach was used. A certificate consisting of a public and a private key is created by the GiraffPlus VPN Certificate Authority, which enables encrypted communication with other computers in the GiraffPlus Virtual Network. To secure communication with the Web Service, the GiraffPlus Certificate Agency is deployed, which creates public and private key pairs for all components and servers in the GiraffPlus ecosystem[10].

The limitation of this principle in the context of the project is that not all aspects of privacy can be built into the technology. As highlighted in relation to the second principle, there are some privacy requirements that cannot be built into the technology. For instance, the requirements related to the number of sensors installed in the home environment or the position of the sensors and of the Giraff-robot. Since these aspects cannot be built in the technical solution, they need to be regulated differently for instance by complementing guidelines for implementation for the SHSEC.

---

[7] D1.2 Technological Component Specifications, http://www.giraffplus.eu/.

[8] D1.3 System Reference Architecture, D2.2 Second Prototype of Sensors, Giraff Platform and Network System, D3.1 Context Inference and Configuration Planning Prototypes.

[9] D4.1 The Interaction and Visualization Service and Personalization Module Alfa Release.

[10] D2.2 Second Prototype of Sensors, Giraff Platform and Network System.

4.4   Principle 4: Functionality—Positive-Sum, not Zero-Sum

The fourth principle means that privacy is an integral part of the system without diminishing its functionality. In the GiraffPlus project, the privacy requirements were formulated in the beginning of the project and were partially treated during the whole development lifecycle of the system going from identifying the end users' needs until the evaluation of the user experiences of the system in its real settings. However, the privacy requirements were not treated as equally important as the services offered by the GiraffPlus system. As we argued in relation to the first principle the project was functionality-driven and defining the main services of the system was always the major focus even if it sometimes meant neglecting privacy. For instance, in the GiraffPlus system both health care professionals (doctors, nurses) and formal caregivers (social assistants, occupational therapist) could access all the data collected by monitoring both physiological as well as environmental parameters at the elderly person's home. According to the collection limitation principle (included in principle 4), the personal data should not be disclosed in a larger extent than necessary for the given and clearly specified purpose. The problem in the project was that the purpose and need for monitoring of the different psychological and environmental parameters was not yet clearly decided. Finding what is relevant to monitor and for what purposes was a part of the research activities of the project. Second, the current implementation was seen as a temporary solution that should be improved in the future versions of the system, since there was only a limited number of secondary users who tested the system. The focus in the project was to make the system work; thus, the functionality was prioritized before privacy.

4.5   Principle 5: End-to-End Lifecycle Protection

The fifth principle relates to the life cycle management of information and stresses that data should be protected in all data handling from its beginning (collection) to its end (destruction). In relation to the GiraffPlus project, this principle means that the right amount of data is collected for a clearly stated purpose, that data is protected during processing, transition and storage and that it is decided where and for how long the data is stored. In relation to principle 3, we described what security measures were implemented to ensure confidentiality of the data processed by the GiraffPlus system. It can be concluded that all sensitive data processed by the system is protected during some parts of the life cycle. The problem with this PbDP in the context of the project is that it is still unknown how the system will be used in practice in the future. During the project, the system was evaluated in home environments, but it was only partially tested by the secondary users (healthcare professionals, formal caregivers and informal caregivers). Thus it is unknown what consequences the implementation of the system can have on privacy in the future use. Many questions related to privacy remain unanswered. For instance: where should the data that is collected through the SHS be saved? Should it be part of the elderly's records or should it be saved somewhere else? How long should the data be kept in the system and for what purpose? How should the data be interpreted? They are important questions that need to be answered before the SHS is implemented.

In the project documents[11], the problem of lacking legislation regarding eHealth in general is also highlighted. It is argued that unclear regulations make it difficult to clearly decide the rules for how sensitive data should be handled when the SHS is in use. It can thus be concluded that in a development project such as GiraffPlus, it is difficult to take care of privacy concerns that may arise when the SHSEC is used in real settings i.e. as a part of regular elderly care.

4.6   Principle 6: Visibility and Transparency

The sixth principle states that data protection should be open to independent examination. This means that the different components and operations should remain visible and transparent to users and providers. In relation to a SHSEC, this principle means that the primary user knows (or can find out) what data is being collected, how the data is being used, and who can access it. In relation to this principle, the users' participation is also emphasized, meaning that the users should be included in deciding about the extent of monitoring and about who will be able to access the collected data.

To involve users in the development process was very important in GiraffPluss project. Significant efforts were made to collect and understand user requirements and preferences regarding the type of services and the system design[12]. Although the focus in the project was on defining the system's functionality and not on understanding the users' preferences regarding privacy, such preferences also emerged during the focus groups meetings, questionnaires and workshops. These privacy preferences were then translated to technical requirements of the system. Users were also involved in the configuration of the GiraffPlus system before the system was deployed at their homes and questions regarding privacy were raised during the evaluation of the system. It was also important to obtain a written permission from the primary users before the system was deployed. Therefore it can be concluded that in GiraffPlus project, the primary users were involved in the design process and they could decide about extent of monitoring that is in line with the sixth PbDP.

A difficulty concerning the elderly users´ participation in the design of the GiraffPlus system was related to their insufficient computer skills and their lacking understanding of the technology involved. In the GiraffPlus project, the developers used different methods to improve the elderly's understanding of the technology and of the consequences the system could have on their lives. For instance, the developers used mockups in order to increase the elderly's understanding of how they could use the GiraffPlus robot in their homes. Scenarios for the GiraffPlus system were also used to aid to the communication and to increase the elderly peoples' understanding of the functionality in the system[13]. Despite all these efforts the elderly users, who had the system installed at home, were surprised when they could see what data about them and their homes were collected by the GiraffPlus system (interview with a developer responsible for test sites in Sweden). They explained that they did not understand that it was possible to measure

---

[11] D1.1 User requirement and Design Principles Report.

[12] Ibid.

[13] D6.1 Preliminary Evaluation Report.

all these parameters using the sensors. They thought that it was only possible by using video cameras. Thus to comply with this PbDP is a challenge in the context of SHSEC because the elderly people have difficulties in understanding the consequences of the implemented technology on their privacy. It was also recognized that in some cases, other stakeholders (relatives, formal caregivers, health care professionals) decided what was relevant to monitor and to what extent without involving the elderly person him/herself. This is also seen as problematic in relation to this PbDP.

4.7 Principle 7: Respect for the Users' Privacy

This principle means that the individual's privacy should be an interest of designers and operators of health systems. As we described earlier, ensuring privacy of the primary users was a high priority during the GiraffPlus project. Thus the users' personal data collected during the project was treated according to current laws and regulations. However, it was recognized during the project that the different stakeholders involved in the design of the GiraffPlus system (developers, health care professionals, formal caregivers, informal care givers) could have different opinions regarding privacy and functionality and could focus on different aspects in this context[14]. For instance health care professionals and system developers most often focused on standardized privacy regulations and preferences that can be applied to the whole population, while caregivers put more attention to what was important for the elderly people they take care of. The general privacy demands are easier to build in the system as default, while the individual needs must remain to be flexible.

5   PbD Principles in the Context of SHSEC

In the previous section several limitations of the PbDPs in the context of the GiraffPlus project were highlighted. In this section, based on this discussion we suggest a set of PbDPs that complement the existing PbDPs and make them more appropriate for the context of SHSEC.

Principle of Holistic Thinking. We described in the case study section that not all aspects of privacy identified as important during the GiraffPlus project could be built into the technology (see Sect. 4.3). Holistic thinking aims at advancing the third PbDP, namely privacy embedded into the design. Although the third principle stays that the privacy must be embedded into the design and architecture of IT system and *business practices*, the focus when applying this principle is all too often on finding technical safeguards that can protect the sensitive data from unauthorized access when processed by the IT-system. This represents a very narrow view on privacy and clearly ignores the other aspects of privacy, such as installing the technology in different parts of the home, choosing the appropriate monitoring technology and the level of detail up to which activities can be monitored. Thus we suggest a principle of holistic thinking.

---

[14] D1.1 User requirement and Design Principles Report.

This principle means that privacy in the context of SHSEC include also aspects beyond data protection that must be considered to be able to ensure the privacy of the elderly person when using a SHSEC. Therefore the measures implemented to protect the elderly person's privacy in the context of SHSEC cannot be limited to technical safeguards. Equally important is establishing adequate procedures and business practices.

Principle of Flexibility. As it is described in the case study section, the elderly person's health situation can change over time and certain privacy-invasive functionality may (no longer) be necessary. Also the elderly person's privacy requirements may change over time and something that was accepted in the beginning may no longer feel comfortable. Hence, we suggest a principle of flexibility. This principle means that privacy implementations in a SHSEC should be adaptable and capable to change over time. This principle is an advancement of PbDP 7: Respect for users' privacy and principle 1: Proactive not reactive; Preventative not remedial.

Principle of Personalization. In the case study section we showed examples of the differences between the elderly users' needs, preferences and expectations. Acknowledging these differences is important to be able to support independent living and ensuring the privacy of the elderly person. Therefore, we suggest a principle of personalization. This principle means that the elderly should have a right to an adjustment of the offered solution (SHSEC) to his/her individual needs and preferences. This principle also means that the SHSEC needs to be configurable due to handle the huge heterogeneity across elderly users. In other words the elderly should have a right to choose the services (time and length of the monitoring) and technologies used (cameras, sensors) according to his/her individual needs and wishes. This principle is an improvement of PbDP 7: Respect for users' privacy.

Principle of Empowerment. The users' involvement in formulating privacy requirements is emphasized in PbD (especially in PbDPs 1, 6 and 7). In the GiraffPlus project special efforts were made to involve elderly users during the design of the GiraffPlus system. However, we could see that sometimes the elderly were persuaded to accept the requirements of the other stakeholders (i.e. the secondary users, relatives), which is not that difficult because the elderly are in a vulnerable position since they are in need of special care, have very low experience with and knowledge about the technology. Therefore, there is a need of empowering elderly people and give them sufficient means to be able to formulate their privacy preferences and to give informed consent regarding time and extent of monitoring services. Thus we suggest a principle of empowerment. This principle can be applied with help of the principle of clarity and the principle of control, described below.

Principle of Clarity. SHSEC involve smart but complex technologies. The different functions of the system are negotiated with the elderly, but they often do not fully understand what they agree to. In the early stages of the design, the system is very abstract and hence, the lack of sufficient (technical) knowledge and awareness makes it difficult if not impossible) to properly assess the consequences on the privacy. Therefore, there is a need for introductory presentations, special methods for collecting the elderly's requirements and usage scenarios that visualize the impact on one's privacy when the system is used. Several of such methods have been successfully used in the GiraffPlus project (as described in the case study section). Thus we suggest the principle of clarity that means that it should be understandable and clear for the elderly what services are implemented, how the data is collected, when and where they are monitored, who has access to the collected data and how the collected data is interpreted. All this aspects should be communicated to the elderly user in a clear way. This principle is an improvement of PbDP 6 and 7 and complements the principle of empowerment presented above.

Principle of Control. Based on the findings from the case study we suggest also the principle of control. This principle means that the elderly should feel that they have control over their life, the implemented technical devices and the data that is collected about them by the SHSEC. To respect this right, formal approval by the elderly regarding these previously mentioned aspects should be required. It is also important that the elderly has a right, capability and/or knowledge to switch off the monitoring when he/she wishes to do so and if it does not jeopardize his/her safety and security. This principle is an improvement of PbDP 6 and 7 and complements the principle of empowerment described earlier.

Principle of Privacy Management in Use. One considerable problem when applying the existing PbDPs during the GiraffPlus project was caused by the fact that the GiraffPlus system was seen as a prototype and therefore, the implementation of the privacy requirements were postponed to the future when the system would be commercialized. Although PbDP 5 emphasizes the importance of considering privacy aspects arising after the system have been developed, this principle is difficult to apply in the context of SHSEC because of lack of experiences, knowledge and regulations with regard to the use of SHSEC in practice. Therefore we suggest the principle of privacy management in use which is an improvement of PbDP 5. The principle of privacy management in use means that privacy aspects regarding the use of SHSEC in real settings should be considered already during the development of SHSEC. It can be done by involving significant stakeholders, such as health care professionals, formal and informal caregivers, politicians in development of a SHSEC. Privacy aspects that may appear when the current SHSEC is in use can be discussed with these stakeholders by using future usage scenarios of the system.

6   Conclusions and Future Research

As argued in the literature, ensuring privacy of the elderly is one of the main concerns in the design of SHSEC. PbD, which helps to build in privacy in technical specifications of IT systems, is seen as a possible solution to this problem. In this paper, we investigated the suitability of existing PbDPs [1] in the context of SHSEC. Through a thorough analysis of the case study, we have identified several limitations of existing PbDPs in this context. Based on these findings, we have suggested seven additional PbDPs which complement Cavoukian's et al. [1] PbDPs and adapted them for the context of SHSEC.

The complementing principles suggested in this paper are based on analysis of a case study. In the future research that is already in progress, we discuss these principles in relation to existing literature in order to find if the experienced limitations were project-specific or if they are general in the context of SHSEC. Based on this discussion we aim to further develop and validate the suggested PbDPs.

References

1. Cavoukian, A., Fisher, A., Killen, S., Hoffman, D.: Remote home health care technologies: How to ensure privacy? Build it in: Privacy by design. Ident. Inf. Soc **3**, 363–378 (2010)
2. Alam, M.R., Reaz, M.B.I., Ali, M.A.M.: A review of smart homes - Past, present, and future. IEEE Trans. Syst. Man Cybern. Part C Appl. Rev. **42**, 1190–1203 (2012)
3. Shankar, K., Camp, L.J., Connelly, K., Huber, L.: Aging, Privacy, and Home-Based Computing: Developing a Design Framework. Pervasive Computing October–December, 46–54 (2012)
4. Demiris, G., Hensel, B.K., Skubic, M., Rantz, M.: Senior residents' perceived need of and preferences for "smart home" sensor technologies. Int. J. Technol. Assess. Health Care **24**, 120–124 (2008)
5. Koch, S., Marschollek, M., Wolf, K.H., Plischke, M., Haux, R.: On health-enabling and ambient-assistive technologies. What has been achieved and where do we have to go? Methods Inf. Med. **48**, 29–37 (2009)
6. Li, K.F.: Smart home technology for telemedicine and emergency management. J. Ambient Intell. Humaniz. Comput. **4**, 535–546 (2013)
7. Zwijsen, S.A., Niemeijer, A.R., Hertogh, C.M.P.M.: Ethics of using assistive technology in the care for community-dwelling elderly people: An overview of the literature. Aging Ment. Health **15**, 419–427 (2011)
8. European Commission: proposal for a regulation of the European Parliament and of the Council on the protection of individuals with regard to the processing of personal data and on the free movement of such data (General Data Protection Regulation) (2012)
9. Nordgren, A.: Privacy by design in personal health monitoring. Health Care Anal. **23**(2), 148–164 (2013)
10. Kosta, E., Pitkänen, O., Niemelä, M., Kaasinen, E.: Mobile-centric ambient intelligence in Health- and Homecare-anticipating ethical and legal challenge. Sci. Eng. Ethics **16**, 303–323 (2010)
11. Bowes, A., Dawson, A., Bell, D.: Implications of lifestyle monitoring data in ageing research. Inf. Commun. Soc. **15**, 5–22 (2012)
12. Frennert, S.A., Östlund, B.: Review: seven matters of concern of social robots and older people. Int. J. Soc. Robot. **6**, 299–310 (2014)
13. Lowe, S.A., ÓLaighin, G.: Monitoring human health behaviour in one's living environment: a technological review. Med. Eng. Phys. **36**, 147–168 (2014)
14. Steele, R., Lo, A., Secombe, C., Wong, Y.K.: Elderly persons' perception and acceptance of using wireless sensor networks to assist healthcare. Int. J. Med. Inf. **78**, 788–801 (2009)
15. Myers, M.D.: Qualitative research in business & management. Sage Publications, London (2009)

An Extension and Validation of the Task-Technology Fit: A Case of a Mobile Phone Voting System

Noluntu Mpekoa[✉] and Aaron Bere

Central University of Technology, Bloemfontein, South Africa
{nmpekoa,abere}@cut.ac.za

Abstract. Literature has emphasized on human computer interaction as the backbone of technology use and acceptance. The authors made use of the task-technology fit theory and argue that any pre-occupation with the theory from the perspective of task and technology characteristics that does not embrace the user technology self-efficacy is unrealistic and unauthentic. Contributing to debates on task technology fit theory; this study provides self-efficacy as an antecedent for mobile phone voting task technology fit. The purpose of this study is to empirically examine the possibility of extending the task technology fit theory by cooperating self-efficacy to the task and technology characteristics within the voting context. The participants voted for their representatives using a mobile phone voting application. Data was collected using a self-completion questionnaire and the partial least squares was employed. The proposed model displayed a good fit with the data and rendered satisfactory explanatory power for mobile phone voting.

Keywords: Mobile phone voting · Mobile phone adoption · Technology use · TTF

1 Introduction

The Unicef [24] report indicates a 30 % growth per annum, for mobile phone adoptions in Africa within the 2002–2012 period. Sanou [22] the director of the International Telecommunications Union (ITU) claim that the number of mobile-broadband subscriptions will reach 2.3 billion by the end of 2014, with 55 % of them in developing countries. Availability of low cost handsets and cheap SIM cards contributed to the 20 % increase in the embracement of mobile phones in South Africa from 2005 to 2010, particularly among the youth [24]. The world's emerging economies are speculated to foster economic and social development through the appropriation of Information Communication Technologies (ICTs) in form of mobile systems. This study identifies voting as one of the essential areas that mobile technologies can foster a quantum leap of evolution in servicing development for the resource constrained nations. The focus of the study is based on mobile technology use and acceptance within the voting environment.

Literature has emphasised on Human Computer Interaction (HCI) as the backbone of technology use and acceptance. Several studies have reported on various technology adoption frameworks that addresses technology use and acceptance. Among these

© Springer International Publishing Switzerland 2015
T. Tryfonas and I. Askoxylakis (Eds.): HAS 2015, LNCS 9190, pp. 538–546, 2015.
DOI: 10.1007/978-3-319-20376-8_48

frameworks include the task technology fit (TTF) theory. Previous studies on TTF have often stressed task characteristics and technology characteristics as the principal determinants of effective TTF. Since any process of TTF cannot be comprehended without considering user self-efficacy and user characteristics. The authors argue that any preoccupation with TTF from the perspective of task characteristics and technology characteristics that does not embrace the individual self-efficacy and user characteristics is unrealistic and unauthentic. Contributing to contemporary debates on TTF within the HCI, this study provides self-efficacy as an antecedent for mobile voting TTF.

The purpose of this study is to empirically examine the possibility of extending the TTF theory by cooperating self-efficacy to the task characteristics and technology characteristics within the voting context. Drawing on these antecedents this study develops a factor model and empirically tests it on South African tertiary students to explore their mobile voting TTF. The study participants voted for the Information Technology (IT) organisation representatives using a mobile voting application developed by the researchers. Data was collected using a self-completion questionnaire from 217 participants at a South African University of Technology. The partial least squares (PLS) was employed for statistical analysis. Overall, the proposed model displayed a good fit with the data and rendered satisfactory explanatory power for mobile voting. Findings of the study suggested that device portability, reliable connectivity, and perceived voting privacy constituted the technology characteristics. Mobile voting efficiency, accuracy, and fairness contributed to mobile voting task characteristics. The study also confirmed the statistical significance of the user self-efficacy on TTF. Perceived ease of use led to electronic voting self-efficacy.

2   Literature Review

2.1   Mobile Phone Voting

Hasty global growth in Internet and mobile applications utilization has stirred numerous creativities directed at applying information and communication advances to develop what many refers to as "digital" or "electronic democracy" [7, 20]. An Internet or Electronic Voting System refers to a polling system that employs an electronic polling scheme that permit electorates to convey their votes to election officials via Information communication infrastructure [7]. According to [2, 25] electronic voting has several advantages which include but not limited to enabling the users to easily express their preferences from any location, exact interpretation of ballots and the virtually immediate publication of the results and these aspects may help to [20] increase the number of voters in public elections.

Soundness, unreusability/uniqueness, completeness are some of the major objectives for electronic voting system [2]. Soundness ensures that member of the electorate cannot invalidate the voting process. This implies that either the final tally is correct or that any error in the final tally can be detected and consequently corrected. Unreusability and completeness contribute to soundness. Unreusability ensures that a voter cannot vote twice. Completeness safeguards against the following (i) forge a vote; (ii) remove a valid vote from the final tally; (iii) add an invalid vote to the final tally [2]. In practice, the property of completeness requires that all and only the valid votes get counted. Other electronic voting objectives are privacy, eligibility, fairness, verifiability, uncoercibility, mobility, efficiency, scalability, deniable authentication [2, 16, 17, 25]. Several previous studies on electronic voting concentrate on technical design and implementation aspects of these technologies [2, 7, 16, 17, 25]. Insufficient studies have examined non-technical HCI aspects that foster adoption of electronic voting systems.

A previous study conducted in the United States of America examined factors that can affect a citizen's intent to vote using electronic devices [20]. The study was underpinned by the Unified Theory of Acceptance and Use of Technology (UTAUT). The results indicated that performance expectancy, effort expectancy, social influence, trust in the internet, and computer anxiety were significantly related to intent to use electronic voting. Trust in the government was insignificant. Performance expectancy, social influence, and computer anxiety were related to intent to electronic voting for both young adults and seniors. Effort expectancy was related to intent to vote for the seniors but not young adults, and trust in the internet was related to intent to vote for young adults but not seniors [20]. However, this study will utilise the TTF theory to establish factors that influence utilization of the mobile phone voting systems.

2.2 Theoretical Framework

With reference to the "Task-Technology Fit Theory" developed by [14], IT becomes useful for one's performance enhancement in cases where technology is accepted and utilised by the users resulting in a fit between technology and the assignments it is meant to support. In other words a fully fleshed TTF environment ensures smooth execution of work facilitated by a match between the technology and tasks involved. Several previous studies have attempted to extend this theory in different IT use settings [8, 18, 26]. Some of the above cited studies [8, 18, 26] attempted to extend the theory using individual characteristics. However, TTF has been insufficiently applied in mobile phone voting contexts. Besides limited studies have attempted to extend it using self-efficacy as an antecedent for TTF.

Self-efficacy. The concept of self-efficacy has been widely used in educational psychology [3, 4, 23]. Various authors within the educational technology context [5, 6, 9, 11] adopted the concept in an effort to explore the technology user's confidence in using Information Communication Technologies (ICTs) in performing teaching and learning tasks. Research suggests that technology self-efficacy plays a significant role in an individual's decision to use technology and how comfortable users are in learning skills related to effective use [5, 6]. Insufficient studies have applied the self-efficiency concept in the mobile phone voting HCI perspectives. This study aims to close this gap by expanding the TTF theory with the self-efficacy antecedent in the mobile phone voting environment (Fig. 1).

Reference [23] argue that an individual's belief in his or her ability to effectively preform a given task in a given context plays a role in that individual's willingness in performing that task continually. Consequently a mobile voter's belief in his or her ability to successfully cast his or her vote using a mobile phone plays a role in stimulating a voter's willingness to vote using such technology in future (Table 1).

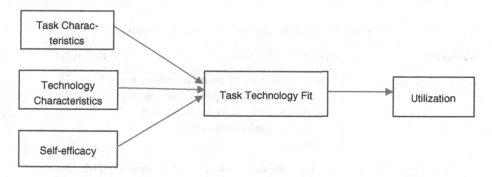

Fig. 1. Proposed research model for the mobile phone voting task technology fit

Research Hypothesis:
H1: Task characteristics significantly leads to TTF
H2: Technology characteristics significantly leads to TTF
H3: Self-efficacy significantly leads to TTF
H4: TTF significantly leads to utilization

3   Research Design

3.1   Participants

The study attempted to systematically investigate the factors which affect utilization of mobile phone voting technology. The participants were IT organisation members. These IT organisation members were registered students at a University of Technology in South Africa. During the 2013 committee member elections, the organisation introduced mobile phone voting which ran parallel with the traditional paper based voting. The IT organisation voters' role had 342 eligible voters. Exactly 301 voters casted their votes, among these voters 217 voted using mobile technologies while 84 voted using the traditional paper based voting system.

3.2   Research Instrument

An online survey was utilized for data collection. The questionnaire items of measure for task characteristics, technology characteristics, TTF and utilization where adopted from previous studies [14, 15]. The questionnaire items of measure for self-efficacy were adopted from [9]. However, all questionnaire items were tailor-made to meet the study's objectives. The questionnaire was based on a 5-point Likert scales ranging from (1) strongly disagree to (5) strongly Agree.

Table 1. The study operational definition contents

Variables	Operational Definition	Reference
Task characteristics	Tasks are actions taken by individuals to turn inputs into outputs. Task characteristics are those tasks that a user might use information technology to perform	[14, 15]
Technology characteristics	Technologies are tools that can be used to execute tasks. Technology characteristics describe the tools, and include whether the information technology is a single system, or a set of systems, policies, or services	[14, 15]
Self-efficacy	It refers to people's perceptions of their capacity to use technology	[5, 6]
Task-technology fit	The degree which technology assists an individual in completing certain assignments	[14, 15]
Utilization	Utilization represents the action of the individual using the technology to complete his or her tasks. It is important to note that in this context, utilization is a measure of whether a system is used, not a measure of duration	[10, 15]

3.3 Data Analysis

Reference [21] argue that PLS is suitable for the establishment of the investigation of the measurement and the structural model. For this reason PLS was employed in this study; particularly for investigating the measurement model with respect to its individual item loadings, construct reliability, convergent validity and discriminant validity. Subsequently, the structural model is assessed, in order to deduce observations regarding the causal relationships and their significance.

The measurement model for this study was assessed using the confirmatory factor analysis (CFA). A total of ten model-fit indices were employed for the purposes of examining the model's overall goodness of fit. Table 2 shows that all the model-fit indices exceeded their respective common acceptable levels as recommended in [5, 13] which demonstrated a good fit between the model and data.

The Composite reliability (CR) and Cronbach's alpha values (α) were employed in this study to estimate the internal consistency. According to [20], a minimum of 0.7 for both CR an α values is acceptable for good internal consistency. In this study all constructs produced values greater than 0.7 indicating a satisfactory internal consistency. With regards to convergent validity [1, 12] proposed that a minimum of 0.5 average variance extracted (AVE) value is adequate to support a good convergent validity. All the constructs in this study produced AVE[1] values ranging from 0.686 to 0.772 indicating satisfactory convergent reliability. Table 3 shows the Cronbach's alpha values and, CR and AVE values for the constructs considered in this study.

Table 2. Fit indices for measurement and structural models

Goodness-of-fit measures	Recommended value	Measurement model	Structural model
χ^2/df	$\leq$3	2.013	2.013
GFI	$\geq$0.8	0.963	0.963
RMSR	$\leq$0.05	0.021	0.021
SRMR	$\leq$0.08	0.053	0.053
RMSEA	$\leq$0.08	0.066	0.066
NFI	$\geq$0.9	0.902	0.902
CFI	$\geq$0.9	0.936	0.936
AGFI	$\geq$0.8	0.901	0.901
PNFI	$\geq$0.5	0.732	0.732
PGFI	$\geq$0.5	0.646	0.046

Structural Model. The bootstrapping technique was used to test the structural model of the study [19]. A total of 500 resamples were conducted. The t-values assessment was based on a two-tail test with statistically significant levels of $p < 0.05$ (*), $p < 0.01$ (**) and $p < 0.001$ (***). Interestingly, the outcomes of the structural model in terms of direct effects, bootstrapping and t-statistics confirmed all the hypotheses of the study, at $p < 0.001$ significance levels. In particular, the technology characteristics construct is associated with the strongest significant relationship with TTF (H2: t-value = 0.454). The self-efficacy construct is associated with a relatively strong significant relationship with TTF (H3: t-value = 0.393). The relationship H1, although significant it has the least strong relationship with TTF construct (H1: t-value = 0.229). Finally, the relationship between TTF construct and technology utilization proved to be significant (H4: t-value = 0.348) (Fig. 2).

---

[1] **Notes:** α = Cronbach's alpha CR = composite reliability. Diagonal elements are the average variance extracted. Off-diagonal elements are the shared variance.

Table 3. The study internal consistency and convergent validity

	α	CR	1	2	3	4	5
1: Task characteristics	0.811	0.923	0.721				
2: Techno characteristics	0.846	0.912	0.700	0.686			
3: Self-efficacy	0.882	0.931	0.701	0.680	0.742		
4: Task technology fit	0.806	0.952	0.682	0.682	0.662	0.772	
5: Utilization	0.823	0.920	0.699	0.621	0.781	0.751	0.693

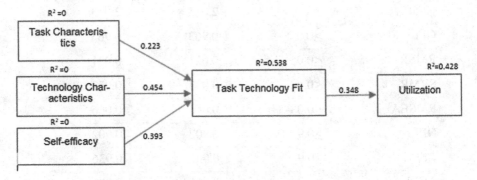

Fig. 2. Structural model for the mobile phone voting task technology fit

4 Discussion

The findings suggest that the relationship between task characteristics and TTF has positive significant, which is in line with the findings of the previous studies [8, 14, 15]. The ability for one to successfully vote remotely, results validated accurately and the fairness of the process are some of the voting characteristics that lead to the relationship being significant.

This study validated TTF hypothesis that states that, there is a positive significance between technology characteristics and TTF. Previous studies [14, 15, 26] also confirmed significance of the relationship in their studies. An application utilised in this study supported the following goals: soundness, unreusability/uniqueness, privacy, eligibility, fairness, verifiability, efficiency, and mobility. These goals have been reported in previous studies as being essential for an electronic voting systems [7, 17, 25]. Mobility, privacy and fairness had the highest ratings contributing to TTF signifying that voters prefer casting their votes in areas of their convenience and not necessarily travel to cast their votes. Furthermore, voters prefer casting their votes in a secure environment in which they are guaranteed that no one will temper with their votes.

The study findings indicate a positive relationship between technology self-efficacy and TTF. Possible reason for this outcome might be associated with the population employed in the study. Since the participants involved were IT students, it might be that their proficiency in the use of technology that contributed to their positive mobile phone voting system self-efficacy. Factors such as ease navigation interface, ease log-in, ease casting of votes, and ease verification of votes contributed to a positive relationship between self-efficacy and TTF.

5 Conclusion

Statistical data presented in this study validated the original TTF relationships (i.e. (1) Technology characteristics have a positive relationship with TTF. (2) Task characteristics have a positive relationship TTF. (3) TTF has positive relationship with utilization. Furthermore, findings of the study reflect that the self-efficacy antecedent extended the TTF theory in the mobile phone voting context. These findings have potential to contribute to the factors that promote mobile phone voting usage within the HCI context.

References

1. Baggozi, R.P., Yi, Y.: On the evaluation of structural equation models. J. Acad. Mark. Sci. **16**, 74–94 (1988)
2. Baiardi, F., Falleni, A., Granchi, R., Martinelli, F., Petrocchi, M., Vaccarelli, A.: Seas, a secure e-voting protocol: design and implementation. Comput. Secur. **24**, 642–652 (2005)
3. Bandura, A.: Self-Efficacy: The Exercise of Control. W. H. Freeman & Company, New York (1977)
4. Bandura, A.: Social Foundations of Thought And Actions. Prentice-Hall, Englewood Cliffs (1986)
5. Bao, Y., Xiong, T., Hu, Z., Kibelloh, M.: Exploring gender differences on general and specific computer self-efficacy in mobile learning adoption. J. Educ. Comput. Rcs. **49**, 111–132 (2013)
6. Bates, R., Khasawneh, S.: Self-efficacy and college students' perceptions and use of online learning systems. Comput. Hum. Behav. **23**, 175–191 (2007)
7. Bouras, C., Katris, N., Triantafillou, V.: An electronic voting service to support decision-making in local government. Telematics Inf. **20**(20), 225–274 (2003)
8. Cane, S., Mccarthy, R.: Analyzing the factors that affect information systems use: A task-technology fit meta-analysis. J. Comput. Inf. Syst. **50**(1), 108–122 (2009)
9. Compeau, D., Higgins, C.: Computer self-efficacy: development of a measure and initial test. MIS Q. **19**, 189–211 (1995)
10. Davis, J., Chryssafidou, E., Zamora, J., Davis, D., Khan, K.H., Coomarasamy, A.: Computer-based teaching is as good as face to face lecture-based teaching of evidence based medicine: A randomized controlled trial. BMC Med. Educ. Med. Teach. **30**, 302–307 (2007)
11. Durndell, A., Hagg, Z.: Computer self efficacy, computer anxiety, attitudes towards the internet and reported experience with the internet, by gender, in an cast european sample. Comput. Hum. Behav. **18**, 521–535 (2002)
12. Fornell, C., Larker, D.F.: Evaluating structural equation models with unobservable variables and measurement error. J. Mark. Res. **18**(1), 39–50 (1981)
13. Gefen, D., Straub, D., Boudreau, M.: Structural equation modeling and regression: Guidelines for research practice. Commun. Assoc. Inf. Syst. **4**, 1–77 (2000)

14. Goodhue, D.L.: Development and measurement validity of a task-technology fit instrument for user evaluations of information systems. Decis. Sci. **29**, 105–138 (1998)
15. Goodhue, D.L., Thompson, R.L.: Task-technology fit and individual peformamnce. MIS Q. **19**, 213–236 (1995)
16. Li, C.-T., Hwang, M.-S., Liu, C.-Y.: An electronic voting protocol with deniable authentication for mobile ad hoc networks. Comput. Commun. **31**, 2534–2540 (2008)
17. Ma, C., Chao, C., Cheng, B.: Intergrating technology acceptance model and task technology fit into blended e-learning. J. Appl. Sci. **13**, 736–742 (2013)
18. Ngai, E., Poon, J., Chan, Y.: Empirical examination of the adoption of webct using tam. Comput. Educ. **48**, 250–267 (2007)
19. Powell, A., Williams, C.K., Bock, D.B., Doellman, T., Allen, J.: E-voting intent: A comparison of young and elderly voters. Gov. Inf. Q. **29**, 361–372 (2012)
20. Roldán, J.L., Leal, A.: A validation test of an adaptation of the delone and mclean's model in the spanish eis field. In: Cano, I.J.J. (ed.) Critical reflections on information systems: A systemic approach. IGI Publishing, Hershey (2003)
21. Sanou, B.: Ict facts and figures. In: 2014, T. W. I. (ed.) The International telecommunications Union (2014)
22. Tschannen-Moran, M., Hoy, A.W., Hoy, W.K.: Teacher efficacy: Its meaning and measure. Rev. Educ. Res. **68**, 202–248 (1998)
23. Unicef: South african mobile generation: study on south african young people on mobiles. In: Beger, G., Sinha, A. (eds.) Digital Citizenship society. Unicef, New York (2012)
24. Weldemariama, K., Kemmerer, R.A., Villafiorita, A.: Formal analysis of an electronic voting system: An experience report. J. Syst. Softw. **84**, 1618–1637 (2011)
25. Yang, H.-D., Kang, S., Oh, W., Kim, M.S.: Are all fits created equal? A nonlinear perspective on task-technology fit. J. Assoc. Inf. Syst. **14**, 694–721 (2011)
26. Yu, T., Lee, Y., Wang, T.: The impact of task technology fit, perceived usability and satisfaction on m-learning continuance intention. Int. J. Digit. Content Technol. Appl. **6**, 35–42 (2012)

Signs of Time: Designing Social Networking Site Profile Interfaces with Temporal Contextual Integrity

Alexander Novotny[✉]

Vienna University of Economics and Business, Vienna, Austria
alexander.novotny@wu.ac.at

Abstract. Social networking sites (SNS) retain status updates, pictures and links on profiles dating back years. Because recent and outdated information intermingle in people's SNS profiles over time, SNS interfaces risk portraying profile owners' biography and true current identity in a false light. Visualizing the passage of time in SNS interfaces can preserve profile information's temporal contextual integrity and a truthful light on people's biographies. Focus groups with SNS users were conducted and digital media experts were consulted to develop temporal interface signs for presenting SNS profiles in a time-sensitive way. Some of the temporal signs were implemented in an SNS interface prototype that was evaluated with users. The usability challenges of implementing the temporal signs in SNS interfaces are discussed. The paper concludes that SNS interfaces presenting people in a truthful temporal light sometimes need to transform the original appearance of profile information itself.

Keywords: Privacy as temporal contextual integrity · Human-computer interaction · Usable privacy

1 Introduction

We approach the age of everlasting personal data retention. From the launch of Facebook's timeline in 2011, it has been envisaged as a personal profile spanning from birth to death. With the increasing amount of status updates, pictures and links shared on social networking sites (SNS), people's profiles fill up quickly over time. But in contrast to the steady inflow of data into profiles, information is sporadically erased or made inaccessible later [1]. In a life's course, an enormous digital profile is piling up, containing information from various episodes. Posts from college are succeeded by pictures of friends in the military service or from one's first job.

With all the personal content from different periods mixed into one profile, viewers risk misinterpreting like the depicted person is now. People's interests, skills, and opinions are constantly changing, but when a SNS profile is visited later, the sum of profile entries looks as if it represents the person's current identity [2]. "Information logged over years, or even decades, may present a record to which a user has a different recollection, but to which they may be held accountable" [3]. Take alcohol-related party pictures posted back from college. After a person's younger, wilder years are long

© Springer International Publishing Switzerland 2015
T. Tryfonas and I. Askoxylakis (Eds.): HAS 2015, LNCS 9190, pp. 547–558, 2015.
DOI: 10.1007/978-3-319-20376-8_49

gone, pictures remaining in SNS profiles may influence how others judge the person and harm his or her reputation. Employers may think of the person as being an irresponsible drunk. Such anachronistic misinterpretations ensue because SNS lack making people's personal development transparent and visible. Without highlighting profile information's (PI) original temporal context, SNS present people in a "false light" [4]. They bias "the way a person is perceived and judged by others" [5].

Privacy theorists emphasize that making PI's original disclosure context visible to recipients is a key building block of user privacy [6]. Visibility around when the information was disclosed (its temporal context) protects PI from being semantically distorted and misinterpreted. That is, to avoid harm to SNS profile owners' privacy, SNS need to preserve the contextual integrity of the displayed information with regard to time [7]. For safeguarding "temporal contextual integrity", SNS user interfaces (UIs) should ostensibly represent the temporal context of PI.

Highlighting PI's temporal context in SNS interfaces requires "unpack[ing] a topic that is often taken for granted: how to represent, or depict, time" [3]. SNS, such as Facebook, Google+ and LinkedIn, take it for granted that PI shall be presented in chronological lists and annotated by timestamps. Facebook heralds this metaphor as the "timeline". But are timestamps and chronologic lists the best way to visualize time? Human-computer interaction research has just started developing metaphors for depicting time in user interfaces [e.g., 8, 9]. For visualizing time in SNS profiles, a thorough discourse on possible design alternatives is still missing.

Drawing on semiotics, this paper contributes a catalog of temporal signs for making the temporal context of PI ostensible. The catalog's design suggestions are developed in focus groups together with SNS users and further elaborated and evaluated with web graphics and digital media design experts. Selected temporal signs are then prototyped into a SNS interface. The temporal signs' usability and implementation suitability are analyzed. Also, the interface signs' influence on profile viewers' risk of later misinterpreting PI is discussed.

The next section outlines how current SNS visualize temporal context, presents related work and, based on semiotic theory, distinguishes between temporal indices and temporal symbols. Section 3 explores the design space for temporal interface signs with user focus groups and expert consultations. Section 4 compiles the results into a catalog of temporal signs for SNS interfaces. Section 5 evaluates a prototype SNS interface implementing selected temporal signs. Section 6 draws conclusions.

2 Related Work

This section argues why SNS interfaces that fail to make temporal context ostensible create a risk to profile owners' privacy. Then, after discussing the semiotics of time, related work on how time can be visualized in user interfaces will be reviewed.

2.1 Temporal Contextual Integrity of SNS Profiles and Privacy

Information integrity is a basic objective for protecting a system's security. The National Institute of Standards and Technology handbook requires systems to take measures that information is "timely, accurate, complete, and consistent" [10]. For SNS, protecting information integrity also entails accurately and truthfully depicting the personal history of profile owners over time. That is, they need to ensure that the integrity of the profile information's temporal context is preserved.

Not surprisingly, accuracy of personal information is a globally guiding principle in regulatory data protection frameworks, such as principle 4 of the FTC Fair Information Practice Principles, and Article 6(d) of the European Data Protection Directive 95/46/EC. The Madrid Resolution on privacy protection renders accuracy as a part of the broader principle of data quality. Inaccurate representations of time in SNS profiles are an instance of poor data quality. They present profile owners in a "false light" [4] and bear the danger of wrong judgments about them. If SNS do not display profiles in a chronologically truthful fashion, they systematically distribute misinformation about profile owners and harm their privacy [5].

SNS aiming to display profile information in a chronologically truthful light should make its temporal context highly transparent and visible [6]. Transparency requires that SNS present the temporal context of profile information to users in a meaningful, veridical, comprehensive, accessible and appropriate way [11]. To convey the meaning of time, SNS can use interface design elements such as symbols, icons and texts serving as temporal signs.

2.2 The Semiotics of Temporal Signs

To elucidate the chronologic meaning of the temporal interface signs that will be developed, semiotic theory is applied. Temporal interface signs denote the temporal context of PI and are interpreted by SNS users. Temporal signs can be indices or symbols [12][1]. Indices have an existential relationship with the PI and are independent of whether they are understood as a sign. For instance, the washed out colors of a portrait are an index of its age. They are a property of the portrait itself. In contrast, temporal symbols have no existential relationship, but depend on whether SNS users understand them as signs. For example, the characters of a textual timestamp of the portrait's creation date written beneath are a symbol of its age.

2.3 Visualizing Time in SNS

In many SNS, time is represented in a fairly uniform way. SNS display PI in temporally ordered lists and are annotated by textual timestamps. Business SNS such as LinkedIn and XING have started to use this curriculum vitae style of user profiles. Also other SNS, including Facebook, Google+, Foursquare, and Instagram, analogically adopted this design that Facebook calls the "timeline". Additionally, Facebook's interface provides a navigation bar enabling profile viewers to directly jump to a specific point in time in the profile. Except for XING, which uses the size of circles in its CV-style list

---

[1] *Icons* are the third category of semiotic signs. However, temporal context has no physically or visually similar image that could be depicted by an icon.

to represent the duration a user has spent on a job, temporally ordered lists are not capable of representing time intervals between PI to scale.

Are textual timestamps and lists enough to make temporal context salient? Text-based cues receive less user attention than picture based or mixed cues [13]. And the lower the visibility of PI's temporal context is in interafces, the greater is the potential of anachronistic misinterpretations. There is unlikely a one-size-fits all temporal sign for various granularities of time, amounts of PI, mixed time intervals and different content type. What other options exist to display time in user interfaces?

Depicting time in interfaces was first addressed in information visualization, which developed static and dynamic visualization techniques for time-oriented data [9]. As these interfaces are not suitable for untrained web users, human-computer interaction (HCI) focused on developing simple time metaphors. Suggestions include group-collaboration pinboards placing newer pins above older layers [8] and desktop time-machines rolling back the state of computer desktops [14]. Other UI designs visualize the time dimension in personal communications archives [15].

For SNS specifically, few suggestions have been made. Facebook "could highlight a post that [a] user had made in the past, either in a sidebar or visually set off from recent content" [16]. SNS may also use metaphors of how people display physical artifacts in their houses, such as adhesive stickers on the fridge for short-lived, and framed wall pictures for long-lived PI [17]. Apart from these initial design ideas, a structured catalogue of possibilities to display time in SNS user profiles is missing.

3 Exploring the UI Design Space for Temporal Signs

SNS users and UI designers were both involved in developing temporal interface signs. Aiming to create rich and well-accepted designs, focus groups were conducted with SNS users. To assess these design suggestions and to create additional ones, experts in web graphics and digital media design were consulted.

3.1 Exploratory User Focus Groups

One pilot as well as two 90 min sessions with 7 and 9 participants (referred to as A1–7, B1–9) have been conducted in German. The focus group discussed the "topicality of information in context of online shopping, web search and social media." Participants were recruited from a university mailing list and paid 12 euros in cash. They were Facebook, XING, or LinkedIn users (2 participants provided no answer). Within-group sex was balanced and the mean age was 23.0 years (group A) and 25.5 years (group B). Group A was making more active use of the web (mean/day: 4.11 h), for instance by reading websites and using the social media, compared to group B (mean/day: 2.94 h).

One task asked participants to come up with interface design ideas for presenting the temporal context of an old, fictitious Facebook post (Fig. 1). The post contained a nine-year-old picture of a person drinking alcohol and a text: "Was alcohol-fuelled at the corporate event yesterday. Was stopped at the way home. Fucking police, driver's license gone…" Participants collected design ideas for 3 min and made notes on an answer sheet: how can Facebook's interface design signal that the profile information relates to an episode that happened a long time ago and can protect the profile owner's reputation? The discussion was audio-taped and transcribed.

Fig. 1. Fictitious Facebook post used in focus groups (Source: http://www.freedigitalphotos.net)

Participants came up with several designs for visualizing time. They proposed to reduce the size of the post, to grey the picture and text making it appear older, and to use outdated technology, such as reducing the picture's resolution to the standard of nine years ago. Moreover, they suggested to edit the post's picture and giving it a retro style, to apply a historic interface look-and-feel and to display the SNS user's historic profile picture at the time of posting. Also graphical time pictograms, watermarks of the post's original publication date and person's age could be added.

Designs based on the characteristics of online media, such as representing time by the screen's dimensions, were not mentioned, though. UI designers were consulted to further extend and assess the design suggestions.

3.2 Expert Consultations

Four web graphics and digital media design experts (1 female (E1), 3 male (E2–4)) with more than 10 years of experience were consulted in person (E1, 2) or by video call (E3, 4). On average, the experts took 61 min to discuss temporal interface signs for SNS. During the sessions following a topic guide, notes were taken. Experts were briefed about the research aims and were asked to assess specific design suggestions. After that, additional suggestions for temporal signs were discussed.

Experts made additional suggestions for temporal signs based on screen dimensions, the dynamic and interactive characteristics of SNS and the typeset used in SNS interfaces. They suggested covering older layers of PI with newer layers, and to arrange PI within horizontal, vertical, concentric, or radial time segments on screen. Further, they proposed displaying new PI in faster motion and degrading old PI's appearance using typefaces perceived as classic (see Sect. 4).

The experts were critical on some suggestions made in the focus grous. Low color contrast and readability could cut into the usability of older PI displayed in light gray color or by outdated display technology (E4). Also, grey color would represent inactivity in interfaces leading SNS users to wrong conclusions (E1). The experts found symbolic objects for time unfavorable, because they require learning a new symbol and may not be intuitive (E2).

3.3   Analysis of Temporal Signs

First, the research participants' proposals for changing the appearance of SNS interfaces for making PI's temporal context ostensible were identified as design suggestions. Second, similar suggestions were grouped and assigned the same label (e.g., "degrading display quality"). Third, drawing on semiotic theory, the temporal signs were categorized into temporal indices and symbols (see Table 1). A second analyst replicated the steps of categorizing design suggestions and assessments (Krippendorff's $\alpha = 0.911$). On the six occasions where disagreement occurred, these have been reconciled.

4   A Catalog of Temporal Signs for SNS Interfaces

Temporal indices and symbols can make time context visible in SNS interfaces (see Table 1). Temporal signs within these two categories are presented in rough order of their suitability for displaying a high to low granularity of time.

4.1   Temporal Indices

Temporal indices make time a visible property of the PI itself. Without requiring additional interface objects, profile viewers can infer a PI's temporal context directly from looking at the content.

Sedimentation. Sedimentation is a natural process in which the testimonials of ancient times settle and are covered by layers of newer material. Archeologists can determine the temporal context of sediments by looking at the cross section of soil. In analogy, SNS interfaces can cover older layers with newer layers of PI (E1, 3).

Display Salience. We have a tendency to make new stuff stand out. Advertising makes big visual statements about brand-new smart phones and web pages highlight upcoming events. In SNS, PI's size and motion can make recent PI more salient.

- *Size:* In mature age, the human body starts to shrink and fruits to shrivel. Similarly, SNS can reduce the size of old PI, by reducing the font size of text, or the size of pictures: "If one would like to leave the photo to mature, I think one should make it smaller." (A4). To ensure readability, full-size PI should be accessible on click.
- *Motion:* Motion is an index of youthful vitality. While youth is agile, seniors are slow moving. SNS can display new PI in faster motion than old PI. For instance, recent PI can flash more frequently or faster. Consuming a high amount of attention, though, motion should be used sparingly (E3).

Table 1. Catalog of temporal interface signs for SNS

Temporal sign	Explanation	High time granularity	High amount of PI	Dynamic generation	Generic representation of UI design
Temporal indices					
Sedimentation	Older PI_{t1} is covered by newer layers of PI_{t2}	x	x	x	PI_{t2} over PI_{t1}
Display salience					
Size	Older PI_{t1} is displayed in smaller size	x	x	x	PI_{t1} PI_{t2}
Motion	Newer PI_{t2} moves faster on screen			x	$((PI_{t1}))$ $(((PI_{t2})))$
Degrading display quality					
Decay	Older PI_{t1} is displayed in decayed state		x	x	PI_{t1} PI_{t2}
Greying	Older PI_{t1} is displayed in lighter gray color		x	x	PI_{t1} PI_{t2}
Outdated display technology	Older PI_{t1} is displayed using earlier technology		x	x	PI_{t1} PI_{t2}
Fashion					
Fashion of content	Fashion of old PI_{t1}'s content is adapted to earlier time		x		PI_{t1} — $Fashion_{t1}$ PI_{t2} — $Fashion_{t2}$
Fashion of UI design	Older PI_{t1} is displayed using old-fashioned UI design		x	x	UI_{t1} PI_{t1} UI_{t2} PI_{t2}
Historic snapshot of the person	Older PI_{t1} is displayed together with old profile picture		x	x	PI_{t1} (t1) PI_{t2} (t2)
Temporal symbols					
Symbolic objects					
Time pictograms	Temporal context is annotated using a graphical symbol	x	x	x	PI_{t1} — [t1] PI_{t2} — [t2]
Textual symbols	Temporal context is annotated using text or dates	x	x	x	PI_{t1} — "t1" PI_{t2} — "t2"
Screen space	Screen areas containing PI are assigned to time segments				
Horizontal	Older PI_{t1} is displayed left of newer PI_{t2}	x	x	x	PI_{t1} PI_{t2} t1 t2
Vertical	Older PI_{t1} is displayed on top or bottom	x	x	x	PI_{t1}^{t1} PI_{t2}^{t2} PI_{t2}^{t2} PI_{t1}^{t1}
Concentric	Newer PI_{t2} is displayed closer to the screen's center	x		x	PI_{t2} PI_{t1}
Radial	Radial sections of the screen are assigned clock-wise to newer PI			x	PI_{t1} PI_{t2}
Typography	Older PI_{t1} is displayed in typefaces perceived as classic		x	x	PI_{t1} — $Font_{t1}$ PI_{t2} — $Font_{t2}$

PI ... SNS profile information, t_i ... temporal context at point in time i

Degrading Display Quality. Old books turn yellow and skin grows wrinkled with age. Similarly, a degenerated appearance of PI can indicate its age to newer PI (E4).

- *Decay:* Desaturated colors in pictures and omitting vowel letters from textual PI can make a decayed appearance of PI in SNS interfaces (E1, E3). On click, PI should be accessible in full quality.
- *Greying:* Lighter gray color tones can indicate older PI. "Make the post light grey [...] Like a button that is disabled. That it is not there, but older" (B1). To ensure readability, greyed PI needs sufficient color contrast (E3).
- *Outdated Display Technology:* SNS can display older PI imitating technically less mature display technologies. For instance, interfaces may mimic low resolution digital photo technology or display text without ClearType rendering. On explicit interaction, access to best available display technologies should be granted.

Fashion. "Fashion follows time" is a credo in the clothing and creative industries. What was "in" yesterday may be already "out" tomorrow. Fashion is an index of its respective time.

- *Fashion of Content:* SNS may adapt the fashion of content to the time it dates back to. "Possible trends on the photo, for instance fashion or design, should be changed and adjusted to the respective period," (A2). Because it is difficult to dynamically adapt a picture's content, such as the style of clothes a person wears, or the language style of a post, dynamically generating these temporal signs is challenging.
- *Fashion of UI Design:* SNS may also adapt the look-and-feel of their interfaces to older PI. Placing white Polariod photo frames around pictures (B7) or visitor counters are interface elements reminding PI recipients of earlier times (E4). On one screen page, only one reminiscent look-and-feel should be applied at once. Users can only spot obvious, gross-grained differences in UI fashion (E2).

Historic Snapshot of the Person. Ten years ago, we were looking younger and presenting aspects of our personality differently. SNS can, in addition to a user's current profile picture, display the profile picture at the time a PI was posted. SNS users, though, have to regularly change their profile pictures.

4.2   Temporal Symbols

Temporal symbols signify PI's temporal context by additional interface elements. These symbols are assigned temporal meaning. SNS users need to learn and pay attention to them.

Symbolic Objects. Pictograms, emblems, and legends provide a quick orientation of the world. Traditionally, interfaces rely on symbolic texts and graphics to represent files, applications, and functionality. Also, SNS can use symbols for time.

- *Time Pictograms:* SNS may display little graphics, calendar symbols and clocks next to PI. Time pictograms may also be added as watermarks to the content (B7).
- *Textual Symbols:* Current SNS use textual characters to display the publication date of posts. SNS may also add textual hints of a person's age at the time of PI

disclosure: "I would note her [the person's] age beneath the name. Her name and how old she was back then. That one can see at first glance that she was 16" (B1).

Screen Space. Verbally, things are "up" recently and "at the center" of interest. We move "back in time" and "forward into the future". SNS interfaces can spatially project time onto available screen areas. PI is placed onto symbolic "maps of time" on which screen areas are assigned to time segments.

- *Horizontal:* In keeping with how Western cultures read left to right, the past is mapped to the left and future to the right. Drawing on this known habit, SNS should place older PI on the left of the screen and newer PI to the right (E1).
- *Vertical:* SNS typically display profiles as temporally ordered item lists. SNS news feeds sort recent PI first, but this convention is not consistently followed in information presentation (E3).
- *Concentric:* Year by year, the rings of a tree grow. In opposite direction to growing trees, SNS can place recent PI at the center and old PI at the periphery (E3).
- *Radial:* Similar to a clock, PI is arranged in radial star segments on screen. Later revealed PI is placed in further clock-wise direction. The 360 degrees of a circle allow SNS displaying PI within closed time intervals.

Typography. Typefaces support the reader's impression of a text. For old PI, SNS may use classically perceived typefaces (e.g., Fraktur) and for new PI modern typefaces (e.g., Antiqua). Temporal associations are induced by typographic characteristics such as the font-family and the presence of serifs (E1) and may vary across users (E2). Thus, type is unsuitable for illustrating fine-granular time differences (E1, 4). Moreover, SNS need to take care of the readability of used typefaces (E1, 2).

4.3   Implementing the Temporal Signs in SNS User Interfaces

Interface designers need to individually select appropriate temporal signs for each SNS interface. Applying the temporal signs in SNS interfaces still requires adherence to web usability guidelines. Designers need to prevent temporal signs causing cognitive overload, interface inconsistency, and reduced learnability of SNS as these degrade user performance [18]. Web usability guidelines, such as WCAG's guideline 2.3, define limits on acceptable user cognitive load when implementing the "display salience:motion" sign, for example: "Web pages do not contain anything that flashes more than three times in any one second period" [19]. Physical interface consistency requires equal visual appearance of the elements comprising the SNS interface [18]. Overusing different screen object sizes, for instance with the "display salience:size" sign, can make SNS profiles look chaotic and inconsistent. Moreover, users learn by analogy from familiar interfaces. Unfamiliar temporal signs, for instance "screen space: radial", may need explanatory textual symbols. Thus, the temporal signs shall not be regarded as mutually exclusive. Often, SNS will need to combine more than one temporal sign – temporal indices and temporal symbols – to raise the visibility of PI's temporal context above obscurity.

The temporal signs have different suitability for varying granularities of time, amounts of PI, and dynamic generation by SNS (Table 1). Some temporal signs, such as "symbolic objects:time pictograms", distinguish between nuanced temporal differences. Other signs, for example "degrading display quality:decay", make gross difference between old and new PI visible. Also, the temporal signs scale up differently to large amounts of PI. Motion-based temporal signs, for instance, are suitable for small volumes, because only a limited number of screen objects can be set in motion simultaneously. Moreover, it's hard for computers to dynamically generate some temporal signs, such as changing the fashion of clothes a person wears.

5   Testing Temporal Signs in a Prototype SNS Interface

Combining one temporal index (display salience: size) and one temporal symbol (screen space: horizontal), a time-sensitive SNS interface prototype was implemented. Both temporal signs are suitable for a high amount of granularity, PI and allows for dynamic generation (see Table 1). The interface arranges PI on a horizontal timeline which is demarcating yearly intervals and displaying PI from the year before last in a smaller size (Fig. 2). Textual timestamps of PI's publication were displayed (symbolic objects: textual symbols).

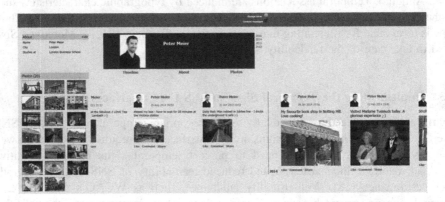

Fig. 2. SNS prototype implementing temporal interface signs (Pictures: http://www. freedigitalphotos.net)

In an audio-taped think-aloud walkthrough, 14 SNS users (indicated by T1–14, 6 females, 8 males, mean age 23.9 years) conducted a task to 'like' PI within a specified time interval of the profile owner's life. They conducted the task with both the timeline interface and a second, traditional SNS interface vertically arranging PI (screen space: vertical) and only displaying textual timestamps. Participants were paid 5 euros. 9 of them are using SNS at least once a day and 5 at least once per hour.

SNS users reported that the timeline interface made them focus on when PI was posted (T2, T12) and helped them spot episodes in the profile owner's life more quickly (T4, T9). In contrast, with the traditional interface "time does not play a big role, but rather the person and what she has experienced" (T3).

Many users were irritated by the timeline interface, because they were expecting familiar SNS interfaces that post vertical content in chronological order. One could become accustomed to the new interface layout (T6, T7). Using the test lab's mouse, most users were disturbed by horizontally scrolling through the timeline (T3, T5, T9, T12, T13, T14). On tablet computers, though, horizontally wiping through the posts on the timeline would cause less usability issues.

Participants said that the small size of older posts does not make them personally relate to these anymore (T8, T11). Actually, this effect where the older posts get less attention is intended to safeguard the temporal contextual integrity of profiles.

6 Conclusions

This paper developed temporal signs for SNS interfaces and tested selected signs in a prototype interface. The temporal interface signs help maintaining the temporal contextual integrity of information displayed in SNS profiles. They were divided into indices and symbols, neither of them having universal merits of utility and usability.

Indexical and symbolic temporal signs present people's identity differently in SNS profiles. Temporal indices have an existential relation with PI's temporal context. As the display of temporal context is entrenched into the PI itself, SNS users cannot perceive the PI without seeing its temporal context. Thus, misjudging the depicted person, because of overlooking the PI's temporal context is unlikely. Temporal indices, however, change and manipulate the PI itself. The content's changed appearance is a novel source of misinterpretations of the person's identity.

Temporal symbols, in contrast, have no existential relation to PI's temporal context. Their display is detached and separated from the PI itself. Consequently, SNS users are at risk because PI without temporal symbols can cause decontextualization and anachronistic misinterpretation. But temporal symbols do not change the PI. When choosing temporal signs, SNS designers need to reconcile PI's display realism with reducing the risks of its misinterpretation in later contexts.

Acknowledgements. I want to thank Martin Heimberger for helping me programming the prototype interface. Moreover, I thank Loretta Neal for editing this paper.

References

1. Novotny, A., Spiekermann, S.: Oblivion on the web: an inquiry of user needs and technologies. In: Proceedings of the European Conference on Information Systems (ECIS 2014), Tel Aviv (2014)
2. Ayalon, O., Toch, E.: Retrospective privacy: managing longitudinal privacy in online social networks. In: Proceedings of the 9th Symposium on Usable Privacy and Security, pp. 1–13. ACM, Newcastle (2013)

3. Lindley, S., Corish, R., Vaara, E.K., Ferreira, P., Simbelis, V.: Changing perspectives of time in HCI. In: Proceedings of the CHI 2013 Extended Abstracts on Human Factors in Computing Systems (CHI EA 2013), pp. 3211–3214. ACM, Paris (2013)
4. Prosser, W.L.: Privacy. Cal. L. Rev. **48**(3), 383–423 (1960)
5. Solove, D.: A taxonomy of privacy. U. Pen. L. Rev. **154**(3), 477–560 (2006)
6. Borcea-Pfitzmann, K., Pfitzmann, A., Berg, M.: Privacy 3.0:= data minimization + user control + contextual integrity. IT **53**(1), 34–40 (2011)
7. Nissenbaum, H.: Privacy in Context: Technology, Policy, and the Integrity of Social Life. Stanford University Press, Stanford (2010)
8. Greenberg, S., Rounding, M.: The Notification Collage: Posting Information to Public and Personal Displays. In: Proceedings of the SIGCHI Conference on Human Factors in Computing Systems (CHI 2001), pp. 514–521. ACM, Seattle (2001)
9. Aigner, W., Miksch, S., Müller, W., Schumann, H., Tominski, C.: Visualizing time-oriented data - a systematic view. Comput. Graph. **31**(3), 401–409 (2007)
10. Guttman, B., Roback, E.A.: An Introduction to Computer Security: The NIST Handbook, NIST Special Publication 800-12. DIANE Publishing, Gaithersburg (1995)
11. Turilli, M., Floridi, L.: The ethics of information transparency. Ethics Inf. Technol. **11**(2), 105–112 (2009)
12. Peirce, C.S.: Phänomen und Logik der Zeichen. Suhrkamp, Frankfurt am Main (1983)
13. Hsieh, Y.-C., Chen, K.-H.: How different information types affect viewer's attention on internet advertising. Comput. Hum. Behav. **27**(2), 935–945 (2011)
14. Rekimoto, J.: TimeScape: a time machine for the desktop environment. In: Proceedings of the CHI 1999 Extended Abstracts on Human Factors in Computing Systems (CHI EA 1999), pp. 180–181. ACM, Pittsburgh (1999)
15. Zhao, O.J., Ng, T., Cosley, D.: No forests without trees: particulars and patterns in visualizing personal communication. In: Proceedings of the 2012 iConference, pp. 25–32. ACM, Toronto (2012)
16. Bauer, L., Cranor, L.F., Komanduri, S., Mazurek, M.L., Reiter, M.K., Sleeper, M., Ur, B.: The post anachronism: the temporal dimension of Facebook privacy. In: Proceedings of the 12th ACM Workshop on Privacy in the Electronic Society (WPES 2013), pp. 1–12. ACM, Berlin (2013)
17. Zhao, X., Salehi, N., Naranjit, S., Alwaalan, S., Voida, S., Cosley, D.: The many faces of Facebook: experiencing social media as performance, exhibition, and personal archive. In: Proceedings of the SIGCHI Conference on Human Factors in Computing Systems (CHI 2013), pp. 1–10. ACM, Paris (2013)
18. AlTaboli, A., Abou-Zeid, M.R.: Effect of physical consistency of web interface design on users' performance and satisfaction. In: Jacko, J.A. (ed.) HCI 2007. LNCS, vol. 4553, pp. 849–858. Springer, Heidelberg (2007)
19. World Wide Web Consortium (W3C). http://www.w3.org/TR/WCAG20/

Poll Workers and Election Integrity: Security as if People Mattered

Whitney Quesenbery[✉] and Dana Chisnell

Center for Civic Design, Cambridge, MD, USA
{whitneyq, dana}@civicdesign.org

Abstract. How do poll workers in tens of thousands of precincts across the nation contribute to (or detract from) election security and integrity? This project aimed to fill a gap in the research and focus in a meaningful way on what must happen to make poll workers truly effective in their vital role in administering elections securely on Election Day. We learned that there are many different ideas about what "security" means in the context of elections, and different patterns about poll workers' attitudes about their responsibilities.

Keywords: Elections · Voting · Civic design · Poll workers · Security · Election integrity · Election administration

1 Introduction

Poll workers are one of the most visible parts of an election, serving as a large temporary corps of "street level bureaucrats" [1]. Every Election Day, hundreds of thousands of poll workers, in tens of thousands of precincts across the nation are responsible for running their local polling places. Without them, elections would not happen.

The work of running a polling place is both pressured and mundane. Poll workers arrive in the early hours to set up their polling places, including opening voting machines for the day. And, at the end of a long day, they report on the results in their precincts and account for ballots and other election materials. They do all this under pressure to work quickly as they open the polls on time in the morning and complete a long day of work at the end of an election day.

This paper contributes to a relatively small body of research on poll workers and their impact on elections. Most of the research is quantitative, conducted through surveys [2–4]. One project [5] included both observations and individual interviews to evaluate how poll workers perceive possible issues of security and privacy. They concluded that poll workers were not familiar with, nor did they understand security procedures, though they had a more intuitive understanding of related privacy issues.

Our team of researchers observed poll workers as they opened and closed their polling places for 19 elections in 12 states from November 2012 to November 2013. These elections included the 2012 presidential elections and a variety of local elections. We chose the elections to include a variety of voting systems, types of elections, counting methods, and other local procedures.

© Springer International Publishing Switzerland 2015
T. Tryfonas and I. Askoxylakis (Eds.): HAS 2015, LNCS 9190, pp. 559–569, 2015.
DOI: 10.1007/978-3-319-20376-8_50

Through studying poll workers and polling places, we learned a lot about what happens in the polling place and how this can affect the security of an election. One of the most important insights for us was that there are many different ideas about what "security" means in the context of elections.

Our research focuses on patterns of poll workers' attitudes about running the election at a polling place and what they believe their responsibilities to be. These attitudes affect many details of how poll worker teams work together and how they solve the inevitable problems that come up on Election Day.

Although there is some variation by individual poll workers, these differences seem to be tied to both the history and culture of elections in each jurisdiction and to the way an election office works with poll workers. The way they are recruited and trained, the procedures and paperwork created for them, and how they are given responsibility for running the polling place all contribute. The teams with the best balance of those elements did best at opening and closing. If they had problems, they were able to use the tools given to them to resolve them well.

2   Method

Our study used ethnographic techniques to systematically study election days from the point of view of the people who make them happen. The project included several phases of work:

- **Preparation.** The researchers reviewed manuals and forms, and reviewed or attended poll worker training where we could. We wanted to see what the materials covered and to what extent. In particular, we wanted to get a measure of how much of the content for poll workers was related to security, and of that, what it covered, including troubleshooting and problem escalation.
- **Observations.** The centerpiece of the project was observing set up and shut down of the polls. To understand the culture of security and how procedures were conducted in a real election, researchers watched without interfering with the poll workers. We also had some opportunity to observe election office operations centers and poll worker training sessions.
- **Interviews.** We conducted both informal discussions during the observation period and semi-structured follow-up interviews with election officials and poll workers.
- **Writing up.** To gather comparable material from our large team of researchers, we created a structured note-taking guide suggesting specific types of activity and materials to observe through the day. We took handwritten "jotted" notes and made sketches of the physical environment. Where allowed, researchers also took photographs of rooms, buildings, setups, and poll workers interacting with technology and materials. Afterwards, we typed up field reports, using a format that allowed easy comparison between locations.
- **Analysis.** We analyzed these field notes to reveal patterns and trends, which led to the insights in this report.

2.1   The Research Team

Because elections happen on a single day, limiting each observer to a single location, we used a large team of usability professionals and political science students to conduct some of the observations at the November 2012 and 2013 general elections. In all, 17 researchers participated in the project.

Most of the observations were conducted in pairs, providing overlap between the two researchers. We conducted training sessions before the observation days, covering the arrangements for the research, guidelines for interacting with poll workers so as not to interrupt their work, and the goals for the observations. The structured note-taking guides and template for reports from each polling place were essential in making it possible compare reports.

2.2   Observation Locations

We observed 19 elections in 12 states (Table 1). Our selection was a purposeful sample to provide a range of different types of jurisdictions.

Table 1. Jurisdictions for election observations

Location	Location type	Election type	Primary voting system
California	Metropolitan	Presidential	Paper: optical scan
Florida	Suburban/ small city	Municipal	Paper: optical scan
Illinois	Metropolitan	Consolidated	Paper: optical scan electronic: DRE + VVPAT
Massachusetts	Metropolitan	Presidential	Electronic DRE
Michigan	Suburban/ small city	Presidential	Paper: optical scan
Michigan	Metropolitan	Municipal	Paper: optical scan
Minnesota (6 polling places in 3 counties)	Metropolitan/ suburban/small city	Municipal	Paper: optical scan
New Jersey	Rural	Presidential	Electronic full face
New York	Metropolitan	Primary	Lever machines
New York	Metropolitan	Municipal	Paper: optical scan
Ohio	Suburban/ small city	Municipal	Paper: optical scan
Rhode Island	Rural	Municipal	Paper: optical scan
Texas	Suburban/ small city	Consolidated	Electronic DRE
Virginia	Suburban/ small city	Municipal	Paper: optical scan electronic: DRE

We looked for polling places:

- Where we could observe poll workers working with a variety of voting systems from paper ballots to fully electronic systems.
- Representing different areas of the country and a range of neighborhood settings from inner city to small cities, suburbs, and rural towns.
- With a variety of approaches to election administration and process.

The selection was also a form of convenience sample, based on the election calendar for local elections and primaries in the spring of 2013 after initial observations in November 2012.

In most locations, we observed in only one polling place, and on one election, but there were exceptions:

- In November 2013, we had teams in six different places in two neighboring cities and the surrounding county, allowing us to see several sites with similar election administration and compare how the polls were run across these sites.
- In two locations, the researcher visited more than one polling place during the day, accompanied by an election official.
- In one state, the same researcher observed in two different locations; in a small town on November 2012 and in a large city on November 2013.
- In two locations, we had researchers who also worked as poll workers, and had additional experience in their polling place, providing more insights into what was different or the same about the elections we include in our observations.
- In one case, the same polling place used different voting systems for the two elections.

Within the broad similarities of elections, we saw many differences in approaches to training and support of poll workers. This is too small a sample to suggest anything other than the wide range of practices that differences in history, local custom and culture, and state law create.

Conducting most of the observations throughout an "off-year" (that is, in 2013, a year without any federal elections) had the disadvantage of being smaller, less pressured events. But it also made it possible to watch poll workers when they were not under the scrutiny and busy-ness of a presidential year. Election offices were also much more willing to allow us to observe in these smaller elections.

3 Security of Elections

We started this research focused on the security of the voting systems, and how poll workers handled them. Our results suggest that the a more nuanced view is needed.

3.1   What "Security in Elections" Means

Most of the discussion about security in elections focused on the hardware and software of voting systems themselves. Our research was designed to study how poll workers manage voting technology at opening and closing of the polls to learn:

- What kinds of common security problems do poll workers encounter at opening and closing of the polls?
- Why do these problems seem to occur? Is it the design of the voting systems, the design of election procedures, the usability of procedures and tools, or something else?
- Are there particular "pain points" where poll workers are more likely to encounter security issues or make mistakes?

We focused on the security implications of interactions between people and technology and materials rather than possible vulnerabilities in the technology, specifically. We

Table 2. Different perspectives on election security

Role	Security goals	Description
Voters	Votes cast as intended, counted as cast	Want to feel secure that they their votes will be counted. Trust in people in many different roles, as well as voting systems and other information technology
Security experts	Votes counted as cast	Concerned about hackers, intruders, and attackers
Election administrators	Election integrity	Focus on the integrity of the whole election, including ensuring that ballots are protected throughout the election

wanted to look at where there might be vulnerabilities as poll workers interact with systems, procedures, materials, voters, and one another.

There are several ways to look at security in elections, depending on your point of view. Voters have one perspective; security experts have another. Poll workers and election administrators approach security differently from either of those (Table 2).

3.2   Poll Worker Attitudes

When we interviewed poll workers and election administrators, one question we asked was, "When I say, 'security in elections,' what comes to mind?" The answers ranged from "being prepared for emergencies in polling places," to personal safety of voters and poll workers. This finding is similar to the experience of Hall et al. [5] who found that poll workers connected the idea of security to either the physical security of the polling place or the equipment.

Some of the administrators we interviewed seemed puzzled about our question. They were surprised that we would separate out security from the rest of the process.

To them, everything about elections was security: all of the procedures and policies were in place to ensure the integrity of their elections. This may help explain why poll workers didn't think of "security" as a separate duty.

There were four broad classifications of attitudes among the poll workers we met,

Table 3. Poll workers attitudes toward responsibility for their polling place

Attitude	Focus of responsibility
I'm responsible for running the polling place	Safety and comfort of voters, and maintaining an orderly polling place
I have to follow procedures	Completing all procedures correctly, as a way of running the polling place well
I have to account for paperwork	Forms and reports as a double-check on equipment tallies and to ensure that all votes are accounted for
I'm responsible for "my election"	The overall results of the election, broadly incorporating the polling place, procedures, and tallies

from a shallower to deeper sense of ownership of the polling place and the election. These attitudes are not directly related to the wide variety of formal or informal leadership structures among the poll workers [5]. For example, in some jurisdictions, there is one poll worker (or a lead and a deputy) who has explicit responsibility for the team, while in others, each poll worker is assigned their own role and responsibilities. Similarly, decision-making processes may be mandated within the team, referred to the election administration, or handled informally within each team (Table 3).

3.3   The Role of Training and Tools

There was a wide variation in the tools and documentation available for poll workers during election day, as well as in the training they received. Some jurisdictions provided thick manuals and many other forms, checklists, and notices. Others took a minimalist approach, with a small manual, a few forms, and the phone number for the elections office. Like the bowls of porridge in the Goldilocks story, some job aids were too much and some too little.

Two factors seem to be at play. First, there is a desire to improve poll worker performance with each election leads to additions aimed at solving the issues in the most recent election. But patching holes in processes and procedures rather than taking a holistic view causes problems as the materials pile up. We saw no evidence that more paper was a sign of a better, more secure election. Nor did we come away thinking that the minimalist jurisdictions were lacking in security. A more important factor is having a polling place culture in which poll workers are encouraged to raise questions. This means that the process in the polling place gets more constructive scrutiny and that questions from poll workers can lead to improvements in the process.

Poll worker training also varied widely from a brief lecture on alternate election years to hands-on training where poll workers learned all of the job responsibilities and roles through scenario-based activities.

3.4   Stress Points During Election Day

As we analyzed the notes from the Election Day observations and the post-election interviews, we identified stress points throughout the process and timeline. Each point is an opportunity for procedures to break down and endanger the integrity of the election. These stress points included:

- Procedures for delivering materials to the polling place.
- The degree to which the polling place is well organized and creates easy traffic paths for voters.
- The stress of the early morning start and rapid setup.
- Documenting and troubleshooting incidents and exceptions during the day.
- Closing the polling place and packing up.
- Inventorying ballots and other materials.
- Reconciling counts from the poll book, ballots, and voting systems.
- Delivering the results and returning materials to the elections office.

In many cases, aspects of how a polling place is run are both good and bad for security. For example:

- A poll worker in the role of a "greeter" can act as a gatekeeper and an obstacle to attacks, but they may also allow known people in who should not be present in the polling place.
- Changing roles during the day makes it easy to check the work at each station as people rotate to different jobs. However, if poll workers are not properly trained, changing roles may leave problems unchecked or unnoticed. Dynamics within teams may make it difficult for some poll workers to challenge the previous workers at a station.
- Law enforcement being present can make voters and poll workers feel more secure but may intimidate some voters, and may send a message that poll workers aren't trusted.
- Relationships outside the polling place lend reputational, social pressure and trust to do the right thing the right way. They may also make it easier to conspire, or to let things go that should be checked and/or corrected.
- Poll workers who know a lot of voters coming into the polling place can tell who belongs and who does not. On the other hand, poll workers with close connection to the neighborhood may be less diligent about some procedures
- Diversity on a team can make voting more approachable for voters of different backgrounds, leading to greater trust in the process. But, if there is racial prejudice, it may cause conflicts within at team.

Knowing that any social setting where people work in a public way, under stress, can include conflicts, we looked for the type of conflicts and how they were resolved. Some

Table 4. Vulnerabilities in process and procedures at the polling place

	Before Election Day	Setup & Opening	During Election Day	Closing & Packing Up	Counting & Reconciling	Delivering Results
People	Volunteer helpers	Relationships among poll workers Staff & trouble-shooting	Relationships between poll workers & voters Poll worker diversity Definition of "order" in polling place Poll watchers Security & law enforcement Changing roles Greeters-as-gatekeepers	Relationships among poll workers Unsupervised poll worker team	Distracted leads Unassigned poll worker team	Party-balanced pairs Attention to safety Police
Procedures	Training style	Trouble-shooting & hotlines	Demonstrating ballot marking Provisional ballots & forms Voter ID questions Election Day registration Continuous audits Trouble-shooting & hotlines	Filling checklists Lack of direction	Trouble-shooting & hotlines Reconciliation steps	Security of transmission channel

(Continued)

Table 4. (*Continued*)

	Before Election Day	Setup & Opening	During Election Day	Closing & Packing Up	Counting & Reconciling	Delivering Results
Paper	Detail in instructions Training manual	Detail in instructions Checklists	Provisional ballots Incident reports Audit forms	Checklists Envelope design & number Seals & closures	Reconciliation forms Checklists	Checklists Envelope design & number Checking paperwork
Polling Place & Policy	Delivering materials and voting systems Troubleshooting	Setting up boundaries Traffic flow & management Closures & seals Crosschecking among precincts	Voter ID Election Day registration Cross-checking Position rotation Entry and exit traffic flow Size of space	Closures & seals Containers with visible contents	Transmitting files Reconciling	Double-checking transmitted tallies

were minor, but others, more serious from the perspective of this paper, were about election procedures. In some places, these disagreements were resolved by the lead, but in most, there was a process of discussion and consensus. In one location, poll workers voted on issues when necessary. Good poll worker teams had established procedures for resolving differences of opinion about their work (Table 4).

4   Conclusions

We learned that election days can be chaotic, with many stress points and that planning for security must take this into account. You don't deploy over a million temporary workers and not get some variation in their diligence and effectiveness.

We especially noticed that the most empowered teams had the easiest time navigating the stress points and places where security issues were most likely to come up.

- The teams worked well together and had ways to resolve disputes.
- The leads were given—and took—strong responsibility for the overall election in their polling place.

- They had forms and checklists that helped the teams catch mistakes before they became big problems.

Training, trust, and constraints contributed to successful poll worker performance. To help poll workers do the best job possible:

- Train well, using scenarios and role-playing to anticipate events that come up at the polling place.
- Trust poll workers and then leave them alone except when they need support.
- Put appropriate constraints in place to guide their work. Good checklists, for example, restrain poll workers by providing models for how to complete procedures correctly.
- Give them responsibility, from picking up the election materials to delivering the final results.
- Have strong expectations (and appropriate penalties) for any indications that they have not reconciled the election results carefully, or not completed the paperwork correctly.

Getting this balance right is all a Goldilocks Problem. Simply adding more and more materials, checklists, training, or other support can be just as bad as not having enough. Each aspect of the process must be balanced. Luckily, this can be done through experimentation over many elections.

In most of the places we studied, poll workers have, and use, procedures designed for security. Security is not a separate layer consciously, explicitly carried out. Election officials approach security as an part of elections and attempt to design election procedures to support trust in the election. Poll workers use those procedures to their best ability. But, when procedures don't make sense, or aren't complete, accurate, or clear, poll workers can rationalize and improvise, which usually results in a good or improved result, but can open the door to unintended vulnerabilities.

4.1   Future Research

The security vulnerabilities in an election are distributed among people, processes, paper, and procedures and training. However, the issues around reconciling after closing the polls deserve specific attention. There has been so much emphasis on getting the polls open on time that our observations suggest that processes and procedures are optimized for opening the polls, with less emphasis on efficient and easy closing and shutdown. Future research should focus on improving poll worker performance, learning best practices in training and support materials [5, 6], and making the end-of-day procedures easier to complete accurately.

Specifically, research could look for answers to these questions:

- How detailed and prescriptive should instructions and procedures be?
- How can materials be designed so their function is easy to understand?
- How much documentation is needed? Should manuals be a reference book or a how-to guide?
- How can checklists and other forms be more helpful both to poll workers as job aids and as a check on the processes in the polling place?

- How can reconciliation forms be more effective in helping poll workers accurately account for the voters and ballots from their polling place?

Acknowledgments. This project was supported by a National Science Foundation EAGER grant CNS-1301887 to the University of Minnesota Humphrey School of Public Affairs. We are grateful for the support of all of the election offices which hosted our researchers. Our team of researchers put in the long hours of an election to conduct the observations. Doug Chapin was invaluable in connecting us to election officials and student researchers.

References

1. Lipsky, M.: Street Level Bureaucracy: Dilemmas of the Individual in Public Services. Russell Sage, New York (2010). (30th Ann. Exp. Edition)
2. Hall, T.E., Monson, J.Q., Patterson, K.D.: The human dimension of elections. Polit. Res. Q. 62(3), 507–522 (2009)
3. Hall, T.E., Stewart III, C.: Voter attitudes toward poll workers in the 2012 election, 4 April 2013. SSRN: http://ssrn.com/abstract=2245353 or http://dx.doi.org/10.2139/ssrn.2245353
4. Glaser, B.E., MacDonald, K., Hui, I., Cain, B.E.: The front lines of democracy. Election Administration Research Center Working Paper 0704, University of California, Berkeley (2007)
5. Hall, J.L., Barabas, E., Shapiro, G., Chesire, C., Mulligan, D.K.: Probing the front lines: pollworker perceptions of security and privacy. In: EVT/WOTE 2012 (2102)
6. Chisnell, D.E., Becker, S.C., Laskowski, S., Lowry, S.Z.: Style guide for voting system documentation. NIST IR 7519 (2008)

From V2X to Control2Trust

Why Trust and Control Are Major Attributes in Vehicle2X Technologies

Teresa Schmidt, Ralf Philipsen[✉], and Martina Ziefle

Human-Computer Interaction Center,
RWTH Aachen University, Aachen, Germany
{schmidt, philipsen, ziefle}@comm.rwth-aachen.de

Abstract. Beyond the increasing quality of car technology in the last decade, road and fast-paced city traffic in metropolises still impose high accident rates. Mostly, drivers' inattentiveness, tiredness or just bad driving abilities are responsible for safety risks. Novel developments such as the combination of in-vehicle systems and vehicle sensors in the environment could lower these risks. While on the one hand the V2X-technologies bare a huge potential for safety and efficiency, on the other hand, the missing trust and concerns about privacy could represent major obstacles for a successful implementation. Hence, historically, trust in new technology is a major issue, which need to be integrated into the technological development. The perceived trust and control in the field of V2X-technology, with a focal point on automated driving, is the main research focus. Using a quantitative approach, users were examined regarding their perception of V2X-technologies. Results reveal an obvious reluctance towards V2X-technologies, independent of user diversity. Data disclosure of personal data is mostly denied homogeneously. Findings hint at a considerable need for a sensitive and individually tailored information and communication strategy regarding V2X-technology.

Keywords: Vehicle2x (V2X) communication · Car2x (C2X) · Vehicular ad hoc network (VANET) · Intelligent transportation systems (ITS) · Trust · Control · Privacy · Technology acceptance · Data handling

1 Introduction

The number of fatalities in traffic situations in Europe is decreasing, but with a total of over 28.000 (in 2012) still not even close to acceptable [1]. In addition, congestion and pollution are also hazards, which need to be taken into account. Therefore, the increasingly aging society needs new strategies in the everyday traffic infrastructure. This is necessary for using all the various mobility options we have today: bus, train, metro or personal car. A combination of in-vehicle systems and vehicle sensors is expected to take part in solving these problems and lowering risks of accidents. Over the last thirty years, this technology was integrated in an automated train operation (ATO) in different countries, like France, Germany or the United States [2].

© Springer International Publishing Switzerland 2015
T. Tryfonas and I. Askoxylakis (Eds.): HAS 2015, LNCS 9190, pp. 570–581, 2015.
DOI: 10.1007/978-3-319-20376-8_51

Now, Sweden started their "Drive Me" project with 100 self-driving cars. The vehicles are able to follow the lane, adapt speed and merge traffic on their own - V2X-technology on public roads with everyday driving situations [3]. A major V2X-center is built since 2014 in Germany (namely the Center for European Research on Mobility, RWTH Aachen University), which will investigate the technology and the user acceptance further.

Those technical solutions are assumed to result in a more efficient and safer transport system by offering the driver a more detailed view of prevailing traffic situations [4]. Another technical solution refers to the connection of transportation means, which can create new opportunities for mobility and be part of the increasing efficiency in traffic [5]. By an exchange of information on the technical level between different road users (cars, signal systems, or intelligent sensor technology in the road surface), a cooperative environment is created, in which an assessment of current traffic situations can be based on more information than there would be available for a single, isolated traffic participant. The more complete situation awareness may be used for an increase of security, for a more energy efficient driving or traffic management. If a traffic situation necessitates a reaction, vehicles or road infrastructure can address this issue either by an autonomous response (takeover of control by the system), or by assisting the human driver by information delivered by the vehicle system (driver control, but information and communication assistance). This could also lead to a safer and easier way of driving, which also feels more relaxing. To achieve such possibilities it is inevitable that the driver is comfortable with handing over control to an automated system [6]. A driver needs to trust the system in order to give up control over a vehicle or the situation. That trust in the technology needs to come from both, the service provider and the user [7].

Hence, the weakening of such positive effects of automation has been identified as e.g. situation awareness [8], misuse or abuse of the technology [9] or over reliance on automation [10]. Further, it is indispensable that users learn about limitations of the technology. As shown in [11], without full knowledge, the over reliability and therefore quickly given trust of drivers in automated systems (adaptive cruise control (ACC)) concluded in collisions. As a result, the increase of information that has to be presented at a time to drivers raises new usability questions. Moreover, acceptance concerns arise: both the sharing of information that may encourage the tracking of users and the possible withdrawal of control may result in privacy and trust issues. Therefore, the consideration of users' abilities, requirements and needs during research and development of future V2X-technology is indispensable in order to reach a positive public perception. While usability issues in traditional in-vehicle system are even more considered due to the increasing integration of multimedia functions [12], in contrast, user-centered research on V2X-communication is still at an early stage. Rudimentary knowledge about the intention to use early V2X-prototypes with, for example, congestion warning functionality or traffic light assistance was already achieved by the COOPERS- and the simTD-project in both simulator and field trials [13, 14].

Hence, trust in and acceptance of V2X-technology is insufficiently explored if not ignored so far. Little is known about the perceived control and risk in driving behaviour or the willingness to share information within transport systems or networks.

Recent work about trust concerns in technology research is wide-ranging, e.g. the various disciplines working on the field of medical devices [15, 16] or car-related topics [6, 17]. Also large enterprises like Google or Volvo have projects on the topic of automation and already started testing self-driving cars [3, 18].

Trust as crucial psychological factor is analysed in all of the following studies throughout the last decades [19–23]. Another study concerning trust in automated cruise control [24] showed that information providing ACCs are perceived more trustworthy by take-over actions than ACCs which take over control without giving the driver information about it. This finding lines to the research of reported by [6], which reported that implications on information is still discussed.

Hence, information and data exchange is a crucible factor in trust-related research, which is why the current study sets a focus on the willingness of the user to share data with an intelligent (V2X-technology) driving assistance. As a key variable for reliance and misuse of automated systems, trust is defined as "...the attitude that an agent will help achieve an individual's goals in a situation characterised by uncertainty and vulnerability" ([23], p. 51). It can be improved by (driving) experience and/or practise with automated systems. However, if the automation fails it entails a decline of trust [23]. A trial and error strategy was tested [25] and concluded as insufficient for building a trust model. Expectations in the systems should also be communicated, as well as the level of information given to the user [23, 25].

2 Method

Using an online survey, we explored users' attitudes towards perceived control and risks, also their willingness to share data as well as opinions with respect to conditions of data handling and storage. Also, a general evaluation of V2X-technologies was collected. Addressing user diversity, we examined age and gender as well as different levels of need of control as an individual trait (Fig. 1).

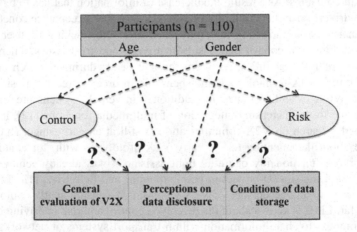

Fig. 1. Structural figure of current questionnaire design

2.1 Questionnaire

In the questionnaire, the trustworthiness in in-vehicle systems and automated driving systems was focused. Traffic situations, which were identified recently [26], were taken as exemplary scenarios. The survey contained the following sections.

Demographic Data. The first part of the questionnaire dealt with demographical data like gender, age and educational level.

Trust and Control in Traffic Situations. The second part introduced beforehand identified traffic scenarios to let the participants envision the active use of V2X-technology (e.g. intersection scenario). A set of different questions about personal data, trust and usefulness of V2X-technology followed (Table 1).

The section closes with questioning duration, storage and handling of the collected information about the user or the vehicle (Table 2).

Vehicle-to-X Technology Evaluation. A set of items questioned a general evaluation of V2X-technology (Table 3).

Table 1. Item example of approval of information collection

What information about you/your vehicle may be collected /would be shared?
– Current motion data (e.g. position, speed, direction)
– Intention to move (e.g. planned route in navigation system)
– Information of past trips (e.g. average speed, preferred routes)
– Type of road user (e.g. personal car, bus, pedestrian)
– Vehicle specifications (e.g. year of construction, safety equipment)
– Demographic data of driver (e.g. age, gender)
– Physiological data of driver (e.g. reaction rate, emotional state)
– Other personal data of driver (e.g. driving experience)

Table 2. Item example of data handling and storage

Who and how long may the collected information about you or your vehicle be used / stored?	
- Local road users.	Capturing and processing
- Local road infrastructure (e.g. traffic light system).	
- Central servers of traffic management and public authorities.	Short-term storage (during a traffic situation)
- Central servers of companies (e.g. car manufacturer or insurance companies).	Long-term/permanent storage

2.2 Sample

Overall, 110 participants took part in this survey. The age range spans from 21 to 66 years (M = 31.5; SD = 10.7). Subjects were divided into four age/mobility need groups:

Table 3. Item example of general evaluation of V2X-technology

General evaluation: Do you agree with the following statements?
– I think V2X-technology is useful
– V2X-technology would help me with daily trips and journeys
– I as a driver must have full and instant control
– V2X-technology has to be strictly regulated
– I would pay a premium to have V2X-technology in my car/on my smartphone
– V2X-technology is threatening

young students (21-25 y., n = 32), young professionals (26-29 y., n = 34), middle-aged professionals (30-40 y., n = 28) and professional experienced (41+ y., n = 16). 67 % men (n = 74) and 33 % women (n = 36) took part. The sample was well educated: 70.9 % had a university degree (n = 78), followed by 18.2 % with a technical college degree (n = 20) and 6.4 % (n = 6) did vocational training plus 4.5 % stated other level of education. For further research, users had to classify themselves according to personal risk or control attitudes: risk-group (n = 39), control-group (n = 89).

3   Results

Data was analyzed by parametric statistical evaluation methods. Analyses of variance (ANOVA) were used to compare groups. The significance level was at p = .05. First we report the general evaluation of V2X technology. The next section is concerned with perceptions on data collection and management, thereby contrasting different data in different sensibilities. Then we report, if there are certain trade-offs in the sensibility of data handling and storage within V2X-technologies; and more detailed, if there are specific situations that are mostly denied while other usage contexts are tolerated. Despite the fact, that the level of disagreement has a strong individual component, we categorized subjects into "Yes-persons" - those being open minded to "V2X open data management" - and into "No-persons" - those who reported to stay disclosed. Also, the conditions for data storage like duration and handling are described.

3.1   General Evaluation of V2X

In a first step, we report on general attitudes towards V2X-technologies (for items see Table 3). As can be seen from Fig. 2, the highest confirmation was found for the need of continuous control over the technology (M = 3.8; SD = 1.5). The next most prominent items are the perceived usefulness of V2X-technology (M = 3.7; SD = 1.6) and the credo that V2X-technology needs a high level of regulation and control (M = 3.7; SD = 1.6).

The question whether V2X-technologies are perceived as threatening was mostly denied (M = 1.4; SD = 1.3). Looking at diversity effects, neither age nor gender did impact the evaluations. Also, the segregation of participants in control-group and risk-group did not make any significant difference for the general evaluation. From this we

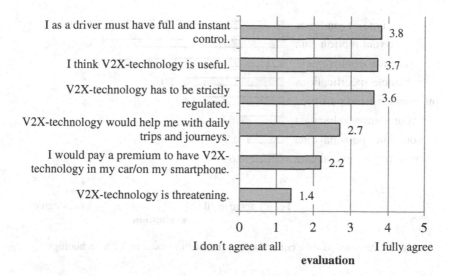

Fig. 2. General evaluations (means, ranked) with respect to V2X-Usage

conclude that the evaluations here represent a quite homogeneous attitude of participants, not impacted by different roles (gender) or biographical points in time (age), not even by different levels of control vs. risk habits of users.

3.2 Perceptions on Data Collection and Data Management

Another important issue in the context of V2X-technology is the question which data might be collected and stored. We presented a set of possible information that could be collected in the actual traffic in order to get a comprehensive picture. Among those there are options that refer to external/distant events (traffic) and options that come close to the person/body (physiological data). Participants were requested to indicate their openness to share the respective within V2X-technology (data disclosure). Descriptive findings can be taken from Fig. 3.

Among the more uncritical information, which participants would mostly agree on sharing is the type of road user (M = 3.9; SD = 1.6) and the current motion data (M = 3.6; SD = 1.6). Participants are willing to disclose data about their movement direction to a lesser extent (M = 2.7; SD = 1.7) and also data about vehicle specifications (M = 2; SD = 1.9). There is overall less willingness to share information about past trips (M = 1.6; SD = 1.7). Most critical are demographic data (M = 0.8; SD = 1.4), other personal data (M = 0.7; SD = 1.1) or even a person's physiological status (M = 0.6; SD = 1). User diversity, again, did not show any single significant influence on the evaluation here. Neither the degree of the self-attributed control vs. risk type, nor age and gender did impact the willingness to share data. We learn from this that there is a considerable susceptibility on the one hand and selectivity on the other hand with respect to the data that may be collected in live traffic.

However, the analysis does not tell something about the individual answering styles so far. In a next step further analyses were run. One analysis refers to the subjects,

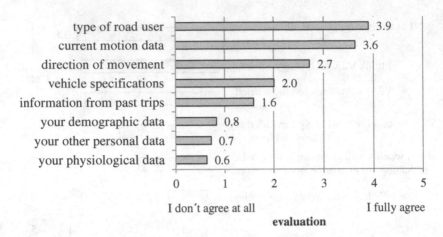

Fig. 3. Perceptions data collection (means) with respect to V2X-technology

which denied collection and storage and those that agreed in the respective data contexts. We divided the sample into two groups: one contained negative answers (black bars) and one positive responses (grey bars). Outcomes can be found in Fig. 4.

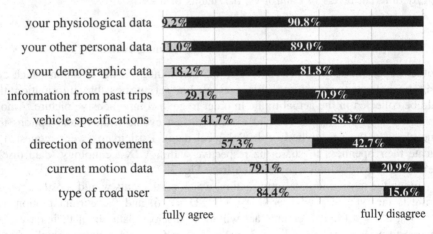

Fig. 4. "Yes" answers (grey bars) in contrast to "No" answers (black bars) in V2X-technology

What can be seen here is a kind of "sensitivity" curve, a trade-off between "yes" and "no" decisions: With decreasing distance to a person, the level of disagreement to disclose data increases. Again, it is astounding how stable the decisions are for the overall group: no gender and age effects showed up as well as no personal needs for risk vs. control effects. If a fair (50 %) cut-off would be applied, only three data contexts reach a higher percentage of yes than no (namely: data on road users, motion data, and direction of movement). In all other contexts the "no fraction" is higher than the "yes fraction".

The other analysis regards the question, whether the data context is predominately impacting the "yes" or "no" decision or rather personal habits ("Yes"/"No" persons). This hypothesis was underpinned by highly significant inter correlations (see Table 4).

Table 4. Intercorrelation matrix of data contexts (N = 110).

Data type	Physio-logical	Perso-nal	Demo-graphic	Past trips	Vehicle	Direction	Motion	Road user
Physio-logical	1	.54**	.68**	.52**	.47**	.36**	.28**	--
Personal	.54**	1	.72**	.43**	.46**	.31**	--	--
Demo-graphic	.68**	.72**	1	.43*	.52**	.36**	.24*	--
Past trips	.52**	.43**	.43**	1	.48**	.63**	.32**	.28**
Vehicle	.47**	.46**	.52**	.48**	1	.28**	.26**	.29**
Direction	.36**	.31**	.36**	.63**	.28*	1	.53**	.50**
Motion	.28*	--	.24*	.32**	.26*	.53**	1	.69**
Road user	--	--	--	.28**	.29**	.50**	.69**	1

* p<0.05; ** p<0.01

Thus, whenever users agreed to disclose data in one context they also tend to agree in other contexts (with few exceptions) and vice versa. This hints at a quite clear-cut personal style to disclose data or not.

Based on this, we analyzed how many persons denied data disclosure in how many contexts (despite of the context, just summarized).

What can be seen from Table 5 is, 11 % of the participants showed a very open-minded attitude to share data (subjects, which agreed in most cases) and considerable 31 % were quite reluctant or rather negative when it comes to sharing data in the V2X context.

Table 5. Personal answer habits to disclose V2X-data (n = 110)

Answer styles	(dis-) agreement to disclose V2X data	Percentage
No	0 times	9,1
	1 time	5,5
	2 times	16,4
	3 times	30,0
	4 times	15,5
	5 times	10,9
Yes	6 times	4,5
	7 times	0,9
	8 times	5,5

3.3   Conditions of Data Storage

Another critical issue for the public is how long which type of data may be stored and which authority may be allowed to store it. Basically, the participants had to indicate the tolerated duration of data storage (only capturing and processing vs. short-term vs. permanent storage) and the authority, which should be allowed to store it (local road users vs. local infrastructure vs. central traffic management vs. companies). Figure 5 shows the findings.

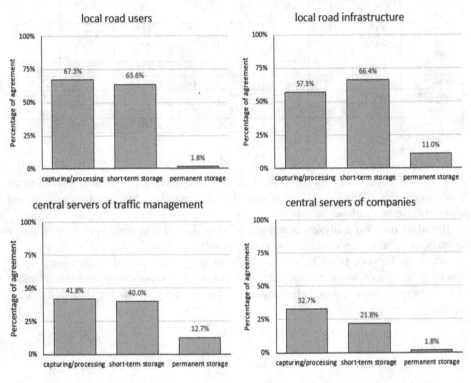

Fig. 5. Perceptions on V2X data handling and storage (percentages of agreement)

As can be seen from Fig. 5, another important issue is the authority, which is in duty of the data storage. Outcomes clearly indicate that a more central (and out of persons' control) location of the server (public authority, or, company) equals a lower openness of participants. Furthermore, long-term storage is generally disliked, independent of which authority might be in duty of data handling and storage.

4   Discussion and Outlook

The study was directed to an understanding of public perceptions regarding automated car traffic and V2X-communication. While V2X-technology gains increasing research attention with respect to technical issues [31, 32], so far sparse knowledge is prevailing about public perception and acceptance of passing over the control to the car, especially when the use case requires a higher degree of automation.

Based on an earlier study [26], which explored acceptance issues (perceived benefits and barriers of V2X-technology), this research concentrated specifically on data privacy and trust in V2X-technology. In order to get a first impression of the prevailing perceptions in this regard, we used a highly technology prone and well-educated sample. As V2X-technologies may be used for a general increase in road safety and effectiveness, they are also especially useful for integrating older road users (e.g. stay mobile at older age, assisting older drivers with medical monitoring during driving), the sample had a wide age range.

In contrast to many other recent studies on technology acceptance in a novel technological field [15, 16], for V2X-technologies were no effects of user diversity identified. Neither age nor gender did affect the evaluations, and also not the personal trait to seek for control vs. risk. Overall, the evaluations were rather homogeneous, at least in this highly educated sample. This is especially notable; as there is substantial empirical evidence that technology acceptance is impacted by the experience with technology, the domain knowledge and technical self-confidence and also with risk perceptions that correlate with gender [27]. Apparently, the question of data disclosure in V2X-technology and the general concerns about protection of intimacy and the fear of losing privacy is dominant and deeply anchored, at least in the western culture to which the sample belongs to [28]. In this context, studies reported on the privacy paradox [29, 30], which is characterized by individuals' intention to information disclosure on the one hand and the willingness to be profiled in cyberspace on the other.

For V2X-technologies (and this was shown here), there is a broad reluctance and aloofness of users to share data. The reluctance is higher the more personal the information is. Or other way round: with decreasing distance to the body (in case of physiological data) or the person (demographics), the level of disagreement to disclose data increases. It is an interesting finding that V2X-technologies seem to cut the sample into two different and diametrical parts. While there is a small group of persons that is willing to share V2X-data (quite irrespective in which context), a larger part is refusing data disclosure (also quite irrespective of the context).

We cannot explain the nature of these two opposite answering styles, or personal attitudes on the basis of the present data. Here, future studies will have to find out, if these perceptions might change in other user groups. In this context, other education levels come into fore as well as a higher experience with V2X-technology. It is most likely that persons without personal experience with a technology tend to overestimate the "risk" or the "threatening" nature of the novel technology and that this might fade with increasing familiarity [16, 27].

Nevertheless, from a social science point of view it is of utmost importance to consider users' perceptions and to integrate users' requirements and information and communication needs in early stages of technology development, in order to shape a sensible information and communication strategy thus to support a broadly accepted attitude towards V2X-technologies in Germany.

Acknowledgements. We would like to thank the anonymous reviewers for their constructive comments on an earlier version of this manuscript. Also, we owe gratitude to the research group on mobility at RWTH Aachen University, which works on the interdisciplinary CERM project (supported by the Excellence Initiative of German State and Federal Government). Many thanks go also to Julia van Heek for her valuable research input.

References

1. European Commision - Directorate General Energy and Transport: Road safety evolution (2014). http://ec.europa.eu/transport/road_safety/pdf/observatory/historical_evol.pdf
2. Erbin, J.M., Soulas, C.: Twenty years of experiences with driverless metros in France. VWT19, pp. 1–33 (2003)
3. Volvo Car Group's first self-driving Autopilot cars test on public roads around Gothenburg (2014). https://www.media.volvocars.com/global/en-gb/media/pressreleases/145619/volvo-car-groups-first-self-driving-autopilot-cars-test-on-public-roads-around-gothenburg
4. Van Driel, C.J.G.: Driver support in congestion: an assessment of user needs and impacts on driver and traffic flow (2007)
5. Picone, M., Busanelli, S., Amoretti, M., Zanichelli, F., Ferrari, G.: Advanced Technologies for Intelligent Transportation Systems. Springer, New York (2015)
6. Helldin, T., Falkman, G., Riveiro, M., Davidsson, S.: Presenting system uncertainty in automotive uis for supporting trust calibration in autonomous driving. In: Proceedings of the 5th International Conference on Automotive User Interfaces and Interactive Vehicular Applications, pp. 210–217. ACM, New York (2013)
7. Duri, S., Gruteser, M., Liu, X., Moskowitz, P., Perez, R., Singh, M., Tang, J.-M.: Framework for security and privacy in automotive telematics. In: Proceedings of the 2nd International Workshop on Mobile Commerce, pp. 25–32. ACM (2002)
8. Endsley, M.R.: Automation and situation awareness. In: Parasuraman, R., Mouloua, M. (eds.) Automation and Human Performance Theory and Applications, pp. 163–181. Lawrence Erlbaum, Mahwah (1996)
9. Parasuraman, R., Riley, V.: Humans and automation: use, misuse, disuse, abuse. Hum. Factors 39, 230–253 (1997)
10. Parasuraman, R., Manzey, D.H.: Complacency and bias in human use of automation: an attentional integration. Hum. Factors: J. Hum. Factors Ergon. Soc. 52, 381–410 (2010)
11. Stanton, N.A., Young, M., McCaulder, B.: Drive-by-wire: the case of driver workload and reclaiming control with adaptive cruise control. Saf. Sci. 27, 149–159 (1997)
12. Harvey, C., Stanton, N.A.: Usability Evaluation for In-vehicle Systems. CRC Press, Boca Raton (2013)
13. Böhm, M., Fuchs, S., Pfliegl, R., Kölbl, R.: Driver behavior and user acceptance of cooperative systems based on infrastructure-to-vehicle communication. Transp. Res. Rec. J. Transp. Res. Board 2129, 136–144 (2009)
14. simTD - Sichere Intelligente Mobilität Testfeld Deutschland: Projektergebnis (2013). http://www.simtd.de/index.dhtml/object.media/deDE/8127/CS/-/backup_publications/Projektergebnisse/simTD-TP5-Abschlussbericht_Teil_B-2_Nutzerakzeptanz_V10.pdf
15. Ziefle, M., Röcker, C., Holzinger, A.: Medical technology in smart homes: exploring the user's perspective on privacy, intimacy and trust. In: 2011 IEEE 35th Annual Computer Software and Applications Conference Workshops, pp. 410–415. IEEE (2011)
16. Wilkowska, W., Ziefle, M.: Privacy and data secrurity in e-health: requirements from users' perspective. Health Inform. J. 18(3), 191–201 (2012)

17. McGuirl, J.M., Sarter, N.B.: Supporting trust calibration and the effective use of decision aids by presenting dynamic system confidence information. Hum. Factors J. Hum. Factors Ergon. Soc. **48**, 656–665 (2006)
18. Google Inc.: Google Self-Driving Car Project (2015). https://plus.google.com/+Google SelfDrivingCars
19. Lee, J., Moray, N.: Trust, control strategies and allocation of function in human-machine systems. Ergonomics **35**, 1243–1270 (1992)
20. Muir, B.M.: Trust in automation: Part I. Theoretical issues in the study of trust and human intervention in automated systems. Ergonomics **37**, 1905–1922 (1994)
21. Muir, B.M., Moray, N.: Trust in automation. Part II: Experimental studies of trust and human intervention in a process control simulation. Ergonomics **39**, 429–460 (1996)
22. Lewandowsky, S., Mundy, M., Tan, G.: The dynamics of trust: comparing humans to automation. J. Exp. Psychol. Appl. **6**, 104 (2000)
23. Lee, J.D., See, K.A.: Trust in automation: designing for appropriate reliance. Hum. Factors J. Hum. Factors Ergon. Soc. **46**, 50–80 (2004)
24. Verberne, F.M., Ham, J., Midden, C.J.: Trust in smart systems sharing driving goals and giving information to increase trustworthiness and acceptability of smart systems in cars. Hum. Factors **54**, 799–810 (2012)
25. Beggiato, M., Krems, J.F.: The evolution of mental model, trust and acceptance of adaptive cruise control in relation to initial information. Transp. Res. Part F Traffic Psychol. Behav. **18**, 47–57 (2013)
26. Schmidt, T., Philipsen, R., Ziefle, M.: Safety first? V2X – Percived benefits, barriers and trade-offs of automated driving. Full paper submitted to the International Conference on Vehicle Technology and Intelligent Transport Systems (Vehits 2015)
27. Ziefle, M., Schaar, A.K.: Gender differences in acceptance and attitudes towards an invasive medical stent. Electron. J. Health Inform. **6**, e13 (2011)
28. Whitman, J.Q.: The two western cultures of privacy: dignity versus liberty. Yale Law J. **113**, 1151–1221 (2004)
29. Awad, N.F., Krishnan, M.S.: The personalization privacy paradox: an empirical evaluation of information transparency and the willingness to be profiled online for personalization. MIS Q. **30**, 13–28 (2006)
30. Norberg, P.A., Horne, D.R., Horne, D.A.: The privacy paradox: Personal information disclosure intentions versus behaviors. J. Consum. Aff. **41**(1), 100–126 (2007)
31. Ardelt, M., Coester, C., Kaempchen, N.: Highly automated driving on freeways in real traffic using a probabilistic framework. IEEE Trans. Intell. Transp. Syst. **13**(4), 1576–1585 (2012)
32. Lefevre, S., Petit, J., Bajcsy, R., Laugier, C., Kargl, F.: Impact of v2x privacy strategies on intersection collision avoidance systems. In: IEEE Vehicular Networking Conference, Bosten, USA (2013)

Security Implications for Personal Assistive Technology in Voting

Sarah J. Swierenga[1(✉)], Rebecca S. Zantjer[1], James E. Jackson[1], Jennifer Ismirle[1], Stephen R. Blosser[2], and Graham L. Pierce[1]

[1] Usability/Accessibility Research and Consulting, Michigan State University,
East Lansing, MI, USA
{sswieren,zantjerr,jamesedj,ismirlej,glpierce}@msu.edu
[2] Resource Center for Persons with Disabilities, Michigan State University,
East Lansing, MI, USA
blossers@msu.edu

Abstract. Voting security and accessibility are important concerns that must be addressed when designing new voting systems or integrating technologies into the voting process, e.g., remote voting, mobile voting, and/or supporting personal assistive technologies in the polling place. We researched the security implications of allowing users with disabilities to vote using their personal assistive technologies, which would significantly improve the accessibility of the voting process, as well as potentially reduce the risks to security, such as data security, data reliability, voter verification, and auditability, among others. Based on this research and feedback from users with disabilities regarding using a tablet device to vote, we proposed using an intermediary device (such as a computer or tablet) to enable the secure use of personal assistive technologies in voting and enhance the user experience.

Keywords: Voting systems · Personal assistive technology · Accessible voting · Voting security

1 Introduction

Although the ability to vote privately and securely in elections is a foundation of many societies, people with physical or cognitive disabilities often find it either impossible or extremely difficult to vote. The 2002 Help America Vote Act (HAVA) recognized these concerns as a significant problem to American democracy. HAVA required that new voting systems be developed to accommodate all users and allocated federal funding to foster the design and development of accessible voting technologies [1].

In order to interact more effectively with technology, users with physical or cognitive, learning, or attention related disabilities (e.g., blindness/vision impairment, hearing impairments, motor/dexterity impairments, dyslexia, ADHD, etc.) use specialized assistive technologies, which are often further modified to meet their unique needs. These personal assistive technologies allow users to input and receive data from devices in formats that are easier for them to control and manipulate. Common examples of assistive technologies

© Springer International Publishing Switzerland 2015
T. Tryfonas and I. Askoxylakis (Eds.): HAS 2015, LNCS 9190, pp. 582–591, 2015.
DOI: 10.1007/978-3-319-20376-8_52

include: screen readers, screen magnifiers, joysticks, touch screens, sip-and-puff, foot pedals, trackballs, and two-button switches. Therefore, the voting process should support the use of personal assistive technologies to allow voters to use devices that are comfortable and familiar to them. These accommodations present security implications that need to be explored and addressed.

2 Security Concerns for Accessible Voting

Because efficient and ethical elections are a cornerstone of democratic societies, questions of both voting security and accessibility need to be addressed. For example, the Committee of Ministers of the Council of Europe published a recommendation to member states on legal, operational, and technical standards for e-voting [2]. In the United States, the Elections Assistance Commission published the Voluntary Voting System Guidelines (VVSG) 1.0 for designing usable voting systems [3]. In the VVSG 1.1, a proposed revision to the 2005 guidelines, the Election Assistance Commission outlined a number of threats to voting security that must be addressed before an election reaches "acceptable levels of integrity and reliability [4]". Security recommendations based on these issues include:

- Identifying voters (e.g., making sure that only authorized voters can vote);
- Controlling access (e.g., making sure that only authorized election officials can access certain processes and/or data within the voting system);
- Maintaining data integrity (e.g., making sure that the selections entered by the voter on the ballot marking device match the data generated by the ballot counting device);
- Preventing data manipulation (e.g., making sure no one is able to modify, insert, or delete data in the voting system after a ballot has been submitted);
- Securing data transmission (e.g., making sure a voter's confidentiality is protected during the transmission of data);
- Ensuring voter privacy (e.g., making sure that a voter's identifying data and election choices cannot be linked at any point during the election process);
- Providing an auditable trail (e.g., making sure that data exist for voters and auditors to validate the results of an election); and
- Protecting against external threats (e.g., making sure that voting systems are protected from any viruses, malware, or hackers).

A number of potential accessible voting technologies have been developed in order to accommodate all users and to maintain the integrity of elections. These designs and ideas can be split into three categories:

1. Designs for building universal voting systems (i.e., designing new voting stations and ballot counting devices that are accessible to all voters);
2. Designs for incorporating voters' personal assistive technologies at polling places (i.e., allowing voters to connect their own technologies and devices to voting systems at the polling place); and
3. Designs for allowing voters to vote remotely using their own devices (i.e., allowing votes to be cast from personal devices outside the polling place).

While each of these designs has the potential to enable more people to vote, they can sometimes effect security. In the sections below, we present examples of designs proposed for each of the categories listed above and discuss security implications these proposed solutions present.

2.1 Security Concerns with Accessible Voting Systems

Most currently deployed systems, including direct-recording electronic systems, do not meet HAVA disability accommodation requirements for a number of reasons, as discussed by Runyan [5], e.g., the lack of dual-switch input control interface for voters with severe manual dexterity disabilities; inadequate audio access features for voters who are blind or have low vision, cognitive impairments, severe motor impairments, or learning or attention related disabilities (e.g., dyslexia or ADHD); lack of simultaneous and synchronized audio and visual outputs; lack of voter-adjustable magnification; and inadequate privacy curtains around the booth, etc. Furthermore, when Swierenga and Pierce [6–8] analyzed several voting systems with accommodations, they discovered considerable issues that would prevent many users with disabilities from being able to successfully use the systems. For instance, users operating one system via the two-button interface designed for people with manual dexterity issues would have to press a button over 1,200 times to complete the NIST Test Ballot without making any errors.

New voting systems and technologies are currently being investigated, and these voting systems would replace existing systems in polling places that do not adequately address accessibility concerns. For instance, the Smart Voting Joystick prototype could be used as a universal input device for an accessible voting system [9], and the Prime III system research project is exploring a multimodal approach for providing equity in access, privacy, and security in electronic voting [10, 11]. In addition, Los Angeles County is attempting to develop a universally accessible system for the nearly 4 million registered voters in Los Angeles [12].

Although questions of security have yet to be specifically addressed in these new designs, it is likely that these new systems can be built using similar security protocols and strategies to those already employed by contemporary voting systems. However, replacing voting systems is a slow process and may be cost inhibitive to many precincts, and it is likely that the implementation of these systems may have a longer timeline due to these financial and infrastructural costs.

2.2 Security Concerns with Personal Assistive Technologies Used at the Polling Place

In order to avoid some of the unique security concerns that stem from remote voting (see next section), some researchers have proposed allowing voters to bring personal assistive technologies and/or their own mobile devices to the polling place to be used in the voting process. In these instances, voters would interface their personal assistive technologies or devices directly with ballot marking or ballot counting machines, reducing the strain on local election officials to provide accommodations and support to all voters. While some alternative input devices (such as two-button switches and sip-and-puff) may be available at polling places, they do not cover the range of needs that potential voters may have, and may in fact make the voting process more difficult for many voters with dexterity impairments. Allowing voters to use their personal assistive technologies has the potential to reduce user error, since users are already familiar and comfortable with the technologies [13].

However, whenever two devices are directly connected, potential security risks of virus transmission and/or hacking exist, especially when one of the devices is a ballot marking or ballot counting machine that may be used by subsequent voters. Most existing designs for directly connecting personal assistive technologies (and their software drivers) to election systems would rely on using a USB connection. Although efficient, USB connections are not immune to attacks (both intentional and unintentional). It is feasible that voters could, knowingly or unknowingly, transmit malicious software from their personal assistive technologies or devices into election systems during the connection, and/or use the direct connection as a means to manipulate election data or election processes, thereby compromising the integrity, privacy, and security of the election.

Assistive technologies also present security risks simply because of how they interact and work with operating systems. Some assistive technologies can programmatically drive the operating system and other applications based on input from the user. In order to do this, assistive technologies need to be able to access processes that run at a higher integrity level (IL), including protected system user interface elements [14]. Allowing assistive technologies to have access to these processes on election machines, therefore, may give users access to otherwise confidential system elements. However, this access would not compromise election integrity if the software is well-designed, or runs on a secure operating system.

2.3 Security Concerns with Remote Voting

To improve accessibility, some engineers and designers are considering products for enabling people to vote using their own mobile devices and personal assistive technologies, remotely. A Pew Research Center survey found that 42 % of American adults own a tablet computer and 58 % own a smartphone [15]. Thus, the prevalence of mobile devices presents a low-cost and immediately implementable pathway for accessible voting. Additionally, enabling remote voting would remove one of the largest constraints imposed by polling places; namely, the need to travel to a particular destination and wait for the necessary equipment in order to vote, which is a significant issue for individuals with disabilities [6, 16].

A number of designers and researchers have attempted to leverage the prevalence of mobile technologies to enable remote voting and the use of personal assistive technologies and devices to vote. Examples of these projects include the Anywhere Ballot [17] and the EZ Ballot [18], and Michigan State University's mobile user interface design specification [19]. However, remote voting poses an additional and controversial burden on security. After the U.S. Department of Defense piloted an Internet voting program with deployed military members called the Secure Electronic Registration and Voting Experiment (SERVE), a number of computer scientists and researchers were quick to point out the security risks posed by such a system [20]. Specifically, they criticized SERVE for: (1) no voter-verified audit trail and the potential for insider attacks, (2) lack of privacy of encrypted voting data, (3) vulnerability to election corruption on a large scale, (4) lack of control over the voting environment, and (5) potential for vote buying and selling. This analysis of security risks concluded that Internet voting cannot be made secure with current technology.

Other computer scientists have echoed similar thoughts, including David Jefferson, who argued that, "There is no way to guarantee that the security, privacy, and transparency requirements for elections can all be met with any practical technology in the foreseeable future" [21]. In 2008, the Verified Voting group released their *Computer Technologists' Statement on Internet Voting* which listed five technical challenges they felt must be overcome before secure internet voting is possible [22]. These challenges include: (1) the voting system as a whole must be verifiably accurate in spite of the fact that client systems can never be guaranteed; (2) there must be a satisfactory way to prevent large-scale or selective disruption of vote transmission; (3) there must be strong mechanisms to prevent undetected changes to votes; (4) there must be reliable, unforgettable, unchangeable voter-verified records of votes; and (5) the entire system must be reliable and verifiable.

It is worth noting that not all of the designs referenced in this remote voting category require the transmission of data over the Internet. Some systems have users vote using telecommunication networks (i.e., televoting). While not identical, televoting faces similar security challenges to Internet voting. Additionally, other systems allow users to vote remotely using their personal assistive technologies or devices and then print a paper ballot that can be counted by already-existing ballot counting devices. These designs still must address security and accessibility questions of auditability for voters with visual impairments (e.g., how do users who are blind ensure that print-outs are accurate?) and questions of voter verification (e.g., how do systems know that the registered voter identified in the system is the one doing the voting?).

3   Designing an Accessible Mobile Voting System User Interface

Because of the complexity and multiplicity of factors surrounding both accessibility *and* security in voting, it is likely that any proposed solution to the question of how to make an accessible, yet secure, voting experience will itself be multi-faceted and complex. We will now discuss research we have conducted using an accessible mobile interface for voting, and how that interface could be used with personal assistive technologies in a polling place to provide a secure and accessible voting experience. While not the only potential solution to this challenge, we believe this can be used to demonstrate ways to move towards an election characterized by both integrity and accessibility.

Our research team at Michigan State University created a specification for an accessible mobile voting user interface [19]. This design specification was based on prior research for creating usable, accessible voting systems, including Laskowski, et al. [23], the U.S. National Institute of Standards and Technology (NIST) [24], Election Assistance Commission (AIGA) [25], Vanderheiden, Treviranus, Ortega-Moral, Peissner, and de

Lera [26], Gilbert et al. [10, 11], Laskowski and Redish [27], Redish et al. [28, 29], and Swierenga and Pierce [6, 7]. These projects examined ballot interaction characteristics (e.g., selecting/deselecting options, multi-selection, overvoting/undervoting messaging), optical scan ballot design (e.g., displaying election information, ballot instructions, ballot navigation), ballot layout (e.g., typeface, type size, distances between elements, etc.), touch screen interaction design, voting using touchpads/button boxes, audio interaction design, plain language ballots and system messages, auto-personalization, usability and accessibility testing methodologies and standards, and more.

There are many challenges in designing an accessible voting system, and many more challenges in designing an accessible *mobile* voting system. Thus, we also drew from other mobile ballot design projects, including the Anywhere Ballot [17], the EZ Ballot [18], the Georgia Tech Research Institute voting ballot testbed [30, 31], Oregon's alternative ballot format [32], Rice University's research on voting using mobile touch screen devices [33], and Michigan State University's voting system design research [6–8, 34]. These mobile voting system design projects focus on small screen design, touch screen design, on-screen instructions, and ballot interaction designs. However, our project was unique in that we specifically focused on making a system that was accessible to persons with dexterity and visual impairments, as well as voters who have limited or no experience with mobile technologies. We also attempted to balance accessibility requirements with security concerns throughout the ideation and design process.

3.1 Requirements for an Accessible Mobile Voting User Interface

Based on our research, we generated a list of general requirements for an accessible mobile voting user interface. The specifications were broken down into 14 design categories, including units and sizing, font and text, button size, button spacing, touch screen and gestures, color, system behavior, user selections, region consistency, focus order, focus visibility, selection visibility, auto-personalization, and hardware buttons. For example, in our research we found that all buttons (including slider and page up/down buttons in scroll bars) must be at least 20 mm in length and width and must have a visible solid border that meets color requirements; all functionality must be available via tap, the preferred and most effective gesture for individuals with motor skill impairments; and the system must support personalization by storing users profiles that hold information about user preferences and the device/assistive technology being used to customize the interface to meet the needs of the user.

The design requirements specified several ways of interacting with the tablet to accommodate different user groups according to their needs. These modes included: default visual layout (which accommodates a wide range of dexterity and visual impairments), screen reader, audio only, five button overlay, sip-and-puff, and external input. The external input mode provides for the use of personal assistive technologies that voters connect to the mobile voting device (in this specification, a tablet computer).

3.2 Design Feedback from Users with Disabilities

Using our interface specification, we built a functional prototype for a tablet computer and invited users with disabilities and assistive technology experts to provide feedback [19].

Both experts with disabilities and assistive technology experts expressed a keen desire to use personal assistive technologies, e.g., headphones, trackball, mouse, and refreshable Braille displays, in conjunction with the prototype. They also preferred to have the option to use the full range of touch screen gestures, instead of a limited set of allowed gestures.

For individuals with reduced dexterity, holding the tablet was determined to be a considerable strain, suggesting the need for a mount, however the angle and position must be customizable to accommodate individuals whose reach or height differs. For individuals with vision impairments, glare due to reflections and ambient lighting causes significant problems, which can be alleviated by allowing the angle of the screen to be adjusted and by providing appropriate shielding and placement. Using a matte screen (or adding a matte screen cover, if it does not interfere with touch screen sensitivity) was also recommended as a means to mitigate glare.

4   Using Intermediary Devices to Make Voting via Personal Assistive Technologies Secure

Based on our research as well as recommendations and feedback from potential users and subject matter experts, it is clear that allowing users with disabilities to vote using their own personal assistive technologies will significantly improve the accessibility of the voting process. However, we acknowledge that this can present significant risks to security. We therefore propose exploring the use of a secure intermediary (such as a computer or tablet) to translate the outputs of voters' assistive technologies into secure inputs for stand-alone electronic voting systems. An alternative input device, such as a joystick, would be connected to the secure intermediary, and the intermediary would be connected to an electronic voting system. Personal assistive technologies would therefore never directly connect to voting systems, allowing these devices to be safely used at the polling place. The intermediary would convert the assistive device's output signals into a simple, secure, and standardized output that can be fed into limited and sanitized (free of security threats) inputs for voting systems.

In addition, the intermediary can provide advanced functionality that would not otherwise be available, including custom control mapping, alternate keyboard support, automatic scanning, single button automatic scanning, user profiles, and can serve as an input device itself. Through the use of an open specification for input translation, simple configuration changes on the intermediary could immediately allow new or customized assistive devices to control existing voting systems.

5   Conclusion

Voting security and accessibility are crucial for enabling voters with disabilities to vote securely, independently, and privately. The three primary strategies for creating an accessible voting experience (i.e., building new voting machines with built-in accessibility components, interfacing personal assistive technologies with current ballot marking/ballot counting systems, and mobile/Internet voting using personal assistive technologies) all pose unique security risks. These risks include data security, data reliability, voter verification, and auditability, among others. Although there has been discussion on security in the mobile/Internet voting community, it has yet to be fully addressed within accessible voting system designs, despite being a major potential roadblock to allowing personal assistive technologies into the voting environment.

We propose the use of an intermediary device (e.g., tablet computer) as a secure "middle-man" between voters' personal assistive technologies and official election machines to mitigate security risks. The intermediary device can also provide an alternative ballot design that adheres to our previously documented user interface requirements for accessible mobile voting interfaces that enhance the accessibility of the user voting experience. Security measures in intermediary devices would filter and prevent malicious attempts to interfere with or alter votes, acting as a firewall between the user and the voting machine. Hardware alterations to USB ports, for example, would enable only the use of control devices and not high speed data transfers.

We feel this concept will help move towards a secure, accessible voting experience for all users, and see the need for further research that explicitly explores the connections between accessibility, security, and voting, as well as a continued discussion about how to balance accessibility and security concerns in mobile/remote voting design.

Acknowledgements. This research was funded through two grants from the National Institute of Standards and Technology to Michigan State University: *Enhancement of Accessible Mobile Voting System Standards* (Grant #70NANB13H150); *Use of Personal Assistive Technologies in Voting* (Grant #60NANB14D265). Principal Investigator: Dr. Sarah J. Swierenga, Michigan State University, Usability/Accessibility Research and Consulting.

References

1. United States Election Assistance Commission: Help America Vote Act (2002). http://www.eac.gov/about_the_eac/help_america_vote_act.aspx
2. Council of Europe Committee of Ministers: Recommendation of the committee of ministers to member states on legal, operational and technical standards for e-voting (2004). https://wcd.coe.int/ViewDoc.jsp?id=778189&Site=CM&BackColorInternet=C3C3C3&BackColorIntranet=EDB021&BackColorLogged=F5D383
3. United States Election Assistance Commission: Voluntary voting system guidelines version 1.0 (2005). http://www.eac.gov/assets/1/workflow_staging/Page/124.PDF
4. United States Election Assistance Commission: Voluntary voting system guidelines version 1.1 (Draft) (2012). http://www.eac.gov/assets/1/Documents/VVSG%20Version%201.1%20Volume%201%20Public%20Comment%20Version-8.31.2012.pdf
5. Runyan, N.H.: Improving access to voting: a report on the technology for accessible voting systems. Voter Action and Dēmos: A Network for Ideas and Action (2007)
6. Swierenga, S.J., Pierce, G.L.: Testing Usability Performance of Accessible Voting Systems: Final Report, Usability/Accessibility Research and Consulting, Michigan State University, East Lansing, MI (2012)
7. Swierenga, S.J. Pierce, G.L.: Testing usability performance of accessible voting systems. Poster presentation at the EAC/NIST Accessible Voting Technology Research Workshop, Department of Commerce, National Institute of Standards and Technology, Gaithersburg, MD (2013)

8. Swierenga, S.J., Pierce, G.L.: Accessible voting system usability measures. J. Technol. Persons Disabil. **1**, 146–154 (2013)
9. Swierenga, S.J., Pierce, G.L., Blosser, S.R., Mathew, A., Jackson, J.: Smart Voting Joystick for accessible voting systems. J. Technol. Persons Disabil. **2**, 144–154 (2014)
10. Gilbert, J., Ekandem, J., Darnell, S., Alnizami, H., Martin, A., Johnson, W.: Accessible voting: one machine, one vote for everyone. In: Proceedings of the International Conference on Human Factors in Computing Systems, CHI 2011, Extended Abstracts Volume, pp. 517–518. ACM, New York (2011)
11. Gilbert, J., McMillian, Y., Rouse, K., Williams, P., Rogers, G., McClendon, J., Mitchell, W., Gupta, P., Mkpong-Ruffin, I., Cross, E.: Universal access in e-voting for the blind. Univ. Access Inf. Soc. **9**(4), 357–365 (2010)
12. McNary, S.: LA County developing a voting system for the digital age (2013). http://www.scpr.org/blogs/politics/2013/04/04/13162/l-a-county-is-reinventing-voting-by-turning-to-the/
13. Cook, D., Harniss, M.: Accessible voting technology: analysis and recommendations (AVTI working paper #004). The Information Technology and Innovation Foundation, Washington, D.C. (2012)
14. Microsoft Windows Development Center: Security Considerations for Assistive Technologies. https://msdn.microsoft.com/en-us/library/windows/desktop/ee671610%28v=vs.85%29.aspx
15. Pew Research Center: Pew research internet project: mobile technology fact sheet (2014). http://www.pewinternet.org/fact-sheets/mobile-technology-fact-sheet/
16. Schur, L., Adya, M., Kruse, D.: Disability, voter turnout, and voting difficulties in the 2012 elections. Report to U.S. EAC and RAAV (2013)
17. Summers, K., Davies, D., Chisnell, D.: Anywhere ballot: why is this ballot the solution for the future? Poster presentation at the NIST/EAC Accessible Voting Technology Conference, Gaithersburg, MD (2013). http://elections.itif.org/resources/posters/poster-anywhere-ballot/
18. Sanford, J.: EZ Ballot. Presentation at the NIST/EAC Accessible Voting Technology Conference, Gaithersburg, MD (2013). http://www.nist.gov/itl/iad/upload/Sanford_avt2013.rtf
19. Pierce, G.L., Jackson, J.E., Swierenga, S.J.: Enhanced user interface and interaction design standards for accessible mobile voting systems. Usability/Accessibility Research and Consulting, Michigan State University, East Lansing, MI (2014)
20. Jefferson, D., Rubin, A.D., Simons, B., Wagner, D.: Analyzing Internet voting security: an extensive assessment of a proposed Internet-based voting system. Commun. ACM **47**(10), 59–64 (2004)
21. Jefferson, D.: If I can shop and bank online, why can't I vote online? (2011). https://www.verifiedvoting.org/if-i-can-shop-and-bank-online-why-cant-i-vote-online/
22. Dill, D.: Computer Technologists' Statement on Internet Voting. http://www.verifiedvoting.org/wp-content/uploads/2012/09/InternetVotingStatement.pdf
23. Laskowski, S.J., Autry, M., Cugini, J., Killam, W., Yen, J.: Improving the usability and accessibility of voting systems and products. NSIT Special Publication 500-256, U.S. Department of Commerce, National Institute of Standards and Technology (2004)
24. National Institute of Standards and Technology: Usability performance benchmarks for the voluntary voting system guidelines (2007). http://www.nist.gov/itl/vote/meeting20070817.cfm
25. United States Election Assistance Commission: Effective designs for the administration of federal elections. AIGA Design for Democracy (2007). http://www.aiga.org/design-for-democracy-eac-reports/

26. Vanderheiden, G.C., Treviranus, J., Ortega-Moral, M., Peissner, M., de Lera, E.: Creating a Global Public Inclusive Infrastructure (GPII). In: Stephanidis, C., Antona, M. (eds.) UAHCI 2014, Part IV. LNCS, vol. 8513, pp. 506–515. Springer, Heidelberg (2014)
27. Laskowski, S.J., Redish, J.: Making ballot language understandable to voters. In: Proceedings of the USENIX/Accurate Electronic Voting Technology Workshop 2006 on Electronic Voting Technology Workshop, p. 1. USENIX Association, Berkeley (2006). http://static.usenix.org/event/evt06/tech/full_papers/laskowski/laskowski.pdf
28. Redish, J., Chisnell, D.E., Newby, E., Laskowski, S.J., Lowry, S.: Report of findings: use of language in ballot instructions. National Institute of Standards and Technology, Gaithersburg (2008). http://www.nist.gov/itl/vote/upload/NISTIR-7556.pdf
29. Redish, J., Chisnell, D.E., Laskowski, S.J., Lowry, S.: Plain language makes a difference when people vote. J. Usability Stud. 5(3), 81–103 (2010)
30. GTRI: Making voting more accessible for veterans with disabilities. Georgia Tech Research Institute, Atlanta (2012)
31. Harley, L., Baranak, A., Bell, C., Ray, J., Fain, B.: Leveraging today's technology to make voting systems usable, accessible, and secure. Poster Presentation at the NIST/EAC Accessible Voting Technology Conference, Gaithersburg, MD (2013). http://elections.itif.org/resources/posters/poster-gtri/
32. Schmitt, J.: Oregon's alternative format ballot: from XP to surface and beyond. Presentation at the NIST/EAC Accessible Voting Technology Conference, Gaithersburg, MD (2013). http://www.nist.gov/itl/iad/upload/Schmitt_avt2013.pdf
33. Campbell, B., Tossell, C., Byrne, M., Kortum, P.: Voting on a smartphone. In: Proceedings of the Human Factors and Ergonomics Society 55th Annual Meeting, pp. 1100–1104. Human Factors and Ergonomics Society, Las Vegas (2011)
34. Decloniemaclennan, R., Nemchick, J., Ismirle, J., Jackson, J., Pierce, G.L., Swierenga, S.J.: Research-based mobile usability and accessibility guidelines. Presentation at the International Technology & Persons with Disabilities Conference, San Diego, CA (2014)

Perceptions of Personal Privacy in Smart Home Technologies: Do User Assessments Vary Depending on the Research Method?

Wiktoria Wilkowska[✉], Martina Ziefle, and Simon Himmel

Human-Computer Interaction Center, Campus-Boulevard 57, 52074 Aachen, Germany
{wilkowska,ziefle,himmel}@comm.rwth-aachen.de

Abstract. Nowadays all Western societies are confronted with the challenges resulting from demographic change, which are (partially) manageable by technical innovations, ranging from sophisticated single devices up to Ambient Assisted Living. However, exceeding the threshold to people's homes evokes diverse privacy concerns. In this paper, aspects of personal privacy are exposed and validated by three different research methods: focus groups, questionnaire, and an experimental study.

The results of the perceived relevance of privacy across the three methodologies showed a decrease of the attributed importance from the focus group to the hands-on experimental study and an increase of the variability of the data. In order to gain genuine exhaustive information about the user's perceptions of (aspects of) new technologies it is therefore insufficient to rely on one single research method. Instead, a multi-method research approach is postulated.

Keywords: Privacy · Ambient assisted living · Ehealth · Multi-method research · Focus groups · Questionnaire · Living-Lab study

1 Introduction

The rapid development in information and communication technology (ICT) and its growing application possibilities in the everyday lives of aging populations have long raised concerns about the individual privacy. Currently, a particular emphasis in this topic is placed onto the use and acceptance of smart home technologies that are meant to support residents especially in their health duties (e.g., measurements of vital parameters, medication, rehabilitation exercises) and in accomplishing their other daily functions. Integration of health-supporting technologies in the domestic area (e.g., health monitoring system) fundamentally changes social and communicative pathways in people's lives, and the users' perceptions of personal privacy in this context may greatly vary from the use of technology in isolated and deliberately determined situations.

The conception of privacy is highly complex and involves different perspectives and dimensions that, depending on social, physical, and cultural factors, considerably vary between individuals. An additional consideration is that the concept of privacy – and the term relates, at this point, to the individual's private sphere and not exclusively to

© Springer International Publishing Switzerland 2015
T. Tryfonas and I. Askoxylakis (Eds.): HAS 2015, LNCS 9190, pp. 592–603, 2015.
DOI: 10.1007/978-3-319-20376-8_53

the privacy in terms of data protection – might be evaluated differently by the users depending on the chosen research method. To examine this phenomenon, in this paper we describe the (potential) users' perceptions of personal privacy in the context of acceptance of medical ambient technology, comparing the results of three different research methods: focus groups, a quantitative survey, and an experimental usability study.

Demographic Change and the Concept of Ambient Assisted Living. It is an obvious fact that most Western societies undergo a demographic change. The decreasing birth rates in the last decades, on the one hand, and the medical improvements, on the other hand, lead to an aging society, recognizable already today and increasing the next 40 years [1, 2]. The present elderly care systems work at their limits regarding human and accommodation resources. The good news is that in addition to all political efforts or the job-related migration [3, 4], there are some technical solutions dealing with the challenge to support the major wishes of the elderly: being healthy and staying in their own four walls as long as possible [5].

Currently, there are several technical applications on the market and under research to support elderly people's staying at home. With the improvement of conventional information and communication technologies and telemedical devices the possibilities to save doctoral consultations for minor checkups are a wide and well researched field of technology [6]. In combination with electronic health devices (eHealth technology), measuring vital parameters connected for telemonitoring even elaborated consultations can be made while staying at home [7]. There are also wearable solutions for emergency calls with buttons on bracelets or necklaces. Currently, the research goes even further, integrating eHealth devices from wearables to implants with an improvement in size, precision, and possibilities [8]. Furthermore, also nursing staff at home – the number of which unfortunately decreases continuously due to the demographic shifts – could one day get support by robot colleagues [9].

Single devices often encompass all of the solutions above. The combination and seamless integration of technology devices into the living spaces, making the home a smart home, leads to the research field of Ambient Assisted Living (AAL) [10]. As we are on the cusp to its commercial realization, current research primarily takes place in living labs [11], where future users can get hands-on experience and the functionality and usability of these technologies can be optimized.

This short introduction from present eHealth systems to Ambient Assisted Living leads to one not yet mentioned, but crucial factor: the user's acceptance. In most of our interdisciplinary research at the Human-Computer Interaction Center the focus lies on the user's point of view. The overall acceptance of health technology, which aims on a quite sensitive area of life, is bound to several key factors. In this work the focus is directed to one currently highly debated topic, dealing with the importance of individual privacy in connection with ambient technologies in home environments [12].

Privacy Concerns as a Key Barrier in Medical Technologies at Home. A specific focus of AAL technologies is naturally directed to the question to what extent such systems respect the fragile trade-off between two different poles: On the one hand, the wish to live independently at home, to feel safe, secure, and fully cared for, and on the other hand, due to a continuous health monitoring the feelings of loss of control, the concerns about the protection of individual privacy and the refusal to tolerate any intrusions in the private sphere.

The omnipresence of information and communication technologies, especially at home, may be perceived as a violation of personal intimacy limits, raising concerns about privacy and loss of control [12, 13]. Recent studies show that this trade-off is not only extremely difficult for individuals, but it is additionally affected by user diversity like e.g., age [14], gender [15, 16], culture [17, 18], or health status [19]. Also, the trade-off varies for different stakeholders: Patients might have a different perspective than family members, caregivers, or medical personnel [20]. So far, privacy issues in technologies are mostly addressed from a legal and technical point of view (e.g., [21]). Though both perspectives are naturally important for the feasibility and broad implementation of such systems, individual perceptions of privacy are an indispensable prerequisite for a vast acceptance and sustainable solution. From this it follows that the perceptions of individual privacy and intimacy limits must be considered from the beginning in the technology development.

Validity of Reported Concerns in Different Methodological Settings. The implementation of the user's privacy and trust perceptions in the technical design is, however, not easy to realize. One reason is the topic itself: The exploration of the medical technology in the context of home environment and the question how far users would tolerate it, is an extremely sensitive and serious issue associated with feelings of being old, ill, dependent of others, and is thus accompanied by stigma and decline [13, 22].

Another reason is the way how privacy perception is examined, i.e., the respective empirical methodology and the validity of the results. In most of the studies, more or less healthy persons of a wide age range and with different professional backgrounds had been requested to evaluate the acceptance of AAL systems in order to learn, which persons would be willing to adopt such systems in their living spaces under which circumstances. Yet, while such approaches are technically sound, there are still some doubts with respect to the validity of the findings. It has been argued that users who are not actually concerned by (chronic) illness and/or old age and the associated consequences of health decline that require medical monitoring system at home, cannot evaluate the "real" situation and thus over- or even underestimate such a situation [19, 22]. This is due to the fact that no experience with smart home technology is present and that persons tend to overemphasize their sensitiveness towards privacy violations if their judgments only rely on the imagination of using it [23, 24].

2 Methodological Concept: A Multi-method Approach

In this paper, privacy concerns in the context of AAL technologies are explored with two major foci: Firstly, privacy and intimacy concerns were empirically assessed among participants of a wide age range (19–98 years of age), both sexes, and with different health states (healthy young, healthy old, more or less diseased young and ill elderly persons). Secondly, different methodology approaches were used: focus groups discussions, a questionnaire study, and an experimental study in a living lab environment (Future Care Lab©, RWTH Aachen University, Germany), in which participants are able interact with an ambient technology integrated in a home.

In focus groups, cognitions and argumentation lines of persons can be collected, allowing an early evaluation of emotional and ethical concerns, like hopes, wishes, and requirements of the users, prior to technology development. Quantitative questionnaires, in contrast, enable to quantify the relative extent of attitudes towards the topic across a broader sample of participants, contrasting thereby positive and negative factors, and allow a screening of the degree to which user factors might influence the evaluations. Finally, a living lab experiment allows studying users in a quite realistic environment, thus enabling to understand evaluations in a socially framed context in which users can touch, feel, and interact with the technology at issue. In Fig. 1, the different empirical approaches are systemized.

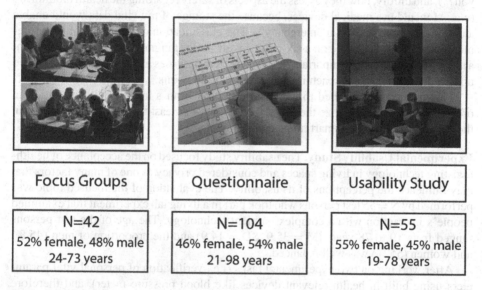

Focus Groups	Questionnaire	Usability Study
N=42	N=104	N=55
52% female, 48% male	46% female, 54% male	55% female, 45% male
24-73 years	21-98 years	19-78 years

Fig. 1. Methodological approaches validating privacy aspects associated with AAL technologies

Focus Groups Study. The focus groups were conducted with N = 42 participants in total, which resulted from five different sessions. According to the topic of the study, the discussion groups were composed of younger and older adults (age range between 24 and 73 years; M = 57.3, SD = 13.7) and assigned to the particular groups considering the users' gender (52 % female). Such composition of the focus groups was meant to support the dynamics of the conversations, allowing better access to the age- and gender-specific perceptions.

The aim was to identify and discuss peoples' ideas of individual privacy when using ambient technology: In the first place, this topic was debated in the context of general use of popular information and communication technology devices (e.g., mobile phone, personal computer), but special emphasis was applied to medical devices and health-related technology systems integrated in home environments. On the basis of the findings derived from this qualitative study, a questionnaire was developed to validate the data in a quantitative way.

Questionnaire Study. In the survey study quantitative data of N = 104 participants aged between 21 and 98 years (M = 46.3, SD = 17.8; 46 % female) were analyzed. The aim was to quantify how relevant the previously identified aspects of individual privacy (e.g., invisibility to outsiders, intimacy, anonymity) are for the acceptance of medical technology on a more representative population level.

One part of the questionnaire surveyed, firstly, how important for the randomly chosen respondents are such issues as for instance discreetness, intimacy, anonymity while using health-supporting devices, secondly, how they perceive the system security of such technology (e.g., "How important is the highest possible data protection to you?"), and thirdly, how they assess the aspects of safety regarding the health monitoring (e.g., "I would use medical devices, because the storage of my vital data would enable a quick access in case of an emergency"). The classification of relevance of the aforementioned items was made on a six-point Likert-scales ranging from 1 ("not important at all") to 6 points ("very important"). For statistical purposes all the items were summed up to a privacy-subscale, reaching a maximum of 66 points.

This method was applied to gather information from a larger adult population in order to be able to generalize the privacy outcomes – at least the investigated ones – in the context of living in a smart home environment.

Experimental Usability Study. The usability study focused on the acceptance of health-assisting technology in living spaces and considered privacy as one of many factors that may influence the perceptions of its usability. The evaluation of the focused topic was performed by N = 55 test persons who took part in a living lab experiment that examined people's interaction with a complex ambient technology. The age of the test persons ranged from 19 to 78 years (M = 35.9, SD = 14.9) and the proportion of men (45 %) and women (55 %) was well balanced.

After working on two experimental tasks (i.e., verification of personal vital parameters using built-in health-relevant devices like blood pressure meter), and therefore extensive interaction with the technology, participants evaluated in addition to the well-known usability criteria (e.g., complexity of the system, learnability, ease of use) the following personal privacy items:

- "It bothers me that my data might be visible and/or accessible by others."
- "I wish for a personal access code for the system to protect my privacy."

The test persons were requested to indicate the degree of their (dis)agreement on a seven-point Likert-scale (1 = "strongly disagree" to 7 = "strongly agree") and a sum of the two items was formed (max. = 14 points) for further statistical analyses.

In the third study, thus, participants assessed the mentioned privacy requirements using yet another method: In contrast to the first and the second research study – which, envisioning the use, solely allow the anticipating of opinions in this subject matter – the evaluation of privacy here was signified after a direct interaction with the technology in a natural setting and performed in context of an everyday activity. It is therefore to be expected that such results are very meaningful.

3 Results

The results of the presented studies regarding opinions of the relevance of personal privacy in using ambient assistive technologies were elaborated from scratch according to the user-centered research. The findings of a previous study, thus, were analyzed and consecutively validated by means of another research method as it was described above.

In this paper, the statistical analyses are mostly left at the level of univariate analyses and the outcomes regarding privacy aspects are presented by means of a central tendency of a variable and its dispersion [mean values (M) and the associated standard deviations (SD)]. Moreover, inferential statistic analyses are used to explore differences between age and gender groups; for this purposes t-tests and analysis of variance are used depending on the nature of the analyzed data. The level of statistical significance is set at 5 %.

Results of the Focus Groups Study. In the introductory part, participants were encouraged to talk about all the technical devices they use in their everyday life. Focusing on such common ICT devices, it was then questioned which information and communication modalities (e.g., integrated camera, microphone, monitor, etc.) the participants would allow in their own homes and where (e.g., living room, kitchen, bedroom, bath). In addition, it was queried what "control" means in the context of (medical) technology, focusing on people's perceptions regarding (health) monitoring and surveillance.

The discussions in all focus groups uncovered different perceptions and aspects regarding personal privacy. Ambient technologies entering private spaces brought up questions addressing intimacy and the control to switch off any technology whenever required. Questions on health-related safety and data security when monitoring individual parameters resulted in heated debates. Who has control over the data and who is watching the observers? How can anonymity be ensured? How is the critical trade-off between autonomous living at home monitored by ambient technology system vs. living in a retirement home evaluated?

The results of a short questionnaire about the valued importance of privacy that was handed out to each participant showed clear results. With a mean of $M = 9.7$ out of 10 possible points ($SD = 0.8$) the importance of privacy was evaluated as extremely important.

Results of the Questionnaire Study. The validation of the privacy aspects that were found by means of focus groups was realized by the quantitative questionnaire. The outcomes regarding the importance of personal privacy appeared somewhat attenuated in comparison to the assessments in the forerun qualitative method. Overall the mean of $M = 48.6$ out of maximum 66 points ($SD = 11.6$) was reached (see Fig. 2, right). This is a high value that makes evident that the individual privacy is in general evaluated quite high. On the left side of Fig. 2 the means of the single aspects of privacy are detailed: The most privacy requirements reached on average a high importance (means

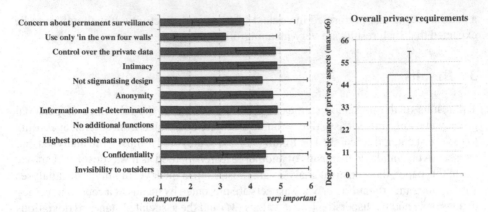

Fig. 2. Assessments of privacy aspects in detail (left) and in general (right) in the questionnaire study (N = 104).

around $M = 5$ out of 6 possible points) – the most pronounced were the highest possible general data protection ($M = 5.1$, $SD = 1.2$), the protection of intimacy ($M = 4.9$, $SD = 1.3$) and the perceived control over the private data ($M = 4.8$, $SD = 1.3$), while no great importance was attributed to the technology use only 'in the own four walls' ($M = 3.2$, $SD = 1.7$).

Additional statistical testing for age [$F(2, 94) = 0.8$, p = n.s.)] and gender effects [$t(93) = -1.4$, p = n.s.)] concerning the presented assessments revealed no significant differences in this regard.

The overall quite high privacy requirements consolidated in a unified privacy-subscale show distinct awareness of this topic in the examined context, but in the end they do not confirm privacy as a main driver for the acceptance of ambient technologies.

Results of the Usability Study. In the experimental study, the importance of the individual privacy topic was examined among other system usability aspects, without putting a strong emphasis on it.

The participants, who in this study assessed the usability of the technology were asked during the experimental setting, firstly, to what extent they feel bothered by the visibility and/or accessibility of their personal health data by third parties. The answers turned out ambiguous reaching in the whole sample a mean of $M = 4.1$ ($SD = 2$) out of 7 points, which in concrete terms means neither unequivocal consent nor unambiguous rejection of this privacy aspect. Secondly, the test persons had to evaluate whether they wish for a protecting code for their personal data. In this case, the analysis revealed rather a rejection than an approval ($M = 2.8$, $SD = 2.1$) of this kind of privacy protection. The mean values of both privacy aspects examined here are presented in Fig. 3 on the left.

Using the experimental research method, the resulting score of privacy not even reached the midpoint of the relevance scale ($M = 6.9$, $SD = 3.6$ out of 14 points), showing overall rather strongly mitigated significance of the individual privacy for the use of health-supporting technology in ambient assisted living.

Furthermore, neither a significant effect of age [$F(2,53) = 3.3$, $p = $ n.s.)] nor gender effect [$t(53) = -0.9$, $p = $ n.s.)] was revealed for the privacy in the usability study.

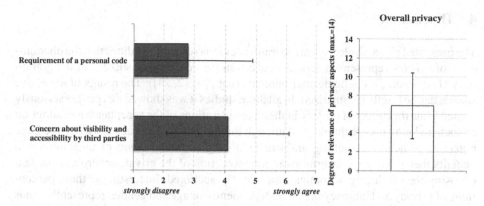

Fig. 3. Assessments of privacy aspects in detail (left) and in general (right) in the experimental usability study (N = 55).

Comparison of the Results of Different Research Methods. In order to "compare" the results for the valued importance of privacy concerns, depending on the respective methodology, a standardization of quantitative outcomes is necessary. Strictly speaking, one could argue that a numerical standardization might not be appropriate in this context, as different persons, scales, and empirical framings had been used across the three methodological approaches. Though, in order to get an impression how far the used method influences and modulates the point at issue, we normalized quantitative results of all approaches and scales to a 10-point scale ranging from −4.5 (= not important) to 4.5 (= very important). The outcomes are depicted in Fig. 4.

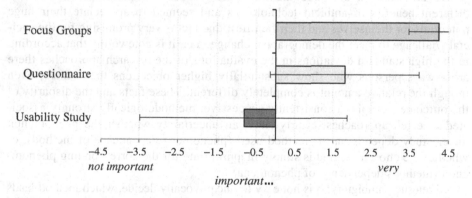

Fig. 4. Comparison of the applied research methods: Mean importance of privacy aspects

As can be seen, it is astounding in how much the relative extent of privacy concerns depends on the research method. The most concerns were collected in focus groups; thus, the individual privacy here was regarded most important, followed by the results from the questionnaire. The lowest degree of concerns was found in the experimental approach in living lab, corroborating that the nature and the extent of concerns naturally decreases with increasing reality of Ambient Assisted Living as a base for the evaluation.

4   Discussion

The presented research clearly corroborates previous scientific findings that the phenomenon of privacy represents a serious concern in the context of a successful integration of AAL technologies in home environments (e.g., [5, 12, 24]). The results of the above studies can be briefly summarized: In all three studies it was showed that people seriously contemplate the aspect of privacy in their considerations of the acceptance and adoption of such an innovative technology. Although the (potential) users acknowledge the huge potential of health-supporting ambient technologies being aware of usefulness and benefits they yield, the concerns about the protection of the private sphere and the fear of losing their intimacy is dominant and deeply anchored. Interestingly, these perceptions of privacy and intimacy prevail independently of age and gender, representing thus an old and profound, even "archetypal" concern.

However, from a methodological point of view the results were astounding, if not alarming. According to the presented findings, the intensity of privacy concerns is dramatically dependent on the respective empirical method with which the focused topics are captured. The more distinct – this means isolated from other contents – the approached topic was within a research method and the more people were allowed to discuss (focus groups) and to envision possible scenarios associated with it (focus groups, questionnaires), the more pronounced were the respondents' concerns about the possible violations of their personal privacy. In contrast, whenever the examined topic was embedded into another matters, or when users were confronted with quite realistic circumstances (in form of living lab experience) and their attention was not only directed to this one topic, the privacy concerns considerably decreased.

Nevertheless, in all three methodological settings participants realized the different benefits of ambient technologies and seemed to appreciate their huge potentials for themselves and their families; this fact is very promising for the societal challenge to meet the demographic change. Yet, it is noteworthy that according to the high standard deviations in the evaluations of the research approaches there are always persons who show substantially higher objections than others, even though the relative amount is completely different. These facts and the disparity of the outcomes, despite a consistently successive, methodologically strongly associated research approaches, clearly show an uncertainty whether the phenomenon under study depends on the method used (phenomena dependence of method), or whether the chosen method is simply inappropriate for the corresponding phenomenon (methods dependence of phenomena).

Given such ambiguity, it is not easy to unequivocally decide, which method leads to the real, genuine, and most valid results. Let us firstly consider focus groups as a method: On the one hand, it could be argued that the possibility for the participants to deliberately discuss the topic of personal privacy is the Via Regia to uncover the relevant motives. Following this line of reasoning, we must assume that the other used methods, evaluating privacy as an aspect among others (survey, experiment) may entirely underestimate the significance of the examined phenomenon. On the other hand, one could polemize that focus group discussions might artificially exaggerate and overestimate the problems, arguing that the more room for discussions is given to the participants in early stages of the developmental process, the more there is space for developing an antagonist position that focuses on potential risks and the uncertainty in connection with a novel technology (according to the motto: if you ask for problems, you will receive them). Such an approach would clearly suggest using additional methods that accordingly validate the results of the initial discussions.

On the base of the present findings no clear statements can be made. The steady weakening of the relevance of the privacy aspects with each research method used complicates a distinct indication of a certain direction in this regard. However, especially in the context of medical technology, there are certain reasons to assume that the potential usage barriers and perceived benefits can be only fully understood and assessed if users are able to actively interact with the ambient technology in a home-like environment [19, 24]. Therefore, an experimental space, like it is given in the surrounding of a living lab, is of central importance for the examination of privacy concerns not only out of validity reasons, but also because patients and caregivers need to experience and "feel" the ambient technology in order to evaluate it properly [25]. As opposed to this, persons may overemphasize their sensitiveness towards privacy violations if their judgments rely only on the imagination of using it (questionnaire method) [22–24].

In view of the results it is evident how much the examination of a research object depends on the chosen scientific method. This paper therefore posits that the application of different research methods is mandatory, especially when investigating or exploring (new) influencing factors in the process of launching technology innovations. In addition, the most important modification in the way traditional technological development in the field of medical engineering is currently accomplished is to systematically include those users in the design process for which the technology is planned. A coherent user-centered research of AAL technologies at home will result in an optimally designed medical technology, which is not only functional, but also addresses fundamental user needs in terms of appearance, ease of use, and last but not least privacy issues.

Acknowledgments. This work was funded by the Excellence initiative of German states and federal government. We would also like to thank Barbara Zaunbrecher for the valuable remarks on this paper.

References

1. European Commission (White paper): The Demographic Future of Europe – From Challenge to Opportunity. Commission Communication, COM, Brussels (2006)
2. Bloom, D.E., Canning, D.: Global Demographic Change: Dimensions and Economic Significance. National Bureau of Economic Research (2004)
3. Koenig, H.G., George, L.K., Schneider, R.: Mental health care for older adults in the year 2020: a dangerous and avoided topic. Gerontologist **34**, 674–679 (1994)
4. Gee, E., Gutman, G.: The Overselling of Population Ageing: Apocalyptic Demography, Intergenerational Challenges, and Social Policy. Oxford University Press, Toronto (2000)

5. Ziefle, M., Himmel, S., Wilkowska, W.: When your living space knows what you do: acceptance of medical home monitoring by different technologies. In: Holzinger, A., Simonic, K.-M. (eds.) USAB 2011. LNCS, vol. 7058, pp. 607–624. Springer, Heidelberg (2011)
6. Koch, S.: Home telehealth—current state and future trends. Int. J. Med. Inf. **75**, 565–576 (2006)
7. Paré, G., Jaana, M., Sicotte, C.: Systematic review of home telemonitoring for chronic diseases: the evidence base. J. Am. Med. Inform. Assoc. **14**, 269–277 (2007)
8. Burns, J.L., Serber, E.R., Keim, S., Sears, S.F.: Measuring patient acceptance of implantable cardiac device therapy: initial psychometric investigation of the florida patient acceptance survey. J. Cardiovasc. Electrophysiol. **16**, 384–390 (2005)
9. Broadbent, E., Stafford, R., MacDonald, B.: Acceptance of healthcare robots for the older population: review and future directions. Int. J. Soc. Robot. **1**, 319–330 (2009)
10. Nehmer, J., Becker, M., Karshmer, A., Lamm, R.: Living assistance systems: an ambient intelligence approach. In: Proceedings of the 28th International Conference on Software Engineering, pp. 43–50 (2006)
11. de Ruyter, B., Pelgrim, E.: Ambient assisted living research in carelab. Interactions **14**, 30–33 (2007)
12. Wilkowska, W., Ziefle, M.: Privacy and data security in E-health: requirements from the user's perspective. Health Inform. J. **18**, 191–201 (2012)
13. Lalou, S.: Identity, social status, privacy and face-keeping in the digital society. J. Soc. Sci. Inf. **47**, 230–299 (2008)
14. Wilkowska, W., Ziefle, M.: User diversity as a challenge for the integration of medical technology into future home environments. In: Ziefle, M., Röcker, C. (eds.) Human-Centered Design of E-Health Technologies: Concepts, Methods and Applications, pp. 95–126. Hershey, PA, IGI Global (2011)
15. Ziefle, M., Schaar, A.K.: Gender differences in acceptance and attitudes towards an invasive medical stent. Electron. J. Health Inform. **6**, e13 (2011)
16. Wilkowska, W., Gaul, S., Ziefle, M.: A small but significant difference – the role of gender on acceptance of medical assistive technologies. In: Leitner, G., Hitz, M., Holzinger, A. (eds.) USAB 2010. LNCS, vol. 6389, pp. 82–100. Springer, Heidelberg (2010)
17. Alagöz, F., Ziefle, M., Wilkowska, W., Calero Valdez, A.: Openness to accept medical technology – a cultural view. In: Holzinger, A., Simonic, K.-M. (eds.) USAB 2011. LNCS, vol. 7058, pp. 151–170. Springer, Heidelberg (2011)
18. Wilkowska, W., Ziefle, M., Alagöz, F.: How user diversity and country of origin impact the readiness to adopt e-health technologies: an intercultural comparison. Work: J. Prev. Assess. Rehabil. **41**, 2072–2080 (2012)
19. Klack, L., Schmitz-Rode, T., Wilkowska, W., Kasugai, K., Heidrich, F., Ziefle, M.: Integrated home monitoring and compliance optimization for patients with mechanical circulatory support devices. Ann. Biomed. Eng. **39**, 2911–2921 (2011)
20. Klack, L., Wilkowska, W., Kluge, J., Ziefle, M.: Telemedical vs. conventional heart patient monitoring – a survey study with german physicians. Int. J. Technol. Access. Health Care **29**(4), 376–383 (2013)
21. Lymberis, A.: Smart wearable systems for personalised health management: current R&D and future challenges. In: Engineering in Medicine and Biology Society, 2003. Proceedings of the 25th Annual International Conference of the IEEE, pp. 3716–3719. IEEE (2003)
22. Ziefle, M., Schaar, A.K.: Technology acceptance by patients: empowerment and stigma. In: van Hoof, J., Demiris, G., Wouters, E.J.M. (eds.) Handbook of Smart Homes, Health Care and Well-being. Springer, New York (2014)

23. Cvrcek, D., Kumpost, M., Matyas, V., Danezis, G.: A study on the value of location privacy. In: Proceedings of the 5th ACM Workshop on Privacy in Electronic Society, pp. 109–118. ACM (2006)
24. Wilkowska, W.: Acceptance of eHealth Technology in Home Environments: Advanced Studies on User Diversity in Ambient Assisted Living. Apprimus, Aachen (in press)
25. Woolham, J., Frisby, B.: Building a local infrastructure that supports the use of assistive technology in the care of people with dementia. Res. Policy Planning **20**(1), 11–24 (2002)

Security Technologies

Risk Modeling and Analysis of Interdependencies of Critical Infrastructures Using Colored Timed Petri Nets

Chrysovalandis Agathangelou, Chryssis Georgiou, Ileana Papailiou,
Anna Philippou[✉], Loucas Pouis, Georgios Tertytchny, and Despina Vakana

Department of Computer Science, University of Cyprus, Nicosia, Cyprus
{fcslab,annap}@cs.ucy.ac.cy

Abstract. Petri Nets (PNs) and their variations are a graphical, mathematical language that can be used for the specification, analysis and verification of discrete event systems, including Critical Infrastructures (CIs). Colored PNs are an extension of classical PNs that are suitable for modeling and analyzing complex interconnected CIs. Timed PNs are another extension of PNs that support timing constraints and events. In this work we present a novel Risk Assessment methodology based on Timed Colored PNs for modeling and analyzing CIs with interdependencies, time-critical events and cascading effects.

Keywords: Risk assessment · Critical infrastructures · Interdependencies · Cascading effects · Timed colored petri nets

1 Introduction

Motivation: A *Critical Infrastructure* (CI) is an asset, system or part which is essential for the maintenance of vital societal functions, health, safety, security, economic or social well-being of people, and the disruption or destruction of which would have a significant impact as a result of the failure to maintain those functions [3]. Therefore, CIs are vital and must meet their security constrains and specifications (e.g., time constrains) to the highest degree possible. In such infrastructures, *interdependencies* between the various key components (physical or cyber) within or across infrastructures, and *cascading effects* (i.e., a malfunction of one component affects another, and so on) are crucial (see, e.g., [11,12,15,16,18,19]). To this respect, a lot of research has been conducted in developing Risk Assessment (RA) methodologies for CIs dealing with interdependencies, time-critical events and cascading effects (e g , [6,10–12,14]).

The Petri Nets (PNs) formalism [4,13] is a powerful mathematical modeling and analysis method applicable to a wide range of domains. The Colored Petri Nets (CPNs) formalism [9] is an extension of PN's that is particularly suited to modeling

This work is supported by the European Commission under grant agreement HOME/2013/CIPS/AG/4000005093 (MEDUSA: http://medusa.cs.unipi.gr/).

© Springer International Publishing Switzerland 2015
T. Tryfonas and I. Askoxylakis (Eds.): HAS 2015, LNCS 9190, pp. 607–618, 2015.
DOI: 10.1007/978-3-319-20376-8_54

and analyzing complex interconnected systems [1]. In particular, colors can be used to model different interactions between components or transect interdependencies between them. Furthermore, CPNs support a large number of formal analysis methods including verification and model-checking and are associated with a wide range of tools [7,9]. With respect to RA, CPNs are suitable for both system modeling (model the system's behavior) and accident modeling (model the accident sequence of a system) [1,20]. The Timed Colored Petri Nets (TCPNs) formalism [8] enhances the basic CPN framework with timing considerations. From the above, one may conclude that the TCPN framework is a natural choice for developing RA methodologies for CIs with interdependencies, time-critical events and cascading effects. To the best of our knowledge, no such TCPN-based RA methodology has been proposed so far.

Contribution: This work presents a novel application of TCPNs to RA of CIs with interdependencies, time-critical events and cascading effects. Our methodology exploits the power of CPNs in modeling interdependencies and cascading effects as well as the various risks involved in complex CIs, together with the timing considerations offered by Timed CPNs (e.g., for calculating the delay of the process on one component due to the effect of a risk to another component). Although our motivation for this research is to study the interdependencies and cascading effects on sea ports' supply chain, our proposed methodology is suitable for general CIs, and it is presented as such.

Related Work: Extensive research has been conducted for RA of CIs, in general, but also for considering interdependencies and cascading effects (e.g., [5,6,11,12,14–16,18,19]). Also, the PN formalism and its variations (Colored, Timed, Stochastic, etc.) has been used for RA. For example, Vernez et al. [20] discuss the uses and the application perspectives of basic PNs in the field of risk analysis and accident modeling. Aloini et al. [1] argue how CPNs can be used to model risk factors in Enterprise Resource Planning (ERP) projects, focusing on the problem of interdependence in risk assessment. Bernardi et al. [2] propose a method for assessing the risk of timing failures by evaluating the design of a specific software. They use Timed Petri Net (TPN) modeling and analysis techniques, and show the effectiveness of their method, based on a case study of a real-time embedded system. Rossi et al. [17] describe a method for identifying and assessing operational risks in a supply chain. Their approach uses the analogy between logistics networks and dynamical systems and it applies attributed Petri nets and associated tools. However, to the best of our knowledge, our work is the first to combine CPNs and TPNs for developing a RA methodology for CIs while dealing with interdependencies, timing constrains and cascading effects.

Paper Organization: In Sect. 2 we give a brief overview of TCPNs and in Sect. 3 we present our RA methodology. Section 4 presents a case study on a simplified real-world scenario on ports' supply chain. Section 5 concludes the paper.

2 Timed Coloured Petri Nets

Petri Nets (PNs) are a graphical, mathematical language that can be used for the specification, analysis and verification of discrete event systems [13]. They are associated with a formal execution semantics based on which a rich mathematical theory for process analysis has been developed. Since their inception by Carl Adam Petri in 1962, they have been applied to a wide range of applications and they have been extended into a variety of formalisms such as Timed Petri Nets, Stochastic Petri Nets, and Colored Petri Nets [4].

In its basic form, a Petri net is a directed graph consisting of places (denoted as circles), transitions (denoted as bars or rectangles), and directed arcs that connect places to transitions and vice versa, as illustrated in Fig. 1. Places in a Petri net may contain a discrete number of marks called *tokens* which determine the execution/firing of transitions: a condition on a transition determines that the transition is taken if a sufficient number of tokens exists on the place preceding the transition in which case it will consume the required number of tokens while creating tokens on the places following the transition.

Colored Petri Nets (CPNs) are an extension of classical PNs in which tokens may be differentiated with the use of colors [20]. Each token is assigned a color from a color set so it is possible to distinguish one from another while modeling complex behaviors. Moreover, CPNs combine the capabilities of PNs with those of the Standard ML programming language. The resulting flexibility and computational power make them a suitable formalism for modeling and analysing risk in critical infrastructures as is the goal of our work. More precisely, since the notion of time is essential in the problem under study, we employ a timed extension of CPNs, namely, Timed Colored Petri Nets (TCPNs) which allows to add timing information to CPN models [8]. A TCPN is defined as follows:

Definition 1. [8] A *timed non-hierarchical Colored Petri Net* is a nine-tuple $TCPN = (P, T, A, \Sigma, V, C, G, E, I)$ where:

1. P is a finite set of *places*.
2. T is a finite set of *transitions* such that $P \cap T = \emptyset$.
3. $A \subseteq P \times T \cup T \times P$ is a set of directed *arcs*.
4. Σ is a finite set of non-empty *colour sets*. Each colour set is either untimed or timed.
5. V is a finite set of *typed variables/tokens* such that $Type[v] \in \Sigma$ for all variables $v \in V$.
6. $C : P \to \Sigma$ is a *set function* that assigns a colour set to each place. A place p is timed if $C(p)$ is timed, otherwise p is untimed.
7. $G : T \to EXPR_V$ is a *guard function* that assigns a guard to each transition t such that $Type[G(t)] = Bool$ and $EXPR_V$ is the set of Standard ML expressions making references to variables in V.
8. $E : A \to EXPR_V$ is an *arc expression function* that assigns an arc expression to each arc α such that
   - $Type[E(\alpha)] = C(p)_{MS}$ if p is untimed;
   - $Type[E(\alpha)] = C(p)_{TMS}$ if p is timed.
   Here, p is the place connected to the arc α.

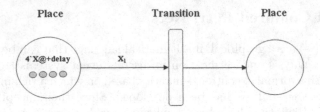

Fig. 1. Simple example of a timed colored Petri net

9. $I : P \rightarrow EXPR_{\emptyset}$ is an *initialisation function* that assigns an initialisation expression to each place p such that
   - $Type[I(p)] = C(p)_{MS}$ if p is untimed;
   - $Type[I(p)] = C(p)_{TMS}$ if p is timed.

A simple example of a TCPN can be seen in Fig. 1. Specifically, there are two places of color-set X and one transition. The initial marking of the first place has four tokens (typed variables) of color-set X which is timed. These tokens will be ready to be removed by the occurring transition at some time delay. Hence, a token starts from the first place and goes to the second through the transition.

3   Methodology

In this section we describe our methodology for risk assessment of critical infrastructures that takes into consideration interdependencies and cascading effects. The proposed methodology is based on TCPNs and it allows to construct models of CIs at various levels of abstraction due to its modularity. It also allows us to model risks and their impact on different components of an infrastructure, interdependencies that may exist between risks and cascading effects of events between different components of an infrastructure. As such, the results obtained can be used to evaluate adopted procedures and modify them as necessary or explore alternative security measures in order to limit the effects of various risks.

The main phases of our methodology are the following: (1) Establish the context. (2) Risk identification. (3) Cascading effects identification. (4) Model construction. (5) Model evaluation. We now proceed to describe each phase.

1. Establish the Context: The goal of this step is to establish the boundaries and characteristics of the process under study. This involves the specification of the infrastructures involved and the entities and activities operating therein. Consider a set *Inf* of infrastructures. For each infrastructure, we identify the *entities* participating in the process. These may involve people, organizations, documents, resources, etc. Once these are identified, the level of abstraction of the model is determined. For instance, if we consider a port supply chain and an associated entity *cargo*, the cargo could be considered as a single unit or as a set of individual containers. Following this consideration, a set $\mathcal{E}_i$ is identified containing all entities appearing in infrastructure $i \in Inf$.

The second component of interest is that of *control points* or *states*. Control points are different states of infrastructures in the process under study. They are characterized by the activities in which they may engage which may take place either within or between infrastructures and are carried out by entities and upon entities involved in the system. Thus states are connected with each other by activities and sequences of activities correspond to procedures and may involve physical or electronic flows, capital flows, information flows, etc. Specifically, for each infrastructure $i \in Inf$, we identify the following:

- the set S_i of states;
- a function *entities* that associates each state $s \in S_i$ with the set of entities from $\mathcal{E}_i$ available to the state;
- a set $\mathcal{A}_i^j$ of pairs of the form (s, s') where s is a state of infrastructure i and s' is a state of some infrastructure j (where possibly i and j coincide) such that state s may execute a transition that provides input to state s';
- for each $(s, s') \in \bigcup_j \mathcal{A}_i^j$ an expression $e_{s,s'}$ that describes the coupling between states s and s' and, in particular, how s manipulates its entities to produce a new set of entities that will be consequently available to state s'.

As an example, consider two control points in some infrastructure i involved in off-loading cargo from a ship, the first, s, being the state where accompanying documentation must be verified and the second, s', being the state where allocation of resources for off-loading is decided. Then we have that $s, s' \in S_i$ and $(s, s') \in \mathcal{A}_i^i$. Furthermore, *entities*(s) should include the relevant accompanying documents and *entities*(s') should include the relevant resources. Finally, an expression $e_{s,s'}$ should be determined stating the conditions under which the presence of the accompanying documents will move the procedure towards the allocation of which resources.

2. Risk Identification: This step concerns the identification of the risks that may affect the CIs under study and characterization of their potential impact. A risk can be any form of threat or vulnerability from external sources such as terrorist attack, or from internal sources such as malfunction of machinery. For each of the identified risks r_i the following parameters must be defined:

- Probability of occurrence, p_i: this is an estimate of the frequency of occurrence of risk r_i.
- Risk effects: the relationships between each risk and the states of the modeled procedure. In particular, we must specify the states of the CIs that are affected by the occurrence of a risk. We denote by S_i^R the set of states affected by risk r_i and, given a state $s \in S_i^R$, we denote by *effect*(s, r) the expression specifying how the entities of state s are affected by risk r.
- Impact duration, d_i: the time during which the risk will be in effect.

Following risk identification and characterization of risk effects, the next step is to consider and determine the relationships between risks. Specifically, this phase concerns the identification of risk interdependencies, that is, cases where the activation of a risk may trigger the activation of another risk. For example, a human error risk activation on the crane may also activate the risk of machinery malfunction because of damage to the machinery as caused by the first risk. The effects, probability of occurrence, and duration of the impact of an interdependency between risks must also be carefully defined as above.

3. Identify Cascading Effects: Following the modeling of the CIs under study and the identification of risks that may affect them, the next step concerns the identification of cascading effects between the various CIs. Note that we have a cascading effect when a disruption/event in one infrastructure has an effect on a component in another infrastructure. In other words, this phase is concerned with the identification of interdependencies between different CIs and characterization of their effects. The output of this phase is (1) a set of pairs (s, s') where s is a state of some infrastructure i and s' is a state of some distinct infrastructure j where a cascading effect exists between the two states and (2) an expression characterizing the effect between the two states for each such pair: given a characterization of the risk-based event in the first state, the expression should be defined so as to characterize the triggering of a risk-based event in the second state. This effect can be modeled depending on the situation as a conditional probability or a fixed event.

For example, consider a port's supply chain, and suppose that there is an electricity disruption in the electrical infrastructure. This may interrupt computer-based activities, such as processing the required forms at the port's customs service, yielding a delay of loading the cargo to a truck and hence a delay of the cargo delivery to its final destination. To model this cascading effect we consider the pair (s, s') where s is the state of failure in the electrical infrastructure and s' is the state of document-processing in the port infrastructure, and the associated expression capturing the effect of this coupling can be modeled either as a conditional probability or as a fixed delay: a conditional probability would capture the probability of additional delay inflicted in the case of the electricity disruption, and, in the case of a fixed delay, the specific amount will be specified and applied to the procedures in place. Similar effects can be considered for the delays in loading the truck or having the cargo reach its final destination.

4. Model Construction as Petri Net: In this step the components that were previously compiled are modeled as a Timed Colored Petri net. We describe how the components of a $TCPN = (P, T, A, \Sigma, V, C, G, E, I)$ are defined following the above analysis.

Beginning with the set of places P of the Petri net, we associate a place with each state $s \in S_i$ for each infrastructure $i \in Inf$, and each risk $r \in R$. Thus, the set P of places is defined as $P = \bigcup_{i \in Inf} S_i \cup R$. Secondly, we must define the set of transitions T and the set of arcs A. These sets correspond to the procedure flows/activities enabled from the various states. In particular, we include a transition and two associated arcs to connect the places corresponding to any two states s, s', with $(s, s') \in \mathcal{A}_i^j$ for some i and j. Here we note that while each CI under study will correspond to a Petri net component describing internal procedures and activities, different infrastructures will also be connected by transitions whenever a state within one infrastructure requires input from another infrastructure.

While these interconnected components constitute the backbone of the Petri net model, another component to be superimposed upon this structure corresponds to the risks identified in Step 3: we include a transition and two associated arcs between the place of each risk r and the states it affects as defined by $\mathcal{E}_r^R$. Finally, we add to the structure a transition and arcs between the associated places between two states related by a cascading effect. In this manner the components T and A of the TCPN are determined.

Moving on to the fourth component pertaining to the color sets to be employed, one must define all the color-types of the tokens/variables that will be used, thus constructing component Σ. Depending on the nature of an entity, its color can have different fields corresponding to the characteristics of interest of the entity as identified in Step 1. For example, a container in a port supply chain can be associated with a color with different fields corresponding to its arrival time, the damage it sustained during transport, its degree of fragility or the presence of accompanying documents.

Next, we must define the set of variables V. Specifically, we employ one variable for each entity defined in the sets $\mathcal{E}_i$ as identified in the first step of the methodology. A variable is associated with an appropriate color set. Similarly, each place is associated with a color set, as required in component C of a TCPN, by merging together the color sets of the entities associated with the state modeled by the place.

Moving on to components G, E of a TCPN, these two functions are used to associate transitions and arcs with expressions as specified by expressions $e_{s,s'}$ and $effect(s,r)$ which determine the conditions and the effects of transitions between places taking place as well as the precondition and the postcondition of the transitions. Here we note that these expressions may associate probabilities of firing transitions (e.g. risk occurrence probabilities will be associated on transitions manifesting a risk) and timed variables will be added in order to measure time passage on transition availability (e.g. duration of the impact of a risk, or duration of a certain activity).

Finally, component I is used to initialize the system by associating each place of the composed Petri net with initial conditions (initial number of tokens in each place and values for all the fields of each token) depending on the scenarios one wants to check. Alternatively, one may define input transitions on places that continuously produce tokens. These transitions can trigger the initial state of the risk chain and they can be programmed to produce tokens according to a function that may depend on time and/or according to a probability distribution. Figure 2 illustrates the skeleton of a Petri net constructed in this step of the methodology. Place $Start$ and transition T_1 illustrate the presence of an initial transition that produces an initial set of tokens as input to the first state of the net, namely $Start_1$, and then further tokens according to its programming.

Once the TCPN is constructed, it can be implemented within one of the various available tools for analysis of timed colored Petri net models.

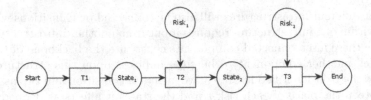

Fig. 2. A representation of the relationships between activities of a CI and risks.

5. Model Evaluation: After the construction of the TCPN model and its implementation within an associated tool, scenarios for analysis must be prepared. These scenarios could include evaluation of the effects of a critical initiating event, evaluation of the effect of interdependencies between risks, or of cascading effects between infrastructures. It is also possible to experiment with different security measures and evaluate the gains and tradeoffs between different approaches.

The above can be carried out by taking into account the different modes of analysis offered by TCPN tools which include simulation and model checking. Using simulation, the user can perform a suite of experiments and reach conclusions based on the resulting executions of the system. In turn, model checking is a powerful technology that performs an analysis of the complete state-space given rise to by the system as opposed to single runs. Using this approach the user must express properties of interest in a suitable language, a *temporal logic*, where a property could be of the form of reachability (is a certain state reachable from the initial state of the system?), safety (a certain state is never reachable from the initial state of the system), liveness (all executions will reach a desirable state), probabilistic properties (the probability that more than 5 % of containers are lost is less than 2 %), temporal properties (no more than 3 % of the containers arrive with a delay greater than 2 times units).

After the simulation or model checking or both, the results must be analyzed. In particular, the acceptable margins for various metrics related to the efficiency of the procedure must be defined. For example, the port operator would accept only 0.001 % of containers to be lost and only a maximum average delay of one day. During this phase, the "weak" parts of the procedure can be identified, therefore it is possible to select or develop security hardening measures, or modify the procedure to be more efficient. Afterwards, analysis can be performed to the improved model to see if the new metrics are now between the accepted margins. This step can be repeated until the results are satisfying. Additionally, evaluation may explore which risks may cause cascading effects on which parts of the procedure and modify the procedure in order to alleviate these effects.

Discussion: We conclude that Petri nets offer a promising approach towards the risk modeling and analysis of interdependencies of critical infrastructures. The graphical part of the language enables a very quick and intuitive representation of the states and activities as well as the interdependencies existing within infrastructures, and to associate risks with parts of a procedure. Simultaneously, the programming language accompanying the graphical language enables the enunciation of complex behaviors pertaining to activities or the effects of a risk. The presence of probabilistic and temporal constructs is particularly useful for specifying relevant aspects of both risks and activities. Moreover, the approach is both modular and scalable: it is easy to add extra flows and connections, or to introduce additional partially independent systems related to the procedure or work at a finer level of abstraction, by implementing nets within nets.

Furthermore, the methodology is supported by any TCPN tool, hence one can select among a number of tools, some of which are freely available. Finally, the methodology is general and not application-specific, and it can be used to model and evaluate any type of critical infrastructure/risks/dependencies. As such, it is very flexible and one can "flex" it to their needs.

4 Case Study

In this section we demonstrate the applicability of our proposed methodology on a simple port supply chain procedure. This procedure is extracted from a real-world scenario, simplified to serve as a demonstrating example while showing the broad spectrum and capabilities of the proposed methodology: it can easily be extended to cover more complicated procedures. We first present the scenario, then we show how we can model it as a TCPN and apply our methodology to obtain, by simulation, some simple statistics (Table 1).

Scenario: We consider the following scenario. Suppose that a truck-ship docks in the harbor. Afterwards a crane moves the cargo from the truck-ship to a truck and then the truck moves the cargo to a warehouse. For this scenario we consider the following five risks (the probability values are indicative and used for the purpose of our example):

Table 1. Risks of present scenario

Risk Number	Risk Name	Risk Effect	Activation Probability
R1	Work Stoppage	Delay	5%
R2	Untrained Staff	Damage or Lost	2%
R3	Mishandled Operation - Human Error	Damage or Lost	5%
R4	Heavy Weather Conditions	Damage or Lost	3%
R5	Terrorist Attack	Damage or Lost	0.5%

Furthermore, the activation probability of each risk is the same in all phases and the cargo has a possibility of 85% to be destroyed and of 15% to be lost. Also, the occurrence of risk R2 doubles the activation probability of R3.

Modeling: We first identify the four states of the procedure: *truck-ship*, *crane*, *truck* and *warehouse*. Then we establish the risks, namely their relations with the procedure's states as well as their interconnections. In this scenario, for the interest of space, we have not considered cascading effects; however these can be added, for example as conditional probabilities, as explained in Sect. 3.

At this point we have collected all the necessary information, thus we are ready to construct our TCPN. We depict a graphical view of the TCPN derived

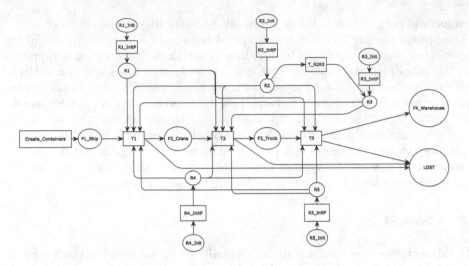

Fig. 3. The model of the case study in CPN tools

using the CPN Tool of [9], which we also use to run our simulations, in Fig. 3. As illustrated in the figure there are fifteen places in total. Specifically, four places represent the states of the modeled procedure and five places represent the risks. In addition, for implementation purposes (as required by the CPN tool) we have created five places for initializing risks and a place in which the lost cargo ends up (terminal case beyond the regular one – warehouse). Hence, component P of the constructed TCPN is the set consisting of these 15 places.

In addition, our TCPN model has ten transitions, where three of which model procedure flow, five deal with the risk initialization flow, one specifies the interdependency between the risks $R2$ and $R3$ and the last one generates the containers. Hence T consists of these 10 transitions.

The depicted arcs represent the flow between places and transitions, e.g., the arc from place $F1\_Ship$ to transition $T1$ as well as the interdependencies among risks, e.g., the arcs between place $R2$ to transition T_R2R3 and then to place $R3$. Thus $A = \{$all depicted arcs$\}$.

We now define the color-sets used. Except from the standard color-sets, like int and bool (integers and boolean types), it was necessary to define two scenario-specific color-sets: one for the representation of the cargo, *containers*, and one for the representation of the risks, *risks*. The *containers* color-set consists of four fields: *ContainerNumber*, *Status* : {*Destroyed, Lost, Arrived, Delay*}, *DelayTime* and *LastReachablePhase*. In turn, the *risks* color-set consists of two fields: *RiskNumber* and *RiskActivationStatus*. A color-set must be assigned to each of these fields; for instance, *ContainerNumber* and *RiskNumber* are of integer color-set. In addition, the *containers* color-set is *timed* because we want to associate containers with delays, while the *risks* color-set is untimed because in our model risks are timeless. These color-sets compose set Σ.

We use different variables in order to represent the different entities, such as cargo and risks. In our case, we assume that each cargo consists of several containers which we associate with individual variables of the *containers* color-set. Similarly, for each risk we declare individual variables of the *risks* color-set. These typed-variables compose set V. Hereafter, we will refer to these variables as *tokens*. Then we assign a color-set to each place based on the entities available to each state. For example, the *containers* color-set is assigned to place $F1\_Ship$ and the *risks* color-set is assigned to place $R1$. Thus, we compose function C.

Next, we assign a guard function for each transition. In general, transitions take as input tokens representing containers and/or risks. Flow transitions check which risks are activated and then calculate and apply the corresponding effects. Risk transitions activate the relevant risks. These guard functions compose function G. Furthermore, at each arc we assign an arc expression function to control the flow of tokens. These functions compose function E. Finally, we assign an initialization expression to the initial risk places such as $R1\_Init$ and transition $Create\_Containers$. In particular, we define the initial tokens of these places and transition. Thus, we compose function I.

Simulation Results: We have run simulations to obtain some simple statistics with respect to the impact of interdependencies on the cargo successfully reaching the warehouse. For this purpose, we have run simulations with an interdependency (between risks $R2$ and $R3$) and without the interdependency (we removed the transition between $R2$ and $R3$); we run each test 6 times obtaining the averages shown in Table 2.

Table 2. Average Results

Container Status	Average With Interdependencies	Average Without Interdependencies
Arrived	76,17%	80,17%
Damaged	10,83%	6,17%
Lost	1,67%	0,33%
Delay	11,33%	13,33%

The derived results are rather expected: the average number of damaged and lost containers are reduced in the absence of the interdependency. Although the simulated scenario is simple, we believe that it sufficiently demonstrates the usability and the potential of our proposed TCPN-based methodology.

5 Conclusions

We have proposed a novel risk assessment methodology based on Timed Colored Petri Nets (TCPNs) for modeling and analyzing Critical Infrastructures with interdependencies, time-critical events and cascading effects. Ongoing work is focusing on applying our methodology on complex real-life scenarios on sea ports and their supply chain. Our analysis, besides simulations will also take advantage of the verification and model-checking capabilities of TCPNs.

References

1. Aloini, D., Dulmin, R., Mininno, V.: Modelling and assessing ERP project risks: a petri net approach. Eur. J. Oper. Res. **220**(2), 484–495 (2012)

2. Bernardi, S., Campos, J., Merseguer, J.: Timing-failure risk assessment of UML design using time Petri net bound techniques. IEEE Trans. Industr. Inf. **7**(1), 90–104 (2011)
3. Council, E.: Council directive 2008/114/EC on the identification and designation of European critical infrastructures and the assessment of the need to improve their protection. Official J. **L345**(3), 0075–0082 (2008)
4. Diaz, M.: Petri Nets: Fundamental Models, Verification and Applications. Wiley, New York (2013)
5. Giannopoulos, G., Filippini, R., Schimmer, M.: Risk assessment methodologies for critical infrastructure protection, part I: A state of the art, JRC Technical Notes (2012)
6. Haimes, Y., Santos, J., Crowther, K., Henry, M., Lian, C., Yan, Z.: Risk analysis in interdependent infrastructures. In: Goetz, E., Shenoi, S. (eds.) Critical Infrastructure Protection. IFIP, vol. 253, pp. 297–310. Springer, Boston (2007)
7. Heiner, M., Herajy, M., Liu, F., Rohr, C., Schwarick, M.: Snoopy a unifying Petri net tool. In: Haddad, S., Pomello, L. (eds.) PETRI NETS 2012. LNCS, vol. 7347, pp. 398–407. Springer, Heidelberg (2012)
8. Jensen, K., Kristensen, L.M.: Coloured Petri Nets: Modelling and Validation of Concurrent Systems. Springer, New York (2009)
9. Jensen, K., Kristensen, L.M., Wells, L.: Coloured Petri nets and CPN tools for modelling and validation of concurrent systems. Int. J. Softw. Tools Technol. Transf. **9**(3–4), 213–254 (2007)
10. Klaver, M., Luiijf, H., Nieuwenhuijs, A., Cavenne, F., Ulisse, A., Bridegeman, G.: European risk assessment methodology for critical infrastructures. INFRA **2008**, 1–5 (2008)
11. Kotzanikolaou, P., Theoharidou, M., Gritzalis, D.: Assessing n-order dependencies between critical infrastructures. Int. J. Crit. Infrastruct. **9**(1), 93–110 (2013)
12. Kotzanikolaou, P., Theoharidou, M., Gritzalis, D.: Interdependencies between critical infrastructures: analyzing the risk of cascading effects. In: Bologna, S., Hämmerli, B., Gritzalis, D., Wolthusen, S. (eds.) CRITIS 2011. LNCS, vol. 6983, pp. 104–115. Springer, Heidelberg (2013)
13. Murata, T.: Petri nets: Properties, analysis and applications. Proc. IEEE **77**(4), 541–580 (1989)
14. U. D. of Homeland Security. Nipp supplemental tool: Executing a critical infrastructure risk management approach (2013)
15. Renda, R.: Protecting Critical Infrastructure in the EU. CEPS Task Force, Brussels (2010)
16. Rinaldi, S., Peerenboom, J., Kelly, T.: Identifying, understanding, and analyzing critical infrastructure interdependencies. Control Syst. **21**(6), 11–25 (2001)
17. Rossi, T., Pero, M.: A formal method for analysing and assessing operational risk in supply chains. Int. J. Oper. Res. **13**(1), 90–109 (2012)
18. Theoharidou, M., Kotzanikolaou, P., Gritzalis, D.: Risk assessment methodology for interdependent critical infrastructures. Int. J. Risk Assess. Manag. **15**(2), 128–148 (2011)
19. Van Eeten, M., Nieuwenhuijs, A., Luiijf, E., Klaver, M., Cruz, E.: The state and the threat of cascading failure across critical infrastructures: the implications of empirical evidence from media incident reports. Public Adm. **89**(2), 381–400 (2011)
20. Vernez, D., Buchs, D., Pierrehumbert, G.: Perspectives in the use of coloured Petri nets for risk analysis and accident modelling. Saf. Sci. **41**(5), 445–463 (2003)

RT-SPDM: Real-Time Security, Privacy and Dependability Management of Heterogeneous Systems

Konstantinos Fysarakis[1]([⊠]), George Hatzivasilis[1],
Ioannis Askoxylakis[2], and Charalampos Manifavas[3]

[1] Department of Electronic and Computer Engineering, Technical University of Crete,
Chania, Greece
{kfysarakis,gchatzivasilis}@isc.tuc.gr
[2] FORTH, Heraklion, Greece
asko@ics.forth.gr
[3] Department of Informatics Engineering, Technological Educational Institute of Crete,
Heraklion, Greece
harryman@ie.teicrete.gr

Abstract. The need to manage embedded systems, brought forward by the wider adoption of pervasive computing, is particularly vital in the context of secure and safety-critical applications. This work presents RT-SPDM, a framework for the real-time management of devices populating ambient environments. The proposed framework utilizes a formally validated approach to reason the composability of heterogeneous embedded systems, evaluate their current security, privacy and dependability levels based on pre-defined metrics, and manage them in real-time. An implementation of Event Calculus is used in the Jess rule engine in order to model the ambient environment context and the rule-based management procedure. The reasoning process is modeled as an agent's behavior and applied on an epistemic multi-agent reasoner for ambient intelligence applications. Agents monitor distinct embedded systems and are deployed as OSGi bundles to enhance the real-time management of embedded devices. A Service Oriented Architecture is adopted, through the use of the Devices Profile for Web Services standard, in order to provide seamless interaction between the framework's entities, which exchange well-formed information, determined by the OASIS CAP standard. Proof-of-concept implementations of all entities are developed, also investigating user-friendly GUIs for both the front-end and back-end of the framework. A preliminary performance evaluation on typical embedded devices confirms the viability of the proposed approach.

Keywords: SOAs · DPWS · Event calculus · Formal methods · Security validation · Metrics composition · JADE · Jess · OSGi · Policy-based access control

1 Introduction

Advances in computing and communication technologies have enabled a new reality where interconnected computing systems, in various forms, permeate our environments,

© Springer International Publishing Switzerland 2015
T. Tryfonas and I. Askoxylakis (Eds.): HAS 2015, LNCS 9190, pp. 619–630, 2015.
DOI: 10.1007/978-3-319-20376-8_55

aiming to enhance all aspects of our everyday lives. These significant changes did not leave the industrial and enterprise environments unaffected, with ubiquitous computing acting as an enabler for new business opportunities and services, but also providing more sophisticated tools for monitoring and managing the existing business functions and infrastructures.

However, the above also introduce significant challenges in terms of the security and privacy of the data processed, stored and communicated by these systems [1]. The complexity and heterogeneity of the underlying infrastructures, systems and networks, along with the limited resources of typical embedded devices, only exacerbate said issues. While existing networking and security mechanisms are updated and adapted to handle the vast population of these resource-constrained devices, higher level, machine to machine interactions, are a requirement in order to effectively monitor and manage the infrastructure, allowing the use of its full potential.

This paper presents RT-SPDM, a framework for supervising the wide range of ubiquitous computing systems, heterogeneous in nature, that are typically found in enterprise and industrial environments (e.g. embedded platforms, devices featuring sensors & actuators, personal computers, smart phones etc.). RT-SPDM leverages the benefits of Service Oriented Architectures (SOAs) to allow real-time monitoring the Security, Privacy and Dependability (SPD) of local and remote systems and their corresponding subsystems, using a formally validated reasoning process to monitor the changes in their SPD states.

This work is organized as follows: Sect. 2 sets the background and highlights related research efforts, Sect. 3 details the framework's components and architecture, Sect. 4 presents the approach followed to produce a proof-of-concept implementation and a preliminary evaluation of its performance, and, finally, Sect. 5 features the concluding remarks.

2   Background

In [2] we have presented a preliminary version of a composition verification and security validation reasoning system, where event-driven model-based methods have been proposed to describe the behavior of a dynamic system in a formal manner.

The work presented here extends this reasoning system by adopting the multi-metric formation and normalization process [3] and the composition evaluation formulas of the medieval castle approach [4]. We propose the use of standardized mechanisms and protocols, both for context-aware modelling as well as real-time control and management of the devices. The resulting system implements a formal methodology in system composition verification and SPD validation, supporting a metric-driven reasoning process, via SOA-based interfaces that enable seamless access to the various devices and their functional elements.

2.1   Service-Oriented Architectures in Embedded Systems

The heterogeneity of ubiquitous devices has compelled researchers and developers alike to focus on mechanisms that guarantee interoperability, providing seamless access to the various devices and their functional elements. SOAs evolved from this need to have interoperable, cross-platform, cross-domain and network-agnostic access to devices and their services. This approach has already been successful in business environments, as SOAs allow stakeholders to focus on the services themselves, rather than the underlying hardware and network technologies.

As SOAs are widely used, there is now an effort to apply this technology on embedded systems as well. To enable these services in such systems, several standards and platforms have been proposed. The Devices Profile for Web Services (DPWS) [5] OASIS standard targets resource-constrained embedded devices and enables secure web service messaging, discovery, description, and eventing.

The Open Service Gateway initiative (OSGi) [6] is a standard module system and service platform in Java and implements a complete and dynamic component model. Components are modeled as bundles for deployment, which can be remotely installed, started, stopped, updated and uninstalled without requiring a reboot.

In the proposed framework, DPWS is integrated into OSGi by implementing operators which are controlled by the relevant system components via an OSGi interface, as will be detailed in later chapters. Embedded devices specify their type and the provided services in DPWS. Each system component implements a component operator bundle that handles its underlying DPWS devices and their services.

2.2 Knowledge Representation and Reasoning

Knowledge Representation and Reasoning (KR&R) is the research field of Artificial Intelligence (AI) that deals with the representation of information about the world in a manner that it is understandable by a machine and can be utilized in order to solve complex tasks. KR&R is strongly related with semantic technologies which encode knowledge to express ontologies, and logic languages which include reasoning rules for processing that knowledge.

Event Calculus (EC) [7] is a logic language for representing and reasoning about actions and their effects as time progresses. An implementation of EC in Java and the rule engine Jess (Jess-EC) is utilized [8]. The whole reasoning model is formed as an agent's reasoning behavior and is implemented on the Java Agent Development framework (JADE) [9], implementing an epistemic multi-agent reasoner. The agents utilize the FIPA standardized Agent Communication Language (ACL) [10] to exchange information; a conflict resolution mechanism between agents' local knowledge is also supported.

The Common Alerting Protocol (CAP) [11], an XML-based data format OASIS standard for exchanging public warnings and emergencies, is used to model semantic information that is exchanged between the entities. The CAP alerts are transformed into Jess-EC events and trigger the rule-based reasoning of CompoSecReasoner and AmbISPDM. The abovementioned two operations are then combined to achieve a holistic metric-driven SPD management.

2.3 Metrics and Methodologies for Quantifying Security

Metrics for evaluating aspects like security and performance are becoming an integral feature in system development. Metrics provide a quantitative assessment of a system's compliance with the application's requirements. This also enables comparisons between different system settings based on objective factors, facilitating the selection of the ones that are more appropriate with respect to the design and/or specific deployment criteria. Moreover, it enables metric-driven management procedures for real-time systems.

In [3] a multi-metric approach is proposed for forming and normalizing different types of metrics in order to compose them and estimate the overall security level of a system. Each metric consists of a triple vector <Security, Privacy, Dependability>, referred to as SPD, where each parameter takes a value from [0–100]. Moreover, each metric has a value-type (e.g. time in ms or security in bits) and takes values from a set (e.g. time from [0.1–5] ms or encryption key length of [128,192,256] bits). Every value in the set is normalized and mapped to an equivalent SPD. All the provided metrics are then composed under a specific formal composition strategy to produce the current overall SPD level of the system.

The medieval castle approach [4] forms the basis of the method adopted to compose the metrics and quantify the security level of the system. Using this approach, a system is considered as a castle and the security mechanisms as the castle's doors. An intruder tries to break through these doors and reach the treasure rooms inside the castle, i.e. the system's assets that must be protected. The difficulty in passing through a door is represented by a relevant metric and the minimum effort to reach a treasure room is the final security level of the system.

3 The Proposed Framework

3.1 Overview

The proposed framework is a multi-agent system, implemented in the JADE platform which, via the OSGi middleware, is able to monitor and manage DPWS devices. The AI reasoning process (CompoSecReasoner and AmbISPDM) is an event-based model checker that is based on EC. The context theory is aware of the security, privacy and dependability aspects of the underlying embedded system (component types and composition, implemented technologies and their different configurations, SPD metrics etc.).

In order to effectively study and model embedded systems and their security characteristics, their architecture is segregated into four layers. These layers, from bottom-up, are: **Node** (represents all the embedded devices themselves), **Network** (consists of nodes connected in networks), **Middleware** (the management-software of the networks) and **Overlay** (formed by RT-SPDM agents, who control distinct sub-systems and exchange high-level security-, privacy- and dependability-related information).

The proposed framework adopts the above layered approach. RT-SPDM agents, implemented using the JADE platform, are part of the overlay, while the necessary DPWS and OSGi mechanisms operate at the middleware.

The framework's entities are deployed using DPWS, allowing each device to expose the services and operations needed to transmit its current status (to allow real-time monitoring) but also to receive commands (for management purposes). DPWS can be used to expose not just the proposed framework's monitoring/management operations, but also those related to their functional elements (e.g. the various sensors and actuators), allowing system owners to leverage the SOA benefits across their whole infrastructure. By exploiting these benefits, the proposed framework facilitates the communication of critical information regarding the secure, privacy-aware and dependable operation of the devices.

This information is then aggregated to a control node, where it is composed using EC-based rules, in a formally validated manner. The system's agents base their reasoning process on Jess-EC, which can perform, among others, automated epistemic, temporal and casual reasoning for dynamic domains with real time events, preferences and priorities; features that are necessary in the context of this work. The various SPD states and properties of each device are modelled as fluents, and the system changes as events of EC, all implemented using the abovementioned extended Jess-EC. Rules that trigger the reasoning process of the agent are also supported, producing a metric-driven management of the infrastructure according to its SPD level. The updates on the current state as well as the changes that need to be enforced by the agent(s) are all realized via appropriate DPWS-based mechanisms present on all devices. These changes can be triggered by human interaction (e.g. from system operators) or by a predefined set of rules. Furthermore, in the case of large organizations or when monitoring facilities in segregated premises, a multi-agent system can be deployed, where each agent monitors the SPD levels of a subset of the infrastructure and communicates with the rest of the agents and/or a central agent to provide enterprise-wide monitoring & management.

The overall state, once calculated, is presented in a form which is usable and simple to understand by the system's operators, enabling real-time assessment of the security and dependability posture of the infrastructure and allowing for a timely response to changes in the system state (either via human interaction or in an automated manner). Thus, the proposed framework simplifies threat assessment and risk management. Moreover, it enables the interfacing with more sophisticated, intelligence-driven, management mechanisms, potentially fully automating the management of the ecosystem (e.g. for automatic incident response).

3.2   Core Components

RT-SPDM consists of two components: CompoSecReasoner and AmbISPDM. The former uses the reasoning system presented in [2] in order to implement an extended composition validation and security verification, while the latter models the management theory of the ambient environment and manages the system in real time.

CompoSecReasoner. In the proposed methodology, technologies and protocols are modeled as attributes. A security analysis is performed for every developed attribute and a relevant SPD is defined for each security level that is provided. Then, the evaluated metrics and properties of the system are determined, including how they may be affected by the underlying attributes at runtime. This information is encoded in the evaluation functions of the relevant metrics and properties.

In order to model metrics and other measurable system parameters in a uniform manner, the previously-cited multi-metric approach and normalization processes are adopted. Each measurable value is modelled as an SPD vector (i.e. <Security, Privacy, Dependability>) and evaluated as in the original approach (i.e. in [3]). These parameters are used to reason about the security, privacy and dependability of a system and whether it can fulfill its specific application requirements. The SPD values are also integrated in the AI reasoning process to accomplish metric-driven real-time management.

For the system composition, verification and security validation, the system is considered as a set of components of four layers (node, network, middleware, overlay) and the components of each layer are composed of sub-components of the adjacent lower layer.

Each component: has a set of sources – data that are processed; a set of attributes – technologies and protocols; performs some operation – a series of attributes; achieves specific levels of SPD – based on metrics and its sub-components; and satisfies a set of properties under some conditions. The components, sources, attributes, operations, metrics and properties attain specific SPD values based on the core evaluation process of the formal methodology. Attributes possess a static SPD for each configuration setting, e.g. encryption with 128-bit keys will have a lower "S" factor in its (S,P,D) triplet compared to encryption with 256-bit keys, assuming a device that can operate with both key lengths. An operation's SPD is derived by evaluation formulas based on the medieval castle approach discussed above. The SPD of a source is the SPD of the last operation that processes it.

The metrics and the properties are layer specific and evaluate their SPD at runtime based on evaluation functions. A component's SPD is the summation of the component's metrics and the minimum SPD of the underlying sub-components (i.e. the weaker inner link). The component's SPD is constrained by the SPD of the higher layer component that contains it (i.e. the weaker outer link). Components are composed to higher layer components by composition operations. In order to perform such an operation, a component must be able to execute the operation's attributes (functional requirements) and achieve specific SPD for relative metrics and properties (non-functional requirements that are determined by the operation). When composition is successful, the composition verification and security validation process are revisited. A similar strategy is followed for decomposition operations.

AmbISPDM. The core of the reasoning process is an event-based model checker which extends EC and is implemented in the Jess rule engine. CompoSecReasoner reasons about the system composition and SPD validation while AmbISPDM models the security and safety related management strategy and the system's administration through real-time technologies. The whole reasoning process is transformed into a JADE agent's reasoning behavior and implemented as a multi-agent epistemic reasoner.

The agents are then encapsulated into OSGi bundles and are deployed on Knopflerfish [12], an open-source implementation of OSGi. Each agent controls a distinct system via the OSGi middleware, while the various agents communicate with each other using the ACL language, with messages containing CAP data exchanged via JADE. The embedded devices specify their type and provided services using DPWS, which is also used to facilitate the exchange of CAP messages between managed devices and agents. Each underlying system component (node, network and middleware) that communicates directly with the agent creates a component-operator that controls the component's services. The agent and the component operators exchange well-formed information determined by the CAP scheme. The DPWS-related components are developed using the WS4D-JMEDS API [13] and are also integrated into OSGi bundles.

3.3 Security Mechanisms

The protection of messages exchanged between RT-SPDM entities is of critical concern. The framework can protect the communication between the managed embedded devices and their respective RT-SPDM agents through the use of the WS-Security standard [14] typically used alongside DPWS. Said standard can provide end-to-end security, non-repudiation, alternative transport bindings, and reverse proxy/common security token in the application layer.

With regard to the protection of the communications between agents, the JADE-S add-on can be used to safeguard the ACL messages exchanged, by providing user authentication, agent actions authorization against agent permissions, as well as message signature and encryption. The OSGi security features can additionally be used to provide inner-platform security on both agents and component operator bundles (i.e. managed devices) by limiting bundle functionality (e.g. which bundles can be started/stopped, when, by whom etc.) to pre-defined capabilities. Figure 1 illustrates the software layers of RT-SPDM.

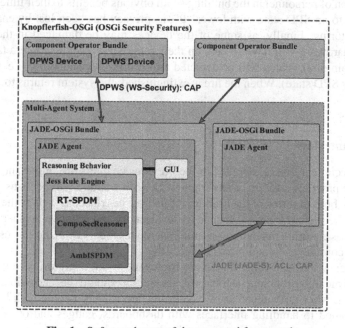

Fig. 1. Software layers of the proposed framework

4 Proof-of-Concept Implementation

As a proof-of-concept example, the proposed framework was developed and used to emulate monitoring and management of an ambient environment, e.g. a smart building, a smart production floor or a critical infrastructure [15].

The agents evaluate the current SPD levels of their underlying sub-systems and the system as a whole (CompoSecReasoner). They also monitor their respective domains, managing them based on SPD levels and the reasoning process (AmbISPDM). The agents can change the configurations of a system in order to increase the security level (e.g. increase the size of the encryption keys) when an attack is detected and then return to the previous state (to conserve resources) when the attack is over.

Moreover, a Policy-Based Access Control (PBAC) mechanism [16] is integrated for managing access to the infrastructure's resources based on the active policy set; said mechanism exploits and extends the DPWS functionality already present on the framework's devices, to realize the necessary mechanisms (i.e. Policy Enforcement Points on the embedded devices and Policy Decision and Information Points on the control nodes). It can be further exploited to allow automatically enforce high-level security requirements (e.g. stemming from risk analysis) [17].

Using these mechanisms, RT-SPDM is able to trigger changes to both the security mechanisms employed to protect the PBAC's messaging but also to the current active policy set. So, for example, in a safety-related incident, the agents can help the personnel in the case of a fire alarm (e.g. enabling them to unlock doors that they were previously not allowed to access), sacrificing security in doing so (thus reporting a lower "S" factor for the current SPD state). Moreover, it could allow system operators to monitor the exact location of personnel in the building (with obvious benefits to their timely rescue), but moving to an SPD state with lower "P", as privacy has been lost by enabling this direct monitoring. Finally, as some of the devices may be damaged in the incident, redundant hardware will have to take up their role (e.g. a backup camera taking over from the main one), which will be depicted as a drop in dependability (i.e. the "D" in the system's SPD state). When the fire is extinguished, the system returns to the normal SPD state.

4.1 User Interface

While the technical aspects detailed in the previous chapters are important, a decisive factor to the practical success of any framework of this nature will be its usability. The accessibility both in terms of the usability of its user interface, as well as the success of visualizing the system's current state in a user-friendly and intuitive manner are important, as well as ensuring that it imposes minimal requirements from the end-user in terms of training, configuration and maintenance [18].

The inner workings of the system are irrelevant to the operator, who may or may not be technically proficient. Moreover, its output should be accessible to higher management, who, in the context of businesses, are usually people with limited time and accustomed to handling interfaces with dashboards, gauges and other high-level representations [19]. The preference to dashboard layouts is not restricted to higher management, but has been shown to be preferable to users in general [20], while recent research indicates there are significant benefits to this approach, helping address various business challenges (e.g. to provide a global view on resource occupation, aiming to enhance decision-making for both human and non-human resource management at run-time [21]). Thus, this is the approach adopted for visualizing the agents' outputs and the corresponding user interface.

The SPD levels derived from RT-SPDM are plain numbers, e.g. (56, 75, 89), since they are the results of the composition process detailed in the previous sections. Though these numbers are appropriate to be transmitted and computed by machines (i.e. 'machine to machine' interfaces), when it comes to presenting them to human operators in user interfaces, there is the need for making their representation more intuitive. That would make the SPD level much easier to understand in order to allow operators to be aware of the situation and possibly operate manual countermeasures wherever appropriate. The appropriate presentation of information is highly dependent on the specific domain and application, however a basic template could be applied to most domains. To this end, and in order to further facilitate the comprehension of the SPD state for a human operator, the use of a graphical scale and appropriate colors should be used (e.g. red for all values below 40, yellow for values from 40 to 70 and green for values from 70 to 100). An example of this approach, chosen for the proof-of-concept implementation of RT-SPDM, appears in Fig. 2.

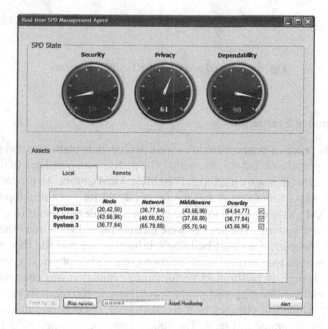

Fig. 2. The proof-of-concept RT-SPDM master agent GUI

Other than the main GUI detailed above which presents the aggregated SPD state of the monitored infrastructure, each RT-SPDM agent also features its own backend GUI. This is aimed to advanced users/system operators, providing low level information of the SPD status changes reported by each subsystem. The events appearing as they happen on the screen, but these changes are also logged in the corresponding files for offline auditing. A screenshot of this user interface appears in Fig. 3.

Fig. 3. The backend GUI of RT-SPDM's agents

4.2 Performance Evaluation

The RT-SPDM proof-of-concept modules were deployed on platforms that are expected to be found in typical ambient environments. The end devices consisted of three Beagle-bone [22] embedded hardware platforms (720 MHz ARM Cortex-A8 processor, 256 MB of RAM). The sub-system agents and the master agent run on a desktop PC (Core i5 CPU, 8 GB RAM), as is expected to be the case in actual deployments (e.g. a command & control backend system). The devices were interconnected via wired Ethernet, as they are assumed to be part of a smart building's infrastructure and the risk of relying on wireless connections to control critical functions (e.g. cyber-physical systems controlling actuators) is high. A preliminary performance evaluation was conducted to investigate the feasibility of the proposed mechanisms. Issuing 200 requests to the monitored devices, while triggering changes to their SPD state in-between, yielded promising performance, as illustrated in Fig. 4. The spikes noted occur when SPD changes take place (thus the agents are informed and the system SPD state is altered).

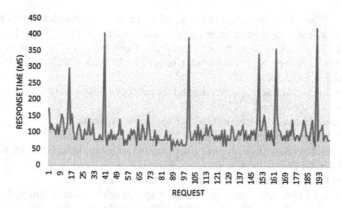

Fig. 4. Response time of the system as the SPD changes occur in the fire-alarm scenario

5 Conclusions

This work presented RT-SPDM, a framework for the real-time management of the Security, Privacy and Dependability of ambient environments. The multi-agent system is implemented in the JADE platform and deployed on OSGi middleware for controlling embedded devices, leveraging the benefits of SOA to provide a platform-agnostic solution with seamless integration across heterogeneous systems. The core of the reasoning process is an event-based model checker which extends the Event Calculus, while security-related theory is modelled and implemented as a formal framework for system composition verification, security validation and metric-driven management of SPD states. The proposed solution is applied to a smart-buildings scenario, where it configures the underlying systems at runtime to counter attacks and perform AI reactive plans to retain the safety of the employees in cases of emergency. A performance evaluation of the proof-of-concept implementation was conducted on typical embedded devices and the results were promising with regard to the feasibility of the proposed framework. An extended performance evaluation will be presented in future work.

Acknowledgments. Part of this work has been supported by the Greek General Secretariat for Research and Technology (GSRT), under the ARTEMIS JU research program nSHIELD (new embedded Systems arcHItecturE for multi-Layer Dependable solutions) project. Call: ARTEMIS-2010-1, Grant Agreement No.:269317.

References

1. Mayes, K., Markantonakis, K.: Information security best practices. In: Markantonakis, K., Mayes, K. (eds.) Secure Smart Embedded Devices, Platforms and Applications, pp. 119–144. Springer, New York (2013). Part II
2. Hatzivasilis, G., Papaefstathiou, I., Manifavas, C., Papadakis, N.: A reasoning system for composition verification and security validation. In: 6th NTMS 2014, pp. 1–4 (2014)

3. Eguia, I., Del Ser, J.: A meta-heuristically optimized fuzzy approach towards multi-metric security risk assessment in heterogeneous system of systems. In: PECCS, pp. 231–236 (2014)
4. Walter, M., Trinitis, C.: Quantifying the security of composed systems. In: Wyrzykowski, R., Dongarra, J., Meyer, N., Waśniewski, J. (eds.) PPAM 2005. LNCS, vol. 3911, pp. 1026–1033. Springer, Heidelberg (2006)
5. Devices profile for web services, version 1.1. http://docs.oasis-open.org/ws-dd/dpws/1.1/os/wsdd-dpws-1.1-spec-os.pdf
6. Open Services Gateway Initiative (OSGi). http://www.osgi.org/
7. Mueller, E.T.: Commonsense Reasoning (2006)
8. Patkos, T., Plexousakis, D.: Epistemic reasoning for ambient intelligence. In: ICAART (1), pp. 242–248 (2011)
9. Java Agent DEvelopment (JADE) Framework. http://jade.tilab.com/
10. FIPA, A.C.L.: FIPA ACL message structure specification. Found. Intell. Phys. Agents. (2002). http://www.fipa.org/specs/fipa00061/SC00061G.html
11. OASIS: Common Alerting Protocol Version 1.2. http://docs.oasis-open.org/emergency/cap/v1.2/CAP-v1.2-os.pdf
12. Knopflerfish - Open Source OSGi service platform. http://www.knopflerfish.org/
13. WS4D-JMEDS DPWS Stack. http://sourceforge.net/projects/ws4d-javame/
14. Lawrence, K., Kaler, C., Nadalin, A., Monzilo, R., Hallam-Baker, P.: Web Services Security: SOAP Message Security 1.1. https://www.oasis-open.org/committees/download.php/16790/wss-v1.1-spec-os-SOAPMessageSecurity.pdf
15. Petroulakis, N.E., Askoxylakis I.G., Tryfonas T.: Life-logging in smart environments: challenges and security threats. In: IEEE ICC 2012, pp. 5680–5684 (2012)
16. Fysarakis, K., Papaefstathiou, I., Manifavas, C., Rantos, K., Sultatos, O.: Policy-based access control for DPWS-enabled ubiquitous devices. In: 2014 IEEE ETFA, pp. 1–8 (2014)
17. Tsoumas, V., Tryfonas, T.: From risk analysis to effective security management: towards an automated approach. Inf. Manag. Comput. Secur. **12**, 91–101 (2004)
18. Lahlou, S. (ed.): Designing User Friendly Augmented Work Environments. Springer-Verlag, London (2009)
19. Beuschel, W.: Dashboards for management. In: Adam, F., Humphreys, P. (eds.) Encyclopedia of DecisionMaking and Decision Support Technologies, pp. 116-123. Information ScienceReference, Hershey, PA (2008). doi:10.4018/978-1-59904-843-7.ch014
20. Read, A., Tarrell, A., Fruhling, A.: Exploring user preference for the dashboard menu design. In: 42nd Annual Hawaii International Conference on System Sciences, HICSS (2009)
21. Linden, I.: Proposals for the integration of interactive dashboards in business process monitoring to support resources allocation decisions. J. Decis. Syst. **23**, 318–332 (2014)
22. BeagleBone System Reference Manual, RevA3_1.0. http://beagleboard.org/static/beaglebone/a3/Docs/Hardware/BONE_SRM.pdf

Putting a Hat on a Hen? Learnings for Malicious Insider Threat Prevention from the Background of German White-Collar Crime Research

Ulrike Hugl[(⊠)]

School of Management, Innsbruck University, Innsbruck, Austria
ulrike.hugl@uibk.ac.at

Abstract. Mainly based on an increasing dependence on ICT, the protection of crucial assets has become increasingly important for organizations. Beside external hacker attacks and malware, malicious insider threat continues to be one of the main security issues facing organizations. This article presents motives, characteristics and other influencing factors of employees to commit to criminal behavior. Therefore, results from the background of German economic offenders' research and related theories of crime are analyzed. The work closes with recommendations for further research and starting points for insider threat prevention management.

Keywords: Malicious insider threat · Criminal psychological profile · Criminal motive structures · Theories of crime

1 Introduction

According to the results of the 2013 US State of Cybercrime Survey [1], attacks of trusted employees respectively malicious insiders cover about 30 % of all cyber-attacks (broadly stayed consistent since 2004), whereby the total number of such attacks has increased dramatically, resulting in $2.9 trillion in employee fraud losses globally per year. In addition, the results show that it is hard to know who these malicious insiders are – normally they are acting within the boundaries of trust necessary to perform normal duties - and how to prevent attacks.

The CERT Insider Threat Center (Carnegie Mellon University) defines a malicious insider as "…a current or former employee, contractor, or other business partner who has or had authorized access to an organization's network, system, or data and intentionally exceeded or misused that access in a manner that negatively affected the confidentiality, integrity, or availability of the organization's information or information systems" (http://www.cert.org/insider_threat/, accessed on Jan. 8, 2014).

In this paper, a malicious insider is defined as a current or former employee, (still) having access to the organization's (IT) infrastructure and with specific organizational data, networks' and information systems' access opportunities and privileges and/or with knowledge of processes, services and persons, enabling the individual to gather, misuse or steal an organization's crucial assets (e.g. customer data, production and

T. Tryfonas and I. Askoxylakis (Eds.): HAS 2015, LNCS 9190, pp. 631–641, 2015.
DOI: 10.1007/978-3-319-20376-8_56

product secrets, etc.), either causing solely harm to the organization and/or benefiting him-/herself.

In fact, based on new technical opportunities, data theft has become much easier: for example, mobile trends like BYOD (bring your own device), cloud services with related security vulnerabilities, the ability to work from home and access an organization's data when on the road, as well as more and more malware opportunities have increased the potential of related attacks. Other main security obstacles may be budget constraints, the complexity of the internal (IT) environment, competing priorities, a lack of top-level direction and leadership, as well as a lack of awareness training, and others.

The remainder of the paper is organized as follows. The next section reviews some risk factors for organizations due to malicious insider threat. This is followed by a description of two process models relating to an offenders' (potential) criminal behavior and related decision issues. In a next step, several related theories of crime as well as recommendations for further insider threat research are discussed.

2 Current Risk Factors Companies Face from Malicious Insider Threat

An analysis of the changing nature of internal offenders can help organizations stiffen their defenses against malicious activities. A study of KPMG [2], covering 596 fraudsters companies investigated between 2011 and 2013 highlights that the typical fraudster in 2013 is very similar to the typical one in 2011: the attacker is middle-aged (36–45 years old), mostly employed in an executive operations, marketing or finance (senior) position, whereby many of them are employed in the victimized organization for more than six years. A report of the British Centre for the Protection of National Infrastructure [3] show significantly more males (82 %) engaged in insider activity than females (18 %), whereby motivating personal factors are financial gain (47 % of cases), ideology (20 %), desire for recognition (14 %), loyalty to friends, family or country (14 %) as well as revenge (6 %).

The results of a current PWC [4] study points out that used fraud detection methods can be differentiated into three elements: corporate control (all in all 55 %), corporate culture (23 %), as well as issues beyond the influence of management (21 %) like accidents, law enforcement, or investigative media. Moreover, most crimes by trusted former or present employees are perpetrated for financial or personal gain [5]: The top threat action varieties within insider misuse are privilege abuse (88 %), unapproved hardware (18 %), bribery (16 %), e-mail misuse (11 %), and data mishandling (11 %).

In general, current well-known cases, communicated in mass media in the US and Europe, show that beside the technological detection and prevention also behavioral-oriented aspect are playing a crucial role. In the field of technological-oriented prevention and detection diverse applications and efforts are used to avoid related attacks from malicious acting employees: anti-fraud management with big data analysis, cloud service methods for managing insider threat, opportunity-reducing techniques, IT security incident systems, event detection methodology and correlation analysis, and methods to audit USB device usage [see e.g. 6–11].

Typically, a malicious insider has a specific goal in mind, motives like financial needs, a method (actions and tools to achieve the goal) and an opportunity (for example based on a lack of the internal control system). In this context, Magklaras and Furnell [12] highlight a human-centric approach of insider threats, ranging from misbehaviour of individuals to issues of the reason for misuse, system role, and system consequences. According to Parker [13], other factors can be knowledge and skills, resources, authority, and motives.

To summarize, beside technical and behavioural factors, insider threats may also be triggered by some organizational issues like the organizational structure and culture [14], official stated and 'internalized' corporate policies [15], environmental factors like relationships (relating to so-called 'social bonds'), societal norms and values, as well as by ideas of legitimacy and (borders of) legal norms.

Nevertheless, beside all above presented aspects and studies, in point of fact, activities of malicious insiders certainly are designed for non-detection - as a consequence, the dark figure of related crime is hard to value.

According to estimates of experts, losses conducted by economic offenders (including undetected malicious insiders) encompass between €50 and 75 billion per year in Germany, but because of the dark figure of crime this vague span cannot be related to a valid data base. Especially immaterial damages like a loss of reputation are rarely gathered. Furthermore, many organizations do not make public or solely report related cases to governmental institutions responsible for national information security strategies in economic crime defense. Such governmental institutions are mainly aiming on an analysis of new attack forms of malicious insiders and external offenders. From the background of malicious insider threat, attack forms may occur from when working alone, cooperating with colleagues, but also may be initiated by organized criminal groups, searching for a cooperation with an internal employee or blackmailing an internal offender.

3 Leanings from Economic Offenders' Research in Germany

3.1 A Process Model of Economic Delinquency

Mainly based on the work of Coleman's [16] integrated theory of white-collar crime, focusing on situational and motivational factors for an appearance of a criminal act, Schneider [17–19] developed a process model of criminal acting employees inside an organization. RölfsPartner and Schneider [18] conducted a study with economic criminals and analyzed their related social aspects. The authors highlight that such offenders are (social) unobtrusive, higher educated than average, are married, societal integrated, and often have (as managers in a middle or higher position) a reputable societal status. The authors analyze the emergence of criminal activities based on both, a progression of events and personality factors. Thereby, a previously loyal employee is being plunged into a personal crisis (e.g. because of a fear of job loss, financial problems, etc.), discovers occasionally a crime opportunity inside the organization, and grabs the chance (for example to let out his/her frustration). From this time on, based on a non-detection of the human's criminal former activity, and inspired by the first sense of achievement, from now on the human actively searches for crime opportunities to conduct further criminal acts. The authors differentiate between a situational level (in the context of the offender and a potential opportunity) as well as situational vulnerability and related risk constellations (in the context of an offender's personality or characteristics). On the situational level, the results of the analyzed convicted economic criminals highlight so-called opportunity seekers and opportunity takers. Opportunity takers are long-term employed, loyal and highly trusted employees who have the chance to commit a crime, mainly based on poor organizational control systems. Without being stopped, this kind of offender may become an (actively criminal activities planning) opportunity seeker. Due to the personal risk constellations, the authors point out four favorite types of offenders: such with a high stress disorder, crisis offers (most frequent), dependents, and unsuspicious offenders.

Schneider's [17] process model starts with a potential situation for a criminal act, followed by a perception filter with two opportunities: potential influences at this stage are a puristic individual basic attitude (like correctness, blamelessness, righteousness) and knowledge of organizational processes. The model continues with three steps (see Table 1): The first step leads to the 'awareness of a situation', either as a blockade or a so-called 'clear view' due to an opportunity and towards a (potential) criminal behavior. At this stage, a blockade as well as a clear view is influenced by different individual risk factors. Positive factors leading to a blockade are for example personal satisfaction, estimation of others (supervisors, colleagues, etc.), and an adequate (financial) aspiration level; main triggers for a clear view (towards a criminal act) may be frustration and grievance, an inadequate (intended or existing) aspiration standard of living, as well as individual neutralization (justification) strategies to downplay a (potential) criminal behavior and decrease cognitive dissonance. The second step deals with the 'evaluation of a situation' and its individual interpretation: on the one hand, an employee can detect a lack of the organizational control system and make suggestions to eliminate the security gap or (in the worst case) he/she can value the situation as a change (opportunity) for a criminal act (with supporting impact of mentioned main triggers due to the clear view). The third step relates to 'acting in the situation' with two influencing aspects: fantasy (an individual detects an opportunity but does not act criminal) and the criminal activity (an employee may take the opportunity to act criminal). In this last step, mentioned negative triggers of step two, but also aspects like workplace-related sub-cultures or external relationships (family, friends) can play a crucial role to commit a crime.

To summarize, the model integrates different theoretical approaches and offers reference points for a possible new theory of economic delinquency in the future [20, p. 85]. In addition, based on a typology of offenders (expert interviews, n = 47 male, 3 female), an organization can try to identify 'endangered' individuals and find starting points for intervening measures.

Table 1. Process model of criminal economic behavior [19]

Criminological Situation			
'Puristic' value orientation	Perception filter		Knowledge of processes
Step 1	*Blockade* - Satisfaction, appreciation - Adequate aspiration level - Realistic relation to money and property - Modern idealistic or traditional values	**Awareness of a situation** Individual risk factors ←――――――→	*'Clear view'* - Frustration, grievance - inadequate aspiration standard of living - neutralization strategies
Step 2	*Lack of control system* Alternatives of behavior	**Evaluation of a situation** Compression of the individual risk	*Change for a criminal activity* 'Crucial' relevance aspects
Step 3	*Fantasy*	**Acting in the situation**	*Commit a crime*

3.2   A Process Model of Relevant Motive Structures of White-Collar Crime Offenders

Beside general factors like socio-demographic data of white-collar crime offenders, Cleff et al. [21] aimed in their study on deeper connections of the emergence of white-collar crime, especially regarding a better understanding of the interplay of emotional, motivational and cognitive perception processes on the way to commit a crime. Furthermore, they wanted to figure out possible consequences for a prevention and control of white-collar crime attacks. The authors conducted 13 unstructured interviews with prisoners (economic offenders; each interview took about five to six hours). In addition, they got the permission to analyze 60 court papers of convicted offenders in Germany.

According to the authors, an offender passes through a process with five main phases (see Table 2) [21]: In the first phase, an individual tries to achieve his/her objectives on a legal way. In the second phase, the individual experiences no success when trying to achieve specific objectives. At this stage, the individual is confronted with negative emotions like fear of failure, fear of loss, or existential fear. To overcome this emotional deficiency state, in a third phase, the individual searches for new and also illegal ways to achieve the intended objectives; the person explores legal borderlines. In the case of first successes (fourth phase), a person's behavior is being confirmed and strengthened; the wish for further successes is higher than the fear of potential sanctions. At the end of the process (fifth phase), something like a point of no return exists: to justify or neutralize misbehavior, the person tries to bring his/her behavior and personal sense of right and wrong into harmony. Persons concerned increasingly suffer from a loss of reality. In this last phase, offenders already are deeply involved in their illegal activities – hence, a way back seems to be impossible. With the disclosure of the illegal behavior an individual reality shock occurs.

According to Cleff et al. [21], this process has not necessarily to end with an illegal activity. In fact, an emergence of a criminal act is always dependent on a complex

Table 2. Process model of white-collar crime [21]

Phase 1: Achieving objectives on a legal way

↓

Phase 2: Bad success experienced on a legal way

↓

Phase 3: Searching for new ways to achieve objectives

↓

Phase 4: First successes

↓

Phase 5: 'Point of no return' Process-oriented loss of control

↓

Confrontation with the illegality of an activity

Illegal activity not disclosed	Illegal activity disclosed
↓	↓
Strengthening, disinhibition	Shock

framework of diverse influencing factors: on the one hand, internal factors involve the personality structure, individual motives, values as well as a related rating of money, and the intra-individual sense of right and wrong influences the human; on the other hand, external factors encompass organizational- or industry-specific influences, negative emotions (resulting from bad success) as well as the subjective perception of potential opportunities to act illegal. In the case of committing a crime, the person concerned develops diverse neutralization strategies to justify his/her bad behavior.

4   Reflection and Recommendations for Malicious Insider Threat

4.1   Theoretical Reflection of the Presented Models

Prevention and countering of malicious insider threat has to consider concurrent causes. In general, both presented models try to find such causes and effects in the field of white-collar crime. Nevertheless, there have to be considered some strengths and weaknesses.

In his model, Schneider [19] refers to Coleman's [16] (above mentioned) integrated theory of white-collar crime, especially considering that "motivation and opportunity are often closely associated in a particular setting". But his model is also based on several other theories from the background of criminology, for example on strain, for example on Merton's anomie theory [22] as well as on control and social theories. In this connection, Hirschi's social bond theory [23] relates to informal social control of colleagues, family and friends (so-called "social bonds"). Furthermore, Coleman's [16] "work-related subcultures" as well as control theories like Gottfredson's and Hirschi's [24] self-control theory of crime (often referred to as the General Theory of Crime) with its lack of a human's self-control as a crucial factor behind criminal behavior seem to play a fundamental role in Schneider's model.

According to strain theories, Schneider [17] developed criminal act-supporting or - preventing personal risk factors (see step one) like emotions (negative or positive), the kind of lifestyle (inadequate or adequate), and personal crisis (with a related retention or lowering level of demand). The background of control theories leads to further risk constellations like value orientation (modern and/or materialistic values), and control theories respectively 'social bonds' relate in the model to personal contacts, relationships and especially the kind of work-related subcultures [see e.g. 16] as 'social capital' of an offender. Not least, the routine activity theory of Cohen and Felson [25] is a central aspect of the model: crime occurs when there exists an intersection in time and space of a motivated offender, an attractive target, and a lack of capable guardianship (e.g. a lack of the internal control system). In general, this theory focuses on the question how to discover and prevent opportunities for criminal behavior in the routine activities of potential attackers.

Schneider's model also relates to results from other scholarly work, especially focusing on the fact that economic offenders normally are higher educated, are so-called 'latecomers to crime' [see e.g. also study results from 2] and their profile does not correspond with other stereotypes of criminals like the typical street offender [see e.g. 26]. Furthermore, perpetrators are influenced by a specific situational context [27], and – according to Schneider's main category of offenders, namely 'crisis responder' - for example, by a personal crisis based on a fear of losing what one has worked so hard to obtain [28].

In order to describe causes of white-collar crime, Schneider considers in his process model socio-structural as well as personal risk factors, especially based on the concept of neutralization strategies. Neutralization strategies refer to one specific and helpful aspect of the model: Schneider [18] states a survey of Buzzell [29], analyzing different techniques of neutralization adapted from research of Lanier and Henry [30], as well as from basic research of the founders of this theory [31]. For example, such neutralization strategies refer to justifications like "I didn't have a choice" and "the defense of necessity" or "I deserve this, they owed me" as "the claim of entitlement" [32], or "I'm not as bad as others" as "justification by comparison" [33].

Other considered approaches in the course of the development of Schneider's model of economic delinquency are the (above-mentioned) routine-activity approach of Cohen and Felson [25], relating to a motivated offender meeting a suitable target in the absence of a capable guardian, and general strain theory [34] or anomie theory [22], relating to a goal blockade (no fit between goals and resources available) and a maintenance of social success. For example, the latter may occur in a highly competitive economic environment and therefore demanding for high-level objectives from their employees which are extremely hard to achieve. In this context, Agnew et al. [34] state that "[c]rime may be used to achieve monetary goals, obtain status in the eyes of one's peers, seek revenge against the perceived source of goal blockade or other targets, and alleviate frustration and other negative emotions" [also relating to results of 2, and partially 5].

To summarize, Schneider's model considers diverse theories from the background of criminology. Nevertheless, beside positive aspects of Schneider's model like the process-oriented character and diverse starting points like personal risk factors to describe a potential emergence of bad behavior, also some weaknesses can be mentioned. Some aspects refer to general questions of such models, namely a demand for universality; and: what about a (potential) offender's available level of information at the time of a conscious decision between legal and illegal behavior (see step 3: fantasy or commit a crime)? In fact, in specific working situations, it is sometimes crucial to balance or find the 'right' (legal) way of behavior, especially in a complex organizational and legal environment. Another crucial point seems to be that the main stream of argumentation lines is based to the background of theories coming from the field of criminology. However, the model only marginally considers issues from the organizational background like structural issues, (kind of) business processes and collaboration, the specific role of leadership, as well as (implemented) strategies or policies regarding information security, governance and ethics, all of them with related effects on employees' awareness.

In addition, Cleff et al. [21] refer to another weak issue of Schneider's model: individual strategies of (potential) offenders in dealing with 'loss-making' and negative emotional conditions and implying motivational issues and anticipated problem solving strategies. The authors argue that related details disappear in a kind of 'melting pot with totalitarian demand'.

The second presented model of Cleff et al. [21] mainly focuses on offenders and their value systems. Dependent on the opportunity to translate their motives and values successfully, offenders develop personal benefit and emotional approval or fear and frustration, and in the latter case are motivated to commit a crime. The authors state that a financial benefit of an offender merely expresses something like a 'quasi need' - an instrumentalization for deeper existing essential needs (beyond money). Furthermore, the authors' qualitative results show that offenders have a subjective and biased sense of justice. In the worst case, different influencing factors (internal and external) with crucial intensity are coming together and concentrate the risk for a decision towards bad behavior.

In comparison to Schneider's [19] model, Cleff et al. [21] also mention some external influencing factors like branch- and organizational-specific issues (e.g. corporate culture and 'value management', internal structure, strategic relevance of compliance management, whistleblowing-systems, and the role and intensity of other internal control systems). Hence, the study of Cleff et al. [21] brings up some additional aspects, opening up a huge field of new empirical work with regard to motives and surrounding issues like value management or ethics in organizations.

Similar to Schneider's [18] research in the field of offenders' typology, Cleff et al. [21] analyzed all 60 court papers of offenders (cluster analysis) and developed a typology of perpetrators: the "visionary" (15 persons of 60) with the main categories "egocentric" and "frustrated"), the "dependent" (26) and the "naive" (10).

To summarize, the work of Cleff et al. [21] identifies first critical motive structures of economic offenders, personal characteristics and benefiting determining factors of (potential) white-collar crime activities. Notably the analysis of different types of offenders points out the interaction of emotional, motivational as well as cognitive perceptual processes on the way to a criminal behavior. The authors summarize that successful prevention of white-collar crime has to consider the different types of offenders, respectively specific positive or negative signs regarding the likelihood of a potential misbehavior.

4.2   Recommendations and Further Research Efforts

The National Cybersecurity and Communications Integration Center of the US Department of Homeland Security [35] states (besides patterns of frustration, financial needs and greed) some further behavioral risk factors of insiders: for example, introversion, a tendency to minimize mistakes and faults, ethical 'flexibility' (as mentioned in both presented models) and an inability to assume responsibility for their actions (both may refer to mentioned neutralization strategies), a lack of empathy, a history of managing crisis ineffectively, intolerance to criticism, reduced loyalty, and compulsive behavior.

However, such indicators are hard to identify, especially if they do not occur for a longer period. Nevertheless, also such factors could be considered to development a corporate insider threat prevention program. Therefore, the theory of planned behavior [36], referring to environmental psychology, as well as the situational crime prevention approach, making crime activities more risky [37] and focusing on specific ways to modify the social (and physical) environment [38], could be opportunities to consider.

Furthermore, relevant studies in the field show that offenders are so-called late-comers to crime. Hence, the age of employees also can be a specific starting point when managing target group-oriented' insider threat prevention (e.g. in the field of personal development-oriented measures). Also the kind of leadership, referring to issues like satisfaction, fairness in dealing with difficult situation (e.g. regarding an employee's poor achievement of objectives in a highly competitive business), and the quality and culture of working groups may play a crucial role. In the worst case, all these aspects can influence and trigger a personal decision for misuse.

Anyhow, for a development of insider threat measures, an identification of potential crisis responders (as opportunity seekers and takers) seems to be important. In this connection, executives should be trained to recognize different personal drug, gambling or other serious crisis or negative life events like a relationship break, a death of a family member or close friend with related financial needs.

One opportunity could be to transfer such an exposed employee to a working place with a less vulnerable work profile (reduced opportunities to commit a crime) and/or to offer specific arrangements to support a difficult personal situation (for example via financial support).

5   Conclusion

Typically, the responsibilities for prevention, detection and interventions in managing insider threat are shared among diverse departments inside an organization (e.g. IT, information security, HR, legal affairs). The problem may be to bring up an internal insider threat program together and to split responsibilities in a proper way. Such a program should be designed in accordance to the likelihood of committing misuse – especially on focusing on potential crisis responders. In current malicious insider research scholarly work mainly focuses on technical detection measures; related research efforts focusing on the human factor should be increased.

References

1. PwC, Key findings from the 2013 US State of Cybercrime Survey, pp. 1–20. PricewaterhouseCoopers (co-sponsored by: CERT/Carnegie Mellon University, CSO Magazine, United States Secret Service), June 2013
2. KPMG, Global profiles of the fraudster, pp. 1–124. KPMG International (Headquarters), Amstelveen, November 2013
3. CPNI, CPNI Insider Data Collection Study. Report of Main Findings, pp. 1–15. Centre for the Protection of National Infrastructure, UK (2013)
4. PWC, Global Econoic Crime Survey 2014, pp. 1–860. PricewaterhouseCoopers (2014)
5. Verizon, 2014 Data Breach Investigations Report, pp. 1–60. Verizon, USA (2014)
6. Capelli, D., Moore, A., Trzeciak, R.: The CERT Buide to Insider Threat. Pearson, Westford (2012)
7. Flynn, L., Porter, G., DiFatta, C.: Cloud Service Provider Methods for Managing Insider Threats: Analysis Phase II, Expanded Analysis and Recommendations, pp. 1–46. Technical Report, CMU/SEI-2013-TN-030, CERT Division, Carnegie Mellon University (2014)
8. Padayachee, K.: A Framework of Opportunity-Reducing Techniques to Mitigate the Insider Threat: Towards Best Practice. UNISA (University of South Africa) (2014)
9. Grimaila, M.R., et al.: Design and analysis of a dynamically configured log-based distributed security event detection methodology. J. Def. Model. Simul. Appl. Methodol. Technol. 9(3), 219–241 (2012)
10. Silowash, G.J., King, C.: Insider Threat Control: Understanding Data Loss Prevention (DLP) and Detection by Correlating Events from Multiple Sources. Carnegie Mellon University/Software Engineering Institute, Research Showcase (paper 708) (2013)
11. Silowash, G.J., Lewellen, T.: Insider Threat Control: Using Universal Serial Bus (USB) Device Auditing to Detect Possible Data Exfiltration by Malicious Insiders, pp. 1–35. Carnegie Mellon University/Software Engineering Institute, Research Showcase (paper 728) (2013)
12. Magklaras, G.B., Furnell, S.M.: Insider Threat Prediction Tool: Evaluating the probability of IT misuse. Comput. Secur. 21(1), 62–73 (2001)
13. Parker, D.B.: Fighting Computer Crime: A New Framework for Protecting Information. Wiley, New York (1998)
14. Hugl, U.: The malicious insider: approaching organizational crisis management, culture and management's role on employees' behaviour. In: Sarrafzadeh, M., Petratos, P. (eds.) Strategic Advantage of Computing Information Systems in Enterprise Management, pp. 305–316. Athens Institute for Education and Research (ATINER), Athens (2010)
15. Predd, J., et al.: Insiders behaving badly. IEEE Secur. Priv. 6(4), 66–70 (2008)
16. Coleman, J.W.: Toward an integrated theory of white-collar crime. Am. J. Sociol. 93(2), 406–439 (1987)

17. Schneider, H.: Person und Situation. Über die Bedeutung personaler und situativer Risikofaktoren bei wirtschaftskriminellem Handeln. In: Löhr, A., Burkatzki, E. (eds.) Wirtschaftskriminalität und Ethik, pp. 135–153. Hampp, München/Mering (2008)

18. Schneider, H.: Der Wirtschaftsstraftäter in seinen sozialen Bezügen. In: RölfsPartner, (ed.) Der: Wirtschaftsstraftäter in seinen sozialen Bezügen. Aktuelle Forschungsergebnisse und Konsequenzen für die Unternehmenspraxis, pp. 4–19. Universität Leipzig, Leipzig (2009)

19. Schneider, H.: Wirtschaftskriminalität (§25). In: Bock, M. (ed.) Kriminologie, pp. 418–436. C.H Beck, München (2008)

20. Homann, D.: Betrug in der gesetzlichen Krankenversicherung. Eine empirische Untersuchung über vermögensschädigendes Fehlverhalten zulasten der Solidargemeinschaft, Godesberg, Mönchengladbach (2009)

21. Cleff, T., et al.: Wirtschaftskriminalität. Eine Analyse der Motivstrukturen, pp. 1–54. PricewaterhouseCoopers (PWC) (2009)

22. Merton, R.: Social structure and anomie. Am. Sociol. Rev. 3, 672–682 (1938)

23. Hirschi, T.: Causes of Delinquency. University of California Press, Berkeley (1969)

24. Gottfredson, M.R., Hirschi, T.: A General Theory of Crime. Standford University Press, Standford (1990)

25. Cohen, L.E., Felson, M.: Social change and crime rate trends: a routine activity approach. Am. Sociol. Rev. 44(4), 588–608 (1979)

26. Leeper Piquero, N., Weisburd, D.: Developmental trajectories of white-collar crime. In: Simpson, S.S., Weisburd, D. (eds.) The Criminology of White-Collar Crime. Springer, New York (2009)

27. van Koppen, M.V., et al.: Criminal trajectories in organized crime. Br. J. Criminol. 50(1), 102–123 (2010)

28. Leeper Piquero, N.: The Only thing we have to fear is fear itself: investigating the relationship between fear of falling and white-collar crime. Crime Delinquency 58(3), 362–379 (2012)

29. Buzzell, T.: Holiday revelry and legal control of fireworks: a study of neutralization in two normative contexts. West. Criminol. Rev. 6(1), 30–42 (2005)

30. Lanier, M., Henry, S.: Essential Criminology. Westview Press, Boulder (2004)

31. Sykes, G.M., Matza, D.: Techniques of neutralization: a theory of delinquency. Am. Sociol. Rev. 22, 664–670 (1957)

32. Coleman, J.W.: The Criminal Elite: Understanding White-Collar Crime. Worth, New York (2006)

33. Cromwell, P., Thurman, Q.: The devil made me do it: use of neutralizations by shoplifters. Deviant Behav. 24, 535–550 (2003)

34. Agnew, R., Piqueroleeper, N., Cullen, F.T.: General strain theory and white-collar crime. In: Simpson, S.S., Weisburd, D. (eds.) The Criminology of White-Collar Crime, pp. 35–60. Springer, New York (2009)

35. NCCIC, Combating the Insider Threat, pp. 1–5. National Cybersecurity and Communications Integration Center (NCCIC/Homeland Security), Washington, D.C., May 2014

36. Ajzen, I.: The theory of planned behavior. Organ. Behav. Hum. Decis. Process. 50(2), 179–211 (1991)

37. Clarke, R.V.: Situational Crime Prevention: Successful Case Studies. Criminal Justice Press, Monsey (1997)

38. Homel, R.: The Politics and Practice of Situational Crime Prevention. Criminal Justice Press, Monsey (1996)

Business and Threat Analysis of Ports' Supply Chain Services

Spyridon Papastergiou[1](✉), Nineta Polemi[1], and Ioannis Papagiannopoulos[2]

[1] Department of Informatics, University of Pireaus, Karaoli & Dimitriou 80,
18534 Pireaus, Greece
{paps,dpolemi}@unipi.gr
[2] Piraeus Port Authority, Miaouli, 10, 18538 Pireaus, Greece
ypapagiannopoulos@olp.gr

Abstract. Maritime supply chain is a dynamic system in which a set of organizations, people, activities, information and resources are involved aiming at delivering a service or a product to the final users. The paper describes the business processes of a representative example of a cross-border supply chain service, namely the "Vehicles Transport Chain"; analyses its interdependencies and threats; revealing the limitations of existing risk management methodologies in terms of addressing the cascading effects and the complexity of the maritime security ecosystem; highlights and underlines the need for a targeted risk assessment approach applicable to maritime supply chains.

Keywords: Supply chain · Security · Critical infrastructures

1   Introduction

The maritime supply chains consist of interconnected business partners (port authorities, ministries, maritime companies, ship industry, customs agencies, maritime/insurance companies) other CIs (e.g. airports, energy, telecommunication), people, processes, services, products, and other elements. This complex chain has become lately highly dependent upon ICT in order to provide innovative services in the highly competitive maritime digital trade [1].

The ports play a major role in the maritime supply chain and their infrastructures have interdependencies at multiple levels (local, national, international). In this context, they interact closely with all actors in the complex maritime eco-system. As a result, port stakeholders (notably port security operators and port facilities operators) have to deal with internal, external and diffused cyber/physical threats rising from the whole maritime supply chain.

The paper aims to present a systematic analysis of an important cross-border supply chain service (SCS), namely the *"Vehicles Transport Chain"*. This SCS has been selected based on specific criteria: (i) *European level nature*: most of the biggest commercial ports in Europe (e.g. Piraeus and Valencia Port Authorities) offer or are involved in this service; (ii) *Economic enablers*: this operation has a high economic

© Springer International Publishing Switzerland 2015
T. Tryfonas and I. Askoxylakis (Eds.): HAS 2015, LNCS 9190, pp. 642–653, 2015.
DOI: 10.1007/978-3-319-20376-8_57

impact on the ports as well as the European economy as a whole, for example in the port of Piraeus, the traffic of local and transit vehicles from 2009 to 2014 ranges from 276 k to 459 k per year; and (iii) *Environmental importance*: the transit of vehicles through the ports can cause dangerous water or environmental pollution events.

The analysis follows specific four (4) stages: description of business goals, business partners involved in the provision of the service, types of interdependencies among business partners and threats and risks related to the processes. Finally, the paper highlights the need for a new, targeted multi-dependency approach to risk assessment to deal with the cascading effects risks, threats and vulnerabilities, associated with the maritime supply chain.

2   State of the Art

2.1   Dependencies Analysis Approaches

A dependency or interdependency is a relationship between two entities involved in the maritime supply chain. This relationship can be considered as an interaction between two maritime entities which is either unidirectional or bidirectional. This relationship depicts how one process, activity or resource relies upon another. In this case, a supply chain actor may depend on another entity in order to perform a critical business process.

A framework to study interdependencies was proposed by Rinaldi et al. [2]. In this paper the authors separate the important factors that need to be taken into account in risk assessment, into six dimensions. These dimensions are: types of interdependencies, infrastructure, environment, coupling and response behavior, infrastructure characteristics, types of failures, and state of operations. In addition, these six dimensions are further analyzed to subtypes and substates. The infrastructures that are studied in this paper have wide impact in everyone and include electric power, natural gas and petroleum production and distribution, telecommunications (information and communications), transportation, water supply, banking and finance, emergency and government services, agriculture, and other fundamental systems and services. Furthermore, they present the most vital classes of interdependencies, which are: physical, cyber, geographic, logical and social. Moreover, environmental changes have crucial implications for interdependencies and how they affect the states of infrastructures and how they operate.

According to [3] the methodologies for dependency modeling, simulation and analysis have been recently categorized in the following broad categories:

i.   *Empirical approaches*: they focus on the study of the impact (e.g. [4]) and/or the risk related with the dependencies between CIs [5, 6] and their potential cascading effects according to historical accident or disaster data and expert experience [5, 7];
ii.   *Agent-based approaches*: they treat the CIs as complex adaptive systems and adopt an agent-based model to simulate their behaviors [8–12];
iii.   *System dynamics* based approaches: they analyze the CIs and model their dependencies by capturing important causes and effects under disruptive scenarios [13–18];
iv.   *Economic* based approaches: they provide a representation and interpretation of the CIs' interdependencies in terms of economic models [19–23];

v.   *Network* based approaches: they focus on the flow of products or services exchanged between CIs describing the topologies and flow patterns of the interdependencies[24–26]; and

vi. *Other:* they aim at capturing and analyzing the characteristics of the CIs using different models such as the hierarchical holographic modeling (HHM) method [27–33]

All the above-mentioned methodologies follow diverse approaches to capture CIs' behavior and analyze their interdependencies.

The paper follows a network based approach in order to analyze and depict the dependencies among the entities involved the Vehicles Transport Chain scenario described in the following Section. In particular, each entity is represented as a node and their physical and cyber connections are represented as links.

3   Supply Chain Service: Vehicles Transport Chain

This Section describes a representative example of a maritime supply chain that involves the shipment and receipt of various types of vehicles and equipment such as trucks, vans, truck trailers, threshing machines etc. The Vehicles Transport Chain is a relatively long and complicated process that involves domestic and international transportation, warehouse management, order and inventory control, materials handling, import/export facilitation, and information technology.

3.1   Vehicles Transport Chain Entities

The Vehicles Transport Chain is a massively complex system with numerous players, including shippers, transport operators. The key **business partners** (port related entities) involved in the chain are the following:

- *Importer*: entities that initiate the vehicles transport supply chain, who owns the vehicles to be transported, both to be exported or imported.
- *Industry*: The automobile industry that produces the vehicles and equipment such as automobiles, trucks, semi-trailer trucks, trailers, and railroad cars etc.
- *Ship Agents*: a business partner that is responsible for the transports of the vehicles by the sea (via ships). Usually, the Agent does not own ships and acts as charterers; the chartering contracts are for long periods or even without a time prescription.
- *Ship-owners*: the owner of a merchant vessel (commercial ship). The ship-owner is someone who equips and exploits a ship, for delivering cargo at a certain freight rate, either as a per freight rate (given price for the transport of a certain cargo between two given ports) or based on hire (a rate per day).
- *Public Administrations*: Local Authorities represent a number of local public stakeholders that are involved and play a crucial role in the Vehicles Transport Chain process including:
  - *Port Authorities*: manages the areas where port operations take place. These port operations usually involve physical operations (stevedoring, loading, unloading,

storage, transportation, inspection, etc.) as well as information and data flow operations through networks, document management systems, databases, portals, etc. (forwarding, invoicing, pre-arrival notifications, customs clearance documentation management, ISPS declaration, etc.) between the port operators and the other entities involved in these operations in any way.

- *Customs Authorities*: responsible to overview the implementation of the customs clearance procedures for the clearance of the vehicles from customs control of an importer's consignment.

- *Local Agent*: has primary responsibility to complete shipping and customs documentation, and arrange for vehicles transportation. Agents assist businesses and individuals (Importers) who need to ship the vehicles from one country to another.

- *Insurance Company*: provides coverage to the Importer for damages to the vehicles resulting from incident during their transportation, loading, unloading, or storage.

3.2 Vehicles Transport Chain Processes

This Section describes the main interactions among the entities engaged in the vehicles transport chain. This process can be divided into the following four (4) sub-processes:

A. Purchase and Shipment Phase (Fig. 1). The *Importer* sends a purchase order to the *Industry* that contains its orders for a number of vehicles. When both *Importer* and *Industry* have agreed upon the terms and conditions of the contract like pricing, documentation, freight charges, currency etc., the latest proceeds to complete the order. The *Industry* is seeking to contract a *Ship Agent* or a *Ship Owner* to deliver the vehicles to the destination port defined by the *Importer*. Also, the *Industry* makes the arrangements with the *Public Administrations* (port and customs authorities etc.) and transfers the vehicles to the *Port* for loading. The *Ship Agent* or the *Ship Owner* makes the arrangements with the *Public Administration* (management of the ship formalities including the Manifest) related to the authorization processes which take place from the entry of the ship into the port until its exit and then proceed to load the vehicles into the vessel for shipment to the destination *Port*. Finally, they undertake the responsibility to send the relevant documentation to the Importer's *Local Agent* which has the responsible for the ship arrival and the regional procedure of receiving and delivering the vessel to the importer.

B. Pre-arrival Phase (Fig. 2). In this phase, the Local Agent of the Importer has to arrange various details about the vessel docking and unloading of the vehicles at the Port terminals. In this context, it has to interact with the following entities:

- *Customs Authority*: the Local Agent submits the manifest of the vessel and receives the Manifest Registration Number (MRN).
- *Public Administrations*: the Local Agent submits the ship formalities requesting docking clearance. Once the agent grants permission for the vessel to dock at the port, informs the ship (captain) about the docking arrangements.
- *Insurance Company*: the Local Agent negotiates and signs a contract with the Insurance Company for the provision of insurance cover for damages to the vehicles.

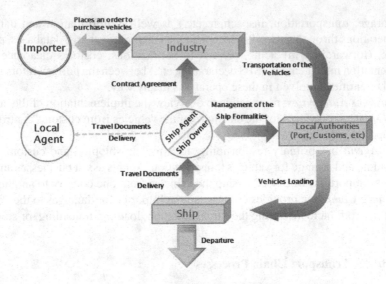

Fig. 1. Purchase and shipment phase

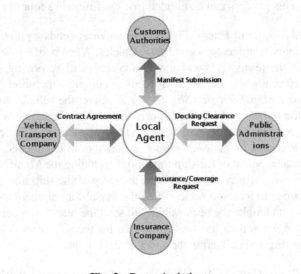

Fig. 2. Pre-arrival phase

- *Vehicle Transport Company*: the Local Agent employs a Transport Company to transfer the vehicles from the docks to the Importer's yard.

C. Port's Services Requested Phase (Fig. 3). The *Local Agent* submits the Manifest Registration Number (MRN) received from the Custom to the *Port Authority* requesting services for the vessel such as, mooring, lacing, personnel (drivers for transferring the cars from the ship to storage area, etc.). This process is performed via the Port Community System (PCS) that is an electronic platform which connects the multiple

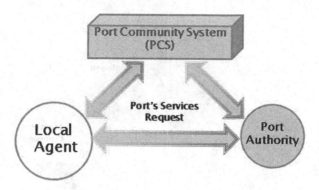

Fig. 3. Port's services requested phase

systems operated by a variety of organizations involved in the port's supply chain. Actually, this system facilitates the secure and efficient electronic exchange of information between the public and private stakeholders and allows the automatisation and the smooth operation of the port and logistics processes through a single request submission. In this context, the following steps should be followed:

i. The Local Agent shall prepare and submit an application form to the Port Community System (PCS).
ii. The Local Agent follows the prepayment procedures using e-Banking through the PCS.
iii. An Email or SMS is sent by the Destination port to the Local Agent, referencing the newly received request.
iv. The submitted request is processed by the representatives of the Port Authority.
v. The necessary resources and services are allocated by the Port Authority.
vi. Finally, a notification (via Email or SMS) is dispatched to the Local Agent containing the status of the whole process.

The PCS acts as a centralized system for the collection, dissemination and management of the information related to the request and provision of ports' services.

D. Port's Requesting Services and Delivery Phase (Fig. 4). In this phase the vessel approaches the port and receives all services requested by the *Local Agent*. In this context, the port's equipment (ship-to-shore cranes, yard tractors, forklifts, etc.) and port personnel should be available to unload the vehicles and store them to the port's facilities. Then, the *Transport Company* has the responsible to transfer the vehicles from the port to the *Importer*. The *Insurance Company* oversees the whole process in order to identify possible damages to the vehicles occurred during transportation process and report them to the *Local Agent*. The Latest informs the *Importer* about the status of the process

3.3 Entities Dependencies

According to the Vehicles supply chain scenario described in the previous section, the interaction of the involved entities could be through physical or non-physical flows.

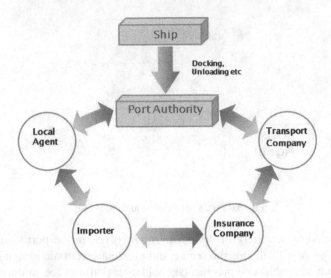

Fig. 4. Port's requesting services and delivery phase

Theses interactions can be classified into four (4) main types of interdependencies as follows:

1. Access to cyber-systems: The access could be to a database, to operational systems, networks, etc.
2. Interaction with cyber-systems: The interaction could be by sharing information, the offer of common services, etc.
3. Access to physical facilities: These facilities are buildings, terminals, etc.
4. Usage of physical facilities: The use could be for warehousing, offering a service, for hosting an installation, etc.

In general, the interdependencies among the key entities can be summarized in Table 1.

4   Threats and Consequences to Vehicles Transport Chain Service

The rise of crime, cybercrime and terrorism poses significant threats to supply chain continuity. Therefore, if a security incident or a failure occurs in a supply chain actor (supply chain link), this will affect the normal operation of the whole Vehicles supply chain, partially or completely leading to disruptions or outages it its operation. In the literature, three types of failures [2] have been identified:

- *Cascading failure*: a disruption in the operation of a supply chain actor may cause the failure of a component/element in an interconnected entity.
- *Common-Cause failure*: an incident may cause the disruption of the operation of two or more supply chain actors simultaneously.
- *Escalating failure*: a disruption in the operation of a supply chain actor may trigger an independent disruption of an interconnected entity.

Table 1. Dependency among the main entities involved in the "vehicles transport chain" service.

Dependency Direction: From rows to columns (Entity in the 1st column depends on an entity in the 1st row)

Entities / Dependencies	Importer	Industry	Ship Agent	Ship Owner	Public Administrations	Port Authority	Customs Authority	Vehicle Transport	Local Agent	Insurance Company
Importer		1						2, 3	2	2
Industry	1, 2		2	2	2	2, 3, 4			2	
Ship Agent		1		2	2, 3	2			2	
Ship Owner		1, 2	2		2, 3	2			2	
Public Administrations		1, 2, 3, 4	2	2					2	
Port Authority		2	1, 2, 3, 4	1, 2, 3, 4	2, 3, 4		2, 3, 4	3, 4	2	3
Customs Authority			2	2	1, 2	2			2	
Vehicle Transport Company									2	
Local Agent	2	2	2	2	2	2	2	2		2
Insurance Company	2								2	

The identification of the threats and risks in the Vehicles Transport Chain is a difficult process. The difficulties are partly due to the complexity induced by the large number of related and interdependent activities (data flows and physical operations) in the supply chain. Thus, understanding the interdependencies and the complex causal relationships in the supply chain is therefore crucial to the successful management of these activities as well as to the assessment of the corresponding threats.

Based on the analysis of the Vehicles Transport Chain flows and relationships the threats can be classified in the following categories based on the target of an examined threat:

- *TC-1: Infrastructural Threats.* This category includes threats targeted to the infrastructure elements of a business partner (buildings, gates, warehouses, tracks, CCTV systems etc.). Notable examples of threats are the destruction of the warehouse of the stored vehicles due to a deliberate action (e.g. bombing attack) or a physical threat or a physical disaster (e.g. earthquake).
- *TC-2: Information & ICT Threats.* This category includes threats targeted to the information and ICT elements of a business partner (data, systems, software,

hardware etc.). Representative example is the unauthorized access to the supply chain's information/documentation systems for the purpose of disrupting operations or facilitating illegal activities.

- *TC-3: Threats related with Personnel Security & Safety.* This category includes human centric threat scenarios. This category includes threat against the life of people involved in the Vehicles Transport Chain.
- *TC-4: Threats related with Goods and Conveyance Security.* By good we consider any item, exchanged or delivered via the Vehicles Transport Chain, e.g. various types of vehicles and equipment such as trucks, vans, truck trailers, threshing machines etc. Including threats related to operations aiming to facilitate a terrorist incident including using the mode of transportation as a weapon.
- *TC-5: Other.* Under this category fall all other threats targeting the broader Vehicles Transport Chain environment e.g. economical, security, commercial, and political instability.

Note that this categorization is not distinctive and several threat scenarios may partially belong to more than one category.

5   Conclusions

The Vehicles Transport Chain can be considered as a dynamic system in which a set of organizations, people, activities, information and resources are involved aiming at producing and delivering various types of vehicles and equipment such as trucks, vans, truck trailers, threshing machines etc. to the last link of the supply chain (Importer). In this context, this system includes business processes, which begin with the submission of the purchase order to the *Industry* and extends through the delivery of the vehicles to the *Importer* through different transport means.

Thus, the analysis of the interdependencies among the entities involved in the Vehicles Transport Chain as presented in Sect. 3 reveals that the processes are classified in two categories. The first one includes the physical operations which involve stevedoring, loading, unloading, storage, transportation and inspection procedures and the information and data flow operations performed through networks, document management systems, databases, portals, etc. (purchase order submission, pre-arrival notifications, customs and docking clearance documentation management, etc.).

Nevertheless, despite the digital and physical interactions among the entities involved in the abovementioned operations in any way, these entities currently handle their security and safety issues and threats independently. In particular, they adopt and follow risk assessment methodologies, methods and techniques that fail to capture and evaluate the whole picture of the maritime supply chain. Actually, they do not support effective and efficient processes that enable, facilitate and promote the identification, assessment and treatment of the spectrum of threats and their various cascading effects that are associated with security incidents occurring from interacting entities, cross-sectoral, cross border interdependencies and massive interconnectivity.

In this context, the paper acknowledges the limitations of existing risk management methodologies in terms of addressing the cascading effects and the complexity of the maritime security ecosystem. Also, it highlights and underlines the need for a targeted risk assessment approach that incorporate well-defined, precise and clear procedures that are able: (a) to identify, document and model the key dependencies of all entities involved in the maritime supply chain. (b) to support an effective algorithm for capturing multi-order dependencies among the supply chain actors (e.g. comprising the supply chain operation). (c) to adopt predictive mechanisms that assess the potential impact of security incidents on the supply chain process, given their various mutual dependencies.

Acknowledgments. The authors are grateful to the E.C. Programme "Prevention, Preparedness and Consequence Management of Terrorism and other Security related Risks for the Period 2007–2013". for their support in funding the CYSM and MEDUSA projects. The authors also thank all partners of CYSM (Port Institute for Studies and Co-Operation in the Valencian Region – FEPORTS, Singular Logic, Electrical, Electronics and Telecommunication Engineering and Naval Architecture Department (DITEN) - University of Genoa (UNIGE), University of Piraeus Research Centre, Piraeus Port Authority (PPA), Fundacion Valencia Port (VPF)) and Medusa (University of Piraeus Research Centre, Singular Logic, University of Cyprus (UCY), EUROPHAR EEIG, Austrian Institute of Technology) projects for their contributions.

References

1. ENISA report: Cyber security aspects in the maritime sector. ENISA (2011). http://www.enisa.europa.eu/activities/Resilience-and-CIIP/critical-infrastructure-and-services/dependencies-of-maritime-transport-to-icts
2. Rinaldi, S.M., Peerenboom, J.P., Kelly, T.K.: Identifying, understanding, and analyzing critical infrastructure interdependencies. Control Syst. IEEE **21**(6), 11–25 (2001)
3. Ouyang, M.: Review on modeling and simulation of interdependent critical Infrastructure systems. Reliab. Eng. Syst. Saf. **121**, 43–60 (2014)
4. Franchina, L., Carbonelli, M., Gratta, L., Crisci, M.: An impact-based approach for the analysis of cascading effects in critical infrastructures. Int. J. Crit. Infrastruct. **7**(1), 73–90 (2011)
5. Utne, I.B., Hokstad, P., Vatn, J.: A method for risk modeling of interdependencies in critical infrastructures. Reliab. Eng. Syst. Safety **96**(6), 671–678 (2011)
6. Kjølle, G.H., Utne, I.B., Gjerde, O.: Risk analysis of critical infrastructures emphasizing electricity supply and interdependencies. Reliab. Eng. Syst. Safety **105**, 80–89 (2012)
7. Franchina, L., Carbonelli, M., Gratta, L., Crisci, M.: An impact-based approach for the analysis of cascading effects in critical infrastructures. Int. J. Crit. Infrastruct. **7**(1), 73–90 (2011)
8. Bernhardt, K.L.S., McNeil, S.: Agent-based modeling: approach for improving infrastructure management. J. Infrastruct. Syst. **14**(3), 253–261 (2008)
9. Rinaldi, S.M.: Modeling and simulating critical infrastructures and their interdependencies. In: Proceedings of the Hawaii international conference on system sciences (HICSS-37), Big Island, Hawaii, pp. 54–61 (2004)
10. Haimes, Y.Y.: Models for risk management of systems of systems. Int. J. Syst. Syst. Eng. **1**(1–2), 222–236 (2008)
11. Kaegi, M., Mock, R., Kröger, W.: Analyzing maintenance strategies by agent- based simulations: a feasibility study. Reliab. Eng. Syst. Safety **94**, 1416–1421 (2009)

12. Ehlen, M.A., Scholand, A.J.: Modeling interdependencies between power and economic sectors using the N-ABLE agent based model. In: Proceedings of the IEEE conference on power systems. San Francisco (2005)
13. Kollikkathara, N., Feng, H., Yu, D.: A system dynamic modelling approach for evaluating municipal solid waste generation, land fill capacity and related cost management issues. Waste Manag. **30**, 2194–2203 (2010)
14. O'Reilly, G.P., Jrad, A., Kelic, A., LeClaire, R.: Telecom critical infrastructure simulations: discrete event simulation vs. dynamic simulate on how do they compare? In: Proceedings of the IEEE global telecommunications conference, Washington, DC, pp. 2597–2601 (2007) http://dx.doi.org/10.1109/GLOCOM.2007.493
15. Stapelberg, R.F.: Infrastructure systems interdependencies and risk informed decision making (RIDM): impact scenario an alysis of infrastructure risks induced by natural, technological and intentional hazards. J. Syst. Cybern. Inf. **6**(5), 21–27 (2008)
16. Santella, N., Steinberg, L.J., Parks, K.: Decision making for extreme events: modeling critical infrastructure interdependencies to aid mitigation and response planning. Rev. Policy Res. **26**(4), 409–422 (2009)
17. Min, H.J., Beyeler, W., Brown, T., Son, Y.J., Jones, A.T.: Toward modelling and simulation of critical national infrastructure interdependencies. IEEE Trans. **39**, 57–71 (2007)
18. Brown, T.: Multiple modeling approaches and insights for critical infrastructure protection. In: Skanata, D., Byrd, D.M. (eds.) Computational Models of Risks to Infrastructure, NATO Science for Peace and Security Series D: Information and Communication Security, vol. 13, p. 329. IOS Press, Amsterdam
19. Santos, J.R., Haimes, Y.Y.: Modeling the demand reduction input–output (I–O) inoperability due to terrorism of interconnected infrastructures. Risk Anal. **24**(6), 1437–1451 (2004)
20. Haimes, Y.Y., Horowitz, B.M., Lambert, J.H., Santos, J.R., Lian, C., Crowther, K.G.: Inoperability input–output model for interdependent infrastructure sectors. I: theory and methodology. J. Infrastruct. Syst. **11**(2), 67–79 (2005)
21. Rose, A.: Economic principles, issues, and research priorities in hazard loss estimation. In: Okuyama, Y., Chang, S. (eds.) Modeling Spatial and Economic Impacts of Disasters, pp. 13–36. Springer, New York (2004)
22. Zhang, P., Peeta, S.: A generalized modelling framework to analyze interdependencies among infrastructure systems. Transp. Res. Part B: Methodol. **45**(3), 553–579 (2011)
23. Zhang, P., Peeta, S.: Dynamic analysis of interdependent infrastructure systems. In: Proceedings of the 90th Annual Meeting of the Transportation Research Board, Washington, DC (CD-ROM) (2011)
24. Lee, E.E., Mitchell, J.E., Wallace, W.A.: Restoration of services in interdependent infrastructure systems: a network flows approach. IEEE Trans. Syst. Man Cybern. Part C Appl. Rev. **37**(6), 1303–1317 (2007)
25. Svendsen, N.K., Wolthusen, S.D.: Connectivity models of interdependency in mixed-type critical infrastructure networks. Inf. Secur. Tech. Rep. **12**(1), 44–55 (2007)
26. Ouyang, M., Duenas-Osorio, L.: An approach to design interface topologies across interdependent urban infrastructure systems. Reliab. Eng. Syst. Saf. **96**(11), 1462–1473 (2011)
27. Becker, T., Nagel, C., Kolbe, T.H.: Integrated 3D modelling of multi-utility networks and their interdependencies for critical infrastructure analysis. In: Kolbe, T.H., König, G., Nagel, C. (eds.) Advancesin 3D Geo-Information Sciences. Lecture Notes in Geoinformation and Cartography. Springer, Heidelberg (2011). http://dx.doi.org/10.1007/978-3-642-12670-3_1
28. Bernhardt, K.L.S., McNeil, S.: Agent-based modeling: approach for improving infrastructure management. J. Infrastruct. Syst. **14**(3), 253–261 (2008)

29. Brummitt, C.D., D'Souza, R.M., Leicht, E.A.: Suppressing cascades of load in interdependent networks. In: Proceedings of the National Academy of Sciences, vol. 109, no. 12 (2011)
30. Eusgeld, I., Nan, C.: Creating a simulation environment for critical infrastructure interdependencies study. In: Proceedings of the IEEE International Conference on Industrial Engineering and Engineering Management (IEEM), pp. 2104–2108 (2009)
31. Eusgeld, I., Nan, C., Dietz, S.: System-of systems approach for interdependent critical infrastructures. Reliab. Eng. Syst. Saf. **96**, 679–686 (2011)
32. Polemi, D., Ntouskas, T., Georgakakis, E., Douligeris, C., Theoharidou, M., Gritzalis, D.: S-Port: collaborative security management of Port Information systems. In: 2013 Fourth International Conference on Information, Intelligence, Systems and Applications (IISA), vol. 1, no. 6, pp. 10–12 (2013)
33. Kotzanikolaou, P., Theoharidou, M., Gritzalis, D.: Interdependencies between critical infrastructures: analyzing the risk of cascading effects. In: Bologna, S., Hämmerli, B., Gritzalis, D., Wolthusen, S. (eds.) CRITIS 2011. LNCS, vol. 6983, pp. 104–115. Springer, Heidelberg (2013)

Insider Threats: The Major Challenge to Security Risk Management

Teresa Pereira[1]([⊠]) and Henrique Santos[2]

[1] Polytechnic Institute of Viana do Castelo, Viana do Castelo, Portugal
tpereira@esce.ipvc.pt
[2] University of Minho, Guimarães, Portugal
hsantos@dsi.uminho.pt

Abstract. Security risk management is by definition, a subjective and complex exercise and it takes time to perform properly. Human resources are fundamental assets for any organization, and as any other asset, they have inherent vulnerabilities that need to be handled, i.e. managed and assessed. However, the nature that characterize the human behavior and the organizational environment where they develop their work turn these task extremely difficult, hard to accomplish and prone to errors. Assuming security as a cost, organizations are usually focused on the efficiency of the security mechanisms implemented that enable them to protect against external attacks, disregarding the insider risks, which are much more difficult to assess. All these demands an interdisciplinary approach in order to combine technical solutions with psychology approaches in order to understand the organizational staff and detect any changes in their behaviors and characteristics. This paper intends to discuss some methodological challenges to evaluate the insider threats and its impacts, and integrate them in a security risk framework, that was defined according to the security standard ISO/IEC_JTC1, to support the security risk management process.

Keywords: Information security risk · Security risk management · Insider risk · Insider threats and insider behavior

1 Introduction

Information systems security and communication technologies have received a significant attention, especially in the last decade. This includes various dimensions of computer and network security and several application domains (e.g. critical infrastructures such as banking, energy, transportation systems and networks). Information security (or cyber security) has been recognized increasingly critical to society today, since its well being is highly dependent on the performance of information systems and communication technologies [1]. However, more and more citizens and businesses are likely to suffer security breaches, which not only damage reputation but can also cause heavy financial losses, usually difficult to recover from. Such security breaches may be

© Springer International Publishing Switzerland 2015
T. Tryfonas and I. Askoxylakis (Eds.): HAS 2015, LNCS 9190, pp. 654–663, 2015.
DOI: 10.1007/978-3-319-20376-8_58

IT related, for example through computer viruses or other malicious software, system failure or data corruption, or may be socially motivated, for example through theft of assets or other incidents caused by direct human action.

Security risks arise from multiple sources and motivations, are very dynamic and consequently demand a proper management. In general, organizations are more focused on being protected against external attacks and threats to ensure the confidentiality, integrity and availability of their information assets, often without considering insider threat. In fact, there are several studies [1, 20] arguing that there are more threats coming from the inside then from anywhere else. It is undoubtedly the risks raised from insider threat are an important issue, with severe consequences to an organization. Therefore insider threat has to be included and treated in the security risk management process, the same way the traditional technical vulnerabilities are handled. Due to the different organizations' environments and the diverse natures of human behavior, it is required to consider the involvement of psychological approaches in combination with technological mechanisms, to understand and observe any changes in employees' behaviors and characteristics. In fact, it is important to know how well a particular set of technological controls is functioning, but it is much more important for decision makers to be able to "know what they don't know", or what is hidden in the human behavior, which can derive in a security risk.

In this context, the goal of this paper is to discuss some methodological challenges to evaluate the insider threats and its impacts, and integrate them in a security risk framework, that was defined according to the security standards ISO/IEC_JTC1, to support the security risk management process. This paper is structured as follows: in Sect. 2, some reflections regarding the risk evaluation of insider threats and its role in the risk management process are presented; Sect. 3 focuses on an overview of current approaches to address insider threats; in Sect. 4 a security risk framework and proposed methodological challenges to be included in the security risk management process are highlighted; and conclusions are presented in Sect. 5.

2 Risk Insider Threat and Security Risk Management

Nowadays, the security risk management process is well accepted and widely used by organizations. Security standards guide the information security administrator to identify critical assets and processes, to define objectives and to identify proper security controls as a main input to the risk management model. Nevertheless, security managers consider these standards not covering all the organizational security needs, mostly because they fail to address the requirements concerning assessment, which is fundamental to measure efficiency. Despite some guides towards characterization of what a good metric is, there is a long way to find models enabling objective and helpful assessments, especially within human-oriented security controls [3].

Risk is defined by the standard ISO/IEC FDIS 27000 - Information technology - Security techniques - Information security management systems - Overview and vocabulary [4], as the relation between the probability of occurrence of an event and its impacts.

In simple terms, when modeling risk, human threat can be decomposed into the factors of motivation, opportunity and capability. This approach is generally referred to as CMO Model asserting that to commit an attack, the perpetrator must first have the [5]:

- Capability: the skills to commit the attack.
- Motive: the reasons to commit an attack.
- Opportunity: the time-window and/or settings required to commit an attack.

These factors should be included in insider threat management, because the impact of insider threats can occur in multiple dimensions, such as financial loss, disruption to the organization, loss of reputation, and long-term impacts on organizational culture. These impacts are extremely difficult to measure or quantify. For example, an organizational bonus distribution may result in actions taken with angry, revenge, compensation, et cetera, with severe impacts on diverse levels of an organization. Thus, a minor or meaningless motivation can have a huge impact. In the same way, the impact may not be strictly dependent on motivation, since an accidental or unintentional act can have the same dramatic effect as a malicious motivated attack. Therefore, the main goal should be focused on avoiding crucial consequences regardless the motivation. These aspects as well as other risk accelerators should be represented in a security risk management process.

Lastly, it still remains unclear how efficient are the indicators used to assess the various prevention, detection and response techniques, in mitigating and reducing insider threat and consequently in reducing related vulnerability. In practice, there is a lack of data and studies that enable to evaluate the efficiency and effectiveness of different security policies against acts stemming from different motives.

3   Current Approaches

Currently a number of independent bodies have developed well-documented methodologies for assessing risk. In IT security, perhaps the best well known is Carnegie-Mellon's OCTAVE method [6]. Other worthy methods include (or are part of) COBIT [7], ITIL [8], CORAS [9], ISRAM [10] and CRAMM [11], as well as others that are presented and listed by ENISA [12]. However, the studies about these practices implemented in real environments reveal a poor effectiveness of the information security management processes [13, 14]. Moreover, Sadok and Spagnoeletti demonstrate with their studies that enterprises implementing widely used security practices continue to experience difficulties regarding assessing and managing their security risks, implementing appropriate security controls, and preventing security threats. This is because the available information security risk management models and frameworks mainly focus on the technical aspects of security, and do not pay much attention to the influence of environmental and insider-related problems, such as users motivation and behavior, on the reliability of the provided solutions [13, 15, 16].

In the scope of insider threats, several models have been proposed in the literature review. Some models are more focused on the prevention and detection of insider threats and others are following technical approaches. Facing a more prevention and detection-oriented approach, Schultz [2] proposes a framework for understanding and predicting insider attacks essentially based on personality traits and verbal behavior. Another model brought up by Wood [5], uses the attributes of users' knowledge, privileges and skills metrics. Moreover, Hidden Markov Models [17] have been aligned with other activity models to infer divergence activity patterns of a user. Other sciences such as psychology have been drawn up, in order to achieve the identification of an insider profile through the identification of personnel attributes, such as introversion and depression. From the background of psychology, Caputo *et al.* [18] investigate the relation between intent and user action based on the development of experimental tests. In addition, Theoharidou *et al.* [19] relates to criminology theories, designed to measure insider misuse and explore the possible enhancements to the standard ISO17799 [19]. Finally, Kandias *et al.* [20] present a model aim to predict insider behavior, through the use of user taxonomy, psychological profiling and a decision algorithm in order to identify potentially dangerous users. This model introduces a more interdisciplinary approach, since it combines technical solutions with approaches that draw upon psychology [20].

On the technical approach, Intrusion Detection Systems (IDS), in various technological architectures, are widely used, in particularly on the detection of insider violations of security policies in place. An IDS system intents to monitor the abnormal activity within the information system on a regular basis. This can be achieved using several technologies from the AI (Artificial Intelligence) area, such as the system presented by Cappelli *et al.* [21], which is based on machine learning algorithms, to analyze collected search events to detect anomalous user search behavior. Moreover, Duran [22] presents a system that models the user life cycle to analyze user interaction with insider security protection strategies. Other approaches are based on the production of baits, in order to detect potential insider abuses. The main goal is to detect derivations from an expected behavior, usually described in a security policy. However, the ultimate threats are those that don't leave a technological detectable trail in the system or make use of normal activities to undertake malicious actions.

There are multiple well-known direct sources that enable the analysis and anomalous behavior and from where a risk alert may result. This information is available from tools that an organization may already possess and use, such as security information and event management tools, like OSSIM, McAfee Enterprise Security Manager, UmbroData, Digital Attack Map, Unisys Security Index, IP reputation, among others. In addition, we can extend this list to indirect sources that typically publish information related with security threats, such as CERT repositories, CAPEC (Common Attack Pattern Enumeration and Classification enumerations and classifications), Google Help Net Security, CVE, ATLAS threat index, among others. From this information sources, it is expected that several security indicators emerge. However, to automatically process these information, it is important to (1) understand exactly what is being measured and give (useful) meanings to values; and (2) develop and define a flexible enough model framework aiming on machine based processing, as similarly seen in security policies computational enforcement frameworks. Since information security, by definition, imposes restriction to flexibility and consequently may impact business negatively, it is also desirable to carefully align security policies with business objectives. This dimension should also be part of the set of metrics used to assess risks and security controls' efficiency.

Despite there exists a substantial number of models addressing insider threats, they tend to solve the problem in a limited point of view, focusing on dedicated metrics which are very difficult to integrate in a unified risk assessment approach [20, 23]. In the following section, we present a model that structure a hierarchy of security concepts, in order to facilitate a proper management of information security risks, emphasizing some methodological challenges due to organizational insider threat.

4   A Conceptual Model Developed in the Context of IS Security Risk Management

The study work in the field of attacks, threats and assets' vulnerabilities concerning information systems continues to grow because they are evolving and have a significantly impact. Managing such an environment requires both a detailed understanding of security concepts and their relationships. The concepts defined in the conceptual model are based on a wide recognized standard, produced by ISO/IEC_JTC1 (the ISO/IEC 27000). The hierarchical relation between the concepts assists organizations with regard to an implementation of the right combination of protection controls to mitigate security risks. In practice, the implementation of a conceptual model, richly represents security concepts and their relationships in terms of threats, attacks, vulnerabilities, assets and countermeasures, and thus facilitates a more efficient management of information systems security [24].

The advantages of this approach to organizations are:

1. a proper identification of the valued or critical assets
2. an accurate identification of the assets vulnerabilities
3. to be able to identify and mitigate potential threats
4. a proper evaluation of organizational risks
5. an adequate evaluation of the efficiency and effectiveness of the security policies and safeguards defined and therefore analyze and implement the necessary adjustments to security policy adopted.

The defined conceptual model comprises 8 concepts and 16 relationships, and is built up as a hierarchy structure, as illustrated in Fig. 1. These concepts are described as follows [26]:

Incident: a single or series of unwanted or unexpected events that might have significant probability to compromise the information system security.

(Security) Event: an identified occurrence of a particular set of circumstances that changed the status of the information system security.

Asset: any resource that has value and importance to the organization, which includes information, programs, network and communications infrastructures, software, operating systems, computers and people.

Confidentiality, integrity, availability properties (CIA): the information properties to be ensured, namely confidentiality, integrity and availability; besides these aspects, main security properties, and depending on the context, other security properties may need to be addressed, such as authenticity, accountability and reliability.

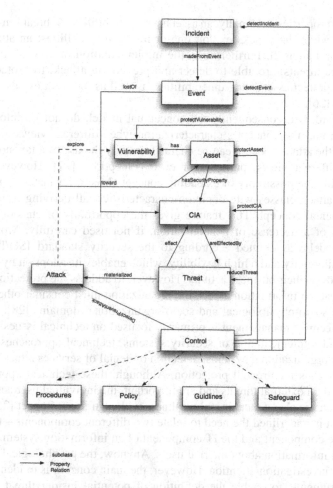

Fig. 1. Hierarchical concepts defined in the conceptual model [26]

Threat: the types of dangers against a given set of properties (security properties). The attributes defined in this concept follow the Pfleeger approach [25], which includes an attacker (insider or external), actions or a position to perform an interception, fabrication, modification and interruption, over a resource.

Attack: a sequence of actions executed by some agents (machine-aided or manual) exploring any vulnerability.

Control: mechanisms used to detect an incident or an event, to protect an asset and security properties, to reduce a threat and to minor or prevent the effects of an attack.

Vulnerability: represents any weakness of the system.

In short, the rationale behind this model is structured as follows: an incident is made from – *madeFromEvent* – events; the occurrence of an event can lead to a loss of – *lostOf* – a set of security properties (CIA); an asset has security properties – *hasSecurityProperties* – and each one can be affected by a threat, while a threat can affect one or more security properties and finally, an asset has vulnerabilities. A threat is materialized by an attack, while the attacks exploit one or more vulnerabilities; an attack is also triggered toward an asset. Furthermore, the implementation of control mechanisms help to reduce threats, are able to detect and prevent an attack, to protect security properties, to protect assets and vulnerabilities, as well as to detect events, in order to protect assets [26].

The standard, and consequently the conceptual model, do not go into fine grain details concerning the concept's characterization when different views are possible. For instance, the attack concept can be characterized by the use of a taxonomy, taking in account different views, purposes or even perceptions [27]. However, there is nothing limiting the possibility of extending concept classes, for instance, regarding a definition of attack classes with common characteristics, all deriving from the same main fundamental concept. This feature gives the opportunity of customization, but with the risk of a decrease of generalization, if not used carefully. Moreover, the developed model was defined according to the security standard ISO/IEC 27000, exhibiting a simplicity and a high flexibility, which enables its adoption by any organization, regardless their business activity. However, to address the protection and mitigation of threats to information assets, the organization must consider other domains, including the socio-physiological and socio-organizational domains [28]. In general, information security management is primarily focused on technical issues concerning the design and implementation of security systems, technical approaches to prevent intrusion into organizational systems, detection of denial of services attacks, and more advanced solutions for firewall protection. Although, these technical approaches are highly focused on external threats and are important, the individual user actions inside an organization are also a meaningful weakness with significant impact [2, 17–22]. In this context, it is underlined the need to relate two different components – the psychological profile component and the IT component of an information system, in order to collect useful information about internal users. Anyhow, the psychological component needs further investigation/attention. However, the main concern is to identify a set of relevant instruments, to enable the definition of potential insider threat profiles. In practice, it must be considered an analysis of organizational users' behavior related to information security, their attitudes concerning the use of technologies and their estimations about risks in the context of their daily work. This analysis must be framed (and supported) by the organization's business strategy, including an alignment with other regulations and/or obligations.

After the risk assessment, the Chief of the Information Security Officer has all the information required to define an adequate security policy. However, aiming on the necessary managerial aspects of information security, he/she also needs to put in place the measuring process to (1) keep risk evaluation under surveillance; and (2) evaluate the efficiency of security controls chosen in order to validate the prior decisions. Desirably, this evaluation should be carried out continuously but can be an impossible task, especially concerning the aspects depending on user behavior. Indeed, if we use interviews or surveys to measure the desirable indicators and since the application of such instruments collides with the usual working tasks, we can easily figure out a negative impact on business, which will not be admissible. So we need to look for alternative ways of measuring the same behaviors, which may be achieved, at least partially, by profiling users' interaction with the help of information systems, for example through logs and events. This information is already available and used mainly for intrusion detection purposes [29], but it is possible to explore it for a more general users' behavior evaluation.

In practice, the methodological challenges include the following research tasks:

- Specification of the psychological and behavioral indicators on well-being, as well on stress/disorders of users, in accordance with the organization's security policy, its culture and legal structure. In practice, a related analysis focuses on the assess of the user's predisposition to malicious behavior;
- Evaluation of IT skills of a user. The goal is to evaluate the user's practical computer, his/her knowledge of organizational networks, databases, and techniques implemented, familiarization with specific technologies, et cetera. These information will enable the organization to identify the users' sophistication attributes;
- Development of an assessment protocol to collect users' information regarding their perceptions, meanings, attitudes and feelings, their security behavior and related risks in their daily work;
- Development of measurement indicators.

An analysis of the mentioned measures will facilitate the identification of unusual behavior within an organization, as well as other measurable insider-related characteristics, which will serve as input to responsible managers, enabling them to assess whether a user is potentially dangerous or not.

Finally, all this activities should be framed by standards used to certify organizations concerning their attitude, towards the growing risks of information security. And since organizations are increasingly interconnected and interdependent, being certified becomes a relevant management goal.

5   Conclusions

It should be accepted that employees are an important organizational' asset, but also probably causing multiple vulnerabilities that must be handled (managed and assessed) as others security vulnerabilities. However, these vulnerabilities involve people and their behaviors, which require an interdisciplinary approach to combine technical solutions with psychological approaches. A better understanding of the psychological behavior of employees and the detection of changes in their behavior and characteristics will enable organizations to gain a better understanding of the real risks and thus face them more efficiently. Meanwhile organizations must be prepared for the cultural, technological, social and economic environment changes, and be able to perform evaluations in a continual basis in order to protect their information assets.

Technology is an essential tool that supports the control accesses to information, and helps in monitoring and detecting malicious activities. Nevertheless, it is the working environment and the organizational staff that will provide the real foundations to success. The security controls must be agile and workable in multiple environments and preferably with end user cooperation, because it will certainly contribute to a better understand of the reasons for security controls implementation.

Insider risks need to be moved up in importance and discussed by decision makers prior to attacks, and not after the occurrence of a significant security incident. Currently, for any business, particularly in the security domain it is important to take proactive measures to stop the occurrence of insider attacks, instead of reactive measures. Risk management and compliance should be extended to create means of recognizing, capturing, assessing and testing insider behavior and its impact. However it is extremely difficult to measure and quantify malicious insiders' behavior unlike the measures of IT components' performance. The security benefits will certainly be higher in a longer-term rather than in a shorter-term. This must be weighted against the organizational priorities. The investments spend to face insider threats may require a substantial justification, but this is the challenge.

Acknowledgements.   This work has been supported by FCT - Fundação para a Ciência e Tecnologia in the scope of the project: PEst-UID/CEC/00319/2013.

References

1. Whitman, M., Mattord, H.: Management of Information Security, 4th edn. Cengage Learning, Boston (2013)
2. Schultz, E.E.: A framework for understanding and predicting insider attacks. Comput. Secur. **21**(6), 526–531 (2002)
3. Cohen, F.: How do we measure security? INCOSE Insight **14**(2), 30–32 (2011)
4. ISO/IEC_JTC1: ISO/IEC FDIS 27000 information technology - security techniques - information security management systems - overview and vocabulary. ISO Copyright Office, Geneva, Switzerland (2009)
5. Wood, B.: An insider threat model for adversary simulation. In: Anderson, R.H. (ed.) Research on Mitigating the Insider Threat to Information Systems. RAND (2000)
6. Alberts, C., Dorofee, A.: Managing Information Security Risks: the OCTAVE (SM) Approach, 1st edn. Addison Wesley, Boston (2002)
7. ISACA (2011) COBIT 4.1: Framework for IT governance and control [on-line]. ISACA. http://www.isaca.org/Knowledge-Center/cobit/Pages/Overview.aspx
8. ITIL 2000. Official ITIL® Website [on-line]. itSMF International. The IT Service Management Forum. http://www.itsmfi.org/content/official-itil®-website
9. Stolen, K., den Braber, F., Dirmitrakos, T.: Model-based risk assessment –the CORAS approach (2002). http://www.nik.no/2002/stolen.pdf
10. Karabacaka, B., Songukpinar, I.: ISRAM: information security risk analysis method. Comput. Secur. **24**(2), 147–169 (2005)
11. Yazar, Z.A.: Qualitative risk analysis and management tool – CRAMM. SANS Institute InfoSec Reading Room (2011)
12. ENISA. Inventory of risk management/risk assessment methods [on-line]. European Network and Information Security Agency (2011). http://rm-inv.enisa.europa.eu/rm_ra_methods.html
13. Sadok, M., Spagnoletti, P.: A business aware information security risk and analysis method. In: D'Atri, A., Ferrara, M., George, J.F., Spagnoletti, P. (eds.) Information Technology and Innovation treads in Organization, pp. 453–460. Springer, Heidelberg (2011)

14. Asosheh, A., Dehmoubed, B., Khani, A.: A new quantitative approach for information security risk assessment. In: IEEE International Conference on Intelligence and Security Informatics 2009 (ISI 2009), pp. 229–239, 8–11 June 2009. http://ieeexplore.ieee.org/stamp/stamp.jsp?tp=&arnumber=5137311&isnumber=5137253. doi: 10.1109/ISI.2009.5137311

15. Posey, C., Roberts, T.L., Lowry, P.B., Bennett, R.J., Courtney, J.: Insiders' protection of organizational information assets: development of a systematics-based taxonomy and theory of diversity for protection-motivated behaviors. MIS Q 37(4), 1189–1210 (2013)

16. Posey, C., Roberts, T.L., Lowry, P.B., Hightower, R.T.: Bridging the divide: a qualitative comparison of information security thought patterns between information security professionals and ordinary organizational insiders. Inf. Manag. 51(5), 551–567 (2014). doi: 10.1016/j.im.2014.03.009. http://dx.doi.org/

17. Thompson, P.: Weak models for insider threat detection. In: Carapezza, E.M. (ed.) Sensors & Command, Control, Communications & Intelligence (C3I) Technologies for Homeland Security & Homeland Defense III, vol. 5403, pp. 40–48 (2004)

18. Caputo, D., Marcus, A., Maloof, M., Stephens, G.: Detecting insider theft of trade secrets. IEEE Secur. Priv. 7(6), 14–21 (2009)

19. Theoharidou, M., Kokolakis, S., Karyda, M., Kiountouzis, E.: The insider threat to information systems and the effectiveness of ISO17799. Comput. Secur. 24(6), 472–484 (2005)

20. Kandias, M., Mylonas, A., Virvilis, N., Theoharidou, M., Gritzalis, D.: An insider threat prediction model. In: Katsikas, S., Lopez, J., Soriano, M. (eds.) TrustBus 2010. LNCS, vol. 6264, pp. 26–37. Springer, Heidelberg (2010)

21. Cappelli, D.M., Moore, A.P., Trzeciak, R.F., Shimeall, T.J.: Common Sense Guide to Prevention and Detection of Insider Threat, 3rd edn. Carnegie Mellon University, Pittsburgh (2009)

22. Duran, F., Conrad, S., Conrad, G., Duggan, D., Held, E.: Building a system for insider security. IEEE Secur. Priv. 7(6), 30–38 (2009)

23. Beres, Y., Mont, M.C., Griffin, J., Shiu, S.: Using security metrics coupled with predictive modeling and simulation to assess security processes. In: 3rd International Symposium on Empirical Software Engineering and Measurement, pp. 564–573 (2009)

24. Onwubiko, C., Lenaghan, A.P.: Challenges and complexities of managing information security. Int. J. Electro. Secur. Digit. Forensics 2(3), 306–321 (2009)

25. Pfleeger, C., Shari, L.: Security in Computing, 4th edn. Prentice Hall PTR, Upper Saddle River (2007)

26. Pereira, T.: Conceptual framework to support information security risk management. Ph.D thesis, University of Minho (2012)

27. Hansman, S., Hunt, R.: A taxonomy of network and computer attacks. Comput. Secur. 24(1), 31–43 (2005)

28. Crossler, R., Johnston, A., Lowry, P., Hud, Q., Warkentin, M., Baskerville, R.: Future directions for behavioral information security research. Comput. Secur. 32, 90–101 (2013)

29. Oliner, A., Ganapathi, A., Xu, W.: Advances and challenges in log analysis. Commun. ACM 55(2), 55–61 (2012)

Framework for Cloud Usability

Brian Stanton[1(✉)], Mary Theofanos[1], and Karuna P. Joshi[2]

[1] National Institute of Standards and Technology, Gaithersburg, MD, USA
{bstanton,maryt}@nist.gov
[2] Department of Computer Science and Electrical Engineering,
University of Maryland Baltimore County, Baltimore, MD, USA
kjoshi1@umbc.edu

Abstract. Organizations are increasingly adopting cloud-based services to meet their business needs. However, due to the complexity and diversity of cloud systems, it is important to evaluate the user experience within a framework that encompasses multiple characteristics. In this paper, we propose a cloud usability framework to provide a structure to evaluate the key attributes of the cloud user experience. The framework includes five attributes and 20 elements. Generally these describe the consumer's expectations of the cloud. The framework can be foundation for developing usability metrics for organizations interested in measuring the user experience when adopting cloud-based services.

Keywords: Usability · Cloud · Framework

1 Introduction

Cloud computing[1] is a model for enabling ubiquitous, convenient, on demand network access to a shared pool of configurable computing resources (e.g., networks, servers, storage, applications, and services) that can be rapidly provisioned and released with minimal management effort or service provider interaction [1]. Organizations are increasingly adopting cloud-based services to address their information technology (IT) needs for software, hardware or network speed [2]. To date, the driving forces behind the cloud have been technological advances and business needs that often outpace the needs of the end-user. In order to better enable ready adoption (acceptance and utilization), users' needs (and their goals) must be incorporated into the process of cloud implementation. Fundamentally, users' needs and goals drive usability.

Various cloud service providers use different models and deployment types of cloud services and so there is no consistency to the user experience. Moreover, cloud services deployed via the web or mobile device are limited by the capabilities of the browser or mobile app interface and may provide user interfaces that are of lower quality than that

---

[1] Specific hardware and software products identified in this report were used in order to perform the evaluations described. In no case does such identification imply recommendation or endorsement by the National Institute of Standards and Technology, nor does it imply that the products and equipment identified are necessarily the best available for the purpose.

© Springer International Publishing Switzerland 2015
T. Tryfonas and I. Askoxylakis (Eds.): HAS 2015, LNCS 9190, pp. 664–671, 2015.
DOI: 10.1007/978-3-319-20376-8_59

provided by traditional client server applications on a desktop platform. It is being increasingly recognized by the cloud user community that there is a need for developing cloud usability standards to ensure consistency among different cloud services purchased from different vendors [3]. Lack of a consistent user experience (see Fig. 1) in an enterprise cloud environment can result in longer time to on-board an application into the enterprise cloud, more training requirements and more technical assistance for the end users. This lack of consistency will affect the actual cost of the application to the organization. If an organization with hundreds of end users can reduce their training requirements by a day, they can improve their organizational productivity and realize cost savings.

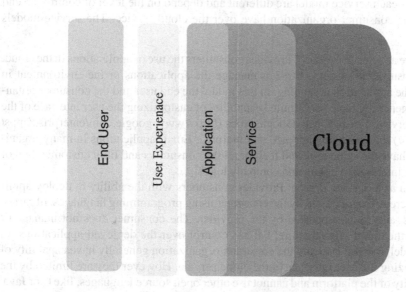

Fig. 1. The cloud user experience

The cloud pushes us to examine the user experience beyond the standard desktop computing environment of well-established usability principles, guidelines, and metrics. Thus, we have developed a framework to provide a structure to evaluate key attributes of the cloud user experience. The framework identifies five attributes further compartmented into elements and associated measures to ensure that critical usability areas are not overlooked.

2 Background

The complexity and diversity of cloud systems has made it difficult to evaluate the user experience using typical usability evaluation techniques.

2.1 Cloud Standards

National Institute of Standards and Technology (NIST)'s cloud computing initiative was aimed at standardizing the definition of cloud computing, its various models and deployment strategies. NIST's definition of the cloud mandates five essential characteristics of on-demand self service, broad network access, resource pooling, rapid elasticity, and measured service [1]. The NIST deployment models, including Private, Public, Community, and Hybrid cloud models, do not specifically address the human computer interaction or usability attributes that make up the user experience of a cloud service.

The NIST cloud model enumerates three service models. Usability elements to consider for each service model are different and depend on the level of control the end user and the consumer organization have over the cloud service. The service models include:

- Software as a Service (SaaS): Provides consumers the use of applications in the cloud. The consumer does not control or manage the applications or the environment in which the application is running. In this model the end user and the consumer organization generally have very limited capability of customizing the user interface of the cloud service. For instance, Google Apps (http://www.google.com/enterprise/apps/business/) that are being adopted as Enterprise Email applications in many organizations have the same look and feel for all the consumers and limit customization of the user interface to colors and company logos.

- Platform as a Service (PaaS): Provides consumers with the ability to deploy applications created or acquired by the consumer using programming languages, libraries, services, and tools supported by the provider. The consumer does not manage or control the cloud infrastructure, but has control over the deployed applications. In this model, the end user and the consumer organization generally have capability of customizing the user interface of the cloud service. However they are limited by the capability of the platform and cannot use other open source languages, like C or Java, to develop custom applications. For instance, Salesforce.com provides 'Salesforce1 Platform' application [4] as a PaaS cloud model that allows end users to develop apps on the salesforce platform. However, they are limited to the tools provided by Salesforce on that offering and so might be limited in getting the same user interface as other applications in their enterprise cloud that are purchased from other vendors.

- Infrastructure as a Service (IaaS): Provides consumers with the ability to provision processing, storage, networks, and other fundamental computing resources where the consumer is able to deploy and run arbitrary software, which can include operating systems and applications. The consumer does not manage or control the underlying cloud infrastructure but has control over operating systems, storage, and deployed applications. For instance, Amazon Web Services (http://aws.amazon.com/) provide a IaaS environment to their consumers who can develop personal applications using languages and tools of their choice. This model provides end users with the maximum flexibility of customizing their cloud services and so facilitates development of a consistent user interface. However, IaaS cloud services also require consumer organizations to develop in-house expertise to be able to utilize the benefits of the cloud.

As these cloud computing environment characteristics and components demonstrate decisions about moving to the cloud can be overwhelming to organizations/consumers [5]. Many frameworks and taxonomies have been developed to assist enterprises as they consider the use of the cloud [6–8]. These frameworks generally focus on technical capabilities and measure business services. Usability features have only been mentioned in passing, if at all.

3   Proposed Framework for Cloud Usability

Any usability framework should start with a good understanding of what usability is. For our purposes, we used the International Organization for Standardization (ISO) definition of usability:

> Usability is the extent to which a system, product, or service can be used by specified users to achieve specified goals with effectiveness, efficiency, and satisfaction in a specified context of use [9].

The definition provided us with a roadmap for developing the framework. It first talks about users but their goals have often been left out when considering the cloud. The definition then goes on to state three metrics: effectiveness, efficiency, and satisfaction. All of which occur within a specified context of use. It is during the development of the context of use that users' needs (and their goals) are first identified in the User Centered Design (UCD) process [9]. As can be seen in Fig. 2 User Needs are central to developing a usable system, product, or service. It is these user needs that form the basis of our framework.

Figure 3 is a pictorial representation of the NIST Cloud Usability Framework. This figure lists the various usability attributes that are of interest to cloud users.

3.1   Cloud Usability Framework

In a similar vein as the cloud Services Measurement Initiative Consortium (CSMIC) who created a framework to establish measures for quality of cloud services (Service Measurement Index (SMI) [7] we independently created a framework that characterizes the usability attributes that the cloud should contain. The framework's attributes and elements are based on other usability frameworks [10] and ISO usability standards. Consumers should expect the cloud to be Capable, Personal, Reliable, Valuable, and Secure. Each of these attributes are described below.

Cloud consumers can expect their cloud services to have certain capabilities. The four main features that they should look for in a capable cloud service are:

1. **Current:** Consumers must be able to tell if the cloud service is based on current technology. Providers upgrade their services to stay current with the state-of-art of the technology. To stay compatible with the latest release of hardware, operating system (OS) and related software applications on which it is dependent. Currently providers upgrade the technology of their services every 18 to 24 months. In the coming years, we may see a reduction in this time span.

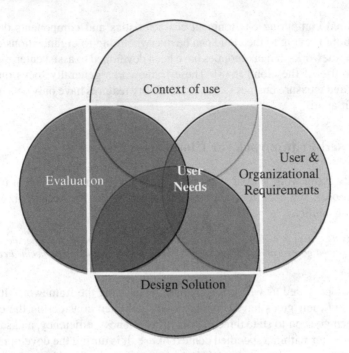

Fig. 2. The User Centered Design process

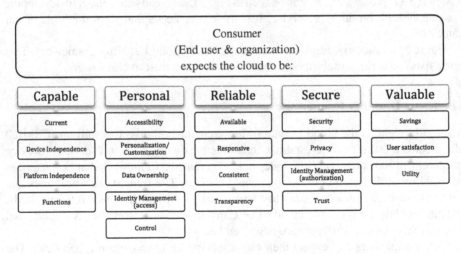

Fig. 3. Cloud usability framework

2. **Platform:** Consumers who use IaaS services want to be able to define the exact hardware specifications of the service they wish to purchase. For SaaS services, consumers want the cloud service to be independent of the cloud hardware, Operating System, etc. so that the service can function correctly on any device hardware and software setup.

3. **Device:** For a cloud service to be capable, consumers may need to be able to access the cloud service using any device type – fixed/mobile etc.
4. **Cloud Functionality:** Cloud services can be considered capable for the consumers if they provide cloud functionality, like elasticity, scalability; rapid provisioning etc., that is not possible in other platforms.

Personal. Cloud Services should allow consumers (organizations and end users) to change the look and feel of the user interface and customize service functionality to suit their needs. At times, an organization's IT policy may not allow the end users to personalize the user interface of any enterprise application; however, they may still customize the basic solution for the whole organization. There are five main elements that make up the Personal attribute:

1. **Accessibility:** Accessibility is the degree to which a product or system can be used by people with the widest range of characteristics and capabilities to achieve a specified goal in a specified context of use [11]. Cloud services should be accessible to consumers with a variety of needs.
2. **Customization:** Customization is adaptation of a software product to the needs of a particular audience [12]. Cloud services can allow consumers to change their user interface to suit their needs. Along with consumers, organizations may choose a standard customized interface for all their end users to ensure lower maintenance needs.
3. **Control:** The consumer should have a sense of control over the functionality of the cloud service. For instance, they may need to be able to determine what cookies are set by the cloud service, or be able to switch off GPS tracking if the service is accessed as a mobile application.
4. **Data Ownership:** Consumers must have ownership over the data they store in the cloud services they use. Users should be able to declare the policies on its usage (in advertisements, other services etc.). For instance, if a consumer uploads pictures to a cloud service, the consumer should be able to determine how that image is used or who has access to it.
5. **Identity Management (Access):** To ensure ease of use, multiple access authentications will have to be implemented in a seamless manner so that the consumer is not aware of the number of authentication/authorization steps they have to go through to access their applications on the cloud.

Reliable. Reliability is the ability of a system or component to perform its required functions under stated conditions for a specified period of time [11]. There are four main elements that cloud consumers look for under the Reliable attribute:

1. **Available:** Availability is defined as the ability of a service or service component to perform its required function at an agreed instant or over an agreed period of time [13]. Cloud users can expect high availability and it is not unusual to find providers advertising over 99 % availability.
2. **Responsive:** Cloud consumers may want the cloud services to have high degree of performance. The main performance measure that is of interest to the end user is the response time, which is the time it takes the service to respond to a user's request/ instruction.

3. **Consistent:** A cloud service may exhibit the same functionality under every situation, when that functionality is available. The service should also have no conflicts with the user device type (e.g., different types of desktops) accessing the service.
4. **Transparency:** The cloud service provider's service policies and technology can be transparent to the cloud consumer organization. Organizational users (like managers, database administrators, etc.) should have access, as needed, to the cloud datacenter and have details about the cloud p`latform's capabilities and planned changes. This feature is important for building trust between cloud providers and cloud consumers.

Valuable. Cloud consumers should expect cloud services to provide value to them and their organization. The three main features that can measure this value include

1. **Savings:** By using the cloud Service, users will be able to save on the costs it would take to run the same application on their personal infrastructure. In addition they will be able to consolidate and save resources they might need if they ran the same application on their personal infrastructure.
2. **User Satisfaction:** User satisfaction measures the affective experience of the service. The user satisfaction measure should be high for the user to continue consuming the service.
3. **Utility:** cloud services will be valuable to the consumers if they can provide new features that are not possible with any other IT setup. For instance, cloud services are proving to be very valuable in –
   a. Distributed computing with large datasets (Big Data Applications)
   b. Mobile /pervasive computing.

Secure. Cloud consumers want their cloud services and its data to be secure. The three main features that they are looking for in cloud services under this category are

1. **Security:** The cloud service must be resistant to attacks from unauthorized users, other cloud services, malicious software and attacks on cloud hardware and Internet network. Security attacks on a service by cloud based attackers compromise the functionality of that Service. While these attacks may not directly harm the user's private data; they will make the cloud service more vulnerable to Privacy attacks.
2. **Privacy:** The cloud service can prevent leakage of data that compromises end user's private data like personal information, financial accounts, geo-location (if not desired by the user) etc. Privacy Attacks compromise a cloud user's personal information. These attacks may not directly harm the cloud service's security, but can affect its performance. To ensure a cloud user's privacy, cloud providers authenticate or validate a user's credentials. Tools, patches, utilities and applications are deployed by the cloud providers to ensure the cloud User's privacy.
3. **Identity Management (Authorization):** The cloud service shouldn't allow unauthorized users to access user data or execute any process. The organization will designate an administrator who will be able to maintain the list of users and their authorization levels.

4. **Trust:** Cloud consumers can have confidence in the cloud service to, at least, fulfill the conditions set forth in the SLA. Trust is highly correlated with other elements such as privacy, security, and data ownership.

4   Conclusions and Ongoing Work

We have presented a framework for evaluating the user experience of the cloud. The framework builds on techniques, metrics, and guidelines from desktop computing and more recent work in ubiquitous computing. The goal of the cloud usability framework is to provide a structure to ensure that key areas of evaluation and consumer needs are not overlooked.

Finally we believe the framework is the foundation for developing usability metrics for organizations adopting the cloud. Thus our goal is to develop a method of measuring the elements in the framework and defining an associated set of usability metrics.

References

1. Mell, P., Grance, T.: The NIST Definition of Cloud Computing, (Special Publication 800-145). National Institute of Standards and Technology, Gaithersburg MD (2011)
2. Gartner predicts infrastructure services will accelerate cloud computing growth. http://www.forbes.com/sites/louiscolumbus/2013/02/19/gartner-predicts-infrastructure-services-will-accelerate-cloud-computing-growth/ (19 February 2013). Accessed 12 Sept 2013
3. Singleton, D.: It's time for a cloud UI standard. http://blog.softwareadvice.com/articles/enterprise/its-time-for-a-cloud-ui-standard-1021412/. Accessed 18 Nov 2013
4. Salesforce1 Platform. http://www.salesforce.com/platform/overview/. Accessed 18 Nov 2013
5. Goyal, P.: Enterprise usability of cloud computing environments: issues and challenges. In: 2010 Workshops on Enabling Technologies: Infrastructure for Collaborative Enterprises, pp. 54–59 (2010)
6. Garg, S.K., Versteeg, S., Buyya, R.: SMIcloud: a framework for comparing and ranking cloud services. In: 2011 Fourth IEEE International Conference on Utility and Cloud Computing (UCC), pp. 210–218, 5–8 Dec 2011. doi:10.1109/UCC.2011.36
7. Cloud services measurement initiative consortium, the service measurement index. http://csmic.org/. Accessed 6 Sept 2013
8. Vaquero, L.M., Rodero-Merino, L., Caceres, J., Lindner, M.: A break in the clouds: towards a cloud definition. SIGCOMM Comput. Commun. Rev. **39**(1), 50–55 (2008). doi:10.1145/1496091.1496100
9. ISO/IEC 9241 -210:2010 Ergonomics of human-system interaction – Part 210: Human-centred design for interactive systems
10. Scholtz, J., Consolvo, S.: Toward a framework for evaluating ubiquitous computing applications. Pervasive Comput. **3**(2), 82–88 (2004)
11. ISO/IEC 24765:2010 Systems and software engineering vocabulary
12. ISO/IEC 26514:2008 Systems and software engineering requirements for designers and developers of user documentation
13. ISO/IEC 20000-1:2011 Information technology service management

Using Logical Error Detection in Software Controlling Remote-Terminal Units to Predict Critical Information Infrastructures Failures

George Stergiopoulos[1], Marianthi Theocharidou[2], and Dimitris Gritzalis[1(✉)]

[1] Information Security and Critical Infrastructure Protection (INFOSEC) Laboratory, Department of Informatics, Athens University of Economics and Business, Athens, Greece
{geostergiop,dgrit}@aueb.gr
[2] European Commission, Joint Research Center (JRC), Security Technology Assessment Unit, Institute for the Protection and the Security of the Citizen (IPSC), Via E. Fermi 2749, 21027 Ispra, Italy
marianthi.theocharidou@jrc.ec.europa.eu

Abstract. A method for predicting software failures to critical information infrastructures is presented in this paper. Software failures in critical infrastructures can stem from logical errors in the source code which manipulates controllers that handle machinery; i.e. Remote Terminal Units and Programmable Logic Controllers in SCADA systems. Since these controllers are often responsible for handling hardware in critical infrastructures, detecting such logical errors in the software controlling their functionality implies detecting possible failures in the machine itself and, consequently, predicting single or cascading infrastructure failures. Our method may also be tweaked to provide estimates of the impact and likelihood of each detected error. An existing source code analysis method is adjusted to analyze code able to send commands to SCADA systems. A practical implementation of the method is presented and discussed. Examples are given using open-source SCADA operating interfaces.

1 Introduction

An Industrial control system (ICS) is a general term that encompasses several types of control systems, including supervisory control and data acquisition (SCADA) systems, distributed control systems (DCS), and others, such as Programmable Logic Controllers (PLC) and Remote Terminal Units (RTUs). ICSs are typically used in industries such as electrical, water, oil and gas, chemical and others [20].

An industrial control system usually has a central unit and a number of control locations. Data and commands are exchanged as messages. Many Critical Infrastructures (CIs) use Remote Terminal Units (RTUs) and Programmable Logic Controllers (PLCs) as control locations, in order to handle the machinery and functionality of an infrastructure (e.g. valves, sensors, breakers, etc.). Thus, a failure on any one of them may affect the operation of the entire infrastructure and start a cascading event, where multiple CIs fail due to their dependencies.

© Springer International Publishing Switzerland 2015
T. Tryfonas and I. Askoxylakis (Eds.): HAS 2015, LNCS 9190, pp. 672–683, 2015.
DOI: 10.1007/978-3-319-20376-8_60

A *Programmable Logic Controller* (PLC) is a microprocessor-based controller, which implements functions such as logic, sequencing, timing, counting to control machines and processes [18]. Logical rules in the form of `"if (A and B) occurs, switch on C"` are used to program this type of controllers. Similar to PLCs, *Remote Terminal Units* (RTUs) are in charge of representing the communication interface between the remote substation and the SCADA master control [2]. *Supervisory Control and Data Acquisition* (SCADA) control systems operate with coded signals over communication channels and provide control of RTU equipment [19]. RTU/PLC logical rules provide a fertile ground for logical errors, especially if business logic restrictions are imposed incorrectly when handling processes and advanced control functions.

Motivation. When industries connected SCADA systems with the Internet, these control systems were exposed to various vulnerabilities and threats [1]. Built as stand-alone, isolated control systems, they lacked the proper security measures needed to support a robust and safe functionality over the Internet. For example, an over-the-Internet, man-in-the-middle attack on a green diesel generator that led to a total melt-down has been presented in the literature [2].

Obviously, the consequences of maliciously operating SCADA systems can be devastating. Modern implementations are using the internet and allow common programming languages (such as Java) to send and receive data and commands through the central control unit to RTUs. Such implementations include, amongst others, open-SCADA [4], MODBUS4 J [17] and JAMOD [5], which uses the MODBUS protocol. The added complexity coupled with open-source components resulted in an increase in software weaknesses, vulnerabilities and failures in these types of systems [6]. A number of logical threats have been registered in public databases [7]. Source code analysis of programs that remotely control RTUs opens a path to prevent software failures. Such failures may lead to malfunction in individual controllers or infrastructures, or even initiate cascading failure to dependent infrastructures. Yet, to our knowledge, no effort has been made in detecting logical flaws in the functionality of software that controls RTUs; flaws due to erroneous implementation of the intended functionality in source code.

Example 1. Consider an RTU that controls the gas supply in an infrastructure, using coils; a faulty implementation can lead to sending the same "increase flow" command more times than what the pipe system can handle, eventually making pressure reach critical levels. Automated detection of such program behavior is a relatively uncharted territory.

Contribution. In this paper, we adjust a recently developed method for detecting logical errors in software [8–11, 33], in order to detect logical errors in high-level source code controlling Critical Infrastructure field devices (e.g. temperature sensors, valves etc.) through SCADA which implements RTUs at remote locations. We aim to detect software flaws that may create malfunctions to infrastructure control systems due to erroneous implementation of functionality into source code that controls field sensors. The presented methodology is based on static and dynamic source code analysis.

Our contribution is threefold: (a) We introduce a way to detect logical flaws in software that may lead to failures in CIs. (b) Detected flaws are classified according to their severity and likelihood of causing a failure; more dangerous failures (i.e. failures that affect critical functionality) get higher Risk values than others. (c) To support the applicability and efficiency of this approach, we present proof-of-concept example tests on appropriate software, using common, open-source implementations. Tests demonstrate the ability of this method to detect software flaws in real-world scenarios, under reasonable parameters (i.e. tests were based on plausible, albeit small, software testbed examples).

2   Related Work

Concerning control systems, research has focused mainly on securing SCADA systems through the use of alternate communication links, robust devices and added security measures [1, 2, 7]. Yet, published research suggests that software does play an important factor in cyber physical systems' stability.

An empirical analysis of software-induced failure events in the nuclear industry shows that software faults and human errors are inevitable in complex systems [31]. Recently, approaches have focused on demonstrating the effect of cyber-attacks on the physical components of cyber-physical systems. The demo presented in [32] showcases the effectiveness of attacks on terms of voltage instability to power grid and possible cascading effects to other infrastructures, as railway transport and power mark. Moreover, [14] depicts how an error in one of these systems could have a cascading and catastrophic impact on the whole infrastructure. More specifically, a software-implemented fault injection technique is used to induce errors/faults inside devices used in power grid substations. A single error in a substation device is proven able to render the operator in the control center unable to control the operation of a relay in the substation.

The method used in this paper is based on previous research [8–11, 33]. In [8], the authors describe how they used the Daikon tool [15, 16] to infer a set of behavioral specifications called likely invariants that represent the behavioral aspects during the execution of web applets. They use NASA's Java Pathfinder (JPF) [12] for model checking the application behavior over symbolic input, in order to validate whether the Daikon results are satisfied or violated. The analysis yields execution paths that, under specific conditions, can indicate the presence of certain types of logic errors that are encountered in web applications. The described method is applicable only to single-execution web applets. A variant of the method is used in [9–11], where we presented a first implementation of the APP_LogGIC tool. In [9], we specifically targeted logical errors in GUI applications. We presented a preliminary deployment of a Fuzzy Logic ranking system to address the problem of false positives and applied the method on lab test-beds. In [10], the Fuzzy Logic system was formally defined. Finally, in [11], preliminary results of a real-world application of the method were presented. The research in [13], focuses on flaws found in web applications.

The output of the method presented here can be used as partial input to risk analysis and dependency analysis methods for CIs. Research has suggested several methodologies of this type, either focusing on cascading consequences [28] or on the risk derived from potential failures in CI dependencies [3, 22–24]. Many of these methods rely on CI operators' assessment as input. Thus, they could benefit from the analysis performed in this paper; albeit only for software failure threats.

3 Building Blocks

This section describes the three building blocks of the methodology that will be developed later in this paper: (i) the methodology for modelling the functionality of software, (ii) the testing method that detects contradictions that indicate the existence of logical errors and (iii) the fuzzy system used to classify detections. These techniques are implemented as steps when detecting logical errors in software [9, 11].

3.1 Intended Functionality Model Using Dynamic Invariants

A representation of a program's behavior can be inferred in the form of dynamic invariants, i.e. source code rules in the form of assert statements. Invariants are inferred by dynamic analysis of source code using MIT's Daikon tool [15, 16]. Dynamic invariants are logical rules for variables, such as p!=null or var=="string" that hold true at certain point(s) of a program in all monitored executions. They represent program behavior.

If executions monitored by Daikon are representative use case scenarios, based on Business Logic documentation, and cover all functionality of the software under test, then the generated dynamic invariants refer to the program's intended functionality and the extracted programmed behavior matches the programmer's intended behavior [8, 9]. An example dynamic invariant generated is:

Daikon observes the values that the program computes during execution and reports, as in Fig. 1, assertions about source code variables that hold true throughout all SUT executions (much like "laws of conduct" for correct execution [10, 11]). For example, the dynamic invariant of Fig. 1 shows that, upon invocation of method exec(), the value of the variable TopLevel_Chart_count equals' 2.0'.

```
rjc.Chart.Wait_for_stable_rate_100000203_exec():::ENTER
this.TopLevel_Chart_count == 2.0
```

Fig. 1. Dynamic invariants produced by daikon dynamic analysis

3.2 Testing Invariants Against Program Executions

A possible *logical error* exists if two different versions of the same execution path are detected (i.e. same instructions executed in the same order implemented in a source code method), which differ in some state, such that one path satisfies a Daikon's dynamic invariant while the other version violates it [8].

Example 2. Consider the code in Fig. 2: Let's say that the path/state depicted in Fig. 2 shows the beginning instruction of the aforementioned method. Figure 1's invariant must hold *true* every time execution enters the rjc.Chart.Wait_for_stable_

`rate_100000203_exec()` method. Yet, it is clear from the memory read in Fig. 2, that the invariant is *violated* (false), since variable `TopLevel_ Chart_count = 1`. In this case, this path violates the corresponding dynamic invariant. If a different version of this path is found to have `TopLevel_ Chart_count = 2` in the same execution path, then a logical error is probably manifesting at that point, since two same executions lead to different states of a program [8–11, 33]. This contradiction, if present, signifies a logical error inside `exec()`.

```
[rjc/Chart.java:342] : if(this.TopLevel_Chart_count == 1)
          STATE VARIABLE: this.TopLevel_Chart_count -> 1
```

Fig. 2. Execution path output state: instruction executed and variable content

To do the aforementioned test, we need as many executions of a program's functionality as possible, in order to test its possible paths-states. Someone can do that by hand but, in realistic situations, that is not feasible. Instead we use NASA's Java Pathfinder (JPF) tool [12]. JPF is a static analysis tool able to verify Java programs and collect runtime information of a program and more [12]. Using custom-made extensions, our method symbolically executes a program's source code and analyzes multiple execution paths and states along these paths, over a wide range of input. JPF allows us to test multiple execution paths of a program against inferred dynamic invariants, in search for contradictions and violations in the description of a program's logic. Figure 2 depicts an example execution record from JPF.

3.3   Classification of Detections – Fuzzy Logic System

Verifying Dynamic Invariants - Logical Error Detection. Yet, not all possible detections are dangerous for causing unstable execution of software and, consequently, manifest failures in infrastructure controls. If a program error located in some execution path does not cause unstable execution of the software, it does not manifest as a failure [10, 11]. For this reason, this method adopts a notion of risk for classifying logical error detections. Risk is quantified by means of a fuzzy logic system based on two measuring functions, namely Severity and Vulnerability. These functions complement invariant verification and act as filters. Severity, with values from a [1, 5] Likert scale, quantifies the impact of a logical error with respect to how it affects execution. Vulnerability, with values from the same scale, quantifies the likelihood of a logical error to appear.

Severity. It refers to the impact of a source code point on execution. By measuring the Severity of a point in source code, we assign a Severity rating to the accessed variables. Source code points that affect the execution flow of software are considered dangerous, since logical errors tend to manifest on the variables used in them [8, 9, 11]; for example, the IF-statement `if(isAdmin == true)` represents a check on `isAdmin:`. This conditional branch is a control flow point where un-intended execution deviations may occur [10]. Thus, the involved transition is classified as important (rating 3–5 on the scale) and rated as **Medium (3)**. A variable is assigned only one rating, depending on how the variable is used in transitions (Table 1).

Table 1. Severity ranks in the Likert scale

Linguistic value	Condition	Severity level
Low	Random variable Severity	1
Low	Random variable Severity	2
Medium	Severity for variables holding data originated from **user input**	3
Medium	Severity for variables used <u>once</u> on an **"IF" branch**	3
High	Severity for variables used in a conditional branch <u>twice or more</u> on an **"IF" branch** and/or a **"SWITCH" branch**	4
High	Severity for variables used as a **data sink** <u>and</u> in a conditional branch on an **"IF" branch** and/or a **"SWITCH" branch**	5

Vulnerability. By measuring the Vulnerability of a source code point, we also assign the given Vulnerability rating to the accessed variables used in its transition. A variable is assigned only one overall Vulnerability rating, depending on how the variable is used. Rating conditions are presented in Table 2 below.

Table 2. Vulnerability levels in the Likert scale

Linguistic value	Condition	Vulnerability level
Low	No invariant incoherencies / No improper checks of variables.	0
Medium	Multiple propagation of input data.**No RTU functionality affected.**	2
Medium	*Multiple propagation* to method variables with improper checks. (**Might affect other functionality indirectly**).	3
Medium	*Improper/insufficient checks* on input data – Variables also used branch conditions. **Functionality doesn't involve field devices.**	4
High	*Improper/insufficient checks* on input data – Variables also used branch conditions. **Functionality involves field devices.**	5
High	*Invariant enforcement AND invariant violation* in alternate versions of same execution path. **Functionality controls field devices.**	5

Risk. Risk represents a calculated value assigned to each source code point and its corresponding variables, by aggregating the aforementioned Severity and Vulnerability ratings. It is calculated using Fuzzy Logic's linguistic variables in the form of IF-THEN rules, e.g. *"IF Severity IS low AND Vulnerability IS low THEN Risk IS low"*. For clarity, all scales (Severity, Vulnerability and Risk) share the same linguistic characterization: *"Low"*, *"Medium"* and *"High"*. A complete analysis of the Fuzzy Logic system is provided in [11]. Table 3 depicts the Risk matrix used.

4   A Method to Predict Failures in Infrastructure Software

The techniques presented in the previous section has been proven effective in detecting a subset of possible logical errors in both laboratory test-beds and real-world source code alike [8–11, 33]. Since logical errors violate the functionality of software as intended by its programmers, if that functionality corresponds to a RTU, then it is obvious that these logical errors *will* create failures in controls.

Table 3. Risk for each variable = Severity x Vulnerability

Severity Vulnerability	Low	Medium	High
Low	Low	Low	Medium
Medium	Low	Medium	High
High	Medium	High	High

The aspects presented previously in Sects. 3 and 4, can be summarized using the following sentence: If an execution path of a program controlling an RTU violates a (combination of) dynamic invariant(s) but a different version of the same path is found to enforce the same invariants, then this means that a possible logical error exists, due to the contradiction between two executions and that source code point must be analyzed to see which RTU functionality it affects. The detailed proposed method consists of the following steps to detect such logical errors in high-level code:

1. **Gather Business Logic documentation** for the *software under test* (SUT), along with any functionality restrictions and prerequisites. Since this a white box program audit, we consider that both the source code and relevant documentation is available.
   a. Model functionality into flowcharts, depicting all software interactions with hardware control systems and RTUs.
   b. Break flowchart into multiple flows, one for each intended functionality.
2. **For each flow, perform dynamic analysis** of the SUT using the Daikon tool.
   a. Sum of executions must cover the SUT's intended functionality.
   b. Gather dynamic invariants inferred in executions (invariants are rules that effectively describe the functionality analyzed during execution).
3. **Filter dynamic invariants** and keep those referring to source code methods with high risk functionality.
   a. Source code methods that manipulate control systems (such as coils). Failure in this part of the code may result in field device malfunctions.
   b. Methods imposing confidentiality, availability or integrity measures to the program communication (e.g. authentication methods etc.). Failure in this part of the source code compromises the overall security and communication between the software and the RTU.
4. **Instrument the SUT's source code with the dynamic invariants** of interest.
   a. Invariants are embedded into code as Java Assertions. An *assertion* is a statement in the Java language that enables to test assumptions about programs [27].
5. **Symbolically execute** the instrumented source code using the JPF tool.
   a. Covers a broad magnitude of possible SUT execution paths using backtracking.
   b. Tests numerous combinations of input and execution (i.e. all possible functionality; not only the intended one).
6. **Check for assertion violations**.
   a. Flag invariants detected to be both enforced and violated in a different version of the same execution path. This indicates of a logical error.

7. **Classify each detection** into <u>Severity</u> and <u>Vulnerability</u> levels. The more a source code point affect the SUT's execution, the higher it scores in the system.
   a. If detection ratings are above <u>medium (3)</u>, classify detection as high risk.
   b. If functionality affected causes a failure to a <u>component or the entire control system</u>, classify this detection as a possible initiating factor for cascading failures in depended infrastructures.

The original methodology has been previously implemented in a prototype tool with successful results in [9–11]. Briefly, the tool accepts input from Daikon (step 2) and automate steps 3 to 6 using step 2's output and the source code files.

5 Experiments and Practical Use

To the best of our knowledge, there is no commercial test-bed or open-source revision of an SUT with a reported set of existing logical errors. Since, the purpose of this article is to introduce a novel method and display its applicability, our experiments are based exclusively on formal fault injection into two different open-source test-bed examples of manipulating a RTU using Java software.

5.1 Open-Source SCADA Control Implementations

As mentioned earlier, the Internet is now widely used to connect web-based SCADA systems, since it is a cheap, efficient way to deploy geographically unrestricted control systems. Software able to communicate with such systems is being developed in high-level languages, using common open-source implementations of system protocols.

For the purposes of this article, we focus our analysis a Java library able to communicate and control SCADA systems, named JAMOD [5]. JAMOD applies the MODBUS protocol to connect software interfaces with RTUs in SCADA systems, using registers that manipulate control circuits (coils, holding registers etc.). This test utilized the tools and extensions from previous research [13].

The code found in Figs. 1 and 2 can be used with real RTUSs, like the L75 RTU unit [26]. The L75 RTU unit is an RTU that provides remote control actuation of quarter-turn valves and other rotary devices. Here, this RTU is not responsible for failure realizations; the flaw manifests in the Java code which controls the RTU.

Software-to-RTU Command Code – A Realistic Example. Let Coil 1 be the valve shaft motion control circuit. A write data command sending "FF00" will either start or continue valve movement; a write data of "0000" will stop valve movement. Other data values will return an exception response [26] Using this realistic example, we wrote a MODBUS command able to do just tha, using the function "Write Coil" on bus 5: The hexadecimal version of the command would be: 05, 05, 00, 00, FF, 00, 8D, BE. Figure 3 depicts high-level sample instructions able to control the flow of a valve, using the aforementioned command. When variable `stopFlow` is false, an "open valve" request is sent, otherwise a "close valve".

```
// MODBUS Request to open valve in Coil 0000 (hex)
if (!stopFlow) {
  hi = Integer.parseInt("FF",16); // open valve
}else {
  hi = Integer.parseInt("00",16); // close valve
}
low = Integer.parseInt("00",16);
reges = new SimpleRegister(hi, low);
write_sreq = new WriteSingleRegisterRequest(ref , reges);
trans.setRequest( write_sreq ); trans.execute(); }
```

Fig. 3. High-level code able to manipulate a gas shaft in an L75 RTU unit

The Logical Error. The logical error utilized is a real-world error taken from [29]. It is a classified CWE-226 error in the Common Weakness Enumeration database [30].

The control system must not utilize more than a specific amount of gas pipes, otherwise high pressure will cause a rupture, leaks and, consequently, a failure to the distribution system. Each time the program sends an RTU request to open a valve, it must check if the pressure in pipes has reached a maximum or not. If true, it should stop the flow. Variable "stopFlow" controls this functionality. Thus, the logical error manifests when StopFlow is updated. The software checks a pressure sensor to see if it should allow further increase in gas pressure or not. This check should take place each time a valve shaft is ordered to open. Yet, a higher number of pipes than the allowed maximum can be opened, by bypassing the aforementioned pressure check using alternate execution routes, due to sensitive information that remains unclear in objects.

To better understand this execution deviation, refer to Fig. 4. Due to an erroneous initialization of variable checked, the check can be bypassed if two consecutive "increase flow" instructions are sent within 3–4 s (i.e. before connection resets).

```
if (choice.equalsIgnoreCase("1")) {
  StopFlow = readRegisterPressure(con);
  checked = true;
  System.out.println("---    Information:    Max    pressure
reached");}
else if (choice.equalsIgnoreCase("2")) {
  if (checked) increaseFlowBugged(size, cushion);
  else System.err.println("--- Error: Check pressure"); }
```

Fig. 4. Source code example - checks imposed to handle pressure limits

5.2   Method Execution Results on the Faulty Example

To test our method on the example above, a simulator is used to emulate an RTU, since acquiring a fully operational SCADA control was not feasible. For our needs, we used the PLCSimulator [27], originally created to allow testing of Texas Instruments 500 MODBUS RTU serial driver without the need for physical equipment. It supports MODBUS over TCP, so this makes it ideal for testing purposes. We deployed the method presented in Sect. 5. The results for each step were the following (only output concerning the flaw is presented due to space limitations):

Step 1. Functionality in this example has two flows currently available:

```
A. Exec choice(1), Exec choice(2).
B. Exec choice(2), Exec choice(1), Exec choice(2).
```

Steps 2–3. Dynamic analysis of flows yielded 40 dynamic invariants for the selected functionality. Amongst them, the next invariant refers to the hidden logical error:

```
Bug.readRegisterPressure():::ENTER
this.checked == false
```

meaning that, upon entering execution of method `readRegisterPressure()`, variable `checked` should always be FALSE.

Steps 4–6. Dynamic invariants where instrumented inside the source code in their corresponding points and the software was executed symbolically. An assertion violation was detected for method `readRegisterPressure()`: Two execution were found where checked was TRUE and FALSE respectively, implying a logical error.

Step 7. Our method classified this invariant with **Severity = 3** (*variables used in a conditional branch once*) and **Vulnerability = 5** (*Invariant enforcement AND invariant violation in alternate versions of same path - Functionality controls RTUs*), thus yielding a **total Risk value of ~4.5** for the specific dynamic invariant and its variable.

6   Conclusions and Limitations

Results show that detecting logical error in software that may lead to CI failures is indeed feasible (up to a certain complexity level) even in real-world implementations. The use of Fuzzy Logic can exclude errors in non-critical points of the source code which do not divert execution. Risk output can be used as input to existing risk analysis methods. Currently diverse methodologies rely on expert opinion to estimate the likelihood and impact of possible threats [3, 21–24]. Introducing technical results contributes to the accuracy of assessments (albeit only for software threats).

Yet, the method suffers by the same limitations as its original form. Complex invariant rules need deep semantic analysis and loops are not supported [11]. Daikon's dynamic execution must cover as much SUT functionality as possible, otherwise, dynamic invariants inferred will not correctly describe the source code's behavior, as intended by its programmer. Logical errors that are not software-based, such as programmable circuits, cannot be analyzed using the current method.

Acknowledgment. This project has received funding from the European Union's Seventh Framework Programme for Research, Technological Development and De-mon-stration, under grant agreement no. 312450. The European Commission's support is gratefully acknowledged.

References

1. Krutz, R.: Securing SCADA Systems. Wiley, Indianapolis (2005)
2. Alcaraz, C., Lopez, J., Zhou, J., Roman, R.: Secure SCADA framework for the protection of energy control systems. Concurrency Comput. Pract. Experience **23**(12), 1414–1430 (2011)
3. Theoharidou, M., Kotzanikolaou, P., Gritzalis, D.: Risk assessment methodology for interdependent critical infrastructures. Int. J. Risk Assess. Manag. Special Issue on Risk Analysis of Critical Infrastructures **15**(2/3), 128–148 (2011)
4. OpenSCADA: Open-source supervisory control and data acquisition system. http://openscada.org/. Accessed 2014
5. Wimberger, D.: Jamod - Java modbus implementation (jamod.sourceforge .net). http://jamod.sourceforge.net/ (2004). Accessed 2014
6. Cardenas, A., Amin, S., Sastry, S.: Research challenges for the security of control systems. In: 3rd USENIX Workshop on Hot Topics in Security (HotSec 2008), USA (2008)
7. Chikuni, E., Dondo, M.: Investigating the security of electrical power systems SCADA. In: AFRICON (2007)
8. Felmetsger, V., Cavedon, L., Kruegel, C., Vigna, J.: Toward automated detection of logic vulnerabilities in web applications. In: Proceedings of the 19th USENIX Symposium, USA (2010)
9. Stergiopoulos, G., Tsoumas, B., Gritzalis, D.: Hunting application-level logical errors. In: Barthe, G., Livshits, B., Scandariato, R. (eds.) ESSoS 2012. LNCS, vol. 7159, pp. 135–142. Springer, Heidelberg (2012)
10. Stergiopoulos, G., Tsoumas, B., Gritzalis, D.: On business logic vulnerabilities hunting: the APP_LogGIC framework. In: Lopez, J., Huang, X., Sandhu, R. (eds.) NSS 2013. LNCS, vol. 7873, pp. 236–249. Springer, Heidelberg (2013)
11. Stergiopoulos, G., Katsaros, P., Gritzalis, D.: Automated detection of logical errors in programs. In: Lopez, J., Ray, I., Crispo, B. (eds.) CRiSIS 2014. LNCS, vol. 8924, pp. 35–51. Springer, Heidelberg (2015)
12. The Java PathFinder tool. NASA Ames Research Center. babelfish.arc.nasa.gov/trac/jpf/
13. Doupe, A., Boe, B., Vigna, G.: Fear the EAR: discovering and mitigating execution after redirect vulnerabilities. In: Proceedings of the 18th ACM Conference on Computer and Communications Security, pp. 251–262, ACM (2011)
14. Kuan-Yu, T., Chen, D., Kalbarczyk, Z., Iyer, R.: Characterization of the error resiliency of power grid substation devices. In: 42nd Annual IEEE/IFIP International Conference on Dependable Systems and Networks, pp. 1–8, 25–28 June 2012
15. Ernst, M., Perkins, J., Guo, P., McCamant, S., Pacheco, C., Tschantz, M., Xiao, C.: The Daikon system for dynamic detection of likely invariants. Sci. Comput. Program. **69**, 35–45 (2007)
16. The Daikon invariant detector manual. http://groups.csail.mit.edu/pag/daikon/
17. MODBUS4J. http://sourceforge.net/projects/modbus4j/. Accessed January 2014
18. Bolton, W.: Programmable Logic Controllers. Elsevier, Amsterdam (2009)
19. IEEE Standard C37 1994. Definition, Specification and analysis of systems used for supervisory control, data acquisition and automatic control

20. Stouffer, K., Falco, J., Kent, K.: Guide to supervisory control and data acquisition and industrial control systems security. NIST (2008)
21. EAR/Pilar-risk analysis environment. http://www.ar-tools.com/en/index.html
22. Kotzanikolaou, P., Theoharidou, M., Gritzalis, D.: Interdependencies between critical infrastructures: analyzing the risk of cascading effects. In: Bologna, S., Hämmerli, B., Gritzalis, D., Wolthusen, S. (eds.) CRITIS 2011. LNCS, vol. 6983, pp. 104–115. Springer, Heidelberg (2013)
23. Kotzanikolaou, P., Theoharidou, M., Gritzalis, D.: Assessing n-order dependencies between critical infrastructures. Int. J. Crit. Infrastruct. **9**(1/2), 93–110 (2013)
24. Kjølle, G., Utne, I., Gjerde, O.: Risk analysis of critical infrastructures emphasizing electricity supply and interdependencies. Reliab. Eng. Syst. Saf. **105**, 80–89 (2012)
25. Oracle Java SE documentation. http://docs.oracle.com/. Accessed 2014
26. FlowServe L75 series electric actuator. FCD LMAIM7502-00 – 07/05
27. PLCSimulator. http://www.plcsimulator.org/. Accessed 2014
28. Kotzanikolaou, P., Theoharidou, M., Gritzalis, D.: Cascading effects of common-cause failures on critical infrastructures. In: Butts, J., Shenoi, S. (eds.) Critical Infrastructure Protection VII. IFIP AICT, vol. 417, pp. 171–182. Springer, New York (2013)
29. Boland, T., Black, P.: Juliet 1.1 C/C++ and JAVA test suite. Computer **45**(10), 88–90 (2012)
30. The common weakness enumeration initiative. MITRE Corporation. cwe.mitre.org/
31. Fan, C., Yih, S., Tseng, W., Chen, W.: Empirical analysis of software-induced failure events in the nuclear industry. Saf. Sci. **57**, 118–128 (2013)
32. Soupionis, Y., Benoist, T.: Demo abstract: demonstrating cyber-attacks impact on cyber-physical simulated environment. In: ACM/IEEE International Conference on Cyber-Physical Systems, p. 222, 14–17 April 2014
33. Stergiopoulos, G., Katsaros, P., Gritzalis, D.: Source code profiling and classification for automated detection of logical errors. In: Proceedings of the 3rd International Seminar on Program Verification, Automated Debugging and Symbolic Computation, Germany (2014)

Applying the ACPO Guidelines to Building Automation Systems

Iain Sutherland[1,3(✉)], Theodoros Spyridopoulos[2], Huw Read[1,4], Andy Jones[3,4], Graeme Sutherland[5], and Mikhailia Burgess[1]

[1] Noroff University College, 4608 Kristiansand S, Vest Agder, Norway
Iain.sutherland@noroff.no
[2] Faculty of Engineering, University of Bristol, Bristol, UK
[3] Security Research Institute, Edith Cowan University, Perth, Australia
[4] Faculty of Computing, Engineering and Science, University of South Wales, Pontypridd, UK
[5] North Building Technologies, 95 Ditchling Road, Brighton, UK

Abstract. The increasing variety of Internet enabled hardware devices is creating a world of semi-autonomous, interconnected systems capable of control, automation and monitoring of a built environment. Many building automation and control systems that have previously been limited in connectivity, or due to cost only used in commercial environments, are now seeing increased uptake in domestic environments. Such systems may lack the management controls that are in place in commercial environments. The risk to these systems is further increased when they are connected to the Internet to allow control via a web browser or smartphone application. This paper explores the application of traditional digital forensics practices by applying established good practice guidelines to the field of building automation. In particular, we examine the application of the UK Association of Chief Police Officers guidelines for Digital Evidence, identifying the challenges and the gaps that arise in processes, procedures and available tools.

Keywords: Building control system · Forensics · ACPO · Embedded systems

1 Introduction

Building Automation Systems (BAS)[1] have been around for a number of decades with the technology used in commercial premises such as hotels and shopping centers to monitor and control various aspects of the building. Provided functionality includes environmental controls (air conditioning, lighting), security systems (alarms, security shutters and fire control systems) and transport systems (lifts, escalators and walkways) [1]. One advantage of building automation is that it enables the most efficient use of buildings' environmental controls, so reducing costs for owners. In addition to being commonly used in office and retail structures these automation systems are also used in specialist settings such as law enforcement and prison access systems. These systems

---

[1] Sometimes also referred to as Building Control Systems, Intelligent or Smart buildings.

© Springer International Publishing Switzerland 2015
T. Tryfonas and I. Askoxylakis (Eds.): HAS 2015, LNCS 9190, pp. 684–692, 2015.
DOI: 10.1007/978-3-319-20376-8_61

are now being gradually adopted into domestic environment [2]. However, due to the increasing use of BAS systems, they form an attractive target for cyber attacks. The disruption or destruction of such systems due to malicious actions can have a significant impact. Although there has been some research [3, 4] on the security analysis and protection of such systems there is still much to be done, especially in the field of post-incident analysis where information from past incidents can help strengthen the system against future events.

This paper presents a first step towards a digital forensics investigation process in BAS systems, exploring the application of commonly accepted digital forensics investigation guidelines [5] in BAS systems. We present the current threat landscape and security risks in this area and identify the challenges that arise when traditional digital forensics is applied.

The rest of the paper is structured as follows: Sect. 2 presents key concepts building automation systems along with utilized technology. In Sect. 3 we present the current threat landscape and security risks. Section 4 investigates the application of the ACPO guidelines in a BAS, presenting the challenges that arise in each step. Finally, Sect. 5 presents the conclusions of our work.

2 Building Automation Systems

In addition to reduced costs, building automation provides additional smart functionality; emergency systems are being developed for commercial premises that, for instance, highlight exit signs based on the location of a fire to provide a safe method of evacuation [6, 7]. The increasing production of the 'Internet of Things' is heading toward an accelerated growth in the adoption of building automation systems in domestic environments. Current home automation systems can be divided into two types. The first is simple systems that allow the users to monitor and control devices via a web interface or through their smart phones and are now available on the consumer market. At present these relate to controlling entertainment systems, lighting or domestic energy consumption, for example the Nest thermostat [8]. The second alternative is a fully automated system for domestic use from a supplier specialising in domestic systems [9–14]). It is estimated that the US market alone will grow by 40% between 2014 and 2019 with 6% of homes in the USA already having some degree of automation [2].

The increasing uptake of building automation and the expanding capabilities raises the probability of these systems having the potential to appear in an investigation. The question must therefore be asked as to how these systems would be analysed if deemed necessary in a digital investigation.

2.1 BAS Technology and Implementations

There are a variety of different organisations in the market looking at standards and industry practices concerning commercial building control systems [15–17]. The most commonly used commercial communication protocols are BACnet, LonTalk and Modbus (with Modbus being a popular and free protocol). Commonly "two-wire"

RS485 networks are used in the field bus due to its large range (1000 m). Shorter range connections from a controller to a computer (usually a standard desktop PC) are made using an RS232 connection which is limited to a 15 m range.

More recently, the IP network of the building has been utilized allowing for greater flexibility in installation and reducing the wire costs by using one common network supporting multiple protocols at the same time. Although [18] recommend that commercial building control systems use a separate network infrastructure to ensure security on the system, the end customer may not necessarily mandate this requirement. It remains to be seen if this practice is adopted in domestic systems.

IP Connectivity also has the advantage of buildings in different cities or countries being able to communicate with each other over the Internet [19].

Within a building, different devices have varying amounts of storage capacity. For example a smaller device such as a ceiling air conditioning unit may be limited to holding only current settings and active alarm data. Multiple units may then be managed by a larger master unit which would collect information over a field bus and hold a limited 'event log' e.g. one Programmable controller used to integrate devices, the North Commander, holds 500 alarms and 2000 log entries [20].

Utilising the protocols above, or manufacturers' proprietary protocols, an additional piece of hardware could be used to interface different systems within a building. This would allow different products on different networks to share information. The additional hardware interface scans the different devices on the network according to a specified rate, which is configured at the time of installation. The installing engineer then elects how often each system is queried for available data. Systems might be queried for alarms, which are then stored, thus expanding the events logs (into the thousands) to allow for a detailed history of system activity.

In larger building networks, a PC is used to collect information from the interface hardware or directly from systems. The storage capacity of the PC is now the only limitation on the size of the event log. A desktop PC also tends to be used as a GUI so that the user can adjust system settings rather than being limited to settings pre-specified by the installation engineer. The PC or interface hardware can transmit critical information to users via an SMS or email, providing them with notifications of events within a building based on tailored user requirements.

The focus of building automation systems is communication and control. The protocols currently used are inherently insecure [21] as security was not a major concern when these protocols were conceived. Consequently, most systems do not make use of encryption and most end devices do not support encryption. Commercial building automation systems typically communicate in ASCII format and controlling computer systems may store alert logs, configurations and settings also in ASCII within comma-separated formatted files (CSV) which are stored, unencrypted, on the controlling PC. Some aspects of security systems may however use encryption. Door access controls are encrypted inside the door or access system, but messages from the door systems to the BAS are not encrypted. Access to the controlling computer on the building network could therefore potentially enable access to door and alarm systems.

Current home automation systems use a number of proprietary protocols depending on the supplier [9, 10, 12, 14]. However, there are standards such as Zigbee and KNX.

The Zigbee system [22] is wireless and based on 802.15.4. KNX [23] which uses a number of different physical communication methods, has been recognised as an open standard and formalised as an international standard: ISO/IEC 14543-3-10:2012. The divide between commercial and home automation standards is somewhat artificial as it is possible to find combinations of the systems running in both domestic and commercial settings. Manufacturers of certain home entertainment automation systems are unable to interface into other commercial devices e.g. air conditioning units and therefore may use the service of an integration company to connect these systems. Zigbee [21] is high-lighting the advantages of using the Zigbee standard in commercial premises when refurbishing commercial property as it avoids the expense related to rewiring.

3 Threats -Security Risks/Misuse

Concerns on security issues with possible use of botnets inside building control systems have already been raised. Wendzel [4] has already highlighted the possibility of these systems being breached and the theoretical risk of the building control system being incorporated into a Botnet. Fisk [3] recommended the hard wiring of some systems to enable them to continue to function without intelligent control in the event of an attack. Rios [24] has highlighted the ease with which some building systems can be compro-mised. The Shodan search engine [25] highlights the risk of these systems being online as this provides a facility for searching for online systems and thus potentially providing a catalogue of systems vulnerable to attack. The increased use in home systems broadens the target landscape for the attackers and increases the potential impact of a successful attack.

A few examples of successful attacks have already been highlighted: In 2013 researchers [26] uncovered a vulnerability that would have allowed them to control the Heating, Ventilation, and Air Conditioning (HVAC) systems within Google's Wharf 7 building in Sydney, Australia. There are therefore concerns regarding the security stance used in these systems, for example the Tridium Niagara system in use in Google. In a Washington Post interview in 2012 [27], Tridium executives were quoted as saying:

> "...attacks seemed unlikely, because hackers had not traditionally targeted such systems. In interviews, the executives said they and their customers generally assumed that control systems were buffered somewhat by their obscurity..."

A potential problem of BAS is that devices may not have been designed to be indi-vidually secure, although newer standards like Zigbee include security, albeit limited, within the system. Additionally, integrators may install systems in an insecure manner as system performance is determined by the customers' specification, which then leave the system vulnerable to being compromised [27]. Issues may also arise due to the information provided to the company when installing the devices. For example, a company was requested to automate a swimming pool system and implemented the system according to the provided specification. However, during testing it was noted that although this had been implemented according to the specification provided, this equated to the maximum values supported by the plant systems and not the maximum desirable settings i.e. this would enable the entire chlorine reservoir contents to be delivered into the pool in one dosage. A similar oversight when specifying a security system may leave a building vulnerable or even hazardous.

Information on specific BAS systems may also be easy to obtain. For instance, they may be released as part of the tender/contractual process and it should be noted that organizations might specify features of an existing system for integration purposes. This is the case with the Los Angeles Airport Terminal building [28]. If the manufacturer and model of the devices used in BAS are known, then publicly available engineering documents can provide details on how to control the devices and, in some cases, provide default passwords. Connecting these systems to smart phones and enabling Internet connectivity to support control and maintenance exposes them to additional security risks.

4   Forensic Practices

The expansion of the number of BAS systems in use, coupled with the threat of cyber attack or misuse suggests that at some point there will be the need to investigate these types of systems. Their interconnectivity and complexity, along with their domestic use, renders them an attractive target, particularly when domestic systems may also include other smart systems such as entertainment devices or fitness/health monitoring systems that may collect personal data [29]. The ability to respond to critical cyber-security incidents is crucial, but the question remains as to how these systems are analysed. Therefore, the application of the traditional digital forensics practices as they are presented through good practice guidance would appear to be the first logical step in proposing a system of analysis. The ACPO [5] guidelines are issued by the Association of Chief Police Officers of England, Wales and Northern Ireland and put forward four principles to ensure the accuracy and admissibility of evidence:

1. *No action should be taken that could change data that will later be relied upon in court.*
2. *Where live evidence must be accessed it should be done so only by experienced competent personnel.*
3. *An audit trail must be kept of all processes applied to evidence such that an independent party can follow and achieve the same results.*
4. *The case officer ensures that the law and these principles are adhered to.*

Principles 3 and 4 mainly relate to the way in which a case is processed. Principles 1 and 2 require a detailed understanding of the systems functionality and this may pose a number of challenges during an investigation. These challenges are described according to the recommendations put forward in ACPO [5] concerning the stages related to the acquisition and processing of digital evidence: *Plan, Capture, Analyse, Present.*

4.1   Plan

Planning requires investigators to *"develop appropriate strategies to identify the existence of digital evidence and to secure and interpret that evidence throughout the investigation"* [5]. Investigators are expected to understand the systems they are called to analyse and to apply resources to the most appropriate areas. There are then some potential difficulties in the planning stage:

Challenge 1: Most digital forensics investigators have little experience on BAS devices or the range of protocols present in a BAS.

Challenge 2: It is quite difficult to preserve the integrity and authenticity of evidence while conducting a digital forensics analysis in such systems. Due to the potential complexity of such systems there is the potential for a single investigative action within such an environment of increased interconnectivity to inadvertently alter evidence across the whole BAS system. A live analysis under such circumstances therefore presents some significant challenges.

4.2 Capture

In the planning stage, the investigator determines the specific types of hardware and software they are likely to face and selects the tools that will be used in the investigation process. In a BAS relevant data may reside in:

- The end device - 'slave system' in the Modbus protocol, or part of the mesh network in a Zigbee based system.
- Intermediate systems if information is buffered within the system
- Wired and wireless network communication devices that might have buffering or logging capabilities.
- The controlling computer system, if present, in logs, configuration files and other Security devices, such as Intrusion Detection Systems (IDS) or Intrusion Prevention Systems (IPS).

Challenge 3: A challenge that arises when capturing data is the wide variety of different protocols and standards potentially utilised within one building installation. This, along with the additional manufacturer specific commands used by end systems can make the collection stage time consuming.

The capture phase is the collection of evidence from data sources using the appropriate tools. This may cover both 'live' forensics and 'static' forensics, based on the nature of the data that needs to be captured. Live forensics is the process of data capturing from volatile storage media from end devices. The investigator has to be both careful and fast in order to capture data related to the incident without compromising integrity and authenticity.

Challenge 4: In a BAS system live forensics can involve highly volatile data constantly produced by the end devices, along with the perpetual function of those devices. This may result in the loss of evidence, especially when the system is not forensically ready. Additionally, dealing with network systems where evidence may only exist for short periods of time in buffers or in "live" data flows are also a consideration.

Challenge 5: The physical end devices may neither be readily accessible nor easily locatable by the investigator. Systems mounted in difficult to access areas will be a challenge to acquire data from, potentially making some sources unobtainable. This also assumes an accurate and complete record of all devices within the BAS is available, which may not be the case for those systems that have evolved and increased in complexity over time.

4.3 Analyse

This stage includes identifying data of potential evidential value, evidence of exploits or actions from specific users. Eventually, a timeline of activities is constructed that represents all actions relative to the incident, giving the investigator the ability to correlate events that took place within the system. In this way the investigator gathers additional knowledge regarding the vulnerabilities of the system and the identity of the perpetrator.

Challenge 6: Analysing evidence from various data sources can be time-consuming. In an environment of disparate embedded systems and IoT devices the vast volume of data created can be difficult to analyse. Additionally, correlating the evidence from multiple data sources further complicates the situation.

Challenge 7: The correlation of data that come from a large network of devices requires high synchronisation capabilities among the end devices. A lack of synchronisation may result in false evidence and a misleading timeline of events.

4.4 Present

It is imperative that the investigator keeps track of the whole process and documents all steps taken as the investigator may be required to present the final results of the investigation in court as an expert witness. Due to the specialised nature of the system, this may also pose a number of challenges when explaining the evidence uncovered from this type of system to a jury.

5 Conclusions

Building automation systems enable a wide variety of different devices to be connected to facilitate the management of different environmental conditions. There can be a broad range of different types of technology and protocols used to implement building control systems. The complexity and lack of familiarity can pose a problem when analysing a BAS as part of an investigation. The use of good practice guidelines (ACPO) can help to clarify the challenges and improve analysis. Such analysis may also disclose the system's vulnerable points in order to avoid future events. Furthermore, the adoption of automated mechanisms and techniques for the evidence collection and analysis will eventually lead to improved incident response times. However, collecting and analysing evidence will not only reveal information regarding the system's vulnerabilities, but may also provide useful information regarding the culprit's identity. The whole process of evidence collection, analysis and presentation is realised in traditional systems through the digital forensics investigation process and the same processes and methods can be applied to BAS.

Acknowledgments. The authors would like to thank EBS for proof reading the final version of the paper.

References

1. Kwona, O., Leea, E., Bahnb, H.: Sensor-aware elevator scheduling for smart building environments. Build. Environ. **72**, 332–342 (2014)
2. Berg Insight AB: Smart Homes and Home Automation—3rd Edition (2014). http://www.berginsight.com/ReportList.aspx?m_m=3
3. Fisk, D.: Cyber security, building automation, and the intelligent building. Intell. Build. Int. **4**, 169–181 (2012). doi:10.1080/17508975.2012.695277
4. Wendzel, S., Zwanger, V., Meier, M., Szlósarczyk, S.: Envisioning Smart Building Botnets. In: Sicherheit LNI 228, pp. 319–329, GI Vienna (2014)
5. Association of Chief Police Officers (ACPO): Good Practice Guide for Digital Evidence, Version 5, October 2011. http://www.acpo.police.uk/documents/crime/2011/201110-cba-digital-evidence-v5.pdf
6. Chen, C.Y.: The design of smart building evacuation system. Int. J. Comput. Technol. Appl. **5**(1), 73–80 (2012)
7. Cho J., Lee G., Won J., Ryu E.: Application of Dijkstra's algorithm in the smart exit sign. In: The 31st International Symposium on Automation and Robotics in Construction and Mining (ISARC 2014)
8. Nest (2015). https://nest.com
9. AMX Corporation (2015). http://www.amx.com/
10. Control4: Home automation (2015). http://www.control4.com/
11. LeGrand Building Control Systems. http://www.legrand.co.uk/building-control
12. Crestron. http://www.crestron.com/markets/corporate_boardroom_and_building_automation/
13. Lutron residential solutions. http://www.lutron.com/en-US/Residential-Commercial-Solutions/Pages/Residential-Solutions/WholeHomeSolutions.aspx
14. SAVANT systems. https://www.savant.com/
15. Continental Automated Buildings Association (CABA): About Us. http://www.caba.org/about
16. Modbus: About Modbus Organisation. http://www.modbus.org/about_us.php
17. IEC: About the International Electrotechnical Commission: Vision and Mission (2015). http://www.iec.ch/about/?ref=menu
18. NIST: Guide to Industrial Control System (ICS) Security, Special Publication 800-82 (2011)
19. Canzler: Deutsche Telekom AG MUlti-property Building Management (2015). http://www.canzler.de/images/stories/3_Referenzen/3.4_Downloadbereich/EN/Liegenschaftsuebergreifendes%20Gebaeudemanagement%20E%2020131218.pdf
20. North Building Technologies: North Commander (2015). http://www.northbt.com/products/commander/
21. Hayes G., El-Khatib K.: Securing modbus transactions using hash-based message authentication codes and stream transmission control protocol. In: Third International Conference on Communications and Information Technology (ICCIT), pp. 179–184 (2013)
22. Zigbee Alliance. http://www.zigbee.org/
23. KNX association. http://www.knx.org/knx-en/index.php
24. Rios, B.: Owning a Building: Exploiting Access Control and Facility Management Systems. https://www.blackhat.com/asia-14/archives.html#Rios

25. Shodan Metadata Search Engine. http://www.shodanhq.com/
26. Rios, B.: Google's Buildings Hackable (2013). http://blog.cylance.com/blog/bid/297050/Google-s-Buildings-Hackable
27. O'Harrow Jr., R.: Tridium's Niagara Framework: Marvel of connectivity illustrates new cyber risks. 12 July 2012, Washington Post (2012). http://www.washingtonpost.com/investigations/tridiums-niagara-framework-marvel-of-connectivity-illustrates-new-cyber-risks/2012/07/11/gJQARJL6dW_story_1.html
28. FBI: Vulnerabilities in Tridium Niagara Framework Result in Unauthorized Access to a New Jersey Company's Industrial Control System, 23 July 2012. Situational Information Report, Federal Bureau of Investigation, Newark Division, SIR-00000003417 (2012). http://www.wired.com/images_blogs/threatlevel/2012/12/FBI-AntisecICS.pdf
29. Los Angeles World Airport: Terminal Building Automation System (2012). http://www.lawa.org/uploadedFiles/LAXDev/Construction_Handbook/Guide_Specs/25%2020%2000%20Terminal%20Building%20Automation%20System%20%28BAS%29.pdf
30. Petroulakis, N.E. Askoxylakis, I.G. Tryfonas T.: Life-logging in smart environments: challenges and security threats. In: 2012 IEEE International Conference on Communications (ICC), pp. 5680–5684 (2012). doi:10.1109/ICC.2012.6364934

Visualizing BACnet Data to Facilitate Humans in Building-Security Decision-Making

Jernej Tonejc[1]([⊠]), Jaspreet Kaur[1,2], Adrian Karsten[1,2], and Steffen Wendzel[1]

[1] Fraunhofer FKIE, Bonn, Germany
{jernej.tonejc,steffen.wendzel}@fkie.fraunhofer.de
[2] Rheinische Friedrich-Wilhelms-Universität Bonn, Bonn, Germany
{kaur,karstena}@informatik.uni-bonn.de

Abstract. Building automation systems (BAS) are interlinked networks of hardware and software, which monitor and control events in the buildings. One of the data communication protocols used in BAS is Building Automation and Control networking protocol (BACnet) which is an internationally adopted ISO standard for the communication between BAS devices. Although BAS focus on providing safety for inhabitants, decreasing the energy consumption of buildings and reducing their operational cost, their security suffers due to the inherent complexity of the modern day systems. The issues such as monitoring of BAS effectively present a significant challenge, i.e., BAS operators generally possess only partial situation awareness. Especially in large and inter-connected buildings, the operators face the challenge of spotting meaningful incidents within large amounts of simultaneously occurring events, causing the anomalies in the BAS network to go unobserved. In this paper, we present the techniques to analyze and visualize the data for several events from BAS devices in a way that determines the potential importance of such unusual events and helps with the building-security decision making. We implemented these techniques as a mobile (*Android*) based application for displaying application data and as tools to analyze the communication flows using directed graphs.

Keywords: BACnet · Building automation · Visualization · Data analysis · Directed graphs · Treemaps

1 Introduction

Building Automation Systems (BAS) aim at controlling, monitoring and administrating services such as heating, ventilation, air-conditioning and lighting in the buildings. While managing various building systems, they ensure the operational performance of the facility as well as the comfort and safety of the building's inhabitants. They also aim to decrease the energy consumption and reduce the operational costs of a building.

One of the data communication protocols used in BAS is Building Automation and Control networking protocol (BACnet) [6]. It is an internationally adopted

© Springer International Publishing Switzerland 2015
T. Tryfonas and I. Askoxylakis (Eds.): HAS 2015, LNCS 9190, pp. 693–704, 2015.
DOI: 10.1007/978-3-319-20376-8_62

OSI Layer	BACnet Stack Protocol						
Application	BACnet Application Layer						
Network	BACnet Network Layer						
Data Link	BACnet/IP over ISO 8802-2 LLC	MS/TP	LONTalk	PTP	BVLL	BZLL
Physical	Ethernet	ARCNET	RS485		RS232	UDP/IP	ZigBee

Fig. 1. BACnet OSI layers as defined in the ISO standard [6].

ISO standard for the communication between BAS devices and implemented in products by more than 800 vendors worldwide. The BACnet protocol defines a number of services that are used to communicate between building devices and works over a number of data link/physical layers, including ARCNET, Ethernet, BACnet/IP, Point-To-Point, Master-Slave/Token-Passing, LonTalk etc. as shown in Fig. 1.

BAS are responsible for taking care of many services in the buildings but the BAS operators face a significant challenge while effectively monitoring BAS due to modern-day building's complexity. BAS operators generally possess only partial situation awareness, i.e., the perception of the *current situation* within the building and how it might change in the near future. Especially in large and inter-connected buildings, the operators face the challenge of spotting meaningful incidents within large amounts of simultaneously occurring events. For example, slight temperature changes can occur throughout the day, and even hardware failures and access events for rooms can occur hundreds of times each day. On the other hand, if a usually closed window is opened at night, it should raise the attention of the BAS operator: opening a window at night is probably linked to a more important cause than slight temperature changes over the day.

In this paper, we present the techniques to analyze and visualize the data for several events from BAS devices in a way that determines the potential importance of such unusual events and helps with the building-security decision making. First, we explain the concept of processing and selecting the data from BACnet traffic to carry out the data analysis. Second, we discuss the visualization methods that can be implemented in BAS to increase situation awareness among the operators and users, while handling the events effectively. These methods can improve the detection of the anomalies in BAS. We implemented these techniques as a mobile (*Android*) based application to efficiently visualize the application data and created tools for visualizing and analyzing message flows between different devices in a BAS network. The tools generate directed graphs that illustrate the network topology, allowing the operators to quickly identify unusual communication.

The rest of the paper is structured as follows. In Sect. 2, we summarize the related work in the field of network analysis and visualization techniques for BAS. In Sect. 3, we explain the methods used for collecting the BAS data. Section 4 discusses the visualization techniques for network data. This is followed by the discussion on techniques for visualizing application data along with the usability study in Sect. 5. The conclusions and future work are presented in Sect. 6.

2   Related Work

Traffic flow measurement has been known in IP networks for quite some time, but observing the traffic flow in BACnet networks has been done only recently [9]. The methods were later improved in [13] to include entropy-based analysis of the traffic flow. However, these papers focused on the volume of the packets and packet rates and no attempt was made to classify the traffic between individual BACnet devices, making the methods unsuitable for detecting anomalies within the BACnet networks.

There has been some research on visualizing events in BAS. Wendzel et al. proposed one such approach for visualization of simultaneously occurring events in [12] and implemented it in a tool named Chronos [10]. Chronos provides temporal mosaic charts for events which provide good representation of details and make efficient use of screen real-estate, unlike Gantt charts. The temporal mosaic charts possess the capability of combining parallel occurring events into a single stream so as to use the provided screen space more efficiently. In [12], the authors make use of entropy to highlight the important events. However, while a lot of research has been done in the context of visualizations on limited screen space, no attempts have been made to transfer this to the context of mobile applications in the area of BAS networking data.

Chittaro [3] investigated general aspects of visualizations on mobile devices, stressing the importance of data selection, efficiency of space usage and inter-activity. Games et al. [5] proposed focus-plus-context approach, showing that it outperforms bar graphs or scatter plots in certain scenarios. Our approach on visualizing BAS data on mobile devices originates from a method called *treemaps*, first introduced by Shneiderman in 1992 [11]. It maps a tree to rectangles for each node, filling the available space. The rectangle sizes can be connected to some attributes of the nodes, e.g., weights. This technique is more space efficient than conventional graph visualizations.

3   Collecting the BAS Data

In this section, we describe the experimental lab setup, our methods of obtaining the BAS data, and the sources of BAS data that were used to obtain the results.

3.1   Lab Setup

To evaluate our methods, we used two BACnet labs, each with several BACnet devices. A generalized scheme of the labs is shown in Fig. 2.

The first lab setup has 16 wireless EnOcean sensors, which includes door and window sensors, motion sensors (wall and ceiling) and temperature sensors. It also has 16 actuators/binary output devices. All the devices are connected to the BACnet network via a BACnet gateway module. The second lab setup has various BACnet devices, sensors (CO_2, light, motion, presence, air pressure, moisture, temperature) on MS/TP bus, together with 32 binary outputs.

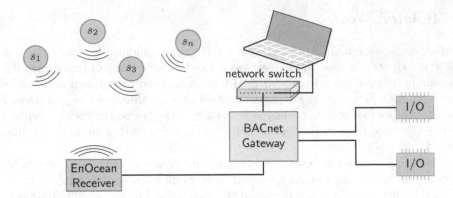

Fig. 2. A generalized scheme of our BACnet labs. EnOcean sensors $s_1, \ldots, s_n$ connect wirelessly to the EnOcean receiver which is connected to a BACnet gateway device. The binary input/output devices are connected to the gateway via MS/TP.

3.2   Collection Methods

We analyzed two types of data: network data and application data. The methods of obtaining data differ between the two types. For collecting the application data from BAS devices we used the log export functions of the BACnet gateway module. Module's internal software maintains the logs of data and allows them to be exported in the form of `csv` files for each individual sensor. In general, there are two ways of obtaining sensor data: by periodically polling the sensors for data or by subscribing to sensor's notifications about changes in value. We use the latter approach, i.e., the sensors were configured to report the *Change-of-Value* data. The door, window and motion sensors record their state using binary values, while the temperature sensor records every change in the room temperature of more than 0.1°C. The states of the actuators are also recorded as binary values. The values from different sensors can be combined together and correlated to analyze and visualize the events in BAS.

We used `Wireshark` [4] to capture the network data. Wireshark is an open-source network protocol analyzer. It allows examining the data from a live network or from a saved capture file. The captured data can be interactively browsed, delving down into all the levels of packet details. It supports hundreds of protocols and media types including BACnet. Wireshark also has the functionality of filtering the captured packets. In case of BACnet, packets can be filtered by using keywords *bacnet, bvlc* etc. The captured packets are saved in .pcap format. In addition to our own `Wireshark` recordings from the two labs, we used the network traffic recordings from Steve Karg's collection [8] to test the performance of our code.

4   Visualizing the Network Data

In this section, we focus on the network-related data, more specifically, on BACnet/IP over Ethernet. In this case, the BACnet data is encapsulated in

User Datagram Protocol (UDP) layer. BACnet data is transmitted as packets and each packet contains communication and control values. BACnet standard requires that there exists exactly one message path between any two nodes on an interconnected BACnet network. Therefore, a *flow* between two BACnet devices is well-defined and can be identified by the BACnet addresses of the devices in question.

4.1 Selection and Processing

An important aspect of any raw data analysis is a selection of the relevant features, together with pre- and postprocessing. Since the data are captured using `Wireshark` and stored in a raw `pcap` format, a fair amount of preprocessing is needed. The preprocessing was done using the Python library Scapy [2], together with the open source Scapy BACnet extension [7] which we substantially extended to enable full network and application layer parsing. Figure 3 shows the structure of a typical BACnet/IP packet. For a detailed explanation of the structure of NPDU and APDU, we refer the reader to the ISO standard [6].

Fig. 3. Structure of a typical BACnet/IP packet. The outermost layer is the Ethernet layer, which encapsulates the Internet Protocol (IP) and User Datagram Protocol (UDP) layers. BACnet/IP is encapsulated within the UDP datagram as a BACnet Virtual Link Layer (BVLL), containing the BACnet Virtual Link Control (BVLC) that indicates the function of the BACnet packet. The presence of the Network layer Protocol Data Unit (NPDU) and the Application layer Protocol Data Unit (APDU) within NPDU depends on the particular BVLC function and the values in the Network Protocol Control Information (NPCI), which is the second octet of NPDU.

One piece of data that is important for analysis but is not explicitly contained in any of the layers is the timestamp of the captured packet. However, this is recorded by `Wireshark` and is stored for each packet along with the packet contents inside the `pcap` capture files. We use the timestamps to estimate the packet rates and determine whether certain types of packets are periodic or sporadic, e.g., network layer message packets with a specific message type or application layer packets with specific PDU type for a given pair of source/destination addresses.

We next describe the features we select from each layer, starting with the outermost layer and working towards the inner layers.

Ethernet Layer. Two features are of interest here: *destination MAC* and *source MAC*. These are the physical addresses of the communicating devices, or in the case of a broadcast message, `FF:FF:FF:FF:FF:FF` (only as destination).

BVLC Layer. Although this layer can contain broadcast distribution table data, we only focus on the *BVLC function* field and the total *BVLC length*. Both serve the purpose of characterizing the message flows.

The last two layers, NPDU and APDU, are present and can be analyzed only if the BVLC function is 0x04 (*forwarded NPDU*), 0x0A (*original unicast NPDU*), or 0x0B (*original broadcast NPDU*).

NPDU Layer. The fields in NPDU layer depend on the values of the NPCI control octet, which is the second octet within the NPDU. In particular, bit 7 of the NPCI control octet indicates whether the NPDU contains a network layer message or application layer data. We extract the *source address, destination address,* and *message type,* when they are present. For BACnet/IP, the source and destination addresses are always 6 octets long and are encoded according to Annex J of the standard [6] as 4-octet IP address and 2-octet port number. For MS/TP, the addresses are 1 octet long. The addresses are needed to map the flows within the BACnet network.

APDU Layer. If the indication bit of the NPCI control octet is 0, the data portion of the NPDU contains application data within an APDU, from which we only consider one parameter, the *PDU type.*

The chosen fields allow us to detect and map message flows, characterize these flows, and create an overview of the communication within a BAS network. Characterizing individual flows also provides a means to detect certain traffic anomalies and attacks. For example, the packet length for a specific PDU type usually does not deviate much from the average size, so unusually small or large packets can indicate an attack or other kinds of anomalies.

In the postprocessing step we aggregate and export the data in a form suitable for visualizing the flows and creating the model for anomaly detection.

4.2   Analysis

To analyze the flow data, we group the packets based on their source and destination addresses and call each such group a *connection*. For each such connection, we divide the packets into two sets: packets containing network layer messages and packets containing application layer data. Within each set we further group the packets based on the network message type and PDU type (for network layer messages, respectively application data). For each set we analyze the timing data to detect whether the packets are sent periodically or sporadically. We detect this by computing the average inter-arrival time τ between the packets and its standard deviation. If the standard deviation is suitably small (comparable to a fraction of the mean, e.g., less than 20 %), we classify such traffic as *periodic*. If the standard deviation is comparable to the mean (e.g., between 0.5τ and 2τ), we treat such traffic as *sporadic* and we model it using a Poisson process with parameter $\lambda = \frac{1}{\tau}$. If the standard deviation does not fit in these two cases, we do not attempt to classify the packets based on their arrival time.

After computing these parameters for all connections from the sample traffic data, we create a probabilistic flow map, which we later use to analyze each incoming packet by checking whether it fits in the constructed flow map. We do this by computing the likelihood of observing such a packet at the given time. If the probability of observing such a packet is smaller than some pre-defined threshold (which can be connection-dependant), we flag such packet as anomalous.

4.3 Directed Graphs for Flow Data

In addition to analyzing the flow data, we visualize the connections between the BACnet devices in the form of a directed graph. Each source and each destination address represents a node, with edges being the observed directed message flows. Both network layer messages and application layer data can be used for this pupose and lead in general to different graphs. The weights of the edges are computed from the number of packets on each connection as a fraction of the total traffic. The data are processed using a Python script and the graph information is exported in the *Graph Exchange XML Format* (GEXF). We then visualize this flow map using the open source program `GePhi` [1]. The program has several tools to process graph data, including optimal node placement based on edge weights and node degrees, finding clusters of more tightly connected nodes, etc. This allows us to visualize the intrinsic network features of a BAS. An example of a flow map is shown in Fig. 4. The corresponding flow classification (the top 5 flows) is shown in Table 1.

We construct the directed graph representation from traffic recordings for a sample period, e.g., one week. We then regenerate the representation every day by adding the newly recorded data from that day and observing the changes in the graph. If new nodes or edges appear, the operator is notified. The new nodes and edges can be confirmed and become part of the reference representation from that point on. Additionally, packets can also be analyzed in real time by checking whether they fit the individual connection distribution and timing parameters.

Fig. 4. An example of a flow map for BACnet network using the application layer data. The thickness of the edges is determined by the weight, which corresponds to the fraction of the traffic belonging to that edge.

Table 1. Flow classification of the 5 most frequent flows for the network in Fig. 4. The PDU types are 0x00-BACnet-Confirmed-Request and 0x03-BACnet-ComplexACK.

Source	Destination	PDU type	τ	σ	Flow type
73:c3	5c:ce	0x00	0.96743	1.75864	sporadic
5c:ce	73:c3	0x03	1.02827	1.88999	sporadic
73:c3	c1:eb	0x00	1.48328	2.93323	sporadic
c1:eb	73:c3	0x03	1.48876	2.97395	sporadic
73:c3	5f:44	0x03	60.9053	0.07921	periodic

5   Visualizing the Application Data

The application-related data are the actual sensor values and actuator states. No special selection is performed on the application data, we simply collect all the values that are available. Since the application data come from internal logs, no preprocessing is needed on our part. For the postprocessing, we convert the extracted csv data from internal logs in a format that is more appropriate for our visualization application. In particular, since most sensors report Change-of-Value data and our visualization methods are based on fixed time intervals, we extrapolate the data so that there is at least one data point within each 15 min interval, by repeating the previous known sensor value.

5.1   Weighted Tree for Application Data

The BACnet application data is transformed into a weighted tree for each day as shown in Fig. 5. The root represents the total set of BACnet events on that day, while its children separate the data into a specific cluster for each sensor type. Each cluster vertex has 24 children, representing the 24 h of a day. In [12], the authors already considered entropy for highlighting events in BAS. We expand on their work as follows. The weight $W(h)$ for an hour h is a function of the information content $I(h)$ and the number of changes in value $N(h)$ in that hour. The events which deviate in value from the events in the past are associated with higher

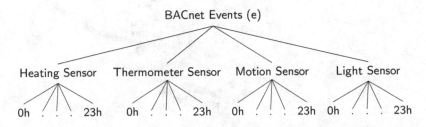

Fig. 5. Weighted tree for BACnet application data. Events for each day are clustered by sensor type and subdivided in individual hours within each cluster.

weights. The calculation differentiates between floating point and boolean values. For a boolean event e with value v, the probability $p(v)$ is calculated by comparing it to the values of events in the past at around the same time of the day.

The information content $I(e)$ is computed as

$$I(e) = -\log_2(p(v)).$$

For a floating point event e, the deviation of its value v from the mean of the values in the past at around the same time is considered. $I(h)$ results from the maximum of $I(e)$ in hour h. The number of changes in value in hour h is also compared to the number of changes in the past and $N(h)$ is the deviation from the resulting mean. Finally, $W(h)$ is the maximum of $I(h)$ and $N(h)$. These calculations result in weights that are higher for data whose fluctuation deviates significantly from the average or whose values are unusual for the specific time. However, since real BACnet traffic will always show some form of irregularity or inconsistency which is not caused by malfunctions, the weight calculation will generally produce noise which might lead to false conclusions. The weight for a cluster vertex $W(c)$ is the mean of the weights $W(h)$ of its 24 children.

The visualization of the weighted tree, representing one day of data, is implemented using a 2D-grid. Figure 6 shows two screenshots of our implementation. Every column is associated with a cluster of sensors and there is a row for each of the 24 children. The details of data events associated with a row can be expanded separately for every cluster and viewed in a list below the grid. We implemented two methods for the visualization of the weights, namely, the *size coding* and the *color coding*. Both methods are illustrated in Fig. 6. In the size coding method, we link the weights to the heights of the individual cells and the widths of the

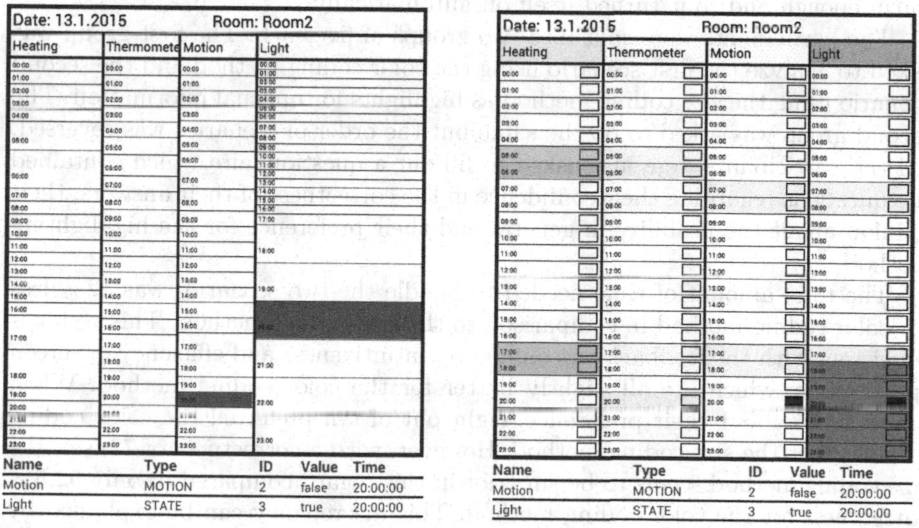

Fig. 6. The size coding method (*left*) and the color coding method (*right*).

whole columns. This results in bigger rectangles for interesting data. In the color coding method, we use uniform grid size while visualizing the weights using colors. The background of a row is linked to the weight of that row, giving it darker shades of color for higher weights. The weights for the clusters are visualized by colored backgrounds of the column headings. We implemented both visualization methods of the BACnet application data for Android phones. Due to the limited display space available on these devices, we focused on a space efficient arrangement of the data, providing a good display of values in the grid along with the feature to go into details for each cell value. The potentially interesting data are highlighted (either by using the size coding method or the color coding method, as shown in Fig. 6) in the grid to make the detection of anomalies easier.

5.2 Usability Study

We conducted a user study with ten participants to test our Android implementations. The participants had background in the field of Computer Science but had no deeper knowledge or practical experience in operating building management systems. The goal was to compare the two highlighting methods (as presented in Sect. 5.1) for interesting data and to prove that the visualizations enable fast and reliable error detection while being restricted to a small screen space.

We simulated data for two typical scenarios of malfunctions in a BAS. The first scenario represented a *light* that usually gets switched on or off in connection with the measurements of a motion sensor. From a certain point onward the light stayed switched on all the time, even if the motion sensor did not detect any motion because the automatic regulation was broken. In the second scenario, a *thermometer* got stuck at a certain value and did not measure the real temperature any more. This caused the heating to detect that the room was warm enough and so it turned itself off automatically.

The participants were split into two groups of five each. The first group was asked to analyze the first scenario using the color coding method and the second scenario using the size coding method as highlights for unusual information. The second group was asked to do the same but the order of scenarios was reversed. All the participants were also asked to fill out a questionnaire which contained the questions regarding their confidence in the correctness of their answers, their opinion about the usability in general and their preference for the highlighting method.

The total amount of time needed to handle the two scenarios was 12 % less for color coding method in comparison to the size coding method. This result is consistent with the feedback on confidence, intuitiveness and efficiency of screen space usage, which are all slightly better for the color coding method. When being asked about their preference, eight out of ten preferred the color coding method over the size coding method. However, with a correctness of 72.5 %, the size coding method seems to be superior in this regard compared to only 52.5 % correctness for the color coding method. This discrepancy can be explained by the users relying too much on the colored highlights and neglecting to verify the underlying data. Since there will always be some highlights which do not correspond to actual errors in the system, neglecting the real data can lead to false conclusions. In addition to being less obtrusive, size coding method has an advantage that interesting rows are bigger and can be selected easier for looking at the data list. This supports a more thorough analysis and requires longer time but leads to better conclusions. Due to the variable row sizes, a disadvantage of size coding method is that the rows in different columns are not aligned, which makes the comparison across different sensors harder.

6   Conclusions and Future Work

Visualizing network message flows and computing probabilistic flow maps to study the traffic patterns allows us to detect various kinds of anomalies and attacks that could be present within a BACnet network. By focusing solely on BACnet traffic, the amount of data is reduced, which makes it more manageable for analysis. However, our current models support only two time-based types of traffic, periodic and sporadic, without the capacity to characterize diurnal, weekly or seasonal cycles which are common in BAS. We therefore intend to incorporate these more advanced classifications of flows in our future work to improve anomaly detection.

The usability study has shown that the visualization techniques for application data work. Considering that the participants had no practical experience in the BAS field, 72.5 % and 52.5 % correctness is a satisfying result. The feedback in general supports this conclusion. However, there is still some room for improvement. A combination of both highlighting methods is possible, combining the advantages of both and reducing the disadvantages to a minimum. In addition, further testing has to be done to improve the highlight calculations, reduce their noise and increase their significance.

References

1. Bastian, M., Heymann, S., Jacomy, M.: Gephi: an open source software for exploring and manipulating networks (2009). http://www.aaai.org/ocs/index.php/ICWSM/09/paper/view/154
2. Biondi, P.: The Scapy community: Scapy documentation, Release 2.1.1 (2010). http://goo.gl/nPEUFx
3. Chittaro, L.: Visualizing information on mobile devices. Computer **39**(3), 40–45 (2006)
4. Combs, G.: Contributors: Wireshark (2015). https://www.wireshark.org/
5. Games, P.S., Joshi, A.: Visualization of off-screen data on tablets using context-providing bar graphs and scatter plots, vol. 9017, pp. 90170D–90170D-15 (2013)
6. ISO: Building automation and control systems - part 5: data communication protocol. In: ISO 16484-5:2012, International Organization for Standardization, Geneva, Switzerland (2012)
7. Jähnigen, C.: A BACnet layer for Scapy. https://github.com/desolat/scapy-bacnet (2014). Accessed November 2014

8. Kargs, S.: BACnet traffic captures. http://kargs.net/captures/ (2014). Accessed November 2014
9. Krejčí, R., Čeleda, P., Dobrovolný, J.: Traffic measurement and analysis of building automation and control networks. In: Sadre, R., Novotný, J., Čeleda, P., Waldburger, M., Stiller, B. (eds.) AIMS 2012. LNCS, vol. 7279, pp. 62–73. Springer, Heidelberg (2012)
10. Luz, S., Masoodian, M., McKenzie, D., Broeck, W.: Chronos: a tool for interactive scheduling and visualisation of task hierarchies. In: 2009 13th International Conference Information Visualisation, pp. 241–246, July 2009
11. Shneiderman, B.: Tree visualization with tree-maps: 2-D space-filling approach. ACM Trans. Graph. 11(1), 92–99 (1992)
12. Wendzel, S., Herdin, C., Wirth, R., Masoodian, M., Luz, S., Kaur, J.: Mosaic-chart based visualization in building automation systems, pp. 687–690. MEV Verlag/Fraunhofer Verlag (2014)
13. Čeleda, P., Krejčí, R., Krmíček, V.: Flow-based security issue detection in building automation and control networks. In: Szabó, R., Vidács, A. (eds.) EUNICE 2012. LNCS, vol. 7479, pp. 64–75. Springer, Heidelberg (2012)

XACML Privacy Policy Editor
for Critical Infrastructures

Nils Ulltveit-Moe[1]([⊠]), Henrik Nergaard[1], Terje Gjøsæter[1], and Jennifer Betts[2]

[1] Universitetet i Agder, Jon Lilletuns Vei 9, 4879 Grimstad, Norway
{nils.ulltveit-moe,henrin10,terje.gjosater}@uia.no
[2] School of EEECS, Queens University Belfast, Belfast, Northern Ireland, UK
jbetts01@qub.ac.uk

Abstract. This paper describes a Scratch-based eXtensible Access Control Markup Language (XACML) editor ViSPE that can be used for designing authorisation and anonymisation policies, as well as how these policies can be enforced by using the Reversible anonymiser. Private and confidential information can be protected based on identified security requirements, as described in two case studies. The first case covers privacy-enhanced IDS-alarm handling in a traffic control centre, and in the second case, we mitigate insider threats with a secure configuration deployment policy.

Keywords: XACML · Privacy · Security · Anonymisation · Critical · Infrastructure

1 Introduction

This paper demonstrates modelling of privacy and trust policies using a novel high-level graphical policy editor. The privacy requirements are based on the results of two case studies, done as part of two EU-projects. The results of these analyses are then used to propose how policies can be implemented using the eXtensible Access Control Markup Language (XACML) [1], enhanced with the reversible anonymisation protocol in [2, 3]. The policies are modelled using our visual policy editor ViSPE [4], which is implemented in Smalltalk based on the children's programming language Scratch [5, 6]. ViSPE focuses on providing an easy to use interface for defining XACML policies for access control, anonymisation and encryption of information in XML documents or messages. The paper demonstrates how the policy editor can be used for mitigating insider threats as well as protecting private or confidential information.

The rest of this article is organised as follows: Sect. 2 covers issues of privacy in Critical Information Infrastructures (CII), and presents the tools and technologies used to mitigate the issues in the two case studies. Section 3 presents the two cases, including the policies created to support them. Section 4 provides a brief discussion of ViSPE and its applicability to the cases, and in Sect. 5 we make our conclusions. Finally, Sect. 6 presents some ideas for future work.

© Springer International Publishing Switzerland 2015
T. Tryfonas and I. Askoxylakis (Eds.): HAS 2015, LNCS 9190, pp. 705–716, 2015.
DOI: 10.1007/978-3-319-20376-8_63

2 Privacy in Critical Infrastructures

There are several important objectives for privacy regulation. Personal data and similar information must only be collected using legitimate means and for legitimate purposes to comply with data protection legislation. Access to personally identifiable information (PII) and/or confidential information must only be granted to those with appropriate authorisation. Identities must not be compromised by any action of the system. No change in ownership, responsibility, content or collection of personal data must take place without the knowledge and consent of the data subject. An audit trail of all actions having an impact on personal data and confidential information must be maintained within the system to allow for forensic analysis in the event of a data breach.

Our long-term goal is to build and extend the ViSPE policy editor combined with our reversible anonymisation scheme to model such privacy requirements. We can already model a range of scenarios, however other remain as future work, for example adding policy controlled secure logging obligations. The privacy enforcement tool is based on the reversible anonymisation scheme [3]. It has been integrated with the Prelude-IDS Security Incident Event Management (SIEM) system[1] in order to demonstrate privacy-enhanced intrusion detection services, as shown in Fig. 7.

2.1 Privacy Enforcement Mechanism

Figure 1 gives a high-level overview over the XACML based anonymisation scheme for anonymising XML documents or messages [2]. The scheme consists of an initial authorisation policy with a set of XACML Obligations, which amongst others define multiple XPath resource definitions identifying XML elements or attributes that need to be authorised. The XACML Policy Enforcement Point (PEP) of the anonymiser will subsequently loop through all resource definitions and extract and authorise each match of the XPath resource against the XACML Policy Decision Point (PDP).

The PEP sends the resource identifier with each resource to be authorised, so that the respective XML element authorisation policy is evaluated to decide whether the given XML element should be authorised or not. If the XML element is authorised, then an XACML Obligation describes how the element should be anonymised, for example whether the data should be replaced with a fixed string (e.g. "confidential") or whether it should be padded using a character (e.g. pad-with X). The anonymisation scheme supports a decision caching protocol in order to improve efficiency [2], and can also describe cache timeout values and similar parameters from the XACML Obligations.

The anonymisation scheme has been extended to support XACML controlled reversible anonymisation of XML documents or messages based on storing the anonymised information encrypted in different security levels, so that only authorised users or roles can access this information [3].

---

[1] https://www.prelude-ids.org.

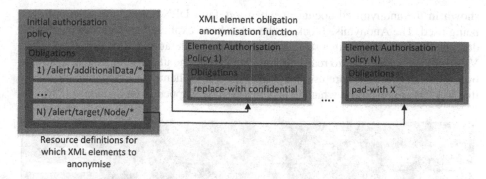

Fig. 1. Overview over XACML anonymisation scheme

The reversible anonymisation protocol is based on a hybrid encryption scheme where a user can unlock an encryption key using her secret key, and this encryption key is furthermore used to unlock an authorisation mapping which contains the encryption keys for the security levels the user has access to. The reversible anonymiser supports advanced functionality, such as default *PERMIT*, or default *DENY* anonymisation policies, multiple security levels and policy defined key sharing, so that several users or roles must collaborate to reverse the anonymisation. This paper shows how we have created a high-level abstraction for creating XACML-based anonymisation policies using the Scratch-based policy editor ViSPE [4].

2.2 ViSPE's Graphic Primitives for XACML Policy Elements

XACML is an XML-based policy-definition language. The syntax is human/machine-readable, but not trivial to write without comprehensive editor support. While there are editors that support writing of XACML policies, like UMU-XACML[2] or the WSO2 Identity Server[3], the novel editor ViSPE takes a new approach by presenting XACML elements as graphical blocks [4]. ViSPE allows non-programmers like policymakers to implement privacy, anonymisation and authorisation policies using a high-level graphic XACML-like policy language, which is generated into XACML XML policies.

The blocks follow the same structure as the underlying XACML syntax. This makes it easy to visualise the containing element of a tag. The colour differentiation between blocks is also a helpful tool for quickly orienting the start and end of a tag element.

The editor also includes specialised blocks tailored to present the obligations and their assignments. This means that the user does not need to have knowledge of the underlying XACML syntax, e.g. for the different obligations supported by the anonymiser.

The editor is shown by Fig. 2, and includes two example XACML Obligation blocks in ViSPE, while Fig. 3 shows the more verbose XACML implementation of the first block. The Declassify block implements an obligation to declassify the content of an entire XML element or attribute from a security level *secret*, so that this attribute is

---

[2] UMU-XACML editor: http://umu-xacmleditor.sourceforge.net.
[3] WSO2 Identity Server: https://docs.wso2.com/display/IS450/Creating+an+XACML+Policy.

shown in the anonymised document when a default DENY anonymisation policy is being used. The Anonymise block on the other hand explicitly anonymises data in the document and stores this in a security level *secret* for default PERMIT protocols. The ViSPE block is far easier to read and understand than the underlying XACML Obligation. The editor furthermore uses a consistent colour scheme for Obligation blocks, so that it is easy to recognise which blocks that will be mapped to Obligations.

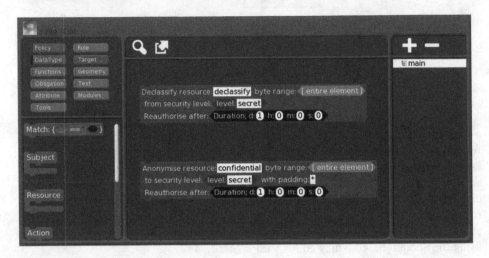

Fig. 2. The ViSPE editor with resource definition examples

```
<Obligation FulfillOn="Permit" ObligationId= "urn:prile:org:resource:declassify:restrictions">
  <AttributeAssignment AttributeId= "urn:prile:org:resource:declassify:policy:declassify"
    DataType="urn:ogc:def:dataType:geoxacml:1.0:geometry">
    <gml:MultiPoint srsName="http://www.prile.org/ByteRanges">
      <gml:pointMember><gml:Point><gml:coordinates>
      0,-1</gml:coordinates></gml:Point></gml:pointMember>
    </gml:MultiPoint>
  </AttributeAssignment>
  <AttributeAssignment AttributeId= "urn:prile:org:resource:declassify:authorisation:levels"
    DataType="http://www.w3.org/2001/XMLSchema#string">level:secret
  </AttributeAssignment>
  <AttributeAssignment AttributeId= "urn:prile:org:resource:declassify:cache-timeout"
    DataType="http://www.w3.org/TR/2002/WD-xquery-operators-20020816#dayTimeDuration">
    PT1H</AttributeAssignment>
</Obligation>
```

Fig. 3. XACML obligation corresponding to the *Declassify resource* block

XACML is very verbose and not easy to read or write. While the graphical block representation is much more compact, the readability is also better, since it highlights the important parts of each block while hiding the verbose syntax.

3   Case Studies

Here, we will present two use cases that highlight the issues at hand. The first is a critical infrastructure network related to a traffic control centre, and the second is a multinational smart grid demand/response operator.

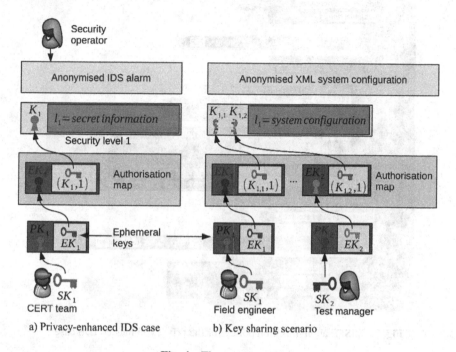

Fig. 4. The two scenarios

3.1   Case 1: Privacy in Critical Cyber-Infrastructure

This case describes how to define a default *DENY* privacy policy for an outsourced managed security service provider, so that a first-line security analyst can only see information defined as non-sensitive in the privacy policy, while an authorised Computer Emergency Response Team (CERT) doing attack investigations is authorised to de-anonymise the information in the Intrusion Detection System (IDS) alarms. An advantage with such a policy, is that only information that is explicitly allowed will be presented to the first line security analyst, effectively implementing privacy by default [7]. In this scenario, the operators on the critical infrastructure network of the traffic control centre may trigger IDS alarms that may in turn leak PII if they are not anonymised.

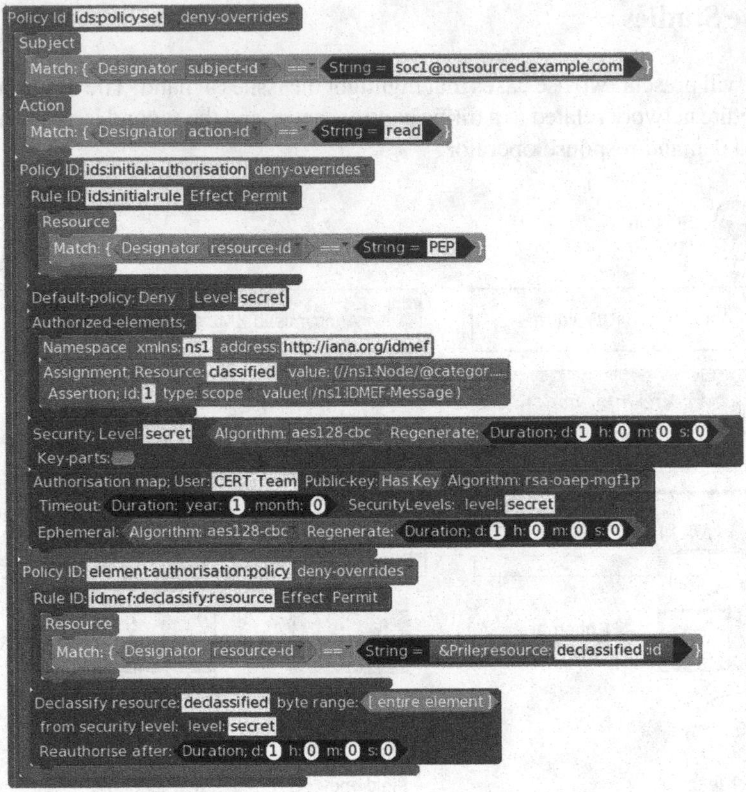

Fig. 5. ViSPE anonymisation policy for the privacy-enhanced IDS case

IDS Alarm Anonymisation Policy for a Traffic Control Centre. In the traffic control centre, security monitoring using IDS is outsourced to a managed security service company. It is assumed that possible exposure to PII sampled in IP packets from the traffic control center must be avoided, so that this information does not leave the network perimeter of the traffic control center. This means that IDS alarms normally will be anonymised, however it will be possible for a trusted Computer Emergency Response Team (CERT) to investigate suspected attacks on the traffic control network when necessary.

This case assumes that the security operator escalates suspected attacks to the Computer Emergency Response Team (CERT), which is trusted to de-anonymise the secret information in order to perform a more in-depth forensic analysis. This is implemented using the encryption key schema in Fig. 4a, where the *CERT Team* first needs to decrypt the ephemeral key EK_1 using its secret key SK_1. EK_1 is then used to decrypt the encryption key K_1, which can be used to decrypt the secret information in security level 'secret'. The de-anonymiser then replaces the anonymised content in the IDS alarm with the decrypted information. EK_1 is regenerated after a given time interval (one day), which allows for reusing it for subsequent de-anonymisation operations for the given user, as long as the key is valid.

Figure 5, shows the full anonymisation policy, created in ViSPE. The policy allows for using symbolic names (for example security level *secret*), which is easier to understand than the numeric IDs used in the mathematical notation in [3]. Some parts of the obligation attributes are optional for the user to define. These are presented as an oval placeholder which generates the default values if left alone.

The anonymisation specification/decision cache declaration consists of two visual blocks *Default policy* and *Authorized-elements* that are mapped to XACML Obligations. The first block specifies the default policy, which is set to default *DENY* in order to ensure that all information by default is being anonymised (privacy by default). The second block is an XACML Obligation with id *authorize-elements*, which is performed on successful initial authorisation. This obligation consists of a set of one or more *Resource* declarations defining XPath expressions of XML resources to be authorised, and *Assertion scope* declarations which are XPath expressions that can be used for conditional policy evaluation based on document content. These are mapped to XACML *AttributeAssignments* (simplified to Assignments in ViSPE). The XPath expressions identify XML resources and attributes in the input document which need to be authorised. The next block is the security level declaration, which defines the name of the security level 'secret', and the encryption key used to encrypt the security level. The security level 'secret' corresponds to level '1' in the mathematical notation in Fig. 4. The encryption key block also contains the time duration until the key needs to be regenerated, in order to reduce the effect of compromised security level keys. The Authorisation map defines the connection between an authorised user or role, the public key associated with this user or role, and the security levels that this user or role has access to. We use an intermediate encryption key (ephemeral key) which acts as an alias for the user[4]. The authorisation map can be defined for a set of one or more users/roles, security levels or key shares.

3.2 Case 2: Reducing Insider Threats

Insider threat is a common problem, particularly for critical infrastructures, where they can have severe consequences. It is important to emphasise that insider threats are not necessarily malicious, but may be the result of responding to a phishing email, or from a simple error. This case study investigates how a critical infrastructure, for example a Smart grid Demand/Response system, can reduce the risk of accidental or malicious deployment of faulty system configurations by implementing a security policy using the graphical XACML editor. Staff may not always have background checks performed before hiring, even in critical infrastructures, and may not receive training in security and privacy. In a pilot study conducted among critical infrastructure providers for the privacy impact assessment developed for the PRECYSE project, it was found that less than half of respondents carried out employee background checks, and half conducted staff training in security and privacy, at least annually.

One way to mitigate both types of insider threat is to implement a multi-party authorisation (MPA) policy; that is to require more than one authorised employee to

---

[4] Note that this only is a truly ephemeral key if the renegotiation time is set to zero.

co-sign for deployment of security-critical configuration changes. If there is a mistake made by an inexperienced employee, or an intentionally malicious change in the new configuration, it should be detected by one of the co-signing parties. This will discourage malicious attacks, as well as encourage employees to do a careful examination of a policy. In the secure policy deployment scenario of this case, a changed policy needs to be examined and co-signed by 2 authorised persons before deployment.

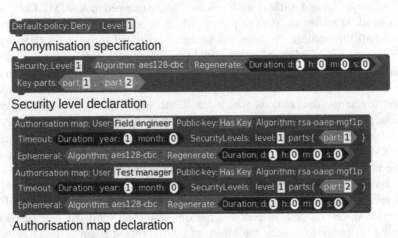

Default-policy: Deny   Level: **1**

Anonymisation specification

Security; Level: **1**   Algorithm: aes128-cbc   Regenerate: Duration; d: **1** h: **0** m: **0** s: **0**
Key-parts: part: **1** ,   part **2**

Security level declaration

Authorisation map; User: Field engineer   Public-key: Has Key   Algorithm: rsa-oaep-mgf1p
Timeout: Duration: year: **1** . month: **0**   SecurityLevels: level: **1** parts:{ part: **1** }
Ephemeral: Algorithm: aes128-cbc   Regenerate: Duration; d: **1** h: **0** m: **0** s: **0**
Authorisation map; User: Test manager   Public-key: Has Key   Algorithm: rsa-oaep-mgf1p
Timeout: Duration: year: **1** . month: **0**   SecurityLevels: level: **1** parts:{ part: **2** }
Ephemeral: Algorithm: aes128-cbc   Regenerate: Duration; d: **1** h: **0** m: **0** s: **0**

Authorisation map declaration

Fig. 6. Encryption scheme for secure deployment of security configurations

Policy for Secure Deployment of Configurations in a Smart Grid D/R system. The anonymisation specification consists of a default *DENY* policy, without declassifying any information, which means that a resource authorisation policy will not be necessary. The security level declaration defines one security level, and the security level encryption key is split into two parts as shown in part (b) of Figs. 4 and 6.

The authorisation map defines the two users/roles: a *field engineer* who has access to the first key share $K_{1,1}$, and a *test manager* who has access to the other key share $K_{1,2}$. This means that the field engineer and test manager must collaborate on deploying a given system configuration, which reduces the risk of accidentally or maliciously deploying the wrong system configuration. It is necessary that the system configuration file is signed, so that the application installing it can verify and enforce that only trusted system configurations are installed. The signing can either be done explicitly, or one can use the inner signature created by the Anonymiser PEP, which contains a signature of the original document before anonymisation (not shown in the figures). This adds another layer of security in case the field engineer attempts to install the wrong system configuration, or even worse, that a malicious field engineer attempts to install a fake system configuration using a forged digital signature. This is not only a theoretical assumption, since RSA signature forgery attacks based on implementation weaknesses have been demonstrated [8].

Figures 4b, and 6 shows how the encryption scheme works. The field engineer first needs to decrypt his ephemeral key EK_1 using his secret key SK_1. EK_1 is then used to decrypt the first key share $K_{1,1}$. The test manager unlocks her key share in a similar way by decrypting $K_{1,2}$ using EK_2 decrypted with SK_2. The deanonymiser will now add the two keys modulo the key size using the Karnin, Greene and Hellman scheme [9], in order to retrieve the encryption key for security level l_1 which stores the encrypted parts of the system configuration file. The deanonymiser then decrypts security level 1, and replaces the anonymised text with the decrypted text. It then verifies that the inner signature of the system configuration is OK and deploys the system configuration. This allows for policy controlled secure deployment of system configurations, in order to reduce the risk of insider threats. This shows one of the simplest key sharing schemes. More elaborate schemes are possible, involving more stakeholders, more key shares, several security levels and more complex policies.

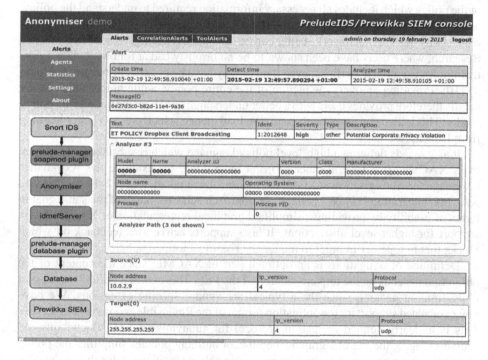

Fig. 7. Anonymiser test scenario

3.3 Experiments

We have implemented and tested the privacy-enhanced IDS scenario using the policy in Fig. 5. ViSPE can generate policies for both use cases, but the reversible anonymiser needs some extensions to handle deployment of configuration files. This will be implemented as future work in the SEMIAH project. Figure 7 shows an alarm triggered by the policy from the IDS case, running in the Reversible anonymiser and presented by the PreludeIDS/Prewikka SIEM console. ViSPE is implemented in the Pharo Smalltalk environment. We have previously shown that it has sufficient performance for advanced policy scenarios [4]. The performance of the reversible anonymiser is satisfactory for small to medium-size IDS deployments, as discussed in [3].

4 Discussion

This article illustrates how privacy requirements identified during a privacy impact assessment can be implemented as XACML policies using the Visual Policy Editor (ViSPE). Our graphical editor provides a high-level user interface for designing authorisation and anonymisation policies. This approach works better than existing general purpose XML editors or specialised XACML editors by providing an overview picture of the policy which includes all necessary information required to understand the policy, while hiding much of the syntactic verbosity and complexity of XACML. Another reason why this approach works better can be drawn from analogies in Design Science Research, where users have been shown to be notoriously bad at following deep information, for example hyperlinks, even though they have been explicitly instructed to do so [10]. Providing an overview picture of the entire policy, while hiding unnecessary details therefore provides users with a better understanding of how the underlying policy works. This is also consistent with cognitive load theory, which predicts better learning from leaner presentations [11].

It also avoids defining a high-level policy language which is substantially different from XACML, like several other projects have done, for example the Axiomatics Language for Authorisation (ALFA), the non-technical notation in [12–14] or Ponder2 XACML integration [15]. We believe our approach achieves much of the same goal in terms of usability by providing a simplified graphical representation of XACML, with support for higher level abstractions. It also supports active user feedback on which blocks that fit together in order to reduce the risk of ill formed policies.

Definition of obligations is an optional part of XACML, since the content of the obligation depends on the implementation of the PEP. This makes it difficult to support obligations in general, since these typical are vendor specific extensions. We have however added support for the obligation format of the Reversible anonymiser to ViSPE. This is a clearly defined obligation protocol for anonymising XML documents. As shown in Fig. 5, the use of a graphical editor for building policies simplifies the policy creation process and clarifies the purpose of the policy significantly for the reader.

5 Conclusion

The paper illustrates designing policy-maker-friendly XACML authorisation and anonymisation policies for XML documents or messages using the ViSPE policy editor. The editor implements a novel blocks-based anonymisation language implemented in Smalltalk, and is based on the visual programming language Scratch. The policy editor has been adapted to support the PEP interface of the reversible anonymiser, amongst others by adding specific blocks for anonymising and deanonymising information. The policies can subsequently be enforced using the Reversible anonymiser [3]. This allows for complying with identified security and privacy requirements in order to control access to private or confidential information.

6 Future Work

Future work includes adapting the reversible anonymiser and ViSPE to XACML 3.0 which offers better support for target matching, and obligations. We also plan to extend the reversible anonymiser with logging functionality so that policy makers can give polices different logging obligations, accessible only having correct authorisation. Furthermore, we plan to enhance ViSPE to support GeoXACML, in order to enable location based policies [16], as well as location-aware role-based access control [17, 18]. ViSPE is still an early prototype. We have therefore left usability testing as future work.

Acknowledgements. The project has been sponsored by the FP7 EU projects:
• SEMIAH - Scalable Energy Management Infrastructure for Aggregation of Households, ICT-2013.6.1-619560 (http://semiah.eu).
• PRECYSE - Protection, prevention and reaction to cyberattacks to critical infrastructures, FP7-SEC-2012-1-285181 (http://www.precyse.eu).

References

1. Moses, T. (ed.): OASIS eXtensible Access Control Markup Language (XACML) Version 2.0 (2005)
2. Ulltveit-Moe, N., Oleshchuk, V.: Decision-cache based XACML authorisation and anonymisation for XML documents. Comput. Stand. Interfaces **34**(6), 527–534 (2012)
3. Ulltveit-Moe, N., Oleshchuk, V.: A novel policy-driven reversible anonymisation scheme for XML-based services. Inf. Syst. **48**, 164–178 (2014)
4. Nergaard, H., Ulltveit-Moe, N., Gjøsæter, T.: A scratch-based graphical policy editor for XACML. In: ICISSP 2015 Proceedings of the 1st International Conference on Information Systems Security and Privacy ESEO, Angers, Loire Valley, France, pp. 182–191 (2015)
5. Malan, D.J., Leitner, H.H.: Scratch for budding computer scientists. In: Proceedings of the 38th SIGCSE Technical Symposium on Computer Science Education, pp. 223–227, New York, NY, USA (2007)
6. Resnick, M., Maloney, J., Monroy-Hernández, A., Rusk, N., Eastmond, E., Brennan, K., Millner, A., Rosenbaum, E., Silver, J., Silverman, B., Kafai, Y.: Scratch: programming for all. Commun. ACM **52**(11), 60–67 (2009)
7. Cavoukian, A., Taylor, S., Abrams, M.E.: Privacy by design - essential for organizational accountability and strong business practices. Identity Inf. Soc. **3**(2), 405–413 (2010)
8. Intel Security: BERserk vulnerability part 1: RSA signature forgery attack due to incorrect parsing of ASN.1 encoded DigestInfo in PKCS#1 v1.5. Intel (2014)
9. Karnin, J.G.E., Hellman, M.: On secret sharing system. IEEE Trans. Info Theor. **IT-29**, 35–41 (1983)
10. Kuechler, B., Vaishnavi, V.: On theory development in design science research: anatomy of a research project. Eur. J. Inf. Syst. **17**(5), 489–504 (2008)

11. Mayer, R.E., Jackson, J.: The case for coherence in scientific explanations: quantitative details can hurt qualitative understanding. J. Exp. Psychol. Appl. **11**(1), 13–18 (2005)
12. Stepien, B., Matwin, S., Felty, A.: Advantages of a non-technical XACML notation in role-based models. In: 2011 Ninth Annual International Conference on Privacy, Security and Trust (PST), pp. 193–200 (2011)
13. Stepien, B., Felty, A., Matwin, S.: A non-technical user-oriented display notation for XACML conditions. In: Babin, G., Kropf, P., Weiss, M. (eds.) E-Technologies: Innovation in an Open World. LNBIP, vol. 26, pp. 53–64. Springer, Heidelberg (2009)
14. Stepien, B., Felty, A., Matwin, S.: A non-technical XACML target editor for dynamic access control systems, pp. 150–157. IEEE (2014)
15. Zhao, H., Lobo, J., Bellovin, S.M.: An algebra for integration and analysis of ponder2 policies. In: IEEE Workshop on Policies for Distributed Systems and Networks 2008, POLICY 2008, pp. 74–77 (2008)
16. Matheus, A. (ed.): OGC 07-026r2 geospatial extensible access control markup language (GeoXACML) version 1.0. Open Geospatial Consortium, Inc. (2007)
17. Ulltveit-Moe, N., Oleshchuk, V.: Enforcing mobile security with location-aware role-based access control. Secur. Commun. Netw., p. n/a–n/a (2013)
18. Ulltveit-Moe, N., Oleshchuk, V.: Mobile security with location-aware role-based access control. In: Prasad, R., Farkas, K., Schmidt, A.U., Lioy, A., Russello, G., Luccio, F.L. (eds.) MobiSec 2011. LNICST, vol. 94, pp. 172–183. Springer, Heidelberg (2012)

Author Index

Printed in the United States
By Bookmasters